BUSINESS
ENGLISH
AND
COMMUNICATION

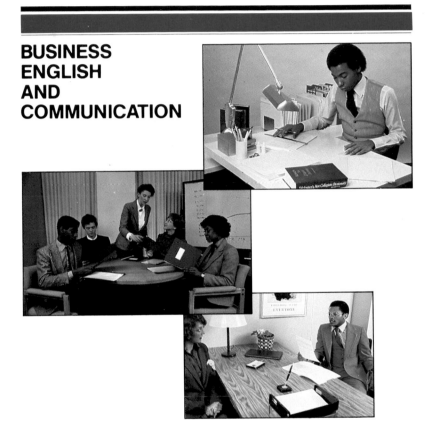

BUSINESS ENGLISH AND COMMUNICATION

SIXTH EDITION

MARIE M. STEWART, Ph.D.
Late Head of Business Education
  Department
Stonington High School
Stonington, Connecticut

KENNETH ZIMMER, Ed.D.
Professor of Business Education and
  Office Administration
California State University
Los Angeles, California

LYN R. CLARK, Ed.D.
Professor of Business
Los Angeles Pierce College
Woodland Hills, California

GREGG DIVISION/McGRAW-HILL BOOK COMPANY
NEW YORK • ATLANTA • DALLAS • ST. LOUIS • SAN FRANCISCO • AUCKLAND • BOGOTÁ • GUATEMALA • HAMBURG
JOHANNESBURG • LISBON • LONDON • MADRID • MEXICO • MONTREAL • NEW DEHLI • PANAMA • PARIS • SAN JUAN
SÃO PAULO • SINGAPORE • SYDNEY • TOKYO • TORONTO

Sponsoring Editor:	**Marie Orsini Rosen**
Editing Supervisor:	**S. Goldfarb**
Production Manager:	**Frank Bellantoni**
Design and Art Supervisor:	**Nancy Axelrod**
Photo Editor:	**Mary Ann Drury**
Interior Design:	**Delgado Design Associates**
Cover Photo:	**James Nazz**
Technical Studio:	**Fine Line, Inc.**

Photographs on chapter-opening spreads appear courtesy of the following: Chapters 1 and 6: IBM Corporation; Chapters 2, 3, 4, 7, 9, 10, and 11: Kip Peticolas/Fundamental Photographs; Chapter 5: Jacquard Systems; Chapter 8: Dictaphone Corporation; Chapter 12: Jane Hamilton-Merritt.

Line illustrations and excerpted material appearing on the following pages were reprinted or adapted courtesy of the following: pages 27–28: Walt Disney Productions, Burbank, California; pages 56–57: G. & C. Merriam Co., Springfield, Massachusetts; pages 59–60: Houghton Mifflin Company, Boston, Massachusetts; page 220: *Wordwatching,* Bryn Mawr, Pennsylvania; page 398: The Franklin Mint, Porcelain Division, Franklin Center, Pennsylvania; page 409: University of Illinois College of Medicine, Chicago, Illinois; page 417: Carnation Company—Health and Nutrition Division, Los Angeles, California; page 440: JC Penney Company, Inc., Northridge, California; page 446: Dow Jones & Company, Inc., New York, New York; page 459: California Federal Savings & Loan Association, Los Angeles, California; page 479: Creative Travel Planners, Inc., Woodland Hills, California.

Library of Congress Cataloging in Publication Data

Stewart, Marie M., date
  Business English and communication.

  Rev. ed. of: Business English and Communication/
Marie M. Stewart . . . [et al.] 5th ed. c1978.
  Includes index.
  Summary: Emphasizes the English and communication
skills that are necessary in the business world, including
speaking, listening, reading, and writing.
  1. English language—Business English. [1. English
language—Business English. 2. Business education]
I. Zimmer, Kenneth, date. II. Clark, Lyn.
III. Title.
PE1115.S78 1984b   428.2′02465   83-14912
ISBN 0-07-061420-2 (pupil's ed.)

Business English and Communication, Sixth Edition
Copyright © 1984, 1978, 1972, 1967, 1961 by McGraw-Hill, Inc. All rights reserved. Copyright 1953 by McGraw-Hill, Inc. All rights reserved. Printed in the United States of America. Except as permitted under the United States Copyright Act of 1976, no part of this publication may be reproduced or distributed in any form or by any means, or stored in a data base or retrieval system, without the prior written permission of the publisher.

1 2 3 4 5 6 7 8 9 0 DOCDOC 8 9 0 9 8 7 6 5 4 3

ISBN 0-07-061420-2

P · R · E · F · A · C · E

Think about all the time you spend communicating. You may not even realize how much of your day is spent this way. Whether you are the secretary to the president of a company, a word processing operator, a marketing representative, an information systems manager, or a corporate executive, much of your work involves reading, writing, listening, and speaking. Even though technology helps you function more efficiently and across long distances, you must still have polished communication skills to succeed at what you do. In fact, your value as an employee and your very promotability may depend, in large part, on your ability to communicate.

The *Business English and Communication* program has been designed to provide you with the broad, thorough training necessary to develop competence on the job in each of the communication skills: reading, writing, speaking, and listening.

The Sixth Edition

The Sixth Edition begins by introducing you to the fundamentals of business communication skills and describing the impact of technology on these skills. Then, after you have learned how to develop good reading—and proofreading— skills, you will start to improve your general word skills and study how mastery of grammar, punctuation, and style can make the difference between effective and ineffective communication. Before studying how to develop your speaking and writing skills, you will study the enormous impact human relations and communication psychology have on your job. Finally, you will learn how to apply all your communication skills and talents toward getting a job. In addition to having developed your communication skills, you will also have been introduced to the language of business, for the textbook emphasizes business vocabulary throughout.

Business Communication and Technology. The Sixth Edition addresses one of the most interesting aspects of business communication: office technology. Right away, in the first chapter of the text, the communication skills of reading, writing, speaking, and listening are identified and illustrated through practical examples. Then, in new coverage, you are shown how technology does not eliminate the need to master these skills; technology only makes communicating faster and easier. In Chapter 1, office technology and its relation to communication skills are discussed. Also, throughout the text photographs depict business communicators in both the traditional and the electronic office.

Reading. Your reading and—more important—proofreading skills are developed early in the text, in Chapter 2. This way, you may apply these skills throughout the course. Also, starting in Chapter 2 and continuing throughout the grammar, punctuation, and style coverage (Chapters 4 and 5), you will find oral Class Practice and Proofreading Practice exercises. These short exercises are designed to provide immediate reinforcement of principles just learned.

Word Skills. Because words are the basic elements that make up both written and oral messages, Chapter 3 offers a broad overview for developing word skills. In this chapter, you learn how to expand your vocabulary and how to use a dictionary and other word references. Of special interest in Chapter 3 is Unit 7, on spelling, which offers a three-step approach for mastering a basic business vocabulary. In addition, you learn to distinguish differences in meaning of many of the most commonly confused words.

Grammar and Punctuation. A solid foundation in English grammar is essential for successful communication, and Chapters 4 and 5 offer you all the grammar and punctuation know-how you will need to succeed on the job. Developed over several editions, these chapters stress the practical principles of grammar and punctuation—the ones that you *must* know. Much of the confusing, complex terminology has been eliminated. Moreover, Quick Trick sections are frequently offered immediately after those rules that are most confusing. These Quick Tricks take difficult principles and change them into easy-to-remember rules. Many practice exercises are provided throughout each unit in the grammar and punctuation chapters—after every Quick Trick section, for example—to help you understand each principle and to reinforce your understanding.

Communication Psychology. Having mastered the fundamentals of business communication, you are then introduced to the basic principles of human relations in Chapter 6. Armed with a fundamental knowledge of what motivates people to act, you will be able to apply the principles of communication psychology to your oral and written communications and will therefore be able to communicate more successfully.

Writing Craft. Expert writers do more than write messages that are correct. They create messages that are explicit and polished, and their ability to do so is what distinguishes their messages from everyday, routine messages. Chapter 7 helps you develop expertise in joining words, phrases, and clauses into communications that receive special attention and that get results. This chapter develops your awareness of cold, unpleasant, and obsolete language, for example, and explains how to transform it into warm, cordial, up-to-date writing.

Business Letters. Chapter 8 offers you a thorough training program on business letters, from the general to the specific. It begins with general business letter formats and proceeds to cover almost every specific type of letter, each in an individual unit. You learn to write not only routine letters such as transmittals and requests, which would be assigned to beginning employees, but also more specialized letters such as sales and credit letters. Thus this chapter prepares you for real-life, on-the-job writing assignments.

Memos and Reports. Because memos are the primary means of written communication within an organization, in Chapter 9 you are introduced to the ways in which memos are used in business, and you are given in-depth procedures for planning and writing effective memos. Also included in this chapter are a discussion of other types of form messages that you will use on the job, a thorough treatment of report writing, and an introduction to minutes of meetings and news releases.

Listening Skills. In Chapter 10, the important skill of becoming a good listener is discussed. You will learn techniques that will help you master this crucial skill. In addition, ways that listening may bear on your job are discussed.

Speaking Skills. Chapter 11 prepares you to speak effectively by offering practical guidance on planning and giving a talk, meeting the public in person and by telephone, and participating in group discussions. In this chapter you will also learn some of the common pitfalls of enunciation and pronunciation and how to avoid them.

Résumés and Job Applications. The effectiveness with which you can prepare résumés and employment letters will have an immediate, direct impact on your success in seeking employment. Chapter 12 prepares you for all the employment messages you may write—application letters, résumés, reference letters, acceptance letters, and so on. In addition, it offers helpful suggestions that will prepare you for employment interviews.

Communication Laboratory

At the end of every unit within the text is a Communication Laboratory section, which provides exercises that will help you apply the principles learned in the unit. Each Communication Laboratory offers a series of three different exercises.

Application Exercises. These exercises test your understanding of the principles presented in the current unit and review those presented in previous units.

Vocabulary and Spelling Studies. This section of each Communication Laboratory emphasizes the development of spelling and vocabulary skills.

Communicating for Results. Each Communication Laboratory ends with Communicating for Results, a thought-provoking exercise that tests your ability to apply communication skills in realistic business situations. Not only do these exercises require you to apply the principles of language usage, but they also test your ability to solve problems in human relations, social business etiquette, and so on.

Supporting Materials

In addition to this text, the *Business English and Communication* program includes a workbook of projects and activities for students, a set of objective tests, and teacher's editions of both the textbook and the workbook.

The Workbook. A complete teaching-learning aid, *Student Projects and Activities for Business English and Communication* provides application exercises closely correlated with the principles covered in each of the corresponding units of the textbook. These worksheets offer enrichment, reinforcement, and review exercises covering spelling and vocabulary development, reading comprehension, listening comprehension, proofreading, editing, rewriting, note-taking, and composing letters and other types of business communications. All the exercises offered in this workbook differ from those given in the text.

Teacher's Edition of the Textbook. New to this edition, *Business English and Communication* offers a page-for-page teacher's edition of the textbook. Short teaching suggestions and short exercise solutions appear, in a second color, right on the page of the text to which they refer. In addition, grouped at the back of the teacher's edition are explanations of how to use the program; additional detailed unit-by-unit teaching suggestions; schedules and grading guidelines; and longer solutions to exercises in the text, carefully cross-referenced to the actual exercises.

Teacher's Edition of the Workbook. Another teaching aid is the teacher's edition of the workbook. Not only does it include a page-for-page facsimile key of all the workbook exercises, it also includes objective tests for the students (see below).

Tests. Thirty-two pages of test masters are included at the back of the teacher's edition of *Student Projects and Activities for Business English and Communication*. Ten progress tests cover all the units of the textbook. In addition, an inventory test for use at the beginning of the course and a final examination for the end of the course are included. A facsimile key to the tests follows the tests at the back of the teacher's edition of *Student Projects and Activities for Business English and Communication*.

Acknowledgments

We would like to thank the following educators for their invaluable review comments on our program: Carolyn Fingar, East Bay High School, Gibsonton, Florida; Jeanette Hesse, Fountain Valley High School, Fountain Valley, California; Ann Hittle, Hinsdale Central High School, Hinsdale, Illinois; and Dorothy Querry, Altoona Senior High School, Altoona, Pennsylvania.

Kenneth Zimmer
Lyn R. Clark

C · O · N · T · E · N · T · S

FINAL MODULE   AUG 26, 1986

[handwritten: BEFORE OCT 29 SUBMIT ARTICLE FOR INDIVIDUAL PRESENTATION IN FRONT OF CLASSROO. (PUBLIC SPEAKING)]

CHAPTER 9   **Memos, Reports, and Other Communications   482**

PART 7   **DEVELOPING LISTENING
AND SPEAKING SKILLS   515**

CHAPTER 10   **The Art of Listening   516**

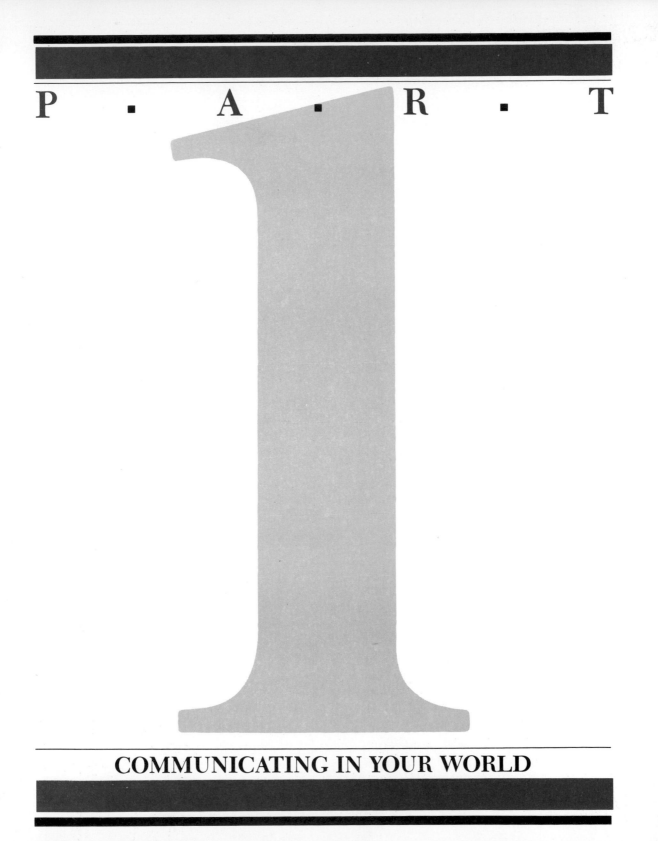

P . A . R . T

1

COMMUNICATING IN YOUR WORLD

Think about how much time you spend sending ideas *to* others or receiving ideas *from* others. When you are reading a report, listening to instructions, filling out an application form, or speaking about your interests, you are spending your time communicating.

Communication activities take skill. When you send a message to others, you want to be sure that the receiver of your message understands exactly what you mean. When you are receiving a message from someone, you want to be sure *you* understand what that person means. And how you send or receive messages is affected by modern technology.

To be an effective communicator, you need to know the importance of communication skills, both in your personal life and in your career. You also need to know how new and evolving technologies can affect your ability as a communicator. Given a situation requiring speaking, listening, reading, and writing skills, your mastery of the units in this chapter will enable you to do the following:

1. *Define the importance of effective communication in your personal and professional life.*

2. *Identify the kinds and levels of communication skills needed for success in your personal life, your personal business activities, and your chosen career.*

3. *Describe the impact that computer technology has made and will further make on all your roles as a communicator.*

4. *List ways that office technology—such as word processing, information processing, networking, and telecommunications—affects the communication process.*

1

Your Personal Need For Communication Skills

The ring of the telephone—someone wishes to speak with you. A knock at the door—the person on the other side is asking you to open it. The utterance of your name—the person speaking wants your attention. All these sounds are signals that someone wishes to communicate with you. That person has a message to convey.

The exchange of messages between and among human beings is known as communication. We send and receive messages in a variety of ways. The examples given above rely on sounds to send messages; other methods of message transmission include speaking, writing, gestures, and facial expressions. Listening, reading, and observing are the means we use to receive the messages sent. The most difficult task involved in the communication process is ensuring that the receiver interprets the message as the sender meant it to be interpreted.

This process is not so simple as it seems. Take, for example, the following case. Bill, a seventeen-year-old high school junior, received a telephone call from his friend John. John informed Bill, "I can't go to the beach with you tomorrow because I have to look for another job." "OK," responded Bill, "give me a call when you can go." So ended the conversation! When Bill hung up, he told his parents that John had lost his job at Reliable Pharmacy and had to look for another one. It was not until a few days later that the true circumstances were uncovered. John had not lost his job at the pharmacy; he was just looking for *another* part-time job to supplement the too few hours he was working at Reliable.

Why did this breakdown in communication occur? Both the sender and the receiver were at fault. The sender, John, gave too little information; he was not specific or concrete in conveying his message. Too many details were left to the imagination of the receiver. Bill, the receiver, was at fault too because he reached an unwarranted conclusion based upon the information given. Just because John was looking for another job, Bill should not have assumed that John had lost his previous one.

Miscommunication can occur easily in any situation—especially in our electronic age, where even the pressing of a button can send an incorrect message. That is why it is important for you to study the entire communication process and sharpen your verbal skills. To communicate effectively, you need to develop your abilities in speaking, writing, listening, and reading. You also need to understand the principles of communication psychology. This unit begins your study of the communication concepts necessary for success in your personal and business life.

Your Personal Communication

Communication begins early in life. The baby's cry provokes the parents' response. Is the baby hungry? Does he or she need to have a diaper changed? Is the cry for attention? The fact that the baby has a need is communicated by a simple cry. As children grow older, however, the communication process becomes more complex. Words become the means of communication, and to a considerable degree the extent of a person's vocabulary governs his or her ability to send and receive messages. Besides communicating with family members and friends, the child must learn to communicate effectively in school in order to prepare properly for later life.

Verbal Skills for Everyday Life. Communication skills are not important just for functioning among family members and friends and in school; they are also essential for functioning in everyday life. Reading, writing, speaking, and listening all play an integral part in our contemporary lifestyle. Take, for example, the communication involved in obtaining a driver's license.

Reading plays a prominent role. You must read the directions to fill in the application form. You must also read the driving manual issued by the motor vehicle department, since a knowledge of the rules and regulations of the road is essential to pass the written test. Reading skills are also necessary for actually taking the written test. Intricate questions, sometimes with tricky choices for answers, require critical reading skills. Road signs, too, not only require interpretive skills, but may also require reading skills.

Writing skills are needed to fill out the license application form. Correct information must be supplied clearly. Speaking skills come into play in asking questions, providing answers, and following through in the application process. Listening plays an especially important role in the practical test. If the examiner were to instruct you to turn left at the next intersection and you instead turned into the first driveway, you would decrease your likelihood of passing the examination. If you did not hear the instruction and continued to drive straight ahead, points would be deducted from your score. Equally serious results would occur if you were to misinterpret the instruction to turn left and instead turned right. Careful listening and appropriate interpretation govern your success in this and many other endeavors.

Skills to Avoid Misunderstanding. As you can see, the entire communication process plays a vital role in acquiring a driver's license. Communication skills are essential in many other aspects of the young adult's world. As an additional example, note the difficulties that can result from a communications breakdown in applying for a social security card.

Betty White, a sixteen-year-old high school sophomore, went to her local social security office to apply for a card. She already had obtained her first part-time job but needed the card to begin work. As instructed, Betty brought with her a copy of her birth certificate. She carefully filled out the application, using the name shown on her birth certificate, Elizabeth Jean White. Satisfied that she had completed all the requirements, Betty signed her application and went home.

A week later Betty's application was returned to her by mail with the request to resubmit it. You see, Betty had signed her application "Betty White" instead of "Elizabeth Jean White." Yet the instructions had clearly stated, "Sign name as shown on application." If Betty had signed her name correctly, she could have started her job a week earlier. Not reading the instructions carefully had cost Betty the wages she would have earned if she had signed the application correctly and begun work the prior week.

Your Personal Communication in the Business World

Even though you may never work in a business organization, you cannot escape communicating with business and government in conducting your personal business. Routine purchases of food, clothing, gas, and household supplies require reading, listening, and speaking skills. Reading labels and instructions carefully enables you to make proper and economical selections. Asking questions, making requests, giving instructions, and describing your needs all require precise and distinct speaking skills. Listening, too, is required to follow directions in meeting your personal purchasing needs.

Satisfying Your Needs as a Consumer. Purchasing a car, a home, life insurance, medical insurance, or a major home appliance requires communication skills. So do contractual agreements for home improvements, installment buying, or investment. Solving problems generated by faulty merchandise, insurance claims, legal matters, and medical concerns requires even more advanced communication skills. Not only will you rely on speaking, listening, and reading, but you also will draw on your writing skills for such tasks.

Notice how Steve Meister, a twenty-nine-year-old architectural drafter, solved this problem. The Itsumi electronic game he had purchased nearly two years ago was no longer working; one of the circuit boards was broken. Itsumi had no authorized repair stores in the city where he lived, so Steve had to write a business letter to solve his problem. This meant writing to Itsumi, explaining the nature of the problem, requesting shipment of the appropriate replacement part, and making arrangements for payment. This information needed to be stated simply, exactly, and clearly in his letter. To do this, Steve called upon his knowledge of spelling, grammar, writing style, message organization, and business-letter format—all areas you will be studying in this textbook.

Communicating With Government. Writing skills are essential for solving problems that may arise with government. Bertha Granados, a twenty-six-year-old nurse's aide, was shocked when she opened a letter that stated, "If the enclosed parking ticket is not paid within 30 days, a warrant will be issued for your arrest." Upon examining the enclosed parking ticket, Bertha saw that it had been issued in a city more than 90 miles from her home on a day that she had been working. After closer scrutiny, she noticed that the cited vehicle had the license plate number PUC 718. Bertha's license number was PUC 719! Evidently someone had made an error in entering the license number into the computer to locate the owner's name and address—a perfect example of miscommunication in our electronic age.

Nevertheless, Bertha was still faced with the problem of having to correct this situation. She could take a day off from work and drive 90 miles to this city's courthouse to rectify the situation, but why waste so much time and money when a well-written letter could achieve the same results? Bertha chose to write the letter. Again, skillful and clear expression was needed to ensure that the reader understood the circumstances and took the action requested.

Business Communication in the World of Work

No matter what occupation you select—office worker, accountant, electronic technician, business executive, nurse, flight attendant, construction worker, mail carrier, or computer programmer—you will need to deal with communications in the world of work.

Interactions in the Work Environment. In your work environment you will interact with co-workers, superiors, subordinates, customers, suppliers, and machines. You will be involved with face-to-face dialogues, telephone conversations, conferences, and committee meetings. All these activities will require you to exercise your speaking and listening expertise.

Media such as forms, letters, memorandums, reports, bulletins, news releases, meeting minutes, newsletters, and employee handbooks require reading and writing skills. At this point you may view yourself only as a reader of these documents, but your job may also involve your writing some of them. You may be asked to generate letters to customers and suppliers, memos to co-workers or subordinates, reports to superiors, or any of the other written documents that an organization produces.

Responsibilities for Written Communications. Take, for example, the array of written communiqués originating at the desk of a secretary. Simple phone messages may not seem too important; but think of the communication breakdowns that could occur if the secretary forgot to ask the name of the caller, jotted down the phone number incorrectly, misinterpreted the message, or even neglected to place the message on the recipient's desk.

One Monday a secretary took a phone message for a clothing department manager that read, "The shipment of dresses you inquired about should arrive by next Wednesday." Well, "next Wednesday" was too late for the weekend sale planned by the store, so the department manager removed this item from the newspaper ads announcing the bargains to be offered during the coming weekend.

When the dresses arrived on Wednesday in time for the sale, the department manager was confused. That is when she discovered that "next Wednesday" to her secretary meant "the next Wednesday occurring." To the department manager "next Wednesday" meant "not this immediate Wednesday but the one following it." Are you confused? Then there is little wonder that this message was misinterpreted. If the message had been written to say, "The shipment of dresses you inquired about should arrive by Wednesday, May 12," surely there would have been no doubt about the day in question.

Besides being responsible for preparing all kinds of written communiqués, a secretary sometimes must originate letters, memorandums, bulletins, and meeting minutes. The types of letter a secretary is asked to write frequently include acknowledging receipt of a document while the supervisor is away on a business trip, answering a routine inquiry or request, and writing a nonroutine order. A memo to the personnel department requesting a replacement for a terminating employee or a bulletin to other staff members informing them of telephone directory changes might be initiated by a secretary. And meeting minutes are more often than not the total responsibility of the secretary.

Persons in other occupations, too, are faced with originating a myriad of written documents. Salespeople draft letters to customers and suppliers, accountants prepare reports for clients, nurses chart patients' progress, insurance agents complete claims, and engineers write specifications. Almost all occupations require some kind of writing skill, and virtually all occupations require oral communication skills. Your success as a communicator may well measure your success in a chosen field. That is why it is important for you to improve your personal communication skills constantly.

COMMUNICATION LABORATORY

APPLICATION EXERCISES

A. Describe a situation, humorous or otherwise, in which you were involved and miscommunication occurred. What were the consequences? How could the misunderstanding have been prevented?

B. Select a person you know whom you would classify as an expert communicator. In your opinion, what skills does this person possess that make him or her successful?

C. Search your local newspaper for an article that cites a language barrier or misinterpretation as the cause of a problem (or at least a contributory cause). Summarize and report the circumstances to your class.

D. Keep a log of your significant communication activities for a day, two days, or a week. Prepare it in tabular format, using headings such as the following: "Date," "Time," "Persons Involved," "Summary of Content," "Communication Processes," and "Evaluation." Under "Evaluation," rate the effectiveness of the communication in the incident by using terms such as *Excellent, Good, Fair,* and *Poor.* The log can best be kept on 8½- by 11-inch paper, using the 11-inch side as the width. Note the details of any important conversations, telephone calls, business transactions, written materials, social encounters, or instructional programs in which you were involved. For each activity, determine which processes (listening, speaking, reading, writing) were used, and evaluate your success in completing the communication process.

E. Select a well-known local, national, or international personality. Describe why you feel this individual is a good or poor communicator. Give concrete examples to substantiate your judgment.

F. Select a friend, family member, or co-worker whom you have the opportunity to observe frequently. Evaluate that person's ability to communicate effectively. Give specific incidents to justify your opinion.

G. Communication skills are essential for job success. Choose one of the following occupations and discuss the various kinds of written communications needed to carry out the duties and responsibilities of this job classification.

1. salesperson
2. manager
3. nurse
4. electrician
5. accountant
6. word processor

H. Interview a member of your family or a member of a family close to you. Discuss the kinds of personal-business correspondence written by this family and the circumstances that prompted the correspondence. Inquire specifically about claim letters, inquiry letters, order letters, and letters to correct problems. Describe in detail at least two situations that resulted in specific letters or that could be resolved through letters.

I. Choose two activities in which you are presently involved—one that usually attracts your interest and one that rarely does so. Analyze the factors that contribute to making one activity so interesting and the other less so. Which of these factors can be related to the presence or absence of effective communication?

J. Select an occupation in which you are interested. Discuss the oral and written communication skills necessary for success in that job.

VOCABULARY AND SPELLING STUDIES

A. The following words were used in the text in this unit. Locate them in the dictionary and write the definition that relates to the word as it was used in the unit. Then construct a sentence using each word to show that you understand its meaning and use.

1. transmission
2. superiors
3. subordinates
4. expertise
5. generate
6. array
7. communiqués
8. recipient
9. originate
10. terminating

B. Words are not always spelled as they sound. For example, the sound of *f* in our language may be spelled *f, ff, ph,* or *gh.* The sound of *s* is prefaced with a silent *p* in *psychology.* Likewise, a number of other alphabetic sounds use different letters in the formation of words. Complete the spelling of the following words. Use the correct combination of letters to complete the alphabetic sound shown in parentheses.

1. al (*f*)abet
2. (*n*) eumonia
3. le (*j*) er
4. (*f*) nomenon
5. (*a*) rial
6. (*f*) armacy
7. bu (*j*) et
8. h (*i*) giene
9. (*s*) issors
10. s (*i*) ndicate

COMMUNICATING FOR RESULTS

Avoid a Mistake. You overhear the new salesclerk promise a customer that the latter's new dress will be delivered the following evening. As an experienced clerk, you know that the alterations will not be completed for three days and that it will take still another day for delivery. How can you convey the correct information to the customer without causing the new clerk to lose face?

2

Applying Communication Skills in the Business Network

Today's advancements have made it possible to send oral and written messages around the world in just a matter of seconds. Computers and electronic transmission systems have enabled business and government to speed up and improve the communication process. Data, voice, and graphic networks supply the technology for rapid communication and decision making.

These networks are composed of computer-based systems that "talk" to each other so that voices, images, and written data can be transmitted electronically and instantaneously. Within the last quarter century, this emerging new technology has caused a revolution in human communication. Think about the pace of human progress during the centuries of the past and compare it with the developments that have taken place during the last twenty-five years, and even the last ten years.

Early Communication

Human beings have communicated from the beginning of time. Communication probably began with grunts, gestures, and expressions. The origins of speaking and writing are unknown, but signs and symbols were added very early in the time line of human development.

Even in early times, people began to keep records. The Egyptians developed a picture language called *hieroglyphics*, while at the same time the Sumerians were writing on clay tablets with a system that used wedge-shaped signs. The Semites were the first to devise an alphabet, around 1500 B.C., and the Assyrians and Babylonians established libraries around 600 B.C.

Many historians attribute the invention of writing to the priests in these early societies. The need to recall the rituals and the secrets of healing provided the impetus for developing written records. Writing also allowed messages to be sent over considerable distances without revealing their contents to the messengers.

Writing was once taught only to scribes and priests. It was such a laborious and time-consuming process that it belonged only to a privileged few. Even with the development of the pen and quill, writing was such a chore that few people had ever seen a book, let alone owned one. Just imagine how long it would take you to copy by hand the pages of this textbook!

It was not until the invention of the printing press in the fifteenth century that knowledge was opened to everyone. Printing provided a more rapid and easy way to communicate. Although type needed to be set by hand, multiple copies could be run once the type had been set. Then, in the middle of the nineteenth century, a vehicle appeared that would speed up the printing process. Little did Christopher Scholes realize when he invented the typewriter that this machine would be the forerunner of the sophisticated equipment used in publishing and modern offices today. Some contemporary typewriters permit materials to be revised easily during and after the typing process, have printers that produce copies at thousands of words a minute, and are connected with systems that reproduce copies in seconds.

The New Technology

Civilization has progressed from the sign and symbol tediously chiseled into rock to our highly advanced technology, where the written word can be obtained almost instantaneously through machines. Human beings, however, must still generate the messages processed by these machines. People are responsible for the content, organization, wording, and format of the information processed. Therefore, users of modern technology must be skilled in the communication process. Your study of the principles and concepts in this textbook will prepare you to make effective use of the communication technology found in modern offices today.

The advanced technologies that have emerged during the last quarter century include word processing, information processing, and telecommunications. These new developments are combined in various degrees in the business communications network. Each is defined and briefly described for you in the following sections. In addition, the proposed merging of information processing and telecommunications that will result in single-terminal networking is previewed.

The Word Processing Concept

People have been processing words since the Semites developed the first known alphabet, but the concept of word processing as we know it today was introduced by the IBM Corporation in the early 1960s.

Word processing began with the release of the IBM typewriter known as the MT/ST. Since then, IBM and many other companies have introduced more sophisticated and advanced versions of this original design. Today the MT/ST may be viewed in the word processing industry as the Model T Ford is viewed in the automobile industry. The Model T Ford got you where you were going, but the modern-day Lincoln Continental will get you there faster, more comfortably, and with greater ease. Modern-day *word processing* now involves the use of a standardized set of procedures combined with text-editing equipment to produce written documents.

What Word Processors Can Do. To obtain a better understanding of word processing equipment, let us first look at its special components. Word processors have a typewriter keyboard. As data is entered into the word processor, each keystroke is recorded on a magnetic medium, much in the same manner as a voice is recorded on a cassette tape. If you wish to make a change on a cassette tape, all you need to do is erase and record over the present material. Similarly, if you make a keyboarding or typing error, all you need to do is backspace to erase the error from the magnetic medium and then retype the correct stroke in its spot.

With word processors you can also easily add and delete complete sentences and paragraphs. Once you have made all the corrections and revisions you wish in a letter, memorandum, report, or other document, you are ready to prepare the finished copy. Word processing printers read the magnetic medium and type out its contents error-free at speeds ranging from hundreds of words a minute to over a thousand words a minute.

What are the advantages of using word processing equipment to record typewritten material for playback to obtain finished copy? The equipment saves time in the production of business documents. Word processing operators can type at fast rates, just backspacing and retyping to correct keyboarding errors. No longer does a typist who makes a so-called "uncorrectable error" during the typing process have to start over.

Many times the same originally typed document must be sent to a number of different people or the same paragraph must be repeated in different documents. By recording these materials on word processing equipment, they may be played back as many times as necessary to obtain the number of originally typed copies needed.

Reports provide information that is often the basis for important decisions. The person who writes a report may rewrite it several times before it is ready for distribution. In the past the report had to be retyped with each rewrite, thereby necessitating the tedious process of keyboarding and proofreading the entire document. By recording the report on word processing equipment, only the changes need to be keyboarded and proofread; the remainder of the report remains unaltered, just waiting to be played out with the changes to form a revised final copy.

Word processing offers reduced costs and improved quality in written communications. Because it eliminates repetitive keystroking, reduces the time needed for proofreading, and prints error-free copy at hundreds of words a minute, word processors are playing a dominant role in American business and industry. What many experts in the late 1970s termed "the office of the future" is already the office of today in the 1980s.

The Modern Technology at Work. Who uses word processing equipment? For what purposes is it used? Frequent users include law firms, where many documents that require precise wording are produced. In addition, many legal documents contain large sections of wording that do not need to be changed for each new client. These standardized paragraphs are recorded on word processing equipment and recalled for the preparation of contracts, wills, trusts, agreements, dissolutions, testimonies, and many other legal documents.

Banks and savings and loan associations use word processing equipment to communicate with their current and prospective customers. Standardized form letters are entered into and stored by the word processing equipment. When a single letter needs to be sent to a list of customers, the standardized form can be retrieved and merged with the list of names to produce an originally typed letter for each name on the list. Similarly, many companies use word processing equipment to send collection letters to their delinquent accounts.

Hospitals and other health care facilities are large users of word processing equipment. The equipment is used to maintain lists of patients, prepare patients' files, and compile reports of diagnoses and examinations. Standardized examination reports are stored for each specialty, so the doctor need only dictate any abnormal conditions that may exist. Word processing equipment is also used for preparing financial statements, government and insurance reports, professional papers presented by staff members, public service bulletins, applications for special projects, and a variety of other documents.

Insurance companies use word processing equipment to keep track of and to communicate with their tremendous number of clients. Specialized types of communication are sent to those clients who carry certain kinds of insurance. Personalized letters prepared on word processors are also used to solicit additional business.

Businesses such as those in the aircraft industry, whose major revenue comes from government contracts, use word processing equipment to prepare proposals. Volumes of paperwork describing specifications, costs, and procedures need to be prepared before a contract can be awarded. Thousands of hours of editing and revision are required to prepare a proposal for submission, and word processing equipment eases the typing burden.

These are just a few applications of word processing equipment currently in use. In 1978 the market for word processing equipment reached $780 million. International Data Corporation, an independent consulting firm, estimated that the market would reach $4.2 billion in the United States by the mid-1980s.* Managers wish to boost the productivity of their office staff while communicators are eagerly awaiting new technologies to assist them in their jobs.

Information Processing— A Broader Perspective

Word processing in most instances refers to equipment that is capable of being used to edit and revise text. Many organizations use word processing equipment until they realize that their needs exceed the capabilities of this equipment; then these companies acquire equipment with information processing capabilities added.

*"Business Communication Alternatives for the Eighties," International Data Corporation, supplement to *Fortune*, December 14, 1979.

Information processing is the movement of words, symbols, or numbers from the origination of an idea to its destination. It is the manipulation of data by electronic means to collect, organize, record, and store information for decision-making purposes. Information processing equipment retains the text editing and revision function but has the capability to use the data in a wider range of applications. For example, the hospital that uses word processing equipment to prepare and maintain patients' records can upgrade its technology to obtain a list of patients with a specific disease or disorder, sort its patients' files according to admitting doctor, locate the patients admitted on a certain date, or compile information from the records for a research report. Expanded applications and capabilities can be achieved by *interfacing* (connecting) word processing equipment with computers or installing computer-based information processing equipment.

Picture the checkout stand of a modern supermarket. Notice how the clerk skims each product over a certain section of the counter top. Listen for the high-pitched beep as the name of the item and its price are recorded on the cash register tape. You, as a customer, may like this new procedure because it provides you with an itemized tape listing the specific product purchased and its price. To the grocery store, however, the new system provides information that was not as readily available before information processing technology. Now the store has complete inventory records on which to make purchasing decisions. How many frozen turkeys should be purchased for Friday? How many cases of a certain brand of canned peas are needed to restock its shelves? What products move slowly and should be discontinued? These questions and many more can be answered accurately and quickly to cut costs and increase profit—all through information processing technology.

The World of Telecommunications

The documents produced by word and information processing equipment discussed so far have been printed on paper and carried to their destinations by intracompany mail systems, the U.S. Postal Service, and private mail carriers. Since paper is associated with slow delivery and high costs, more companies are turning to electronic methods for transmitting information. Any information distributed electronically over telephone lines is called *telecommunication*.

You already know that information can be sent electronically through voice communications. Every time you make a telephone call, you are using a form of telecommunication. Perhaps you did not know, though, that printed words can also be sent electronically through telephone lines. It is possible to type a document on a terminal at one location, transmit it over telephone lines to another location miles away, and have it play back on a terminal at the destination. In just minutes, data can be communicated from city to city and from coast to coast.

Like printed words, graphic data may also be sent electronically. Copies of charts, graphs, maps, and diagrams may be sent from one location to another. An electronic device called a facsimile scans the copy to be sent, sends it over telephone wires, and produces a replica at the destination.

Teleconferencing is a type of video communication that involves sending pictures of people as well as voice and print communications. Once a teleconferencing room with the proper electronic equipment is rented, people in various locations can exchange ideas with gestures and facial expressions as well as through speaking, listening, and writing.

Presently the major carriers of telecommunication in business are telephone lines. However, scientists are continually experimenting with new technologies to move information more rapidly. Lasers, fiber optics, and satellites are all being explored further to speed up such business applications as teleconferencing and facsimile transmission.*

The Case for Networking

Computer communications will be the key to the office of this and future generations. There will be multiple lines that enable word processors and minicomputers to "talk" with big computers. In other words, computers will communicate with each other. Although it will still be possible to use word processors and small computers as isolated pieces of equipment, almost all such equipment will be capable of communicating with other computers.

Office workers will be able to generate all their communication from a single terminal. Small groups of terminals will be connected to a local computer, which in turn will be connected to one or more combinations of computers in national or even international networks.

What does all this mean to office workers? It means that communicators will be able to plug in to any computer within their network and gain access to any data stored by any of the computers in the network. It will be possible for office workers to have access to data stored anywhere in this country, and perhaps anywhere in the world. Business communicators and decision makers will be able to work at home and use a microcomputer to gain access into the network and retrieve any needed information.

Think of the networking process in much the same way as you think of the telephone. Today you can call anywhere in the world to obtain information. Tomorrow, with a terminal, you will be able to obtain information from computers throughout the world.

The communicator's terminal will not only provide access into computers, but it will also contain sophisticated text-editing equipment for processing messages electronically. Words and graphic data will take only seconds to be sent from one location to another on the same terminal that is used for all other communication processes. Separate pieces of equipment for each function will no longer be needed; all functions will be performed on a single terminal.

---

*Fiber optics are thin, transparent fibers of glass or plastic used to transmit light through internal reflections.

Networking is the newest dimension in communication technology. It opens up to the business communicator avenues never before explored. With such expanded access to information, however, the businessperson of the future must develop keen skills of analysis, organization, and verbalization to sort through the resources being made available by technology. Your study of the communication skills and knowledge in this textbook will better prepare you to deal with the office of today and the office of the future.

COMMUNICATION LABORATORY

APPLICATION EXERCISES

A. Visit your local public library or school library. Locate from a business periodical an article on any phase of word processing or information processing. Summarize in writing the important points brought out by the author of this article. Be prepared to share this article orally with the rest of the class.

B. Visit a local business or industry that uses word processing equipment. Describe briefly the equipment in use and the purposes for which it is used. Analyze whether the equipment is performing only word processing functions or whether it has been expanded to include information processing functions.

C. Visit your local Western Union office to inquire about telecommunication services. Describe the kinds of services offered by Western Union.

D. Collect mail samples prepared on word processing equipment or computers that have been sent to your home or to the homes of neighbors and friends. Although these materials have been prepared through electronic means, analyze their effectiveness as communication devices. Which of these devices were effective in accomplishing their purposes?

E. Visit your local public or school library. Locate at least one magazine article that discusses personal or home computers (microcomputers). Summarize the contents of this article. What impact do your foresee these computers having on your personal life?

VOCABULARY AND SPELLING STUDIES

A. Many words in computer language are fast becoming everyday words. Because a knowledge of certain terms will be necessary for successful communication, locate the definitions of the following terms. Copy the term and its definition on a separate sheet of paper.

1. communicating computer
2. microcomputer
3. minicomputer
4. interface
5. program
6. software
7. compatibility
8. intelligent word processor

B. What letter should appear in the blank space in each of these words?

1. perc___late
2. attend___nce
3. sep___rate
4. controver___y
5. p___rsuade
6. vet___ran

C. The following words are spelled as they are often incorrectly enunciated. A letter or syllable has been added or dropped. Respell all words correctly.

1. Wednesdy
2. canidate
3. filim
4. labratory
5. strenth
6. sophmore
7. probly
8. sufferage
9. naturly

COMMUNICATING FOR RESULTS

Urgent Message. You receive this telephone message: "Tell Ms. Takei I've been called out of town and can't see her until Thursday." Ms. Takei, your boss, is on the way to the airport to board a plane to the city of the caller. The plane is to leave in 45 minutes. How would you relay this urgent message to your boss? List alternative methods in case your first attempt fails.

P · A · R · T

2

DEVELOPING READING SKILLS

Reading many types of written communications will be part of your business experience, no matter what your job may be. As a reader, your success will be judged by how quickly you understand written messages. But reading written communications will be only part of your business experience. You will have to write many communications as well. As a writer, your success will be judged by how well you communicate your ideas. Since errors—even typographic ones—reduce your message's effectiveness, your skill in proofreading what you write relates directly to your success as a communicator.

It is easy to see why, then, that improving your reading and proofreading abilities will improve your effectiveness at your job. Given a situation that requires reading and proofreading, your mastery of the units in this chapter will enable you to do the following:

1. *Judge and explain which reading technique most benefits the purpose for which you are reading.*

2. *Increase your reading speed through timed practices.*

3. *Improve your reading comprehension.*

4. *Develop techniques to remember better what you have read.*

5. *Apply a systematic method for proofreading typewritten or printed documents.*

6. *Use editing symbols to indicate revisions in rough-draft materials.*

U · N · I · T

3 Improving Your Reading Skills

You already know the importance of reading in your personal life. Take a moment to reflect how your life would be if you were not able to read. You would be unable to drive a car, read your favorite magazine, understand the contents of your mail, or even follow instructions to play the latest in video games. The pleasure found in books, newspapers, and magazines would not be available to you. You wouldn't be able to install parts to repair your car, follow a new recipe, or select a menu item from your favorite restaurant.

As a student, you are aware that there is a close connection between school success and the ability to read well—but have you taken the time to consider that your reading ability may be even more important to you *after* you have completed your formal education? Whether you continue your education by attending college or decide to accept a business position after high school, reading will still contribute significantly to your life. Successful business and professional people spend much of their time reading all types of material—books, magazines, notices, bulletins, reports, memorandums, and letters, as well as other written materials that provide them with information that is essential to performing their jobs. Therefore, the greater your reading skill, the better equipped you will be to succeed in your chosen career.

Purpose Determines Reading Technique

The way in which you read should be determined primarily by your purpose in reading. When you read for pleasure alone, your reading is different from those situations in which you read to absorb information, as in studying. Therefore, you should always know your reading purpose so that you can better determine *how* you should read. Among the many purposes in reading, the following are probably the most used.

Reading for Pleasure. When reading for pleasure, it is not necessary to absorb every detail, to remember all facts, or to read critically. Therefore, you may read at a rapid rate such material as most novels and biographies and many magazine articles. Try to target your pleasure reading at 400 words a minute.

Reading for Specific Information. When hunting for information such as a name or date that is somewhere within a block of reading material, you should skip and skim in order to make the best use of your reading time. Skipping merely means jumping over large portions of material that are not needed to serve your reading purpose. Skimming means moving your eyes rapidly down a page of type, stopping to read only significant facts and phrases. When you wish to gain the main ideas and details of an article but are not sure beforehand what the article contains, you should both skim and skip. Most people read newspapers largely by skipping and skimming. They simply can't take the time to read every single word.

Reading to Absorb Information. Reading to study—to absorb information—is always required of you as a student, whether the reading is from a textbook or from some resource material. It calls for your active participation, since you must read for meaning and must remember what you read.

Reading for Copying and Checking. Most business writers, secretaries, typists, accountants, and clerical workers do a great deal of this kind of reading. Every prepared business document or typing job, every set of inventory figures that must be checked, and every invoice that must be compared with receiving reports and purchase orders requires careful reading. When such reading is done without concentration and without attention to meaning, errors may not be detected and corrected. So important to the student and the business worker is this type of reading that it will be discussed fully in the next unit.

Setting the Stage

Research has shown that the average executive spends half the business day reading, and reading experts say that two hours could be cut from this load by learning to read faster and with greater understanding. What about you? Does it take you longer than it should to read your assigned work? Do you dread reading because you have a feeling of plowing your way through? Do you have to spend so much time reading for some courses that you do not have enough time for others? If you said yes to any of these questions, then you *can* and *should* do something to improve your reading skills, beginning now. The suggestions in the remaining part of this unit will help you to get off to the right start.

Your Eyes. The first step in your reading improvement program is to make certain that your eyes are in good condition. There are many differences in different people's ability to see. One person may have difficulty seeing objects that are close, whereas another may find it difficult to see objects that are some distance away. If you must hold ordinary written material either very close to your eyes or at arm's length to read it, if the material you are reading seems blurred, or if your eyes tire easily, then you should consult an eye doctor. You may need to wear glasses, perhaps only for reading. If you already wear glasses, you may need to have them changed.

Whether or not you wear glasses, you should practice good eye hygiene. Here are a few suggestions:

1. Rest your eyes every half hour or so by looking into the distance or by closing your eyes for a few minutes.
2. Exercise your eyes from time to time, particularly after doing close work. One good eye exercise is to rotate the eyes slowly, without moving your head. Move your eyes far to the right; then to the left; then up; and finally, down. These exercises will help to strengthen your eye muscles.
3. Avoid reading in bright sunlight or while riding in a car, train, or other vehicle.
4. Have eye injuries or sties attended to at once by a doctor.

Reading Conditions. Poor lighting contributes to eye fatigue and blurry vision. Of course, nonglaring daylight provides the best light for reading, and light-colored walls permit the best use of daylight. Indirect lighting, rather than semidirect or direct lighting, is the best artificial lighting. Therefore, make certain that there are no glaring lightbulbs visible to the eyes or any other glaring spots anywhere near where you are reading.

For the best reading conditions, sit comfortably in a well-ventilated (not overheated) room that is free from distracting sights and sounds. Above all, do not attempt to do serious reading with the radio, television, or stereo on.

Increasing Your Speed

As discussed earlier, how rapidly you should read depends upon the type of material you are reading and the purpose for which you read. Most "light" reading should be at a rate of at least 400 words a minute. Most studying and other serious reading should be at a rate of at least 200 to 250 words a minute.

There are technical aids for improving reading speed, and reading specialists may be consulted for assistance. However, there are a number of things you can do on your own to improve your reading speed. If you follow these six suggestions, you should soon note an increase in your reading speed. (If you already are a fast reader, these suggestions will help you to read still faster.)

Read in "Thought Units." When you read in phrases, or thought units, rather than word by word, your eyes take in more words before each pause. Since you make fewer pauses on each line, you automatically read faster. To illustrate, read these short lines and notice the difference in your reading time for each line:

1. f d z r t m
2. climbing of spell
3. read for meaning

You probably read each line with ease, but reading the first line took longer than reading the second line, and the second line took longer than the third. Why? Because in the first line, you read *six* individual letters; in the second, you read *three* individual words; but in the third, you read *one* entire phrase.

You should be able to read a newspaper column line with one or two eye pauses and a book-width line with not more than four or five pauses. Now read the following sentence, noticing the difference in speed when you read it word by word and when you read it in phrases.

You / are / more / likely / to / understand / and / remember / what / you / read / if / you / actively / participate / in / what / you / read.

You are more likely / to understand and remember / what you read / if you actively participate / in what you read.

Reading in phrases means reading in *units of thought*. Reading this way enables you to understand better what you read, because sentences—complete thoughts—are made up of these smaller thought units.

Phrase reading will also increase your understanding of what you read. Because slow readers usually *think* much faster than they can read, their thoughts often wander. On the other hand, phrase readers receive ideas from the printed page more rapidly and thus keep their minds so busy that they do not have time to let their thoughts wander. Therefore, the fast reader—the phrase reader—usually gets better results from reading.

Keep Eyes Moving From Left to Right. Once you have read a phrase, do not allow yourself to go back and read it a second time. Such backward movements of the eyes are called *regressions*, and they slow the reader considerably. For the untrained reader, these regressions become a habit. Force yourself to get the meaning of a phrase the first time; force yourself to concentrate. This forcing yourself calls for practice and discipline, as well as for eliminating all distractions that might interfere with your reading.

Keep Lips and Tongue Motionless. Don't spell or pronounce the words you are reading, not even inwardly. Such vocalization slows down your reading; it makes you read silently only as fast as you can read aloud.

Read Word Beginnings. You can identify the following portions of words without seeing the entire word: *undoub——, remem——, partici——.* (You can tell from the rest of the sentence whether the last word should be *participate, participating,* or *participation.*)

Keep Building Vocabulary. Follow the suggestions made in Unit 5 for increasing your vocabulary. The more words you have at your command, the fewer pauses you will have to make to check the meanings of words and the faster you will read. Also, when your mind instantly recognizes words, you will understand better what you are reading.

Constantly Practice. Continual increase in reading speed means exercising your willpower and continually practicing rapid reading. If you force yourself always to read a little faster than is comfortable, rapid reading soon will become a habit.

Increasing Your Understanding

Reading speed is very important to both students and business workers. However, even more important than speed is understanding (comprehension) and remembering (retention) what you have read. Some of the suggestions made for increasing your reading speed will also contribute to your greater understanding. Developing a wide vocabulary is one example. Reading in thought units is another. Both contribute a great deal to understanding and to speed. The following suggestions will further help to improve your reading comprehension, as well as your ability to remember what you read.

Scan or Preview the Material. First look over the material to be read, noting the main headings and subheadings, looking at the illustrations, and reading captions and numbered portions. This preliminary survey will help you to determine your purpose in reading, and it will also reinforce important points that you want to remember.

Think As You Read. You will understand what you read more fully if you read actively—if you try to relate what you are reading to what you already know. You must also constantly keep in mind the problem you wanted to solve when you started to read. This takes a high degree of concentration. It demands that you be on the lookout for main ideas and also for the way in which the author arranges these ideas to reach a conclusion.

Study all illustrative material, such as pictures, graphs, and charts, as well as the footnotes; all these are designed to explain and to expand the main ideas. Be sure, too, to read examples presented by the author. Often these examples will help to clarify an idea that at first may seem hazy to you. They will also help you to remember main ideas.

Make Brief Notes. If you own the book or magazine you are reading, you may wish to underline or circle some key words or phrases. Or you may wish to make marginal notes. If the publication is not yours, you may want to make notes in a notebook to use for future reference.

How do you select the essential material for notes? Just record main ideas and related ideas. Never take verbatim (word-for-word) notes, even if you know shorthand.

How do you find the main ideas? Usually writers convey only one idea in each paragraph. Often this main idea is in the first sentence, but sometimes it may be in the last sentence. Occasionally there may be two central ideas expressed in a key phrase or sentence within the paragraph. If you have difficulty in finding a central idea, you may need to read the paragraph carefully two or three times.

Reread and Review. How often you reread or review the material will depend upon its difficulty and the use you plan to make of the material. Often a quick skimming or rereading of your notes will be adequate for review if the first reading was done carefully.

If you immediately put into practice the suggestions made in this unit, not only will you reap dividends in terms of improved schoolwork but also you will see these dividends assist your professional growth.

COMMUNICATION LABORATORY

APPLICATION EXERCISES

A. Everyone does some reading every day. Make a list of your typical reading activities, including reading for school and reading that you do for your own personal reasons. After each activity, indicate the approximate percent of total reading time you spend on that particular activity. An example of a reading activity with a percent of total reading time would be: "Textbook reading for school—40 percent."

B. On another sheet of paper, indicate your professional goal. Then write a short essay (about 350 words) telling how you will use reading in your professional life and how your reading can contribute to your professional growth.

C. To get an idea of your reading speed, have someone time you with a stopwatch as you read the following excerpt from a report issued by the Disney Corporation to introduce its popular feature at Disney World, Epcot Center.

Disney World's Epcot Center—Spaceship Earth

The architecturally unique Spaceship Earth globe forms a breathtaking entrance to Epcot Center. Entering Future World, visitors pass directly beneath this glistening geosphere which reaches a height surpassing that of the Walt Disney World Contemporary Resort Hotel. Within this theme structure, a swirling time journey retraces the increasingly important role of communications in mankind's survival.

Upon entering Spaceship Earth, guests become time travelers taken back to the age of Cro-Magnon man. The caveman's attempts to record his experiences are seen as the earliest contribution to the development of written communication. We'll survey other communication milestones such as the Egyptians' development of hieroglyphics and the Phoenician alphabet which established the foundation for modern alphabets.

Dramatic communication is born in the Greek theater, becoming a poetic expression of ideas and philosophy. Another stopping point in the journey, Gutenberg's 15th century print shop, is the setting for a communications revolution.

More centuries pass and we're propelled into the Age of Invention. A stream of inventions—the telegraph, telephone, radio, motion pictures, television—bring the dream of instant communication to reality.

Accelerating into space-age technology, we find ourselves within a maze of computer impulses and are electronically transmitted into space aboard a burst of telemetry. Momentarily suspended in the heavens, we gaze down upon our small planet, our Spaceship Earth, adrift in the midnight sky. Having relived our past and eyed our future, we time passengers are ready to become captains, to chart our earth's course toward tomorrow and determine our own destinies.* (250 words)

Note the time it took you to read the above selection. Then locate this time in the following chart. Your reading speed will be opposite the time. For example, if you read the above paragraphs in 50 seconds, your reading speed is 300 words a minute; if it took you one minute, your speed is 250 words a minute. Most material such as this should be read at a rate no slower than 300 words a minute. How does your speed compare?

Reading Time	Reading Rate
30 seconds	500 wam
40 seconds	375 wam
50 seconds	300 wam
1 minute	250 wam
1 minute 10 seconds	215 wam
1 minute 20 seconds	190 wam
1 minute 30 seconds	165 wam
1 minute 40 seconds	150 wam
1 minute 50 seconds	135 wam
2 minutes	125 wam

D. Without rereading the paragraphs in Exercise C, write a brief synopsis of them. Use your own words. Then compare your summary with the selection. Were you accurate? complete?

E. Be prepared to read aloud in class the paragraphs in Exercise C, thus demonstrating your ability to read for meaning.

F. One good reading habit that will help you gain speed is to look only at the beginnings of familiar words rather than at the entire words. Test your ability to do so by reading as rapidly as possible the following paragraphs in which the endings of some familiar words have been omitted.

Your abil____ to read is of____ taken for gran____. Aren't you, there____, surp____ when you hear someb____ make the state____ that read____ is and prob____ always will be one of the most useful and most impor____ skills taught in sch____?

*Copyright © 1982, Walt Disney Productions.

Your work in elem_____ school, high sc_____, and col_____ is great_____ affec_____ by your abil_____ to read. As a stu_____, you must be able to read qui_____ and thoro_____. You must be ab_____ to read fast enough so that you will have ti_____ for some pers_____ relax_____.

In busi_____ you will have to read corres_____ and other writ_____ mater_____ rela_____ to the busi_____ activ_____ in which you eng_____ ev_____ day.

VOCABULARY AND SPELLING STUDIES

A. A skillful reader should have a well-developed vocabulary. Indicate whether the italicized word has been used correctly in each of the following sentences. If not, what is the correct word?

1. The committee *past* the motion quickly.
2. No one will *except* the responsibility for the error.
3. I drove 15 kilometers *further* than you did.
4. Joan and Phil followed the *recipe* for making that dip.
5. We need your *presents* at the meeting today.

B. Should *ance* or *ence* be added to the following?

1. accord_____
2. dilig_____
3. experi_____
4. resembl_____
5. appli_____

6. remembr_____
7. correspond_____
8. abund_____
9. evid_____

C. Should *er, or,* or *ar* be added to the following?

1. counsel_____
2. gramm_____
3. betray_____
4. collect_____
5. propell_____

6. advertis_____
7. supervis_____
8. profess_____
9. prosecut_____

COMMUNICATING FOR RESULTS

Reducing Reading Time. Larry managed to get through high school, but when he got to college, Larry began to have difficulty passing his courses. He had a great many reading assignments and often had to stay up until after midnight. Even then, he often could not complete all the required reading. What advice would you give Larry so that he will not have to spend so much time on reading assignments and neglect both his much-needed sleep and some opportunity for recreation?

4 Transferring Your Reading Skills to Proper Proofreading

In business, writers are responsible for their own communications. If an error appears that results in misunderstanding, it is the fault of the business writer, regardless of who may have typed the letter, memorandum, report, or other written communication. The ultimate responsibility for the content and presentation of a document lies with the business writer. That is why it is important for the document originator to be able to proofread accurately.

Just because business writers carry the major responsibility for the documents they generate, this does not mean that secretaries, typists, word processors, or clerks who assist with the preparation are blameless for any errors that are not corrected. Such administrative support personnel will not hold their jobs long if they allow many errors to go undetected. They, too, must become expert proofreaders to ensure that the communication process will function smoothly, efficiently, and professionally.

Imagine the consequences of a simple typing transposition. What if you were a building contractor and wrote a client saying that you could complete a room addition for $23,450? The client accepts your offer. However, when you check your original records containing your calculations, you find that the correct quotation for this particular job should have been $32,450—$11,000 more than the cost you submitted! A simple transposition error not caught in the proofreading process can result in a substantial financial loss.

Other errors may not have such direct consequences. Incorrect spellings, strikeovers, improper formatting, typographical errors, capitalization errors, and other such mistakes, though, can create a poor image in the mind of the receiver. Errors in written documents diminish the reader's confidence in the writer and create communication barriers. You, as a business communicator, need always to present your most positive image. By developing keen proofreading skills, your documents will be error-free and assure the reader of your abilities.

Proofreading skills can be acquired through study and practice. A thorough knowledge of grammar principles, correct spelling, proper punctuation, capitalization, number-usage rules, and word division principles is needed to exercise precise proofreading techniques. These principles are all part of your study of business English and communication and are thoroughly covered in the units that follow. In addition to having the needed knowledge, the expert proofreader must approach the task in an organized and methodical fashion. A recommended procedure includes the following steps: (1) skim and check for format errors, (2) read carefully for typographical and content errors, and (3) review for inconsistencies. Each of these important steps is discussed fully in the following sections.

Skim and Check for Format Errors

The first step in the proofreading process is to skim the document for any format errors. For example, if you were proofreading a business letter, you would need to check the placement of the various letter parts: the date, the inside address, the complimentary close, the signature lines, the reference initials, and any enclosure or copy notations. Are the margins even? If indented paragraphs were used, are all new paragraphs indented uniformly? Is the letter placed properly on the page? These questions could be answered quickly by skimming the document.

All the parts separate from the body of a document need to be checked individually. In a report, the title, subtitles, and footnotes need to be reviewed. Introductory "To," "From," and "Subject" lines in the memorandum require special attention, and in the business letter the inside address must be scrutinized carefully. To illustrate the appropriate approach, let us examine a method for checking the following business-letter inside address:

Ms. Carol Irwin
9543 Black Hawk Street
Albuquerque, NM 87122

Ask yourself the following questions. Has the correct courtesy title been used? Is the name spelled correctly (Carole or Carol, Irwin or Erwin)? Are the numbers in the street address and ZIP Code accurate? Are the street and city names spelled correctly? And don't forget to make sure that you have used the correct two-letter abbreviation for the state. By verifying step by step all the information in the inside address, you can ensure that it is correctly written.

Read for Typographical and Content Errors

The second step in the proofreading process is to read the body of the document for a variety of typographical and content errors. You need to develop an awareness of the kinds of errors for which you are looking and a skill in spotting them during a single reading.

Typographical Errors. Probably one of the easiest kinds of typographical errors to recognize is the error of transposition. Notice how this type of error stands out in the following sentence.

Mail your check in hte enclosed envelope.

As a proofreader, you need to indicate that the letters *h* and *t* must be reversed. Standard revision marks provide the tool to show easily the adjustments needed, and these symbols should be learned by the business writer. See how the transposition error in the previous sentence is marked for correction.

Mail your check in t͡he enclosed envelope.

The transposition symbol may be expanded in use to indicate a reversal of words, phrases, clauses, or even sentences.

Other obvious typographical errors include omitted letters, extra letters, and incorrect letters. Corrections for these kinds of errors are shown below:

omi^t̲ed letter

e͡xtra letter

in^c̲orrect letter

To show an insertion, use a caret (∧) to indicate where the additional letter should be placed. This mark may also be used to show the insertion of entire words or word groups. For letter deletions use a left-slanted diagonal line (\ ) through the unwanted letter; close up the extra space with loops above and below (◯). Incorrect letters can be changed easily by running the left-slanted diagonal through the incorrect letter and then writing the correct letter directly above the diagonal.

Less obvious typographical errors can be hidden because they seem to blend in with the rest of the typewritten material. Read the following sentences carefully:

Several of the nightstand were damaged in transit.

May we hear form you by May 20.

Only by reading for meaning can you locate the errors in the above examples. That is why the accurate proofreader not only must look at the words but also must read the content for meaning and make the necessary corrections. Would you have changed the sentences like this, based on your knowledge of revision marks?

Several of the nightstand∧ˢwere damaged in transit.

May we hear f͡rom you by May 20.

PROOFREADING PRACTICE 1

In this unit, and in all the other grammar, punctuation, and style units in this text, Proofreading Practice exercises are provided to help you master the principles you are studying.

Check your understanding of the proofreading techniques discussed so far. On a separate sheet of paper, write the numbers from 1 to 8. Read the following sentences and locate any typographical errors; write the incorrect word as it is shown in the sentence. Then use the appropriate revision mark to show the needed change. If a sentence is correct as shown, write *OK* on your paper.

1. Please order an additional supply of gauze adn bandages for our first-aid kit.
2. We have stilll not received the signed forms from your agent.
3. When do you expect the reprt to be completed?
4. Some of our client should be notified of the higher insurance premiums.
5. As soon as we receive your approval, we will ship your order.
6. Please credit my acsount for $35.85, the cost of the dress I returned on January 7.
7. Be sure to renew you subscription to *Time* magazine by returning the enclosed postcard today.
8. The tour group will spend one week in Callifornia.

As you are reading for content, be alert for omitted words. Make sure that each sentence makes sense.

For further information please your local sales representative.

This sentence does not make sense without the missing word; the reader does not know what action is to be taken. Should the reader write, telephone, see, contact, or ask the local representative? Notice how this error of omission can be corrected.

For further information please~telephone~ your local sales representative.

Sometimes errors cannot be detected just by reading the copy. The finished typewritten copy needs to be compared with the rough draft. Can you locate the error in the following sentence?

The balance in your account will earn interest at the rate of 7 percent compounded daily.

Probably not! You see, the omitted word does not obviously cloud the meaning. The sentence was supposed to have read, "The balance in your *checking* account will earn interest at the rate of 7 percent compounded daily." The word *checking* is necessary because it clarifies which account, but this error might not have been discovered unless the proofreader checked the final copy against the rough draft. Therefore, in the proofreading process, be sure to check the revised copy against the original copy for errors of omission. Do not limit this check to single-word omissions, but look for omissions of word groups and sentences as well.

Delete repeated words and lines by drawing a straight horizontal line through them. Some single repeated words may appear within the same line, but they generally occur at the end of one line and at the beginning of another. Notice the corrected example that follows.

> We plan to install the new word processing equipment, the laser printer, and and the central dictation unit next week.

Repeated lines are usually caused by an identical word appearing elsewhere in the copy. Study the following example to see how this error occurred and how the correction was handled.

> Line repetition errors usually occur when vocabulary in a document is repeated. The typist often shifts focus and returns to the inappropriate spot. The document is ~~repeated. The typist often shifts focus and returns to the inappropriate spot.~~ ~~The document is~~ then typed with an extra line, one repeated from earlier copy.

PROOFREADING PRACTICE 2

On a separate sheet of paper, copy the following sentences. Use the proper revision marks to show your corrections.

1. We hope to open our new in January.
2. Who will be manufacturing the movable parts for our new line of exer-exercise equipment?
3. When is the new hospital wing scheduled to be be completed?
4. Our attorney has promised to the contracts prepared by June 7.
5. All our salespeople were asked to work overtime to complete the inventory January 4.
6. Two of our older stores and our new warehouse need to have more up-up-to-date security systems installed.

Number Errors. All figures should be checked for accuracy. First, ask yourself, "Does the number make sense?" If you saw the weight of a newborn infant stated as 70 pounds, you might suspect that this was an error and that the typist may have meant to type 7 pounds. If the price of a 21-inch color television set was stated as $195, you might conclude that the first digit had been mistyped. Likewise, if a ZIP Code appeared as 911135, you would know that an error had occurred; ZIP Codes contain five digits, not six. Reading for sense helps you locate obvious numerical errors.

Other errors need to be checked against copy to be identified. To make sure the numbers in the rough draft and final copy coincide, follow these procedures. For a long number, count the digits in the original copy and make sure the same number of digits appears in the copy being checked. Then compare in groups of three the digits in the original with the digits in the copy.

In some cases it may be necessary to verify computations and recalculate totals. Be sure to think through each calculation so that errors in reasoning will not be duplicated. Approach the verification process as if it were a new problem. This outlook will enable you to find errors that otherwise might be overlooked.

PROOFREADING PRACTICE 3

On a separate sheet of paper, write the numbers from 1 to 12. Compare the figures in Column A with those in Column B; use revision marks to make any necessary corrections in the figures appearing in Column B. If no corrections are needed, write *OK* on your paper.

A	B
1. PL 873569213	1. PL 873569123
2. 567-45-7479	2. 567-45-7749
3. (212) 985-8421	3. (213) 985-8421
4. San Diego, CA 92143-1896	4. San Diego, CA 921143-1896
5. November 12, 1968	5. November 21, 1968
6. Serial No. 8968437291	6. Serial No. 8968437291
7. (805) 998-5481	7. (805) 998-5471
8. 9845 West 82 Street	8. 9846 West 82 Street
9. $13,847.96	9. $13,874.96
10. JK54321876	10. JK84321786
11. 8259467831	11. 825946831
12. 432-82-8987	12. 432-882-8987

Spelling Errors. Keep handy an up-to-date dictionary as you proofread, and look up any words whose spelling you doubt. Use the appropriate revision symbols to show any corrections that need to be made.

Sometimes spelling errors may be viewed as typographical errors and vice versa. It does not matter what kind of error has occurred; the important consideration is that the error is noted and corrected. See how the following error was changed:

Your busⁱness cards will be ready for delivery on May 24.

Punctuation Errors. Internal punctuation marks may be added to copy by using the insertion mark; just place the comma, semicolon, or colon inside the caret at the point of insertion. Closing punctuation marks (periods, question marks, and exclamation marks) may be added to copy without insertion marks; periods are circled to make them more visible.

Vans⸍campers⸍and trucks are prohibited from parking in Lot A⊙
Your brother was here Friday⸍when may we expect you⸘

Extra or incorrect punctuation marks may be deleted by using the left-slanted diagonal. If another punctuation mark must be substituted, just delete or change the incorrect mark and follow the procedures for inserting the correct one.

ORIGINAL: The sale ended last week, therefore we are unable to fill your order at the sale prices?

REVISION: The sale ended last week, therefore we are unable to fill your order at the sale prices?

ORIGINAL: On April 3, may we send you the following items; 12 boxes printed letterhead, 8 boxes printed memorandum forms, and 24 boxes legal-sized envelopes.

REVISION: On April 3, may we send you the following items: 12 boxes printed letterhead, 8 boxes printed memorandum forms, and 24 boxes legal-sized envelopes.

Grammar Errors. Pay close attention to the grammatical construction of sentences in the copy you are proofreading. Watch for errors in subject-verb agreement, noun plurals and possessives, compound adjectives, and other such commonly misused principles of grammar. Use the revision marks you have learned so far to make any necessary changes.

PROOFREADING PRACTICE 4

Recopy the following sentences on a separate sheet of paper. Then make any necessary corrections using the revision marks presented in this unit.

1. On several occassions we have tried to contact you personally about your overdue account.
2. You may wish to visit our showroom, on Benton Street.
3. We was very surprised to learn that Dr. Sanchez is not accepting any new patients.
4. When may we expect to hear from you.
5. The hotel cannot accomodate an organization the size of ours.
6. Please fill in your name address and telephone number on the enclosed form.
7. When will the latchs on the cupboard door be repaired?
8. As soon as we recieve the information, we will send it to you.

Capitalization Errors. While you are proofreading, look for those words that should be capitalized and are not. At the same time, be alert for those words that have been capitalized but should appear in lowercase letters. A good source for determining whether a word should be capitalized is *The Gregg Reference Manual*, Fifth Edition, by William A. Sabin (Gregg Division, McGraw-Hill Book Company, New York, 1977).

To show that a letter should be capitalized, place three short lines under it; to capitalize entire words, underline the word or word group three times.

Please contact the American supply company for further information today!

Mr. Desoto will be flying to the west coast tomorrow.

Use a right-slanted diagonal through a capital letter that should appear in lowercase form. Words appearing in all-capital letters that should be written in a combination of capital and lowercase letters may be changed by using the right-slanted diagonal in conjunction with a straight horizontal line.

Your Martinsville China Cabinet will be delivered by AVERY AIR FREIGHT SERVICES the week of December 2.

Number-Usage Errors. Number-usage rules dictate that some numbers be written in figure form and others be written in word form. When proofreading copy, check to see that each number is expressed in the proper format. If a figure should be spelled out, merely circle it. If a number in word form should be expressed in figure form, draw a horizontal line through the incorrect expression and above it write the correct figure or figures.

Last week 5 of our sales personnel each sold over $30,000 thirty thousand dollars in video recording accessories.

PROOFREADING PRACTICE 5

Proofread the following sentences. On a separate sheet of paper, write the error or errors as they are shown in each sentence. Use revision marks to make the necessary corrections.

1. We have only 1 suggestion to offer you for this next sales period.
2. How many english classes have been scheduled for this semester?
3. Please purchase new Refrigerators, OVENS, and Ranges for the apartments in this complex.
4. Because she applied for a sensitive government job, the fbi had to interview her.
5. We received one hundred thirty-two applications for the sales position.
6. These records must be sent to pacific indemnity insurance company by this afternoon.

Review for Inconsistencies

Once a document has been proofread carefully, it should be checked an additional time for any inconsistencies. Some of these inconsistencies may have been recognized in the initial reading. Less conspicuous ones, though, need to be located through a separate inspection after the document has been read thoroughly.

Check to make sure that courtesy titles have been used consistently throughout. If "Dr. Guffey" is used in one place, "Mrs. Guffey" in another, and "Ms. Guffey" in still another, then revisions are in order. More than likely, "Dr. Guffey" is correct and should be used in all three places.

Spellings of names and references to companies and associations should be consistent. Is the spelling Guffey or Guffy? Clark or Clarke? McDonald or MacDonald? Whichever one it may be, be sure it is correct consistently throughout the document. If California State University, Los Angeles, is generally referred to as CSULA, then make sure that any "Cal State" references are changed to CSULA. Similarly, if a company called Midwest Medical Equipment and Supply is generally referred to as Midwest Med, then any attempt to also call this company MMES would be incorrect. Be consistent in the use of shortened forms for the same company, group, association, or government body.

Check for inconsistencies in number usage. For example, if a certain set of numbers is presented in figure form in one section, be sure that similar sets of data are presented in figure form also. Double-check the accuracy of dates and times. If you plan to meet someone on Monday, August 10, be sure your calendar shows August 10 to be on a Monday. If you will arrive at your hotel by ten on Thursday, June 23, be sure to let the reservations clerk know whether you mean 10 a.m. or 10 p.m.

Once you have checked the document for inconsistencies, the proofreading process has been completed. The material is now ready to be prepared in final form if you have followed the procedure recommended in this unit.

Revision Marks

Revision marks provide a concise, organized method for noting changes on rough drafts, manuscripts, and other documents. By using consistently the same symbols to indicate certain changes, you are minimizing the opportunities for communication failure with the preparer of the final document. Whether the preparer is a printer, a typist, or even yourself, these symbols will convey a uniform set of instructions that will result in error-free copy.

The revision marks you have learned so far, as well as several others you will need as a proofreader, are shown below. Learn them and practice using them as often as you can.

Transpose letters	thier
Transpose words	to directly call you
Insert letter	leter
Insert word or words	charge account / a customer
Delete stroke	typewriterk
Delete stroke and close up space	typewritter
Delete punctuation mark	on May 5, we
Change stroke	correspondance
Omit word or word group	charge account customer
Change word or word group	book which we sent / that
Capitalize letter	bushnell corporation
Use all capitals	stop sign

Use lowercase letter	the ₵ompany
Use a series of lowercase letters	FDI C∅RPORATION
Insert comma, semicolon, or colon	now⋀not Friday⋀so do the following⨀
Insert period, question mark, or exclamation mark	⨀ ? !
Spell out	⑩
Close up space	sales‿person
Insert a space	in⋀addition
Hyphenate	up⸗to⸗date files
Underscore	call me <u>collect</u>.
Restore word or words deleted	stock ~~and bond~~ certificates
Start new paragraph	¶ May we have your
Delete paragraph	No¶ This information is
Indent five spaces	5] In the future
Single-space	When we receive your report⌉SS we will
Double-space	One of our sales representa-⌉DS tives
Move as indicated	(at your discretion)
Move to the left	[Send in your report
Move to the right	] Send in your report
Center	] January 25, 1986 [

COMMUNICATION LABORATORY

APPLICATION EXERCISES

A. On a separate sheet of paper, write the numbers from 1 to 20. Proofread the following sentences. If a sentence contains an error, write the error on your paper. Then use the appropriate revision mark to make the necessary correction. If a sentence does not contain an error, write *OK* on your paper.

1. We should have your test results by September Fifth.
2. Several customers their receipts at the counter.
3. When will you return from your vacation.

4. Your apointment with Dr. Eckles has been changed to May 3.
5. Be sure to have copies of your records mailed to oklahoma state university.
6. Did you receive a signed reciept for the payment?
7. We do not except any second-party checks.
8. It appears that the ammount of this check has been altered.
9. Lisa is the eldest of eihgt children.
10. Give the report to John Ellen or Chris.
11. Our local High School is sponsoring a bake sale to help build the new auditorium.
12. Only three of our salespersonnel have met their quotas for this month.
13. We can not guarantee that interest rates will not rise during the next three months.
14. None of the offices, in our building, are vacant.
15. The florist is unable to deliver the flowers as you requested.
16. Please send us you answer by the end of next week.
17. Because of her outstanding recomendations, we are offering Ms. Scott a full-time teaching contract.
18. Our offices have been moved to the medical arts building.
19. Have you asked Proffessor Jackson to send a copy of his résumé to our main office?
20. We will need your check for for $60 by November 14 to hold your reservation.

B. Proofread the following excerpt from a business letter and on a separate sheet of paper make a list of the errors. Then rewrite the excerpt, correcting the errors.

> We received you letter of Febuary 15 and the check for $165 enclosed. Every store appreciate the patronage of it's customers. We have credit your account for $165 and hope that their will be many more opportunity to serve you.

C. Reading carelessness when checking amounts of money and other figures often leads to problems. Compare the following two lists. On, a separate sheet of paper, indicate which pairs of numbers do not agree. Follow the style used in the example.

	List A	List B		Do *Not* Agree
0.	1234567	1235467	0.	X
1.	$768,967	$786,967	1.	_____
2.	987654	986754	2.	_____
3.	$3,232.33	$3,232.33	3.	_____
4.	654A765	654A765	4.	_____
5.	897898V	897889V	5.	_____
6.	R787899T	R787989T	6.	_____

D. Proofread the following letter. On a separate sheet of paper, list the errors that appear. Then use revision marks to show the needed corrections.

Dear Msr. Rosennelli:

We welcome you as a charge acount customer of marsha's department store. Enclosed is your charge card and a broshure discribing our charge plan. We hope that you will take advantage of our many bargins and use you card often.

This month we are featuring a sale on famous-brand stainless steel cookware. All pots and frying pans inthis line have been from 25 to 50 persent. If you need to replace your cookware now is the time to do so. Also, if your need a wedding gift for the June bride, consider giving this fine cookware.

What ever your needs in the department store line maybe, be sure to visit marsha's first. We are eager to serve you with our complete line of high quality merchandize.

Sincerly,

VOCABULARY AND SPELLING STUDIES

A. Without consulting your dictionary, indicate which of the two spellings shown for the following words is preferable. Then check your selections in the dictionary.

1. acknowledgment, acknowledgement
2. instalment, installment
3. quartet, quartette
4. anaemic, anemic
5. realize, realise
6. usable, useable
7. accidently, accidentally
8. loveable, lovable

B. The following brief definitions indicate frequently used words that contain silent letters. Spell the words. To help you, the number of letters in each word is given.

1. A body of land surrounded by water (6 letters).
2. To strike or rap (5 letters).
3. Unruffled; still (4 letters).
4. The opposite of day (5 letters).
5. The branch of medicine that deals with mental disorders (10 letters).
6. The opposite of right (5 letters).
7. A lien on property by which the property is made security for a loan (8 letters).
8. A religious song (4 letters).
9. A twenty-fourth part of a day (4 letters).
10. A visitor (5 letters).

COMMUNICATING FOR RESULTS

Following Instructions. Laura got into difficulty because she failed to read correctly the memorandums that came from her supervisor regarding changes in procedures. When her supervisor finally had to speak to Laura regarding her failure to follow instructions, Laura replied, "Oh, we get so many memos that I can't keep all of them straight in my mind." If you were Laura's supervisor, what advice would you give to help keep the memorandums "straight"?

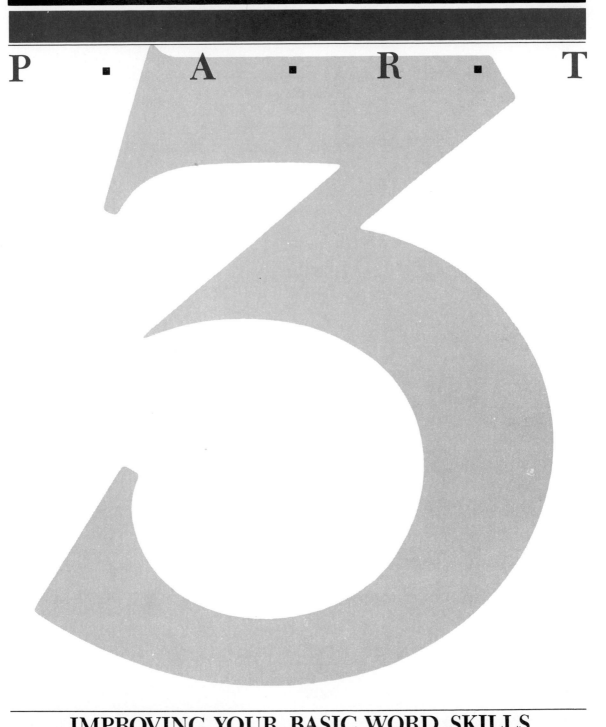

P · A · R · T

3

IMPROVING YOUR BASIC WORD SKILLS

Expressing yourself well is the key to effectively communicating with others. Think about how a situation can become complicated because someone does not understand what you are expressing. In business, such misunderstandings can be costly.

The words you select will determine whether you can communicate your ideas exactly as you mean to. An expanded vocabulary will provide you with accurate and precise words. This can only help promote the understanding that is critical to effective communication. Given a situation that requires you to express yourself, your mastery of the units in this chapter will enable you to do the following:

1. *Choose the most accurate, the most effective, and the most meaningful words to express your ideas.*

2. *Understand and use up-to-date and acceptable vocabulary to describe your thoughts.*

3. *Use reference books such as a dictionary and a thesaurus to increase your knowledge of words.*

4. *Use words that are commonly confused in a sentence to show you understand their different meanings and spellings.*

5. *Make a list, with correct spelling, of many of the words frequently used in business writing.*

5 Words—The Basic Medium of Communication

What are words? They are the symbols all of us use to share our experiences, feelings, and ideas with one another. We use words to think. We use words to read and write. We use words to listen and speak. When you stop to think about it, words are one of the basic things we depend upon for survival.

Have you ever been at a loss for words? For example, have you ever tried to describe a sunset over the ocean? Or have you ever tried to thank a friend for saving you from danger or for doing you a very special favor? In such situations, words are the tools that will enable you to share a beautiful sight or to express your heartfelt thanks. How well you are able to do so depends on the tools—the words—you select.

In business situations, words are the tools for hiring and managing employees, buying and selling merchandise, reporting and receiving information, and giving clients good service. Therefore, your ability to use words will be the key to both your success and the success of your organization.

Vocabulary—The Foundation for Business Success

All business employees are expected to have good vocabularies. What is a good vocabulary? It is more than a large store of words. Your vocabulary may be described as good when it enables you (1) to understand fully what you hear and read and (2) to say and write precisely what you mean. The key words are *fully* and *precisely*. Weakness in either area results in mistakes and in embarrassment. The following examples will demonstrate how the lack of a good vocabulary may be a handicap.

Two candidates for the same job were asked to list in writing their previous experience. One applicant wrote "Office work." The other candidate wrote "General clerical: typing letters and reports, using adding machines, distributing mail, checking inventories." Which applicant probably made the more favorable impression? *The possessor of a good vocabulary uses precise words to express meaning.*

Two supervisors told an employee to leave a memo on the manager's desk saying that they had gone out to inspect two sites that had been suggested for their new factory building. The manager found this memo: "Ms. Ortiz and Mr. Galvin have gone out to inspect sights for the new factory." Would the manager or the supervisors be likely to feel that the writer of the memo had a good vocabulary? *The possessor of a good vocabulary is familiar with words that are pronounced exactly alike but are spelled differently and have different meanings (homonyms).*

Jennifer wondered why people smiled when she said she thought the speaker's remarks were "inflammable." They knew, of course, that she meant "inflammatory,'" but her embarrassing blunder was not soon forgotten. *The possessor of a good vocabulary distinguishes between words that look or sound somewhat alike.*

A thank-you note read: "Thank you for a great time. You were so great to everyone there." The substitution of "kind" for the second "great" would have varied the wording. *The possessor of a good vocabulary achieves variety by using synonyms (words that have the same or very nearly the same meaning).*

Bill introduced a customer's wife as "Mizzuz" Nosaka. A mispronunciation like this instantly reveals slovenly habits of speech. *The possessor of a good vocabulary pronounces words correctly.*

A stenographer's transcript contained the phrase "seperate accomodations." When the misspellings were noticed, the stenographer had to retype the entire letter to insert the correct "separate accommodations." *The possessor of a good vocabulary spells words correctly.*

Vocabulary in Your Personal Life

Most of the examples you have just read relate to office experiences. However, your ability to use words effectively is just as much an asset in school, personal, and social situations. Many business transactions take place in a social situation. If you can say or write exactly what you mean so that others will not misunderstand you, your ability to communicate successfully will be recognized and admired.

As a member of a group or association, you probably will have many occasions to express opinions or to make suggestions during meetings. The person who can word a recommendation clearly or can summarize the feelings of a group precisely will probably be elevated to a position of leadership. If you could read material written by the top people in organizations, you would probably find that they write in clear, concise, concrete language. They are easy to understand. They are admired for their ability to speak and write effectively. The ability to communicate can be the vehicle that gets you to the top of the organization. Activities such as keeping minutes of meetings and writing correspondence as secretary to an organization are excellent preparation for the business world.

Building Your Vocabulary

How do you build a good vocabulary? Reading is one of the best ways. Newspapers, books, magazines—all can help you build a good vocabulary. Whenever you read, jot down any words you do not fully understand so that you can learn their meanings and add them permanently to your vocabulary. (How to use the dictionary and other word reference books will be discussed in the next unit.)

Studying another language will also introduce you to new words in your own language. In addition, meeting and talking with new people—especially people from different backgrounds—can help you improve your vocabulary. Two other important vocabulary building techniques are reviewed below.

Words—A Source of Curiosity. If you are word-conscious, you are curious about and interested in words, especially words you don't know. The more you know about words—their origins, their development, their synonyms—the more swiftly your word supply will grow and the more words you'll promote from your passive vocabulary (words that you merely recognize) into your active, or working, vocabulary (words that you use).

Studies of successful people show that they have this in common: a large vocabulary. It is logical, then, that you can increase your vocabulary by listening intently to the speech of such people. Listen to your teachers and—when you start working—to the executives in your office. Observe their choice of words. Take note of any word or expression that is not in your active vocabulary. Also, pay special attention to radio and television commentators. Since broadcasts and telecasts are carefully prepared, they offer excellent examples of well-chosen words. In addition, most commentators have had speech training, so their pronunciation is usually correct.

Surrounding Words—A Source of Help. Discovering the meaning of a word or an expression from the surrounding words in its sentence is called finding meaning from context. From the context we are usually able to figure out about half the words that we don't know. Using our common sense, we guess at the meaning of a word from the clues given, particularly when we do not have easy access to a dictionary. This kind of detective work can be fun.

For example: In reviewing a new novel, a literary critic referred to the author's "pedestrian style of writing that lacks the excitement deserved by the subject matter." To you, *pedestrian* probably means "walker." This definition is a partial clue to the meaning of *pedestrian* in this sentence, but it obviously is not sufficient. Probably the best clue here is the phrase *lacks excitement*. Put the clues together and you have "a writing style that lacks excitement." Now you're close. Referring to a dictionary, you learn that *pedestrian* may mean "unimaginative" or "commonplace." These latter meanings are the proper ones in this context.

Our Living Language

Just as the words you use change as you grow in knowledge and experience, the words in the English language change too. It is a living language, and language must change and develop to keep pace with the people who use it. As people invent new things, make discoveries, enter into new relationships, and otherwise add to their store of experiences, they coin new words to express these experiences. They also borrow words from other languages, and they add new meanings to already existing words. As these new words and meanings are used more and more, they gradually find their way into the dictionaries.

Growth Spurts. Every year, thousands of new words are added to our dictionaries. Our space program is an example of an activity that has added many entries to our dictionaries. In fact, English is now considered *the* major language throughout the world simply because scientific advances have forced us to coin new words to support modern technology. Thus people are learning English because their own language does not include the terminology of American science and technology, making translations into their own language nearly impossible. Since English is a living language, we who speak it must build our vocabularies to keep up with the constant changes.

Here are a few examples of new words and of old words with newer meanings found in the eighth edition of *Webster's New Collegiate Dictionary: bioinstrumentation, lunar excursion module, noise pollution, biodegradable, minicomputer, body shirt, domino theory, cinematize, urbanology, COBOL, software,* and *programmer.*

Usage and Acceptability. New words and new meanings are absorbed into our language through usage. If enough people use them over a long enough period of time, the new words become an accepted part of the language. For example, some words that were once looked down on, such as *mortician* and *beautician,* are now accepted as real words. Certain abbreviations—like *auto, plane, taxi, gym, phone*—also have come to be accepted as words. Note that, unlike real abbreviations, these shortened words are not followed by a period. Another example refers to changes in verb-subject agreement. The word *data* is a plural word meaning several pieces of information; *datum* is the singular form. Therefore, *data* should take a plural verb: "The data are correct." However, so many people have used *data* with a singular verb— "The data is correct."—that the dictionary now says that *data* can be used with a singular or a plural verb.

It may surprise you to learn that some of our commonly used words were originally considered slang. For example, *mob* and *sham,* once not considered "good" words, are now acceptable.

Changing Styles in Words. Changes in the meanings of words are nothing new in the development of our language. The English language has always been shifting. Who would think that *silly* once meant "good" or "happy"? that *fond* meant "foolish"? that *curious* meant "careful"? that *fascinate* once meant "to influence in some wicked and secret manner"?

In addition, the ways in which many words were used in sentences long ago differed from the ways in which they are used at present. Once, if the pronoun *you* referred to one person, a singular verb was used. (Today, of course, we always say "you *were*," never "you *was*.") Many words have been dropped from our working vocabularies because they no longer apply to our modern way of life. When gentlemen ceased to wear high boots, they no longer required bootjacks to help remove that type of footgear. Hence *bootjacks* is rarely used except in museum catalogs. Under our democratic way of life it is no longer fitting for the writer of a business letter to close it with "Your obedient servant." Yet it was common long ago. Words like *erstwhile* and *quoth*, once in common use, just do not fit the direct speech and writing needed today.

Keeping in Step

How are you to keep your vocabulary in step with changing times? How are you to judge which words, meanings, and pronunciations are up to date? Which are acceptable? There are three answers: First, listen and observe. Second, adapt your language to the occasion, the audience, and your purpose. Third, clarify confusing words—ask as many questions as necessary to eliminate possible misunderstanding.

Listening and Observing. To enlarge your vocabulary, you should listen to the speech of those people who use language well—experts in various fields, like professional speakers, executives, teachers, and newscasters. Also observe the language used in well-written newspapers and magazines. Through such observation and listening, you will learn to judge what is appropriate in language—what is suited to the times and to the people you communicate with—and that's the key to using language well.

Adapting Your Language. The English language is flexible: most of the time you will need—and use—conversational English, but when you must, you can adapt a more formal style of writing or speaking. Thus you must learn to adapt your language to the occasion, the audience, and your purpose.

Use Conversational English. The trend in speaking and writing is definitely toward a more conversational tone. When appropriate, adapt a conversational tone in writing letters and memos so that they sound natural—as if you were talking. Reserve your more formal English for those special occasions that require it. For example, instead of beating around the bush by saying, "I wish to take this opportunity to thank you for . . . ," go ahead and say "thank you" just as you would if you were facing your reader. A straightforward "thanks" is just as sincere, courteous, and correct, as well as more human and lifelike. Remember, however, that "conversational" means language that sounds natural and straightforward, not language that is loaded with slang and colloquialisms.

Avoid Slang Expressions. Although slang can be used effectively, its use should be avoided—especially in writing. The phrase *clip joint* (a dishonest business) is an example of slang; another is *prof* (for "professor"). Remember: (1) Always set off slang in quotation marks, and (2) avoid overusing slang.

Watch for Colloquialisms. Colloquialisms are simply word patterns that are commonly used in everyday speech. An example of a well-known colloquial expression is "get on the ball." Since colloquialisms are considered substandard English, however, they should be avoided in writing. Moreover, a colloquial phrase that is understood by someone in California may have no meaning to someone from New York or Texas.

Limit Attempts at Humor. Humor can enhance communication, but what is humorous in one part of the country may not be humorous in another part of the country. Also, humor can often offend people, even though no offense is intended. Many a contract has been lost over the misuse of humor.

We should ask ourselves these questions before using slang, colloquialisms, or humor: Is this slang really necessary? Will this phrase make sense to someone else? Can this joke hurt someone's feelings? To answer these questions, we must constantly put ourselves in the other person's shoes.

Clarifying Confusing Words. If you are not sure of a word someone has said, ask a question. An occasional question can fill a vocabulary gap. One day Louis answered the phone and then left the following note on the boss's desk: "Call Bill Farns of Clocksville Tendency." Luckily the boss knew Bill and realized that "Clocksville Tendency" should have been "Clarksville, Tennessee." But had he not known Bill, valuable business could have been lost for lack of a returned phone call.

COMMUNICATION LABORATORY

APPLICATION EXERCISES

A. Larry has gotten into the habit of describing as "fantastic" whatever he likes or is excited about. Suggest a more exact adjective to describe each of the following.

1. a job offer	**6.** a baseball player
2. a good teacher	**7.** a large building
3. an interesting book	**8.** a new car
4. a musical concert	**9.** a big park
5. a vacation	**10.** a good secretary

B. The words at the top of the next page are either new words or old words with new or added meanings. Refer to an up-to-date dictionary like *Web-*

ster's New Collegiate Dictionary for the most recent definitions. Then for each word write a sentence using the word appropriately.

1. printout
2. hardware
3. motel
4. input
5. module
6. binaural
7. broadcast
8. condominium

C. In each of the following sentences, choose the word in parentheses that correctly expresses the meaning.

1. The mining company discovered a new (vain, vein) of ore.
2. The reactor was surrounded by a (lead, led) shield.
3. Some airlines offer a special (fair, fare) between New York and Orlando.
4. Our seats were in the third (tier, tear) of the stadium.
5. The (soul, sole) on this shoe is badly worn.
6. A number of small (aisles, isles) were scattered about the bay.
7. The sound of the pounding (surf, serf) grew louder as the wind increased.
8. Once a year the ranchers (sheer, shear) their sheep.
9. This week we will (sew, sow) the corn in the field beside the road.
10. Clarissa learned the German songs by (wrote, rote).

D. Here are ten frequently used words. Which are misspelled?

1. acountant
2. approval
3. transaction
4. profitible
5. guarante
6. impliment
7. instalation
8. assessment
9. collateral
10. accomodate

E. For each of the following words, name another word with a similar meaning. The hints in parentheses may help you.

1. initiate (a 5-letter word starting with *b*)
2. resign (a 4-letter word starting with *q*)
3. acknowledge (a 5-letter word starting with *a*)
4. substantial (a 5-letter word starting with *l*)
5. endorse (a 4-letter word starting with *s*)
6. authentic (a 4-letter word starting with *r*)
7. negotiate (a 7-letter word starting with *b*)
8. assist (a 4-letter word starting with *h*)
9. evaluate (a 4-letter word starting with *t*)
10. prevent (a 4-letter word starting with *s*)

F. The following words were used in this unit. Try to determine the meaning of each from its context. You will need to find and reread the sentence in which each word appears and, in some instances, the sentences around it. Check your guesses in a good dictionary.

1. express
2. enable
3. recommendation
4. precisely
5. intently

6. access
7. coin (*verb*)
8. absorb
9. appropriate
10. enhance

COMMUNICATING FOR RESULTS

Avoiding Slang. A new co-worker has asked you to read and correct the first memo she has written on the job. How would you suggest she revise her draft copy?

> Contemporary Printers has suggested some nifty ink colors for our new brochure. As you can see from the enclosed samples, the deep purple and dark orange inks are really out of sight, but the lighter ink colors do not make it, in my opinion. May I have your green light to use the deep purple and dark orange inks?

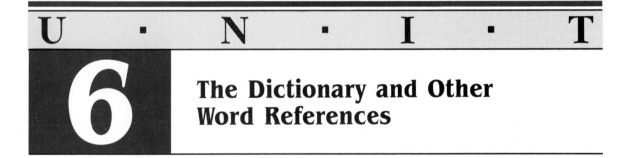

U · N · I · T

6

The Dictionary and Other Word References

Is the noun *prophecy* or *prophesy?* Is the plural of *radio* formed by adding *s* or by adding *es?* When word division is necessary at the end of a line, should *describe* be divided into *des-cribe* or *de-scribe?* What does *moratorium* mean? Is it correct to pronounce *adult* either '*ad-ult* (with emphasis on *ad*) or *a-'dult* (with the emphasis on *dult*)? If you end a sentence with *in*, is *in* a preposition or an adverb? These are the kinds of questions that often confront even the most accomplished speakers and writers. The answers to such questions about words are to be found in the dictionary and other word references. You will find out more about these references in this unit.

The Alphabet—A Useful Tool

There are many extremely fine word references available and most—if not all—are arranged in alphabetical order. Although we all "know" the alphabet, we must all develop the ability to find words *quickly* using the alphabet. Have you ever suffered from "alphabet blackout"? To test yourself, try finding in the dictionary at least ten words that you already know how to spell. You should be able to find each of those words in not more than 20 seconds. When taking this self-test or when using the dictionary at any time, be sure to make use of the guide words (the first and last words on each page) appearing at the top of the page.

Quality References

Today there are many quality references available in both hardback and paperback. Because our language is constantly growing and changing, our references should be up to date. You can depend on your library to have the large, expensive, up-to-date word references.

Occasionally, references may differ as to the spellings, pronunciations, or syllabications for some words. Regardless of the reasons for such differences, you should remember that language is constantly changing in all respects and that differences among references do not make one reference wrong and the other one right. Any established, up-to-date reference can properly be cited as the authority for acceptable word usage.

Dictionaries

Many of the differences among dictionaries are of little consequence to the ordinary user. For example, one dictionary may show abbreviations, biographical names, and geographic names in separate sections at the end of the book; another dictionary may include all this information arranged alphabetically with the words in the main vocabulary list. Also, different dictionaries use different systems for indicating pronunciation and for showing definitions, word origins, and other information about words. See pages 56–57 for the system used in one popular dictionary.

The most nearly complete dictionaries are unabridged, such as *Webster's Third New International Dictionary* and *Funk & Wagnalls New Standard Dictionary of the English Language*. These comprehensive works contain approximately 450,000 words in the main vocabulary list.

For personal use at home, in the office, or at school, a good standard desk dictionary is the best choice. Among these are *Webster's New Collegiate Dictionary*,* *The American Heritage Dictionary of the English Language, The Winston Dictionary for Schools, The American College Dictionary, Funk & Wagnalls Standard College Dictionary, Webster's New World Dic-*

*Webster's New Collegiate Dictionary (G. & C. Merriam Co., Springfield, Massachusetts, 1981) is the source for spelling and syllabication for all words in this book as well as for the definitions and pronunciations given.

tionary of the American Language. The Random House College Dictionary, Chambers Twentieth Century Dictionary, The Doubleday Dictionary: For Home, School, & Office, and *The Thorndike/Barnhardt Advanced Dictionary.*

Every dictionary, no matter how small or how large, whether paperback or hardback, shows the spelling, word division, pronunciation, and meaning or meanings of each word listed. A good standard desk dictionary also gives the part of speech of a word, its origin, the ways in which it is used, any synonyms, and certain irregular forms: for example, the principal parts of the verb (*did, done, do, doing*), the plural of the noun *alumna* (*alumnae*), and the comparative and superlative forms of the adjective *gluey* (*gluier, gluiest*). In addition, it helps you determine whether a word should be capitalized.

Determining Capitalization and Noun Plurals. The dictionary is an important source for capitalization and noun plurals. Suppose you are writing advertising copy for a sale of women's bathing suits—one-piece, skirted, and bikini types. You happen to know that Bikini is an atoll of the Marshall Islands, so you think you should capitalize the word. You check to make sure.

As you open the dictionary, you recall that each word entry is printed in small letters unless the word almost always or more often than not begins with a capital letter. Therefore, when you see *bikini* and read the definition, you know that the word as you are using it does *not* begin with a capital letter. The main part of your dictionary, then, will help you with capitalization, but you may get further help from the rules for capitalization in the reference section.

The dictionary supplies any out-of-the-ordinary plural forms. It does not show regular plurals—those formed by adding *s* or *es* or by changing a final *y* to *i* and adding *es*. If you need to know the plural of *fungus*, for example, you would look in the dictionary and see this information after that word: "*n, pl* **fun · gi** also **fun · gus · es.**" And if it is the plural of *mother-in-law* that bothers you, you would find after that word: "*n, pl* **mothers-in-law.**"

Following the Pronunciation Guide. As we have said, not all dictionaries agree on preferred pronunciations. Since the standard of English pronunciation is based on the usage that prevails among educated people, this collective usage is hard to measure. When a word has more than one pronunciation, the "preferred" pronunciation is generally the first one listed. In one dictionary you may find two pronunciations for *lever:* 'lev-ər, 'lē-vər. In another, you may find the opposite arrangement. Thus it is essential that you know how your dictionary denotes pronunciation.

Each dictionary offers a pronunciation guide that explains the use of stress marks (') (ˌ) for accented syllables and the meaning of the vowel and consonant symbols that stand for all the sounds in our language. This pronunciation guide usually appears at the front of the dictionary. To help users

Word origins help you understand the meaning of a word.

Run-on entries list words that are derived from the main entry.

Principal parts of verbs are often listed, especially when the verb ending changes or when the verb is irregular.

Main entries show whether a term is spelled as one word or two words and whether a term is hyphenated.

Plurals of nouns are given when the plural is formed irregularly.

Parts of speech (in abbreviated form) label each main entry.

Example phrases show how the main entry is commonly used.

Pronunciations — even of foreign terms — are listed for each main entry.

corrected time *n* : a boat's elapsed time less her time allowance in yacht racing
cor·rec·tion \kə-'rek-shən\ *n* **1** : the action or an instance of correcting: as **a** : AMENDMENT, RECTIFICATION **b** : REBUKE, PUNISHMENT **c** : a bringing into conformity with a standard **d** : NEUTRALIZATION, COUNTERACTION (~ of acidity) **2** : a decline in market price or business activity following and counteracting a rise **3** **a** : something substituted in place of what is wrong (marking ~s on the students' papers) **b** : a quantity applied by way of correcting (as for adjustment or inaccuracy of an instrument) **4** : the treatment and rehabilitation of offenders through a program involving penal custody, parole, and probation; *also* : the administration of such treatment as a matter of public policy — usu. used in pl. — **cor·rec·tion·al** \-shnəl, -shən-ᵊl\ *adj*
cor·rec·ti·tude \kə-'rek-tə-ˌt(y)üd\ *n* [blend of *correct* and *rectitude*] : correctness or propriety of conduct
cor·rec·tive \kə-'rek-tiv\ *adj* : tending to correct (~ lenses) (~ punishment) — **corrective** *n* — **cor·rec·tive·ly** *adv* — **cor·rec·tive·ness** *n*
¹cor·re·late \'kȯr-ə-lət, 'kär-, -ˌlāt\ *n* [back-formation fr. *correlation*] **1** : either of two things so related that one directly implies or is complementary to the other (as husband and wife) **2** : a phenomenon (as brain activity) that accompanies another phenomenon (as behavior), is usu. parallel to it (as in form, type, development, or distribution), and is related in some way to it **syn** see PARALLEL — **correlate** *adj*
²cor·re·late \-ˌlāt\ *vb* **-lat·ed; -lat·ing** *vi* : to bear reciprocal or mutual relations ~ *vt* **1** **a** : to establish a mutual or reciprocal relation of **b** : to show a causal relationship between **2** : to relate so that to each member of one set or series a corresponding member of another is assigned **3** : to present or set forth so as to show relationship (he ~s the findings of the scientists, the psychologists, and the mystics —Eugene Exman) — **cor·re·lat·able** \-ˌlāt-ə-bəl\ *adj*
cor·re·la·tion \ˌkȯr-ə-'lā-shən, ˌkär-\ *n* [ML *correlation-, correlatio,* fr. L *com-* + *relation-, relatio* relation] **1** **a** : the act of correlating **b** : the state of being correlated; *specif* : a relation of phenomena as invariable accompaniments of each other (the assumption that there is a positive ~ between performance and pay —Kermit Eby) **2** : reciprocal relation in the occurrence of different structures, characteristics, or processes in organisms **3** : an interdependence between mathematical variables esp. in statistics — **cor·re·la·tion·al** \-shnəl, -shən-ᵊl\ *adj*
correlation coefficient *n* : a number or function that indicates the degree of correlation between two sets of data or between two random variables and that is equal to their covariance divided by the product of their standard deviations
cor·rel·a·tive \kə-'rel-ət-iv\ *adj* **1** : naturally related : CORRESPONDING **2** : reciprocally related **3** : regularly used together but typically not adjacent (the ~ conjunctions *either . . . or*) — **correlative** *n* — **cor·rel·a·tive·ly** *adv*
cor·re·spond \ˌkȯr-ə-'spänd, ˌkär-\ *vi* [MF or ML; MF *correspondre,* fr. ML *correspondēre,* fr. L *com-* + *respondēre* to respond] **1** **a** : to be in conformity or agreement : SUIT (fulfillment seldom ~s to anticipation) **b** : to compare closely : MATCH — usu. used with *to* or *with* **c** : to be equivalent or parallel **2** : to communicate with a person by exchange of letters (frequently ~s with his cousin) **syn** see AGREE
cor·re·spon·dence \-'spän-dən(t)s\ *n* **1** **a** : the agreement of things with one another **b** : a particular similarity **c** : association of one or more members of one set with each member of a second — *compare* FUNCTION, MAPPING **2** **a** : communication by letters; *also* : the letters exchanged **b** : the news, information, or opinion contributed by a correspondent to a newspaper or periodical
correspondence school *n* : a school that teaches nonresident students by mailing them lessons and exercises which upon completion are returned to the school for grading
cor·re·spon·den·cy \ˌkȯr-ə-'spän-dən-sē, ˌkär-\ *n, pl* **-cies** : CORRESPONDENCE
¹cor·re·spon·dent \ˌkȯr-ə-'spän-dənt, ˌkär-\ *adj* [ME, fr. MF or ML; MF, fr. ML *correspondent-, correspondens,* prp. of *correspondēre*] **1** : CORRESPONDING (each advantage having ~ disadvantage) **2** : FITTING, CONFORMING — used with *with* or *to* (the outcome was entirely ~ with my wishes)
²correspondent *n* **1** : something that corresponds **2** **a** : one who communicates with another by letter **b** : one who has regular commercial relations with another **c** : one who contributes news or comment to a publication (as a newspaper) or a radio or television network often from a distant place (a war ~)
cor·re·spond·ing *adj* **1** **a** : agreeing in some respect (as kind, degree, position, or function) (the figures are large but the ~ totals next year will be larger) **b** : RELATED, ACCOMPANYING (all rights carry with them ~ responsibilites —W. P. Paepcke) **2** **a** : charged with the duty of writing letters (~ secretary) **b** : participating or serving at a distance and by mail (a ~ member of the society) — **cor·re·spond·ing·ly** \-'spän-diŋ-lē\ *adv*
cor·re·spon·sive \ˌkȯr-ə-'spän(t)-siv, ˌkär-\ *adj* : mutually responsive
cor·ri·da \kȯ-'rē-thə\ *n* [Sp, lit., act of running] : BULLFIGHT
cor·ri·dor \'kȯr-əd-ər, 'kär-, -ə-ˌdo͝o(ə)r\ *n* [MF, fr. OIt *corridore,* fr. *correre* to run, fr. L *currere* — more at CURRENT] **1** : a passageway (as in a hotel) into which compartments or rooms open **2** : a usu. narrow passageway or route: as **a** : a narrow strip of land through foreign-held territory **b** (1) : a restricted lane for air traffic (2) : a restricted path a spacecraft must follow to accomplish its mission : WINDOW 3 **3** : a densely populated strip of land including two or more major cities (the Northeast ~ stretching from Washington into New England —S. D. Browne)
cor·rie \'kȯr-ē, 'kär-ē\ *n* [ScGael *coire,* lit., kettle] : CIRQUE 3
Cor·rie·dale \-ˌdāl\ *n* [*Corriedale,* ranch in New Zealand] : any of a dual-purpose breed of rather large usu. hornless sheep developed in New Zealand
cor·ri·gen·dum \ˌkȯr-ə-'jen-dəm, ˌkär-\ *n, pl* **-da** \-də\ [L, neut. of *corrigendus,* gerundive of *corrigere* to correct] : an error in a

Every dictionary shows the spelling, word division, and meaning or meanings of each word listed. A good standard desk dictionary also gives the part of speech of the word, its origin, the ways in which it is used, any synonyms, and certain of the

printed work discovered after printing and shown with its correction on a separate sheet bound with the original

cor·ri·gi·ble \'kȯr-ə-jə-bəl, 'kär-\ *adj* [ME, fr. MF, fr. ML *corrigibilis*, fr. L *corrigere*] : capable of being set right : REPARABLE ⟨a ~ defect⟩ — **cor·ri·gi·bil·i·ty** \ˌkȯr-ə-jə-'bil-ət-ē, ˌkär-\ *n* — **cor·ri·gi·bly** \'kȯr-ə-jə-blē, 'kär-\ *adv*

cor·ri·val \kə-'rī-vəl, kō-, kȯ-\ *n* [MF, fr. L *corrivalis*, fr. *com-* + *rivalis* rival] : RIVAL COMPETITOR — **corrival** *adj*

cor·rob·o·rant \kə-'räb-ə-rənt\ *adj, archaic* : having an invigorating effect — used of a medicine

Synonyms offer words that are similar in meaning to the main entry. **Antonyms** (words that mean the opposite) are sometimes listed as well.

cor·rob·o·rate \kə-'räb-ə-ˌrāt\ *vt* **-rat·ed; -rat·ing** [L *corroboratus*, pp. of *corroborare*, ... *cor*—, *robur* strength] : to support with evidence or authority : make more certain ... **syn** see CONFIRM **ant** contradict — **cor·rob·o·ra·tion** \-ˌräb-ə-'rā-shən\ *n* — **cor·rob·o·ra·tive** \-'räb-ə-ˌrāt-iv, -'räb-(ə-)rət-\ *adj* — **cor·rob·o·ra·tor** \-'räb-ə-ˌrāt-ər\ *n* — **cor·rob·o·ra·to·ry** \-'räb-(ə)rə-ˌtōr-ē, -ˌtȯr-\ *adj*

cor·rob·o·ree \kə-'räb-ə-rē\ *n* [fr. native name in New South Wales, Australia] **1** : a nocturnal festivity with songs and symbolic dances by which the Australian aborigines celebrate events of importance **2** *Austral* **a** : a noisy festivity **b** : TUMULT

cor·rode \kə-'rōd\ *vb* **cor·rod·ed; cor·rod·ing** [ME *corroden*, fr. L *corrodere* to gnaw to pieces, fr. *com-* + *rodere* to gnaw — more at RAT] *vt* **1** : to eat away by degrees as if by gnawing; *esp* : to wear away gradually usu. by chemical action ⟨the metal was *corroded* beyond repair⟩ **2** : to weaken or destroy gradually ⟨manners and miserliness that ~ the human spirit —Bernard DeVoto⟩ ~ *vi* : to undergo corrosion ⟨the bare metal will ~ after a few weeks of exposure to the weather⟩ — **cor·rod·ible** \-'rōd-ə-bəl\ *adj*

cor·ro·dy *var of* CORODY

Main entries also show syllable breaks for word division.

cor·ro·sion \kə-'rō-zhən\ *n* [ME, fr. LL *corrosion-, corrosio* act of gnawing, fr. L *corrosus*, pp. of *corrodere*] **1** : the action, process, or effect of corroding **2** : a product of corroding

cor·ro·sive \-'rō-siv, -ziv\ *adj* **1** : tending or having the power to corrode ⟨~ acids⟩ ⟨~ action⟩ **2 a** : weakening or destroying by a gradual process ⟨the ~ influence of industrialization —Louise C. Hunter⟩ **b** : bitingly sarcastic ⟨~ satire⟩ — **corrosive** *n* — **cor·ro·sive·ly** *adv* — **cor·ro·sive·ness** *n*

corrosive sublimate *n* : MERCURIC CHLORIDE

cor·ru·gate \'kȯr-ə-ˌgāt, 'kär-\ *vb* **-gat·ed; -gat·ing** [L *corrugatus*, pp. of *corrugare*, fr. *com-* + *ruga* wrinkle — more at ROUGH] *vt* : to form or shape into wrinkles or folds or into alternating ridges and grooves : FURROW ⟨*corrugated* his brows in thought —John Buchan⟩ ~ *vi* : to become corrugated

corrugated iron *n* : usu. galvanized sheet iron or sheet steel shaped into straight parallel regular and equally curved ridges and hollows

cor·ru·ga·tion \ˌkȯr-ə-'gā-shən, ˌkär-\ *n* **1** : the act of corrugating **2** : a ridge or groove of a corrugated surface

Numbers separate different main entries that are spelled the same way. **Numbers** also separate different meanings *within* a main entry.

¹cor·rupt \kə-'rəpt\ *vb* [ME *corrupten*, fr. L *corruptus*, pp. of *corrumpere*, fr. *com-* + *rumpere* to break — more at REAVE] *vt* **1 a** : to change from good to bad in morals, manners, or actions; *also* : BRIBE **b** : to degrade with unsound principles or moral values **2** : ROT, SPOIL **3** : to subject (a person) to corruption of blood **4** : to alter from the original or correct form or version ~ *vi* **1 a** : to become tainted or rotten **b** : to become morally debased **2** : to cause disintegration or ruin **syn** see DEBASE — **cor·rupt·er** *or* **cor·rup·tor** \-'rəp-tər\ *n* — **cor·rupt·ibil·i·ty** \-ˌrəp-tə-'bil-ət-ē\ *n* — **cor·rupt·ible** \-'rəp-tə-bəl\ *adj* — **cor·rupt·ibly** \-blē\ *adv*

²corrupt *adj* [ME, fr. MF or L; MF, fr. L *corruptus*, fr. pp. of *corrumpere*] **1 a** : morally degenerate and perverted : DEPRAVED **b** : characterized by bribery, the selling of political favors, or other improper conduct ⟨~ judges⟩ **2** *archaic* : PUTRID, TAINTED **syn** see VICIOUS — **cor·rupt·ly** \kə-'rəp-(t)lē\ *adv* — **cor·rupt·ness** \-'rəp(t)-nəs\

Usage labels identify words that are archaic or obsolete.

cor·rup·tion \kə-'rəp-shən\ *n* **1 a** : impairment of integrity, virtue, or moral principle : DEPRAVITY **b** : DECAY, DECOMPOSITION **c** : inducement to wrong by bribery or other unlawful or improper means **d** : a departure from what is pure or correct **2** *archaic* : an agency or influence that corrupts **3** *chiefly dial* : PUS

cor·rup·tion·ist \-sh(ə-)nəst\ *n* : one who practices or defends corruption esp. in politics

corruption of blood : the effect of an attainder upon a person which bars him from inheriting, retaining, or transmitting any estate, rank, or title

cor·rup·tive \kə-'rəp-tiv\ *adj* : producing or tending to produce corruption — **cor·rup·tive·ly** *adv*

cor·sage \kȯr-'säzh, -'säj, 'kȯr-\ *n* [F, bust, bodice, fr. OF. bust, fr. *cors* body, fr. L *corpus*] **1** : the waist or bodice of a woman's dress **2** : an arrangement of flowers to be worn by a woman

cor·sair \'kȯr-ˌsa(ə)r, -ˌse(ə)r\ *n* [MF & OIt: MF *corsaire* pirate, fr. OProv ... fr. OIt *corsaro*, fr. ML *cursarius*, fr. L *cursus* course — more at COURSE] ... *esp* : a privateer of the Barbary coast

corse \'kȯ(ə)rs\ *n* [ME *cors*, fr. OF ...] *archaic* : CORPSE

Variant spellings are preceded by the word *or*.

corse·let \ *for 1* 'kȯr-slət, *for 2* ˌkȯr-sə-'let\ *n ... or* **corslet** [MF, dim. of *cors* body, bodice] **a** : a piece of armor covering the trunk but usu. not the arms or legs **b** : a pikeman's armor including helmet **2** *or* **cor·se·lette** [fr. *Corselette*, a trademark] : an undergarment combining girdle and brassiere

¹cor·set \'kȯr-sət\ *n* [ME, fr. OF, dim. of *cors*] **1** : a usu. close-fitting and often laced medieval jacket **2** : a woman's close-fitting boned supporting undergarment that is often hooked and laced and that extends from above or beneath the bust or from the waist to below the hips and has garters attached

²corset *vt* **1** : to dress in or fit with a corset **2** : to restrict closely : control rigidly

Pronunciation guides are handy charts that explain the pronunciation symbols.

ə abut	ᵊ kitten	ər further	a back	ā bake	ä cot, cart
aů out	ch chin	e less	ē easy	g gift	i trip	i life
j joke	ŋ sing	ō flow	ů flaw	oi coin	th thin	th this
ü loot	ů foot	y yet	yü few	yů furious	zh vision	

irregular forms. By permission. From *Webster's New Collegiate Dictionary*, copyright ©1981 by G. & C. Merriam Co.,

quickly find the meanings of these symbols, most dictionaries offer a short list of the most frequently used symbols at the bottom of every two-page spread:

ə abut ᵊ kitten ər further a back ā bake ä cot, cart au̇ out ch chin e less
ē easy g gift i trip ī life j joke ŋ sing ō flow ȯ flaw ȯi coin th thin <u>th</u> this
ü loot u̇ foot y yet yü few yu̇ furious zh vision*

Assume that you want to know how to pronounce the verb *mediate*. Is the first *e* long (as in *easy, meet,* and *beat*), or is it short (as in *less, bet,* and *bed*)? By referring to the mark above the vowel and then checking the handy guide at the bottom of the page, you would find that the first *e* is long.

Understanding the Explanatory Notes. To save you time and promote accuracy, study the explanatory notes before you use your dictionary. These notes explain the different typefaces and labels, the significant symbols and punctuation, and the other means by which a dictionary can achieve compactness. Take just one example, that of word division.

Suppose you want to know if the noun *blackout* is one word, two words, or a hyphenated word. When you look it up, you see *black · out*. The explanatory notes tell you that a centered period denotes a syllable break only; therefore, *blackout* is one word. If you looked up *self-conscious*, you would find *self-con · scious*. This word, then, is hyphenated after *self* and syllabicated after *con*.

Knowing the Abbreviations and Symbols. So much information must be packed into a dictionary that abbreviations and symbols frequently are necessary. To get full use of your dictionary, you should read and know where to find the explanations of these abbreviations and symbols. For example, it is important for you to know that *obs* stands for *obsolete*, which means that the word listed is no longer in current usage. Knowing the abbreviations for the parts of speech—*n., v., adj., adv.,* and so on—may save you from making embarrassing errors when you speak and write.

Although you need not memorize all the abbreviations, you should learn those most commonly used. You should also know where to find the meanings of those used less often.

Finding Synonyms. Your writing will be more interesting if you can use a varied supply of words. To do so, you will frequently have to use synonyms.

A synonym is a word that has the same or nearly the same meaning as another word. Although a dictionary is not primarily a book of synonyms (like a synonym dictionary or a thesaurus), it does offer synonyms for some words. Therefore, when you have a synonym problem you ordinarily reach first for that good old reliable reference, the dictionary. Suppose you are writing a memo recommending a "new plan." Since you have already used

*By permission. From *Webster's New Collegiate Dictionary* copyright © 1981 by G. & C. Merriam Co., Publishers of the Merriam-Webster Dictionaries.

the word *new* twice, you don't want to repeat it a third time. Looking in a dictionary you might find these four substitutes listed: *novel, modern, fresh original.* For a more detailed list of synonyms, see a thesaurus or a synonym dictionary.

The Thesaurus

A thesaurus is a collection of words and phrases arranged according to ideas. The function that it serves is different from that of a dictionary. A dictionary gives the meaning of the word that one has in mind. A thesaurus enables one to find the word with which to express an idea one has in mind. In other words, a thesaurus goes one step further than a dictionary. In using the dictionary or a book of synonyms, you must have at least one word in mind; in using a thesaurus, you can start with a general idea from which comes one word that will start you on the hunt for the exact word you need.

Suppose, for example, that you want to change your job and job location. You know very little about the area to which you want to move. To find out what businesses are there, you decide to write to the local chamber of commerce. When writing the letter, you find that you are using the word *business* so often that your language sounds repetitious. So you turn to a thesaurus for help.

A thesaurus usually gives three types of information about a word: which part of speech it is, its definition or definitions, and a synonym or synonyms. Sometimes it will even give you an example of how the word is used in a phrase or sentence. When you look up the noun *business* in a thesaurus, you will find something like this:

business   *noun*

1. Activity pursued as a livelihood: *Her business is advertising.*

2. Commercial, industrial, or professional activity in general: *laws regulating business, when business is slow.*

3. The commercial transactions of customers with a supplier.

4. A commercial organization.

5. Something that concerns or involves one personally: *Do you think that's any of your business?*

1. **Syns:** calling, employ (*Archaic*), employment, job, line, occupation, pursuit, racket (*Slang*), trade, vocation, work.

2. **Syns:** commerce, industry, trade, trading, traffic.

3. PATRONAGE.

4. COMPANY.

5. **Syns:** affair, concern, lookout.*

From this, you decide that definition 4 and its synonym are helpful. Using *company* at times instead of *business* in your letter is an improvement in

*By permission. From *Roget's II: The New Thesaurus,* copyright © 1980 by Houghton Mifflin Company, Boston, Massachusetts.

style. However, you would like to have more words to use than *business* and *company*. Therefore you look up *company* in the thesaurus. When you look up the noun *company* in a thesaurus, you will find something like this:

company *noun*

1. A commercial organization: *a new computer company.*

2. A number of persons who have come or been gathered together.

3. A person or persons visiting one: *had company for dinner.*

4. A pleasant association among people: *enjoyed their company.*

5. A group of performers.

1. *Syns:* business, concern, corporation, enterprise, establishment, firm[2], house, outfit.

2. ASSEMBLY.

3. *Syns:* guest, visitant, visitor.

4. *Syns:* companionship, fellowship, society.

5. BAND[2] *noun.**

After finding *company* in the thesaurus, you decide that definition 1 and its synonyms will help your letter to sound less redundant.

By using a thesaurus here, you have learned much about the word *business:* you verified what part of speech it was; you learned of its many definitions as a noun; and you acquired knowledge of several of its synonyms. Accomplishing all this took little time and helped you learn a lot about the meanings and usages of words.

Other References

Biographical and Geographical Names. Suppose you need some information about a famous person. For example, say you read or hear the name Amelia Earhart and want to know more about her. For fast identification, you might check the Biographical Names section of your dictionary and find under *Earhart:* "Amelia 1898–1937 Am. aviator." For more information, you would check *Webster's Biographical Dictionary* (G. & C. Merriam Company, Springfield, Massachusetts) or some other comprehensive listing of biographical names.

Have you ever been confused as to the pronunciation of faraway places and strange-sounding names? Suppose your boss asks you to make travel arrangements to San Juan and Ponce, Puerto Rico, and neither you nor your boss knows how to pronounce *Ponce*. Checking the Geographical Names section of your dictionary or a source such as *Webster's New Geographical Dictionary* (G. & C. Merriam Company) you would learn that Ponce, pronounced 'pȯn(t)-(ˌ)sā, is a city and a port in southern Puerto Rico; it has a population of 128,233.

Abbreviations and Acronyms. Commonly used abbreviations such as *FHA* (for Federal Housing Authority) and *UFO* (for unidentified flying object) are usually listed in standard desk dictionaries. To find the meaning of abbrevia-

*Ibid.

tions that are not listed in your dictionary, refer to a reference such as *Abbreviations Dictionary, Sixth Expanded Edition*, by Ralph DeSola (American Elsevier Publishing Co., Inc., New York, 1981).

An acronym is a word formed from the initial letter (or letters) of other words. *Radar* is an acronym derived from the words "*radio detecting and ranging*"; *sitcom* is formed from "*situation comedy*." To find the meaning of an acronym, see a reference such as *Acronyms, Initialisms, and Abbreviations Dictionary, Eighth Edition*, edited by Ellen T. Crowley (Gale Research Company, Detroit, Michigan, 1982).

Foreign Words and Phrases. Foreign terms often become popular in our language. For example, we hear the word *détente* in news discussions of our foreign policy. To understand our state department's actions, we need to know what *détente* means. It is "a relaxation of strained relations or tensions (as between nations)." To find the meaning of a puzzling foreign term that is not listed in your dictionary, you should use a reference such as *The Dictionary of Foreign Terms in the English Language*, by David Carroll (Hawthorn Books, Inc., New York, 1979).

Style Manuals. Everyone who writes or types will occasionally require a style manual to answer the common (and uncommon) questions that arise in ordinary written communications. Should you use a period at the end of a polite request, or should you use a question mark? When do you spell out numbers? When do you use numerals? How do you set up personal or confidential notations, mailing notations, and postscripts? The answers to these and many more questions can be found in a good style manual.

Among the style manuals available today are *The Gregg Reference Manual, Fifth Edition*, by William A. Sabin (Gregg Division, McGraw-Hill Book Company, New York, 1977); and *How: A Handbook for Office Workers, Third Edition*, by James Clark and Lyn Clark (Wadsworth Publishing Company, Inc., Belmont, California, 1982).

COMMUNICATION LABORATORY

APPLICATION EXERCISES

A. Do you really know the exact order of the letters of the alphabet? In your dictionary, locate the following fifteen words, taking each one in the sequence shown. Note the exact time you start your search for the words and the exact time you finish.

1. affect	6. inquest	11. expenditure
2. amend	7. phosphor	12. periscope
3. acquaint	8. interfere	13. consolidate
4. realist	9. submission	14. envelope
5. executive	10. complicate	15. remit

How many minutes did it take you? If it took you more than five minutes, you ought to brush up on the alphabet.

B. Now write the words that are listed in item A above in alphabetical order, without consulting a dictionary.

C. The following words are to be found on consecutive pages of a dictionary. Without using a dictionary, write them in alphabetical order. Note your starting and finishing times. How long did it take?

1. mantis	7. marrow	13. manual
2. manufacture	8. marmalade	14. maroon
3. manor	9. market	15. marriage
4. mariner	10. masonry	16. margarine
5. maple	11. mantel	17. marigold
6. marry	12. manner	18. maritime

D. Among the following words are several misspellings; a few of the words are spelled correctly. Correct the words that are wrong.

1. krafty	6. preferd
2. dauter	7. mesage
3. necessary	8. apeel
4. numerous	9. acomodate
5. ninedy	10. laughible

E. Here are ten common words. You should know how to break them down into syllables so that you can divide them properly at the end of a line. Without consulting your dictionary, indicate the syllable divisions for each word. In words of more than one syllable, place a primary stress mark (') *before* the accented syllable. Check your decisions in the dictionary.

1. compensate	6. graph
2. obsolete	7. estimate
3. opportunity	8. assurance
4. illuminate	9. magnetism
5. contradict	10. rectify

F. The following words were used in this unit. If you are not already familiar with them, try to guess their meaning from the context of the sentences in which they are used. Then check your guesses in the dictionary.

1. accomplished	6. reliable
2. respects	7. function
3. consequence	8. appropriate
4. comprehensive	9. standard
5. prevail	10. require

COMMUNICATING FOR RESULTS

Using the Dictionary. Your supervisor leaves a note on your desk. In the note are several abbreviations and acronyms. Use your dictionary to find the meaning of each one.

> As you know, later this year we will participate in state book fairs throughout the country—in Mo., N.C., Tenn., Okla., Miss., N.J., Vt., and Fla. For each meeting I would like you to ship a min. of 300 journals that we have printed for various societies and organizations, especially the latest journals for the AMA, ANA, NRC, LWV, and NCAA.
> Package the samples in boxes that can withstand NTP.
> Make sure the boxes arrive three days bef. each fair.

U · N · I · T

7

Do on own.

Spelling

One of the keys to successful communication is correct spelling. In business writing a misspelled word can detract the reader from the content of the message and cause misunderstanding. Incorrect spelling may also cause embarrassment because it lowers the writer's image in the reader's mind. Proper spelling, therefore, is basic to effective communication.

What spelling skills are needed to communicate effectively? How can a person learn to become a good speller? The purpose of this unit is to help you gain those skills needed to spell correctly as you write.

To become a good speller, you should be able to spell automatically those words used frequently in business writing. Your basic spelling vocabulary should include some of those "tricky" words that often cause problems—those that are used frequently enough to warrant your memorizing them.

You should also have an awareness of the basic spelling rules commonly used in our language. These rules will help you distinguish among common confusions.

Finally, you should have a knowledge of the common spellings of word beginnings and commonly used secondary sounds. Then you can use your dictionary effectively to locate the spellings of words you do not readily know.

In this unit the following three-step process will be your basis for study to improve your spelling of business vocabulary: (1) memorizing a basic vocabulary, (2) reviewing important spelling rules, and (3) learning the various spellings of word beginnings and frequently used secondary sounds.

Mastery of a Basic "50"

Even if most commonly used words do not cause you any spelling difficulties, there may be a few tricky ones that do. Some of these tricky words, however, are so frequently used in business writing that you should master their spelling. For your minimum spelling vocabulary, you should master the spelling of the 50 words emphasized, if you have not already done so.

Double-Letter Combinations. Some words are misspelled because one or more of their double-letter combinations are not written in their entirety. Study the following words and note that each word has *two* or more sets of double letters.

a_cco_mm_o_date	o_cc_u_rr_ed
b_ookkee_ping	su_ccee_d
co_mmittee_	emba_rrass_

Note the single set of double letters in the following words:

o_cc_asion	pro_cee_d
questio_nn_aire	di_ss_atisfaction
o_ff_ered	profe_ss_or
reco_mm_endation	

One Word or Two Words? Some words are misspelled because they are written as separate words instead of as a single word; other words are misspelled because the reverse is true.

Single Words	**Separate Words**
cannot	all right
nevertheless	home owner
percent	a lot

CLASS PRACTICE I

In this unit and in all the grammar, punctuation, and style units of this text, oral Class Practice exercises are provided to help you learn the principles you are studying. In the following sentences, select the correct spelling of the words shown in parentheses.

1. What kinds of (questionaires, questionnaires) were mailed to our suppliers?
2. These modern warehouses can (accommodate, acommodate, acomodate) at least 3,000 pieces of furniture.

The exchange of messages between and among human beings is known as communication. Electronic technology has made it possible to send these oral and written messages both near and far, quickly and efficiently.

Common methods of message transmission include writing, speaking, gestures, and facial expressions.

Listening, reading, and observing are the means we use to receive the oral or written messages sent to us.

Computer-based systems, called business
networks, "talk" to each other so that written
data, voices, and images can be sent
electronically and instantaneously.

Businesses such as supermarkets and department stores often use information processing technology to collect, organize, record, store, and retrieve sales, revenue, date and time, and inventory data on a daily basis.

Word processing operators can write business letters, memos, and reports on the equipment and can type, edit and correct them there at fast rates.

Intracompany mail systems, private mail carriers, and the U.S. Postal Service use telecommunications technology to transmit information quickly and efficiently across great distances.

Teleconferencing technology allows business people in different locations to speak, listen, and observe facial expressions and gestures when exchanging ideas across the miles.

3. Mrs. Mercado has (offered, offerred) a large donation to boost our hospital drive.
4. Our appraisers have evaluated office space in the city on several (ocasions, occasions, ocassions).
5. Did any of our customers express (disatisfaction, dissatisfaction, disattisfaction) with our service contract?
6. The Family Pet Shop (cannot, can not) be extended any further credit.
7. Only one (proffessor, proffesor, professor) requested a copy of this book.
8. What (percent, purcent) of the survey sample did not respond?

Dropped Letters or Sounds. Some words are misspelled because letters or syllables in the words are omitted. Such words often include the following:

conv*en*ient	(*not* convient)	th*o*rough	(*not* through)
sincer*e*ly	(*not* sincerly)	We*d*nesday	(*not* Wenesday)
int*e*rest	(*not* intrest)	mor*t*gage	(*not* morgage)
knowle*dg*e	(*not* knowlege)	bankrup*t*cy	(*not* bankrupcy)
colum*n*	(*not* colum)	itiner*ar*y	(*not* itinery)
manufact*ur*ers	(*not* manufacters)	a*c*quire	(*not* aquire)
g*u*arantee	(*not* garantee)	nin*e*ty	(*not* ninty)
Feb*r*uary	(*not* Febuary)		

CLASS PRACTICE 2

Select the correct spelling of the words shown in parentheses.

1. Meet us there only if it is (convient, convenient) for you.
2. Your travel agent will send you your (itinery, itinerary) next week.
3. Our company filed for (bankruptcy, bankrupcy) last week.
4. Her (knowlege, knowledge) of real estate values in this area will be of considerable help to us.
5. We (sincerly, sincerely) appreciated your recommending our firm to your colleagues.
6. Mr. Wong will (aquire, acquire) ownership of the property on (Wednesday, Wenesday).
7. Our lease expires in (Febuary, February).
8. Approximately (ninty, ninety) people applied for the position.

Additional Letters. Sometimes words are misspelled because letters are added. Here are some words commonly misspelled for this reason.

realty	(*not* real*i*ty)
usable	(*not* us*e*able)
privilege	(*not* privile*d*ge)
regarding	(*not* reg*u*arding)
similar	(*not* simili*a*r)
ninth	(*not* nin*e*th)

Changed Letters. Words are also misspelled because one vowel is substituted for another or letters are transposed. Some words commonly misspelled because of changed letters are shown below.

sep*a*rate	(*not* sep*e*rate)
superintend*e*nt	(*not* superintend*a*nt)
likel*i*hood	(*not* likel*y*hood)
congra*t*ulations	(*not* congra*d*ulations)
d*e*scribe	(*not* d*i*scribe)
defin*i*te	(*not* defin*a*te)
curr*e*ncy	(*not* curr*a*ncy)
gr*ate*ful	(*not* gr*eat*ful)
fin*ally*	(*not* fin*ely*)
v*e*rify	(*not* v*a*rify)

CLASS PRACTICE 3

Select the correct spelling of the words shown in parentheses.

1. The (usable, uzable) floor space in this plan is 10,000 square yards—about 8,371 square meters.
2. May we have the (priviledge, privilege) of serving you in the near future?
3. (Congradulations, Congratulations) on being elected president of the Chamber of Commerce.
4. There is little (likelihood, likelyhood) that your order will be shipped before July 15.
5. I have contacted two other (realty, reality) companies.
6. We have not yet received a (definate, definite) commitment from either agent.
7. Your daughter is (ninth, nineth) on the waiting list for admission to Brentview Dance Academy.
8. Please (verify, varify) all these calculations.

Three Basic Spelling Rules

There are many spelling rules that can help you improve your spelling. Only three rules are discussed in this unit because they are the ones that can be applied most consistently. These three basic rules do have some exceptions, but they are few, as you will see. Whenever you doubt the spelling of any of these words, be sure to consult a dictionary.

Ie or *ei*? Generally speaking, use the *ie* combination to represent the sound of long *e* (the sound in *meet*).

ch*ie*f	y*ie*ld	p*ie*ce
f*ie*ld	n*ie*ce	gr*ie*f
bel*ie*ve	th*ie*f	p*ie*rce

EXCEPTIONS: either, neither, weird, seize, leisure.

After *c*, however, use the *ei* combination.

| rec*ei*ve | conc*ei*t | dec*ei*t |
| c*ei*ling | rec*ei*pt | dec*ei*ve |

EXCEPTION: financier

The *ei* is also used when the combination is sounded like long *a* (the sound in *may*).

w*ei*gh	fr*ei*ght	v*ei*n
n*ei*ghbor	th*ei*r	h*ei*r
v*ei*l	sl*ei*gh	*ei*ght

CLASS PRACTICE 4

Use *ie* or *ei* to complete the correct spelling of the words in the following sentences.

1. We bel___ved that we would be awarded the contract.
2. The doctor had difficulty locating the child's v___n.
3. Be sure to obtain rec___pts for all your expenditures.
4. You may select ___ther model.
5. Please ask the rel___f crew to wash all the counters before closing.
6. The painters will spray the c___lings before they paint the walls.
7. The w___ght of each package must not exceed 10 kilograms.
8. Circulars were distributed throughout the n___ghborhood.

Double the Final Consonant. When adding an ending to a one-syllable word ending in a consonant, double the final consonant if it is *preceded* and *followed* by a single vowel.

ship + ed	ship*p*ed	ban + ed	ban*n*ed
bag + age	ba*gg*age	trim + est	trim*m*est
plan + ing	plan*n*ing	wrap + er	wrap*p*er

EXCEPTION: The final consonant of a word ending in *x* or *w* is not doubled.

| tax + ed | taxed | saw + ing | sawing |
| wax + ing | waxing | bow + ed | bowed |

Drop the *e* or Keep the *e*? Words that end in silent *e* usually drop the *e* before an ending that begins with a vowel (such as *able* or *ing*).

desire + able	desirable	use + age	usage
decorate + or	decorator	advise + ing	advising
enclose + ure	enclosure		

EXCEPTIONS:

shoe + ing	shoeing	acre + age	acreage
mile + age	mileage	eye + ing	eyeing
dye + ing	dyeing		

When adding an ending that begins with a consonant (such as *ful* or *ment*), retain the silent *e*.

entire + ty	entirety	cease + less	ceaseless
use + ful	useful	bare + ly	barely
state + ment	statement	tire + less	tireless
gentle + ness	gentleness	absolute + ly	absolutely

EXCEPTIONS:

wise + dom	wisdom	acknowledge + ment	acknowledgment
whole + ly	wholly	judge + ment	judgment

CLASS PRACTICE 5

Select the correct spelling of the words shown in parentheses.

1. Three dresses must be (hemed, hemmed) about 4 centimeters higher.
2. The floors in this building were (waxed, waxxed) this morning.
3. It would not be (adviseable, advisable) for you to invest in this property.
4. Our (safety, safty) record is one of the best in the county.
5. She is, in my (judgment, jugment), one of our most loyal employees.
6. His store is located in a (desirable, desireable) location.

Spellings of Common Sounds

All the words that may cause you spelling difficulties are listed in your dictionary. Even though these words are included in the dictionary, they may not be found easily because many sounds have a variety of spellings. Thus the business writer who is not familiar with these spellings will not know where to look in the dictionary.

By learning the various spellings for commonly used word sounds, you can become a better speller. Your dictionary will become a more valuable tool to help you locate the correct spelling of all the words you use. This section focuses on the spellings of commonly used word sounds that appear at the beginning or in the middle of words.

Double Letters. Sometimes certain consonant sounds are expressed with single letters; other times these same sounds are expressed with double letters. In looking up words in your dictionary, remember that a consonant sound may be expressed with either a single letter or a double one. Study the following examples:

Single Consonant	Double Consonant
a<u>p</u>ologize	a<u>pp</u>oint
i<u>n</u>oculate	i<u>nn</u>ocent
i<u>m</u>itate	i<u>mm</u>ediate
e<u>l</u>ate	e<u>ll</u>ipse
a<u>c</u>oustic	a<u>cc</u>ordion

o*p*eration	o*pp*osite
me*l*ody	me*ll*ow
ga*l*oshes	ga*ll*on
defe*r*ence	defe*rr*ed

Vowel Variations. Words are often misspelled because they are mispronounced. Word beginnings that have identical consonant sounds but different vowel sounds fall into this category. When trying to locate such words in the dictionary, keep in mind the possibility that the word may be spelled with a vowel other than the one you have in mind. Notice, for example, the similarity within the following groups.

des	des/cription		mon	mon/ey
dis	dis/tribute		mun	mun/dane
fer	fer/ocious		per	per/suade
for	for/eign		pur	pur/sue
fur	fur/lough		pre	pre/cision
def	def/inite		in	in/sure
dif	dif/ferent		en	en/large
dev	dev/astate		un	un/pleasant
div	div/idend		im	im/prove
men	men/ace		em	em/ploy
min	min/eral			

CLASS PRACTICE 6

Select the correct spelling of the words shown in parentheses. Use your dictionary, if necessary, to locate the correct spelling.

1. This location is more (desirable, disirable) than the one selected by Mr. Hughes.
2. We are quite (aprehensive, apprehensive) about investing in the stock market at the present time.
3. Have you taken every necessary (percaution, precaution, purcaution) to avoid such accidents in the future?
4. Please obtain another legal (opinion, oppinion) before we take any further action.
5. Who is in charge of our (endowment, indowment) fund?
6. I am not allowed to (devulge, divulge) that kind of information.

Common Beginning Sounds. To locate words in the dictionary, you must know the different possible spellings for the common sounds used at the beginning of words—that is, the most common first and second sounds. See pages 70–71 for a list of these sounds and their spellings.

SOUND	SPELLINGS	SOUND	SPELLINGS	SOUND	SPELLINGS
a	a (*a*bout)	ē	ae (*ae*on)	k	c (*c*riminal)
	ai (pl*ai*d)		e (*e*gotist)		cc (o*cc*ur)
	au (l*au*gh)		ee (st*ee*l)		ch (*ch*emistry)
	ea (h*ea*rt)		ei (perc*ei*ve)		k (*k*imono)
			eo (p*eo*ple)		q (li*q*uidation)
ā	a (*a*ble)		i (mach*i*ne)		
	ai (*ai*lment)		ie (rel*ie*ve)	m	lm (ca*lm*)
	au (g*au*ge)				m (*m*edicine)
	ea (br*ea*k)	er	ar (li*ar*)		
	ei (n*ei*ghbor)		ear (*ear*nest)	n	gn (*gn*arled)
	eigh (sl*eigh*)		er (*er*osion)		kn (*kn*itwear)
			err (*err*oneous)		mn (*mn*emonic)
ä	a (f*a*ther)		ir (*ir*ksome)		n (*n*atural)
	eau (bur*eau*cracy)		or (w*or*thless)		pn (*pn*eumonic)
	o (*o*bligation)		our (j*our*nal)		
			ur (*ur*gency)	o	o (*o*rdinary)
ak	ac (*ac*robat)				oa (b*oa*rd)
	acc (*acc*laim)	f	f (*f*easible)		
	ack (*ack*nowledge)		ff (e*ff*ective)	ō	eau (b*eau*)
	acq (*acq*uire)		gh (lau*gh*ter)		o (n*o*table)
	aq (*aq*ueduct)		ph (*ph*otograph)		oa (thr*oa*t)
					oe (t*oe*)
ār	ar (*ar*ea)	g	g (*g*rievance)		ou (s*ou*l)
	aer (*aer*ial)		gh (*gh*etto)		ough (th*ough*)
	air (*air*port)		gu (*gu*arantee)		ow (kn*ow*)
as	as (*as*bestos)	h	h (*h*oliday)	oi, oy	oi (f*oi*l)
	asc (*asc*end)		wh (*wh*olesale)		oy (env*oy*)
	ass (*ass*embly)				
		i	e (*e*nlist)	o͞o	eu (man*eu*ver)
aw	aw (*aw*kward)		i (*i*diom)		ew (thr*ew*)
	au (*au*dience)		ie (s*ie*ve)		ieu (ad*ieu*)
	augh (t*augh*t)		y (m*y*stery)		o (rem*o*ve)
	ough (th*ough*t)				oo (f*oo*lish)
		ī	ai (*ai*sle)		ou (s*ou*)
e	ae (*ae*sthetic)		eigh (sl*eigh*t)		ough (thr*ough*)
	e (*e*stimate)		i (*i*dentical)		u (r*u*le)
	ea (br*ea*kfast)		ie (l*ie*)		ue (bl*ue*)
	ei (h*ei*fer)		igh (fl*igh*t)		ui (fr*ui*t)
	eo (l*eo*pard)		y (h*y*peractive)		
	ie (fr*ie*nd)			ow	ou (pron*ou*nce)
		j	dg (bu*dg*et)		ough (b*ough*)
			g (*g*enerate)		ow (br*ow*se)
			gg (exa*gg*erate)		
			j (in*j*ure)		

SOUND	SPELLINGS	SOUND	SPELLINGS
r	r (_r_elaxation) rh (_rh_etoric) wr (_wr_inkle)	ū	eau (b_eau_tiful) eu (f_eu_d) ew (p_ew_ter) u (_u_seful) ue (c_ue_)
s	c (_c_ivil) ps (_p_sychology) s (_s_table) sc (_sc_enic) ss (pe_ss_imist)		yu (_yu_le) o (ch_o_ir)
		w	u (q_u_artile) w (_w_edding) wh (_wh_arf)
sh	ch (ma_ch_ine) ci (spe_ci_al) s (_s_ure) sc (con_sc_ious) sch (_sch_illing) se (nau_se_ous) sh (_sh_ampoo) si (ten_si_on) ss (i_ss_ue) ti (par_ti_al)		
t	pt (_pt_omaine) t (_t_arnish)		
u	u (_u_pper)		

CLASS PRACTICE 7

Use the preceding chart to find the various spellings for the sounds in parentheses. Then find the correct spelling in your dictionary, and rewrite each word.

1. Did the manager (ak)uiesce to the sales representatives' request for salary increases?
2. The washing instructions on the label state specifically that the electric blanket should not be squeezed or (r)ung out.
3. Can this furniture wax be purchased in an (ar)osol can?
4. Dr. Moran's field of specialty is (s)(i)chiatry.
5. Will the customer accept our Model 18 radio in l(oo) of the discontinued model he ordered?

6. Ms. Bronson is a very con(sh)ien(sh)ous employee; she works hard and is always on time.
7. José missed three weeks of school last year because he was in the hospital with a serious case of (n)eumonia.
8. Ms. DiBona asked the butcher for a kilogram of roast beef, and she watched him carefully as he w(a)ed it.

COMMUNICATION LABORATORY

APPLICATION EXERCISES

A. On a separate sheet of paper, provide the correct spellings for the sounds shown in parentheses. Then rewrite each word.

1. The robbery o(k)u(r)ed nearly three months ago.
2. We were given permission to proc(e)d with the original plan.
3. We have already rec(e)ved eight 20-liter and five 50-liter drums of lubricating oil.
4. The mor(g)age on these homes is for thirty years.
5. Ni(n)ty-three applications were received for the position.
6. Thank you for the privile(j)e of serving you.
7. Please include the fr(a)t charges in the invoice.
8. Smugglers cannot easily dec(e)ve our customs agents.
9. The contract copy had sli(p)ed down behind the files.
10. You may pick up your mil(e)ge check in the bursar's office.
11. Ms. Avery appears to be pe(s)imistic about the potential of our new line.
12. The employees complained about the (mon, mun)otony of the task.
13. What system did you use to c(aw)dify these materials?
14. The advertisement pictured a dog (n)awing a bone.
15. Our latest production is a science fiction movie regarding mar(sh)ian life.

B. On a separate sheet of paper, write the correct spelling of any words misspelled in the following sentences. If a sentence does not contain a misspelled word, write *OK* on your paper.

1. Our secretary is hospitalized with a serious case of neumonia.
2. How many people are imployed by your corporation?
3. Will we be forced to ferclose on this property?
4. Rita has inate athletic ability.
5. When may we expect to recieve your final payment?
6. We are grateful for your help in settling this claim.
7. Have you received any additional information reguarding the status of my appeal?
8. Your account will acrue interest at the rate of 7 percent.

9. The tax assesment on your property has risen 30 percent.
10. His report of the accident is destorted.
11. Mr. Corey has a tendency to exagerate the effectiveness of our paint products.
12. Did the city council approve the proposed erban renewal project?
13. A number of the insurance claims we have received have been for cyclone damage.
14. The witness was found guilty on three counts of purgery.
15. Please post a sign that prohibits children from loytering in the shopping center.

C. Correct any spelling errors in the following paragraph.

The finance committe met yesterday to review the proposed budgets for the various departments in our devision. The requests from the departments far exceed the ammount budgeted to our operation. Therefore, this committe must decide which items should recieve priority consideration and which items should be deferred. Our deliberations yesterday determined that the number of personel should be kept at its present level. Additional requests for equipment and office supplies, however, can not be accomodated through this year's funding.

VOCABULARY AND SPELLING STUDIES

A. The spellings of some commonly used words may not be easily located in the dictionary because the spellings of their sounds do not follow usual spelling patterns. Look up in your dictionary the pronunciation and meaning of the following words:

1. hors d'oeuvre
2. quay
3. sergeant
4. faux pas
5. indict
6. sew

B. These words are often confused: *extent, extant, extinct; collision, collusion.* Explain the meaning of each.

C. To each of the following, add the ending pronounced *shun.*

1. illustra_____
2. provi_____
3. electri_____
4. repeti_____
5. coer_____
6. aver_____

COMMUNICATING FOR RESULTS

Poor Speller. Assume that you work in a word processing center as a correspondence secretary. Most of your typing involves letters that are sent to customers. Another correspondence secretary with whom you work has the same reference initials as you. He is careless and a poor speller, and since he does not consult a dictionary, the letters he types are full of mistakes. This is the third time this week you have been blamed for spelling errors made by your co-worker. What would you do to correct this situation?

8 Choosing the Right Word

An amazing number of words in the English language are confused because they sound alike or look alike but have different spellings and different meanings. Some words are pronounced exactly alike, as *break* (to shatter) and *brake* (a device to stop motion). Some sound somewhat alike, as *respectively* (in the order given), *respectfully* (courteously), and *respectably* (in a conventionally correct manner). Others look somewhat alike. They may contain the same letters but in different order, as *diary* (a daily record) and *dairy* (a business that produces milk and milk products). One may have one letter where the other has two, as *ad* (the shortened form of *advertisement*) and *add* (to increase). Or they may have other superficial resemblances, as *facetious* (witty) and *fictitious* (like fiction).

How to Study Word Confusions

In this unit are groups of words that are often confused because they either sound or look exactly alike or sound or look similar. You will easily distinguish between these kinds of words if you will do the following:

1. Examine carefully how each word is spelled, noting whether the same letters occur but in different order, whether a letter is doubled in one word but not in another, and so on.
2. Learn how each word is pronounced. Consult the dictionary to be sure. Note the phonetic spelling, which indicates the correct sounds, together with the stress marks that tell you which syllables are to be accented.
3. Determine the part of speech of each word. This will save you time in locating the precise meaning in the dictionary. It is very important to do this when words are spelled alike, as *desert* (barren land) and *desert* (to abandon).
4. Study how the word is used in a sentence. This method of finding meaning from context often reveals the distinctions between words more easily than do dictionary definitions.
5. If you have any doubt about the meaning of a word, always look it up in a dictionary. Sift through the various meanings; become acquainted with the word's possibilities for use.

6. Make a habit of entering in your personal notebook any new group of words that are often confused. Head one section of your notebook "Word Confusions" and include brief definitions for each entry. Enter any sentences you find that illustrate how these words are used. Some students find it helpful to underscore the letters that are the keys to the differences in meaning of the words in a group; for example, a<u>cc</u>ept, ex<u>c</u>ept, exp<u>ec</u>t.

Words Commonly Confused

The spelling or meaning of the following combinations of words are commonly confused. Study them carefully. Be sure to look up the pronunciation of any word that is unfamiliar.

accede (*v.*) To comply with. "We must *accede* to this customer's request."
exceed (*v.*) To surpass. "Our sales this quarter will *exceed* our projections."

accent (*n.*) A stress in speaking or writing. "Where is the *accent* in the word *profit?*" (*v.*) To stress; emphasize. "The manager's remarks *accented* the need to control expenses."
ascent (*n.*) A rising or climbing. "Her *ascent* in the department was swift because of her qualifications."
assent (*n.*) Agreement. "The customer's written *assent* is necessary before we can charge an account." (*v.*) To agree. "Did Ms. Mendoza *assent* to your request?"

accept (*v.*) To approve; receive with favor. "We *accept* your decision."
except (*prep.*) Other than. "All employees must work this Saturday *except* those with over ten years of service." (*v.*) To exclude. "We can *except* no one from the need to arrive at work on time."
expect (*v.*) To look forward to. "I *expect* our sales to increase soon."

all ready (*adj.*) Prepared. "The reports are *all ready* for the meeting."
already (*adv.*) By this time. "I have *already* met my quota."

advice (*n.*; rhymes with *ice*) A recommendation regarding a course of conduct. "Mr. Sims' *advice* will help your career."
advise (*v.*; rhymes with *skies*) To counsel. "What do you *advise* me to do about this overdue account?"

affect (*v.*) To influence. "How will the new procedures *affect* our budget?" (*v.*) To pretend. "He *affects* busyness and overwork."
effect (*v.*) To bring about. "We expect this new computerized system to *effect* an upturn in our business." (*n.*) A result. "What *effect* has the new word processing system had upon efficiency?"

altar (*n.*) Table used in worship. "The *altar* dominated the cathedral."
alter (*v.*) To change. "If we *alter* the schedule, our customers will be glad."

assistance (*n.*) Support. "Do you need *assistance* with the payroll?"
assistants (*n.*) Those who help. "Our company president has three *assistants.*"

bare (*adj.*) Uncovered. "This report looks *bare* without graphs and charts."
bear (*v.*) Carry. "She *bears* the responsibility for the entire department."

capital (*adj.*) Chief; principal. "Carson City is the *capital* city of Nevada." (*n.*) The value of accumulated goods. "We used all our *capital* to start this company."
capitol (*n.*) The building in which a legislature meets; capitalized when it refers to the building in which the U.S. Congress meets. "Industry representatives will testify in the Capitol on August 4."

chews (*v.*) Masticates. "I noticed that our dog *chews* his food very well."
choose (*v.*) To select; to prefer. "We must *choose* a word processing system that will serve our needs."
chose (*v.*; past tense of *choose*; chōz) Selected. "You *chose* the best system."

cite (*v.*) To quote; to refer to. "She *cited* our poor delivery record."
site (*n.*) A location. "This is the new *site* for our company headquarters."
sight (*n.*) Vision. "Jane's well-kept ledgers are a *sight* to see." (*v.*) To see. "If all goes well, we will *sight* land tomorrow morning."

close (*v.*; klōz) To shut. "The office will *close* at noon tomorrow." (*n.*) The end. "We balance all accounts at the *close* of the business day."
close (*adj.*; klōs) Stuffy. "The air in this room is *close*." (*adj.*) Tight. "It will be a close fit, but the copy machine will go in that corner." (*adv.*) Near. "The water cooler is too *close* to my office."
clothes (*n.*) Wearing apparel. "Appropriate *clothes* should be worn in an office."
cloths (*n.*) Fabrics. "Are there any more *cloths* in the supply room?"

commence (*v.*) To begin. "We shall *commence* contract negotiations today."
comments (*n.*) Remarks. "Your *comments* on our marketing problems are most helpful." (*v.*) To mark distinctly. "My supervisor always *comments* on my performance."

complement (*n.*) Something that completes. "Without a full *complement* of workers, we can't handle that contract." (*v.*) To make whole. "The new employees *complement* our staff nicely."
compliment (*n.*) A flattering remark. " A *compliment* for a job well done is most welcome." (*v.*) To express approval. "A wise supervisor always *compliments* good workers."

correspondence (*n.*) Letters. "We answer all *correspondence* immediately."
correspondents (*n.*) Persons conducting correspondence or commercial relations. "Each of our sales *correspondents* works for five representatives."

council (*n.*) An assembly that deliberates. "An advisory *council* sets industry guidelines."
counsel (*n.*) Advice. "The company's legal staff provides management with good *counsel*." (*v.*) To give advice, especially on important matters. "Our personnel department will *counsel* employees on career choices."
consul (*n.*) A government official who represents a nation in a foreign country. "If you need help in negotiating with companies in Germany, notify the American *consul* in Bonn."

defer (*v.*) To postpone. "May I *defer* my payment until next month?" To yield. "When it comes to a knowledge of procedures, I always *defer* to the older workers."

differ (*v.*) To disagree; to be unlike. "Successful salespeople often *differ* in their approach to a customer."

dense (*adj.*) Thick. "The *dense* smoke drove us from the building."
dents (*n. pl.*) Depressions in a surface. "This old file cabinet has a lot of dents."

dependence (*n.*) Reliance; trust. "The company's *dependence* upon a single supplier frightened the purchasing department."
dependents (*n. pl.*) Persons who rely on others for support. "The tax witheld from your check will depend on the number of *dependents*."

desert (*n.*; 'dez-ərt) Arid, barren land. "The new agricultural company hoped to make the *desert* bloom."
desert (*v.*; di-'zərt) To abandon. "This is a good financial plan, and we will not *desert* it." (*n.*; usually plural) Deserved reward or punishment. "He got his just *deserts* for being too greedy."
dessert (*n.*) A sweet course at the end of a meal. "We had chocolate cake for *dessert*."

dye (*n.*) A stain or color. "Will this *dye* run when it is washed?" (*v.*) To stain or color. "I *dyed* this coat last month."
die (*n.*) A tool for molding or shaping. "We will need new *dies* if we change the product's design." One of a pair of dice. "One die is red." (*v.*) To cease living. "That tree will *die* unless it is fertilized."

formally (*adv.*) In a formal manner. "She has not *formally* accepted."
formerly (*adv.*) Previously. "He formerly worked for a competitor."

lead (*n.*; rhymes with *bed*) A heavy metal. "It took three people to lift that large *lead* pipe."
lead (*v.*; past *led*) To guide. "She will *lead* the company into new markets."

loose (*adj.*) Unfastened; not compact. "The *loose* parts will get all mixed up." (*v.*) To set free. "Don't let the dog *loose*."
lose (*v.*) To mislay; to fail to win. "Please don't *lose* that important report."

patients (*n.*) Persons under medical care. "The physician examined the *patients* carefully."
patience (*n.*) The quality of enduring without complaint. "If you have *patience*, you can work with and for anyone."

personal (*adj.*) Belonging to a particular person. "Never leave your *personal* belongings on the top of your desk."
personnel (*n.*) Staff of people. "All our *personnel* know how to use a desk-top computer."

precede (*v.*) To go before. "My name should *precede* Ms. Castella's in the company telephone directory."
proceed (*v.*) To advance. "After the meeting in Denver, we will *proceed* to the conference in Seattle."

precedence (*n.*) Priority in time or rank. "That rush project takes *precedence* over everything else."

precedents (*n.*) Established rules; things done that may serve as examples for later actions. "There are several *precedents* to guide us in this kind of sales campaign."

principle (*n.*) General truth. "The basic *principle* of finance does not change." Rule of conduct. "His company has always been guided by the highest *principles*."

principal (*adj.*) Chief. "Electronic computers are the company's *principal* product." A chief person or thing. "She is one of the *principals* in the company." Money on which interest is paid or income received. "We can spend the interest, but we cannot touch the *principal*." One who hires another to act for him or her. "An agent has power to make contracts for a *principal*."

reality (*n.*) That which is real. "The *reality* is that certain skills are more in demand."

realty (*n.* and *adj.*) Real estate. "Our *realty* company is looking for a new office site for us."

residence (*n.*) A house; dwelling place. "Is your *residence* close to where you work?"

residents (*n. pl.*) Those living in a place. "The *residents* of the apartment started a bowling league."

right (*adj.*) Correct. "After weeks of searching, he found the *right* job." (*n.*) Privilege. "You have the *right* to find a better job."

rite (*n.*) Ceremony. "We observe the *rite* of opening each meeting with The Pledge of Allegiance."

write (*v.*) To inscribe. "Please *write* your account number on each check."

stationary (*adj.*) Fixed in position. "A *stationary* lamp gives better light."

stationery (*n.*) Writing paper and envelopes. "Our company *stationery* was redesigned last year."

superintendence (*n.*) Management. "We work directly under the *superintendence* of a district manager."

superintendents (*n. pl.*) Supervisors. "The *superintendents* of our company's power plants spoke at the energy conference."

COMMUNICATION LABORATORY

APPLICATION EXERCISES

A. Now that you have studied the meanings of the words most commonly confused, see if you can apply them correctly. Study the list of words given here. Select from the list the appropriate words to insert in the blank spaces within the sentences and write those words on a separate sheet of paper. No word should be used more than one time.

advise	principle	complement
advice	principal	compliment
formally	accept	all ready
formerly	except	already

1. Today I received a nice _____ on this outfit.
2. Please _____ the members that the meeting will begin promptly.
3. The firm used the interest from its investments but kept the _____ intact.
4. The representatives are _____ to begin the sales campaign.
5. It is _____ too late to improve sales in this quarter.
6. Ms. Aston _____ worked in our regional office.
7. The Board of Directors always takes the _____ of the company's attorney.
8. I would willingly _____ the responsibility that goes with the job.
9. Everyone _____ Carl spoke in favor of the plan.
10. This product is a fine _____ to our line of tools.

B. Follow the instructions in Exercise A.

stationary	cite	basis
stationery	site	bases
desert	precede	accede
dessert	proceed	exceed

1. The sales staff believes it can _____ last year's performance.
2. A transformer in a power plant is a _____ machine.
3. The company is searching for a _____ for its new manufacturing facility.
4. In the manufacturing process, painting must _____ the final inspection.
5. Ralph lost ten pounds by avoiding _____.
6. This color ink looks good on our new ivory _____.
7. After we make this strong case, the general manager is sure to _____ to our request.
8. Can you _____ the law that governs the labeling of hazardous material?
9. Quality and service are the _____ upon which our company was built.
10. We certainly don't want to _____ our solid financing plan.

C. Follow the instructions in Exercise A.

dependents	residence	bare
dependence	residents	bear
alter	assistance	lead
altar	assistants	led

1. The shipping supervisor has just hired three new _____.
2. The amount withheld from your pay for taxes depends upon the number of _____ you have.
3. A large number of the _____ of our town oppose any increase in taxes.
4. That invention allowed the company to take the _____ in its industry.
5. Our operators are trained to give _____ to any caller.

6. Since sales have not increased, perhaps we'd better _____ our advertising plans.
7. This budget will allow us to purchase only the _____ essentials.
8. The fire insurance on a private _____ is not very expensive.
9. _____ upon past successes will not help us in the future.
10. I can't _____ to visit that difficult customer.

D. Follow the instructions in Exercise A.

affect   council   patience
effect   counsel   patients
precedence   personal   commence
precedents   personnel   comments

1. Our _____ will accompany us to court.
2. The higher postal rates _____ every business.
3. The city _____ has discussed this legislation many times.
4. I had to go to New York on _____ business.
5. Your _____ on this plan would be most welcome.
6. The _____ who work in a business are its most important asset.
7. The attorney tells us that there are many _____ for the action we took.
8. It takes time to _____ a change in any large organization.
9. To supervise people demands a lot of _____.
10. The ceremony will _____ right after the governor's speech.

COMMUNICATING FOR RESULTS

Selecting the Right Word. Assume that the following sentences are taken from an office memorandum. Rewrite them, using correct words for those that have been used incorrectly or misspelled.

The time is rite for us to decrease our dependents upon suppliers who chews to meet their schedules rather than ours. We must comments at once to search for an appropriate cite where we can manufacture our own electrical parts. We have the necessary capitol available. If we were to decide to push ahead, the affect of such a decision would be to positively altar our method of operating.

P · A · R · T

4

DEVELOPING YOUR LANGUAGE SKILLS

More than ever before, job applicants today must have superior grammar skills, because employers are aware that an understanding of grammar provides an excellent basis for good writing, speaking, listening, and reading skills—skills that help businesses succeed.

This chapter will help you choose the correct words and put them together expressively and meaningfully, thereby enhancing your ability to communicate well and making you an attractive prospective employee. Given a situation that requires polished grammar skills, your mastery of the units in this chapter will enable you to do the following:

1. *Construct complete sentences that will describe your ideas fully.*

2. *Use verbs correctly to give your writing the proper direction.*

3. *Use nouns and pronouns precisely, so that who does what is always clear.*

4. *Choose the correct verb form to agree with any noun or pronoun, so that your sentences are always easy to understand.*

5. *Select exact descriptive words—adjectives and adverbs that will convey your thoughts.*

6. *Use conjunctions and prepositions to join words clearly and correctly.*

9

An Overview of Grammar

If you have not already been exposed to word processing equipment, you may not be familiar with words such as *cursor, wraparound,* and *scroll.* These words are mysterious to those who have not had the opportunity to use a word processor. But those who have know that a *cursor* is only a blinking light on a television screen. *Wraparound* is simply the machine's ability to start a new line without being told to do so. And *scroll* is just a way of saying "turn the page."

The concepts behind this jargon, as you can quickly see, are not in any way mysterious or difficult to understand. These words are difficult to understand only if they are unfamiliar.

Likewise, the principles of grammar and punctuation are not difficult to understand. Some grammatical terms, however, may be unfamiliar. Others you may have heard of but may not fully understand. The best way to demystify such jargon is simply to learn what the words mean—which, of course, is the goal of this introductory unit.

The Parts of Speech

All the thousands of different words we use can be categorized into one of eight groups, which are discussed below. Knowing these terms will simplify your understanding of all that follows, so give this your undivided attention.

Nouns and Pronouns. The names of people, places, and things are called *nouns.*

PEOPLE:	manager	Fred
	boss	Amy
	friend	Glen
	brother	Bert
PLACES:	city	Ames
	store	Sid's
	state	Iowa
	county	Hunter County
THINGS:	car	Buick
	television	Zenith
	bike	Schwinn

Obviously, such words are *very* commonly used—almost all our sentences contain nouns.

My *manager* bought a *bike* at *Sid's Department Store*.

Her *friend* fixed his *car*.

Hunter County is where *Ed* lives.

As often as we use nouns, however, we also use *pronouns,* which are noun substitutes:

Singular	Plural	Singular	Plural	Singular	Plural
I	we	me	us	my	our
you	you	you	you	your	your
he		him		his	
she	they	her	them	her	their
it		it		its	

Each of these pronouns is commonly used to replace a noun.

Miriam sent the free-lance work to John.

She sent the free-lance work to *him*.

Glenn left early, but the store was closed.

He left early, but *it* was closed.

Yes, Georgia is the state where Hugh and Diane lived.

Yes, *it* is the state where *they* lived.

Remember that *pro* means "for," and you will be sure to remember that pronouns are substitutes *for nouns*.

Verbs. You may have heard verbs referred to as *action words,* because verbs do indeed depict the motion or the activity of a sentence.

Jethro *bought* a van.

Allison *is playing* tennis.

Ms. Pike *signs* all checks over $500.

Besides depicting action, however, verbs also show condition or state of being.

Jason *is* tired.

Ms. Brunner *has been* away on a busin   trip.

I *am* the assistant director.

Verbs can be just a single word, or they can consist of several words.

Our company *has* a pool on the fourth floor.   (*Has* is the verb in this sentence.)

Grace *has been swimming* during her lunch hours.   (The verb is *has been swimming*.)

Ms. Millerton *should have been* here for this meeting.   (The verb is *should have been*.)

Ms. Millerton *should have been asked* to this meeting.   (The verb is *should have been asked*.)

CLASS PRACTICE 1

As you learned in Units 4 and 7, oral Class Practice and Proofreading Practice exercises are provided throughout Units 9 through 33 to help reinforce the principles you learn in each unit.

To test your skill in identifying nouns, pronouns, and verbs, label each word in parentheses in the following sentences *N*, *P*, or *V*. Use a separate sheet of paper.

1. Two (managers) in our department (insisted) that (they) required comprehensive data bases.
2. Veronica and Joy (have been requisitioning) the (supplies) for the meeting (they) planned.
3. (He) and (I) already (are prepared) for the next conference with our (editors in chief).
4. The pamphlets (she) wrote on Friday (have been returned) by the (printer).
5. (He) and (Carolyn) (should have been) ready, but (they) left the sales reports in the (hotel).

Now fill in a word for each blank (marked *a* and *b*) in the sentences below. Identify whether your choices are nouns, pronouns, or verbs.

6. Our ___*a*___ obviously ___*b*___ more money.
7. Please give ___*a*___ a copy of the summary sheet that I ___*b*___.
8. Alex ___*a*___ extra copies of the ___*b*___.
9. ___*a*___ retyped the entire ___*b*___.
10. Only ___*a*___ has returned the completed ___*b*___.

Adjectives. Modifiers are words that *clarify* the description or the quality of something. The most commonly used modifiers are *adjectives* (which we will discuss here) and *adverbs* (which we will discuss immediately after adjectives).

Adjectives are words that modify, describe, or define a noun or a pronoun. They tell what kind, which one, or how many. Note how adjectives change the descriptions of nouns in the following sentences.

The *new* building is a *tall, modern* structure.   (*New* describes the noun *building*; *tall* and *modern* describe the noun *structure*.)

It is a *new, tall, modern* structure. (Here, the adjectives *new, tall,* and *modern* describe the noun *structure.*)

It is *new, tall,* and *modern.* (Here, the three adjectives modify the pronoun *it.* What is new, tall, and modern? *It* is.)

Helen is a *successful, innovative* designer. (The adjectives *successful* and *innovative* modify or describe the noun *designer.*)

She is *successful* and *innovative.* (Here, the adjectives *successful* and *innovative* modify the pronoun *she.*)

Other adjectives include the italicized words below:

this magazine	*these* vans
that agency	*those* stores
Florida hotel	*Kansas* office
three sales	*first* client
one-week delay	*up-to-date* file

As you can see, then, adjectives do indeed *describe.*

Adverbs. Like adjectives, adverbs are also modifiers.

1. Adverbs modify adjectives:

his *nearly* fatal accident

a *fairly* long table

her *obviously* expensive car

The adverbs *nearly, fairly,* and *obviously* modify the adjectives *fatal, long,* and *expensive.*

2. Adverbs modify verbs:

Jack ran *quickly.* (The adverb *quickly* modifies the verb *ran.*)

The committee *unanimously* approved the plan. (The adverb *unanimously* modifies the verb *approved.*)

3. Adverbs modify other adverbs:

Jack ran *very* quickly. (The adverb *very* modifies the adverb *quickly.*)

The committee *almost* unanimously approved the plan. (The adverb *almost* modifies the adverb *unanimously.*)

Perhaps you noticed that except for *very* and *almost,* all the adverbs above end in *ly.* Indeed, many adverbs are formed by adding *ly* to adjectives:

quiet	quietly
bad	badly
sudden	suddenly
careful	carefully

But there are others that do not end in *ly*, including *very, almost, never, here, there,* and many, many more.

To identify adverbs, most students generally try to remember that adverbs answer such questions as How? When? Where?

Put that carton *there*.   (Where? There. *There* is an adverb.)

Joanne draws *beautifully*.   (Draws how? Beautifully.)

Ms. Clemson will arrive *soon*.   (Arrive when? Soon.)

CLASS PRACTICE 2

A. Identify the words in parentheses as either adjectives or adverbs.

1. Karen (quietly) discussed the issue with the group for more than (three) hours.
2. Ms. Campbell returned the (broken) packages (immediately).
3. Jerry said that an (important) order will be delivered to us (soon).
4. Mr. Youngquist (strongly) argued against the (ridiculous) suggestion.
5. A (new) cathode-ray tube will be shipped (there) as soon as possible.

B. On a separate sheet of paper, rewrite the following sentences, filling in the blanks as you do so. Identify each of your fill-ins as an adjective or an adverb.

6. Sean always submits _____ work.
7. Sean always works _____.
8. Leroy generally arrives _____.
9. Barbara Conroy was _____ happy to hear the news.
10. Mark Lindstrom recently bought a _____ car.

Prepositions. Prepositions are words that connect and describe relationships. They include these very commonly used words:

in	to	for
by	from	with
of	after	before
out	on	over

Prepositions are always used in prepositional phrases such as the following:

in the morning	in April
by the door	by Hills Department Store
of the owners	of Mrs. Henson
to the company	to Collins Chemical Company
from her	from Rebecca
for him	for Scott
with them	with Rebecca and Scott

Now read the following pairs of sentences and notice the prepositional phrases in the second sentence in each pair.

We plan to meet.
We plan to meet *in the morning*.

Please give me the package.
Please give me the package *by the door*.

The request was to provide an itemized estimate.
The request *of the owners* was to provide an itemized estimate.

The price was 10 percent higher than we anticipated.
The price *to the company* was 10 percent higher than we anticipated.

The letter did not include a purchase order.
The letter *from her* did not include a purchase order.

A gift was delivered early this morning.

A gift *for him* was delivered early this morning.

We went later.
We went *with them* later.

In each case, the preposition helps to connect words in the form of a prepositional phrase, and it serves to connect that prepositional phrase to the rest of the sentence.

Some other commonly used prepositions are:

about	above	behind
before	except	between
into	until	among

Conjunctions. Conjunctions are the most commonly used connectors. The words *and, but, or,* and *nor* are conjunctions.

Glenn *and* Kyle demonstrated the computer's capabilities to a small audience. (The conjunction *and* joins two nouns, *Glenn* and *Kyle*.)

Glenn, Kyle, *and* Mark demonstrated the computer's capabilities. (The conjunction *and* joins three nouns.)

The books were stacked behind the cabinets *and* on the floor. (The conjunction *and* joins two prepositional phrases, *behind the cabinets* and *on the floor*.)

Andy always works quickly *but* neatly. (The conjunction *but* joins two adverbs, *quickly* and *neatly*.)

Other conjunctions that are used to join clauses in a special way are discussed later.

CLASS PRACTICE 3

On a separate sheet of paper, identify the words in parentheses as prepositions (*P*) or as conjunctions (*C*). For each preposition, identify the prepositional phrase.

1. Ms. McGrath (and) her assistant are (in) the auditorium.
2. Kenneth (or) Blanche will probably be (at) the booth (in) the afternoon.
3. In January (and) again in June, Marsh Industries led the fight (against) pollution.
4. All the sales representatives (except) her wanted to go (to) the national convention.
5. (For) next week's status meeting, Amy has prepared an agenda (and) minutes (of) our last meeting.
6. Melissa went (into) the conference room (at) 9 a.m.
7. Mr. Kreske divided most (of) the work (between) them.
8. The discount offer (for) certain items is valid (until) April 30.
9. Fill in your credit card number, (or) send us your check—but act (before) June 1!
10. Raymond (and) Elsa found the contracts (among) old papers.

Interjections. Interjections are words that express strong feeling; they are usually independent of the rest of the sentence.

Great! Joan succeeded in getting the Wilson account.

No! We certainly cannot approve the terms of this agreement.

Subjects and Predicates

Sentences consist of subjects and predicates. Simply put, the *subject* is that part of the sentence that tells (1) who is speaking, (2) who is spoken to, or (3) who or what is spoken about.

1. Who is speaking:

   I prefer an afternoon flight.   (The subject *I* identifies the person speaking.)

   We prefer an afternoon flight.   (*We* identifies the persons speaking.)

2. Who is spoken to:

   You are one of the best salespeople in our company, Betty.   (The subject *you* identifies the person spoken to.)

   You are two of the best salespeople in our company.   (Here the persons spoken to are two people, identified by the subject *you*.)

3. Who or what is spoken about:

   Jenny is the person in charge of sales promotion.   (Who is spoken about? *Jenny*, the subject of the sentence.)

She is the person in charge of sales promotion. (Who is the person spoken about? *She,* the subject of the sentence.)

Now notice how these sentences can be rephrased:

The person in charge of sales promotion is Jenny. *The person in charge of sales promotion* is she. (In both sentences, the subject is now *The person in charge of sales promotion.*)

This text editor performs a global search in just a few seconds. (What is spoken about? *This text editor,* the subject of the sentence.)

It performs a global search in just a few seconds. (What is spoken about? *It,* the subject of the sentence.)

Now notice how the person or thing spoken about can be compounded—that is, notice how two or more people or things can be spoken about:

Jenny and Carl are the people in charge of sales promotion. (The subject is *Jenny and Carl,* the people spoken about.)

Jenny, Carl, and Richard are the people in charge of sales promotion. (The subject is *Jenny, Carl, and Richard,* the people spoken about.)

Once you have identified the subject correctly, remember that the predicate is simply the rest of the sentence.

CLASS PRACTICE 4

Identify the subjects in the following sentences. Can you tell whether the subject is the person speaking, the person spoken to, or the person or thing spoken about?

1. Helen is ready to leave for Australia.
2. This machinery is no longer under warranty.
3. You must be sure to deposit the money before the bank closes today.
4. They are ready to leave.
5. I will be on vacation during the first week of August.
6. Helen and Rebecca have completed the sales analyses that Mrs. Gulden had requested.
7. Cars and vans are leased for our staff.
8. Jerry, Nina, and Kay were assigned to develop the advertising campaign for the Sperry account.

Phrases and Clauses

When words are grouped together, those word groups may be categorized as phrases or as clauses. A *clause* is a group of words that has both a subject and a predicate. A *phrase* does *not* have a subject and a predicate. Let's look at clauses first.

Independent Clauses. As we have seen, a complete sentence is a clause. Because the clause in a complete sentence can stand alone, we call that clause an *independent clause.*

Jenny is the person in charge of sales promotion. (The subject is *Jenny.* The predicate is the rest of the sentence. This is an independent clause. It can stand alone as a sentence.)

This text editor can perform a global search in a few seconds. (The subject is *This text editor.* The predicate is the rest of the sentence. This clause is independent; it can stand alone as a sentence.)

Dependent Clauses. Not all clauses can stand alone as a sentence. Clauses that are incomplete—that cannot stand alone as sentences—are called *dependent clauses.*

if you need more information (The subject is *you;* the predicate is the rest of the clause. Read the clause aloud. Does it make sense by itself? No. What should you do *if you need more information?*)

when Ms. Block returns the merchandise (Is this a clause? Does this group of words have a subject and a predicate? Yes. The subject is *Ms. Block,* and the predicate is *returns the merchandise.* But what will happen *when Ms. Block returns the merchandise?* This is a dependent clause.)

Because they cannot stand alone as sentences, dependent clauses must be joined to independent clauses, as in the following sentences.

If you need more information, you should call your regional benefits office. (Here the dependent clause, *if you need more information,* is joined to an independent clause, *you should call your regional benefits office.*)

When Ms. Block returns the merchandise, Henry will give her a credit voucher. (Again, the dependent clause, *when Ms. Block returns the merchandise,* is joined to an independent clause.)

CLASS PRACTICE 5

Some of the following groups of words are sentences. Others are dependent clauses that are incorrectly treated as sentences. Identify each, and then add independent clauses to the dependent clauses to create sentences.

1. Edward misplaced the original contract file.
2. Because he misplaced the original contract file.
3. When Harry bought this store.
4. Mr. Marshall submitted this report to the committee.
5. If we do not finish by Friday.
6. Kenneth and Lauren may be asked to attend the convention in San Francisco.
7. Before Janet leaves for the airport.
8. Blaine has applied for a position with Ampex Chemicals Inc.

Phrases. Unlike clauses, phrases have neither subjects nor predicates. Three kinds of phrases are discussed below: prepositional phrases, infinitive phrases, and verb phrases.

Prepositional Phrases. Prepositional phrases such as *from her, with them, to the store, at the meeting,* and *on the plane* generally serve as adjectives or adverbs.

Theresa went *with them.* (Went where? With them. Adverbs usually answer the question Where? Therefore, *with them* serves as an adverb.)

The customer *with the umbrella* is Mr. Sinclair. (*With the umbrella* describes the noun *customer;* because it describes a noun, this prepositional phrase must be an adjective.)

Infinitive Phrases. An infinitive is the *to* form of a verb: *to run, to go, to write, to be, to see, to have,* and so on. Infinitive phrases include the infinitive plus its subject, object, or modifiers. Infinitive phrases are most often used as nouns or as adjectives.

To become the president of the company is Beatrice's goal. (The complete infinitive phrase is *To become the president of the company;* it is the subject of the verb *is.*)

My supervisor is the person *to see for information on medical benefits.* (The infinitive phrase *to see for information on medical benefits* modifies the noun *person;* therefore, this infinitive phrase is an adjective.)

One pitfall in identifying infinitives is to confuse an infinitive with a prepositional phrase that begins with *to.* To avoid this trap, study the following Quick Trick.

QUICK TRICK ▏ INFINITIVE OR PREPOSITIONAL PHRASE?

Compare the following infinitives with the prepositional phrases next to them.

Infinitive	Prepositional Phrase
to run	to the store
to type	to them
to control	to us
to write	to many customers

Now try to use each infinitive as a verb: *I run, you type, we control, they write,* and so on. Using these infinitives as verbs works because infinitives are verbs! Prepositional phrases do not include any verbs. Thus if you were to try to use any of the words in the prepositional phrase as a verb, you would get nonsense. Try it to see for yourself.

Verb Phrases. Verb phrases consist of two or more verbs—a main verb plus one or more helping verbs—joined to function as one verb within a sentence. REMEMBER: The main verb is always the last verb in the verb phrase.

John *has been asking* for volunteers. (*Has been asking* is a verb phrase. *Asking* is the main verb; *has* and *been* are helpers.)

Our company *will be moving* to new quarters soon. (*Will be moving* is the verb phrase. *Moving* is the main verb; *will* and *be* are helpers.)

Ms. DeCamp *should have been notified* of the change in schedule. (The verb phrase is *should have been notified.* Which is the main verb? Which are the helpers?)

Do not be misled when the verb phrase is interrupted by any other words, as in the following examples.

John *has* already *been asking* for volunteers. (The adverb *already* interrupts the verb phrase *has been asking.*)

Our company *will* soon *be moving* to new quarters.

CLASS PRACTICE 6

Identify the words in parentheses in the following sentences. On a separate sheet of paper, write *PP* for each prepositional phrase, *IP* for each infinitive phrase, or *VP* for each verb phrase.

1. Harriet (has been working) here (for about 10 years).
2. Jennifer wants (to work) (for a large computer company).
3. The meeting (with the lawyers) (has been canceled).
4. When we display these products, we must be sure (to stress the key benefits) and (to emphasize the value) (of the five-year warranty).
5. Elko Chemicals has laboratories (in the South) and distribution plants (across the country).
6. Ms. Hazeltine divided the work (between Audrey and me) and asked us (to give her) a progress report.
7. We are waiting (for the results) (of the recent union election).
8. A customer survey (has been developed) and (has been submitted) to the committee, which (will review) the survey next Friday.

COMMUNICATION LABORATORY

APPLICATION EXERCISES

A. Identify the words in parentheses in the following sentences. On a separate sheet, for each choice write the part of speech (*noun, verb, conjunction,* and so on) or the kind of phrase (*VP, IP,* or *PP*).

1. Marietta (and) George (have been invited) (to the banquet).
2. Mr. Nye wants (to review the proposal), and he wants (to share a copy) with Ms. Russell.
3. (They) have decided to reject the offer (from) Hastings Production.
4. Our (manager) has developed an (excellent) system for ensuring that we follow up on all customer (requests).
5. James (has) only one copy of the manual, (but) he (thinks) that he can get more.
6. Laura's flight should be arriving (soon); when she gets (here), we will take a (taxi) to the city.
7. (Marion) is on vacation (until May 30); while she is out, Sylvia will help you (with this problem).
8. All of us think that this product (will be) a (tremendous) success, (but) its development is (very) expensive.
9. Bart is (exceptionally) happy (about his promotion), and he (is) eager (to begin) his new job.
10. Each (executive) in our division is responsible (for) his or her (budget).
11. Barbara (has) an (expert) assistant, James Henley, who (may be) able to help you.
12. Mr. Red Eagle (has requested) that we estimate the value of his property (for him).
13. (We) prefer the (old) system, (but) we admit that the (new) system is faster.
14. Angela Rossi's suggestion is (very) interesting, (but) Ms. Damstra said it (would be) expensive to put into effect.
15. Send this (package) to Lawton Manufacturing (by messenger).

B. Which of the following clauses are dependent, and which are independent? On a separate sheet, write *D* or *I* to identify each clause. (REMEMBER: Independent clauses can stand alone as complete sentences; dependent clauses cannot.)

1. When Ms. Baxter asked us to help her with that project.
2. If you would like to speak with one of our customer service agents.
3. You and I should work together to proofread this long report.
4. Edna Gabler is a senior auditor for our firm.
5. Which we requested from the warehouse.
6. While they were in the auditorium this morning.
7. Lyle Owens is the supervisor of the data processing staff.
8. The J & L Corporation is a major supplier of building materials in the East.
9. Because Sharon and Mike are working on a high-priority project.
10. Frank and Andrea are in the auditorium.
11. That we need to complete this report.
12. You should discuss these benefits with someone who is familiar with personnel policies.

3. Although Mr. McCoy is not in the office this week.
4. They are now working on an important new account.
5. As Mrs. Louis said in our meeting yesterday afternoon.

VOCABULARY AND SPELLING STUDIES

A. Distinguish between the meaning and the spelling of each of the following groups of words, which are often confused: *recent, resent; reference, reverence.*

B. Add a short prefix to each of the following words to change the meaning of the word to a negative one.

1. polite
2. pure
3. certain
4. reliable
5. apt
6. logical

COMMUNICATING FOR RESULTS

A Matter of Publicity. You work for Lockhart Productions, a large company with an excellent reputation for high-quality products and for fairness to its employees. Lockhart, through its supervisors, always encourages its employees to take advantage of tuition-refund programs, supports employees' favorite charities, makes available a physical fitness center after work and on weekends, and has an annual Christmas party and a summer picnic for employees and their families. Because of these policies, Lockhart is generally regarded as a good place to work.

Recently there have been various rumors concerning a possible merger of Lockhart with another company. One day you receive a phone call from a local newspaper editor who asks you what you know about the merger. You have heard quite a bit.

A lot of the information you have heard is unflattering to Lockhart and its management. You have heard this information from many different sources and feel confident that most of it is true. You and your family have been very friendly with your Lockhart colleagues and with some of Lockhart's management. Given this and your satisfaction in working at Lockhart, you don't know what to do.

What should you tell the editor?

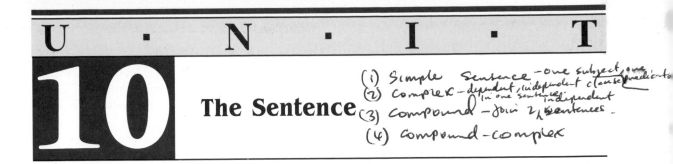

U · N · I · T

10

The Sentence

[handwritten annotations:]
(1) Simple Sentence - one subject, one predicate
(2) Complex - dependent, independent clause in one sentence
(3) Compound - join 2 independent sentences.
(4) Compound - complex

When we answer someone's question with a simple "yes" or a simple "no," our one-word response says a lot. For example, assume that a friend asks, "Do you want to come with me to the game tomorrow?" and that your response is "Yes." Your one-word answer really includes some *understood* words. Your answer really is "Yes, *I do want to go with you to the game tomorrow.*" However, a simple "Yes" says it all!

Except when answering such questions, we seldom can communicate complete messages with single one-word responses. To express ourselves precisely, we must know how to use sentences expertly. The first step, of course, is to learn what a sentence is.

The Sentence Defined

You have probably heard a *sentence* defined as "a group of words that expresses a complete thought." Note the word *complete*. If the thought is not complete, then the group of words is not a sentence but a fragment.

It is important that you learn to write and speak in sentences—that is, learn to express yourself in complete thoughts, not in fragments. To be able to distinguish between complete thoughts and incomplete thoughts, look at the Quick Trick below.

QUICK TRICK | **NO SENSE, NO SENTENCE**

Whenever you must decide whether a group of words is a sentence, consider whether the words make sense. If they do make sense, then the group of words is a sentence. If they do not make sense, the group of words is not a sentence.

We will receive a 10 percent discount for early payment. (These words make sense; they express a complete thought. Therefore, they make up a sentence.)

Jessica Owens is planning to attend the seminar next week. (Again, the words make sense. They express a complete thought; therefore, this is a sentence.)

If we do not receive the equipment within the next ten days. (This group of words is not complete; it doesn't express a complete thought. This is *not* a sentence.)

CLASS PRACTICE 1

In the following groups of words, tell which ones are sentences and which ones are not. Just say "sense" or "no sense." Then, for additional practice, take each group of "no sense" words and add words as necessary to make sense of them.

1. Working as hard as she could.
2. To order a copy of this catalog.
3. Their check was received at our Los Angeles branch office.
4. Because we forgot to send the payment.
5. Our end-of-year sale ended last Tuesday.
6. If you need more information.
7. Since this store opened last year.
8. Alice Hill was appointed group vice president.
9. This building will be painted during the month of April.

Subjects and Predicates

The subject is that part of the sentence that shows (1) who is speaking, (2) who is spoken to, or (3) the person or thing spoken about. In the following examples, note that the complete subject may be one word or several words. Also notice that all the other words in the sentence make up the predicate of the sentence.

The predicate is that part of the sentence that tells you something about the subject. The core of the predicate is the verb, which can also be one word or more than one word.

Study these examples:

1. The person speaking is generally *I* or *we*, as shown in these examples:

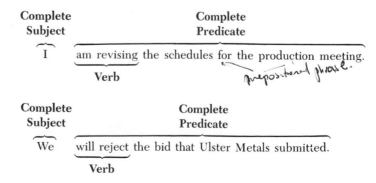

Complete Subject	Complete Predicate
I	am revising the schedules for the production meeting.
	Verb prepositional phrase.

Complete Subject	Complete Predicate
We	will reject the bid that Ulster Metals submitted.
	Verb

2. The person *spoken to* is generally addressed *you:*

Complete
Subject

Complete
Predicate

You   should inform your supervisor of the change in schedule.

Verb

3. The person or thing *spoken about* can be any number of subjects, two of which are shown here:

Complete
Subject

Complete
Predicate

One accountant whom we consulted was especially helpful.

Verb

Complete
Subject

Complete
Predicate

Our new training materials will be delivered later today.

Verb

Once you identify the subject, you know that the rest of the sentence is the predicate. As you can see, then, identifying subjects and predicates is not a difficult task, but it will become simpler yet with practice.

CLASS PRACTICE 2

Identify the *complete subject* of each sentence below. (Remember that the rest of the sentence must, of course, be the *predicate*.)

1. Increases in our prices must be approved by our marketing manager.
2. Most of the applicants had excellent communication skills.
3. You will receive an automatic increase at the end of your probationary period.
4. The findings of the report have been shared with all the members of the committee.
5. Mrs. Lloyd is the manager of our West Coast sales office.
6. One of the clerks will be transferred to our annex.
7. These invoices must be processed no later than Monday.
8. The instruction book for using this word processing program is very simple and easy to follow.

Simple and Compound Subjects

Once you are able to identify the complete subject, you must next be able to tell whether that complete subject is a *simple* or a *compound* subject. In later units the importance of this distinction will become clear.

A *simple subject* is the single most important word in the complete subject.

The *supervisor* of these two departments is now on vacation. (The complete subject is *The supervisor of these two departments*. The most important word in this complete subject is *supervisor*; therefore, *supervisor* is the simple subject.)

A *compound subject* consists of two or more words that are equally important. Usually these words are joined by *and, or,* or *nor.*

The *supervisor and* her *assistant* are now on vacation. (The complete subject is *The supervisor and her assistant.* In this complete subject the two most important words are *supervisor* and *assistant.* Therefore, the compound subject is *supervisor and assistant.*)

The *supervisor,* her *assistant, and* their *secretary* are all on vacation. (The complete subject is *The supervisor, her assistant, and their secretary.* This complete subject has three equally important words—*supervisor, assistant, and secretary.* Thus the compound subject is *supervisor, assistant, and secretary.*)

CLASS PRACTICE 3

Select the simple or the compound subject in each sentence below. (HINT: Identify the complete subject first.)

1. The experience of each sales representative is a key factor in determining the annual bonus that he or she will receive.
2. A thesaurus and a dictionary are invaluable tools when you are preparing a report.
3. A restaurant near the hotel has been selected for the luncheon.
4. The calculator on my desk is available to you if you need it.
5. This word processor and that printer belong to our Personnel Department.
6. An updated report and a revised price list were the only items in the envelope.
7. Dr. Geraldine D. Dubrow is the head of our Medical Department.
8. Beth and Jeff were both selected to attend the convention in Puerto Rico.
9. Arnold or Emily has the only copy of the revised five-year marketing plan.

Sentence Order

The *normal order* of the sentence is complete subject followed by complete predicate, as in all the examples that you have seen so far.

None of the customers were aware of the special discount for cash payments. (The complete subject is *None of the customers;* it is followed by the complete predicate, *were aware of the special discount for cash payments.* This sentence is in *normal* order.)

Whenever the complete subject does *not* precede the complete predicate, the sentence is said to be in *inverted order.*

During the third-quarter sales period just ended, two representatives in our sales division received cash bonuses of $5,000 each. (This sentence is in inverted order because part of the predicate appears before the complete subject. The complete subject is *two representatives in our division.* As you see, part of the complete predicate, *During the third-quarter sales period just ended,* appears before the complete subject. Therefore this sentence is in *inverted* order.)

The normal order of the sentence is as follows:

Two representatives in our sales division received cash bonuses of $5,000 each during the third-quarter sales period just ended.

Some of the most common—and the most serious—errors in grammar occur because writers and speakers are not able to identify the simple subjects of sentences, especially in inverted sentences. Thus the ability to recognize normal order is important. Likewise, it is important to be able to change inverted order to normal order.

To change inverted sentences to normal order, simply find the complete subject and then rearrange the sentence so that the complete subject is first and is followed by the complete predicate.

When he signed the contract, Mr. Gorski received a $2,000 advance payment. (Inverted order.)

Mr. Gorski received a $2,000 advance payment when he signed the contract. (Normal order.)

During the months of July and August, our business generally drops about 15 to 20 percent. (Inverted order.)

Our business generally drops about 15 to 20 percent during the months of July and August. (Normal order.)

Have you ever noticed that questions are usually phrased in inverted order?

Will Ms. Diaz be one of the engineers invited to the conference? (Inverted order.)

Ms. Diaz will be one of the engineers invited to the conference. (Normal order.)

When will the invitations be mailed? (Inverted order.)

The invitations will be mailed when? (Normal order.)

You will notice that some sentences will sound odd when you change them to normal order, but do not let this bother you. You are merely using this as a technique to identify subjects of sentences.

CLASS PRACTICE 4

Which of the following sentences are in normal order, and which ones are in inverted order? Identify each; then change the inverted-order sentences to normal order. In addition, identify the complete subject of each sentence.

1. When will you arrive?
2. In February Miss Higgins will be appointed vice president.
3. When Mrs. Raub comes, Adam will give her this package.
4. Were all the new brochures distributed?
5. Ms. Newton-Smith is responsible for the Toronto office.
6. We found the contract Mr. Tristram had been searching for after he left.
7. In the fall, our sales representatives focus on telephone campaigns.
8. We found only Miss Depree and Mrs. Curme in the conference room.
9. One copy of the letter was sent to Leonard.
10. Does this carton weigh more than 5 kilograms?

COMMUNICATION LABORATORY

APPLICATION EXERCISES

A. On a separate sheet of paper, number from 1 through 13. For each of the following sentences (*a*) change to normal order any sentence that is inverted, (*b*) write the complete subject, and (*c*) draw a line under the simple or the compound subject.

1. A car and a van were leased for our district office.
2. When Sarah arrives, John will ask her to sign these vouchers.
3. A new brochure will be written and mailed to all customers.
4. Arthur and Mary Jo are coordinating the seminar.
5. On the dais were the three speakers.
6. By completing all the courses in the evening program, she created an opportunity for a promotion.
7. Next Monday Evelyn will begin her two-week trip across the country.
8. Does one of the supervisors know the revised schedule for evening courses sponsored by the company?
9. All employees must call in before 9 a.m. whenever they will be absent for any reason.
10. By noon on Friday we should know whether the court approved our request for an extension.
11. Lunch and dinner are included in the daily rate.
12. Will Ms. Gilmore be able to attend the first session?
13. Within the next year or so, Frank or Stephanie will probably be given the opportunity to manage a branch office.

B. On a separate sheet of paper, (*a*) identify each complete sentence below or (*b*) add the words necessary to make any sentence fragment a complete sentence. Then (*c*) indicate the normal order of any inverted sentence, and (*d*) identify the complete subject and the simple or compound subject for each sentence, labeling each as simple or compound.

1. William does not understand these directions very well.
2. Were all managers and supervisors supposed to attend the meeting to discuss new ventures?
3. Ms. Rickles the audiovisual equipment for our sales-training courses.
4. Do you know where we can buy good-quality diskettes for less than $5 each?
5. One of the CPAs in our department.
6. During the busy season our district managers travel from one store to another.
7. Time and money are the two most important criteria, according to Mr. Bentley.
8. We write more interoffice memorandums and reports than letters in our department.
9. In our department we write more interoffice memorandums and reports than letters.
10. Her application for the sales job has been accepted.
11. One of the reasons why we discontinued these products is that the cost of manufacturing them is excessive.
12. This is the principal reason for switching our insulation material to poly-vinyl chloride.
13. The high cost of leather is the principal reason for switching to another material.
14. Nitrogen and oxygen are two of the gases that are stored in these containers.
15. Are nitrogen and oxygen stored in these containers?
16. One of the causes of the strike.
17. Will Ms. Furjanic be able to design the brochures that we need within a week?
18. Will one of the artists complete all the sketches we need by Wednesday on schedule?
19. The cost of printing and binding 2,500 copies of the catalog.
20. The estimate and the actual bill were more than $4,000 apart!

VOCABULARY AND SPELLING STUDIES

A. Because the following groups of words are so similar, they are often confused: *device, devise; precede, proceed, proceeds; mood, mode; command, commend.*

Distinguish between the meaning and the spelling of the words in each group; then write a sample sentence using each word.

B. Which of the following words are misspelled?

1. apologize   4. advertise
2. merchandize   5. exercise
3. realise   6. analyse

COMMUNICATING FOR RESULTS

Understanding Industry Jargon. During his first day at work for the World-Wide Film Corporation, Ken Grier is asked by his supervisor to "Get two *OKs* and send them to Pamela McClintock." Ken is embarrassed to ask, but he does not know what an *OK* is. What should he do?

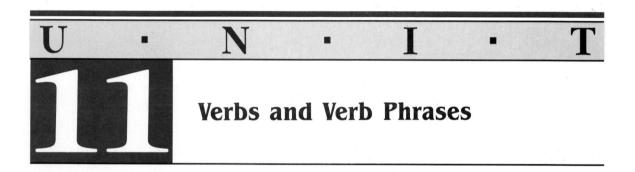

U · N · I · T

11

Verbs and Verb Phrases

As you remember from the last unit, verbs are the core of the predicate. Verbs tell something about the subject of the sentence. Because they often show an action or a movement by the subject, verbs spark a sentence and bring it to life.

Your ability to use verbs correctly will help you avoid some of the most common and most serious errors in speaking and writing. Thus you should pay special attention to this unit and the next.

Verbs—The Motors of Sentences

A verb describes a subject's action, condition, or state of being. Therefore, you may find it helpful to think of verbs as the "motors" of sentences.

Fred *lifted* the projector.   (*Lifted* is the verb. It describes Fred's *action*.)

Fred *looks* tired.   (*Looks* is the verb. It tells Fred's *condition*.)

Fred *is* in the auditorium.   (*Is* is the verb. It tells Fred's *state of being*.)

Now read the above sentences *without* the verbs. Do you see how the verbs serve as motors—how they describe an action, a condition, and a state of being? Here are some sentences without verbs. Note how they are incomplete without their motors.

> Ms. Styles one of the applicants for the position of word processing supervisor.

> The Stelton Corporation the contracts for the construction project.

> Helene and Frank the conference on sales techniques.

Do you understand these messages? Without verbs, the above groups of words express no message because they are incomplete. Now watch how these words come to life with the addition of verbs:

> Ms. Styles (*interviewed, rejected, accepted, is*) one of the applicants for the position of word processing supervisor.

> The Stelton Coporation (*signed, returned, revised, reviewed*) the contracts for the construction project.

> Helene and Frank (*enjoyed, attended, sponsored, coordinated*) the conference on sales techniques.

CLASS PRACTICE 1

Underline the verb in each of the following sentences. If the sentence has no verb, supply a verb for it.

1. Maria the agenda for the upcoming seminar.
2. Several copies of the minutes are in this file.
3. Mrs. Alvarez the executive vice president in charge of personnel.
4. The word processing equipment is on this floor.
5. Gregory and Eleanor the brochures for this product.
6. This catalog the features of each machine.
7. My manager a monthly production report.
8. A dictionary the meanings of words.
9. Lloyd Flynn gave a presentation entitled "The Electronic Office."
10. Luis and Bernard accepted the invitation to the luncheon.

Verb Phrases

Two or more verbs are sometimes joined in a sentence. Two or more verbs that work together as one verb are called a *verb phrase*. Verb phrases such as *will be, will be going, has been asked, is working, has been working,* and *will have been approved* allow speakers and writers to express their meanings exactly.

In a verb phrase, the last verb is the main verb; any other verbs are considered *helping* (or *auxiliary*) verbs.

> You *should have* another copy of the contract in your files. (Main verb: *have;* helping verb: *should.*)

> I *should have asked* Miss DiMartino for her recommendations. (Main verb: *asked;* helping verbs: *should* and *have.*)

In the above examples, note that *have* is the main verb in the first sentence, but *have* is a helping verb in the second sentence. Remember that the main verb is always the last verb in the phrase and you will have no difficulty finding the main verb in any phrase.

The following chart gives some typical verb phrases. Note that in all cases the main verb is the *last* verb in each phrase.

Helping Verb	Main Verb
is	walking
are	dancing
do	deliver
will	be
will be	finished
has been	accomplished
did	explain
should have	insisted
might have	listened
had been	returned
will have	received
will have been	budgeted

In questions, a verb phrase is often separated.

Is Martin *working* on his report? (The verb phrase *is working* is split by the subject, *Martin*. The normal order is *Martin is working* . . . .)

Will the latest sales report *be included* in your analysis? (The verb phrase *will be included* is separated by the complete subject, *the latest sales report*.)

Adverbs also split verb phrases, as shown in these examples:

She *has* always *taken* her vacations in July. (The verb phrase *has taken* is split by the adverb *always*.)

We *will* often *remember* her inspiring speech. (The verb phrase *will remember* is split by the adverb *often*.)

CLASS PRACTICE 2

In each of the following sentences, identify the verb phrase and the main verb in each phrase. (HINT: Be on the lookout for split verb phrases!)

1. Marsha Gurr has already received her new credit card.
2. Can he install this equipment before noon?
3. All checks must be signed by the treasurer.
4. Has Ms. Brantley been informed of the new procedures?
5. Eric has often requested help in preparing catalog copy.
6. We are still waiting for the revised price list.
7. Andrew has been making all the arrangements for our trip to the West Coast.

8. You should have asked us for an additional copy of the agenda.

9. Have you proofread these letters?

10. Is Daniel waiting for Mrs. Lopes?

Principal Parts of Regular Verbs

The principal parts of verbs are the forms we use to express the time of action, or *tense*, of a verb. The four parts are the present, the past, the past participle, and the present participle. For most verbs, these parts are very easily formed, as shown in the table here.

PRINCIPAL PARTS OF SOME REGULAR VERBS			
PRESENT	**PAST**	**PAST PARTICIPLE**	**PRESENT PARTICIPLE**
type	typed	typed	typing
prepare	prepared	prepared	preparing
use	used	used	using
return	returned	returned	returning
answer	answered	answered	answering

Verbs that end in *e* just add *d* to form the past tense and the past participle. The present participles of verbs ending in *e* are formed by dropping the *e* and then adding *ing*.

For verbs that do not end in *e*, add *ed* to form both the past tense and the past participle. Add *ing* to form the present participle.

Because most of the verbs in our language form their principal parts in one of the ways described above, such verbs are called *regular verbs*.

Present Tense and Past Tense. Study the present tense and past tense forms of the verb *type* below:

Present Tense		Past Tense	
I type	we type	I typed	we typed
you type	you type	you typed	you typed
he		he	
she types	they type	she typed	they typed
it		it	

As you can see, there are only two present tense forms—*type* and *types*. There is only one past tense form—*typed*. This is standard for all regular verbs.

I *type* my own reports. (Present tense.)

Scott *types* about 95 words a minute. (Present tense.)

I *typed* all my own reports. (Past tense.)

Scott *typed* about 95 words a minute. (Past tense.)

Past Participle and Present Participle. In verb phrases, participles are always the main verbs—the last verbs in the phrases.

> I *have typed* all my own reports. (The past participle *typed* is the main verb; *have* is the helping verb.)

> Scot *has been typing* about 95 words per minute. (The present participle *typing* is the main verb; *has* and *been* are helping verbs.)

CLASS PRACTICE 3

In the sentences below, identify the present tense and past tense forms and the present participles and past participles. (REMEMBER: Past tense and present tense forms never have helping verbs.)

1. Louise generally submits her expense account report once a month.
2. Mr. Speigel wants another copy of the full-page ad.
3. Dr. Mandel has been submitting her claim forms to the regional benefits office.
4. Yes, Mr. Compo, I completed the invoices on Friday, July 15.
5. For many years I have wanted a job with the Millbury Corporation.
6. For your convenience, we have enclosed an envelope.
7. Has Gail answered all your questions?
8. An estimate form has already been requested.
9. Rosemary always completes her work on time.
10. Mr. French was presented with a special award for his charitable work.

Principal Parts of Irregular Verbs

You have seen that regular verbs form their past tense and past participle forms by adding *d* or *ed* to their present tense forms. A number of other different verbs form their principal parts in various ways—often by changing to a different word. Note, for example, the verbs in the table here.

PRINCIPAL PARTS OF SOME IRREGULAR VERBS			
PRESENT TENSE	**PAST TENSE**	**PAST PARTICIPLE**	**PRESENT PARTICIPLE**
am	was	been	being
begin	began	begun	beginning
do	did	done	doing
go	went	gone	going
have	had	had	having
write	wrote	written	writing

Obviously, these verbs deserve special attention, as do all the irregular verbs in the table on pages 109–110. Study these irregular verbs. Memorize them if you don't already know them. Always consult the dictionary for those verbs whose forms you do not know. (The dictionary lists at least the past tense and past participle forms of irregular verbs.)

PRINCIPAL PARTS OF IRREGULAR VERBS

PRESENT	PAST	PAST PARTICIPLE	PRESENT PARTICIPLE
am	was	been	being
become	became	become	becoming
begin	began	begun	beginning
bid (to offer)	bid	bid	bidding
bite	bit	bitten	biting
blow	blew	blown	blowing
break	broke	broken	breaking
bring	brought	brought	bringing
burst	burst	burst	bursting
buy	bought	bought	buying
catch	caught	caught	catching
choose	chose	chosen	choosing
climb*	climbed	climbed	climbing
come	came	come	coming
do	did	done	doing
drag*	dragged	dragged	dragging
draw	drew	drawn	drawing
drink	drank	drunk	drinking
drive	drove	driven	driving
drown*	drowned	drowned	drowning
eat	ate	eaten	eating
fall	fell	fallen	falling
fight	fought	fought	fighting
flee	fled	fled	fleeing
fly	flew	flown	flying
forget	forgot	forgotten	forgetting
freeze	froze	frozen	freezing
get	got	got	getting
give	gave	given	giving
go	went	gone	going
grow	grew	grown	growing
hang	hung	hung	hanging
hang (to put to death)*	hanged	hanged	hanging
hide	hid	hidden	hiding
know	knew	known	knowing
lay	laid	laid	laying
leave	left	left	leaving
lend	lent	lent	lending
lie	lay	lain	lying
lose	lost	lost	losing
pay	paid	paid	paying
ride	rode	ridden	riding
ring	rang	rung	ringing

*These are regular verbs, but their past tense and past participles are often misused.

PRINCIPAL PARTS OF IRREGULAR VERBS (Continued)

PRESENT	PAST	PAST PARTICIPLE	PRESENT PARTICIPLE
rise	rose	risen	rising
run	ran	run	running
see	saw	seen	seeing
set	set	set	setting
shake	shook	shaken	shaking
shine†	shone	shone	shining
shrink	shrank	shrunk	shrinking
sing	sang	sung	singing
sit	sat	sat	sitting
speak	spoke	spoken	speaking
spring	sprang	sprung	springing
steal	stole	stolen	stealing
strike	struck	struck	striking
swear	swore	sworn	swearing
swim	swam	swum	swimming
take	took	taken	taking
tear	tore	torn	tearing
throw	threw	thrown	throwing
wear	wore	worn	wearing
write	wrote	written	writing

†When *shine* means "to polish," the parts are *shine, shined, shined, shining.*

As with regular verbs, always be sure to use a helping verb with the past participle. On the other hand, *never* use a helping verb with the past tense. Note, for example, the correct uses of the verbs below.

Past Tense	Past Participle
She *went.*	She has *gone.*
He *did* a good job.	He has *done* a good job.
We *broke* the vase.	We have *broken* the vase.
I *flew* to Denver.	I had *flown* to Denver.
They *gave* us a discount	They have *given* us a discount.

In each case, note again that the past participle always has a helper and that the past tense never has a helper. Thus it is always wrong to say or write *she gone, he done,* and so on, because these past participles must have helping verbs.

PROOFREADING PRACTICE 1

In the following sentences, correct all errors in the use of verb forms.

1. Ms. Farrow has already did her sales charts for the meeting.
2. Two hours later we had chose the design for the newspaper ads.
3. Anna has wrote the report on telemarketing.

4. We returned to the office after we had ate lunch.
5. The customer had incorrectly took a 10 percent discount.
6. Leo, my assistant, seen these products at the exhibit.
7. By the time the messenger arrived, Mrs. Erhlich had went home.
8. You should have began your work on this project last week.
9. Congratulations! You have broke the sales records for May.
10. Carla has often spoke of the need for cooperation.

COMMUNICATION LABORATORY

APPLICATION EXERCISES

A. Find the verb or verb phrase in the following sentences. Then identify the main verb in each phrase. Supply a verb or verb phrase for any group of words that has none.

1. Does Mrs. Fasano want a copy of the procedures manual?
2. Have you and Robert approved the budget for this project?
3. All applicants have been interviewed by Jack Hood and me.
4. When did Alan make his decision?
5. Yes, the errors were corrected by the word processing operator.
6. The customer the brochures.
7. All our sales representatives have been complaining about the new policy.
8. Only Mr. Jackson's name is on the list of approved signatures.
9. Did you ask Bart for more information?
10. Our networking system saves time for all of us.
11. Several assistants next year.
12. By 1992 our company will be earning $1 million a year.
13. An incentive compensation plan by the president.
14. Mr. Pearlman, do you have a receipt for the merchandise that you bought this morning?
15. Between you and me, I do not have confidence in his plan to increase profits by lowering production standards.

B. Correct any errors in the following sentences. If a sentence has no error, write *OK*.

1. Last month, interest rates finally begun to drop.
2. This machine is broke, but you may use mine if you wish.
3. Yes, we have wrote to the City Council concerning these restrictions.
4. Of course, Miss d'Amato, we have already spoken to our attorneys.
5. Harold generally type about 75 words a minute.
6. I'm sorry—I had forgotten about our 9 a.m. appointment.
7. The meeting had begun about 15 minutes before we arrived.
8. Marion become quite an authority on microprocessors.

9. Sheila drove about 10 miles (16 kilometers).
10. That stock had fell to $25 a share by midday!
11. Has Mr. Morrison gave us his new address yet?
12. Our parking lot was dangerous because all the rain had froze.
13. Ms. Constantine has frequently flown to Chicago's O'Hare Airport.
14. Our engineers had knew that the structure needed additional support.
15. I seen Mrs. Derek at this morning's production status meeting.

C. The blanks within the following sentences should contain some form of these verbs: *begin, break, drink, drive, go, grow, know, see, speak,* or *write.*

1. Ms. Weathers has already _____ her speech, hasn't she?
2. During the break this morning, we _____ all the cold juices on the coffee wagon.
3. Helen and I have _____ each other since we graduated from high school.
4. We _____ Mr. Hansen earlier today when he was keyboarding information at this terminal.
5. The delivery will be late, but we have already _____ to the dispatcher.
6. Market research has shown that consumer demand for software has _____ tremendously.
7. Our interest in buying word processors such as this one _____ a few months ago.
8. After we have _____ Ms. Mackenzie to the airport, we will return to the hotel.
9. Unfortunately, this equipment has been _____ for several weeks.
10. Edna generally _____ to work on Saturdays during the busy season.

VOCABULARY AND SPELLING STUDIES

A. Distinguish between the meaning and spelling of the following words, which are often confused: *fineness, finesse; leased, least.* Then write a sample sentence using each word.

B. Some of the following words contain silent letters: *listen, strength, night, island, candidate, doubt.* List the words and tell which letters (besides *e*) are silent. Use the pronunciation guide in your dictionary.

C. Should *ancy* or *ency* be added to the following words to complete the correct spellings?

1. effici___   4. flu___
2. hesit___   5. buoy___
3. emerg___   6. occup___

COMMUNICATING FOR RESULTS

Remembering Names. Businesspeople often meet several new clients or co-workers at a time. How well can you remember names when several people are introduced to you at the same time? Have six of your classmates assume fictitious names; then introduce yourselves to one another. As you meet each person, ask a question of each that will help you fix that person's name in your memory. (HINT: Try to associate face, appearance, dress, speech, and so on, with each name.)

U · N · I · T

12 Troublesome Verbs

The "being" verbs are the most commonly used verbs in our language. Unfortunately, they are also among the most misused. In this unit you will have an opportunity to master the forms of the verb *to be* in a simple and practical way. In addition, as you will see later, understanding the difference between transitive and intransitive verbs will help you avoid errors in a few other commonly misused irregular verbs. Therefore, this unit will focus on (1) "being" verbs, (2) transitive verbs, and (3) intransitive verbs.

"Being" Verbs

The "being" verbs are all the forms of the verb *to be: am, is, are, was, were, been,* and of course, *be.* Now let's see how they are used.

To begin, make sure you know the present tense and the past tense forms of the verb *to be:*

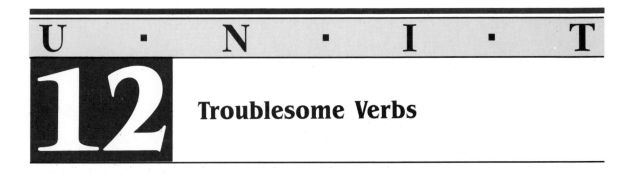

Present Tense		Past Tense	
I am	we are	I was	we were
you are	you are	you were	you were
he ⎱		he ⎱	
she ⎬ is	they are	she ⎬ was	they were
it ⎰		it ⎰	

As you can see, then, the verb *to be* is unique. Its present tense has three forms—*am, are,* and *is.* Its past tense has two forms—*was* and *were.* Memorize these forms, because you will certainly use them often.

I *am* now in charge of this project.

We *are* on the accounting staff.

Miss Graham *is* on vacation.

You *were* not at this morning's meeting, *were* you?

Carl *was* responsible for the delay.

Past Participle and Present Participle. The past participle *been* can be used as a main verb with a helper or helpers, as in *has been, have been, had been, should have been, will have been, could have been, might have been,* and so on. In addition, *been* can be used as a helper in a verb phrase—but only with other helpers. Note that a verb *phrase* is not considered a being verb unless the *main* verb is the "being" verb.

Sheila *should have been* here hours ago.   (*Been* is the main verb; *should* and *have* are helpers. Therefore, this verb phrase is a "being" verb.)

Sheila *should have been called* hours ago.   (*Called* is the main verb; *should, have,* and *been* are helpers. Therefore, this verb phrase is *not* a "being" verb.)

Likewise, the present participle *being* can be used as a main verb, as in *am being, is being, are being, was being,* and *were being.* It can also be used as one of two or more helping verbs, as in *is being planned, are being reviewed, was being discussed,* and so on. Again, to find out whether *being* is the main verb in a verb phrase, be sure to isolate the entire phrase; then see whether *being* is the *last* word in that phrase.

Our attorneys *are being* extremely cautious.   (The main verb is *being; are* is a helping verb.)

The jurors *are being cautioned* by the judge.   (The last verb, *cautioned,* is the main verb; *are* and *being* are helping verbs. This verb phrase is *not* a "being" verb.)

Are the jurors now *being cautioned* by the judge?   (Do not be tricked by inverted sentences. The verb phrase here is exactly the same as in the previous example.)

Be. The last form is the word *be* itself. *Be* can also be used as a helper or as a main verb.

Tomorrow *will be* the last day of our vacation.   (*Be* is the main verb; *will* is the helper.)

Each payment *will be checked* by our treasurer.   (*Checked* is the main verb; *will* and *be* are helpers.)

CLASS PRACTICE 1

In each of the following sentences, identify the verb or the verb phrase. Then determine whether that verb or verb phrase is a "being" verb. (HINT: Remember that a verb phrase is a "being" verb only when the *last* verb in the phrase is a "being" verb.)

1. Yes, Mr. Van Heusen, this machine can be very efficient in our operation.
2. In fifteen years our company will be the largest manufacturer of semi-conductors.
3. No, Ms. Bogart, we were not expecting so many replies.
4. All these inquiries from customers must be answered within two days.
5. Arnold, is this procedures manual up to date?
6. Wendy's new microprocessor was delivered to her office today.
7. When are you expecting Mr. and Mrs. Quimby to arrive?
8. Of course, Denise should have been at that meeting.
9. Pamela O'Brian might be our next marketing director.
10. Pamela O'Brian might be chosen as our next marketing director.

Transitive and Intransitive Verbs

A *transitive* verb is a verb that has an *object*—a word that tells what or who receives the action expressed by the verb.

> Mario *typed* the *report*. (The object of *typed* is *report*, so *typed* is a transitive verb.)

> Mario *travels* to the West Coast once a month. (The verb *travels* has no object; therefore, it is intransitive.)

For a shortcut in identifying transitive and intransitive verbs, study the Quick Tricks below and on the following page.

QUICK TRICK | **ASK "WHAT?" OR "WHOM?"**

After saying the verb, ask the question "What?" or "Whom?" If you can supply a noun or pronoun that makes sense, then the verb is transitive.

> Ms. Enrico asked me for a revised expense budget. (Asked what? No answer. Asked whom? Answer: *me*. *Asked* is a transitive verb because it has an object.)

> Ms. Enrico sells office equipment in the metropolitan area. (Sells what? Answer: office equipment. *Sells* is a transitive verb.)

> Ms. Enrico frequently speaks at sales conventions. (Speaks what? No answer. Speaks whom? No answer. *Speaks* is an intransitive verb.)

QUICK TRICK | **ALWAYS TRANSITIVE**

Whenever you see a past participle that has a "being" verb helper, the verb phrase is automatically transitive. Remember this rule:

Being Verb Helper + Past Participle = Transitive Verb Phrase

This combination automatically makes the subject the receiver of the action. Because there is always a receiver of the action, such verbs must therefore be transitive.

Ms. Díaz *should have been promoted* a long time ago. (*Promoted* is a past participle, and *should have been* is a phrase with a being verb helper. Thus *should have been promoted* is automatically a transitive verb.)

CLASS PRACTICE 2

Identify the verbs and the verb phrases in the following sentences; then label each as *transitive* or *intransitive*. (Remember to use the "always transitive" formula as a shortcut.)

1. Jonathan should have been told about the cancellation of this afternoon's meeting.
2. Mrs. Rosenwald was speaking into the microphone too loudly.
3. Our Bath, Maine, office was built three years ago.
4. We have analyzed the monthly sales reports very carefully.
5. The monthly sales reports have been analyzed very carefully.
6. The proposal was reviewed by Mr. Banks and Ms. DeKoonig.
7. My supervisor, Doris Truscott, seems especially happy this morning.
8. Lenora practices every day.
9. Has Elton been informed about the budget cuts?
10. Gail has been traveling for the past two weeks.

Your knowledge of transitive and intransitive verbs will simplify the process of using these troublesome verbs properly: *lie* and *lay*, *sit* and *set*, and *rise* and *raise*. As you will see in the following Quick Trick, the secret is to remember that *lie*, *sit*, and *rise* are *in*transitive.

QUICK TRICK | **THE *I* VERB IS INTRANSITIVE**

First, study the principal parts of these troublesome verbs. As you do so, note that the three verbs with the short or long sound of the letter *i* are *lie*, *sit*, and *rise*.

Present	Past	Past Participle	Present Participle
lie	lay	lain	lying
lay	laid	laid	laying
sit	sat	sat	sitting
set	set	set	setting
rise	rose	risen	rising
raise	raised	raised	raising

Now let's review them one pair at a time.

LIE–LAY. Which verb has the *i* sound? Answer: *lie*. Let the sound in *lie* remind you that the word *intransitive* begins with *i*. *Lie* is intransitive.

SIT–SET. Which verb has the *i* sound? Answer: *sit*. Let the *i* sound in *sit* remind you that the word *intransitive* begins with *i*. *Sit* is intransitive.

RISE–RAISE. Which verb has the *i* sound? Answer: *rise*. Let the *i* sound in *rise* remind you that the word *intransitive* begins with *i*. *Rise* is intransitive.

This simple, foolproof method will help you remember that *lie, sit,* and *rise* are *i*ntransitive. Also remember that the other verb in each verb pair (that is, *lay, set,* and *raise*) is transitive. Now let's see how you can put this knowledge to use in choosing the right verb.

I will (lie, lay) the briefcase on your desk tomorrow.

To decide whether the intransitive *lie* or the transitive *lay* is correct, just ask whether the verb in this sentence has an object. Answer: Yes, *briefcase.* Therefore, a transitive verb is required. Which verb is transitive? Answer: *lay*.

Let's try another example:

Paul (lay, laid) the papers on my desk.

This is the tricky part, so pay strict attention. Here, *lay* is the past tense form of *lie; laid* is the past tense form of *lay*. Thus in this example *lay* is intransitive and *laid* is transitive. Now let's proceed with our analysis of this sentence.

Does the verb in this sentence have an object? Answer: Yes, *papers.* Which verb is required: a transitive verb, or an intransitive verb? Answer: a transitive verb is required. Which is the transitive form, *lay* or *laid?* Answer: *laid*.

As you can see, then, you must know the forms of these troublesome verbs—especially the forms of *lie* and *lay*. *Lie* and *lay* are particularly tricky because it is so easy to confuse the present tense of the transitive verb *lay* with the past tense of the intransitive verb *lie*.

Present Tense of *Lie*	Past Tense of *Lie*
I *lie* down after work.	I *lay* down after work yesterday.
You *lie* down after work.	You *lay* down after work yesterday.
He *lies* down after work.	He *lay* down after work yesterday.
We *lie* down after work.	We *lay* down after work yesterday.
They *lie* down after work.	They *lay* down after work yesterday.

Present Tense of *Lay*	Past Tense of *Lay*
I *lay* packages on this table.	I *laid* packages on this table.
You *lay* packages on this table.	You *laid* packages on this table.
She *lays* packages on this table.	She *laid* packages on this table.
We *lay* packages on this table.	We *laid* packages on this table.
They *lay* packages on this table.	They *laid* packages on this table.

As with regular verbs, *lie* has only two present tense forms (*lie* and *lies*) and one past tense form (*lay*). Likewise, *lay* has only two present tense forms (*lay* and *lays*) and one past tense form (*laid*). The same is true of *sit, set, rise,* and *raise.*

I usually *sit* near the window.   (Present.)

Yolanda always *sits* in the front of the room.   (Present.)

Yesterday we *sat* in different places.   (Past.)

You generally *set* the prices for these products, don't you?   (Present.)

Sometimes Ms. Greer *sets* the prices.   (Present.)

We *set* these prices last May.   (Past.)

We always *rise* to applaud the speaker.   (Present.)

Gene *rises* to greet all his visitors.   (Present.)

They *rose* in order to see the screen more clearly.   (Past.)

I often *raise* money for charitable causes.   (Present.)

Fran still *raises* money for the United Fund.   (Present.)

Together we *raised* several thousand dollars last year.   (Past.)

CLASS PRACTICE 3

Select the correct verb for each of the following sentences. (Be sure to determine whether a transitive or an intransitive verb is required.)

1. Your draft copy was (lying, laying) on the file cabinet.
2. Marlene generally (sits, sets) the policy for performance evaluations.
3. Enough money has been (risen, raised) to buy new uniforms.
4. Joan (lies, lays) in the sun all morning on weekends.
5. Has a new schedule been (sat, set) for printing the manual?
6. No, Ms. Darness, the water has not (risen, raised) to a dangerous level.
7. When will the foundation of the building be (lain, laid)?

8. Please (sit, set) all the materials on the table in the conference room.
9. If the price (rises, raises) above $10, I will not buy this item.
10. Unfortunately, these expensive products had (lain, laid) in the supply room for months.

If I Were . . .

Sometimes it is correct to use *were* where ordinarily you would expect to use *was*. Usually this use of *were* occurs after *if, as if, as though,* and *wish*. Follow this rule: If the expressed condition is not true, is not possible, or is highly doubtful, use *were*.

> Our Denver office manager sometimes acts *as if he were* the president of the company. (He is not the president of the company; he is the Denver office manager. Thus the condition expressed is not true.)

> *If I were* John, I would reject this proposal. (But I am not John.)

> Ms. Barcellona is in Europe. *If she were* here in Chicago, she would gladly speak at the conference. (But she is not in Chicago.)

> However, use *was* if the condition expressed is true or could be true.

> If the package *was* delivered this morning, it was probably sent to the receiving dock. (The package may indeed have been delivered.)

> If Mrs. DeSoto *was* at the exhibit, she left before I arrived. (There is the possibility that she was at the exhibit and that I did not see her there.)

CLASS PRACTICE 4

Which is correct in the following sentences, *were* or *was?*

1. Mr. Graystoke acts as if he (was, were) the vice president of sales instead of the district manager.
2. If my former boss (was, were) to come out of retirement, she would find that our company has changed drastically.
3. I wish that it (was, were) possible to grant you credit, but company policy prohibits our doing so.
4. If Daryl (was, were) in the building this morning, he left before I arrived.
5. I wish that Mrs. Owens (was, were) still working in New York.

COMMUNICATION LABORATORY

APPLICATION EXERCISES

A. On a separate sheet of paper, write the complete verb in each of the following sentences and indicate whether each verb is transitive, intransitive, or a "being" verb. Use *T* for *transitive*, *I* for *intransitive*, and *B* for *"being."*

1. The last applicant might be a competent word processing supervisor.
2. We purchase all electrical supplies from Shelton Inc.

3. Karen and Sean should have been at the Miami conference.
4. This microcomputer uses 13-sector diskettes, not 16-sector diskettes.
5. The audience was applauding loudly for almost 10 minutes.
6. Electronic mail equipment will be installed in these offices in May.
7. The cables will be laid within the next two or three weeks.
8. Eleanor sat quietly throughout the presentation.
9. Apparently, enough money has been raised for the building fund.
10. Yes, Mrs. Castagna has returned from her trip to Kentucky.
11. Both Mary Anne and Paul dislike the new credit policy.
12. The total weight of both packages was approximately 10 kilograms.
13. The briefcase was returned to its owner.
14. Anthony and Michael are coordinating those projects.
15. Lisa Landau is the new supervisor of the data processing center.

B. Correct any errors in the following sentences and identify the transitive and intransitive verbs. Write *OK* on your paper if the sentence is correct.

1. If it was earlier in the season, I would be happy to accompany you.
2. With the help of a crane, the sign was risen within 30 to 40 minutes.
3. Henry said that the chemicals have laid in the storeroom since last January.
4. Now that the foundation has been lain, we can proceed with this project.
5. Will you please help me sit these cartons onto the loading platform?
6. The nurse immediately asked Ms. Jenkins to lay down.
7. Before you assemble everything, we suggest that you lay all the parts out on a flat surface.
8. My new assistant already acts as if he was the president of the company!
9. These prices have been risen since last year, haven't they?
10. Mrs. Jefferson rised some serious questions that we had not considered.
11. Now that the policies have been set, all employees will have better guidance in hiring the handicapped.
12. The mason has been lying bricks nonstop for nearly ten hours.
13. The price has been rising steadily for the past few months.
14. Our total travel budget has been risen about 10 percent.
15. Mr. Poland has been setting in the reception area since 9 o'clock.

C. For each sentence, write the correct form of the verb in parentheses.

1. The photographs are usually (hang) to dry for several minutes.
2. The reference materials that you'll need are (lie) on the credenza.
3. While recuperating from the accident, Morgan had (lie) in bed for over three weeks.
4. We (lay) the handouts on a table in the front of the room.
5. Last night I (lie) in bed for hours before I finally fell asleep.
6. Of course, I do wish that I (was) earning more money so that I could return to school.

7. I (set) all the graphs on the conference room table, just as Ms. Wilson had requested.
8. Dave has already (speak) to his staff about the increase in work load that he expects next year.
9. Although all of us were careful, the new monitor for the word processor (break).
10. After several years of hard work and long hours of study, Agnes finally (become) a department head.

VOCABULARY AND SPELLING STUDIES

A. The spellings and meanings of word pairs such as *feet/feat* and *aisle/isle* are often confused. Give the meaning of each of these four words; then write a sample sentence using each correctly.

B. Which of the following words is *mis*spelled: *signify, testify, liquify, classify?*

C. Which of the following words is spelled correctly: *accomodate, privelege, embarrass, aquiesce?*

COMMUNICATING FOR RESULTS

Business Courtesy. Read each of the following statements to judge whether it is correct. Explain your answer.

1. To save time when placing a telephone call, the caller should always ask a secretary to get the other party on the line first.
2. An employee who must be out for sick leave should call the office to let the supervisor know.
3. After completing the required work for the day, an employee may then visit co-workers.

U · N · I · T

13

Plural Nouns

The words *managers*, *manager's*, and *managers'* are all pronounced precisely the same. In speaking, therefore, we need not specify which of these three forms we intend to use. But in writing, errors in using such forms of nouns are obvious because these three words cannot be used interchangeably. We must know whether the plural form *managers* is correct or whether one of the possessive forms, *manager's* or *managers'*, is correct.

In this unit you will review forming plurals of nouns. Then, in the next unit, you will review forming possessives of nouns. Together, these two units will help you avoid many of the obstacles to correct spelling.

Forming Routine Plurals

Most Nouns. Most plural nouns end in *s*. To form these plurals, we simply add *s* or *es* to the singular forms.

Add S

clerk	clerk*s*	Smith	Smith*s*
building	building*s*	Brown	Brown*s*
car	car*s*	Freid	Freid*s*
attorney	attorney*s*	Donnelly	Donnelly*s*
machine	machine*s*	John	John*s*

Add Es

boss	boss*es*	Adams	Adams*es*
tax	tax*es*	Marx	Marx*es*
bench	bench*es*	Lidz	Lidz*es*
blitz	blitz*es*	Tench	Tench*es*
wish	wish*es*	Walsh	Walsh*es*

As you can see, for nouns that end in *s, x, z, ch,* and *sh* you must add *es* to the singular form. For all other nouns (exceptions are discussed later in this unit), just ad *s*. Note that the same rule applies to common nouns and to proper nouns. A *common noun* is the name of a person, place, or thing, such as *attorney, building,* and *car*. A *proper noun* is the name of a *specific* person, place, or thing, such as *Clarence Darrow, Empire State Building,* and *Oldsmobile*.

Nouns Ending in *Y.* In the list above, you see that the plural of *attorney* is *attorneys* and that the plural of *Donnelly* is *Donnellys.* But not all nouns that end in *y* form their plurals by adding *s.* Note the following rules:

For Common Nouns. For common nouns, if the final *y* is preceded by a vowel (*a, e, i, o,* or *u*), then just add *s* to the singular form. If the final *y* is preceded by a consonant (that is, by any letter other than *a, e, i, o,* or *u*), then change the *y* to *i* and add *es:*

Add *S*		Change *Y* to *I* and Add *S*	
day	day*s*	quantit*y*	quantit*ies*
valley	valley*s*	secretar*y*	secretar*ies*
toy	toy*s*	compan*y*	compan*ies*
ray	ray*s*	facilit*y*	facilit*ies*
key	key*s*	territor*y*	territor*ies*
relay	relay*s*	factor*y*	factor*ies*

For Proper Nouns. For proper nouns ending in *y,* just add *s* to form the plural, regardless of whether the *y* is preceded by a vowel or not.

Connelly	Connelly*s*
Delaney	Delaney*s*
Haggerty	Haggerty*s*
Pauly	Pauly*s*

There are very few exceptions to this rule, but note the following three common ones:

Complete Name	**Shortened Name**
Alleghen*y* Mountains	the Alleghen*ies*
Rock*y* Mountains	the Rock*ies*
Smok*y* Mountains	the Smok*ies*

Both the complete and the shortened names are plural forms, but for the shortened names change the *y* to *i* and add *es.*

PROOFREADING PRACTICE 1

Now that you understand how most plurals are formed, correct any errors in the use of plurals in the following sentences. HINT: Some sentences have no errors.

1. One summer we went to Knoxville for the World's Fair and visited the Smokys.
2. Several concerned citizens complained about the increases in taxs over the past two years.
3. All lunchs are included in the total price for the five-day conference.
4. Only three of our subsidiaries are represented at this meeting.

5. For her fiftieth anniversary with the company, we presented her with a ring studded with rubys.
6. Because these gasses are very dangerous, we take special precautions with them.
7. Were the Basses—Mike Bass, Angela Bass, and their children— invited?
8. To remove this pipe, I will need at least two 14-inch wrenchs.
9. Apparently, the waxes we used on this cabinet ruined the finish.
10. Most factorys owned by Consolidated Metals are in Kentucky and West Virginia.
11. Ask Mary Ellen for the address where Mr. and Mrs. Jones are now staying; then send this package to the Jones.
12. Our sales representatives have already set up the displays of brushs and polishs.
13. Mr. Blainy said that all the Blainies would be happy to accept our invitation.
14. So far, about 25 different business have agreed to display their products.
15. Several offices in various districts have their own warehouses and plants.

Forming Special Plurals

In addition to the routine plurals that you learned to form earlier in this unit, you must learn how to form the plurals of such special words as *woman*, *man*, and *child*. You already know that they do not form their plurals in any regular way. You must also learn to form the plurals of compound nouns and of titles used with names. Finally, there are a few plurals that are formed using the apostrophe, and you must also master these.

Vowel Changes. Some nouns form the plural by vowel changes.

man	men	woman	women
tooth	teeth	mouse	mice
foot	feet	goose	geese

Note, however, that the plural of *German* is *Germans*.

Compound Nouns. A compound noun is a noun in which two or more words have been combined. When the compound is written as one word (no hyphen), then form the plural at the end of the word.

cupful	cupfuls
toothbrush	toothbrushes
textbook	textbooks
stepchild	stepchildren
courthouse	courthouses
letterhead	letterheads

EXCEPTION:

passerby	passersby

When the compound is written with either a space or a hyphen between the words, make plural the main word in the compound.

bulletin board	bulletin board<u>s</u>
general manager	general manager<u>s</u>
editor in chief	editor<u>s</u> in chief
vice president	vice president<u>s</u>
daughter-in-law	daughter<u>s</u>-in-law
court-martial	court<u>s</u>-martial
notary public	notar<u>ies</u> public
attorney-at-law	attorney<u>s</u>-at-law
lieutenant colonel	lieutenant colonel<u>s</u>

When there is no main word in the hyphenated compound, form the plural at the end of the noun.

follow-up	follow-up<u>s</u>
write-in	write-in<u>s</u>
hand-me-down	hand-me-down<u>s</u>
tie-up	tie-up<u>s</u>
trade-in	trade-in<u>s</u>

Titles With Names. Sometimes it is necessary to form the plural of a name with a title such as *Miss, Ms., Mrs.,* or *Mr.* In such cases make either the title or the name plural—not both. Note the plurals of these common titles:

Singular	**Plural**
Miss	Misses
Ms.	Mses.
Mrs.	Mesdames (*Mesdames* is a French word, meaning "more than one *Mrs.*")
Mr.	Messrs. (*Messrs.* is the abbreviation for *messieurs,* the French word for *"misters."*)

Now compare the alternative ways to make a name with a title plural. In each case note that only one word, the title *or* the name, is made plural.

Singular	**Plural**
Send this contract to Miss Klein.	Send this contract to the *Misses* Klein. Send this contract to the Miss *Kleins.*
We invited Ms. Hander to lunch.	We invited the *Mses.* Hander to lunch. We invited the Ms. *Handers* to lunch.
Only Mrs. Wilson attended.	Only the *Mesdames* Wilson attended. Only the Mrs. *Wilsons* attended.
This belongs to Mr. Ford.	This belongs to the *Messrs.* Ford. This belongs to the Mr. *Fords.*

Plurals With Apostrophes. As you will see in Unit 14, apostrophes are used in possessive forms of nouns. In rare instances, however, an apostrophe prevents possible misreading of certain plurals—for example, plurals of capital or lowercase letters that could be misread.

No Apostrophe Needed	Apostrophe Prevents Misreading
several M.D.s	learning your abc's
two CPAs	counting the c.o.d.'s
all Bs	earned three A's

Plurals such as *pros* and *cons*, *ins* and *outs*, and *dos* and *don'ts* are not likely to be misread.

PROOFREADING PRACTICE 2

Correct any errors in the following sentences. Write *OK* for any sentence that has no error.

1. Ms. Van Gleason requested that we post these notices on all the bulletins board.
2. All the woman in our district office are planning to attend next month's convention.
3. The three M.D.s on our staff work on a rotating-shift basis.
4. Be sure to explain to the new clerk that the I's on these invoices mean "incomplete."
5. Ask the Messrs. Jordans to attend next Wednesday's session.
6. Emma, Larry, and Francine are the three Ph.D.'s in our research laboratory.
7. If the Mesdames Colliers agree, we will submit a bid for the property.
8. Her sister-in-law and my former supervisor, both of whom are attorney-at-laws, own this shopping mall.
9. Many passerbys crowded around the scene, creating a traffic snarl at rush hour.
10. This car dealer gives fair value for trades-in.

Forming Tricky Plurals

Because there are so many exceptions to the rules for forming plurals for nouns ending in *o* and *f* or *fe*, you should develop the habit of using the dictionary to check the spellings of such plurals. In addition, you will find the dictionary especially helpful for checking nouns that originated in foreign languages and nouns that have only one form for both the singular and the plural. All these troublesome plurals are covered below.

Nouns Ending in *O*. When a singular noun ends in *o*, its plural is usually formed by adding *s*. In the examples below, note that all musical terms ending in *o* are included in this category.

dynamo	dynamo<u>s</u>	tobacco	tobacco<u>s</u>
studio	studio<u>s</u>	Eskimo	Eskimo<u>s</u>
zero	zero<u>s</u>	ratio	ratio<u>s</u>
radio	radio<u>s</u>	memento	memento<u>s</u>

piano	piano<u>s</u>	soprano	soprano<u>s</u>
solo	solo<u>s</u>	banjo	banjo<u>s</u>
trio	trio<u>s</u>	alto	alto<u>s</u>

However, some nouns ending in *o* preceded by a consonant form the plural by adding *es:*

echo	echo<u>es</u>	motto	motto<u>es</u>
tomato	tomato<u>es</u>	veto	veto<u>es</u>
hero	hero<u>es</u>	cargo	cargo<u>es</u>
embargo	embargo<u>es</u>	potato	potato<u>es</u>

Nouns Ending in *F* or *Fe*. For some singular nouns ending in *f* or *fe,* change the *f* or *fe* to *v* and add *es.* For others, simply add *s.*

Change *F* or *Fe* to *V;* Then Add *Es*

wi<u>fe</u>	wi<u>ves</u>	shel<u>f</u>	shel<u>ves</u>
li<u>fe</u>	li<u>ves</u>	loa<u>f</u>	loa<u>ves</u>

Just Add *S*

plaintiff	plaintiff<u>s</u>	belief	belief<u>s</u>
proof	proof<u>s</u>	chcf	chef<u>s</u>

Foreign Nouns. Nouns of foreign origin such as *agenda* and *prospectus* may form their plurals by adding *s* (*agendas*) or *es* (*prospectuses*). But many foreign nouns have both an "English plural" and a "foreign plural," as shown below.

Singular	Plural	English Plural
addend<u>um</u>	addend<u>a</u>	
alumn<u>a</u>	alumn<u>ae</u>	
alumn<u>us</u>	alumn<u>i</u>	
analys<u>is</u>	analys<u>es</u>	
ax<u>is</u>	ax<u>es</u>	
bas<u>is</u>	bas<u>es</u>	
cris<u>is</u>	cris<u>es</u>	
criter<u>ion</u>	criter<u>ia</u>	criter<u>ions</u>
curricul<u>um</u>	curricul<u>a</u>	curricul<u>ums</u>
dat<u>um</u>	dat<u>a</u>	
formul<u>a</u>	formul<u>ae</u>	formul<u>as</u>
hypothes<u>is</u>	hypothes<u>es</u>	
ind<u>ex</u>	ind<u>ices</u>	ind<u>exes</u>
medi<u>um</u>	medi<u>a</u>	medi<u>ums</u>
memorand<u>um</u>	memorand<u>a</u>	memorand<u>ums</u>
nucle<u>us</u>	nucle<u>i</u>	nucleus<u>es</u>
oas<u>is</u>	oas<u>es</u>	

parenthes*is*	parenthes*es*	
stadi*um*	stad*ia*	stadi*ums*
stimul*us*	stimul*i*	
vertebr*a*	vertebr*ae*	vertebr*as*

In some cases, the preferred form is the English plural (for example, *memorandums*); in other cases, the preferred form is the foreign plural (for example, *criteria*). Sometimes the two plural forms may have entirely different meanings, as with *indexes* and *indices*. Obviously, there is no one rule that will simplify your using these words correctly. Be sure to consult your dictionary whenever you are uncertain about the plural form of a noun of foreign origin. If two different plural forms are given, use the form that appears first, since this is the preferred plural. NOTE: The plural noun *data* is now commonly followed by a singular verb.

The data that we compiled *proves* that our customers prefer monthly billing.

For this and other usage principles, learn to use a comprehensive, up-to-date reference manual.

Always Singular	Always Plural	One Form for Both Singular and Plural	
news	thanks	deer	salmon
genetics	trousers	fish	politics
mathematics	proceeds	odds	economics
aeronautics	pants	sheep	statistics
	riches	corps	
	tidings	Chinese	
	credentials	moose	
	belongings	Japanese	

The recent news about decreasing unemployment *shows* some hope. (Not *news show*.)

Her credentials *make* Clara an excellent candidate. (Not *credentials makes*.)

One rare deer *was* acquired by the zoo.

A Japanese *is* the inventor of this computer equipment.

Three Japanese *are* the principal owners of the firm.

Economics *is* my favorite subject.

The economics of the situation *are* discouraging.

Note, too, how words such as *hundred, thousand,* and *dozen* are used in the following sentences.

One *hundred* people are expected.

Three *hundred* customers requested credit cards. (Not *Three hundreds*.)

Several *dozen* complaints were received. (Not *Several dozens*.)

CLASS PRACTICE 1

Select the correct word in each of the following sentences.

1. Use (parenthesis, parentheses) to indicate the page numbers.
2. Hundreds of husbands and (wifes, wives) are expected at the stockholders' meeting.
3. The carpenters will have all the (bookshelves, bookshelfs) installed over the weekend.
4. Each (analysis, analyses) supported our original premise.
5. All the (datum, data) will be shared with our marketing staff.
6. Two (pianos, pianoes) will be delivered to the auditorium tomorrow.
7. John and Thomas emerged as the (heros, heroes).
8. Wearing seat belts has saved many (lifes, lives).
9. Universal Instruments manufactures guitars and (banjos, banjoes).
10. The news from financial circles (is, are) that interest rates will soon decrease.

PROOFREADING PRACTICE 3

Correct any errors in the following sentences.

1. The United States threatened embargoes against both nations.
2. The proceeds from the special drive is expected to top $1 million!
3. Economics have always been a required course for all business students.
4. The company choir is seeking two more altoes for the upcoming Christmas show.
5. Increased prices of potatos and tomatos will affect the consumer price index.
6. In both cases, the plaintives claimed high damages.
7. The formulas they developed were remarkably similar.
8. To avoid such crisis in the future, our security staff is taking special precautions.
9. Has Rory completed all the addendum he was typing?
10. Only one analyses had been completed as of this morning.

COMMUNICATION LABORATORY

APPLICATION EXERCISES

A. On a separate sheet of paper, write your corrections for any errors in the following sentences. Write *OK* for any sentence that has no error.

1. The Mr. Osborns are programmers who have developed excellent educational materials for us.
2. The attornies agreed to settle the dispute out of court.
3. Mr. Kent said, "There is only one criteria worth considering—cost."

4. The owners of MarshLand Enterprises are the Marshes.
5. Mrs. Hammond's will left a substantial sum to her four stepchilds.
6. To store all the books that we had in the supply room, we will need at least three more shelfs on this wall.
7. A handwriting expert proved that the writing belonged to Mr. Talbot by the unique way that he dotted his is.
8. Jerry will reimburse the Fitchs for the damaged merchandise.
9. According to the newspaper report, politics are not an issue.
10. About 85 percent of the alumnuses live within the tristate area.
11. Both senator-elects refused to discuss their opinions with the press.
12. Memorandums from the head of our Zurich office are very well written, but she often confuses a's and an's.
13. Three countys in our state have already begun to use the new system.
14. Her credentials for handling maritime law is well known.
15. Most of the radioes that we import are from Japanese manufacturers.

B. Beginning with this exercise and continuing through Unit 23, each Application Exercise B will be a review. The following sentences will help you review the grammar principles you have studied so far. Correct sentences with errors; write *OK* for any sentence that has no error.

1. Among the major stockholders are the Ms. Gordon, whose grandfather was the founder of Gordon Chemicals.
2. The Brown & Lund Travel Agency handles all the Marxes' tickets.
3. Long before she became an engineer, mathematics were Sherry's favorite subject.
4. One customer claimed that these waxs are harmful to human skin, but tests do not support that contention.
5. Over the weekend some of the chemicals had froze.
6. In January his two daughter-in-laws plan to submit their bid to Hamilton Real Estate.
7. The fragile porcelain pieces were slowly lain on the countertop.
8. Because used cars are in such demand, we are trying to encourage trades-in.
9. Use parenthesis to enclose metric equivalents; for example, 10 yards (9.14 meters).
10. We recommended to the Johnson's several excellent investment possibilities.
11. My boss' office is being painted while she is away on vacation.
12. Do these figures represent thousands? If so, then be sure to add three zeroes to each numeral.
13. Eventually we will merge both halfs of the manuscript onto one diskette.
14. Since 1984 our investment has grew approximately 15.5 percent annually.

15. Because Mrs. Yelburton has retired, Mr. Herndon is handling two terri-
torys temporarily.

C. Correct the errors in the following paragraph.

To make sure that all agreements with foreign countries are legal, we asked the
attornies and the CPA's in our tax department to inspect the documents carefully.
Their analyses will be completed within the next few week's. Then, when the
various embargos against these countrys are lifted by our government, we will be
able to resume our business in Europe and Asia.

VOCABULARY AND SPELLING STUDIES

A. These words are often confused: *adverse, averse; preposition, proposition*. Distinguish between the pairs, and write a sentence using each word.

B. What does the suffix *ish* (as in *bookish, bluish,* and *devilish*) mean:
(1) "resembling," (2) "full of," or (3) "made of"?

C. What does the suffix *ee* (as in *employee, lessee, mortgagee,* and *nominee*)
mean: (1) "a native of," (2) "state or quality of," (3) "the recipient of an
action," or (4) "having the characteristics of"?

D. How do you spell:

1. The verb meaning "to be before"?
2. The number that follows *one?*
3. The adverb formed from *full?*

COMMUNICATING FOR RESULTS

Your employer, Carolyn Watts, is in Chicago on a business trip. While her
secretary is away from the desk, you answer Ms. Watts' phone. The caller is
a good customer, Mr. Jeffries, who asks for a number where he can call
Ms. Watts. Assuming that you know Ms. Watts' number at her hotel in
Chicago, what should you tell Mr. Jeffries?

14 Possessive Nouns and Pronouns

Possessive forms of nouns and pronouns cause writers undue anxiety. As you saw in Unit 13, some difficulties arise, for example, because the plural *managers* is pronounced precisely as the possessives *manager's* and *managers'* are pronounced. Now that you know how to use plural forms correctly, you will learn how to use possessive forms correctly.

The rules for using possessives are few, and fortunately they are not difficult to master. By giving your attention to the rules presented in this unit, studying the examples, and practicing your skill on the exercises provided, you can quickly end—once and for all!—any problems in using possessive forms of nouns and pronouns.

Possessive Nouns—Basic Uses

When used with a noun, the apostrophe is the symbol of possession: one *woman's* briefcase, several *employees'* records, Ms. *Walters'* promotion. The apostrophe helps us take a shortcut from the longer possessive expressions "the briefcase of one woman," "the records of several employees," and "the promotion of Ms. Walters."

Follow these three rules for using apostrophes to form noun possessives:

1. Add an apostrophe plus *s* to a noun that does not end in *s:*

   One *woman's* suggestion developed into a new product.

   Five *women's* handbags were turned in to the police.

   Because neither *woman* nor *women* ends in *s,* add an apostrophe plus *s* to form the possessive of these nouns. This rule applies to all nouns, singular and plural, that do not end in *s.*

2. Add only the apostrophe to a plural noun that ends in *s:*

   Three *managers'* transfers were approved by our vice president.

   A *ladies'* lounge will be built in the southwest corner of the building.

   We estimate that we'll need two *years'* time to get these items into production.

The *Collinses'* lease expires at the end of 1994, doesn't it?

Managers, ladies, years, and *Collinses* are all plural forms.

3. **a.** Add an apostrophe plus *s* to a singular noun ending in *s* if the resulting possessive form is pronounced with an additional syllable.

One *actress's* script did not have the revised pages. (*Actress's* has one more syllable than *actress.*)

His *boss's* solution was to file a lawsuit against the manufacturer. (*Boss's* has one more syllable than *boss.*)

    b. Add only the apostrophe to a singular noun ending in *s* if the possessive form is *not* pronounced with an additional syllable. The key to this rule is to determine whether the possessive form would sound awkward if pronounced with the additional syllable. This rule applies mainly to proper names.

Ralph *Saunders'* request for a franchise has been approved. (The pronunciation of *Saunders's* would be awkward.)

To make sure that you always place the apostrophe (or the apostrophe plus *s*) correctly, study the following Quick Trick.

QUICK TRICK   **FIND THE OWNER!**

Reword the possessive phrase to be sure that you know which word is the "owner" and which word is the object of ownership:

that customer's account (the account of that customer: object, *account;* owner, *customer*)

several manufacturers' bids (the bids of several manufacturers: object, *bids;* owner, *manufacturers*)

the boys' gymnasium (the gymnasium of the boys: object, *gymnasium;* owner, *boys*)

With this method, you will be sure to locate the correct object and the correct owner. When you know the owners, of course, you will then know that *customer, manufacturers,* and *boys* are the words that you must make possessive.

NOTE: In the official names of certain organizations, banks, or buildings, apostrophes may be omitted from the possessive forms; for example, *the Woman Executives Association, Manufacturers Bank,* and *the Theatrical Agents Building.* In all cases, however, always use the official spelling.

CLASS PRACTICE 1

Once you are confident that you can apply the rules for forming noun possessives, select the correct word in parentheses in the following sentences.

1. (Martha's, Marthas') suggestion was innovative and practical.
2. Several (applicant's, applicants') résumés were sent to Personnel.
3. There are four insurance (agent's, agents') offices on this floor.
4. Hawaiian Surf designs both (women's, womens') and (girl's, girls') swimwear.
5. Westcott Lumber requested 30 (day's, days') notice to submit its bid.
6. Barbara (Hastings', Hastings's) law office is now in the Lincoln Building.
7. My (boss's, bosses') husband also works for our company.
8. Matt (Walters', Walters's) report concerned the effect of the proposed construction on the water supply for the community.
9. Only one (applicant's, applicants') résumé was sent to Personnel.
10. We asked for Dr. (Jennings', Jennings's) expert opinion on solar energy.

PROOFREADING PRACTICE 1

Do the following sentences have any errors in the use of apostrophes? Find and correct each error.

1. A special fund has been set aside for childrens' aid in our community.
2. The presidents' signature is required on checks over $10,000.
3. One real estate agent's bid for the property was $100,000.
4. Myra Young handles the trust fund for the Nelsons' children.
5. This new law will raise home owner's taxes about $10 a year.
6. Only one employee's vacation request was rejected.
7. Ralphs' car insurance policy does not cover loss by fire.
8. New Yorks' financial center is Wall Street.
9. Oil importers' demands for lower gasoline taxes have been refused.
10. Billy Joes' new company car is an Oldsmobile Cutlass.

Possessive Nouns—Special Uses

Here are some additional rules for using the apostrophe with nouns to show possession. Study them carefully.

Compound Nouns. Form the possessive of a compound noun on the last word of the compound.

my *brother-in-law's* investments   (The investments of my brother-in-law. Because *law* does not end in *s*, add an apostrophe and *s* to form the possessive.)

both general *managers'* assistants   (The assistants of both general managers. Because *managers* is a plural noun ending in *s*, add only an apostrophe.)

an editor in *chief 's* budget   (The budget of an editor in chief. Because *chief* does not end in *s*, add an apostrophe plus *s*.)

Joint Ownership. When two or more "owners" possess something jointly, place the apostrophe (or the apostrophe plus *s*) on the last owner's name.

Janet and *Andrew's* summer home is on Long Beach Island. (Janet and Andrew own the home jointly—that is, they share it as owners. Place the apostrophe plus *s* on the latter owner's name, *Andrew.*)

Audrey and *Jerry's* assistant is a highly qualified worker. (Audrey and Jerry share the same assistant, as indicated by placing the apostrophe plus *s* on *Jerry.*)

Separate Ownership. When two or more owners possess things individually or separately, place the apostrophe (or the apostrophe plus *s*) on the name of *each* owner. REMEMBER: Make *separate* possessives to indicate *separate* ownership.

Janet's and *Andrew's* summer homes are on Cape May and Long Beach Island, respectively. (In other words, "Janet's summer home and Andrew's summer home . . . ." Separate ownership, separate possessive forms.)

Audrey's and *Jerry's* assistants are highly qualified workers. (That is, Audrey's assistant and Jerry's assistant—*both* are highly qualified workers. Separate ownership, separate possessives.)

The key to using possessives correctly to show joint ownership and separate ownership is to analyze the context of each sentence.

CLASS PRACTICE 2

Select the correct word in parentheses for each of the following sentences.

1. Ask for a copy of (Steve and Laura's, Steve's and Laura's) report to their supervisor on projected sales for next year.
2. The estimated income for my (mother-in-law's, mother's-in-law) business next year is $500,000.
3. (Ms. Paulson and Mr. McCreedy's, Ms. Paulson's and Mr. McCreedy's) new franchise operations, which each purchased within the past three months, are doing very, very well.
4. Have you asked for (someone's else, someone else's) opinion on this proposal?
5. In 1984 (Webster & Abbott's, Webster's & Abbott's) total sales exceeded $1.5 million—its best year ever!

PROOFREADING PRACTICE 2

Read the following sentences to correct any errors in the use of possessives.

1. My son and my daughter's new car is the one that I bought them for Christmas.
2. New York and New Jersey's governors criticized the plan to decrease aid for the unemployed.

3. Perhaps Frank and Joseph's new supervisor, Ms. Abercrombie, can help us with this problem.
4. Leo's and Fred's new business is an interesting co-venture.
5. As you know, Marshall's and Randolph's newest store is the one in the Tucker Avenue Mall.
6. My father-in-law's and my brother-in-law's ideas for increasing business were very similar.

Possessive Personal Pronouns

The personal pronouns are *I, we, you, he, she, it,* and *they.* In the following chart, note the possessive forms of these personal pronouns—and note that they do *not* have apostrophes.

Personal Pronouns	Possessive Forms
I	my, mine
you	your, yours
he	his
she	her, hers,
it	its
we	our, ours
they	their, theirs

As you can see, the possessive pronouns *my, your, her,* and *his* are always used as adjectives. The pronouns *our, their,* and *its* are also used as adjectives.

My plane leaves at 2 p.m. *His* flight is scheduled to leave at 3 p.m., but *her* flight may be delayed until 4:30.

The pronouns *mine, yours, hers, his, ours,* and *theirs* replace possessive phrases such as *my book, your desk, her car,* and so on.

This is *my book.* OR: This is *mine.*

Is this *your pen?* OR: Is this *yours?*

She parked *her car.* OR: She parked *hers.*

As you see, the pronouns *mine, yours, hers, his, ours,* and *theirs* may never be used as modifiers; they always stand alone. Using personal pronouns correctly is tricky not because their usage is confusing (the opposite is true) but because some of the possessive forms of personal pronouns sound precisely like other words. Review the following pairs, remembering as you do so that personal pronouns never have apostrophes. The first word in each heading is the personal pronoun.

Its, It's. The possessive pronoun *its* means "of it" or "belonging to it." *It's* is a contraction—a shortened form of "it is."

We prefer the Rapitron Printer because of *its* ability to handle all standard paper sizes.   (*Its ability,* or "the ability of it." *Its* is a possessive form of a personal pronoun.)

It's essential that we increase our production. (*It's*, a contraction meaning "it is." *It's* is not a personal pronoun.)

Their, They're, There. *Their* means "of them" or "belonging to them." *They're* is a contraction, a shortened form of "they are." *There* may mean "in that place"; it may also be used as an introductory word and in some other ways.

Mr. Edwards manages one of *their* stores. (Stores *belonging to them.*)

Yes, *they're* planning to attend Friday's session. (*They are* planning.)

I'm positive that I left the briefcase *there*. (Left it *in that place.*)

There is reason to believe that sales will drop in June. (Introductory word.)

Your, You're. *Your* means "belonging to you." *You're* is a contraction, a shortened form of "you are."

While *you're* here in the bank, why not pick up *your* new charge card? (While *you are* here. Charge card *belonging to you.*)

Whose, Who's. *Whose* is a possessive pronoun meaning "belonging to whom." *Who's* is a contraction for "who is."

Do you know *whose* calculator this is? (Calculator *belonging to whom.*)

Who's in charge of the accounting staff? (*Who is* in charge.)

QUICK TRICK | **TEST THE CONTRACTION**

To choose between *its/it's*, *their/they're*, and so on, test the sentence by reading it with the full form of the contraction. If the sentence makes sense, then the contraction is correct. If the sentence does not make sense, then the pronoun is correct.

Do you know when (they're, their) supposed to arrive? (Read the sentence with the full form of the contraction: Do you know when *they are* supposed to arrive? Does the sentence make sense? Yes, so *they're* is correct.)

Please give me (they're, their) new address. (Again, read the sentence with *they are*: Please give me *they are* new address. Does the sentence make sense? No, so the personal pronoun *their* is correct.)

PROOFREADING PRACTICE 3

In the following sentences, find all the errors in the use of possessive personal pronouns.

1. One benefit of this equipment is that its easy to operate.
2. Do you know whether this diskette is her's?
3. Alan, who's signature is on this check?

4. According to the report, there van was damaged only slightly.
5. As soon as you're ready to leave, just call me.
6. No, its not too late to order the ScreenWriter II program for your word processor.
7. Their is one easy way to check this release date: call the West Coast office.
8. While you're working at the microcomputer, please make a backup copy of this diskette.
9. Who's voice is that on the loudspeaker?
10. When you're ready to distribute your handouts, just let me know.

Possessive Before a Gerund

A *gerund* is a verb form ending in *ing* and used as a noun. A noun or a pronoun before a gerund should be in the possessive case.

I heard about *Jack's* winning the monthly sales contest.   (Not *Jack winning*.)

I heard about *his* winning the monthly sales contest.   (Not *him winning*.)

We appreciated *Bob's* calling us and *his* sending us the new text on BASIC programming.   (Not *Bob calling*. Not *him sending*.)

CLASS PRACTICE 3

Select the correct word in parentheses.

1. Dr. Roberts, (you, your) teaching us to use this text-editing equipment is much appreciated.
2. Of course, we enjoyed (you, your) telling us about this special sale.
3. None of us had heard about (Ann, Ann's) promoting her assistant.
4. (Us, Our) working with mechanical calculators is time-consuming.
5. Mr. Hopkins was justifiably angry at (Ed, Ed's) leaving early.

COMMUNICATION LABORATORY

APPLICATION EXERCISES

A. Choose the correct word in each of the following sentences. HINT: For each possessive noun, make sure that you know which word is the owner.

1. (Girls, Girl's, Girls') ten-speed bikes will be put on sale during our Labor Day Special.
2. Jerome asked for both (companies, company's, companies') proposals.
3. Of course, we were proud of (Jenny, Jenny's, Jennys) receiving a special award from the mayor.
4. Because there was a (months, month's, months') delay in receiving the merchandise, we were not able to sell the entire stock before Christmas.

5. All the (secretary's, secretaries, secretaries') in our division have learned to operate Wang, Lanier, IBM, and Digital word processors.

6. The (Harrington's, Harringtons, Harringtons') original store was opened in Knoxville in 1980.

7. (Nancy and Roberta's, Nancy's and Roberta's, Nancys and Robertas) husbands work for an oil refinery.

8. Please be sure that (your, you're) prepared for our meeting with Mrs. Vance tomorrow.

9. One (district's, districts, districts') solution was to close their old warehouse.

10. Did you already try to find out (whose, who's) manual this is?

11. Several (manager's, managers, managers') budgets were cut more than 30 percent.

12. Employees should give the management at least (two weeks, two weeks') notice when leaving for another job.

13. (Bob's and Tom's, Bob and Tom's) plan is to resell both the building and the land within two years.

14. The (Jacobson's, Jacobsons, Jacobsons') recently acquired the rights to these trade names.

15. Obviously, the (Nelson's, Nelsons, Nelsons') profit from the sale of their stock exceeded $1 million.

B. On a separate sheet of paper, write your corrections for any errors in the following sentences. Write *OK* if a sentence has no error.

1. We are interested in learning more about you developing this software program, Ms. Quimby.

2. The contracts for Bethel and Company have laid here for almost two weeks!

3. One editor's in chief comment was that such action would be unconstitutional.

4. How long has Harold knew about the plans to close three of our stores?

5. As soon as we receive approval from the president, send these specifications to the Rodriguezes.

6. Joe's and Martha's typing skill has improved steadily since they started using a microprocessor.

7. We looked for the master diskette for hours; all the while, it was laying right there on the monitor.

8. She said, "If I was you, I would ask Ms. Kutcher for her advice."

9. Phil and Marion's clothing helps make them successful-looking stockbrokers.

10. The receptionist said, "I been asking the operator to connect me to the payroll clerk."

11. As you probably know, we have chose San Francisco as the site for our newest distribution center.

12. Now that the Anderson's have canceled their trip to California, perhaps they can attend our June seminar.
13. Both my assistant's have completed training courses sponsored by IBM, Honeywell, and Xerox.
14. If your going to take vacation in August, you should complete a vacation-request form now.
15. By tomorrow we should know whether its necessary to destroy all the booklets that were printed incorrectly.

C. Write the correct plural or possessive form of each word or phrase in parentheses.

1. El-Tee Designs, Inc., is a well-known manufacturer of (woman) clothing.
2. This request for information was received from the (attorney general) office.
3. Ms. Nugent is the researcher (who) study is now receiving much nationwide publicity.
4. Try to use (someone else) terminal to see whether you have the same problem.
5. Dr. (Hastings) account is handled by Hugh Moore.
6. We plan to sign a (year) lease for the district office.
7. All (executive) stock options must be exercised before December 31.
8. Among the (CPA) in our office is Anne W. Powell.
9. All the (Bench) have already returned their response cards.
10. Miriam received all (A) last semester.

VOCABULARY AND SPELLING STUDIES

A. These words are often confused: *finely, finally, finale; expensive, expansive*. Explain the differences.

B. Do you know the difference between the following homonyms: *overdo, overdue; prophet, profit; hear, here?* Define each.

C. The following words can either have one *l* or two, but most American dictionaries list one spelling as preferred. Write the preferred spelling of each word.

1. cancellation
2. cancelled
3. traveler
4. skilful
5. marvellous
6. installment

COMMUNICATING FOR RESULTS

Conflicting Interests. You are a member of the advertising staff at Bentley Toys. One of your close co-workers, Louise Cooper, an advertising copywriter in the same department, confides that in order to save money to buy a car, she is doing free-lance writing for Nu-Day Toys and Novelties, one of Bentley's competitors.

Do you see a conflict of interest in working for two different companies that are in the same business? What advice do you have for Louise about working for a competitor?

U · N · I · T

15 Other Forms of Pronouns

The skilled business communicator knows enough not to say "Him and I worked on the report together" and "Between you and I." Such incorrect constructions mark the writer or the speaker as ill prepared for business.

In Unit 14 you studied the possessive case forms of personal pronouns. Personal pronouns also have other case forms, which you will study in this unit and the next.

Case Forms of Pronouns

The pronoun cases are *nominative*, *objective*, and *possessive*. *Case* refers to the relationship of a word to other words in the sentence. You have already learned, for example, that a noun or pronoun in the possessive case shows ownership. A pronoun in the nominative case shows a different relationship to the other words in the sentence, and a pronoun in the objective case shows yet another relationship.

Compare the following pairs of sentences.

Nominative

Henry asked for this pamphlet.   (*Henry* is a nominative case noun.)

He asked for this pamphlet.   (*He* is a nominative case pronoun. *He* substitutes for *Henry* in the sentence above.)

Objective

Give *Henry* this pamphlet.   (*Henry* is an objective case noun, object of the verb *give*.)

Give *him* this pamphlet.   (*Him* is an objective case pronoun, object of the verb *give*.)

Possessive

This is *Henry's* pamphlet.   (*Henry's* is a possessive case noun.)

This is *his* pamphlet.   (*His* is a possessive case pronoun.)

These sentences show the basic relationships of the nominative, the objective, and the possessive cases of nouns and pronouns to other words in the sentence. Note that nouns have the same form for the nominative and the objective cases. Note, too, how pronouns substitute for nouns—*he* for *Henry* in the first pair of sentences, *him* for *Henry* in the second pair, and *his* for *Henry's* in the third pair.

Here is a list of nominative and objective pronouns. Review them before you continue.

Nominative Pronouns		Objective Pronouns		Examples
I	we	me	us	*I* gave; *we* went; for *me*; hired *us*
you	you	you	you	*you* are; with *you*
he she it	they	him her it	them	*he* has; *she* has; *it* will be; *they* know; to *him*; promoted *her*; on *it*; gave *them*
who	who	whom	whom	*who* has; appointed *whom*

Nominative Case

The most common uses of the nominative case are as subjects of verbs and as complements of "being" verbs.

Subject of a Verb. Pronouns that are the subjects of verbs must be in the nominative case.

We requested an extra copy, and *they* delivered it promptly.   (*We* and *they* are nominatives. *We* is the subject of the verb *requested; they* is the subject of the verb *delivered.* Obviously, *us requested* is wrong; *them requested* is also wrong.)

I prefer meeting with Ms. Johnson on Monday, but *she* is not available then.   (*I* is the subject of the verb *prefer; she* is the subject of the verb *is.* Both *I* and *she* are nominative case.)

Complement of a "Being" Verb. A noun or a pronoun that completes the meaning of a "being" verb is called a *complement.* As you know, of course, the "being" verbs are *am, is, are, was, were, be, being,* and *been.* A pronoun that follows a "being" verb must be in the nominative case.

It was *I* who recommended changing these procedures. (*I* completes the meaning of the being verb *was*. As a complement of a being verb, the nominative *I* must be used.)

The vice president in charge of marketing is *she*. (*She* completes the meaning of the being verb *is*; therefore, the nominative case is required.)

Could it have been *they* in the auditorium? (*They* completes the meaning of the being verb *could have been*; therefore, the nominative case is required.)

Complement of Infinitive *To Be* When *To Be* Has No Subject. Any pronoun that follows and completes the meaning (is a complement) of the infinitive *to be* when *to be* has no subject of its own is in the nominative case. For correct application of this rule, there are two things you must remember:

1. This rule applies only to the infinitive *to be*. Do not try to use the rule in any other situation.
2. The infinitive *to be* will have a subject *only when a noun or a pronoun immediately precedes it*.

Look at two sentences where the infinitive *to be* does not have a subject.

I would not wish to be *he*. (Is there a subject—a noun or pronoun—immediately preceding *to be?* No. Then this *to be* has no subject and the complement *he* is correct, because the pronoun must be in the nominative case.)

The owners appeared to be *they*. (Since *to be* has no subject immediately preceding it, the complement of the infinitive *to be* must be *they*, not *them*, because *they* is in the nominative case.)

Now study the following sentences, in which the infinitive *to be* does have a subject:

Mr. Richards thought *her* to be me. (*Her* is the subject of *to be*.)

The nurse mistakenly believed the *patients* to be us. (*Patients* is the subject of *to be*.)

QUICK TRICK   **NO SUBJECT—NOMINATIVE CASE**

For a memory hook on which to hang the *to be* rule, make this connection:

NO subject—*NO*minative case

NO is the word you must remember, and *NO* starts the word *NO*mina-*tive*.

Think this over. You will be amazed to see that the Quick Trick promotes immediate application of the *to be* rule.

CLASS PRACTICE 1

Choose the correct pronoun in parentheses.

1. (We, Us) will not have the final report until May 15.
2. Apparently, (they, them) thought that the cash discount was greater than 2 percent.
3. Ask Mr. Novak whether (he, him) has the new appraisal forms.
4. No, it was not (I, me) in the conference room this morning.
5. Ms. Rourke was in Newark yesterday, so perhaps the woman you saw at Newark Airport was (she, her).
6. We would not want to be (they, them).

PROOFREADING PRACTICE 1

Now correct any errors in the use of the nominative case in the following sentences.

1. On October 3 him will begin visiting all our branch offices.
2. No, it could not have been him in the lobby this morning because Jack is now in Europe.
3. The representatives who most opposed changing the plan were they.
4. Do you know whether it was her who rejected the engineers' report?
5. I told John, "When a caller says 'I'd like to speak with John Mays,' you should respond by saying 'This is he.'"
6. The recruiter thought they to be us.

James and I or James and Me?

Nouns and pronouns are commonly joined by *and* or *or* in compound subjects and compound objects.

Compound Subject	Compound Object
James and *I* will go . . .	. . . to James and *me*
Ms. Chan or *he* is . . .	. . . for Ms. Chan and *him*
She and *I* wrote . . .	. . . written by her and *me*

To be sure that you always use the correct pronoun in compounds such as these, follow this Quick Trick:

QUICK TRICK   USE THE PRONOUN BY ITSELF

For compounds that include pronouns, test the pronoun *by itself*, as shown here:

Louis and (I, me) may go with Dr. Trent.   (Omit *Louis and* and the answer becomes clear: "*I* may go . . . .")

Dr. Trent invited Louis and (I, me). (Again, test the pronoun by itself. Omit *Louis and:* "Dr. Trent invited . . . *me.*")

Note that pronoun choice in the following constructions can be tested in a similar manner:

(We, Us) proofreaders enjoy working overtime. (Read the sentence omitting the noun *proofreaders* and the answer becomes clear: "(We, Us) . . . enjoy working overtime." Obviously, you would say "*We* enjoy," not "*Us* enjoy."

They have asked (we, us) proofreaders to work overtime. (To decide between *we proofreaders* and *us proofreaders,* omit the noun *proofreaders:* "They have asked *us* . . . to work overtime.")

CLASS PRACTICE 2

Choose the correct pronoun in the following sentences.

1. Ms. Gwyn asked Carolyn and (I, me) to assist her.
2. Your word processing operators certainly give (we, us) reporters excellent help.
3. As you know, (we, us) editors must work under very tight deadlines.
4. The CPAs and (they, them) have devised a new tax schedule.
5. (We, Us) translators generally check one another's work.
6. Was Mrs. Daley or (he, him) among the final candidates?

PROOFREADING PRACTICE 2

Correct any errors in the use of pronouns in the following sentences.

1. Anna and I tried to encourage Jack and her to apply for that position.
2. Gail, my supervisor, asked Marie and I to submit these reports by the 10th.
3. Ms. Soderheim and him will discuss the effect of the new government policy on imports.
4. We celebrated when we heard that Mr. Braun had appointed Gary and I assistant vice presidents.
5. Only Brenda and her are on the list of interviewees.
6. If you give us sales representatives enough time, we will be able to develop an effective sales promotion campaign.

Objective Case

The objective case of personal pronouns is used when a pronoun is the object of a preposition or the object of a verb. The following rules also apply to *whom* and *whomever,* the objective case forms of the pronouns *who* and *whoever.*

Object of a Preposition. A preposition is always used in a *prepositional* phrase. Every prepositional phrase has a noun or a pronoun as an object.

Preposition	Prepositional Phrase	Examples
to	to the manager to her	Give the film *to the manager.* (The noun *manager* is the object of the preposition *to.*) Give the film *to her.* (The pronoun *her* is the object of the preposition *to.*)
from	from Ann and Bill from them	The message *from Ann and Bill* was vague. (The compound noun *Ann and Bill* is the object of the preposition *from.*) The message *from them* was vague. (The pronoun *them* is the object of the preposition *from.*)
against	against the proposal against it	We heard comments *against the proposal.* (The noun *proposal* is the object of the preposition *against.*) We heard comments *against it.* (The pronoun *it* is the object of the preposition *against.*)
for	for Joe, Gloria, and me for us	Get copies *for Joe, Gloria, and me.* (The object of the preposition *for* is *Joe, Gloria, and me,* which includes the nouns *Joe* and *Gloria* and the pronoun *me.*) Get copies *for us.* (The pronoun *us* is the object of the preposition *for.*)

Object of a Verb. Now notice how objective pronouns are used as objects of verbs.

We hired *her* yesterday. (The pronoun *her* is the object of the verb *hired.*)

Invite Stu, Betty, and *him* to the luncheon. (The pronoun *him* is the object of the verb *invite.* The nouns *Stu* and *Betty* are also objects of the verb *invite,* of course.)

COMMUNICATION LABORATORY

APPLICATION EXERCISES

A. From the choices in parentheses, select the correct form. For each nominative form you select, give the reason for your choice—write *sub* for subject of a verb and *comp* for complement of a "being" verb.

1. Are you sure that it was (he, him) who ordered this material?
2. When you have finished using this book, please return it to (he, him).
3. Between you and (I, me), I have little confidence that the economy will recover within the next two months.
4. The new manager asked Kenneth and (she, her) to prepare a flowchart.
5. Among the attendees was (he, him).
6. All of us were surprised when Ms. Rooney appointed Gladys and (I, me) to head the committee.
7. Jack and (he, him) always handle the Weston account.
8. Agnes asked, "If you were (I, me), would you sue for damages?"
9. Whenever you answer the phone, Louise, say "This is (she, her)."
10. From here, that gentleman looks like Mr. Ashe, but I'm not sure whether it is (he, him).
11. Barry and (I, me) interviewed several more applicants early this morning.
12. Veronica promised to send extra copies of her column to you and (I, me).
13. Mrs. Lewis encouraged Helen and (he, him) to continue their education in the evenings.
14. (We, Us) agents always work extra hours during the busy season.
15. Mr. Goldberg often depends on (we, us) printers to handle his "rush" projects.

B. Correct any errors in the following sentences. Write *OK* for any sentence that has no error.

1. Since this new carpet was lain, we have more static electricity than ever!
2. The monthly executive's meeting is attended by all general managers and vice presidents.
3. Have you already requested Kuhn & Clark latest brochure and price list?
4. Lisa told me that Mr. Faranti has already spoke to his secretary about getting temporary help.
5. Steve and I appreciate you taking the time to help us.
6. Chester behaves as if he were the sole owner of this company!
7. The coupon that was supposed to be there had obviously been tore off.
8. Ask Sandra whether she knows whose responsible for sales in the Atlanta area.
9. Kate and Bart were here earlier; perhaps this portfolio is there's.
10. Elmer been to Europe several times, mostly on business.
11. The clinic (which is on the third floor) has four staff nurses and two M.D.'s.
12. Only the Schwartz's have the combination to the main safe.
13. We must be at the airport by at least 1:30, so call me whenever their ready to leave.
14. How are Arnold and her planning to share the work load on their joint project?

15. Ms. Levesque certainly appreciated me helping her with the end-of-month statements.

C. Select the correct pronoun. Then indicate whether this pronoun is in the nominative or objective case by writing *N* or *O*.

1. Perhaps it was (I, me) who forgot to return the contracts to the company's legal staff.
2. The general manager and (we, us) district managers are concerned that economic conditions will seriously affect sales.
3. Mr. Jenkins, the head of our research staff, has asked (we, us) to draft a marketing survey.
4. The people who are responsible for meeting this tight schedule are (we, us) engineers.
5. Gregory enjoys working with either Margaret or (he, him).
6. Just between you and (I, me), do you really believe that this sales goal is realistic?
7. Frankly, Jack, if I were (she, her) I would not invest in such high-risk stocks.
8. Do you have the software that Angela and (I, me) need to draft this report?
9. Whenever you're ready to discuss this agenda, call Carla and (I, me) to set up an appointment.
10. If you should have any problems understanding these complicated instructions, just ask (we, us) programmers for assistance.

VOCABULARY AND SPELLING STUDIES

A. Explain the differences between these words, which are often confused: *sale, sail; intelligent, intelligible.*

B. What are the plural forms of the following words?

1. teaspoonful
2. gas
3. facility
4. mouse
5. memorandum
6. ratio

C. Which of the following possessives are singular, and which are plural?

1. manager's
2. Walshes'
3. children's
4. women's
5. hotel's
6. Smiths'

COMMUNICATING FOR RESULTS

Robert Weldon has been employed by Danieli Data Systems for over four years. He has established an excellent reputation for completing all his assignments on time and within budgeted costs, and he knows that he is a valued employee.

However, although Robert works long hours, he is seldom in the office on time. The official working hours are from 9 a.m. until 5 p.m. Robert usually works until 7 p.m. or 8 p.m. most days, but he arrives between 10 and 10:30 each morning.

Recently Robert's new supervisor politely discussed with him the need to arrive at work on time, but Robert simply thought the supervisor was trying to establish authority. Robert feels that doing his work is all that matters, regardless of what time he arrives.

Is Robert correct in his thinking?

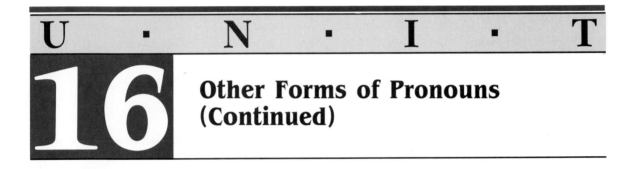

U · N · I · T

16 Other Forms of Pronouns (Continued)

Now that you have learned the case forms of pronouns, you are able to use pronouns correctly in almost all situations. This final unit on pronouns will put the finishing touches on your skill. This unit will cover some troublesome uses of pronouns, including the correct uses of the pronouns *who* and *whom*.

More Than I or More Than Me?

Correct pronoun choice is sometimes clouded because of the shortcuts we take in speaking and writing. For example, in the following sentences we generally omit the words in parentheses because these words are understood in the context of the sentence.

Mrs. Anderson prefers working on microprocessors more than *I* (prefer working on microprocessors). (By completing the sentence, you can easily see that *I*, not *me*, is correct, because *I* is the subject of the understood verb *prefer*.)

The new policy pleases Adam more than (I, me). (To choose between *I* and *me*, supply the understood words: 'The new policy pleases Adam more than *the new policy pleases me* [or *more than it pleases me*].' *Me* is the correct form.)

Choosing the correct pronoun in such sentences often requires an understanding of the meaning of the sentence, because sometimes both the nominative and the objective pronoun could be correct.

Mr. Sarafian enjoys working with Sam as well as (she, her). (Depending on the meaning, either pronoun could possibly be correct. "Mr. Sarafian enjoys working with Sam as well as *she enjoys working with Sam.*" "Mr. Sarafian enjoys working with Sam as well as *Mr. Sarafian enjoys working with her.*" The correct sentence depends on the context, so pay special attention to the meaning of such sentences.)

CLASS PRACTICE 1

Choose the correct pronoun in the following sentences. Be sure to supply the missing words in order to make your choices. (HINT: In some sentences, italics provide the emphasis you will need to understand the meaning of the sentence.)

1. Edward and I work longer hours than (they, them).
2. Has *Harrison* been as satisfied working with Amy as (she, her)?
3. Has Harrison been as satisfied working with *Amy* as (she, her)?
4. Denise has sold as many units this year as (he, him).
5. Does Ms. Franco have as much experience as (he, him)?
6. Is Mr. Van Pelt as articulate a speaker as (she, her)?

Self-Ending Pronouns

Myself, yourself, herself, itself, ourselves, yourselves, and *themselves* are pronouns. They are used (1) to emphasize and (2) to reflect a noun or pronoun already expressed.

To Emphasize. Note how the *self*-ending pronouns add force to the following statements.

Mrs. DePalma corrected the debit statements *herself.* (The sentence reads correctly without *herself.* But do you see how *herself* adds emphasis to the statement?)

I requested those printouts *myself.* (Again, *myself* can be omitted from the sentence, but without *myself* the sentence is a statement without emphasis.)

Be sure that the placement of the *self*-ending pronoun is correct, so that it does not change the meaning of the message.

George *himself* realized that the chemicals were phosphorescing. (The placement of *himself* is correct, but many may have said or written "George realized that the chemicals were phosphorescing *himself.*" Quite a different meaning!)

To Reflect. The *self*-ending pronouns are also used to refer to nouns or pronouns that have already been identified in sentences.

The sales representatives convinced *themselves* that the new product would not be successful. (Here, *themselves* refers to *sales representatives,* the subject of the sentence.)

Morgan asked *himself* whether he should continue with the project. (*Himself* refers to the subject, *Morgan.*)

Self-ending pronouns are often incorrectly used as replacements for nominative and objective pronouns, as in the following examples.

Yes, Mr. Diaz, Roland and *myself* would be delighted to assist you. (The sentence should be "Roland and *I* would be. . . .")

Mr. Diaz asked Roland and *myself* for help. (The sentence should be "asked Roland and *me.* . . .")

CLASS PRACTICE 2

Select the correct pronoun in the following sentences.

1. The board members voted (they, them, themselves) a 10 percent salary increase.
2. Angela Fasano and (I, me, myself) decided to survey all our credit card customers.
3. By reading diligently, Carlos has taught (he, him, himself) the language very well.
4. Would you want Clara or (I, me, myself) to accompany you?
5. Neither Leonard nor (I, me, myself) knew that *NOI* means "net operating income."

PROOFREADING PRACTICE 1

Correct any errors in the following sentences.

1. The general manager herself does not know why the project was canceled by the group vice president.
2. My home economics teacher taught me to sew herself.
3. No, Yvette and myself were not informed that the procedures manual is being reprinted.
4. Allison convinced herself that her plans would be accepted.
5. Paul said that he would leave himself at 4 p.m.

Pronouns in Appositives	In writing and speaking, we often use an appositive, a word or a group of words that explains or gives additional information about a preceding word or phrase.

Ms. Reilly, *my colleague,* is an acknowledged expert in this area. (The words *my colleague* give additional information about the subject, *Ms. Reilly. My colleague* is an appositive.)

The Austin Corporation, *a leader in oil exploration,* is backing the research study. (The appositive is *a leader in oil exploration;* it gives additional information about the subject, *the Austin Corporation.*)

Errors in the use of appositives frequently occur when an appositive includes a pronoun. Remember that the case of the pronoun is the same as the noun with which the pronoun is in apposition. Thus:

Only two agents, Bruce and *she*, sell thermoplastics.   (*Bruce and she* is in apposition with the subject, *only two agents*. Therefore, *she* is correct.)

We sell thermoplastics through only two agents, Bruce and *her*.   (*Bruce and her* is in apposition with *only two agents*, which is the object of the preposition *through*. Therefore, *her* is correct.)

QUICK TRICK USE ONLY THE APPOSITIVE

To test whether the pronoun in the appositive should be nominative or objective case, just cross out the word or words with which the pronoun is in apposition. The correct answer will then be obvious.

Our most successful engineers, Susan and (he, him), have been assigned to the Hong Kong project.   (Cross out *Our most successful engineers* and the sentence then reads: "Susan and (he, him) have been assigned . . . ." Obviously, *he* stands out as the correct pronoun.)

The Hong Kong project has been assigned to our most successful engineers, Susan and (he, him).   (Again, cross out the words with which the pronoun is in apposition and the sentence then reads: "The Hong Kong project has been assigned to Susan and (he, him)." The answer is now clear. *Him* is correct; it is the object of the preposition *to*.)

CLASS PRACTICE 3

Select the correct answers to these sentences.

1. At the end of the ceremony, Ms. Simmons gave special recognition to three outstanding district managers, Lynn, Melanie, and (he, him).
2. Two of our brokers, Mr. Fasano and (she, her), are in charge of GNMA certificates.
3. They explained to the clerks, Dominick and (I, me), that GNMA stands for "Government National Mortgage Association."
4. According to the brochure written by Frank and (she, her), a GNMA certificate is called a "Ginnie Mae" in financial circles.
5. We asked two vice presidents, Mrs. Sontag and (he, him), whether they were interested in investing.
6. Two new applicants, Ron and (she, her) will take the certification exam next Monday.

Who and **Whom,**
Whoever and
Whomever

The pronouns *who* and *whoever* are nominative forms. *Whom* and *whomever* are objective forms.

> *Who* is the supervisor of the information processing staff? (*Who* is the subject of the sentence.)

> *Whom* did she appoint supervisor? (*Whom* is the object of the verb *did appoint*.)

The following Quick Trick will help you find the correct pronoun form immediately in any sentence.

QUICK TRICK	SUBSTITUTE *HE* OR *HIM*

> As you know, *he* is a nominative pronoun and *him* is an objective pronoun. Therefore, when faced with a choice between *who* and *whom* (or *whoever* and *whomever*), mentally substitute *he* or *him*. If *he* could be used, then *who* or *whoever* (the nominative form) is correct. If *him* could be used, then *whom* or *whomever* (the objective form) is correct. To make this even simpler, just let the *m* in *him* remind you of the *m* in *who*m or *whomever!*
>
> > (Who, Whom) has the COBOL book? (Substitute *he:* "*He* has the COBOL book." Thus *who* is correct because *he* can be substituted.)
> >
> > You gave the COBOL book to (who, whom)? (Substituting *he* obviously does not work. Substitute *him:* "You gave the COBOL book to him?" Because *him* works, then *whom* is correct.)

Who and *Whom* in Questions. Most questions containing *who* or *whom* are in inverted order. To apply the Quick Trick, you must (1) change inverted order to normal order and then (2) substitute *he* or *him*. (Review Unit 10 if you do not remember how to change inverted order to normal order.)

1. Change to normal order if necessary.

   (Who, Whom) has the most recent price list? (Normal order? Answer: Yes. Therefore, *who* is the correct pronoun.)

   (Who, Whom) should I ask for the most recent price list? (Normal order: "I should ask (who, whom) for the most recent price list.")

2. Substitute *he* or *him*.

   (Who, Whom) has the most recent price list? (Would you say "*He* has," or would you say "*Him* has"? As you see, "*He* has the most recent price list" is correct.)

   (Who, Whom) should I ask for the most recent price list? (Normal order gives you "I should ask (who, whom) for the most recent price list." Then, substituting *he* and *him* shows that "I should ask *him*" is the only choice. Therefore, if *him* can be substituted, *whom* is correct: "*Whom* should I ask for the most recent price list?")

CLASS PRACTICE 4

Before you select the answers in the following sentences, be sure (1) to check whether each sentence is in normal order and (2) to substitute *he* or *him*. As a double check, give your reason for each answer.

1. (Who, Whom) did you recommend as the main speaker next Friday?
2. (Who, Whom) will serve as the consultant to the owner of this property?
3. (Who, Whom) is the new analyst on the corporate planning staff?
4. (Who, Whom) has Ms. LaMotta selected to replace Otto?
5. (Who, Whom) writes these so-called "boilerplate clauses"?

PROOFREADING PRACTICE 2

Find and correct any errors in the following sentences. Again, be sure to check for normal order before substituting *he* or *him*.

1. Whom did Theresa suggest as the senior project manager?
2. Whom has been interviewed for the inventory clerk position?
3. Who would you invite to make this presentation?
4. Whom has Mr. DiFeo hired to replace Jacqueline Frost?
5. Whom is the present leader in the monthly sales contest?

Who and *Whom* in a Clause. When *who* or *whom* is used in a clause within a sentence, the first step in determining which one is correct is to isolate the clause from the rest of the sentence. Then, as before, check the clause for normal order and substitute *he* or *him*.

1. Isolate the clause. The clause to which the pronoun belongs always begins with *who, whom, whoever,* or *whomever.* Thus your clue is that the pronoun is the first word in the clause.

   Donna is not sure (who, whom) the caller could have been.   (Isolate the clause: "(who, whom) the caller could have been".)

   Dr. Leslie is a physician (who, whom) all of us respect.   (Isolate the clause: "(who, whom) all of us respect".)

   Hand out these brochures to (whoever, whomever) asks for warranty information.   (Isolate the clause: "(whoever, whomever) asks for warranty information".)

   Give this file to (whoever, whomever) you have assigned to the Cleary account. (Isolate the clause: "(whoever, whomever) you have assigned to the Cleary account".)

Why isolate these clauses? Because the choice between *who* or *whom* (or *whoever* and *whomever*) depends on its use *within that clause*. It has nothing to do with any of the other words in that sentence.

2. Change to normal order if necessary.

(who, whom) the caller could have been (Normal order: "the caller could have been (who, whom)".)

(who, whom) all of us respect (Normal order: "all of us respect (who, whom)".)

(whoever, whomever) asks for warranty information (This clause is in normal order.)

(whoever, whomever) you have assigned to the Cleary account (Normal order: "you have assigned (whoever, whomever) to the Cleary account".)

3. Substitute *he* or *him* in each clause.

the caller could have been (he, him) (The pronoun *he* is correct, because *he* "completes" the "being" verb *could have been*. Therefore, the correct choice is "Donna is not sure *who* the caller could have been.")

all of us respect (he, him) (*Him* is correct; it is the object of the verb *respect*. Therefore, *whom* is correct: "Dr. Leslie is a physician *whom* all of us respect.")

(he, him) asks for warranty information (*He* is correct; it is the subject of the verb *asks*. Therefore, *whoever* is correct in the sentence "Hand out these brochures to *whoever* asks for warranty information.")

you have assigned (he, him) to the Cleary account (*Him* is correct; it is the object of the verb *have assigned*. Therefore, *whomever* is correct: "Give this file to *whomever* you have assigned to the Cleary account.")

CLASS PRACTICE 5

A. Isolate the *who* or *whom* clauses in the following sentences.

1. Has Ms. Rubin told you (who, whom) she has chosen to attend the convention?
2. No, I do not know (who, whom) will be coordinating the program.
3. (Whoever, Whomever) provides the best service will get the contract.
4. Beatrice LaGrande, (who, whom) founded this company, is the major stockholder.
5. We suggest that you allocate this extra budget money to (whoever, whomever) Mr. Purdue names to head the Planning Committee.

B. Using the clauses that you isolated in the exercise above, change to normal order any clause that is inverted.

C. Again, using the same sentences, select the correct pronoun for each sentence. Be sure to mentally substitute *he* or *him* before you make your choices.

PROOFREADING PRACTICE 3

Now you should easily be able to proofread for errors in the use of *who*, *whom*, *whoever*, and *whomever*. Apply your skill to the following sentences.

1. Generally, we distribute these complimentary consumer guides to whomever asks us for one.
2. As you know, Ms. Campbell, the award will be presented to whoever sells the greatest number of new cars through December 31.
3. I attended college with one of the attorneys who Mr. Lazlo hired.
4. Of course, I'd be delighted to work with whoever you assign to this project.
5. Yes, Jonathan, I think I know who will be appointed director of research.
6. Agnes asked, "Does anyone in the office know who Ms. Williams was referring to?"

Clause Within a *Who, Whom* Clause. Parenthetical clauses such as *I think*, *we believe*, and *she says* sometimes interrupt the *who, whom* clause, clouding the choice of *who* or *whom*. To make the choice correctly every time, just omit the parenthetical clause and follow the usual procedure for selecting *who* or *whom*.

Is Glenda the representative (who, whom) he said I should see?

1. Isolate the clause: (who, whom) he said I should see.
2. Omit the parenthetical clause: (who, whom) I should see.
3. Change to normal order if necessary: I should see (who, whom).
4. Substitute *he* or *him:* I should see (he, him). If *him* works as a substitute, then *whom* is correct. "Is Glenda the representative *whom* he said I should see?"

CLASS PRACTICE 6

Select the correct pronouns for the following sentences. (HINT: Omit any parenthetical clauses that obscure your selection, and be sure to change the *who, whom* clause to normal order if necessary.)

1. Charles Craig is one of the district managers (who, whom) I think you should notify of the changes.
2. As you know, Dennis is someone (who, whom) we believe will someday become president of the company.
3. Carole is a woman (who, whom) all of us think has tremendous potential for advancement.
4. Is Mr. Wadsworth the engineer (who, whom) you thought I had consulted?
5. The plant employees voted for Ed Waller, (who, whom) I believe they consider their best representative.

COMMUNICATION LABORATORY

APPLICATION EXERCISES

A. Select the correct pronoun for each of the following sentences. Be sure to know the reasons for your choices.

1. For a small charge, we will install this equipment for (whoever, whomever) asks us to do so.
2. Do you know (who, whom) Ms. LaFrance asked to gather the information for the monthly report?
3. Only two supervisors, Janice and (I, me), have already completed the course.
4. Laura and (I, me, myself) explained the benefits of the IRA account to Matthew.
5. Daniel and Carolyn are not as meticulous in their work as (we, us).
6. The copywriters who always work late are Gladys and (he, him, himself).
7. Jonas Paulson, (who, whom) we promoted yesterday, will now be in charge of the Cincinnati office.
8. Mrs. Dougherty knows as much about this business as (he, him).
9. In my opinion, Nancy is as good a sales agent as (he, him).
10. As you suggested, we will give the contract to (whoever, whomever) submits the lowest price.
11. Give the special discount to (whoever, whomever) qualifies for it.
12. Send this government pamphlet to (whoever, whomever) is responsible for equality in employment.
13. No, Gregory has not been a manager as long as (she, her).
14. Of course, she distributed copies to Ms. Murchison and (I, me, myself).
15. Have they announced (who, whom) the winner is?
16. Give the checks directly to the agents, Sal and (she, her).
17. Generally, Emily works longer hours than (he, him).
18. Arnold is a person (who, whom) everyone trusts.
19. The winners of the annual sales contest are usually Kristen and (he, him).
20. Two members of the Executive Committee, Agnes and (she, her), dissented with the majority.

B. On a separate sheet of paper, correct any errors in the following sentences. Write *OK* for any sentence that has no error.

1. I sent one copy to Mr. Hayes, and I kept the last copy for myself.
2. Yes, Gary and myself will be able to help you with this advertising campaign.
3. Give the folders to whomever has the rest of the contract files.

4. Does anyone know to whom this check should be sent?

5. All the cartons have laid there untouched since last week, when the messenger first delivered them.

6. Who will the panel select to represent our company at the international convention?

7. Wilbur has already took all the files he needs to complete his analysis.

8. Is Abigail Williamson the attorney whom you thought we consulted?

9. Who should I ask for more information on pension plans?

10. Does anyone know who the office manager assigned to the Dunbarton account is?

11. Only two sales representatives, Leo and her, have completed their analyses of their territories.

12. All the money was risen from voluntary contributions from our employees.

13. Andrew and me are confident that we can develop an effective proposal to win the Apex Plumbing account.

14. Mario flied to San Francisco for sales meetings many, many times.

15. We hope, of course, that the Marx's agree to the price that we plan to offer them.

16. Ben's and Sam's planned business venture concerns importing raw goods from Japan.

17. "Each managers' budget must be cut by at least 10 percent," said Ms. Young.

18. We have allowed only 15 minutes for the preliminarys—the opening remarks, greetings, and so on.

19. Theirs only one way to handle this sum of money—carefully!

20. As soon as you complete this first draft, please share a copy with James and myself.

C. Read the following paragraph, correcting any errors you find.

The primary business of Fasano & Klimkowski is the marketing of municipal, corporate, and government securitys. The firm has developed a computerized system for handling portfolioes to help it's customer's take advantage of market change's instantly. The firms' network system helps investors' to get access to up-to-the-minute financial information.

VOCABULARY AND SPELLING STUDIES

A. These words are often confused: *lean, lien; deference, difference.* Explain the distinctions between them.

B. Complete these analogies:

1. *True* is to *false* as *perfect* is to _____.
2. *Familiar* is to *strange* as *major* is to _____.
3. *Abundant* is to *scarce* as *natural* is to _____.
4. *Conservative* is to *liberal* as *valuable* is to _____.

C. Words ending in *able*, *ible*, *ance*, and *ence* often cause writers problems. Which of the following are spelled correctly? Correct the misspelled words.

1. intelligible
2. correspondance
3. incapable
4. collectable
5. intelligence
6. grievence

COMMUNICATING FOR RESULTS

Dressing for Results. Henry and Edward are good friends who work together in the Dalton Corporation's new suburban office. One major area of disagreement between the two is the right way to dress for work. Henry believes that dressing for work should be fun; it doesn't really matter what you wear unless you are a sales representative. Why dress up for co-workers?

Ed disagrees. He often tells Henry to wear a suit, dress shirt, and tie rather than jeans and sport clothes because clients often pass through their work area, sometimes stopping to ask for information. In addition, both Henry and Ed often meet with people from other departments within the corporation.

Who is correct?

U · N · I · T
17
Predicate Agreement With Simple Subjects

Movies, television shows, and popular songs have all—in an effort to communicate *feelings*—disregarded many of the rules of grammar. For example, in many popular songs you will hear "he don't" and "it don't" instead of the correct "he doesn't" and "it doesn't" simply because popular song writers do not always feel constrained by the rules of grammar! But remember that although grammatical flaws may not hurt the success of a song, a movie, or a television show, such flaws *can* hurt the chances of success of the business writer and speaker.

In previous units you have learned enough about subjects and predicates to make it easier to master the agreement principles in this unit and in Units 18 and 19. As you proceed through these units on agreement principles, remember that you *must* be able to make subjects and predicates agree if you are to write and to speak correctly.

The Basic Agreement Rule

The principle of subject-predicate agreement is this: *A predicate must agree with its subject in number and in person.* Specifically, those words in the predicate that must agree with the subject are any verbs and pronouns that refer to the subject. Thus you must pay attention to (1) agreement of verbs with the subject and (2) agreement of pronouns with the subject.

Agreement of Verb With Subject. Notice how the verb agrees with its subject in each of these sentences:

Mrs. Janeway *has* those files. (The verb *has* agrees with the subject, *Mrs. Janeway*. How, specifically, do they agree? Both are singular forms.)

Mrs. Janeway, one of the managers, *has* those files. (The subject of the sentence has not changed, and neither has the verb. *Has* still agrees with *Mrs. Janeway*. Do not be fooled by the words *one of the managers,* an appositive that separates the subject from its verb.)

Our manager *insists* that we have weekly status meetings. (The verb *insists* agrees with the simple subject, *manager.* How, specifically, do they agree? Both are singular forms.)

Our managers *insist* that we have weekly status meetings. (Now the verb form is the plural *insist,* to agree with the plural simple subject, *managers.*)

When applying the rules of subject-verb agreement, remember that plural nouns usually end in *s* or *es,* but an *s* ending on a verb indicates that it is a *singular* verb. Thus, in the above examples, "our manager insist<u>s</u>" and "our manager<u>s</u> insist" both illustrate correct subject-verb agreement. Note the following examples:

Singular Noun and Verb	Plural Noun and Verb
the woman is	the women are
an editor in chief has	both editors in chief have
one person says	two persons say
Mr. Hanson does	Mr. and Mrs. Hanson do
one person writes	two persons write

Agreement of Pronoun With Subject. When the predicate includes any pronouns that refer to the subject, those pronouns must agree with the subject.

Mr. Hanson does not want to place *his* order now. (The pronoun *his* must agree with the subject, *Mr. Hanson.*)

Mrs. Hanson does not want to place *her* order now.   (*Her* agrees with the subject, *Mrs. Hanson.*)

Mr. and Mrs. Hanson do not want to place *their* order now.   (The pronoun *their* agrees with the subject, *Mr. and Mrs. Hanson.*)

I do not want to place *my* order now.   (*My* agrees with the subject, *I.*)

Do you want to place *your* order now?   (*Your* agrees with the subject, *you.*)

As you can see, then, making such pronouns agree with the subject is not very difficult. Most agreement problems arise when the subject is not obvious.

CLASS PRACTICE 1

Select the correct verbs and pronouns in the following sentences. Assume that the pronoun refers to the subject.

1. One man (has, have) asked to have (his, her, their) money refunded.
2. Ms. Eaversham (enjoys, enjoy) discussing such problems with (his, her, their) assistants.
3. A young woman (is, are) applying for this position; (his, her, their) résumé (is, are) enclosed.
4. The department heads (does, do) agree that (his, her, their) budgets should be decreased by about 3.5 percent.
5. Olivia (writes, write) most of these brochures in (his, her) spare time.
6. This contract (is, are) supposed to be placed in (its, their) own file folder.

PROOFREADING PRACTICE 1

Now correct any agreement errors in the following sentences.

1. Mr. Stromberg has forgotten their briefcase again.
2. Janet generally answer her own phone.
3. Harry Malone wants a copy of this report for his records.
4. This building have a very impressive view from their fiftieth floor observatory.
5. Apparently it don't matter to John.
6. Pamela Durst create some very impressive ads in their studio.

Agreement Problems

Understanding the following troublesome agreement problems will help you avoid falling into traps as you write. Four specific problems are discussed below.

Inverted Sentences. As you know, the normal order of a sentence is subject first, then predicate. In inverted sentences, part of the predicate precedes the subject. Thus inverted sentences sometimes conceal agreement errors.

(Do, Does) the manager have the original contract? (Change to normal order to find the correct verb: "The manager *does* have. . . .")

(Do, Does) the managers have the original contract? ("The managers *do* have. . . .")

On my desk (is, are) the pamphlet you want. (Normal order: "The pamphlet you want *is* on my desk.")

On my desk (is, are) the pamphlets you want. ("The pamphlets you want *are* on my desk.")

Sentences and clauses that begin with *there* deserve special attention.

There (is, are) only one way to proceed with these estimates. (The subject of the sentence is *way*, a singular noun, so the choice must be "There *is* only one way. . . .")

There (is, are) several ways to correct these problems. (*Ways* requires the plural verb *are:* "There *are* several ways. . . .")

In speaking, many people seem to begin sentences with *there's* or *there is* almost automatically, without considering whether the subject that follows is singular or plural. Beware of this trap in subject-verb agreement.

Words Separating Subject From Verb. When a phrase or a clause separates the subject from its verb, the subject may not be obvious.

The building at the corner of Randall and Elm Streets (is, are) a possible site for our new store. (The prepositional phrase *at the corner of Randall and Elm Streets* separates the subject, *building*, from its verb, *is*. "The building *is*. . . .")

CLASS PRACTICE 2

Choose the correct words for each of the following sentences. Be sure to identify the subjects that your choices agree with.

1. The reason for postponing all these shipments (is, are) that our Denver warehouse is closed.
2. Mr. Yamato, the person who ordered all these supplies, (does, do) not want them shipped until June.
3. The main purpose for requesting so many samples (is, are) to ensure that our survey is complete.
4. Where (is, are) the new fabrics that Tyron & Sharp sent us?
5. The diskette that stores all these files (is, are) on my desk.
6. (Does, Do) your new supervisor (wants, want) you to take this word processing course after work?"
7. Edward asked, "(Is, Are) your assistants coordinating next Monday's sessions?"
8. In my office, on the top shelf of my bookcase, (is, are) the procedures manual you will need.

PROOFREADING PRACTICE 2

Correct any errors in the following sentences.

1. Amy said, "Where's the new catalogs that we recently received?"
2. Sean, the director of marketing and sales, have been developing an audiovisual training program.
3. Apparently there's only one more carton of letterhead paper left in the supply room.
4. The books that are on those shelves, in my opinion, are outdated and useless.
5. Don't Frank agree with Ralph's suggestion to hold the conference in June rather than in July?
6. Mrs. Phelps, who wrote all the product ads and brochures for the past four years, have accepted a transfer to our Toronto office.
7. In the trailer truck parked at the loading ramp is all the new microprocessors for the data processing center.
8. Has the incentive compensation checks been mailed to our sales representatives yet?

Each, Either, and Other Indefinite Pronouns. The following words are always singular: *each, every, either, neither, everyone, everybody, someone, somebody, anyone, anybody, nobody,* and *no one.* Note that whether they are used as subjects or as subject modifiers, they are always singular and their predicates must be singular.

Each of the floppy diskettes *is* packaged in *its* own envelope.   (*Is* and *its* agree with the singular subject *each.*)

Every employee in the company is covered by the pension plan.

Neither of these products *has* a copyright notice on *its* carton.   (*Has* and *its* agree with the singular subject *neither.*)

Everyone on the staff of the magazine *has* been asked to have *his or her* copy for the December issue ready by October 15.   (*Has* and *his or her* agree with the singular subject *everyone.*)

Common-Gender Nouns. Whenever the gender of a noun is obviously masculine (*father, brother, man, boy*) or obviously feminine (*mother, sister, woman, girl*), choosing a pronoun to agree with it is no problem. *Common-gender nouns* are those that can be either masculine or feminine, such as *instructor, supervisor, customer, president, attorney, nurse, secretary, employee, clerk,* and *co-worker.* To agree with common-gender nouns, pronoun combinations such as *he or she, his or her,* and *him or her* must be used.

Each supervisor has guidelines that *he or she* must follow.   (*He or she,* singular, to agree with the singular subject *supervisor,* a common-gender noun.)

Each supervisor has already received *his or her* guidelines. (*His or her*, to agree with *supervisor*.)

Ask each supervisor to bring the guidelines with *him or her* to tomorrow's meeting. (*Him or her*, to agree with *supervisor*.)

When *he or she* and similar combinations are used too often—especially within the same sentence—the message will be awkward. In such cases, the sentences could easily be revised by changing the subjects and the pronouns that agree with them to plurals.

The supervisors have guidelines that *they* must follow.

All the supervisors have already received *their* guidelines.

Ask all the supervisors to bring the guidelines with *them* to tomorrow's meeting.

CLASS PRACTICE 3

Choose the correct words in the following sentences.

1. Someone in your department (has, have) requested a change in (his or her, its, their) tax deductions.
2. Each manager in our branch office (answers, answer) (his or her, its, their) own phone.
3. Every secretary in the entire corporation (has, have) (his or her, its, their) salary reviewed every six months.
4. Anyone who (wishes, wish) to return merchandise must bring (his or her, its, their) receipt.
5. The president of a company must learn to depend on the information (he or she, it, they) (receives, receive) from (his or her, its, their) managers.

PROOFREADING PRACTICE 3

Correct any agreement errors in the following sentences.

1. Neither of the assistants are eligible to join the retirement plan until May 1995.
2. We believe that every secretary in the United States and Canada will want to have her own subscription to this magazine.
3. An executive always finds that they must observe strict time-management principles in order to be effective.
4. Anyone who submit their résumé should address it to our personnel recruiter.
5. No one, in our opinion, should invest more in stocks than they can afford to lose.
6. We are now seeking a secretary who knows how to manage his or her time well.

COMMUNICATION LABORATORY

APPLICATION EXERCISES

A. Choose the correct verbs and pronouns in the following sentences. Also, identify the nouns and pronouns with which your choices agree.

1. For one month, some drivers in our union (is, are) donating (his, her, their) overtime pay to a fund for handicapped children.
2. In the folders on her desk (is, are) the list of films we are distributing next month.
3. One of the managers (has, have) suggested a better way to process all these requests.
4. Each applicant (was, were) asked to bring (his, her, his or her, their) résumé to the interview.
5. One of the reasons for supporting the measure (is, are) to increase the demand for American-produced goods.
6. (There's, There are) probably only three people on our research staff who do not have Ph.D.s.
7. Each of the microprocessors in our division (has, have) a set of instructions beside (it, them).
8. Everyone who (enters, enter) this area must wear (his, her, his or her, their) employee badge.
9. No, every visitor (doesn't, don't) need (his, her, his or her, their) guest pass to enter the building.
10. In the top drawer of my desk (is, are) the graphs that you are looking for.
11. The offices in this building (is, are) tied in to this speaker system.
12. One of those women generally (comes, come) to the monthly status meeting with (his, her, his or her, their) assistant.
13. Every employee (is, are) eagerly waiting to hear how the new tax deductions will affect (his, her, his or her, their) take-home pay.
14. Of course, an executive must depend on the accuracy of the reports and the data that (he, she, he or she, they) gets from (his, her, his or her, their) staff members.
15. Where (is, are) all the color swatches that arrived this morning?

B. Correct the errors in the following sentences.

1. Al said, "Us dispatchers are in favor of the proposal."
2. Ask whoever you think has time to help us.
3. According to Sandra, there's a few suppliers who still make this product.
4. Whom do you think will be transferred to the Syracuse office?
5. Jack likes sales jobs more than me.
6. It really don't matter whether the materials are shipped airfreight or not.

7. Every employee in these two district offices are concerned that their job may be affected by increasing imports.

8. Harry and myself are among the people who were asked to work for the charity drive.

9. Needless to say, all of us were surprised to hear about Helen leaving the company.

10. If your sure that Mr. Haynes will approve, I'll increase the quantity to get an additional discount.

11. Has Lisa wrote to all our suppliers to tell them our new address and phone number?

12. Its true that we are the world's largest manufacturer of paper products.

13. These charts are ours; those graphs and tables are their's.

14. The purpose of the meetings are to explore possible ways to cut costs.

15. Has Franklin did all the end-of-month billing yet?

C. What is needed to complete these sentences, a singular or a plural verb? Choose the correct verb for each sentence.

1. Her credentials in the area of tax law (is, are) impressive.

2. Each reporter in Europe and Asia (was, were) asked for (his or her, their) opinion.

3. One of the machines that we recently purchased (is, are) already in the repair shop.

4. An executive who (knows, know) international markets (has, have) great potential in this company.

5. Where (is, are) the call reports from our Minnesota representatives?

VOCABULARY AND SPELLING STUDIES

A. These words are often confused: *staid, stayed; facilitate, felicitate.* Explain the differences.

B. Select the letter that correctly completes each question.

1. What does the French word *résumé* mean: (**a**) something resumed, (**b**) a conversation, (**c**) a summary, (**d**) the main dish of a meal?

2. What does the Latin term *pro rata* mean: (**a**) professional rates, (**b**) according to the rates, (**c**) concerning, (**d**) proportionately?

3. Which of the following means "for each year": (**a**) per capita, (**b**) per diem, (**c**) per annum, (**d**) per se?

C. Which completes the following correctly, *ie* or *ei?*

1. conc__t	6. n__ce
2. bel__ve	7. fr__nd
3. for__gn	8. l__sure
4. ach__ve	9. fr__ght
5. s__ze	10. ch__f

COMMUNICATING FOR RESULTS

First Day on the Job. Georgia Delaney was hired to work for a large bank. On her first day, she spent two hours in an orientation class; then she was to report to her department head, Ms. Carruthers.

Unfortunately, Ms. Carruthers was out on sick leave. What should Georgia do in this situation?

U · N · I · T

18

Predicate Agreement With Special Subjects

Four more special cases are discussed in this unit. As you learn these principles, be sure to remember the basic rule of agreement: *A predicate must agree in number and person with the simple subject.*

Collective Nouns

A *collective noun* is a word that refers to a group or a collection of persons or things, such as *class, faculty, committee, jury, company, audience,* and *herd.* When a collective noun indicates that the group is acting *as a whole,* the subject is considered singular and takes a singular verb. On the other hand, when a collective noun indicates that the members of the group are acting *as individuals,* the subject is plural and takes a plural verb.

The jury *are* arguing over several issues concerning this case.   (To argue, more than one person is needed. The plural verb *are* is correct because the jury members are acting *as individuals.*)

The jury *has* reached *its* decision.   (Here, the jury is acting collectively; because the group is acting as a whole, the subject is singular and the singular verb *has* is correct. Note, therefore, that the singular pronoun *its* is also correct—to agree with the singular *jury.*)

CLASS PRACTICE 1

Determine whether the collective nouns are singular or plural in the following sentences. Then select the verbs and the pronouns that agree with the collective-noun subjects.

1. The faculty (has, have) different views on these issues.
2. A new committee (is, are) to be established to answer such technical questions.
3. My company (has, have) been in business for nearly one hundred years.
4. The audience (was, were) obviously very pleased, as we could tell by (its, their) reaction.
5. The class (is, are) still debating among themselves the best date for our annual class trip.

PROOFREADING PRACTICE 1

Make any necessary corrections in the following sentences.

1. The committee is now working on their individual reports to the treasurer.
2. The city council have been arguing over this ruling since the members met this morning.
3. Our union have filed a grievance against Jeremy Vendors, Inc.
4. Each department must submit their financial statements to the city auditors by June 30.
5. That company have their headquarters in Knoxville, Tennessee.

Foreign Nouns

You have already seen (in Unit 13) nouns such as the following:

Singular	Plural
alumnus	alumni
alumna	alumnae
criterion	criteria
parenthesis	parentheses
stimulus	stimuli

Review the ways in which such nouns form their plurals so that you will be sure to have no problems with predicate agreement when the simple subject is a noun of foreign origin.

The *basis* for increasing our discount *is* to spark customer buying.   (*Is* is correct because *basis* is singular.)

The *bases* for increasing our discount *are* to spark customer buying and to push out old inventory.   (*Are* is correct because *bases* is plural.)

CLASS PRACTICE 2

Are the foreign nouns in the following sentences singular, or are they plural? Choose the words that agree with the foreign-noun simple subjects.

1. Maryanne's thesis (is, are) to be submitted no later than May 15.
2. The engineers' analyses of the structural defects (shows, show) that the concrete used in the foundation was not mixed properly.
3. The latest crisis in the assembly plant (was, were) caused by a strike in the steel industry.
4. In this report, parentheses (has, have) been used to enclose references.
5. Her criteria for selecting a microprocessor (is, are) price and service.

**A Number,
The Number**

A *number* is a plural subject, and *the number* is a singular subject. Be sure to make their predicates agree accordingly. Note that any modifier immediately before the word *number* (as in *a large number* or *the significant number*) does not affect this rule.

> The *number* of applicants *was* encouraging. (*Was* agrees with the singular *the number*.

> A *number* of word processing operators *have* submitted *their* résumés. (*Have* and *their* agree with *a number*.)

> A *surprising number* of word processing operators *have* submitted *their* résumés. (The modifier *surprising* does not affect *a number*, which is still plural.)

QUICK TRICK	**REMEMBER *P-A-S-T***

Use the word *past* to remember the following:

> PLURAL: a   SINGULAR: the

If you can remember *P-A-S-T*, you can recall the *P*lural term *A* number and the *S*ingular term *T*he number.

PROOFREADING PRACTICE 2

Correct any agreement errors in the following sentences.

1. All the parentheses that is on this page should be changed to brackets.
2. The report showed that the number of potential buyers are significant.
3. The alumnae of Herald College for Women are meeting for their annual reunion on July 22.
4. Of the stimuli that was used to spark economic growth, only tax rebates have been effective.
5. If the number of responses continue to be high, we will reevaluate the need for this product.

"Part," "Portion," or "Amount" Subject

Words such as *all, half, some, two-thirds,* and *none* are used in subjects to indicate a part or a portion of something. Consider such subjects plural when they are followed by plurals; consider them singular when they are followed by singulars. Study these examples:

> Half this book *has* been poorly printed.   (The singular *has* is correct because *book* is singular.)

> Half these books *have* been poorly printed.   (The plural *have* is correct because *books* is plural.)

CLASS PRACTICE 3

Are the following "part," "portion," or "amount" subjects singular, or are they plural? Choose the correct verb for each sentence; be sure to indicate the key word in the complete subject with which each verb agrees.

1. Two-thirds of the payment (is, are) due in advance.
2. Most of this building (contains, contain) valuable store fixtures.
3. All the machine (has, have) been rebuilt.
4. Three-quarters of these payments (is, are) due in advance.
5. Half the supplies (has, have) been stored in this room.
6. None of the building (requires, require) repainting.
7. None of these buildings (requires, require) repainting.

PROOFREADING PRACTICE 3

Correct any agreement errors in the following sentences.

1. Half the area have been sublet to a graphics art studio.
2. Three-eighths of the employees prefer the plan that we submitted to the union last week.
3. All the word processors in our department has been serviced within the past year.
4. Apparently, most of the motor were damaged during shipment.
5. Leonora said, "None of the inventory for these products are now ready for shipment to customers."
6. Two-thirds of the office space for these attorneys are being used as a library.

COMMUNICATION LABORATORY

APPLICATION EXERCISES

A. Select the correct verbs and pronouns in the following sentences. On your paper, indicate the key word in the subject with which each choice agrees.

1. All the materials (has, have) been delivered to the loading platform.
2. A number of people who attended yesterday's session (is, are) planning to return next week when (he, she, he or she, they) will again hear Dr. Peterson speak.
3. The data that we gathered from the survey of television viewers (is, are) very interesting.
4. Emily said the bases of the decision (was, were) explained in Paul's report.
5. Surprisingly, the number of employees who opted for Plan A (is, are) smaller than we had anticipated.
6. None of the reasons that she gave (is, are) convincing, in my opinion, although (it, they) (was, were) explained very clearly.
7. None of this building (was, were) affected by the fire.
8. A number of tenants (is, are) planning to file a suit against United Realty; in fact, (he, she, he or she, they) (has, have) already consulted an attorney.
9. Ms. Grosvenor said, "From now on, all criteria (is, are) to be specified more concisely."
10. The primary basis for the decision to build another warehouse (is, are) that the cost of renting space elsewhere is uncontrollable.
11. Her analyses of the situation (has, have) convinced our general manager to hire more data processing personnel.
12. The jury (has, have) found the defendant innocent of all charges.
13. A committee (is, are) to be established to study the problem and suggest possible solutions.
14. The alumni, all of whom graduated in 1984, (is, are) scheduling (its, their) next reunion for May 29.
15. A number of respondents (was, were) exceptionally pleased with (his, her, his or her, their) gifts.

Correct any errors in the following sentences.

1. From this distance, we thought that that woman was her.
2. Our insurance premiums were raised after a customer had fell on some materials accidentally left in an aisle.
3. One mans' suggestion was to store on our computer all customer transactions for a period of at least one year.
4. There's more cassettes in the storage cabinet, if you need them.
5. Each of the recipients are going to get a $500 prize.
6. Both Trent and myself agree that the cause of the problem is poor quality control.
7. Has everyone already gave Kathy his or her completed registration form?
8. Yes, we have experienced difficultys trying to set up the equipment.
9. When you need assistance, ask whomever is available in the computer room.

10. Please let me know whether its necessary to pay in cash.
11. I would appreciate you getting a copy of the bulletin for me.
12. My managers' home is about 10 minutes or so from our Navato office.
13. Sue and Richard's new book will be the third book that they have co-authored.
14. As soon as you find out who's calculator this is, bring it to the security desk.
15. As far as I can tell, that woman at the corner is definitely she.

C. Write one sentence with each of the following: (1) *there is,* (2) *there are,* (3) *neither,* (4) *none,* (5) *a number,* and (6) *the number.*

VOCABULARY AND SPELLING STUDIES

A. These words are often confused: *billed, build; deduce, deduct.* Explain the differences.

B. Identify the letter of the answer that correctly defines *agenda:* (**a**) a list of company officers, (**b**) a special financial statement, (**c**) a list of topics to be discussed at a meeting, (**d**) a legal agent.

C. Spell the following as directed.

1. The plurals of *alumnus, parenthesis, basis, criterion.*
2. The past tense of *take, grow, write, know, buy.*
3. The past participle for each verb in the item above.

COMMUNICATING FOR RESULTS

A Time and a Place for Everything. Your friend and co-worker Rosalind has just returned from a two-week vacation. Early on Monday morning she begins to give you a detailed description of everything that happened, but you have a deadline to meet.

What should you say to Rosalind?

U · N · I · T

19

Predicate Agreement With Compound Subjects

Subjects joined by *and, or,* or *nor* are compound subjects. The special treatment of compound subjects is discussed in this unit. In addition, in this unit you will learn the principles governing agreement in relative-pronoun clauses.

Subjects Joined by *And*

A compound subject joined by *and* is clearly a plural subject and takes a plural predicate.

> One disk drive *and* one video display monitor *are* included in this sale price. (The two parts of the compound subject are *disk drive* and *monitor. Are* is the correct verb to agree with this plural compound subject.)

> Mr. Anselm *and* Mrs. Greco *have* been coordinating the word processing seminars. (Again, two subjects are joined by *and*. The plural verb *have* is correct.)

EXCEPTIONS: Certain subjects can be joined by *and* to identify *one* person or thing. When both parts of the subject identify the same person or thing, the subject is singular and its predicate must be singular.

> My coauthor *and* business partner *receives* half the royalty on these books. (Here the subject refers to one person, who is both coauthor and business partner to the speaker. The singular verb *receives* is correct.)

> My coauthor *and* my business partner *receive* half the royalty on these books. (This is a genuine compound subject because two different people are referred to.)

> Ham *and* eggs *is* the breakfast that will be served. (*Ham and eggs* is *one* breakfast; thus the singular verb *is* correct.)

Another exception to the compound subject rule occurs when a compound subject joined by *and* is modified by *each, every,* or *many a*. In such cases, the subject is considered singular and takes a singular predicate.

> *Each* diskette *and* cassette *is* on sale until August 30. (*Is* is correct because *diskette and cassette* is modified by *each*.)

173

Every district manager *and* regional manager *has* been invited to dinner with *his or her* spouse. (The singulars *has* and *his or her* are correct because the compound subject is modified by *every*.)

Many an author *and* agent has asked for more information about this script.

CLASS PRACTICE 1

Apply the agreement rules concerning compound subjects to the following sentences.

1. Every man and woman in the company (is, are) covered by this insurance policy.
2. The students and their instructor (was, were) invited to visit our word processing facilities.
3. Eunice and Francine (does, do) not consider this project important to their careers.
4. Many a secretary and clerk (has, have) become an executive through (his or her, their) hard work.
5. Every inventory clerk and warehouse manager (has, have) been bonded.
6. His agent and advisor (is, are) his wife, Karen.

Subjects Joined by *Or* or *Nor*

Whenever a compound subject is joined by *or* or *nor*, make the predicate agree with that part of the subject that is closer to the verb.

Neither *Janice nor* her *assistants have* the master diskette. (Which part of the subject is closer to the verb? Answer: *assistants*. Therefore, the verb *have* is correct.)

Her *assistants or Janice has* the master diskette. (Which subject is closer to the verb? Answer: *Janice*. Therefore, the verb *has* is correct.)

Are you or Jack responsible for the inputting error? (Which part of the subject is closer to the verb? Answer: *you*. Therefore, the verb *are* is correct.)

Remember to find that part of the subject that follows *or* or *nor* and you will be sure to simplify predicate agreement in such cases.

CLASS PRACTICE 2

The following sentences have compound subjects joined by *or* or *nor*. Choose the words in parentheses that correctly agree with the subjects.

1. The president or his vice presidents (has, have) the authority to sign checks over $5,000.
2. For each audit, the auditor or the company treasurer (receives, receive) the original copy of the report, and (his or her, their) immediate supervisor always gets a copy.

3. At least once a month Jacqueline or Sam (purchases, purchase) supplies.
4. Neither Mrs. Garcia nor we (wants, want) to take this case to court.
5. Wendell or his sister (is, are) responsible for buying these bonds.
6. Either an attorney or an accountant (is, are) to be asked for (his or her, their) opinion.

PROOFREADING PRACTICE 1

Correct the predicates in the following sentences to make sure that they agree with their compound subjects.

1. Joanne, Rosalyn, and William have his or her tickets already, haven't they?
2. Heidi said, "Neither Mr. Owens nor the sales representatives in this district has received his or her issues.
3. My car and my van is available to you if you need it.
4. Ellen or Tony has generally allowed me to use her or his equipment whenever mine is being serviced.
5. Arnold or his partners usually does attend these public hearings.
6. Either wood or plastic have been used in similar cases.

Relative-Pronoun Clause

The last agreement rule that you will study concerns agreement in clauses that begin with the relative pronouns *who*, *which*, and *that*. Although this rule does not concern only simple and compound subjects, it is presented here to round out your understanding of predicate agreement.

To begin, review these few statements:

1. A clause is a group of words having a subject and a verb.
2. The relative pronouns are *who*, *which*, and *that*. They are called *relative* because they *relate to* another word in the sentence. This other word is called an *antecedent*.
3. The *antecedent* is a noun or a pronoun usually occurring immediately before the relative pronoun.

Study the following examples to make sure that you are able to recognize a relative pronoun and to identify its antecedent. In each sentence, the relative pronoun is in italics, and an arrow points to its antecedent.

The inspector *who* checks these machines is Mrs. Kinder. (The relative pronoun *who* begins the clause *who checks these machines*. What is the antecedent of *who*? Answer: *inspector*.)

Send the printouts by Monday, *which* is the deadline. (The relative pronoun *which* begins the clause *which is the deadline*. What does *which* refer to? Answer: *Monday*.)

Please give me the catalog *that* is on my desk. (What does *that* refer to? Answer: *catalog*.)

Notice that in each sentence the verb in the relative-pronoun clause agrees with the antecedent. REMEMBER: The predicate of a clause that is introduced by a relative pronoun *agrees with the antecedent of that pronoun,* not with the relative pronoun itself. For an easy way to apply this rule, study this Quick Trick.

QUICK TRICK	OMIT THE PRONOUN

By omitting the relative pronoun *who, which,* or *that,* you can quickly make the predicate agree with the antecedent of that pronoun. All you must do is use the antecedent as the subject of the clause.

Our Denver office is the one that (is, are) now having (its, their) inventory audited.   (Omit the relative pronoun *that* and use its antecedent, the pronoun *one,* as the subject of the clause: *one is* now having *its* inventory audited. *Is* and *its* are correct, to agree with *one.*)

Our Denver office is one of those offices that (is, are) now having (its, their) inventories audited.   (Again, omit *that* and use its antecedent, the noun *offices,* as the subject of the clause: *offices are* now having *their* inventories audited. *Are* and *their* are correct, to agree with *offices.*)

An employee who (wants, want) to have (his or her, their) vacation schedule changed must see Mr. Helms.   (Again, use the antecedent as the subject of the clause: an *employee wants* to have *his or her* vacation schedule changed.)

Employees who (wants, want) to have (his or her, their) vacation schedule changed must see Mr. Helms.   (Again, use the antecedent as the subject of the clause: *employees want* to have *their* vacation schedule changed.)

CAUTION: *Whom, which,* and *that* are not always *relative* pronouns. In the following sentences, note that *who, which,* and *that* do not relate to anything. They have no antecedents.

Who is the woman talking to Ms. Copeland?   (*Who* has no antecedent in this sentence. It is not a relative pronoun.)

Do you know which restaurant has been selected?   (*Which* has no antecedent.)

Please be sure to treat that microprocessor carefully.   (*That* has no antecedent.)

CLASS PRACTICE 3

In the following sentences, identify the relative pronouns and their antecedents before you make your selections of verbs and pronouns. (Be sure to omit the relative pronoun and use the antecedent as the subject of the clause to make your choice.)

1. Thelma is one of those managers who always (submits, submit) (her, their) budgets one month early.

2. Is this the book that (has, have) become famous for (its, their) effective selling techniques?
3. Anthony is one of those typists who (types, type) more than 100 words a minute.
4. This is one fabric that (is, are) well known for (its, their) comfort and durability.
5. My wife is one of those people who never (forgets, forget) (her, their) appointments.
6. Complete all these forms before the deadline, which (is, are) on Friday, September 13.

PROOFREADING PRACTICE 2

Now correct any agreement errors in the following sentences. Again, be sure that you are able to identify the relative pronouns and their antecedents.

1. Martin is one man who often say that they will never retire.
2. I have already seen all the notices that was posted on the bulletin board.
3. Sheila is one of the most talented agents who is now working for this company.
4. Ms. Zach is the only one in these departments who are authorized to sign checks.
5. Please order one of those calculators that is powered by solar energy.
6. One of the mechanics who is employed by Agro Repairs is Jonas Seton, my former neighbor.

COMMUNICATION LABORATORY

APPLICATION EXERCISES

A. Select the correct verbs and pronouns in each of the following sentences. Also, identify the subjects with which your choices agree.

1. Dr. Vincent is one of those researchers who always (checks, check) (his or her, their) work carefully.
2. Each monitor, disk drive, and printer (is, are) available at a 25 percent discount.
3. Ann Marie is a person who (likes, like) to prepare (her, their) work at the beginning of each day.
4. Every man and woman in these departments (has, have) volunteered (his or her, their) time to the charity drive.
5. Albert or his two supervisors (is, are) going to submit (his, their) recommendations before next Monday.
6. Many a manager and executive in our company (has, have) taken advantage of the stock-option plan.
7. Marjorie or her sister Elaine (has, have) forgotten (her, their) briefcase in the conference room.

8. Let's order one of those how-to books that (gives, give) detailed instructions.
9. Either Mrs. Horowitz or her brothers officially (owns, own) the property.
10. Frances and Phil (rejects, reject) all advertisements for "free" gifts.
11. Is Nathan one of those treasurers who (is, are) always cutting expenses?
12. Waldham Automotive Parts is one of those stores which (offers, offer) below-cost specials during (its, their) Labor Day sales.
13. Either Gail or Donna (finances, finance) (her, their) car loan through the Credit Union.
14. Neither Ms. Adams nor her partners (has, have) shown an interest in developing this land.
15. Rhythm and Blues (is, are) one of the categories of music that Barbara and James (enjoys, enjoy) most.

B. On a separate sheet of paper, correct any errors in the following sentences. Write *OK* if a sentence has no error.

1. Needless to say, both Grant and myself will do our best to complete the project as scheduled.
2. Neither Crista nor the other applicants was given complete instructions for taking the test.
3. As we already mentioned, us managers are willing to work overtime during the busy season.
4. Mrs. Soderberg is one of the quality control supervisors who want to change our entire system.
5. Is this manual one of the six references that was recommended by Ms. Gerber?
6. As of June 30, the Flynn's expenses were already 35 percent higher than last year's expenses during the same period.
7. In an effort to handle this heavy workload, we are hiring three more CPA's next January.
8. Do you know whom on the personnel staff will be assigned to handle medical benefits?
9. Fortunately, consumption of oil and oil-based products has not raised as steadily in the last few years.
10. We try our best to ensure that salary increases and promotions are given to those employees who most deserves them.
11. As you know, there's not enough forms for all of us, so we will photocopy a few more.
12. A sales representative must be sure to establish a feeling of confidence with their clients.
13. Next week we will interview six more applicants; of course, we will then hire the candidate whom we think has the greatest potential.
14. Michael done all he could possibly do to convince Ferris Metals to buy our products.

15. As soon as the Logan's return the completed forms, the trust fund will become official.

C. Identify whether a singular or a plural verb is required in each of the following phrases.

1. either the manager or her assistants_____
2. one of the people who_____
3. Marco and Arthur_____
4. ham and eggs_____
5. the two clerks or their supervisor_____
6. Pearl or Nicholas_____

VOCABULARY AND SPELLING STUDIES

A. These words are often confused: *fair, fare; undo, undue.* Explain the differences.

B. How well can you define the following word processing terms?

1. *Delete* means (**a**) to indent, (**b**) to represent, (**c**) to omit, (**d**) to input copy.
2. *Wraparound* describes the ability of word processing equipment to (**a**) automatically place a word at the beginning of a new line, (**b**) print copy on both the front and the back of a sheet at the same time, (**c**) bind a report in a special wrapper, (**d**) type around the full area of any size sheet.
3. *Hardware* refers to (**a**) the tools that operators must use to adjust or fix equipment, (**b**) the diskettes or disks that are used to store data, (**c**) the mechanical or electronic equipment used in word processing, (**d**) an alternative name for software.

C. Identify the word that is spelled correctly in each of the following groups.

1. wholely, accommodate, symetry
2. specificaly, recolect, Wednesday
3. remembrence, statistical, retreival
4. withold, occasional, aprroximately
5. amateur, expendible, consientious
6. hindrence, necesitate, knowledgeable

COMMUNICATING FOR RESULTS

To Gossip or Not to Gossip? At lunch with a group of co-workers, you hear the conversation suddenly turn to the looks, dress, and other personal characteristics of the manager of your department, Bob. Someone mentions how poorly he dresses, how unfriendly he is, and other equally negative remarks. Because Bob works in your department, everyone is now waiting to hear what you have to say.

What would you say?

U · N · I · T

20 Adjectives

Nouns and pronouns and verbs can be joined together to form complete sentences. But without adjectives, the sentences would be rather boring, and sometimes even imprecise. Adjectives modify nouns and pronouns. To use adjectives correctly is fairly easy—but only if you can identify adjectives accurately.

Identifying Adjectives

Remember that any word that modifies a noun or a pronoun is an adjective. An adjective answers the following questions: What kind? Which one? How many? Now look at the following kinds of adjectives to be sure that you can identify them.

Articles. The words *a* and *an* are called *indefinite articles.* The article *a* is used before a word that begins with a consonant sound, a long *u* sound, or an *h* that is pronounced, as in *a building, a union,* and *a hallway.*

Use *an* before a word that begins with a vowel sound (except long *u*) or an *h* that is not pronounced, as in *an airline, an essay, an item, an odor, an umbrella, an honor, an hour.*

The word *the* is also an article (called the *definite article*). Obviously *the* is one of the most commonly used words in our language.

> *The* instructor brought *the* projector to *the* classroom.

Descriptive Adjectives. When most people think of adjectives, they think of words that describe—descriptive adjectives such as *famous, interesting, intensive,* and *new.*

> A *famous* speaker, Beverly Youngblood, gave an *interesting* presentation. (*Famous* and *interesting* are descriptive adjectives.)

> She took an *intensive* course in business management at a *new* school near her home. (*Intensive* and *new* are descriptive adjectives.)

Possessive Adjectives. The possessive pronouns *my, your, his, her, its, our,* and *their* are used to modify nouns. In addition, possessive nouns (such as *manager's* and *Ralph's*) are used to modify nouns. Therefore, these possessive forms function as adjectives.

180

Your new assistant asked for *our manager's* approval to order *Ralph's* equipment. (*Your, our, manager's,* and *Ralph's* are all possessive adjectives.)

Limiting Adjectives. Adjectives that tell "how many" or "how much" are called *limiting adjectives.* Notice how numbers and words serve to limit the nouns they modify in the following sentences.

One representative in our division was the *first* person to win the award. (*One* and *first* are limiting adjectives.)

Pour *2.6* liters into each of these *four* metal containers. (*2.6* and *four* are limiting adjectives.)

Proper Adjectives. Proper nouns, too, can be used to describe. When they are used as adjectives, they are called *proper adjectives.*

A *New York* hotel advertised special rates for all *West Coast* travelers. (*New York* and *West Coast,* as used here, are proper adjectives.)

Note that words derived from proper nouns are also proper adjectives.

A *European* cruise attracted many *American* tourists. (*European* and *American* are proper adjectives.)

Compound Adjectives. A compound adjective consists of two or more words that act together as a single thought unit to modify a noun or a pronoun.

an *easy-going* person
a *first-class* trip
my *data processing* text
a *high school* student

CLASS PRACTICE 1

A. Choose *a* or *an*, whichever is correct, in each of the following sentences.

1. Gloria's sales presentation lasted for more than (a, an) hour.
2. Do you have (a, an) opinion about the pricing of these goods?
3. After several hours, (a, an) unanimous decision was finally reached.
4. Rita and Bart offered (a, an) unique suggestion for settling the dispute.
5. Please send me (a, an) catalog describing all your products.

B. Identify the adjectives in the following sentences as *descriptive* ("D"), *possessive* ("P"), *limiting* ("L"), *proper* ("PR"), or *compound* ("C"). Disregard the articles *a, an,* and *the.*

1. A long line of eager customers waited for a special sale that had been advertised for two weeks.
2. Two representatives from our Houston office explained their reason for rejecting the huge bid.
3. Ask three or four new employees for their opinions of our plan.

4. A Louisiana company has given us its permission to use its high-speed equipment.
5. An Italian firm accepted our proposal to manufacture merchandise for sale in duty-free shops in six American airports.

Comparison of Adjectives

Adjective forms such as *new, newer, newest* represent three different degrees of a certain quality. The three degrees are called *positive, comparative,* and *superlative.*

Positive Degree. This form is used when the person or thing is not compared to anyone or anything else.

 a new car, an expensive stereo

Comparative Degree. This form is used to express a higher or a lower degree than expressed by the positive degree.

 a newer car, a more expensive stereo

Superlative Degree. This form is used to denote the highest or the lowest degree.

 the newest car, the most expensive stereo

Forms of Comparison of Adjectives. Adjectives may be compared in one of three ways:

1. By adding *er* or *est* to the positive form.

Positive	Comparative	Superlative
large	larger	largest
friendly	friendlier	friendliest

2. By using *more* or *most* (or *less* or *least*) with the positive form.

Positive	Comparative	Superlative
interesting	more interesting	most interesting
	less interesting	least interesting
intensive	more intensive	most intensive
	less intensive	least intensive
successful	more successful	most successful
	less successful .	least successful

3. By changing the form of the word completely.

Positive	Comparative	Superlative
good	better	best
bad	worse	worst
little	less	least
much	more	most
many	more	most

NOTE: Comparatives and superlatives are formed by using *one* of the above three methods. Do not apply more than one method at a time.

This package is *larger* than yours.   (Not *more larger.*)

In the *simplest* terms possible, Jean explained to all of us how to use the new word processor.   (Not *most simplest.*)

Selection of Correct Forms. Adjectives of one syllable are compared by adding *er* or *est;* adjectives of three or more syllables, by adding *more* or *most.* However, adjectives of two syllables may be compared either by adding *er* or *est* or by adding *more* or *most.* Sometimes the sound of the word will guide you in making a choice; often both methods are equally acceptable. If you are in doubt, remember that those two-syllable adjectives not taking *more* or *most* are irregular comparisons. These irregular comparisons are shown in the dictionary under the positive form of the adjective.

Martha is *more ambitious* than Denise.   (You cannot add *er* to *ambitious.*)

Vera is one of the *most courteous* agents in the company.   (You cannot add *est* to *courteous.*)

This word processor is the *costliest* one on the market. OR: This word processor is the *most costly* one on the market.   (Both forms are acceptable.)

Choice of Comparative or Superlative Degree. The comparative degree (*newer, more tired, better,* and so on) is used to compare two persons, places, or things.

Evelyn is tired, but Stu appears *more tired* than she.

Mike's report was good; however, I really consider Bernie's report *better.*

The superlative degree (*newest, most tired, best,* and so on) is used to compare *more than two* persons, places, or things.

Helen appears to be the *most tired* of all the brokers.

Of all the reports that were submitted, Pedro's was the *best.*

CLASS PRACTICE 2

Make the correct choice in each of the following sentences.

1. Paul is considered a very (good, better, best) programmer, but Winnie is certainly (good, better, best); however, everyone agrees that Danielle is the (good, better, best) programmer on our staff.
2. Margaret's argument was (forceful, forcefuler, more forceful, most forceful) than Andrea's.
3. Mr. Rusnak gave the (logicalest, most logical) reasons to explain why our electronic equipment will not work properly.

4. We selected the (whitest, most white, most whitest) paper available to print our sales brochures.

5. Mark's appointment is (early, more early, earlier, most early) than mine, but Charles has the (early, earlier, earliest, most early) appointment with Ms. Hotchkiss.

6. Our attorneys suggested several alternatives, but they agreed that my recommendation might be the (most good, more better, most best, best) of all.

Other and *Else* in Comparisons. When the comparative degree is used to compare a person or a thing with *other* members of the same group, use the word *other* or *else* as shown in these sentences:

> Peter is *more* ambitious than any *other* broker in our company. (Without the word *other*, the meaning of the sentence would be that Peter does not work in our company but that he works for another company.)

> Peter is *more* ambitious than all the *other* brokers in our company. (Again, the word *other* makes it clear that Peter and the other brokers work for the same company. Without the word *other*, the meaning would be that Peter works for a different company than the brokers work for.)

> Peter is *more* ambitious than anyone *else* in our company. (Without the word *else*, the sentence would again imply that Peter does not work in our company.)

With the superlative degree, *other* or *else* is not needed, but *all* is often used.

> Peter is the *most* ambitious of all the brokers in our company. (Note that *other* or *else* is not used in the sentence because the *of* phrase makes it clear that Peter belongs to the group compared.)

Adjectives That Cannot Be Compared. The positive degree of some adjectives already states a quality that cannot be compared. For example, "a *full* glass" tells it all; you cannot have another glass that is *fuller* or a third glass that is *fullest*. *Full* is the absolute degree, so this adjective cannot be compared. Other absolute adjectives are:

accurate	immaculate	sound
complete	level	spotless
correct	perfect	square
dead	perpendicular	straight
even	perpetual	unanimous
final	right	unique

To indicate the degree to which a person or thing approaches the state of being full or complete or correct, use *more nearly* or *most nearly*.

> Louise's estimate ($4,500) proved to be correct. Except for Louise's, Joe's estimate ($4,350) was *more nearly correct* than any of the others.

Only yesterday's vote was unanimous; however, last week's vote was *more nearly unanimous* than any of the others had been.

CLASS PRACTICE 3

Choose the correct words in the following sentences. How well do you understand when to use *other, else,* and *all* in comparisons? How well do you understand how to handle adjectives that cannot be compared?

1. Neil Friedman, my supervisor, gives better raises than (any, any other) supervisor in my company.
2. My new assistant, Sam Brady, delivers clearer presentations than (anyone, anyone else) on my staff.
3. Unfortunately, none of these drawings is accurate; however, Caryl's sketch is the (most accurate, more accurate, most nearly accurate) of all the ones that I've reviewed.
4. New York City has more jewelry stores than (any, any other) city on the Eastern Seaboard.
5. Your secretary types faster than (anyone, anyone else) in your department.
6. Your secretary is the fastest of (all the, all the other) typists in your department.

PROOFREADING PRACTICE 1

This Proofreading Practice will provide you with a cumulative review of this unit. Correct any errors in the following sentences.

1. Veronica's reports are always written more clearly than those of anyone in her company.
2. In your opinion, which district office is best, our Chicago office or our Tampa office?
3. Alice smiled as she said to the audience, "It is indeed a honor to be invited to speak at this convention."
4. Because the air conditioner was off, our room suddenly became more warm than it had been.
5. This tube does not roll off my desk because my desk is more level than yours.
6. After several hours, the committee reached an unanimous decision.

Adjective Pitfalls   Compound Adjectives. As you saw in the beginning of the unit, a *compound adjective* consists of two or more words that act together as a single thought unit to modify a noun or a pronoun. Certain compound adjectives are hyphenated; others are not. Observe these rules:

1. Do not hyphenate compound adjectives that have become very familiar from long use and are considered a single unit. Do not hyphenate compound proper nouns used as adjectives.

   a high school classroom
   charge account customers
   life insurance policies
   data processing texts
   social security benefits
   real estate contracts
   an East Coast convention
   Los Angeles suburbs

2. Hyphenate most other compound adjectives when they precede a noun:

   air-conditioned offices
   first-class tours
   up-to-date equipment
   a 10-mile drive
   one-hour intervals
   well-known speakers

   BUT: a person who is *well known*, an interval of *one hour*

   HINT: To help you decide whether two adjectives that precede a noun do act together as a single unit, try this simple test. Use *long range plans* for an example. The noun is *plans*. Ask yourself, "What kind of plans?" *Long* plans? *Range* plans? No, neither one makes sense. The two adjectives work as a single unit: *long-range plans*—plans that are long-range.

CLASS PRACTICE 4

Decide whether the compound adjectives in the following sentences should be hyphenated.

1. As you know, Pearl is now checking with our (New Hampshire, New-Hampshire) office.
2. Glenda estimates that we have at least a (30 minute, 30-minute) drive during rush hour.
3. A special discount will be offered to (credit card, credit-card) customers who take advantage of this super sale.
4. From her published articles, Ms. Gleason has become (well known, well-known) in the field of tax law.
5. Sales representatives are strictly prohibited from using any (high pressure, high-pressure) tactics.
6. Of course, the methods I just described are now considered (old fashioned, old-fashioned).

Those, Them. Them is never an adjective and should not be used in place of the adjective *those.*

Will you be able to help me carry *those* packages to Ms. Avila? (Not *them pack-ages*. The noun following *those* helps you see that the adjective *those* is needed.)

Note that *those* is the plural of *that; these* is the plural of *this*. Use *that* and *those* to refer to objects that are at a distance from you; use *this* and *these* for objects that are closer to you.

Either, Neither, Any, Any One, No One, Not Any, None. Either and *neither* are used to refer to one of two persons or things. *Any, any one, no one, not any*, and *none* are used to refer to one of *three or more* persons or things.

Either mechanic should be able to help you. (There are two mechanics.)

Any mechanic should be able to help you. (Because *any* is used, there must be three or more mechanics.)

Repeated Modifier. Repeating a modifier such as *a, an, the*, or *my* (as in the following example) shows that two different people are referred to:

The vice president and the general manager approved this addendum to the con-tract. (Two different people—one, the vice president, the other, the general manager—approved the addendum.)

Omitting the modifier *the* before *general manager* shows that one person is referred to:

The vice president and general manager approved this addendum. (Here, one person is referred to. This one person simply has two titles, *vice president* and *general manager*.)

CLASS PRACTICE 5

Select the correct words in the following sentences.

1. Be sure to return (those, them) library books before May 15, please.
2. Those (kind, kinds) of typewriters have been replaced by the new mem-ory machines.
3. If you wish, of course, you may use (either, any) of these three consoles.
4. Maria prefers these (sort, sorts) of projectors.
5. Apparently, (neither, none) of the many applicants met the require-ments.
6. Ms. D'Amico wants (this, these) diskettes duplicated.

COMMUNICATION LABORATORY

APPLICATION EXERCISES

A. Select the correct words in the following sentences.

1. Of all the ideas that the designers presented, Harry's was certainly (unique, the most unique).

2. Bertha is one of the (most tactful, tactfulest) people in the credit office.
3. Paul has already ordered (a, an) uniform, hasn't he?
4. Mrs. Katz always recommends buying (high quality, high-quality) merchandise.
5. The comptroller and the vice president (is, are) now reviewing the tender offer.
6. My supervisor, Joyce Moser, is a better manager than (anyone, anyone else) in the company.
7. Mr. Levesque has planned a number of (60 second, 60-second) commercials to be aired during prime time.
8. Our school is a (ten story, ten-story) building.
9. Ellis and Gomer are both successful agents, but Allison is the (successfulest, more nearly successful, most successful) of the three.
10. If the lease is approved, we will move to the new (Willow Grove, Willow-Grove) Mall.
11. I suggest that you return (those, them) cassettes, Connie.
12. Recently, a (San Francisco, San-Francisco) corporation attempted to buy Inner Vision Inc.
13. For this printer you will need paper in (14 inch, 14-inch) lengths.
14. If you prefer (this, these) kind of frame, you should go to The Frame Shop on High Street.
15. Whenever Maria's workload is (heavier, more heavy) than mine, I volunteer to help her.
16. Jules, my assistant manager, works harder than (anyone, anyone else) in our department.
17. The Postal Service will not insure (this, these) sorts of packages.
18. In financial circles, a (Wall Street, Wall-Street) address is considered prestigious.
19. We prefer this word processor to (any, any other) on the market.
20. Clearly, the diamond she showed us is the (valuablest, more nearly valuable, most valuable) of the jewels on display.

B. Correct any errors in the following sentences. Write *OK* for any sentence that has no error.

1. Our district sent two account executives, Wayne and she, to the Detroit convention.
2. Our advertising agency pays higher wages than any agency in this area.
3. Cecilia always presents us with first-class designs and most unique drawings.
4. In comparing Louise and Joan, I decided that Louise is fastest but Joan is more accurate.
5. Lionel is considered better than anyone in his department.
6. Either Jamison or Dave, two of our well-known chemists, are accepting the award in behalf of the entire research team.
7. There's several reasons for delaying the meeting with Mrs. Mancino.

8. Ask Mr. Mullers' assistant whether he has the file.

9. Who did Ms. Kubick want to talk with?

10. Give these brochures to Mr. Macklin; I'm sure that he needs them more than I.

11. The Bench's are both minors; therefore, their estate is managed by a court-appointed guardian.

12. Until this morning, these boxes had laid here untouched for nearly a year!

13. Perhaps Brenda and myself could help you finish these invoices before closing.

14. On the table in the reception area is the pamphlets that I collected at the exhibit.

15. Theirs only about $2,000 left in the budget for sales promotion.

VOCABULARY AND SPELLING STUDIES

A. These words are often confused: *shoot, chute; desolate, dissolute.* Explain the differences.

B. In which of the following words is the *u not* pronounced as in *human?*

1. gratitude   3. student
2. utterance   4. revenue

C. In which of the following words is the *ou not* pronounced like the *oo* in *noon?*

1. souvenir   3. acoustics
2. cantaloupe   4. coupon

COMMUNICATING FOR RESULTS

Sexist Language. "A Woman's Place Is in the House—and in the Senate Too!" This saying appeared on some signs and bumper stickers across the country. It may be humorous on the surface, but it has a deep, important meaning.

One way in which business and industry can help women to attain equality in the world of work is through language—nonsexist language, which carries with it no bias against women. Discuss how terms such as *firemen, policemen,* and *businessmen* can affect our thinking. What other terms do you consider sexist?

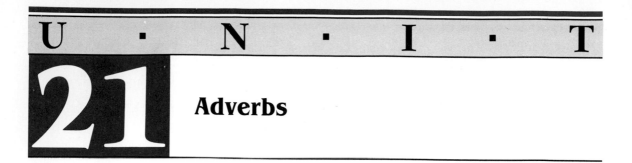

21 Adverbs

In Unit 20 you saw that an *adjective* is a word that modifies a noun or a pronoun. In this unit you will study another kind of modifier—the *adverb*. The adverb can be compared, like the adjective. In fact, you will find that many adverbs are formed by simply adding *ly* to an adjective—*carefully*, *patiently*, *quickly*, and so on. Study each section in this unit carefully, so that you will be sure to use adverbs correctly.

Simple Adverbs

An *adverb* is a word that modifies an adjective, a verb, or another adverb. Adverbs answer questions such as When? Where? How? Why? How much? How little? Many adverbs are formed by adding *ly* to adjectives:

Adjective	Adverb
random	randomly
quiet	quietly
poor	poorly
sole	solely
simple	simply
lazy	lazily
defensive	defensively
productive	productively

Although many adverbs end in *ly*, remember that not all adverbs end in *ly*. Look at the following adverbs:

always	here	now	too
soon	often	then	up
late	there	very	sometimes

Now notice how these adverbs answer the questions When? Where? How? Why? How much? How little? in the following examples:

arrived late   (Arrived when? Answer: *late*.)

sent there   (Sent where? Answer: *there*.)

selected randomly   (Selected how? Answer: *randomly*.)

Comparison of Adverbs. The same general rules that apply to comparison of adjectives also apply to comparison of adverbs. Adverbs are compared in one of three ways:

1. By adding *er* or *est* to an adverb containing one syllable:

Positive	Comparative	Superlative
fast	faster	fastest
late	later	latest
soon	sooner	soonest

2. By using *more* or *most* (or *less* or *least*) with an adverb ending in *ly:*

Positive	Comparative	Superlative
slowly	more slowly less slowly	most slowly least slowly
quietly	more quietly less quietly	most quietly least quietly
poorly	more poorly less poorly	most poorly least poorly

3. By completely changing the form of the adverb:

Positive	Comparative	Superlative
well	better	best
badly	worse	worst
much	more	most

Adverbs That Join Clauses

Adverbs can be used to join clauses. The following adverbs (called *conjunctive adverbs*) are used to join independent clauses, as illustrated in the sentences below.

consequently	moreover
however	accordingly
then	therefore
thus	furthermore
yet	

Mrs. Garrison must be in Pittsburgh on June 13; *consequently,* she cannot attend the monthly status meeting here on that day. (The adverb *consequently* joins two independent clauses—that is, two clauses that can stand alone as complete sentences.)

We need Mrs. Garrison at the next monthly status meeting; we have, *therefore,* changed the date of the meeting to June 16. (Here, the adverb *therefore* joins two independent clauses, but note that it appears not at the beginning of the second clause but elsewhere in that clause.)

Other adverbs (called *subordinating conjunctions*) join subordinate clauses to independent clauses. Among the commonly used adverbs in this category are:

after	because	since
although	before	when
as	if	while

When Larry returns, he will quickly solve this problem. (*When* introduces the subordinate clause *when Larry returns* and joins it to the independent clause *he will quickly solve this problem.* The adverb *quickly* answers the question "will solve *how*?")

Before you mail these contracts, be sure to get Dr. Panov's approval. (*Before* introduces the subordinate clause *before you mail these contracts* and joins this clause to the independent clause *be sure to get Dr. Panov's approval.*)

CLASS PRACTICE 1

Identify the adverbs in the following sentences.

1. Connie Dreschler and I will travel together to Toronto next week; therefore, neither of us will be here to meet with the accountants.
2. While we are in Toronto, we will thoroughly discuss developing a networking system with our home office.
3. Our flight landed earlier than we had expected.
4. Brandon handled the Carlton account well, and he quickly succeeded in selling our services to Carlton Brands Inc.
5. Nancy works more diligently under pressure, doesn't she?
6. Of all the auditors in our firm, Mitch plans his goals best.

PROOFREADING PRACTICE 1

Correct any errors in the use of adverbs in the following sentences.

1. Everyone agrees that Betty coordinates meetings most thoroughly than the other managers.
2. These machines are easy to use, but they operate slowlier than the machines we had.
3. The equipment is functioning worse than we had thought.
4. Of the three applicants whom Andrew interviewed, Ms. Krause responded more candidly.
5. As a general rule, Kenneth proofreads least carefully than Arthur.
6. Mr. Sweeney speaks well; however, Mrs. Camp speaks more well.

Adverb or Adjective?

Should an adjective follow linking verbs such as *look, seem, appear, sound, feel, taste,* and *smell,* or should an adverb follow them? Answer: *Always an adjective!*

The greater your reading skill, the better equipped you will be to perform both personal and professional tasks.

Proofreading skills ensure that communication processes function smoothly, efficiently, and professionally.

Reading is one of the best ways to build a good vocabulary.

Your dictionary is a valuable tool that can help you locate the correct spellings and meanings of all the words you use.

Whether asking for information, looking for a job, buying or selling products or services, or ordering supplies, we must always put ourselves in the place of our receiver, decide what our receiver's needs are, and then phrase our message to meet those needs.

Goodwill is the favor or prestige a business has that causes people to associate with—and keep coming back to—that company.

Showing consideration for others and a genuine desire to help in business goes a long way toward building goodwill.

Building goodwill—and maintaining it—is
an important function of the business letter.

Business people depend on the written word to keep them
in touch with their customers and associates and to
preserve their conversations with them on record.

Words with antagonistic or distasteful
connotations weaken a business's
chances of obtaining goodwill.

Careful business writers select words
that not only convey the intended
meaning but also create positive
images.

This food *tastes* delicious. (*Tastes* is a linking verb—a no-action verb. Therefore, the adjective delicious is correct—not the adverb *deliciously*.)

The cool water *feels* good. (*Feels* is a linking verb. Therefore, the adjective *good* is correct—not the adverb *well*.)

What, then, is the problem? The problem is that verbs such as *look, taste,* and *feel* are not always linking verbs. A linking verb is a no-action verb. Therefore, in the sentence *This food tastes delicious*, the verb *tastes* merely links the adjective *delicious* to the noun it describes, *food*. Of course, an adjective (not an adverb) must be used to modify a noun, so *delicious* is obviously correct. In the sentence *The water feels good*, the verb *feels* is a linking verb; it describes no action. *Feels* merely links the adjective *good* to the noun it modifies, *water*. Again, only an adjective can modify a noun, so *good* is correct.

Now let's see some examples in which these verbs *do* describe action.

Martha *tastes* her food slowly before she swallows it. (*Tastes* is obviously an action verb; it describes something Martha is doing actively—*tasting. Tastes* does not link an adjective to a noun or a pronoun. Tastes how? Answer: *slowly.* The adverb *slowly* modifies the verb *tastes.* Only an adverb, not an adjective, can modify a verb.)

You should *feel* the cloth carefully. (Feel how? Answer: *carefully.* The adverb *carefully* modifies the verb *should feel.* Here, *feel* is obviously an action verb. It does not link an adjective to a noun or pronoun. Therefore, the adverb *carefully* is correct.)

CLASS PRACTICE 2

Determine whether the verbs in the following sentences are action verbs and therefore require adverbs to modify them. If they are linking verbs, of course, adjectives will follow. Then make your choices.

1. As soon as the alarm rang, the guards appeared (sudden, suddenly).
2. All the clerks looked (immediate, immediately) to see whether they could find the error.
3. Both managers appeared (worried, worriedly) when they heard the news.
4. Yes, I did feel (bad, badly) about Ms. Sarafian's accident.
5. Joe seemed (angry, angrily) because he thought he had made a mistake.
6. His voice sounded (nervous, nervously) as he read the bulletin.

PROOFREADING PRACTICE 2

Correct the following sentences.

1. Ms. Graham, who is one of our best customers, seemed angrily at the credit manager.
2. Although all the food tasted well, I was disappointed by the service.
3. As she spoke to the audience, Joanne seemed confidently.

4. Of course, we felt badly when we learned that Mrs. Syms was retiring.
5. The scent of the flowers in your office smells refreshingly.
6. The security guard questioned the man who looked suspicious.

Adverb Pitfalls

The adverb errors that occur most often are (1) positioning the adverb incorrectly in a sentence, (2) misusing *never* for *not*, and (3) using double negatives. All three errors are discussed below.

Position of Adverbs. An adverb should be positioned near the word it modifies. As the following sentences show, misplacing the adverb can change or obscure the meaning of the sentence.

Only my assistant read these computer printouts yesterday. (My assistant was the only one who read them—I didn't; my boss didn't; my secretary didn't.)

My *only* assistant read these computer printouts yesterday. (I have only one assistant. Here the word *only* functions as an adjective meaning "sole.")

My assistant *only* read these computer printouts yesterday. (He didn't do anything else to them. He didn't duplicate them; he didn't mail them; he didn't approve them. He only read them.)

My assistant read *only* these computer printouts yesterday. (He read no other computer printouts, no reports, no magazines, no letters, only these printouts.)

My assistant read these computer printouts *only* yesterday. (He read these computer printouts as recently as *yesterday*: not the day before, not last week, but yesterday.)

My assistant read these computer printouts yesterday *only*. (He didn't read them on any other day; just yesterday.)

PROOFREADING PRACTICE 3

Are adverbs correctly placed in the following sentences? Correct any misplaced adverbs.

1. Harvey just expects Mr. Anderson to arrive in a few minutes.
2. The Frosts' building was not even sold for $100,000, their original purchase price a few years ago.
3. The president and the treasurer have the combination to the safe only.
4. According to Emily, we have nearly received 200 orders for our newest machine.
5. Alexandra has only invoiced 25 or 30 orders.
6. By June 30 Bill had hardly sold three new cars.

Never and Not. *Never* means "not ever; at no time; not in any way." Obviously, it is a strong word.

For 50 years, Bradley Plumbing has *never* had a dissatisfied customer.

The word *not* simply expresses negation. Do not use *never* when a simple *not* will do.

> We have *not* received the check that is due from Jakway Hardware. (Not "We *never* received . . . .")

> Manuel did *not* deliver the materials to us last week. (Not "Manuel *never* delivered . . . .")

Double Negatives. Do not use two negatives to express one negation. Errors occur most often with the negative statements *scarcely, only, hardly, but, never,* and *not*.

> Mrs. Uris had but one suggestion for us. (Not *had not but one.*)

> Horace can hardly believe that we completed all the billing on time. (Not *cannot hardly believe.*)

CLASS PRACTICE 3

Make the correct selections in the following sentences.

1. Gordon (never said, did not say) whether he would definitely be able to attend.
2. Although these bonds were tax-free, they (did not but earn, never earned more than, earned only) 4.75 percent profit.
3. Suzanne can't (help but worry, help worrying) about the rising interest rates.
4. Alicia (has, hasn't) hardly any customer calls arranged for next week.
5. The shipping department (has, hasn't) scarcely any orders backlogged.
6. Ms. Loo (did not say, never said) that she was canceling her service contract.

Adverb and Adjective Confusions

Certain word pairs (*sure, surely; real, really; good, well;* and *some, somewhat*) deserve special attention. As you study them, remember that the first word in each pair is the adjective; the second is the adverb.

Sure, Surely; Real, Really. The most common errors in using these word pairs occur when the adjectives *sure* and *real* are used instead of the adverbs *surely* and *really.* Study this Quick Trick to choose the right word every time:

QUICK TRICK | **SUBSTITUTE *VERY* OR *CERTAINLY***

When faced with a choice between *real* and *really* (or between *sure* and *surely*), substitute the adverb *very* or *certainly* to test whether an adverb is needed.

> Meg (sure, surely) did a great job in landing the Harkovy account. (Substitute *certainly* and you will see that *Meg certainly did* makes sense. Therefore, the adverb *surely* is correct because the adverb *certainly* can be substituted.)
>
> Lawrence did a (real, really) thorough analysis of competitive products. (Substitute *very:* Lawrence did a *very* thorough analysis . . . . Therefore, the adverb *really* is correct.)

Good, Well. Good is the adjective; *well* is the adverb. As an adjective, *good* modifies nouns and pronouns. As an adverb, *well* should answer the question How?

Percy really did a *good* job. (The adjective *good* modifies the noun *job*. It does not answer the question How?)

Percy works very *well* under pressure. (Works how? Well. The adverb *well* modifies the verb *works*.)

EXCEPTION: *Well* can also be an adjective, *but only when referring to health.*

Alger didn't feel *well*, so he left early. (Refers to Alger's health.)

Some, Somewhat. To decide when to use the adjective *some* and the adverb *somewhat*, use the following Quick Trick.

QUICK TRICK   SUBSTITUTE *A LITTLE BIT*

When you can substitute the words *a little bit*, use the adverb *somewhat*.

Marco was *somewhat* nervous about the upcoming licensing exam. (He was *a little bit* nervous.)

Donald and Kitty requested *some* help to complete their end-of-month paperwork. (A *little bit help* makes no sense; thus *some* is correct.)

Most, Almost. The adjective *most* is the superlative of *much* or *many*. The adverb *almost* means "not quite" or "very nearly."

Most employees are delighted with the additional coverage this policy provides. (*Many, more, most* employees.)

The draft of the annual report is *almost* finished. (*Very nearly* finished.)

CLASS PRACTICE 4

Select the correct word from the choices given.

1. Of course, no one does (good, well) work when he or she is not feeling (good, well).
2. Sarah was (sure, surely) happy to hear the (good, well) news.

3. Seymour already received (some, somewhat) of the responses, but he was (some, somewhat) disappointed in the comments.
4. Owen made a (real, really) good deal to buy a new car.
5. Needless to say, Elmer was (sure, surely) pleased that he had been appointed to the mayor's panel.
6. Ask Howard whether he thinks that Ajax Vendors gave him a (good, well) buy; I believe he said that Ajax treated him (good, well).

PROOFREADING PRACTICE 4

Read the following sentences and correct any errors in the use of adverbs.

1. Betty and Rosemary were sure disappointed at the turnout for their presentations.
2. When she was presented with the award, Lynn couldn't help but smile.
3. As of March 15, we had not hardly received any orders for the new products we advertised in that magazine.
4. Most of us agree that price is the real issue.
5. Almost 90 percent of the respondents said that the price of the merchandise is a really important issue.
6. Her managers often tell us that Cynthia works very good and that she has great potential.

COMMUNICATION LABORATORY

APPLICATION EXERCISES

A. Select the right answer for each of the following sentences.

1. If Larry would begin dressing (less casually, least casually), he would present a better image.
2. Karen said that she (had, hadn't) but two hours to prepare her speech.
3. Please look (careful, carefully) at the fabric before you purchase it.
4. As you saw, Mrs. Daly was (sure, surely) happy that she had been chosen to head the committee.
5. Albert always submits (good, well) reports because he writes very (good, well).
6. The art director agreed that Edwin's catalog cover was (real, really) distinctive.
7. Our manager insists that we (buy only, only buy) from Capital Supplies.
8. (Most, Almost) of us were (some, somewhat) shocked to hear that Mr. Warburton had retired.
9. Philip (could, couldn't) hardly wait for the day to end.
10. Terry seemed very (cautious, cautiously) when he discussed next year's budgets.

11. Audrey was (sure, surely) surprised to hear that she had been selected to go to San Francisco.
12. In my opinion, most of the food did not taste very (good, well).
13. Amy showed quite (clear, clearly) that the real problem facing us is the high price of this machinery.
14. We were not surprised to see that Jack did not feel (good, well) after working for more than 12 consecutive hours.
15. Our supervisor, Ms. Pennyworth, always coordinates projects (good, well) and always praises (good, well) work from her staff.

B. Find and correct any errors in the following sentences.

1. At the end of the business day, lie all the important documents in this safe.
2. In the top drawer of my desk is various forms that you will need.
3. Mr. Hendersons' reply startled us, because we thought that he was in favor of the merger.
4. Perhaps it sounds somewhat difficult, but this procedure is really more simpler than it appears.
5. We programmers have been approved to work overtime in order to complete this project by December 1.
6. Alan is one of those accountants who always keep records in order.
7. Its not surprising that sales should decline in summer.
8. The treasurer and her assistant are both CPA's, and their offices are in our headquarters building.
9. All the printing, as you will see, have been smudged.
10. The sales representatives' cars are leased from a dealer in Pittsburgh.
11. Lenny enjoys working with numbers more than I.
12. My assistants and myself will be glad to help if you should have any questions.
13. An executive must be sure to manage their time wisely.
14. The criteria that she outlined in her report is to be reviewed by our general manager.
15. Does anyone know whom Carla appointed to head the task force on customer relations?

C. Select the correct word from the choices in parentheses.

1. Although Joan feels (bad, badly), the error was certainly not her fault.
2. Our attorney said that we had indeed acted (wise, wisely) in refusing the counteroffer.
3. Cheryl said, "Why are you looking at me so (angry, angrily)?"
4. Phyllis hasn't (any, hardly any) money to invest in the franchise.
5. Barton read the data to us very (slow, slowly) so that we could take notes (careful, carefully).
6. Joy appeared to be (real, really) excited over the prospect of speaking at a national convention.

7. Elvira always leads the committee discussions very (good, well); she is a (good, well) group leader.
8. At first we were worried about the success of the project; when we spoke to the loan officer, however, we (sudden, suddenly) became more (confident, confidently).
9. One of the benefits of using a microprocessor is that you can draft and revise letters and reports much more (quick and accurate, quickly and accurately).
10. Yolanda rose to her feet (immediate, immediately) and suggested alternative means.

VOCABULARY AND SPELLING STUDIES

A. These words are often confused: *disburse, disperse; equable, equitable.* Explain the differences.

B. Match each word in Column A with the term in Column B that is nearest in meaning.

A	B
1. repetitious	a. with rainbowlike colors
2. iridescent	b. enduring
3. obscure	c. unreal
4. permanent	d. transitory
5. axiomatic	e. monotonous
	f. indistinct
	g. self-evident

C. How are the following words spelled when *ed* is added?

1. admit
2. acquaint
3. develop
4. appall
5. refer
6. embarrass

COMMUNICATING FOR RESULTS

Business Dress and Grooming. You work for United Banks. Today you have been asked to substitute for Joan Klinitsky, the assistant director of training and development, who is out of the office. Joan was supposed to address a group of ten new employees who are attending an orientation session during their first day working for United Banks. The topic of Joan's speech was to be "Business Dress."

As Joan's substitute, what would you say to these new employees to impress them with the importance of good grooming and appropriate dress on the job?

U · N · I · T

22

Prepositions

Prepositions often go unnoticed as we write and as we speak, but they do important jobs. As you will see, prepositions serve to join words—and joining words is what writing and speaking is all about! Study prepositions carefully so that you will be able to identify them and to use them correctly in your writing and your speaking.

Prepositional Phrases

A preposition is always followed by a noun or a pronoun. In fact, as you look at the word *preposition* you see the word *position* and the prefix *pre*, which means "before." Thus a preposition is a word that is *positioned before* a noun or a pronoun.

Of course, not *every* word positioned before a noun or a pronoun is a preposition. Look at the following list of commonly used prepositions and the examples of prepositional phrases:

Prepositions			Prepositional Phrases
about	between	off	*after* the meeting
above	by	on	*between* those cars
after	down	out	*by* that building
against	except	over	*from* her
among	for	to	*to* them
at	from	through	*with* us
before	in	under	
behind	into	up	
below	like	until	
beside	of	with	

Now let's see how prepositions are used in the following sentences.

We will leave *after the meeting.* (Leave when? After the meeting. Because this prepositional phrase answers the question When? it is an adverbial phrase. It does the job of an adverb.)

The woman *with her* is Mrs. Fetch. (The prepositional phrase *with her* modifies the noun *woman*. Thus this prepositional phrase serves as an adjective because it modifies a noun.)

200

The messenger *from Ajax Messenger Service* is waiting for this package.   (Here, the prepositional phrase describes the noun *messenger*. Which messenger? Answer: The messenger *from Ajax Messenger Service*. Because it modifies a noun, this prepositional phrase serves as an adjective.)

In the above examples, you see that prepositions do indeed join words. They join words to make phrases that can then serve as adjectives or as adverbs. Note, too, that the *object of the preposition* is a noun or a pronoun.

after the meeting (the noun *meeting* is the object of the preposition *after*)

with her (the pronoun *her* is the object of the preposition *with*)

Preposition Combinations

Certain prepositions must be combined with specific nouns or verbs, as shown below:

abide *by* a decision
abide *with* a person

conform *to* regulations
in conformity *with* regulations

enter *on* the record
enter *into* an agreement

wait *for* someone
wait *on* a customer

Now study the following preposition combinations, which are very commonly used. Whenever you have trouble remembering which preposition is correct in a specific instance, refer to a business writer's manual or to a dictionary.

Agree. Agree is used as follows: (1) agree *on* or *upon*—reach a mutual understanding, (2) agree *to* (*accept*) another's plan, (3) agree *with* a person or his or her idea.

They *agreed upon* a solution to the dispute.

Mrs. Wilcox *agreed to* the offer from Wembly Associates.

Mark and I *agreed with* the other programmers.

Angry. Be sure to say "angry *with*" a person, "angry *at*" a thing, or "angry *about*" a condition.

Is Lucy still *angry with* us for delaying her project?

Both of us were *angry at* the machine because we lost so much time.

Everyone was *angry about* the mess the contractors left behind.

Discrepancy. Use (1) *discrepancy in* when the object of the preposition is singular, (2) *discrepancy between* when the object denotes exactly *two* in number, and (3) *discrepancy among* when there are *three or more* things.

I found a *discrepancy in* Carlton's report.

There is a *discrepancy between* Carlton's analysis and mine.

There is a *discrepancy among* our three reports.

In Regard To. The phrases *in regard to, with regard to,* and *as regards* are all correct and interchangeable. But be sure not to say "in regards to" or "with regards to."

Ms. Delaney wants to talk with us (in regard to, with regard to, as regards) our policy for reprinting copyrighted materials. (Which one is correct? All are!)

Miscellaneous Phrases. Memorize the following phrases because they are very commonly used:

different from (not *different than*)
identical with (not *identical to*)
plan to do something (not *plan on* doing something)
retroactive to (not *retroactive from*)

This chart is *different from* the one I expected.

Your car is *identical with* mine.

Does Melanie *plan to* join us in Detroit?

in effect

Is it true that these increases are *retroactive to* January 1?

CLASS PRACTICE 1

Select the appropriate words in the following sentences.

1. Mr. Constantino asked us to make sure that the new manual is in conformity (to, with) company style.
2. As you can see, Harold, the revised agenda is different (from, than) the original one.
3. Mr. Perez immediately noticed that there is a discrepancy (in, between, among) the section on metric measurements.
4. The incentive-compensation policy, once approved, will be retroactive (from, to) March 15 of this year.
5. Anne Williams wants to make an appointment to see you (in regards, in regard) to union regulations.
6. The specifications for the materials for this product are identical (with, to) ours.
7. If Eunice plans (to attend, on attending), then be sure to send her a copy of the outline for the first session.

8. Apparently, Ms. Stephenson was angry (at, with, about) us when we changed our credit policy.
9. We are confident that most of the committee members will agree (on, to, upon) our plan.

PROOFREADING PRACTICE 1

Correct any errors in the following sentences.

1. I studied Jack's and Eileen's reports very carefully, and I found a major discrepancy between them. *(among)*
2. Of course, all the policies of our district and regional offices must also conform with the policies of our home office. *(to)*
3. In your opinion, is this design different than the one that Katherine submitted? *(from)*
4. Several of us agreed with Wanda that holding our present prices would be a smart marketing strategy.
5. Although I personally do not like Mr. Columbo's new policy, I and my staff members will, of course, abide with his decision. *(by)*
6. If the bonus is retroactive to last December, I may earn as much as $1,000 when it becomes effective.
7. Do you know whether our local community college is again planning on offering a course in finance?
8. Ms. Lewing is very strict with regards to lateness.
9. Does Mr. Bell agree to the terms of the proposal that Jenks & Morrison submitted? *(on)*

Troublesome Prepositions

Choosing between certain pairs of prepositions causes writers and speakers some difficulty. Study the following troublesome pairs to make sure that they will cause *you* no difficulty.

Between, Among. Ordinarily, use *between* when referring to *two* persons, places, or things; use *among* when referring to *more than two.*

> *Between* you and me, I am confident that we can finish this assignment at least one week early.

> All commissions will be divided *among* the three agents.

Beside, Besides. Remember that *beside* means "by the side of" and that *besides* means "in addition to" or "except."

> Place these cartons *beside* the credenza. ("By the side of" the credenza.)

> *Besides* pads and pencils, what other supplies will we need for the meeting? ("In addition to" pads and pencils.)

> No one *besides* Gail has the authority to sign checks over $500. ("No one except" Gail.)

Inside, Outside. Do not use *of* after *inside* or *outside*. When referring to time, use *within*, not *inside of*.

> The duplicating machine is just *inside* that door.   (Not *inside of*.)
>
> Our company frowns upon employees' working *outside* regular office hours.   (Not *outside of*.)
>
> Please send your check *within* 10 days after you receive the shipment.   (Not *inside of*.)

All, Both. After *all* or *both*, use *of* only when *all* or *both* is followed by a *pronoun*. Omit *of* if either word is followed by a *noun*.

> In March *all of* us will meet to develop the medium-range plan for our division. *All* managers will participate in that meeting.   (*All of* is followed by the pronoun *us*, but *all* precedes the noun *managers*.)

At, To; In, Into. At and *in* denote position. *To* and *into* signify motion.

> Sarah is *at* the production meeting.   (No action.)
>
> Sarah went *to* the meeting at 9 a.m.   (Action—she *went* to the meeting.)
>
> When I saw the computer *in* the store window, I went *into* the store.   (The computer was *in* position—no action. I went *into* the store—action.)

NOTE: When either *at* or *in* refers to a place, use *in* for larger places; *at* for smaller places.

> Abby lives *in* Boise and works *at* the Office Equipment Shop.

Behind, In Back Of. Use *behind*, not *in back of*. However, *in front of* is correct.

> I sat *behind* Mr. Simmons while the representative displayed the products *in front of* him.

From, Off. Use *from* when referring to persons or places; *off*, when referring to things.

> Thomas received the completed applications *from* Helene.   (Not *off*.)
>
> We want customers to take these applications *off* the countertops.   (*Off* things—correct.)

CLASS PRACTICE 2

How well can you now use prepositions?

1. Do you know whether Mr. Grier has any reference books (beside, besides) these?
2. Get the currency-exchange list (from, off) Ms. Bierney.
3. Was Bill (at, to) his desk when the fire inspector was here?

4. How does Eric plan to distribute the materials (between, among) all the regional offices?
5. Has anyone (beside, besides) Jacqueline read the article "Time Management for the Executive"?
6. Take those supplies (from, off) the table before the next meeting begins.
7. If you're looking for the contract file, it is now (behind, in back of) that storage cabinet.
8. Apparently, (both, both of) the supervisors' budget requests were rejected.
9. (All, All of) the agents agreed that the discount must be 25 percent of the list price.

Preposition Pitfalls

The following are examples of common errors in using a preposition when none is needed or where another word is required.

Of, Have. In speaking, some people tend to pronounce *have* as if it were *of*, as in "I *shoulduv* called earlier." You may hear this from time to time. When you do, remember that the correct phrase is *should have called*, not *should of called*.

At and *In* With *Where.* It is incorrect to use *at* or *to* following *where*.

Where is Maryanne? (Not *Where is Maryanne at?*)

I do not know *where* she *went*. (Not *where she went to*.)

Help, Help From. The word *from* should not follow *help* in sentences such as this:

We cannot *help* being concerned about the situation. (Not *help from being*.)

Opposite, Opposite To. Do not use *to* after *opposite*.

A new office building will be built *opposite* ours. (Not *opposite to ours*.)

Off. Do not use either *of* or *from* with the word *off*.

Please ask the maintenance people to take these machines *off* these tables. (Not *off of*.)

You can probably borrow a calculator from Renee. (Not *off from Renee* or *from off Renee*.)

CLASS PRACTICE 3

Choose the correct word or words to avoid the preposition pitfalls in the following sentences.

1. You can probably obtain a free sample (off, from, off of) Beverly Wilkinson.

2. Ms. Ruck said, "We should not (have, of) postponed the meeting with Halberstram."
3. From where we were sitting, we could hardly (help, help from) hearing their conversation.
4. Do you know who took the monthly sales report (off, off of) my desk?
5. Please ask Danielle where Mrs. Foley (is, is at).
6. Danielle said she doesn't know where Mrs. Foley (went, went to).
7. The Fitch Building is (opposite, opposite to) the Vernon Building.
8. Did Mr. D'Amato say where he is (going, going to)?

PROOFREADING PRACTICE 2

Correct any preposition errors in the following sentences. Write *OK* if a sentence has no error.

1. Ask Robin whether she will be able to complete these forms inside of a week.
2. Perhaps both of the managers will be at tomorrow's session.
3. Let's place these breakable items opposite to my file cabinets.
4. Anthony was the only person who knew where the contract file was at.
5. Ms. Harkavy divided all the work between Carole, David, and me.
6. Do you know whether we may borrow one or two blank diskettes off of Nick or Carolyn?
7. Owen's costs were inaccurate, so we could not help from interrupting him.
8. There were several people beside Mary Jo and Wendy who disagreed with Mr. Fowler.

COMMUNICATION LABORATORY

APPLICATION EXERCISES

A. On a separate sheet of paper, write the correct selections for the following sentences.

1. (Beside, Besides) Mr. Fernandez and Mrs. Spiegel, only two other real estate agents were present at the opening session.
2. As Ms. Wendall suggested, divide all these orders (between, among) the four clerks.
3. Sam said that he would meet us (inside of, within) the hour.
4. Of course, we must abide (with, by) the decision of the board of directors.
5. Please explain the discrepancy you found (in, between) these two market surveys.

6. The assignment was given to (both us, both of us).
7. Our attorney recommended that we not enter (into, upon) such agreements in the future without her advice.
8. The terms of the contract are different (than, from) the old terms, aren't they?
9. In retrospect, I now realize that we should not (have, of) bought such expensive equipment.
10. Frankly, I was slightly angry (at, with) Franklin for not telling us of the planned changes.
11. Is your total for each column identical (to, with) mine?
12. Does Harriet plan (on finishing, to finish) all her follow-up calls before she leaves for Europe?
13. Let's stack all these cartons (behind, in back of) those shelves.
14. Send these notices to (all, all of) our field managers.
15. I'm sure that we can get a free sample (from, from off) our Larkey's sales representative.

B. Correct any errors in these sentences. Write *OK* if a sentence has no error.

1. Give this assignment to either Jennifer or he, whoever has the lighter work load.
2. Are the Adamses the people who bought these municipal bonds?
3. Who is the person in charge of the Albuquerque branch office?
4. The person who is in charge of the Albuquerque office is her.
5. Is Ms. Brill the woman who you thought we hired for the marketing manager position?
6. As supervisor of the department, Sue earns more than him, of course.
7. There's perhaps ten good reasons why we should not renew our service contract.
8. We should hire a full-time worker who does nothing beside keep a log of all orders.
9. A corporate executive must be sure to keep in close contact with their supervisors.
10. Michael's estimate was more precise than mine.
11. During the past three-year period, the Adams's investments have earned an average of 14.5 percent a year.
12. Whoever you ask to help you, be sure that you allow extra time to proofread the entire report.
13. Because the Austin account is so important, we assigned it to our best account executives, Blake and she.
14. As soon as he has wrote his first draft, let's meet to edit the copy and prepare a final version.
15. Jason and I agree that your wasting time by assuming that these costs are still current.

C. Write one sentence using each of the following phrases:

1. different from
2. identical to
3. angry at
4. retroactive to
5. in regard to

VOCABULARY AND SPELLING STUDIES

A. These words are often confused: *pact, packed; facetious, fictitious.* Explain the differences.

B. Give at least one synonym for each of the following:

1. liable
2. ostentation
3. punctual
4. delineate
5. prodigious

C. Correct any misspelled words in the following sentences.

1. It was really a privilige to have such a fine maintenance crew helping us.
2. Mrs. Janson recomended Bert as a possible replacement for Sharon.
3. Caruso & Lombardi, primary contractors for the goverment, won the bid to erect the new building.
4. The acounting firm of Noah and Lambert has been serving as consultants to our company since 1980.
5. We will be begining our work on the project within the next six months.

COMMUNICATING FOR RESULTS

Just 15 Minutes. A co-worker tells you that your supervisor, Jason Verne, has warned her not to be late again. "Next time," he said, "you may lose part of your pay." She thinks Mr. Verne is being unfair, but you have always found him to be very fair.

Your co-worker asks for your opinion. What would you tell her?

U · N · I · T
23 Conjunctions

A *conjunction* is a word that joins sentences or parts of sentences. You have already seen some uses of conjunctions. For example, in Unit 21 you learned how conjunctive adverbs and subordinating conjunctions are used.

In this unit you will review these uses; in addition, you will learn the uses of coordinate conjunctions and correlative conjunctions. Also, you will learn how to achieve *parallel structure*—one of the requisites for clear writing.

Conjunctive Adverbs. In Unit 21 you saw how conjunctive adverbs join independent clauses:

Marilyn had to leave for Mexico City; *consequently*, she will not be available for next week's meeting. (*Consequently* joins two clauses that can stand alone as independent sentences.)

Sales in Jim's territory are falling far behind last year's; *however*, he expects to pick up some very large orders before the end of the year. (*However* is a conjunctive adverb; it joins two independent clauses.)

Other conjunctive adverbs are:

accordingly   moreover
furthermore   then
thus   yet
nevertheless   likewise

As you can see, the conjunctive adverbs serve not only to *join* two independent clauses but also to *modify* the second clause.

Subordinating Conjunctions. Conjunctions that join an independent clause to a dependent (or *subordinate*) clause are called *subordinating conjunctions*.

John will tell us *if he plans to come to the meeting.* (The subordinating conjunction *if* begins a subordinate—or dependent—clause, *if he plans to come to the meeting*, and joins it to an independent clause, *John will tell us*.)

Although Dan ordered 200 copies, we still ran out of manuals. (The independent clause is *we still ran out of manuals.* The subordinating conjunction *although*

209

begins the subordinate, or dependent, clause, *although Dan ordered 200 copies,* and joins it to the independent clause.)

The most commonly used subordinating conjunctions are:

after	since
although	than
as	that
as if	though
as soon as	till
as though	unless
because	until
before	when
even if	whenever
for	where
how	wherever
if	whether
inasmuch as	while
otherwise	why

CLASS PRACTICE 1

Can you recognize the conjunctive adverbs and the subordinating conjunctions in the following sentences? Label each conjunction that you find.

1. If Patricia wants a duplicate, I will be happy to have a photocopy made.
2. Ms. Russo prefers giving such assignments to free-lancers; however, she said that she would abide by our decision.
3. Elaine will give you the complete folder before she leaves for her vacation.
4. As soon as we receive their check, please call our credit manager.
5. We have not paid this bill; nevertheless, this invoice is marked "Paid."
6. Ms. Chelsea said that we will not buy any products from the Diamond Supply Company even if Diamond gives us an additional discount.
7. This bond will yield 14 percent interest each year; therefore, you will receive $1,400 interest in the first year alone.
8. Please tell your supervisor whenever you've completed any assignment.

Coordinating Conjunctions

The coordinating conjunctions are *and, but, or,* and *nor,* and they are used to connect *similar* grammatical elements—two or more words, phrases, or clauses.

1. Two or more words:

   Ralph *or* Cindy
   cheap *but* effective
   Carl, Victor, *and* Ella

2. Two or more phrases:

in the morning *or* in the afternoon
on land, on sea, *and* in the air

3. Two or more clauses:

We did not complete the project on schedule, *nor* did we complete it within the budget.

Mary created the idea, Bill wrote the copy, *and* Jack designed the ad.

We realize that these are difficult times *and* that sales in your district have declined.

Correlative Conjunctions

Correlative conjunctions are used in pairs:

both . . . and   not only . . . but also
either . . . or   whether . . . or
neither . . . nor

Correlatives, too, are used to connect *similar* grammatical elements. (Note that *or* is used with *either* and that *nor* is used with *neither*.)

Both Mr. Dempster *and* Mr. Eisengrim were carnival managers.

Neither Boyd *nor* Ramsey was born in the United States.

Our president *not only* authorized the new product line *but also* authorized manufacturing to begin on March 1.

CLASS PRACTICE 2

Identify the coordinating and the correlative conjunctions in the following sentences and label each.

1. In this chart we identified the weights in both standard and metric terms.
2. Does Paula intend to go to the convention in Panama City, or does she plan to be on vacation at that time?
3. We informed not only Matthew but also Dave that two positions would soon be open in our marketing department.
4. Amos enjoys working here, but his brother does not.
5. Whether Mr. Faversham calls or he comes in person, be sure to apologize to him for our error.
6. As you perhaps have heard, neither Morris nor Courtenay was selected for the manager's job.

Parallel Structure

As used in the term *parallel structure*, the adjective *parallel* means "similar" or "equal." Sentences are considered as having parallel structure (or *parallelism*) when matching ideas are expressed in similar ways. For example, in the parallel sentences below, note how the coordinating conjunctions connect similar elements.

POOR: This product is sturdy, light, and costs very little. (The coordinating conjunction *and* connects three elements: (1) the adjective *sturdy,* (2) the adjective *light,* and (3) the phrase *costs very little.* Do the three items match? No!).

PARALLEL: This product is sturdy, light, and inexpensive. (Now that the conjunction joins three *adjectives,* the sentence *is* parallel.)

POOR: Ms. Kramer said to check the value of the property and that our insurance should be increased. (There are two items after *said,* and both are joined by *and.* The two items are (1) *to check the value of the property* and (2) *that our insurance should be increased.* To be parallel, both should start with *to* or with *that.*)

PARALLEL: Ms. Kramer said to check the value of the property *and* to increase our insurance. (The two elements joined by *and* are parallel.)

PARALLEL: Ms. Kramer said that the value of the property should be checked and that our insurance should be increased. (Again, the two elements connected by *and* match.)

Now let's see how parallelism is achieved in sentences with correlative conjunctions.

POOR: You need *both* a completed medical form *and* to get your supervisor's approval. (The elements that follow *both* and *and* should match. As the sentence now reads, a noun, *form,* follows *both;* and a verb, *to get,* follows *and.* Compare this with the next two examples.)

PARALLEL: You need *both* a completed medical form *and* your supervisor's approval. (Now what follows *both* and *and?* Two nouns—*form* and *approval.*)

PARALLEL: You need *both* to complete a medical form *and* to get your supervisor's approval. (Both elements following the two parts of the correlative *both/and* do match.)

CLASS PRACTICE 3

In the following pairs of sentences, one sentence illustrates parallelism; the other does not. Select the parallel sentence and explain why it is parallel.

1. **a.** She said that you will need both a down payment and an approved loan form.
   b. She said that you will need both a down payment and to have a loan form approved.
2. **a.** Ethel has neither the dedication nor does she have the management experience for that job.
   b. Ethel has neither the dedication nor the management experience for that job.
3. **a.** The training director told us to improve our spelling and that our grammar skills needed improvement.

    b. The training director told us to improve our spelling and our grammar skills.

4. **a.** Our receptionists not only greet visitors but also handling mail is their responsibility.

    b. Our receptionists not only greet visitors but also handle mail.

5. **a.** Gathering sales information and presenting all the statistics in well-written reports are part of her job.

    b. Gathering sales information and to present all the statistics in well-written reports are part of her job.

6. **a.** Before Tuesday, either call Mrs. Mackenzie or meet with her to discuss these stocks.

    b. Before Tuesday, either call Mrs. Mackenzie or we should meet with her to discuss these stocks.

7. **a.** The insurance policy neither covers fire nor theft.

    b. The insurance policy covers neither fire nor theft.

8. **a.** The most important part of this job is to analyze consumer trends and reporting such trends to our Sales Department.

    b. The most important part of this job is to analyze consumer trends and to report such trends to our Sales Department.

PROOFREADING PRACTICE 1

Correct any errors in parallelism in the following sentences. Write *OK* for any sentence that has no error.

1. In my opinion, Dora is capable, reliable, and ought to be promoted.

2. Helen has been not only successful as a store owner but also as a stock analyst.

3. Plaza Supplies has a reputation for being both honest and to be fair.

4. Please let me know when we must submit all this information, why we must have all the forms notarized, and how we will be informed of the decision.

5. Be sure to tell Mr. DeGroat that his flight departure has been changed to 5 p.m. and to allow about 45 minutes for the trip to the airport.

6. Complete the enclosed form and return it to us today, or our toll-free number may be called.

7. Ms. Knudsen said that we should reschedule the meeting for a more convenient time—either in the morning or next Wednesday.

8. Either Henry will fly to Macon or drive there.

Conjunction Pitfalls

Avoiding the following four pitfalls will not only help you use conjunctions correctly but also improve the quality and style of your writing.

1. Use *but*, not *and*, to *join and contrast* two elements:

I immediately called Yvette, *but* she was not in her office.

Andy had an ample supply of these brochures, *but* I think that he distributed most of them yesterday.

2. Say "the reason is *that*," not "the reason is *because*." Say "read in the paper *that*," not "read in the paper *where*." Say "pretend *that*," not "pretend *like*."

The reason Leonard called is *that* he needs the latest prices for the catalog.

Yesterday I read in a magazine *that* the average interest rate in money markets is now about 8.9 percent.

Because she works so well under pressure, Ada often pretends *that* every job is a rush job.

3. There is no such conjunction as *being that*. Instead, use *since*, *because*, or *as*.

Because Ms. Syms was in town, we did not mail the contracts to her.   (Not *being that Ms. Syms . . . .*)

I accomplished a lot today, *since* the office was nearly empty.   (Not *being that the office . . . .*)

4. *Like* is a verb or a preposition, not a conjunction. Yet you will often hear people say "*Like* I was telling Jim . . . ." Use *as*, *as though*, or *as if* when a conjunction is needed, not *like*.

We *like* the new design.   (Here *like* is a verb.)

Sharon needs a modem *like* mine to transmit data via telephone lines.   (The preposition *like* is always followed by a *noun* or a *pronoun*.)

This morning Mike looks *as if* he is ill.   (Not *like he is ill.*)

Gregory said that it does not look *as though* our loan will be approved.   (Not *like our loan will be approved.*)

CLASS PRACTICE 4

Review the uses of conjunctions and conjunction pitfalls before you tackle the following sentences. Then select the correct choice for each sentence.

1. Unfortunately, we had to cancel our appointment (being that, because) Ms. Druin's flight was delayed.
2. In a recent issue of our company newsletter I read (that, where) Mrs. Dirks will soon retire.
3. Miles Supply Company was supposed to deliver everything today, (and, but) several items were missing from the packages we received.
4. Martha said that the secret to selling is to pretend (like, that) each client is a close friend.
5. The reason this microcomputer does not work well in this location is (because, that) it is too close to these motors.

6. If it looks (like, as though) it might rain, we will cancel our game after work this evening.

PROOFREADING PRACTICE 2

Make any corrections needed in the following sentences.

1. Helen often appears like she has more work than she can handle.
2. The reason Richard requested a transfer is because he and his wife prefer the West Coast.
3. Of course, I would like to meet with you next week, and unfortunately I will be out of town.
4. If it doesn't look like you will be able to join us next Thursday, will you please ask your assistant to substitute for you?
5. None of us can take vacation during the month of June, being that June is our busiest season.
6. Recently, I read in an advertisement where Funtime Products is planning to enter the computer game market.

COMMUNICATION LABORATORY

APPLICATION EXERCISES

A. Choose the words that make each sentence parallel.

1. We no longer offer quantity discounts, (and, but) we do grant a 2 percent discount for payments received within 10 days of delivery.
2. For more information, either write to our customer service manager or (our local sales representative should be asked, ask our local sales representative) for help.
3. We asked our attorney to draw up a standard contract and (to explain its terms to our staff, an explanation of its terms to our staff).
4. Valerie prefers either to invest the money in municipal bonds or (to buy another certificate of deposit, in stocks).
5. In our department, each person knows how to type and (giving dictation well, to dictate).
6. Tomorrow (we must either, either we must) call our Phoenix office or send a telex.
7. You must insert the diskette into the disk drive (like, as) the diagram illustrates.
8. These two keys control the movement of the cursor either to the left or (the right, to the right).
9. (Because, Being that) two of your staff members are on vacation, Melissa and I will try to process these orders for you.
10. Recommending promotions is easier than (to convince, convincing) my manager to grant them.

11. The merchandise that was returned was neither the right size nor (the right color, of the correct color).
12. Writing these proposals is simpler than (to get the grants, getting the grants).
13. Mr. DiRoberto neither said that nor (believed it, that he believed it).
14. In such cases, Clinton usually returns the shipment or (a deduction is noted on the invoice, deducts the amount from the invoice).
15. In the mornings, Aaron looks (like, as if) he is totally exhausted.

B. Correct the following sentences. Write *OK* for any sentence that has no error.

1. Janice is intelligent, tactful, and works very effectively.
2. Lou likes using this keyboard, but he prefers her's.
3. There is, as you already know, five or six applicants interested in that job.
4. Ms. Lansbury said that neither the service contract nor the warranty is still in effect.
5. After I read the manual, I realized that the reason for my error was because I had not booted the disk properly.
6. Ms. Carmichael and Ms. Grier, the supervisors of these departments, has the authority to handle the petty cash.
7. Yes, Vera likes to go to school and studying.
8. The Harrises' portfolio is managed by Simone & Trill, a accounting firm.
9. Frankly, between you and I, I have little confidence in their ability to handle this advertising campaign.
10. If its true that our budget must be cut by $25,000, then I suggest that we cut our training programs for next year.
11. Since 1981, when the Davis's opened their first store, Davis Vitamins has quickly grown into a chain of 50 stores.
12. The new parking lot will be located in back of our main building, not next to the warehouse.
13. Because we were sitting so close to the door, we could not help from hearing all the noise in the hallway.
14. Are you sure that the woman whom we saw at the banquet was Ms. Germinder?
15. Yes, I am sure that that woman was her.

C. Edit the following excerpt from a business memorandum.

A comparison of sales through the first six month's of this year with sales through the first six month's of last year show that we are approximately 15 percent ahead of last year. Among the major reasons for this increase are the obvious success of our newest product, Vita-Chews. Parent's are delighted with the high quality and the low price, and children are equal satisfied with the delicious flavor of these chewable vitamins. Indeed, they do taste real well!

VOCABULARY AND SPELLING STUDIES

A. These words are often confused: *fate, fete; census, senses.* Describe the differences.

B. Each of the phrases below can be replaced by one word that has the same meaning. For each phrase, name that word.

1. Without meaning to
2. Of his or her own free will
3. With great emphasis
4. Without thinking
5. From time to time
6. Lost consciousness

C. Give at least one synonym for each of the following:

1. prohibit
2. lucid
3. homogeneous
4. fortitude
5. diminish

COMMUNICATING FOR RESULTS

Chronic Complainers. Emma and Jerry are two of your co-workers at a very successful firm, World Movie Company. From the time they arrive to the time they leave, Emma and Jerry spend most of the day complaining—about the company, your manager, their wages, other employees, the amount of work, and so on, and so on, endlessly throughout each day.

You've tried to overlook their complaints, of course, but after a while their negativism is starting to get to you.

What should you do?

CHAPTER 5

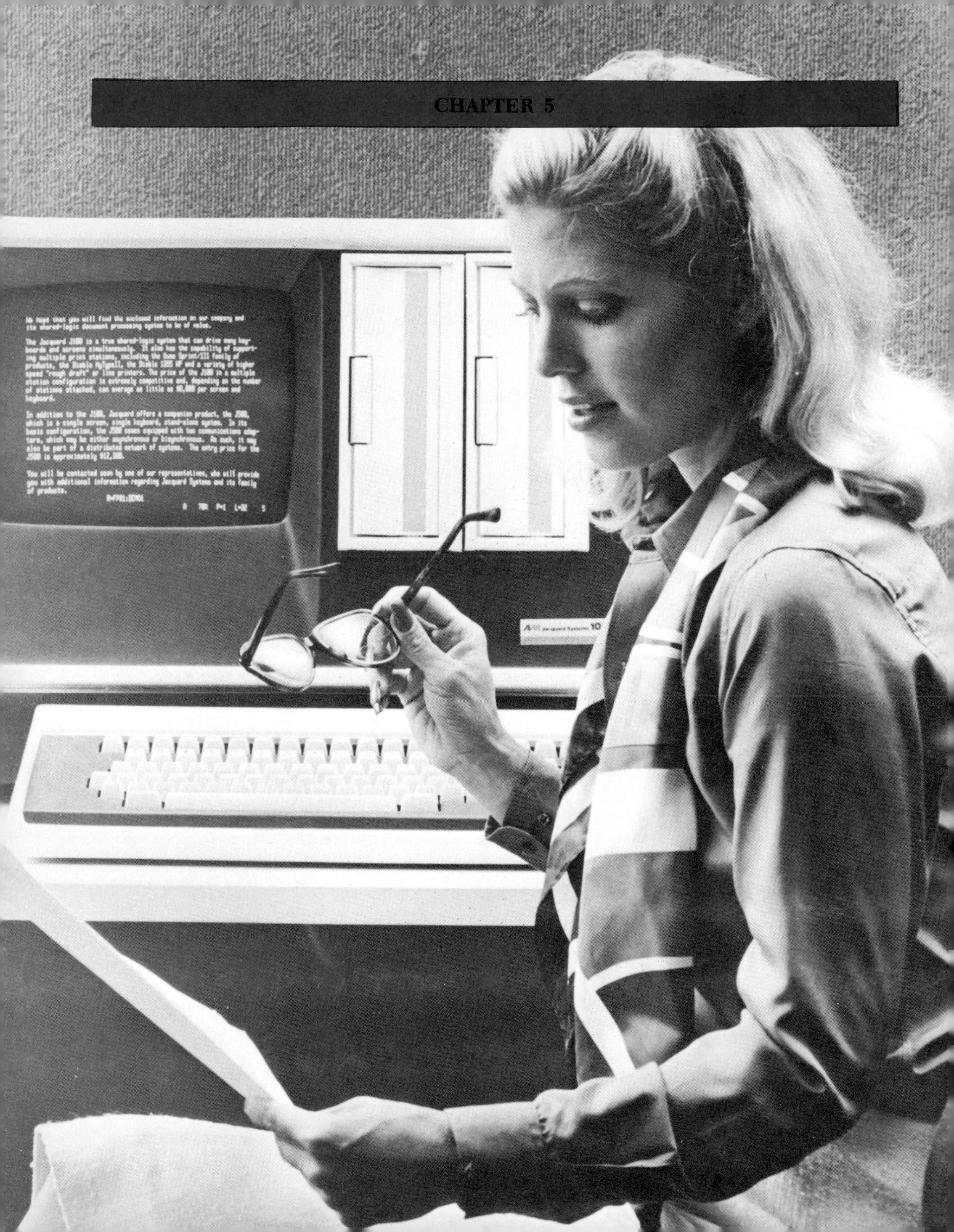

Pauses, gestures, body language, volume—these and many other tools available to us in speaking are not available to us in writing. Instead, as we write, punctuation marks allow us to tell our readers when to pause, which words go where, and so on.

The following units will teach you how to give your readers clear messages by using the appropriate punctuation marks. Given a situation that requires polished punctuation skills, your mastery of the units in this chapter will enable you to do the following:

1. *Use periods, question marks, and exclamation points to end sentences correctly.*

2. *Use commas, semicolons, colons, and dashes to provide pauses for your readers and guide them through your message.*

3. *Identify the exact words of other writers and speakers by using quotation marks to set off quotations.*

4. *Separate and identify additional information by using parentheses.*

5. *Form possessives, contractions, and special plurals correctly by using apostrophes.*

6. *Capitalize words according to accepted standards.*

7. *Use correct abbreviations when abbreviations are appropriate.*

8. *Write numbers in words or in figures, whichever is appropriate.*

The Period, the Question Mark, and the Exclamation Point

A famous pitcher, known to be a man of few words, was asked to comment on his last game. He was quoted as replying ".". History records a few other examples of similar replies. For example, one famous author wrote to his publisher to find out how his book was selling. He simply wrote "?" The book had indeed been selling very well, so his publisher replied "!"*

The period, the question mark, and the exclamation point are the marks used to end sentences. Obviously these are very familiar punctuation marks and easy to master. This unit will review their basic familiar uses and will discuss the few problem areas in using these marks.

The Period

The most commonly used mark of punctuation is the period. You already know the essential uses of the period. Let's review when to use a period and when not to use a period. Then we will review some common pitfalls.

Use a Period. After declarative and imperative sentences, after indirect questions, and after requests phrased as questions, *use a period.*

After Declarative and Imperative Sentences. A declarative sentence makes a statement, and an imperative sentence is an order or a command. Use a period after each.

> Mark Haynes is interested in learning more about daisy wheel printers. (A declarative sentence—it simply makes a statement.)

> Give Mark Haynes some information about daisy wheel printers. (An imperative sentence—it is a polite command. Note that the subject *you* is understood in these constructions.)

After Indirect Questions. An *indirect question* is really a statement, because it simply rephrases a question in statement form. Use a period after indirect questions. Of course, use a question mark after a direct question.

*Adapted from *Wordwatching*, Vol. 5, No. 10, September 1982, copyright © by Kay Powell.

"Do you know," Beth asked, "how to justify the margins on this particular dot matrix printer?" (Beth's actual words are in quotation marks; her actual words comprise a question and require a question mark.)

Beth asked me how to justify the margins on this dot matrix printer. (This is a restatement of Beth's original question. In this form, it is an indirect question and requires a period.)

After Requests Phrased as Questions. Sometimes a request is written in question form. Use a period when such requests clearly indicate that an action is expected. Use a question mark when such requests require a "yes" or a "no" answer (as, for example, for favors).

Will you please send us your check. (An action is being requested. This is just a more polite way of saying "Send us your check.")

Will you be able to send us these supplies in time for our Memorial Day sale? (A genuine question—*can you?*)

CLASS PRACTICE 1

Which of the following sentences should end with periods?

1. Jarrell wants to know when we expect to have all the specifications,
2. Will Ms. Emery be in her office this afternoon at 4 o'clock ?
3. Will you please replace this damaged merchandise as soon as possible ·
4. One agent asked when the revised price list will become effective ,
5. May we have your payment before February 10 ·
6. Will you send me a copy of your furniture catalog ,

Do Not Use a Period. There are a few instances in which writers confuse the rules concerning the uses of periods. Do not use a period after (1) numbers or letters in parentheses, (2) headings or titles that are on separate lines, (3) roman numerals (except when followed by titles, as in outlines), (4) even amounts of dollars, and (5) abbreviations that already end in periods.

Lisa cited three reasons for the delay: (1) the recent strike, (2) the backlog in shipments during summer, and (3) the time needed to check customers' credit accounts. (Not (1.), (2.), ...)

Summary

BIBLIOGRAPHY

Endnotes (No period after headings that appear on separate lines.)

Norman deGroat III will be the new CEO. (Not *III. will be* . . . .)

Ms. Tyson suggested $20 as a fair list price for our new computer game. (Not *$20. as a* . . . .)

Store hours are from 9 a.m. until 8 p.m. (Not *8 p.m.*.)

In addition, do not use a period after items in a list unless the items are long or are essential to complete the sentence that introduces the items.

Nancy discussed three problems:

1. The profit margin
2. Increased competition
3. Government regulation

Now notice how the items in the following example *are* needed to complete the introductory sentence:

Nancy discussed:

1. The profit margin.
2. Increased competition.
3. Government regulation.

PROOFREADING PRACTICE 1

Find and correct any errors in the following sentences.

1. Using the various controls on this word processor, you may delete (1.) a single letter, (2.) an entire word, (3.) an entire line of copy, and (4.) an entire paragraph.
2. Your total purchase price, just $49., will be refunded if you are not completely satisfied.
3. Send this order as a charge to the customer's account, or send it c.o.d..
4. Sandra identified the following possible sites for the distribution center:
   a. Jackson, Mississippi.
   b. Hot Springs, Arkansas.
   c. Mount Hood, Oregon.

Period Pitfalls. One of the common errors in using periods is to use a period *before* the end of the sentence, thereby stranding a group of words and creating a fragment.

Next April we will launch an advertising campaign for our new video recorders. The most expensive and extensive campaign we have ever developed. (You should quickly see that the second group of words makes no sense unless it is joined to the first sentence. See the next example.)

Next April we will launch our advertising campaign for our new video recorders, the most expensive and extensive campaign we have ever developed.

A second common error related to period use is to use a comma where a period should be used. In other words, a sentence that should end with a period is instead joined by a comma to another sentence.

We have been very successful with our new line of men's cosmetics, the colognes and skin creams sell especially well. (Obviously, a period should follow *cosmet-*

ics. Two sentences have been joined—incorrectly—by a comma. Place a period after *cosmetics*.)

PROOFREADING PRACTICE 2

Find the errors in the following sentences and explain why they are errors.

1. Mark these "Fragile" before you ship them, they contain statues worth several hundred dollars.
2. Francine wrote for an application form to Hopkins Industries. Where she would like to apply for a job.
3. Giselle expects to sell out our first printing within one week, the book is one of our best-sellers.
4. Adrienne has a long list of clients, she is a very successful broker.
5. My supervisor has requisitioned a temporary typist. To help us handle all the paperwork we must complete for the upcoming convention.
6. Agnes predicted that prices would rise drastically this year, we were lucky that we bought our supplies last year.

The Question Mark

The question mark is used after a direct question. Note that it is also used after a short direct question that follows a statement.

Who has the order from Owens Chemicals? (Direct question.)

Why did Mr. Haney decide to buy from Newton Falls Plastics? (Direct question.)

This disk drive is expensive, isn't it? (The sentence begins as a statement and ends as a question. Use a question mark.)

All these word processors come with a one-year warranty, don't they? (Use a question mark because a question is joined to the statement.)

When a series of questions is included in one sentence, use a question mark after each question.

Is she still planning to travel to England? to Japan? to Germany?

CLASS PRACTICE 2

In the following sentences, indicate whether a period or a question mark is needed at the point marked by parentheses.

1. Ms. Rubinowitz asked what the total cost would be for the three-year lease(.)
2. Will you please return these samples to us by May 13(.)
3. Mr. Gatto is one of the corporate officers, isn't he(?)
4. Ms. Leonard has already made reservations for herself and her family for our convention in Tampa next October, hasn't she(?)

5. Do you think that we should invite the entire management team—the production manager(   ) the marketing director(   ) the national sales co-ordinator(   )

6. Will you please send future bills to my office address rather than to my home address(   )

The Exclamation Point

To express strong feeling, use an exclamation point after a word, a phrase, or a sentence. But do not overuse the exclamation point—especially in business correspondence.

Congratulations! Henry and I are delighted to hear that you have been promoted to assistant marketing director.   (Exclamation point after a word. Note that the sentence that follows is punctuated in the usual way.)

Another best-seller! How happy I am to hear that your second book . . . . (Exclamation point after a phrase.)

Why didn't we think of this sooner!   (Exclamation point after a sentence.)

Note that the need for the exclamation point must often be determined by the writer. For example, the last sentence could also have been written as a simple question:

Why didn't we think of this sooner?   (Now the sentence does not show as strong emotion as with the exclamation point.)

CLASS PRACTICE 3

Indicate the punctuation at the point or points marked with parentheses in the following sentences. Explain your choices.

1. Another promotion(!) All of us congratulate you(   )
2. What a surprise(!) I am very happy to know that you have returned to Chicago(‘)
3. My sincere appreciation to you for all your help(   ) Thanks(   )
4. I cannot believe it(!) Did you hear that Stephanie and Bridget are opening another store(‘)
5. What a record(‚) Your sales for July set a new company record, and we congratulate you for your achievement(!)
6. Whose idea was this(?)

COMMUNICATION LABORATORY

APPLICATION EXERCISES

A. At the point marked by parentheses, indicate the correct punctuation for the following sentences. If no punctuation is needed, write *None*.

1. As you know, these goods are not duty-free if purchased in the U.S.A.( )
2. Have you heard that Dr. Coronado has been named chief of staff( )
3. The final price that they quoted was incredibly low( )
4. Mrs. Weinstein is in Maine( ) Blanche is temporarily handling her projects.
5. I suggest that you reread Chapter III( ) in this text.
6. I just heard the good news( )
7. Lana asked us to question the messenger about the cartons( )
8. May we have your overdue payment by July 10( )
9. We may work with a new mailing house( ) Allied Mail Service is now out of business( )
10. Will you please give Mrs. LoPresti a copy of this agenda( )
11. Has Stanley heard from our Pasadena office( ) our Portland office( ) our Seattle office( )
12. El-Jay watches are guaranteed for one year( ) AccuWatches are guaranteed for a lifetime( )
13. Are you and Mr. Pina teaching a training course in April( )
14. Why hasn't the messenger arrived yet( )
15. Will you please let me know when Mr. Dietrich calls( )

B. On a separate sheet, correct the following sentences and explain your reasons for making each correction. If a sentence has no error, write *OK*.

1. In Chapter VI., bankruptcy will be discussed in detail.
2. Mail us a check for only $15. for your ten issues of this great magazine.
3. Mary Lou has been working for us since 1980, she has certainly risen rapidly since then!
4. No. Let's not change this procedure.
5. You will find a projector in Mrs. Jones's office, she generally uses it for presentations.
6. What an incredible story.
7. Please let me know whether I am eligible to receive this subscription at a discount?
8. Frankly, between you and I, I doubt that we will get the contract.
9. Has Mr. Robards took all the samples with him?
10. Yes, they're are several more cartons of perforated paper available.
11. According to the builders, the foundation will be lain by March of next year.
12. Be sure to send the entire order quickly, we are almost out of continuous-flow paper.
13. My supervisor and me completed the performance review this morning.
14. The Fondas own nearly half the stock in Fonda Oil Inc.
15. Because there are three Mary Johnson's in our company, the telephone operators sometimes direct their calls incorrectly.

C. Is the punctuation correct in the following paragraph? Correct any errors as you copy the paragraph on a separate sheet of paper.

Congratulations. Your hard work throughout last year has certainly paid off. Your total sales for the year were 155 percent of budget. Everyone here in the headquarters office applauds you for this superb achievement. What do you have planned for *this* year.

VOCABULARY AND SPELLING STUDIES

A. These words are often confused: *expand, expend; interstate, intrastate.* Explain the differences.

B. By adding a short prefix to each of these words, change the word to give it a negative meaning.

1. normal
2. engage
3. proper
4. noble
5. literate
6. enchanted

C. How are the following pairs of words spelled when *ing* is added to each?

1. hop, hope
2. plane, plan
3. mop, mope
4. dote, dot
5. bar, bare
6. pine, pin

COMMUNICATING FOR RESULTS

The Last Minute. Audrey is an administrative assistant for Kent and Roberta. All three are highly skilled, experienced workers with a positive attitude, and all three enjoy working with one another. One problem, however, is that Kent often—almost always—waits until the last minute to give Audrey his work. For example, yesterday at 4:45 he gave her a rather lengthy report that was due to be submitted to the vice president on the same day. Audrey worked until 6:15 to complete and submit that report. What should Audrey do?

25

The Comma—Basic Uses

The period, the question mark, and the exclamation point are *end marks*, as you learned in the preceding unit. The comma never ends a sentence but instead guides the reader within the sentence.

The role of the comma is certainly an important one. In some ways, the comma is the reader's map for each sentence. In any case, as you will see, without properly used commas your writing will often force the reader to take a detour.

In a Compound Sentence

A *compound sentence* is one that has two or more independent clauses (main clauses, each of which could stand alone as an independent sentence). Use a comma between independent clauses joined by *and, but, or,* or *nor.*

> Catherine photographs all our products, but she is out of the office this week. (Note the comma before the conjunction *but.*)

> Our company tries to produce high-quality products, and it expects to get a fair profit for doing so.   (Again, the comma is before the conjunction *and.*)

Now let's take these two examples and omit the word *she* from the first and the word *it* from the second.

> Catherine photographs all our products *but* is out of the office this week.

> Our company tries to produce high-quality products *and* expects to get a fair profit for doing so.

In each case the second clause is no longer *independent* because its subject is missing. Thus the rule about using a comma to separate two independent clauses simply does not apply. Do not confuse such sentences with those that *do* have two independent clauses joined by *and, but, or,* or *nor.*

CLASS PRACTICE 1

Where are commas needed in the following sentences? Explain each answer.

1. Merlin Industries is building a plant in Dayton, and it is planning to build another in Syracuse within two years.

2. Ms. Spears started working for Hemline Clothing five years ago, but she has not worked for Hemline's American division.

3. A & R Homes is known for building low-cost housing, and has had an excellent reputation for many years.

4. Abner & Lipton is going to submit its bid next week and the company is confident that it will get the contract.

5. A French company wanted to export goods to us but it did not meet our requirements.

6. She has worked for our company for several years but has been stationed at one of our overseas operations.

In a Series

A series consists of a minimum of three words, phrases, or clauses. For clarity, always use a comma after each item in the series except the last. Thus the last comma should be immediately before the conjunction that precedes the last item in the series.

> Microprocessors, monitors, and diskettes have been delivered to the computer room.   (Note the comma before *and*.)

> Jim spent most of the week meeting prospective clients, showing them our products, and describing our services.   (Series of phrases.)

> Jim introduced the program, Jan gave a slide presentation, and Greta made the closing remarks.   (Series of clauses.)

If the conjunction is repeated before each item, then no comma is needed to separate the items.

> Our number one sales office may be Denver or Houston or Manchester.

When *Etc*. Ends a Series. Whenever the abbreviation *etc.* ends a series, be sure to use a comma before and after it (unless, of course, *etc.* ends the sentence).

> Sales, profits, revenues, *etc.*, were discussed at this morning's session.

> She gave several reasons for increasing the budget estimate—higher costs, overhead, declining market, *etc.*

Always remember that *etc.* (*et cetera*) means "and so forth" and that, therefore, you must not write *and etc.* (the equivalent of *and and so forth*).

CLASS PRACTICE 2

Where are commas needed in the following sentences? Explain your reason for inserting each comma.

1. Marion, Inge, Charles, and Norman will represent our company at the Frankfurt Book Fair.

2. J & R Tires, Glenn Auto Sales, and the Mobley Tire Company are the prime subcontractors.
3. During the past week we edited the script, photographed all the scenes, and recorded the dialogue for the entire program.
4. Only one store is open late on Mondays and Wednesdays and Fridays.
5. Invoices, orders, returns, etc. are handled by this department.
6. Frank will estimate the manufacturing cost, Joyce will determine the quantity to be produced, and Vera will prepare the approval forms.

After an Introductory Word, Phrase, or Clause

To signal the reader to slow down, use a comma after an introductory word, phrase, or clause.

Introductory Word. Among the most commonly used introductory words are the following. Use a comma after each.

accordingly	moreover
actually	namely
also	naturally
besides	next
consequently	nevertheless
finally	no
first	now
fortunately	obviously
further	otherwise
however	personally
indeed	therefore
meanwhile	yes

Now notice how they are used as introductory words:

First, we must discuss the change in buying patterns. *Second,* we must survey typical customers. (*Fortunately,* we have an excellent mailing list; *however,* the cost of a survey is very high.) *Finally,* we must choose an advertising agency to represent us.

Be sure that you recognize when these words are introductory and when they are not.

Ellen enjoys a challenging project, *however* difficult it may be. (Here, *however* modifies difficult; it is not an introductory word.)

Carlos *personally* delivered the films to the studio. (Here, *personally* modifies *delivered.*)

Introductory Phrase. A comma is needed after an infinitive phrase or a participial phrase that introduces an independent clause.

To qualify, you must be a resident of this state. *To get your copy,* just complete and return the enclosed form. (Introductory infinitive phrases.)

Knowing the exact cost, Karen tried to correct Bill. *Believing he was right,* Bill kept insisting his prices were correct.   (Introductory participial phrases.)

Overwhelmed by the project, the director requested more assistance. *Alerted to the problem,* management assigned help right away.   (Introductory participial phrases.)

A comma is also used after an introductory *prepositional* phrase unless it is a short phrase. Most writers omit commas after *short* introductory prepositional phrases to make the transition to the following clause smoother.

In July we will move to the Dexter Building.   (*In July* is a short prepositional phrase. Read this aloud to see how smoothly the thought flows without a comma.)

During the next month she plans to travel to Europe.   (This phrase, too, flows smoothly into the following clause.)

With the additional clerical help now available to us, our department should no longer have such backlogs.   (This longer prepositional phrase does require a comma after it.)

Introductory Clause. Use a comma after a subordinate clause that introduces the main thought.

If we receive your deposit by February 9, we will reserve one set for you.

Because Everett will be out of town, Sherry did not buy a ticket for him.

While Mrs. Carlisle is here, let's discuss this trust fund.

The following conjunctions introduce subordinate clauses and, therefore, signal you when to use a comma.

after	since
although	so that
as	unless
as soon as	until
because	when
even if	whenever
if	where
in order that	wherever
inasmuch as	while
provided	

NOTE: When these same subordinate clauses *follow* main clauses, a comma may or may not be needed. Use a comma if the subordinate clause provides extra information—that is, nonessential information.

You may charge the entire cost to your account, *if you prefer to do so.*   (The subordinate clause *if you prefer to do so* is not essential to the meaning.)

You may charge the cost to your account *if your balance is under $1,000.*   (The subordinate clause *if your balance is under $1,000* is essential here. No comma.)

CLASS PRACTICE 3

Where are commas needed in the following sentences?

1. To find out how to use this equipment read Chapter 3 of the accompanying manual.
2. Because Ms. Jakowski was delayed at the office she missed her flight to Geneva.
3. During the months of June and December we generally take inventory of all our merchandise.
4. Explaining each point clearly Mr. Ricardo quickly taught us how to use the word processor.
5. Whenever you're ready to discuss these printouts call me.
6. We will be happy to have Ronald with us at next week's session although we know that he will be very busy.
7. Mrs. Rodgers may not purchase any more merchandise until she has paid the complete balance of her outstanding bills.
8. Unless Matthew objects send a free copy of this manual to Alice Dembofsky.

PROOFREADING PRACTICE 1

Are the following sentences punctuated correctly? Correct any errors.

1. When Amy finishes typing this manuscript please ask her to proofread it carefully.
2. If you need any additional information call us at (800) 555-2121.
3. You will receive a 2 percent discount if you pay the total within ten days of the invoice date.
4. Do not approve this schedule unless you are confident that it is realistic.
5. As Mrs. Firenza explained she expects our stock to rise at least 8 points by the end of the year.
6. If you pay the total within ten days of the invoice date you will receive a 2 percent discount.
7. During the meeting with the accounting staff our comptroller explained the organizational changes that are being planned.
8. Knowing our procedures Ms. Kiley submitted an itemized estimate of the costs.

Comma Pitfalls

Including a comma when it is not needed can slow your reader's progress and cause confusion. Observe these rules:

1. Do not separate a compound by one comma. When a compound subject, compound object, or compound verb is interrupted, use two commas to set off the interrupting element.

Madeline's experience and her supervisory skills combine to make her a very effective manager. (Compound subject.)

Madeline's experience and, *of course,* her supervisory skills combine to make her a very effective manager. (The expression *of course* interrupts the compound subject, and *two* commas are needed to set off *of course.*)

2. Do not separate a subject from its predicate by one comma.

Please submit your application and your résumé to our recruiter. (No comma needed.)

Please submit your application and your résumé, *as well as your references,* to our recruiter. (*Two* commas set off the interrupting phrase *as well as your references.*)

3. Do not use a comma before an ampersand (&) in a company name.

Send it to Polski, Trent & McCovey. (Not *Trent, & McCovey.*)

COMMUNICATION LABORATORY

APPLICATION EXERCISES

A. On a separate sheet of paper indicate any punctuation needed in the following sentences. Write OK for any sentence that is correct.

1. Elsa went to the airport but returned immediately.
2. Bert will set up the booth Dana will distribute the handouts and I will run the projector.
3. By Thursday morning all these invoices must be processed.
4. Because this monitor was dropped the insurance policy does not cover the damage.
5. To get her approval we must justify the reasons for the increased expenses.
6. Mrs. Loo is the owner of this property and she has no plans to sell it in the near future.
7. To subscribe to this new magazine send your check or money order today!
8. Having completed the entire report Ms. Mackenzie decided to leave early.
9. Kenneth Tom and Bernice are our resident experts on computers.
10. Alexandra was promoted to manager; naturally she was happy that all her hard work had paid off.
11. Ms. Manning and Mr. Cartwright, of course will be the main speakers.
12. Fortunately Andrea had made a backup copy of each diskette.
13. We now have offices in most major cities—New York, Tampa, Washington, etc..

14. Larry asked for a transfer to our San Francisco office and Lauren requested a transfer to our Montreal branch.
15. Lorna is a field manager and also has her own small territory.

B. Correct the errors in the following sentences. Write *OK* if a sentence has no error.

1. Judd allows about 15 minutes, for questions and answers after his presentation.
2. Keith plans to prepare a survey form send it to all our customers and analyze the results.
3. Such damage is not covered by our policy. Consequently we must pay for the ruined inventory.
4. Edward, Christopher, and I, always play on the company bowling team.
5. To get your passport photo just go to our Travel Department.
6. Send this customer a brochure, if you have not already done so.
7. Yes, her marketing plan has been accepted by the board. Therefore it will be put into effect on January 1.
8. Suspecting that the plane might be delayed Debra and I called the airport before we left.
9. Ms. Shoals has several inventions to her credit and she has patents on nearly all of them.
10. Sacramento, Austin, Boulder and Macon, are among the cities we will use to test-market these products.
11. Freeport Enterprises owns restaurants, supermarkets, clothing stores, bookstores, and etc.
12. Have Allison and Mark wrote their monthly summaries yet?
13. There are, in my opinion, only one reputable supplier of stereo equipment in this area.
14. Every store owner in this city has cast their vote in favor of this tax.
15. A green monitor is more easy to read, according to word processing operators.

C. You have been promoted! Beginning with this lesson, the third set of Application Exercises will require you to edit for all kinds of errors—errors in grammar, spelling, punctuation, and vocabulary. Now that you have this added responsibility, be sure to give your editing special attention. Begin with the following excerpt from a memorandum.

Each customers' opinion of our sales representatives are important to us. Therefore we try to give full attention to the human relations skill, the grooming habits and the speaking ability of our sales representative's. Accordingly we have developed a training program for our sales staff.

VOCABULARY AND SPELLING STUDIES

A. These words are often confused: *lightening, lightning, lighting; respectively, respectfully.* Explain the differences.

B. Which nouns ending in *ty* are related to the following adjectives?

1. rare   4. anxious
2. real   5. facile
3. entire   6. notorious

C. How do you spell the "shun" ending for each of the following?

1. expan_____   4. func_____
2. connec_____   5. discus_____
3. comple_____   6. suspi_____

COMMUNICATING FOR RESULTS

Accepting Criticism. Gloria Ruskin, one of your co-workers, was severely criticized by your supervisor for consistently submitting the weekly sales report late. The report is due at 4 o'clock every Friday afternoon, but Gloria does not usually complete it until mid-morning on Mondays. The main reason that Gloria is late is that she always waits for the district offices to call her, and they often call very late in the afternoon with the statistics that she needs for her report. Gloria has not told this to your supervisor, and now Gloria is angry because she has been scolded. What should she do?

U · N · I · T
26 The Comma—With Nonessential Elements

As we speak and write, we often stop a sentence in midstream to add another thought. The purpose for adding this other thought may vary; however, if we are to communicate our written messages precisely, we must let our readers know when our words provide extra information and when they are essential. The basic tools for communicating the idea of extra information to the reader are commas.

Interrupting Elements

Words, phrases, and clauses that interrupt the flow of the sentence and do not contribute essential information to the message should be set off by commas. Such *interrupters* are not absolutely necessary to the meaning of the sentence. These elements merely provide extra information or an added comment.

Therefore, Anne Kilbride proposed that we sponsor a course on computer graphic arts. (The word *therefore* provides a transition from the preceding thought.)

The agent, *of course*, expected to receive her usual commission. (The phrase *of course* interrupts the sentence.)

Mr. Jefferson has been elected to the board, *as you probably have heard.* (The clause *as you probably have heard* provides additional information at the end of the sentence.)

As you see from the above examples, when such elements appear at the beginning or at the end of the sentence, *one* comma is needed to separate the words from the main part of the sentence. When such elements appear in the middle of the sentence, of course, *two* commas are needed to set them off.

Words. Most of the single words used as interrupters are conjunctive adverbs, such as *accordingly, moreover, therefore, however, nevertheless,* and *consequently.* When they are used at the beginning of a sentence, they are not literally interrupters but transitional words.

Accordingly, we sought the advice of an outside consultant.

James decided, *however,* to accept the terms of the offer.

Ms. Fong approved the purchase, *nevertheless.*

Phrases. We use many phrases such as the ones that follow in our everyday speech:

to say the least
so to speak
after all
for instance
for example
in the meantime
on the other hand

Such phrases often help to make a sentence smoother, to add more information, or to show a contrast; however, these phrases are not *necessary* to complete the meaning of the sentence, and therefore they are separated by commas.

His Denver speech, *for example,* was interesting and informative.

Barbara's rationale, *on the other hand*, was very convincing.

Most of the customers, *not just a few*, favored the cash discount.

Clauses. Among the elements that are commonly used as interrupters are all clauses beginning with subordinating conjunctions (see Unit 21 for a complete list), such as *when, if, as, before, since*, and *because*.

> *When the mechanic finishes his work*, be sure to give him this warranty card. (Subordinate clause at beginning of sentence.)

> We will, *if Mrs. Grimaldi wishes*, review these sales charts. (Subordinate clause in the middle of sentence.)

> Ms. Lindeman has developed the medium-range plan for our division, *as you already know*. (Subordinate clause at end of sentence.)

As with words and phrases, the subordinate clauses can come at the beginning, the middle, or the end of the sentence. The key point is to remember to separate such words, phrases, and clauses with commas when they add extra information (as in the examples above). But *omit* commas when the subordinate clauses contain essential information:

> I will go home *when I have finished my work*.

> She can talk on the phone *as she types*.

> I will help Gina with her work *only if she asks me*.

CLASS PRACTICE 1

Identify the words, phrases, and clauses that should be set off by commas in the following sentences. Remember that such elements may be transitional words or may be interrupters.

1. Jerry said that he'd meet with us on Monday not on Wednesday to finish this schedule.
2. Mona suggested therefore that we try to standardize these specifications.
3. Justin does nevertheless expect a large turnout for the grand opening.
4. Mrs. McQuillan stressed the time-saving techniques of the software of course.
5. Because Eric and Rhonda were using the computer terminals we had to wait until one was free.
6. Mr. Janus as you suggested bought the microprocessor with the 48K memory.
7. Barbara Rodriguez will train you to use these keyboards if you really want to learn.
8. Jordan is convinced nevertheless that the capital expenditure for automation cannot exceed $2.2 million.

PROOFREADING PRACTICE 1

Correct any errors in the following sentences.

1. She was concerned as you can well imagine, about the customer's complaints.
2. Your next statement consequently will show a credit for $150.
3. Betty Jackson, not Bette Janson, is the correct spelling of our supervisor's name.
4. Willis as you already know favors buying a computer known as the "2190."
5. Your representative will if you prefer refund your full deposit.
6. Ms. Neilson's credibility so to speak qualifies her for the position.
7. Mr. McCarthy's actions, to say the least, certainly do betray his feelings.
8. Jonas admitted on the other hand that he prefers working on the K100 machines.

That, Which, and Who Clauses

Among the clauses that deserve special attention are those beginning with *that, which,* and *who.*

essent'l   non-essential

That and *Which* Clauses. Careful writers use *that* to begin a clause with *essential* information and *which* to begin a clause with *nonessential* information. In the following examples, note that *which* clauses are separated by commas because they give extra information.

We sent Mrs. Agronski our latest sales report, *which* shows sales by units. (Because there is only *one* sales report, the *which* clause can obviously give only extra information about it. Compare the following example.)

We have two different sales reports. One shows sales by units; the other shows sales by dollars. We sent Mrs. Agronski the sales report *that* shows sales by units. (Now the *that* clause does not give extra information; it gives *essential* information. Without the *that* clause we would not know which of the two different sales reports were sent to Mrs. Agronski.)

Let us look at another set of examples.

I read Paige Prescott's latest book, *which* was on the best-seller list for six months. (Prescott has only one "latest book," so the *which* clause must give extra information about the book. Compare the next example.)

Paige Prescott's book *that* was on the best-seller list was her most interesting account of World War II. (She has written several books about World War II. The *that* clause identifies one specific book of all the books that she has written.)

Be sure to use *that* when the clause gives essential information and *which* when the clause gives *non*essential information. Consequently, because a *which* clause gives extra information, be sure to separate it with two commas if it interrupts a sentence and one comma if it ends a sentence.

Who Clauses. Question: When should a *who* clause be separated by commas? Answer: When it gives extra information, that is, when it is *nonessential*.

> Mr. Harkavy, *who* is our principal copywriter, formerly worked for Davis & McGuire. (The *who* clause is not intended to differentiate between *two* Mr. Harkavys but to give extra information about Mr. Harkavy.)

> We have two copywriters. The person *who* is our principal copywriter formerly worked for Davis & McGuire. (Here, the clause *who is our principal copywriter* serves to identify one specific person from two possible choices. It gives *necessary* information; thus it is *not* separated by commas.)

Use commas to let a reader know when a *who* clause gives nonessential information: (1) one comma if the clause ends a sentence and (2) two commas if the clause interrupts a sentence.

NOTE: The pronouns *who* and *whom* refer only to people. The pronoun *which* refers only to things. The pronoun *that* can be used to refer either to people or to things.

> The person with *whom* you should speak is Ms. D'Amato. (*Whom* refers to a person.)

> My new personal computer, *which* was on sale for $895, has a 32K memory. (*Which* refers to a thing.)

> He is the kind of person *that* adjusts well. (Here, *that* refers to a person.)

> The personal computer *that* I bought has a 32K memory. (Here, *that* refers to a thing. Compare this essential *that* clause with the nonessential *which* clause in the second sentence.)

CLASS PRACTICE 2

Where are commas missing in the following sentences? Find the nonessential clauses and use commas to separate them from the rest of the sentence.

1. Our new word processing manager who teaches electronic filing courses at Baker Community College reports to a senior partner.
2. The woman who approved this requisition is Mrs. Williams.
3. The manual that explains all these procedures is available in the corporate library.
4. Alan, Fred, and Becky who developed the entire campaign deserve most of the credit for the success of Snack Wafers.
5. In the most recent issue which is on my desk her latest article is featured.
6. The vice president who must approve all dismissals is Henry Fong.

Appositives and Similar Constructions

Appositives. You have already learned how to choose case forms of pronouns in appositives. At that time you probably realized that all the appositives illustrated were separated by commas.

My supervisors, *Daniel Brawley and she*, are in charge of salary administration. (The words *Daniel Brawley and she* are an appositive.)

Now note that an appositive that is very closely related to the preceding noun is *not* separated by commas.

Her brother *Martin* was also graduated from Pine Bluff Academy. (No commas needed to separate *brother* and *Martin*, which are very closely related.)

In the year *1994* Weber Oil will celebrate its 100th anniversary in this town. (*Year* and *1994* are very closely related. No commas needed.)

The term *user friendly* is used to describe the degree to which automated equipment is easy to use.

Degrees, Titles, and Similar Terms. Abbreviations such as *Ph.D.* and *M.D.* following a person's name should be set off by commas. Likewise, abbreviations of courtesy titles such as *Esq.* and of the names of religious orders following a person's name should also be set off by commas.

Brother Arthur James, *F.S.C.*, is scheduled to be the keynote speaker.

Leonora Hopkins, *M.D.*, is the new doctor in our corporate medical department.

Terms such as *Jr.* and *Sr.* and *Inc.* and *Ltd.* are commonly written without commas. However, writers should always follow the style that individuals or companies prefer.

Jason K. Whitman *Sr.* has been named president of Cooperative Research.

The headquarters building for Time *Inc.* is located in Rockefeller Center in New York City. (The actual company name is *Time Inc.*—no comma.)

BUT: Rorden Products, *Ltd.*, has been bought by Giant Brand Toys, *Inc.* (The actual letterheads of these two companies show commas before *Ltd.* and *Inc.*)

Calendar Dates. No comma is needed when a month and a year are given as dates (for example, *May 1992*). But when a day is included, set off the year with commas:

On May 3, *1992*, the president of our company is scheduled to retire. (At the end of a sentence, of course, the comma after *1992* would be replaced by a period.)

City and State Names. Whenever a city and state name are given in consecutive order, commas are needed to separate the state name.

We own a small company in Lexington, *Kentucky*, and are planning to buy another plastics firm in Philadelphia, *Pennsylvania*.

CLASS PRACTICE 3

Where are commas needed in the following sentences? Indicate the elements that must be separated by commas.

1. Patricia's newest store which is located in Manchester opened last July.
2. Her husband Gus is the business manager of her corporation.
3. The first store that she opened was in Kansas City Kansas not Kansas City Missouri.
4. Our former treasurer Andrew K. Clarkston retired and now lives in Pittsburgh.
5. Only John Willard Sr. is among the board members who voted against the measure.
6. Theresa DelGado Ph.D. is the head of our research and development staff.
7. The property was originally purchased by Ford & Savoroski on October 10, 1982 and was sold to Abrams, Westcott & Lordi on January 4 1983.
8. Your cousin Martin was hired by our firm earlier this week.

PROOFREADING PRACTICE 2

Correct any errors in the following sentences.

1. According to these papers, Sophia Burton Esq. became the trustee on April 29 1984.
2. Only her brother Dana owns as many shares of Springfield Metals Inc.
3. The first person to speak at our monthly Executive Committee Pamela Ivorie concisely stated the negative aspects of our marketing efforts in the past.
4. Sheila Owens who coordinated this multimillion-dollar campaign was named a vice president recently.
5. Mark as you know accidentally sent the cartons to Redding California instead of Reading Pennsylvania.
6. This lease became effective on July 1, 1983 and will expire on June 30, 1986.
7. Sabina Clifford CPA will most likely be the next treasurer of Dillon Industries.
8. The forms that you must complete are available in the Benefits Office I believe.

REMINDER: Remember *not* to separate a subject from its predicate by a *single* comma. Use either two commas or no commas (unless the interrupting element comes at the beginning or at the end of the sentence).

Evelyn Cranston is, *I believe*, the person who is most in favor of the merger. (Two commas.)

Evelyn Cranston is the person who is most in favor of the merger, *I believe*. (One comma because interrupter is at the end of the sentence.)

COMMUNICATION LABORATORY

APPLICATION EXERCISES

A. Use commas to separate words, phrases, and clauses as necessary in the following sentences. Correct any errors in comma usage, and write *OK* for each sentence that has no error.

1. One of the companies that we recently purchased Excelsior Foods has its headquarters in Jackson Mississippi.
2. Michael who has been in charge of our data processing operation since May 1983 is an alumnus of the Bell Business Institute.
3. Clara's thorough report which was formally submitted to the legal staff last month has finally been accepted by the court.
4. Among Denise's best sales territories are Ames, Iowa and Overland Park, Kansas.
5. Mrs. Goldenberg indicated that she was favorably impressed after she interviewed my brother Anthony.
6. Robert is confident, that we will meet the March 14 deadline for submitting our bids.
7. Jack promised of course to give Ms. Abercrombie a full refund for the damaged merchandise.
8. Only Nancy Melendez who is in charge of contracts has the authority to sign out such documents.
9. Time Inc. publishes an interesting series of books on this subject.
10. Marcia and Jim in the meantime will estimate the paper, printing, and binding costs.
11. The revenue shown on this report as Rosemary already mentioned, is estimated (not actual) revenue for the remainder of this year.
12. Mr. Freidlander decided consequently to postpone the purchase of the property until the dispute is resolved.
13. Her final proposal which we received only this morning offers the widest service coverage at the most reasonable terms.
14. All the checks were given to Ms. Navarro who is responsible for accounts receivable.
15. The cost of shipping, on the other hand has decreased slightly during the past year.

B. Read the following sentences carefully to correct any errors. Write *OK* for any sentence that has no error.

1. Ms. Cleary may if she prefers assign this project to a consulting firm.
2. Mr. Branch and his family originally indicated that they would attend, but we have not received the Branches' reply card yet.
3. There is, according to the manufacturer, only two or three suppliers of this metal throughout the United States.

4. Each supervisor has already been asked for their suggestions for cutting costs.

5. To receive a copy of the entire study write or call the Research Department.

6. Most of the men and women who work in this department has already indicated that they would pay for extended life insurance coverage.

7. Ronald and myself will probably be able to handle this project before the end of the month.

8. As Ms. Corey has already mentioned, I been exceptionally busy with the Corning account lately.

9. Alex has recently spoke to Mr. FitzGerald about some suggestions for alleviating the congestion in the halls at 9 a.m. and at 5 p.m.

10. Anne will handle your mail, and forward any checks in your absence.

11. Mr. Meltzer will leave on May 23, for Houston.

12. Ask Bonnie Forsythe who is my immediate supervisor, for more information about these requirements.

13. As soon as her oldest brother Justin arrives, let's leave for the airport.

14. Who did Ms. Margolies suggest as a substitute for Stella?

15. If the messenger arrives while I'm at lunch, ask him to lie all the cartons as near to that door as possible.

C. Edit the following excerpt from a business letter.

Are you interested in saving money on your car insurance? If you are, Union Mutual has a new plan which is scheduled to take effect on January 1, of next year.

The details of this plan, are described in the enclosed brochure. After you have read this pamphlet, complete the attached card, and return it to us. An agent will call you to discuss the plan, but you will be under no obligation, of course.

VOCABULARY AND SPELLING STUDIES

A. These words are often confused: *quiet, quite; explicit, implicit.* Explain the differences.

B. Match the choices in Column B with the correct words in Column A.

A	B
1. absurd	a. unstable
2. artificial	b. ridiculous
3. careless	c. inharmonious
4. discordant	d. negligent
5. incessant	e. abusive
	f. diffident
	g. unnatural
	h. unceasing

C. Add the "uhble"sound to each of the following. Be sure to spell each word correctly.

1. detest_____   4. unspeak_____
2. indestruct_____   5. siz_____
3. inexhaust_____   6. reduc_____

COMMUNICATING FOR RESULTS

Crediting Others Fairly. Bob Masterson, your supervisor, leaves a note on your desk to thank you for the great job you did in gathering quickly all the information he needed for his weekly report. He said that he "sincerely appreciated your efforts." But it was really Agnes DePalma, not you, who did the work for Bob's report. What would you say to Bob?

U · N · I · T

27

The Comma—Other Uses

The few remaining principles covered in this unit will complete the basic uses of the comma—the uses that you must know in order to write clear, correct messages.

With Two or More Adjectives

When you use two or more adjectives and *each* modifies the same noun, use a comma to separate the adjectives.

> The *small, sturdy, inexpensive* cabinet is ideal for storing these cassettes. (Each adjective modifies the noun *cabinet:* a cabinet that is small and sturdy and inexpensive. Note that the commas are used *between adjectives;* no comma is used between the last adjective, *inexpensive,* and the noun, *cabinet.*)

> Liza needs a *trustworthy, reliable* assistant to help manage her branch office. (An assistant who is trustworthy *and* reliable.)

If you are not sure whether to use a comma between adjectives, apply the following Quick Trick.

QUICK TRICK   Substitute *And*

To test whether adjectives do indeed modify the same noun, substitute the word *and* between the adjectives:

The small *and* sturdy *and* inexpensive cabinet is ideal for storing cassettes.

Liza needs a trustworthy *and* reliable assistant to help manage her branch office.

Note that the word *and* can obviously be used in place of each comma in the above examples. However, do not use a comma before an adjective that is part of a compound noun.

Marilou just recently bought a red sports car. (Here, *red* modifies the compound noun *sports car.* You would not say "a car that is red *and* sports.")

Likewise, do not use a comma before the last adjective when this adjective is very closely connected to the noun or is thought of as part of the noun.

Arthur is now working on his monthly income statements. (No comma between *monthly* and *income* because they do not separately modify *statements.* You would not say "statements that are monthly *and* income." Here, the adjective *monthly* modifies the compound *income statements.*)

A contractor estimated the costs of renovating that old brick building. (No comma between *old* and *brick* because *old* modifies the compound *brick building.* The meaning is not "a building that is old *and* brick.")

CLASS PRACTICE 1

Use commas as needed to separate adjectives in the following sentences.

1. Marilyn promised to submit a detailed comprehensive report by Friday.
2. We certainly agree that inventorying is a difficult tiresome job.
3. Evelyn bought a modern successful ice cream store.
4. Place the liquid in a large plastic jar.
5. Diana Lemmons writes interesting lively advertising copy.
6. The original warehouse is a run-down shabby old building.

PROOFREADING PRACTICE 1

Test your proofreading skill by correcting comma errors in the following sentences.

1. All the cartons of unsold damaged merchandise were destroyed.
2. The Credit Union provides a safe convenient method to save money through payroll deduction.

3. Ms. Jurado's patient, positive, attitude makes her very popular among her staff members.
4. The Holmes Gallery features expensive unique art objects.
5. Andrea is an intelligent, good-natured, person to work for.
6. For fast efficient service, just call All Night Messengers at 555-2984.

To Indicate Omissions and to Separate Repetitions

Writers sometimes omit words for the sake of brevity. This is fine as long as the meaning is still clear. In the following sentences, for example, note how the commas tell the reader where the *understood* words belong.

> Lena Kutsher was assigned to the Sheilds account; Bill Quince, the J&R account; and Dorothy Franciosa, the Hanover Funds account. (Each comma substitutes for the words *was assigned to.*)

The comma also serves to separate words or phrases that are deliberately repeated for emphasis.

> Last week we received *many, many* requests for more information about municipal bonds.

> When she discussed her project, Margaret was obviously *enthusiastic, very enthusiastic.*

In Direct Address

When we speak directly to someone, we often use that person's name as we address him or her. Such use is called *direct address.* Note how commas are used to separate names in direct address in the following sentences.

> *Mrs. Jarrow,* will you be able to meet with us on Friday, June 11?

> I'm very happy, *Sandy,* that you have been named assistant vice president.

CLASS PRACTICE 2

Punctuate the following sentences.

1. By 1991 we plan to have a nationwide total of 45 stores; by 1994 55 stores; and by 1996 63 stores.
2. All of us appreciate your helping us Mr. Andolini and we look forward to your next visit.
3. Needless to say, Jane was very very happy to hear that she had been selected to represent her co-workers.
4. John is our international sales representative for Italy and France; Gina Great Britain; and Anthony China and Japan.
5. If you wish, we will be glad to help you Laurie with your complicated project.
6. Janet handles all customers whose last names begin with A through J; Carla H through P; and Andrew Q through Z.

In Numbers and in Company Names

Numbers. Commas are generally used to separate thousands, millions, billions, and so on, in numbers of four digits or more.

   1,746   43,649 $2,846,094

However, the comma is not used in the following numbers:

years: 1984, 1989
page numbers: pages 1324 and 1343
house numbers: 1301 Rockaway Parkway
phone numbers: (201) 555-6547
ZIP Codes: 91324
serial numbers: Policy 98475

In addition, the comma is not used in weights and measurements that express *one* total: *11 pounds 3 ounces, 3 hours 23 minutes,* and so on.

Unrelated numbers that are written together should be separated by a comma to avoid misreading.

   By 1992, 34 foreign-language editions will be available.   (The comma prevents the possibility of the reader's seeing *199234* or otherwise confusing these two numbers.)

NOTE: In special cases numbers may get special treatment. For example, in metric terms a space (not a comma) is used to separate groups of three numbers *on both sides of the decimal point!*

   21 435 kilometers
   13 432.875 445 liters

But a four-digit metric number is written with no space (for example, *3425 kilograms*) unless it appears in a table with other numbers that are larger.

Company Names. Many law firms, stock brokerage offices, and other companies are known by the names of the principal partners of the firm, for example, *McLoughlin, Vance, Jones & Ricciuti.* Of course, always write the official name exactly in all details. Use the word *and* or the symbol &, whichever appears on the company letterhead, and use commas exactly as shown in the official name. (Usually, no comma is used before the word *and* or before the symbol &, called an *ampersand.*)

When such company names are shortened, they usually appear as follows:

   Mr. Fasano was named a vice president of *McLoughlin, Vance* just recently. (Note that only the first two names are used—with only *one* comma.)

CLASS PRACTICE 3

Correct these sentences. Write *OK* if there are no errors.

1. Mr. Bacon said that he never never wants to attend another convention.
2. In 1984 87 of our sales representatives met or exceeded their goals—our best year ever!

3. Ms. Franklin was pleased that the meeting lasted only 2 hours, 15 minutes.
4. The precise weight of the merchandise and its package is 7 pounds 9 ounces.
5. The bibliography begins on page 1129.
6. We have dealt with McLoughlin Vance since 1979.

PROOFREADING PRACTICE 2

Correct any errors in the following sentences. Write *OK* if there are no errors.

1. Anne Kiley estimates that we will sell more than 50000 units in the first year.
2. The ZIP Code for Fort Pierce, Florida, is 33,450.
3. On July 29 10,000 brochures were mailed to select customers.
4. Jerry has worked for Hamilton Automotive Parts since 1981; Betty 1980; and Mario 1978.
5. Agnes said that she had never never agreed to that decision.
6. Whenever you return from your trip to DeKalb, please call my office Clark.

COMMUNICATION LABORATORY

APPLICATION EXERCISES

A. Practice applying the comma principles presented in this unit. On a separate sheet of paper, indicate where you would place or remove commas and explain why.

1. Does Mrs. LaCross know that we will be meeting in Room 2,143 at 8 p.m.?
2. The weight of each carton cannot exceed 3 pounds, 4 ounces.
3. Vera have all these purchase requisitions been approved?
4. In July we expect to receive an order worth from $50000 to $60000 from Allied Computer Products.
5. Before you send out these specifications sheets Albert be sure to check each measurement.
6. By March 13 132 representatives had completed our executive techniques seminar.
7. Amanda has a reputation for being an ambitious hard-driving sales manager.
8. Acme Alarms distributes inexpensive home security systems.
9. Ms. Devorak have you confirmed your flight reservations with your travel agent?
10. Steve's reply to that customer was inappropriate very inappropriate.

11. The correct address is 9,343 West 11 Street, not 9,343 East 11 Street.
12. In 1984 745 cars were sold or leased in the same period—a record for our dealership.
13. Last fall we distributed over 40000 of our catalogs, last spring 45000; and this summer 50000.
14. Mr. Polarski has been very very successful in marketing all our new products.
15. We have enclosed Ms. Iovino the price list and the brochure that you requested.
16. Her company is located in Springfield Illinois.
17. Bruce have you revised the copy for the 30-second commercial?
18. Harold is convinced that he has found a low-risk high-return investment.
19. The maximum cargo weight for this vehicle is 12100 pounds.
20. Obviously, he copied the wrong ZIP Code; the correct one is 10,734.

B. Write *OK* on your paper for each correct sentence. Correct each incorrect sentence.

1. If you return your subscription form before May 15 you will receive a free copy of a handy almanac.
2. The fabric that he wants is out of stock but we will immediately place an order directly with the manufacturer.
3. The engine, the transmission, the air conditioner, etc. are covered under the terms of this warranty.
4. One week before the advertising staff will mail out reminders to all charge customers.
5. Halburton Plastics, Inc. is a major importer of polyvinyl chloride.
6. His wife who holds a similar position with Anders & Young Metals has been appointed to the mayor's panel.
7. To find out more about this once-in-a-lifetime offer complete and return the enclosed card today.
8. Henry wants to assign the project to an outside agency but Marietta prefers handling such assignments herself.
9. Ms. Carlysle originally estimated the cost to be approximately $50,000, but now believes it will be closer to $100,000.
10. You may of course have the entire order shipped to your home for only a small delivery charge.
11. Mr. VanPatton decided therefore to reorganize the entire marketing staff.
12. We will purchase new duplicating equipment which should save us a substantial amount when compared with the cost of leasing equipment.
13. Our former supervisor, Jayne W. Franklin is now a regional vice president for our firm.
14. Because Sheldon joined the retirement plan on January 15, 1979 he already has accrued several thousand dollars in his account.

15. The new, executive offices for Jason, Reynolds, Owens & LaRue are located in the Smalley Building.

C. Make the following message clear by correcting all the errors that you find.

Our experience with Lindeman Motors, Inc., has shown that, we can expect fair prices and excellent service on all the vehicles it sells or leases. Our experience with Centurion Auto Sales and Rentals on the other hand has been almost entirely negative. Although Centurion has a reputation for very low prices it also has a reputation for poor service and for hidden costs. When our current lease agreement with Lindeman expires next month therefore we recommend renewing the lease, for an additional 24 months. The 10 percent increase in our total monthly payment (to $15550) will we believe be well worth the small additional price as compared with Centurion's slightly lower price for the same autos ($14995).

VOCABULARY AND SPELLING STUDIES

A. These words are often confused: *manner, manor; emanate, eminent, imminent*. Explain the differences.

B. For each sentence, identify the meaning of the word in italics.

1. Unfortunately, Gerald works with customers in a *perfunctory* way. (*Perfunctory* means (*a*) secretive, (*b*) exhaustive, (*c*) mechanical, (*d*) hasty.)
2. With her knowledge of our procedures, Helen can help you to *expedite* the process. (*Expedite* means (*a*) cancel, (*b*) accelerate, (*c*) understand, (*d*) reverse.)
3. Angela did a *prodigious* amount of work in a very short time. (*Prodigious* means (*a*) sloppy, (*b*) overwhelming, (*c*) formal, (*d*) financial.)

C. Rewrite the following paragraph, correcting spelling and grammatical errors as you do so.

Our superviser, Jim Gormly is teaching a short coarse in the basics of word proceing begining next Wendesday. Sponsored by the corporate training program this course will be offerred again in the spring.

COMMUNICATING FOR RESULTS

Matt Chesterton, one of your co-workers in the word processing center of a large corporation, often calls in to say that he is sick and cannot come to work. In fact, Matt is out about three days a month on a regular basis.

Today Matt confides in you and tells you that he is not really sick when he calls; he just takes a day off when he is in the mood to do so—especially on days when he knows there will be a heavy work load. What advice would you give to Matt?

28

The Semicolon, the Colon, and the Dash

The semicolon, the colon, and the dash have specific uses within the sentence. Knowing these uses will improve your reading skill, and applying them properly will distinguish your writing from the ordinary.

The Semicolon

The semicolon announces a partial stop somewhat stronger than a comma. Thus a semicolon, not a comma, is often required to join the independent clauses in a compound sentence. In addition, a semicolon is often needed before explanatory or enumerating words and in a series of items that already have commas within them.

In Compound Sentences. Before we see how semicolons are used in compound sentences, let's review what a compound sentence is: *A compound sentence is a sentence with two or more independent clauses.* Remember that an independent clause is one that can stand alone and still *make sense*. A compound sentence, therefore, is a sentence with two such clauses (or more than two).

The clauses in a compound sentence (1) may be joined by a comma plus a conjunction, (2) may be joined by a semicolon without a conjunction, or (3) may be written as two separate sentences.

Anne likes the new title, but she prefers the original one. (Two independent clauses joined by a comma plus the conjunction *but*.)

Anne likes the new title; she prefers the original one. (Two independent clauses joined by a semicolon. A comma is not strong enough to join these clauses.)

Anne likes the new title. She prefers the original one. (Two independent clauses written as two separate sentences.)

Now that you have reviewed the compound sentence, study the three uses of semicolons in compound sentences.

1. *To Join Clauses Without Conjunctions.* A semicolon is strong enough to join two independent clauses without a conjunction. A comma cannot do so.

Burt is the senior inventory manager; he has been with our company for five years. (No conjunction joins the two independent clauses. The semicolon signals that the conjunction is omitted.)

2. ***To Join Clauses With Transitional Expressions.*** When the second independent clause includes a transitional word or phrase, a comma is not strong enough to join the clauses. They must be joined by a semicolon.

Benjamin approves all large purchases for the entire division; however, he is now in Europe on business. (A semicolon is needed to join these independent clauses. A comma is *not* strong enough to do so.)

3. ***To Prevent Misreadings.*** If a compound sentence contains commas in either or both clauses *and* a strong break is needed to make the message clear, use a semicolon to separate the clauses even if a conjunction is used. If no misreading is likely, use a comma.

Among the topics to be covered today are general sales techniques, our discount policy, and commissions; and the incentive compensation plan will be discussed next week. (The semicolon provides the break needed to ensure that the reader pauses after *commissions*.)

Before Explanatory or Enumerating Words. Use a semicolon before words and phrases such as *for example, for instance, namely, that is,* and *that is to say* when they introduce an independent clause, an enumeration, or an explanation that is incidental to the rest of the sentence.

To find routine information, you will need to keep up-to-date references handy; for example, a dictionary, an almanac, a ZIP Code directory, and a business writer's manual. (*For example* introduces an enumeration.)

In a Series. Series of items that contain internal commas (such as commas in city and state names or in certain company names) should be separated by semicolons instead of commas to prevent misreading.

Those district offices now participating in the experimental study are in Bloomington, Minnesota; Kansas City, Kansas; Albany, New York; and Seattle, Washington.

NOTE: A semicolon, not a comma, precedes the conjunction before the last item in a series containing internal commas.

CLASS PRACTICE 1

In each of the following sentences, choose the correct punctuation mark within parentheses and explain each of your choices.

1. Several well-known speakers are in the program tomorrow, including Marcia Q. Steinbeck(, ;) director of marketing for Panorama Tours(, ;) Adrian Welch(, ;) publisher of several magazines(, ;) and Jeffrey C. Ulster(, ;) senior designer for Phelps & Morris Clothing.

2. Our warehouse is closed for inventory during the next two weeks(, ;) consequently(, ;) we cannot ship this order until April 20.
3. Any questions concerning the purchase of this property should be addressed to Ms. Lewis, Mr. Judd, or Mrs. Kalbach(, ;) and Mr. Cuomo should be given copies of all correspondence pertaining to the sale.
4. The Glynn Corporation has a virtual monopoly on these products(, ;) Hebner Industries has recently presented a strong challenge, however.
5. Ellen tried to do all that she could to save the Denton account(, ;) for instance, she developed a creative direct-mail campaign.
6. Yuri Urskoff is our representative in the Soviet Union(, ;) he has been selling food products for our firm since last spring.

The Colon

A colon serves a specific function: It tells the reader "Listen to this," or "Here is something important." Study the following uses of the colon.

Colon Before a List. A colon is used to introduce a list within a sentence or a list that is tabulated. Before the colon appears, the reader is often given a hint that a list will follow by such words as *the following, as follows, this,* or *these.*

The total price of $1,596 includes the following:

1. A 48K microcomputer
2. A disk drive
3. A monitor
4. A monitor stand
5. The disk operating system (DOS)
6. Four comprehensive system manuals
7. Accounting and word processing software packages

You may pay for your purchase in any of these convenient ways: by check, by money order, or by credit card.

Colon for Emphasis. A colon may be used to give added emphasis to a word, a phrase, or a sentence.

You know as well as I when we must start this project: immediately.   (Colon to emphasize a word.)

She gave a very good reason for delaying this order: to save the $100 shipping charge.   (Colon to emphasize a phrase.)

Melinda repeated her well-known rule: Each credit application must be checked carefully.   (Colon to emphasize a sentence.)

When a colon precedes a complete sentence, as in the last example, the first word of the sentence is capitalized if the sentence states a formal rule or requires additional emphasis. However, if the sentence following the colon merely completes the main thought, use a lowercase letter.

Lowell explained why he cannot attend the conference: he will be on jury duty for that entire week.   (Lowercase letter because second sentence completes the main thought.)

Remember: No one will be admitted without a company identification card. (Capital letter for added emphasis.)

CLASS PRACTICE 2

Make the correct choices for each of the following sentences.

1. A new developing process will be explained at our next meeting(: . ,) Mr. Fiori will conduct that session.
2. Caution(: . ,) (The, the) chemicals in this cleaner may be harmful if inhaled.
3. A special two-hour seminar will be offered only on these dates(: . ,) May 15, May 22, and June 6.
4. A special two-hour seminar may be offered later in the year(: . ,) May and June are probably the best months for such seminars.
5. Include the following people on your list of guests(: . ,) Marilyn P. Clarkson, James W. Otter, and Ray Dinizio Jr.
6. When you reorder, be sure to specify this catalog number(: . ,) C120-X564.

PROOFREADING PRACTICE 1

On a separate sheet of paper, correct any errors in the uses of semicolons and colons in the following sentences. (HINT: Be sure to look for errors in the use of capitals following colons.)

1. Your car stereo is no longer under warranty, Ms. Richards: however, the total cost of the repair will be only $19.95.
2. Wanda specified where each package is to be sent: The large box, to our St. Louis office; the small carton, to our San Francisco office.
3. Several applicants are now being considered for Brenda's former job, including the following. Henry Sink, Elvera Poole, and Francis Bodine.
4. Be sure to include this information when you return damaged merchandise. The manufacturer's name, the model number, and the serial number.
5. We recently franchised stores in the following areas; Sacramento, California, Newark, New Jersey, and Boulder, Colorado.
6. Remember this. Always insure each package before you ship it to a customer.

The Dash

The dash is an abrupt, emphatic punctuation mark that has a special impact on a sentence. The dash can often be replaced by a comma, a semicolon, a colon, or parentheses. But the dash has a few of its own unique uses. In any case, it is a strong, forceful mark of punctuation and therefore must be used correctly—and sparingly.

As a Substitute for Other Punctuation. Although a dash can often be replaced by other punctuation, the emphasis of the sentence is weaker without the dash. For example, compare the following pairs of sentences, noting how much more emphatic the sentences with dashes are.

Commas vs. Dashes

One new supplier, Acme Typesetters, is very conveniently located.

One new supplier—Acme Typesetters—is very conveniently located.

Semicolons vs. Dashes

The list price of the Electra stereo package is the highest; however, the quality of the Electra is also the best.

The list price of the Electra stereo package is the highest—however, the quality of the Electra is also the best.

Colons vs. Dashes

Buying from Jensen Audio has these advantages: reliable service, low prices, and a wide variety of name brands to choose from.

Buying from Jensen Audio has these advantages—reliable service, low prices, and a wide variety of name brands to choose from.

Parentheses vs. Dashes

Spectrum Appliances has three convenient stores (on Berkely Avenue, in the Howard Mall, and on Sunset Road) for your shopping pleasure.

Spectrum Appliances has three convenient stores—on Berkely Avenue, in the Howard Mall, and on Sunset Road—for your shopping pleasure.

NOTE: When parenthetical material appears at the end of a sentence, only *one* dash is needed to set off the words—as opposed to *two* parentheses.

For your shopping pleasure, Spectrum Appliances has three convenient stores (on Berkely Avenue, in the Howard Mall, and on Sunset Road). (*Two* parentheses.)

For your shopping pleasure, Spectrum Appliances has three convenient stores—on Berkely Avenue, in the Howard Mall, and on Sunset Road. (*One* dash to separate parenthetical copy at the end of a sentence.)

Before a Summarizing Word or a Repetition. Use a dash between a summarizing word that is used as a subject and the listing that precedes it.

Leadership, human relations skill, the ability to communicate well—these are the characteristics of the successful manager. (The word *these* summarizes the items listed before the dash; *these* is the subject of the verb *are*.)

A dash may also be used before a repetition or a restatement.

Congratulations! You have done a fine job in reaching your annual sales goals—a very fine job. (Dash before the repetition.)

With Afterthoughts and Contrasting Statements. Use a dash before a deliberate afterthought to give variety to your writing or to soften a strong statement.

All of us look forward to seeing you at next year's convention—sooner, we hope! (A planned afterthought.)

Your territory was about 15 percent under budget—but economic conditions, of course, seriously curtailed customer buying. (To soften the effect of the main thought.)

Likewise, to give special emphasis to a contrasting statement, use a dash to set it off.

Total revenue for the first quarter was $5.5 million—against a goal of $5.7 million—for all our subsidiaries. (Dashes set off the contrasting statement.)

Punctuating Material Set Off by Dashes. The words that are set off by dashes may be punctuated as described below.

At the End of the Sentence. Whenever "dashed" material ends a sentence, the second dash is omitted and the sentence then ends with the regular end-of-sentence punctuation.

We buy our supplies from Webster Stationers—*all* our supplies. (This is a declarative statement.)

Who is the person standing at the podium—the woman with the briefcase? (This is a question.)

What a tremendous value—a genuine bargain! (This is an exclamation.)

Within the Sentence. Words within two dashes may end in a question mark or an exclamation point, when appropriate; a period is used only if the last word is an abbreviation that requires the period.

Her latest book—a certain best-seller!—is to be made into a movie. (The words within the dashes are an exclamation.)

Analysts predict that Gibbons stock—do you know its present price?—may double by the end of this year. (The words within the dashes are a question.)

We find that leasing equipment—such as cars, trucks, and vans—is less expensive in the long term. (No period before the second dash.)

We find that leasing equipment—cars, trucks, vans, etc.—is less expensive in the long term. (Period before the second dash only because of the abbreviation *etc.*)

Commas are used normally within dashes, as are quotation marks:

Several agents—Carolyn, Frank, Leo, and George, for example—recommended that we review and update the commission plan for all insurance policies.

These executive cars—known in industry jargon as "brass hats"—are being sold at 25 percent below their original list prices.

CLASS PRACTICE 3

Where are dashes needed in the following sentences?

1. At the end of her probationary period, Melissa received a high performance rating a very high rating.
2. Many of our stores our Dallas store, for example have almost no serious competition.
3. Are you planning to register for the finance class the one offered by our Training Department?
4. Phoenix, San Diego, Las Vegas, Austin all are on Ms. Corio's itinerary.
5. A generous discount nearly 33 percent! made this offer too difficult to overlook.
6. United Banks not United Banking has a very helpful Trust Department.

PROOFREADING PRACTICE 2

Test your ability to use dashes correctly by correcting any errors in the following sentences.

1. The liter, the meter, the gram,—these are the basic units for capacity, length, and mass in the metric system.
2. As you can well imagine, Mrs. Edwards has only one thing on her mind her upcoming around-the-world trip.
3. Fast, efficient service, fair prices, high quality all are yours when you deal with Allied Electronics.
4. Ames and Faber—have you ever heard of them—have a wide variety of fabrics for you to choose from.
5. In the past two years, our stock in Wellington Mills has risen more than 300 percent imagine, more than tripled!
6. Please note that your flight is scheduled to depart at 6:30 a.m.—not 6:30 p.m.

COMMUNICATION LABORATORY

APPLICATION EXERCISES

A. Each of the following sentences contains one or more question marks to indicate possible missing punctuation. On a separate sheet of paper, indicate the punctuation you would use at that point. Write *OK* for any sentence that requires no added punctuation.

1. Phyllis requested another copy of the procedures manual (?) one that has the most recent discount policy.
2. Robert Smyth (?) not Roberta Smith (?) is the person you are looking for.
3. Charles Maddigan (?) he's the director of marketing (?) will be speaking at this morning's meeting.

4. In each presentation, you should be sure to do the following (?) explain the features of our products, compare our features with competitors', discuss our credit terms, and try to close the sale.

5. Martha Barone insisted that we can buy these metals at cheaper prices (?) consequently (?) we are exploring other possible suppliers.

6. Remember (?) All purchase requisitions must be signed by your department head and by the controller.

7. In a recent survey, employers indicated that they highly value (?) applicants with good communication skills and positive work attitudes.

8. We plan to air many television and radio commercials for this chain of stores (?) in addition (?) we will have many full-page ads in major newspapers.

9. The reason for the delays is this (?) The warehouse is still out of stock on both items.

10. Only one person (?) Amanda Watt (?) is in favor of the motion.

11. Our latest movie (?) are you planning to see it (?) is drawing standing-room crowds all over the country.

12. Mr. Ewald is not in charge of advertising and promotion (?) however (?) he may be able to answer your questions.

13. Ms. Landis started as a word processing operator (?) she is now director of communications.

14. Please wire our Tokyo office (?) do it immediately.

15. Among the items on the invoice are (?) diskettes, graphic arts supplies, and various standard carbon-pack forms.

B. On a separate sheet of paper, show your corrections for each of the following sentences. (Some sentences may have more than one error.) Write *OK* for any sentence that has no error.

1. As soon as Jerry returns from lunch. Let's get together to discuss this.

2. Cartons, jars, bottles, caps. These are the items that push up our prices.

3. Vincent asked Maria where the blank diskettes are stored?

4. The last day of the sale is Saturday, we expect several hundred customers then.

5. Whenever you need additional information please be sure to call our customer service representative, for help.

6. You have probably already heard that, we will be moving downtown next year.

7. Agnes is in charge of compiling and distributing all the sales statistics, isn't she?

8. We would be delighted to charge the entire amount to your new account. If you prefer, Ms. Chandis.

9. The survey indicates that shoppers are looking for these key things; service, convenience, price, and quality.

10. Three of our account executives—Dorothea Mills, Camille Harper, and Trevor Simms,—will represent us on the panel.

11. In our business the highest expenses are for: salaries, building rent, and travel and entertainment.
12. Caution; Smoking is prohibited beyond this point.
13. All of us are pleased to hear that our new location will be in the Jennings Avenue Mall very pleased.
14. If Mrs. Jamison accepts the overseas position she will be the highest-paid executive in this bank—except for our chairperson.
15. Sylvia Morse, Edwin Mulcahy, Dean Lowry and Darren Chan are members of the committee.

C. Insert the correct punctuation marks in the places with question marks in parentheses.

After we review the entire February issue (?) we should begin laying out our plans for succeeding issues (?) at least for March and April (?) How much ad space have we sold for the March and April issues (?) How many pages will each issue be (?) These and other questions must be answered immediately (?) In addition, I do not like the tentative feature story for March (?) do you (?) We should meet (?) Alan, Evelyn, Bruce, and I (?) before the end of the week to discuss all this.

VOCABULARY AND SPELLING STUDIES

A. These words are often confused: *peace, piece; stationery, stationary.* Explain the differences.

B. On a separate sheet of paper, write the singular forms of the following plural nouns.

1. parentheses
2. teeth
3. CPAs
4. Messrs. Parker
5. notaries public
6. secretaries

C. Column A lists six words containing prefixes, and Column B lists the meaning of many of the most commonly used prefixes. Match the words with the meanings that refer to their prefixes.

A	B
1. subway	a. before
2. contradict	b. against
3. postscript	c. around
4. inconvenient	d. between, among
5. antedate	e. one
6. interstate	f. beyond
	g. under
	h. above
	i. after
	j. not

COMMUNICATING FOR RESULTS

Being Blamed for Others' Errors. Your employer calls to your attention some errors in reports that she believes you prepared. The reports in question are not yours. What should you say or do?

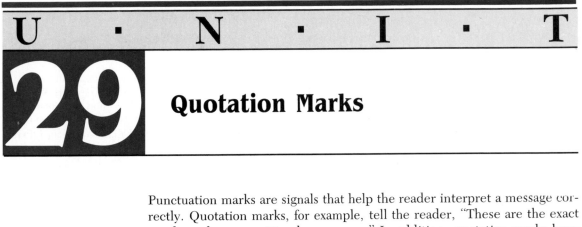

U · N · I · T

29 Quotation Marks

Punctuation marks are signals that help the reader interpret a message correctly. Quotation marks, for example, tell the reader, "These are the exact words spoken or written by a person." In addition, quotation marks have other related uses, all of which are discussed in this unit.

Direct Quotations

Use quotation marks to record the precise words of a speaker or a writer. As you will see below, a comma helps to separate the quotation from the rest of the sentence.

Mrs. Keller said, "The new brochure will be sent to all customers to explain to them the terms of our credit policy and their legal remedies as consumers."

"This new brochure will be sent to all customers to explain to them the terms of our credit policy and their legal remedies as consumers," said Mrs. Keller.

For long quotations (for example, quotations longer than one sentence), use a colon instead of a comma to introduce the quotation.

At the meeting Mrs. Keller said: "Develop a brochure for all our customers. We will send it to them with their charge cards or monthly bills. This new brochure will. . . ."

Because quotation marks identify the exact words someone said or wrote, they must be placed around the quoted words only, even when the quotation is interrupted.

"This new brochure," said Mrs. Keller, "will be sent to all customers to explain to them the terms of our credit policy and their legal remedies as consumers."

Terms and Expressions

Writers use quotation marks to give special significance to certain terms and expressions. In the following discussion, note how quotation marks are used for explanations and definitions, for unfamiliar terms, for slang and humorous expressions, and for translations of foreign words.

Explanations and Definitions. Use quotation marks to give special significance to expressions introduced by *so-called, marked, entitled,* and *signed.*

Their so-called "express service" delayed the delivery by at least six days!

Melissa, please be sure to mark these cartons "Refrigerate: Medical supplies enclosed."

Definitions of words or phrases are also enclosed in quotation marks. Note that the words that are defined are printed in italics (in typewritten copy, underscoring is the equivalent of italics).

The abbreviation *cps* means "characters per second" and refers to the speed with which a word processing printer prints copy.

The abbreviation cps means "characters per second" and refers to the speed with which a word processing printer prints copy.   (Note that underscoring is the same as italics.)

As used in word processing, the word wraparound means "the ability to automatically start a new line of copy."

Unfamiliar Terms. Technical terms and other terms that may be unfamiliar to the reader are generally placed in quotation marks.

Whichever model you choose, you will enjoy the superb performance of our special "EFI" engine.   ("EFI"—for "electronic fuel injection"—may be unfamiliar to many readers.)

Slang and Humorous Expressions. When slang and humorous expressions are used in writing, they are enclosed in quotation marks.

Henry explained that within the next two or three years all these old-fashioned machines would "bite the dust."

When we asked her for the summary, she told us it "ain't ready yet."   (Quotations show that the deliberate grammatical error is intended to be humorous.)

Translations. Foreign words and phrases are underscored in typewritten copy (set in italics in print). Their translations are placed in quotation marks.

Jane did not know that par avion means "by airplane."

PROOFREADING PRACTICE 1

Correct any errors in the following sentences by adding quotation marks. Can you explain your reason for each correction?

1. All folders that are marked Confidential should be placed in the safe at the end of each day.
2. The words *facilitate* and *expedite* are synonymous; both mean to make easier or simplify.
3. If you wish, Ms. Giacone said, you may pay the total in 12 monthly installments.
4. Her exact words were we can no longer afford to offer the same discounts.
5. As Mr. Emmons said, We have the best products; we must now convince our sales staff.
6. We must raise our pay scales, Mrs. Prendergast said, if we are to compete effectively.

Titles

Use quotation marks to enclose the titles of parts or chapters of books, but underscore book titles.

> Make sure that you read carefully Chapter 4, "Estimating Income Taxes," in <u>Personal Finance</u>. (Quotations for the chapter title; underscoring or italics for the book title.)

Also use quotation marks for the titles of lectures, essays, sermons, articles, mottoes, paintings, poems, sculptures, and the names of ships.

NOTE: Underscoring and italics are used for the titles of separately bound works such as magazines, newspapers, long poems, movies, operas, plays, and, of course, books.

> Last July she wrote "Stretching Your Personal Income," an article that appeared in <u>The Wall Street Journal</u>. (Article title in quotations; newspaper title underscored for italics.)

> You will definitely profit from reading Part 3, "The Successful Business Attitude," in his new book, <u>How to Reach the Top of the Corporate Ladder</u>. (Quotations for the title of part of a book; underscore for italic for the title of the book itself.)

PROOFREADING PRACTICE 2

Correct any errors in the following sentences by adding quotation marks or underscores as needed.

1. Among the magazines that we read regularly is U.S. News & World Report.
2. Her speech, Pollution and Your Health, has been well received throughout the country.
3. My supervisor, a former actor, had a minor role in the original Broadway production of The King and I.
4. The director of the Corporate Communications Department writes a weekly question-and-answer column entitled Your Company Benefits.

5. There are, as you know, variant spellings for certain words; for consistency, the spellings in this text are based on Webster's New Collegiate Dictionary.

6. Chapter 11, Preparing Budgets, is perhaps the most important part of this book.

Quotation Within a Quotation

A quotation within a quotation is enclosed in single quotation marks. (On a typewriter, single quotations are made with the apostrophe key.)

> Ms. Romanovski said, "This so-called 'once-in-a-lifetime offer' should be reported to the Consumer Affairs Bureau as a fraud."

> "Each package must be marked 'Fragile,' of course," said Mr. Dunwoody.

Punctuation at the End of Quotations

The positioning of other punctuation marks inside or outside the ending quotation mark sometimes causes confusion. Yet the rules governing such cases are few and easy to understand. Study the following three principles:

1. *Periods and Commas.* Always place periods and commas *inside* the second quotation mark.

> "As you predicted," said Ms. Coleman, "our retail sales have exceeded $1 million this year." (Note the position of the comma and the period *inside* the second quotation mark.)

2. *Colons and Semicolons.* Always place colons and semicolons *outside* the second quotation mark.

> Notice these charts in the article "Tomorrow's Interest Rates": Chart 1.4, Chart 1.9, and Chart 2.5. (Colon *outside* second quotation mark.)

> For quantity orders, the sales agent promised us a "very special deal"; however, we have no room for storing large inventories. (Semicolon *outside* second quotation mark.)

3. *Question Marks and Exclamation Points.* If the words within quotations make up a question or an exclamation, then the question mark or exclamation point belongs *with* those words—that is, it belongs *inside* the second quotation mark.

> Marcia asked, "Does Able Car Rentals still offer us a corporate discount?" (Are the words within quotations a question? Yes. Therefore, place the question mark with those words *inside* the second quotation mark.)

> Jack yelled out, "Congratulations on your promotion, Hilda!" (Are the words within quotations an exclamation? Yes. Therefore, place the exclamation mark with those words *inside* the second quotation mark.)

On the other hand, if the quoted words are just *part of* a question or an exclamation, then the question mark or exclamation point belongs to the entire sentence, not just to the quoted words. In such cases, place the question mark or exclamation point *outside* the second quotation mark.

Is Able Car Rentals the company that offers the so-called "Rent-and-Ride Special"? (Here the quoted words are *part of* the question; thus the question mark is placed *outside* the second quotation mark.)

Believe it or not, Frank again is the leader in our "Million Dollar Club"! (The quoted words are not an exclamation; they *belong to* an exclamation. Thus an exclamation point is placed *outside* the second quotation mark.)

PROOFREADING PRACTICE 3

On a separate piece of paper correct any errors in the use of quotation marks in the following sentences. Write *OK* if there are no errors.

1. Did Harry say he will be leaving "immediately after lunch"?
2. Mrs. Quimby asked, "Does anyone have a copy of the most recent chart of mortgage rates"?
3. Obviously, these two trainees have what we call "the right stuff:" intelligence, ambition, and business acumen.
4. All the cartons had been carefully marked "Fragile", but several had definitely been dropped.
5. "On Monday, January 6," said Ms. Mulrey, "we will move into our new offices".
6. As soon as he saw Mr. Traina, Kenneth cried out "Congratulations!"
7. Do you know why these stocks are called "Blue Chips?"
8. "Before he left for vacation," said Linda, "Martin signed all the contracts, didn't he"?

COMMUNICATION LABORATORY

APPLICATION EXERCISES

A. On a separate sheet of paper, correct any errors in the use of quotation marks and related other punctuation. Write *OK* if there are no errors.

1. In the column marked State Tax, enter the total sales tax for your state.
2. The word principle means "rule"; the word principal means "chief or primary."
3. Reprints of the article that Marla wrote, Advertising and the Intelligent Consumer, are available from her agency.
4. The can is clearly labeled "Warning: Inhaling fumes may cause nausea".
5. One of her several recent articles, 'Investing in Inflationary Times,' won a special journalism award.

6. Michael considered the sale of the company to a multinational conglomerate "an act of treason".

7. Did you know that the official motto for our company is "Products for Better Health"?

8. An assistant attorney general called the matter 'a rip-off—a classic con job.'

9. Is it true, asked Ms. Gilhooley, that the Securities and Exchange Commission has stopped all trading on Spartan Metals?

10. Bill said, "Ask Craig whether he would like to attend the annual Computer Show with us".

11. We have placed several 'Thank You for Not Smoking' signs in the halls and in the reception area.

12. There are several interesting articles in this week's issue of Time.

13. Yes, please do mark each envelope Confidential.

14. When asked whether she had any plans to sell the company, she replied "Absolutely not!"

15. What is the commonly used French expression that means "a social blunder?"

B. Find and correct any errors in the following sentences. If a sentence has no error, write *OK* on your paper.

1. Did Mr. Abrams say that his flight would arrive at 8 a.m. or at 8 p.m?

2. Jeff will probably stay in Denver Colorado for two days on his way to the West Coast.

3. To help us win the Merritt account, Maria submitted a creative ad a very creative ad.

4. Ms. Friedman is looking for an assistant who can: handle correspondence independently, take dictation expertly, and work well with clients.

5. Daniel knows that the equipment is very expensive however he believes it will save us money in the long term.

6. John estimated the total cost to be under $500 but he expects the price of paper to rise sharply within the next six months.

7. As soon as he saw Jenny, Otto said "Congratulations"!

8. A quantity discount is allowed, the terms are printed on the invoice.

9. Among the agents who are invited to the special sales meeting are Sal, Betty and Janice.

10. Anne Carlton who is my supervisor is the person who teaches our finance course in the evening.

11. Our distributor in Indiana reported a gross income of $4.2 million; Iowa, $3.9 million; Kansas, $3.6 million; and Michigan, $4.4 million.

12. These items must still be printed for the convention, invitations, agendas, floor plans, participants' names, and lists of nearby restaurants.

13. Vera thinks that the plan will work very smoothly, Brian is convinced that it will not.

14. Vera thinks that the plan will work very smoothly but Brian is convinced that it will not.

15. Vera thinks that the plan will work very smoothly Brian however is convinced that it will not.

C. Edit the following paragraph.

Please update the attached budget forms and return them to the district office by November 15. As you will see these forms are different than the ones we had been using. For example, one new column ("Percent Change") requires you to compute the change for each budget item as compared with last years' budget. We have enclosed a brief description, of all the changes in the new form to simplify your understanding of the new procedures. Please be sure, to read the entire description before proceeding. If you should have any questions just call the district office at 555-8429. Remember, that the enclosed materials are marked Confidential and should be locked in a safe place at the end of each day.

VOCABULARY AND SPELLING STUDIES

A. These words are often confused: *human, humane; forgo, forego.* Explain the differences.

B. In the following sentences, match the letter of the correct term with the definition in italics.

1. *One who is being taught a job* is *(a)* an instructor, *(b)* an understudy, *(c)* a trainee, *(d)* a jobber.

2. *One who has the authority to represent another in a business transaction* is *(a)* a notary public, *(b)* an agent, *(c)* a financier, *(d)* an author.

3. *One to whom a debt is owed* is *(a)* a creditor, *(b)* a cashier, *(c)* an auditor, *(d)* a referee.

COMMUNICATING FOR RESULTS

Gossip in the Reception Area. In the reception area of your office there are chairs for visitors who are waiting for various people. As you walk by this area you have often noticed employees gathered in twos and threes talking about personal aspects of business—gossip, really—while visitors can clearly overhear their conversations. The nature of the talk often concerns dissatisfaction with a supervisor or with the company in general or similar negative topics.

What effect do you think such talk will have on visitors? Do you think that your co-workers should participate in such gossip—especially within hearing of others? How do you think such talk affects the work of employees?

30 Parentheses and the Apostrophe

Two more signals, parentheses and the apostrophe, will help you improve the effectiveness of your messages. Study their uses in this unit.

Parentheses

Like commas and dashes, parentheses may be used to set off words that give additional information. What, then, are the differences among these three punctuation marks? *nonessential, unnecessary info*

Parentheses for Additional Information. While dashes emphasize the information that they set off, parentheses *de*emphasize the words that they enclose. Commas are generally used to set off additional information that flows smoothly into the sentence—information that does not require the stronger break of dashes or parentheses. The following examples show typical uses of parentheses, dashes, and commas to set off additional (or parenthetical) information.

dash — to emphasize
parentheses — deemphasize
smooth transition to — comma.
a sentence

Sales for January reached $1.2 million—a 27 percent increase over December sales!—according to these figures.   (The dashes provide emphasis to the words set off.)

The cost of paper rose about $2.50 a ream (approximately 11 percent over last year's price).   (The information enclosed in parentheses is considered less important; the parentheses deemphasize these words.)

The cost of paper, as Ms. Jensen explained this morning, is rising at a rate of approximately 11 percent a year.   (The words set off by commas provide information that is obviously additional, unnecessary information. But because these words flow smoothly into the sentence, they are separated by commas. Dashes and parentheses are inappropriate.)

Other Uses of Parentheses. Besides their task of setting off additional information, parentheses are also used to enclose (1) references or directions, (2) numbers or letters in enumerations, and (3) repetitions of dollar amounts in legal writing.

A chart of interest rates (see page 343) is provided to simplify your computations. (Reference.)

Since 1983, Addison Appliances has paid its monthly balance promptly (see the annual credit reports attached). (Direction.)

For your convenience we have enclosed (1) our latest brochure, (2) a handy order form, and (3) a credit application form. (Numbers in an enumeration.)

For and in consideration of the sum of five hundred dollars ($500.00), the party of the first part hereby. . . ." (Repetitions of dollar amounts in legal writing.)

CLASS PRACTICE 1

Insert parentheses wherever they are needed in the following sentences.

1. A more detailed explanation of this procedure is given later see Appendix B for your convenience.
2. Among the multipart forms that we use daily are 1 invoice forms, 2 purchase requisitions, and 3 cash-advance forms.
3. Her new office it's located on the fifth floor occupies about 2,000 square feet of space.
4. Use the example shown earlier page 112 to estimate total tax.
5. She said to call her office 555-6172 if you should have any questions.
6. In estimating the total cost, use the chart provided see page 89 and add the sales tax for your state.

Parentheses With Other Marks of Punctuation. Parentheses can be used (1) to enclose words within a sentence or (2) to enclose a sentence that stands alone. Let's look at each category separately.

To Enclose Words Within a Sentence. Follow these rules when the words enclosed in parentheses are *part of* a sentence.

1. Do not use any mark of punctuation *before* the opening parenthesis.

   If we are able to ship your order before July 18 (and we sincerely hope that it is possible to), we will call to inform you of the new date.

2. After the closing (or *second*) parenthesis, place any punctuation that the sentence ordinarily would require.

   When Ms. Esposito arrives (she will be on a 4 p.m. flight), we will take a taxi to the hotel. (What is the normal punctuation needed after *When Ms. Esposito arrives*? A comma. Therefore, place the comma after the second parenthesis.)

   Have you visited the Computer Store (the one on Main Street)? (After *Have you visited the Computer Store*, what punctuation would you ordinarily use? A question mark. Therefore, place the question mark after the closing parenthesis.)

   Tanya originally managed our district office in Portland (Oregon); in 1983 she moved to our headquarters office as Director of Sales. (After Portland, what punctuation would you use? A semicolon. Therefore, place the semicolon after the closing parenthesis.)

3. Place *inside* the closing parenthesis the following marks only:

   a. A question mark (if the words within the parentheses form a question).

   Bernice said that the standard discount is 25 percent (or did she say 35 percent?) (Are the words within parentheses a question? Yes. Place the question mark inside the closing parenthesis.)

   b. An exclamation point (if the words within parentheses form an exclamation).

   We may be eligible for a substantial discount (perhaps as much as 50 percent off!). (Because the words within parentheses are an exclamation, the exclamation point is placed before the closing parenthesis.)

   c. A period (if the period belongs to an abbreviation).

   Mark left early to meet a client at the airport (his client will arrive at 7:45 a.m.).

4. Do not capitalize the first word within parentheses (unless that word is a proper noun). This rule applies even if the words within the parentheses are an independent clause because the entire parenthetical element is *part of* a sentence.

   Yesterday our new front-wheel-drive vehicles arrived (have you seen them yet?), but they will not be displayed until September 23. (Lowercase for *have*.)

   You will find this reference helpful (Chapter 8 especially). (Capital for *Chapter* because it is the title of a specific chapter.)

   To Enclose a Sentence That Stands Alone. When the words enclosed in parentheses are not *part of* a sentence but are entirely independent, the first word is capitalized and the end punctuation is placed *inside* the closing parenthesis.

   The question of creating a more effective sales-incentive plan arises every year. (Indeed, at our annual sales conventions, this plan is the first item on the agenda!)

   Discuss these personnel problems with Mike Horvath. (He was recently promoted to Director of Personnel.)

CLASS PRACTICE 2

Apply the punctuation principles you have just learned. Insert punctuation marks in the following sentences.

1. The manager of our department cannot handle this problem (she will be in Europe until October 15) but perhaps her assistant can help you.
2. I estimate that you will need at least 2 liters (that is, a little more than 2 quarts) however, you should check the manufacturer's specifications.
3. You may amortize such costs over five years, if you wish. (for more infor-

mation concerning government regulations for amortization, see the enclosed brochure.)

4. Emily prefers investing in bonds (municipal, tax-free bonds) on the other hand, her sister claims that stocks provide greater long-term profits.
5. Next November, Barney will move to Oakland (he will become vice president of our regional office!)
6. He immediately tried to 1) call Ms. Haskells and 2) contact our district office.

The Apostrophe

The primary use of the apostrophe is in forming possessives of nouns. In addition, the apostrophe is commonly used in contractions. Less often, the apostrophe is used to form "special" plurals and to show where numbers have been omitted.

In Possessives of Nouns. As you already learned, the apostrophe is used to indicate the possessive forms of nouns.

Noun	Possessive Form
manager	my *manager's* office
managers	our *managers'* offices
teenager	that *teenager's* subscription
teenagers	those *teenagers'* subscriptions
Mr. Smith	*Mr. Smith's* account
the Smiths	*the Smiths'* account

In Contractions. Contractions are shortened forms of words, such as *won't* for "will not," *shouldn't* for "should not," *isn't* for "is not," and *aren't* for "are not."

The results of the survey *aren't* what we anticipated.   ("Are not.")

In "Special" Plurals. The apostrophe is *not* generally used to form plurals; however, an exception is the plural form of a letter or of a word that might otherwise be confusing without the apostrophe.

For some strange reason, this printer is printing i's and a's very sloppily.   (Without the apostrophes, the plural forms of the letters *i* and *a* might be misread as the words *is* and *as.*)

The apostrophe is not necessary for the plural forms of most capital letters (of course, the plurals of *A*, *I*, and *U* are exceptions). But plurals of lowercase letters (*t's* and *h's*, for example) and lowercase abbreviations (*f.o.b.'s*) could easily be confused without apostrophes.

To Show Omitted Numerals. The apostrophe is used in year numbers such as '79 and '84 to show that the first two numbers—*19*—have been omitted.

CLASS PRACTICE 3

Practice what you have just learned by inserting apostrophes as needed in the following sentences.

1. Both my assistants were graduated in the Class of 85.
2. Customers shouldnt send cash payments in the mail.
3. The overuse of Is in this letter shows that it was written from the writer's, not from the reader's, point of view.
4. We asked Glorias secretary to help us with this small project while Gloria is out of town.
5. My broker said that 80 and 82 were her best sales years ever.
6. Please ask Mr. Fishers agent to review this contract.

COMMUNICATION LABORATORY

APPLICATION EXERCISES

A. On a separate sheet of paper, indicate the correct punctuation for the following sentences.

1. Whenever were ready to proceed, we will set up an appointment with our lawyers.
2. For overseas travel, we suggest that you arrive at the airport at least one hour before your flight is scheduled to depart (that is, no later than 2 p.m.)
3. Because the price of zinc has risen drastically (almost 75 percent over the last two years) our chemists are exploring the possibility of substituting a less expensive metal.
4. Only Anthonys persistence saved us from a costly error—a very costly error.
5. No, employees under the age of 30 arent eligible to join the pension plan.
6. The founder of our company contributes generously to Columbia University (she was a member of the Class of 52).
7. Tomorrow, Sylvia will receive her annual bonus check (for a record-breaking $10,000!)
8. When you have completed a final draft of your résumé (also called a "data sheet") please send me a copy.
9. Mrs. Sparks joined our firm in 1975 (she was then a junior partner) she retired in 1984.

10. Please complete and submit these forms (see the attached envelope) a tax-withholding form, a life insurance form, and a medical history form.
11. To change the number of dependents you now claim, ask the personnel supervisor for a W-4 form (call Extension 6785)
12. Send this copy to Agnes Shields (shes on the 35th floor).
13. Weekly status reports are due on Tuesdays (or are they due on Wednesdays).
14. As Mr. McCauley carefully explained, theres no reason to expect a sudden upturn in the economy.
15. A 50 percent discount (can you imagine that) will be offered until January 30.

B. Find and correct any errors in the following sentences. Write *OK* for any sentence that has no error.

1. Ms. Hancock instructed us as follows: "Our first priority is to explore the possibility of increasing our exports to Asia".
2. The original lease agreement was negotiated in 1979 (it expires in 1989, doesn't it).
3. Mr. Franciosa replied "Our consumer survey indicates a strong preference for a better-quality product."
4. The committee quickly acknowledged, of course, Bruce Greensteins extremely creative efforts.
5. Alvin is the chief product manager for our division, Jason is the director of marketing.
6. Have you already discussed with the ad writers our strategy for promoting this product.
7. Jenora is an experienced, methodical and ambitious programmer.
8. The form that you need (popularly called a W-4) is available from the personnel manager.
9. The messenger service promised us that the packages would be delivered before 5 p.m..
10. Each applicant must complete this form. Before he or she can be scheduled for any interviews.
11. Arthur Paulson is the district manager for California; Eileen Grey, West Virginia; Nancy LaRocca, North Carolina; and Otto VanCamp, Rhode Island.
12. Helen did not agree to the terms of the contract, and returned it immediately.
13. Theodore asked us when we will begin our television advertising campaign?
14. You must submit your bids before March 30. If you want your estimate to be considered.
15. "Our first priority" Ms. Hancock instructed us, "is to explore the possibility of increasing our exports to Asia."

C. Edit and revise the following rough draft paragraph.

The enclosed booklet discusses business ethics for all Blanton employee's. The book clearly tells you, what you can expect of Blanton and what Blanton expects of you. As you will see among the topics covered are conflict's of interest, the rules governing outside employment, handleing confidential information, relations with suppliers, and your responsability to report any violations of this code. Blanton Manufacturing has a worldwide reputation for integraty. All of us make every effort to maintan this reputation.

VOCABULARY AND SPELLING STUDIES

A. These words are often confused: *access, excess; maybe, may be.* Explain the differences.

B. Use your dictionary to look up the two different meanings and pronunciations of each of the following words: *consummate* (adjective and verb), *invalid* (noun and adjective), *refuse* (verb and noun), and *entrance* (verb and noun). Next to each word write the part of speech, the pronunciation, and the meaning for that particular word.

C. Fill in the blanks with *y, i,* or *ie,* whichever is correct.

1. bus___ness
2. dr___ness
3. occup___ing
4. rel___ance
5. territor___s
6. attorne___s

COMMUNICATING FOR RESULTS

Using References. On her first day on the job, Carla was shown her new office and was given the free time to arrange everything in it to her liking. On the shelves Carla has found a dictionary, a thesaurus, a ZIP Code directory, an atlas, an almanac, and a business writer's reference manual. Carla does not have much shelf space, so she decides to put these books in the storeroom. She asks you if you think that is a good idea. What advice would you give to Carla?

31

Capitalization

Capital letters make words distinctive. Because they help words to stand out, capitals are used in special cases—for example, to show the reader where a new sentence starts or which words in a title are the most important words. Writers, therefore, must use these special signals correctly. In this unit you will review some of the well-known basic uses of capital letters. In addition, you will learn to avoid some of the common errors writers make with capital letters.

First Words

One of the routine uses of capital letters is to set off first words. Examples follow.

1. First word in a sentence or a group of words used as a sentence:

   In April Mr. Cohen and Ms. Ways will begin planning our convention for next year. (The word *in* ordinarily is not capitalized; here, of course, it is the first word of the sentence and is therefore capitalized.)

   Andrew asked whether we would cancel the meeting. *Definitely!* (Note that *definitely* is capitalized. Although it is not a complete sentence, it is used as a sentence.)

2. First word in a direct quotation:

   Andrew asked, "*Will* we cancel the meeting with the advertising agency?" (The quotation is part of a sentence, yet the first word of the quotation is capitalized.)

3. First word in a question within a sentence:

   All of us are wondering, *Will* this equipment be shipped on schedule? (An independent question is included within the sentence, and the capital letter for the first word of that question helps set it off.)

4. First word of each entry in a list or an outline:

   The first mailing will include:

   1. *A* covering letter explaining the special offer we are making.
   2. *A* brochure illustrating the entire product line.

3. *Our* credit-application form.
4. *An* order form.
5. *A* service contract form.
6. *A* reply envelope.

Names of Persons

Names of persons are proper nouns and must be capitalized. The capital letter tells the reader that this is the name of a specific person.

Because there are so many similarities in the spellings of names, be especially careful to follow the exact spelling of a person's name. Note, for example, the following common, similar names:

Steven, Stephen
Carol, Carroll, Caryl
Smith, Smithe, Smyth
Macmillan, MacMillan, McMillan
John Von Hoffman, Jon von Hoffman

CLASS PRACTICE 1

Provide capitals for the following sentences. Be sure to explain why each of your choices must be capitalized.

1. the most important question is, can we complete the entire project on time?
2. sherry asked, "is it possible to increase this research budget by about 15 percent?"
3. please call caryl jacobson to tell her about the change in our meeting time.
4. can we deliver the entire shipment by next week? absolutely!
5. of course, we will notify you within ten days of the time we receive your application form.
6. only connie and daniel were asked to attend the conference.

Names of Places

These few rules will help you to capitalize place names correctly:

1. Capitalize the names of countries and major geographic areas, streets, parks, rivers, shopping centers, buildings, and so on.

United States	Canada
Georgia	Ontario
Augusta	Toronto
Fourth Street	Blake Avenue
Raritan River	Modesto Park
Willowbrook Mall	Sears Tower

2. Capitalize the word *city* only when it is part of the official name of the city: *Kansas City* and *New York City,* but *the city of Provo.*

3. Capitalize the word *state* only when it follows the name of a state: *Pennsylvania State,* but *the state of Pennsylvania.*

4. Capitalize the word *the* only when it is part of the official name: *The Dalles* (a city in Oregon), *The Hague* (capital of the Netherlands).

5. Capitalize *North, South, East,* and *West* when they are used to refer to specific sections of the country.

Our headquarters office is in the *South.* We plan to open our first district office in the *North* by next September.   (Referring to specific sections.)

But do not capitalize such names when they are used simply to indicate direction:

The warehouse is about 6 miles *east* of Albany and 2 miles *south* of our store.

CLASS PRACTICE 2

Which place names should be capitalized in the following sentences?

1. Next year our organization is planning to have its annual dinner at a restaurant in the twin towers in new york city.

2. Two districts in the south reported above-average sales in June and July.

3. Most of the time we spend in the state of oklahoma will be in oklahoma city.

4. We have a very successful office in canada—I believe it is in manitoba.

5. The newly constructed oakdale mall, which is only a few blocks north of oakdale park, will be open in two weeks.

Names of Things

You have already seen how some proper nouns (the names of specific persons and places) are capitalized. To complete your understanding of when to capitalize proper nouns, you will now learn when to capitalize the names of specific *things.*

Organization Names. Capitalize the names of specific companies, associations, societies, commissions, schools, political parties, clubs, religious groups, and government agencies and bureaus.

Metropolitan Area Graphic Arts Company
Association of American Publishers
National Society for the Endowment of the Arts
Securities and Exchange Commission
Iowa Central Community College
Democratic Party
Hillside Chess Club
Terrill Road Orthopedic Clinic
Federal Bureau of Investigation

Names of departments in your own organization are usually capitalized unless they are preceded by a word other than *the*. Names of departments in organizations other than your own are not capitalized.

Payroll Department   BUT: our payroll department
Manufacturing Division   every manufacturing division

Product Names. Capitalize the names of commercial products such as *Coca-Cola, Kleenex,* and *Ivory Snow.* But do not capitalize the common nouns that identify the general class of the product.

Ivory soap
Kleenex tissues
Xerox machines
Zenith televisions

Historical Events and Documents. Capitalize the names of historical events or historical periods, specific treaties, bills, acts, and laws.

the Vietnam War
the Bicentennial
the Medicare Act
National Secretaries Week

Holidays, Months, and Days of the Week. Capitalize the names of holidays, months, and days of the week.

Veterans Day   Christmas
Passover   Thanksgiving
Memorial Day   Fourth of July
September   October
Monday   Friday

Do not capitalize the names of the seasons—*winter, spring, summer,* and *fall.*

CLASS PRACTICE 3

Which words in the following sentences should be capitalized? Which words should not be capitalized?

1. Mary Ellen will be attending Mississippi state college for women beginning next september.
2. One of our Country's favorite holidays is the fourth of july.
3. Herman, the supervisor of the production staff, is a member of the rotary club.
4. The United States government printing office offers these brochures at low prices.
5. Last week Ms. Verona presented a case before the supreme court.
6. After Mr. Syms was graduated from Fairfax high school, he attended Kirkwood community college.

7. During the intermission we will serve coke and coffee.
8. For two weeks only we will have a special sale on General Electric Refrigerators.

Proper Adjectives

Because proper adjectives are derived from proper nouns, proper adjectives are also capitalized.

Mexican art   Chinese dialects
German food   Italian operas

Headings

In headings and in titles of books and articles, capitalize the first and last words and all major words. Consider as major words all words except:

1. The articles *a*, *an*, and *the*.

    How to Become an *Expert in* the *Stock Market*   (Book title.)

2. Conjunctions with fewer than four letters, such as *and*, *but*, *or*, *nor*, *as*, and *if*.

    "Stocks *and* Bonds *and* You"   (Article title.)

3. Prepositions with fewer than four letters, such as *at*, *for*, *out*, *up*, and *in*.

    Life *in* the Twenty-First Century   (Heading.)

    "Investments With Potential *for* the Future"   (Article.)

    "What Are We Waiting *For?*"   (Article. Note that *for* is capitalized because it is the last word in the title.)

    For hyphenated words, treat each part of the compound individually.

    "An Up-to-Date System for Controlling Inventories"

    First-Class Travel on a Second-Class Checkbook

CLASS PRACTICE 4

Correct any errors in the use of capitals in the following sentences.

1. She wrote an interesting article entitled "A Foolproof System For Making Lots Of Money."
2. Trent Publications also offers spanish and french editions of its magazines.
3. Martha is currently negotiating a deal with an asian exporting company.
4. You will find the information you need in the section "Up-To-Date Reference Works For The Business Writer."
5. Her latest column is an interview with a yugoslavian diplomat.
6. Sheila wrote a humorous article entitled "What We Really Need In The House Of Representatives."

Personal and Official Titles

Whenever a person has a title that is written before his or her name, capitalize that title.

> Captain M. R. Haggarty
> Professor Marilyn J. Frigosi
> Reverend Carlton Dempster

Titles that are written after names are not capitalized unless:

1. The title is that of a high government official.

> Among the scheduled speakers is Gerald Weems, a *Senator* who is a leader in environmental protection.   (*Senator* is considered a high official.)

2. The title appears not in the context of a sentence but on a displayed line, such as in an envelope address or a signature line in a letter.

> Joan P. Stimpson, Treasurer   (In the signature line of a letter from Ms. Stimpson.)

> Ms. Joan P. Stimpson, Treasurer   (Part of an envelope address or an inside address of a letter to Ms. Stimpson.)

In all other cases, do not capitalize a title that follows a person's name. In addition, do not capitalize *ex-* and *-elect* and *former* and *late* when they are joined to titles.

> A news report stated that *ex*-President Gerald Ford will be in the city later this evening.

> Mayor-*elect* Rubinstein will appoint a task force, she said, within the next two weeks.

> Yes, *former* Governor Hamilton is scheduled to meet the press later this week.

Miscellaneous Rules

Short Forms. Do not capitalize short forms such as *company*, *corporation*, and *college* when they are used in place of full names.

> Edna plans to attend Del Mar College beginning next fall. As you know, the *college* is in Corpus Christi, Texas.

> Tom and I work in the Research Department. The *department* is now conducting some interesting studies, the results of which should aid the general welfare.

However, capitalize short forms that refer to major government bodies, prominent national officials, and well-known places.

> Capitol Hill has been Rosemary's beat since she became a reporter. After several years, she has earned the respect of everyone on the *Hill*.

Other short forms that are capitalized are the *Bureau* (referring to the Federal Bureau of Investigation), the *House* (for the House of Representatives), and the *Coast* (for the West Coast).

Letter Parts. Capitalize the first word and any title in the salutation of a letter (and any proper names, of course). Capitalize only the first word in a complimentary closing.

Dear Ms. Sinclair:
Dear Margaret:

Sincerely yours,
Cordially yours,

Family Titles. Capitalize words denoting family relationships only when they are used as a part of a person's name or as a substitute for a person's name.

Mother   BUT: my mother
Aunt Bernice   your aunt

School Subjects. Capitalize the names of languages and of specific numbered courses. Do not capitalize the names of subjects (proper nouns or adjectives are exceptions).

French   Italian
Accounting 101   mathematics
history   business English

COMMUNICATION LABORATORY

APPLICATION EXERCISES

A. On a separate sheet of paper, indicate the correct capitalization of words in the following sentences.

1. After we meet with the manager of our tokyo office, we will take a two-week tour of the orient.
2. One of the articles that maria suggested is "How To Own And Operate Your Own Business."
3. By March 15 we expect to have all our employees in our new quarters in the henson building on park avenue.
4. About 25 percent of the money will be given to the catholic relief fund and the jewish welfare fund.
5. The head of our Benefits Department, Benjamin Van Buren, is now in puerto rico.
6. Our Spring styles will be slightly delayed, but the brochures will still be available on time.
7. Our television spots were preempted by the president's nationwide news conference.
8. If the senator arrives at 7:30, we will begin the ceremony at 8 p.m.
9. Marla Kregsky, Treasurer of Apex Metals Inc., presented the plan to the Advertising Department on January 14.

10. Among the sponsors of the television series are the manufacturers of Kleenex Tissues and Westinghouse Refrigerators.
11. Our Company offers several interesting personal-development courses, including one course that is called "Time Management For Business People."
12. Our conventions are held on a rotating basis. According to the schedule, next year's meeting will be in the south; the following year, in the east.
13. Theresa very strongly recommends reading this article: "the Secret To Sales Success."
14. In her spare time Ms. Stengel does volunteer work for the willow grove presbyterian church.
15. When we opened this district office, we received invaluable help from the Atlanta chamber of commerce.

B. Correct any errors in the following sentences.

1. The title of her speech is "Creative Planning For Executives."
2. Lowell especially enjoyed visiting our stores on the east coast.
3. Thomas has worked for the Company since 1983, when he was graduated from a Business School.
4. Chicago Illinois is the most convenient site for the meeting.
5. The managers of this division has agreed to meet to discuss these matters further.
6. Ms. Phelps the manager of the vogue department store has an office on the fifth floor.
7. Baron's Pharmaceuticals is one of our largest suppliers, its main office is here in Westfield.
8. Oil exploration is still continuing along the gulf of Mexico.
9. Our first store in the east opened in delaware in January of last year.
10. If Mario had only wrote to the customer sooner, he could have avoided this lawsuit.
11. According to Vernon, the idea to reorganize the department was her's.
12. Perhaps Leon and myself could help you coordinate the first two sessions.
13. Graham works out of the Des Moines office, Larry works out of the Cleveland office.
14. The chairperson of the panel Clarice Brantley is the one who developed this outline for the conference.
15. Is Jenny Langsley the person who is responsible for pensions.

C. Most of the errors in the following paragraph are capitalization errors—but not all. Find and correct each error.

The keynote speaker for next saturdays' dinner meeting of the Glenwood civic <u>association</u> will be Dr. Vanessa Gravilek, a Former Professor of Psychology. The title of Dr. Gravileks' speech is "The Need for Improved Productivity among Office Workers." Admission is free to Members.

VOCABULARY AND SPELLING STUDIES

A. These words are often confused: *credible, creditable; metal, medal, meddle.* Explain the differences.

B. Identify the synonyms in the following groups of words.

1. imminent, professional, volatile, approaching
2. genuine, spacious, commodious, infantile
3. superficial, ridiculous, shallow, serious
4. prestige, fairness, renown, panorama
5. disparage, value, discredit, distrust

C. What is the correct plural form for each of the following nouns?

1. runner-up
2. agenda
3. handful
4. bill of sale
5. go-between
6. analysis

COMMUNICATING FOR RESULTS

Telephone Effectiveness. You overhear your co-worker Edward answering the phone one day. The conversation goes like this:

> Edward: Hello.
> Caller: Who is this?
>
> Edward: Whom do you want to speak to?
> Caller: I was trying to reach someone in the Trust Department.
>
> Edward: This is the Trust Department. May I help you?
> Caller: Yes—is Ronnie Lipton there?
>
> Edward: Yes.
> Caller: May I speak to her, please?

How effective do you think this conversation is? Suggest some ways that it could be improved.

32 Abbreviations

If you look closely at the way we speak and write, you quickly see that Americans certainly enjoy taking shortcuts! Perhaps the most obvious indicator of our preference for shortcuts is our use of abbreviations. *CRT* (for "cathode-ray tube"), *EFI* (for "electronic fuel injection"), and *WP* (for "word processing") are just a few of the abbreviations that have been coined in the recent past and are already becoming common.

As with all the other tools of writing, abbreviations are indeed helpful, but there are rules for their use. As you study this unit, you will master the correct ways to use abbreviations in your writing.

Personal Titles

Because we are so accustomed to using abbreviations such as *Mr.*, *Mrs.*, and *Dr.*, writers are often tempted to abbreviate all titles with names. However, as you will see below, not all titles should be abbreviated.

Titles After Names. Always abbreviate the following titles when they are written after a name:

Jr. (for "Junior")
Sr. (for "Senior")
B.S. (for "Bachelor of Science")
Ph.D. (for "Doctor of Philosophy")
D.D. (for "Doctor of Divinity")

Likewise, abbreviate all other academic titles that follow a name.

Elana Caruso, M.D.
Alan Howell Gray, LL.D.

Titles Before Names. Always abbreviate the following titles when they are used before personal names: *Dr.*, *Mr.*, *Messrs.* (the plural of *Mr.*), *Mrs.*, *Ms.*, and *Mses.* or *Mss.* (plural forms of *Ms.*). The titles *Miss* and *Misses* are not abbreviations and should not be followed by periods.

Miss Jean Moore
Ms. Carlotta Mendez
Mr. Howard Newton
The Messrs. Newton

In general, spell out all other titles used with personal names.

Professor Harris P. Truscott
Senator Lautenberg
Governor McKinley
Officer Jenkins

Military Titles. In formal correspondence spell out long military titles. In informal correspondence you may abbreviate long military titles.

Brigadier General Clay B. Flagg   (Formal)

Lt. Col. Marilyn C. Hoolihan   (Informal)

Titles of Respect. *Reverend* and *Honorable* are titles of respect used in addressing the clergy and government officials of certain rank. In formal usage, spell out these titles and use the word *the* before them. In informal usage, omit the word *the* and use the abbreviation *Rev.* or *Hon.* if you wish.

the Reverend James K. Filbert   (Formal)

Rev. James K. Filbert   (Informal)

the Honorable Clarissa J. Fenimore (Formal)

Hon. Clarissa J. Fenimore (Informal)

Organization Names

The name of an organization should be written precisely as the organization prefers. Thus you should abbreviate *Company, Corporation, Association, Railroad,* and so on, only when the organization itself uses the abbreviation officially (for example, on its letterhead).

All-capital abbreviations, long used as radio stations' call letters, are now very commonly adopted by companies and other organizations of all kinds. The following abbreviations, for example, are seen and heard almost every day:

AT&T	American Telephone and Telegraph
AMA	American Medical Association
YWCA	Young Women's Christian Association
IRS	Internal Revenue Service
NLRB	National Labor Relations Board
AFL-CIO	American Federation of Labor–Congress of Industrial Organizations
AAA	American Automobile Association
WABC	(Radio station call letters)

CLASS PRACTICE 1

Which words should be abbreviated in the following sentences, and which ones should be spelled out? Write *OK* if no changes are needed.

1. Has Doctor Murchison signed all the contracts for this afternoon's meeting?
2. The keynote speaker for the banquet will be Rev. Andrew G. Callahan.
3. Among the candidates for the newly formed position is Robt. Pulaski.
4. If Mister Perlmutter approves this requisition, we can have the equipment delivered within a week.
5. Did you know that Gov. Green is a former partner of this law firm?
6. Anna works at an AT&T branch office in Bedminster, New Jersey.

Punctuating Abbreviations

The usage of punctuation with abbreviations varies, as you will see below. As you read the following discussions, remember to use a business writer's handbook whenever you are not sure how to treat an abbreviation.

Organization Names. You just saw that all-capital organization names such as *ABC*, *IBM*, and *RCA* are usually written solid—no space, no periods. When in doubt, check the official name on the letterhead of that organization, or check a comprehensive reference manual for guidance.

Academic Degrees. Abbreviations of academic degrees are written with a period after each element but no space between elements.

M.A.	Master of Arts
M.B.A.	Master of Business Administration
Ph.D.	Doctor of Philosophy

Business Terms. Besides *Co.*, *Inc.*, *Mr.*, *Mrs.*, and the other abbreviations that were already discussed, the following abbreviations are routinely used in business correspondence. Note the punctuation with each.

a.m.	p.m.
PS:	Enc.
cc:	No.

NOTE: Although the abbreviation *No.* is perfectly acceptable, it should be used only when followed by a numeral (*Policy No. 174-363*), and it should not be used at the beginning of a sentence.

In addition, the two-letter state abbreviations are commonly used in address blocks of letters and envelopes, particularly when ZIP Codes are used. Generally speaking, however, avoid abbreviating words in routine business letters and memos. When space is tight in invoices and other forms, abbreviations may be not only accepted but unavoidable. But in letters and memos the rule is, "Spell it out."

Our policy for deliveries is to post a charge to the customer's account or add the charge to a c.o.d. amount. (The words *charge, account,* and *amount* may be abbreviated *chg., acct.,* and *amt.* in business forms but not in business letters or memos. Note that *c.o.d.*—or *COD*—is perfectly acceptable.)

Units of Measure. In general business correspondence, units of measure (both customary and metric) are spelled out.

Each container holds 9.5 *ounces* of the solvent.

In technical writing, abbreviations such as the following are used:

ft	foot	g	gram
in	inch	kg	kilogram
oz	ounce	m	meter
gal	gallon	mm	millimeter

Refer to an authoritative reference for a comprehensive list of accepted abbreviations.

Chemical Symbols. Do not use periods after chemical symbols.

Na   Cl   H   O

City and State Names. Never abbreviate the names of cities. No matter how long the name of a city, spell it out. In addition, never abbreviate *Fort, Port, Mount,* and *Point* in place names.

For abbreviations of state names, use the U.S. Postal Service's two-letter abbreviations. Refer to a reference book for a complete list of the official abbreviations.

Miscellaneous. Important dates (as in legal documents) are often identified by the abbreviation *A.D.* (for *Anno Domini,* which means "in the year of our Lord"). *A.D.* is always written before the year: *A.D. 1985.*

The abbreviation *B.C.* ("before Christ") is always written after the year.

Archeologists believe that the discovery may date as far back as 250 B.C.

Plurals of Abbreviations

Check a reference manual whenever you are not sure of the plural form of an abbreviation. Note, for example, the following plurals:

No.	Nos.
dept.	depts.
p.	pp.
mo.	mos.
Mr.	Messrs.
Ms.	Mses. (or Mss.)
Mrs.	Mesdames

As you have learned, other plurals may be formed differently:

Ph.D.   Ph.D.s
CPA   CPAs
f.o.b.   f.o.b.'s
c.o.d.   c.o.d.'s

CLASS PRACTICE 2

Are abbreviations used correctly in the following sentences? Should any additional words be abbreviated?

1. We will stay in Dallas for two days; then we will continue on to Ft. Worth.
2. Next Tues. Mister Valdez will give expert testimony at a hearing in N.Y.
3. When Doctor Franklin approves this purchase order, we will send the orig. copy to the Order Dept.
4. One attorney, Clara Rheinhold, wants to review Policy No. 1-576-982; send a copy to her at our Calif. office.
5. Among the computer comps. that have agreed to display their products are Apple, Wang, I.B.M., and Radio Shack.
6. Because Mister Jamison is away on an emergency, his 2 PM meeting has been changed to Thurs. at 4 PM.
7. Grace estimates that we'll need no more than three yds of cloth for the display table.
8. An interpreter translated the words as "signed this seventh day of May, 1100 A.D."

COMMUNICATION LABORATORY

APPLICATION EXERCISES

A. On a separate sheet of paper, make any corrections needed in the following sentences. Write *OK* for each sentence that has no error.

1. Francis X. Simmons, PhD, is the director of the Training Department.
2. Full payment of all outstanding premiums on Policy Number 83-1334-8475 must be received no later than June 14.
3. Our CPA checked the policy with the I.R.S., of course, and received full approval.
4. The person who was named to chair the committee is William Carlos McKenzie Junior.
5. To emphasize our support of the legislation, we have written to Sen. Stern.
6. Dr. Mulholland has been a member of the A.M.A. since 1983, when he was graduated from medical school.

7. He plans to visit Pt. Arthur on his return from Beaumont, Texas.
8. John Warburton, LLD, will meet with us to discuss union-related matters at 3 PM today.
9. If your package weighs more than 5 lbs., then you should consider sending it by another method.
10. In these chemical equations, the symbol Fe. represents iron.
11. Gov. Claybourne is scheduled to attend the fund raiser on Sat., isn't she?
12. Because the Apex Chemicals account is now several mos. overdue, we have turned the matter over to our lawyer.
13. Sandra is now working toward her M.B.A. degree, which she expects to complete next June.
14. Our agency represents W.K.O.K. and W.N.F.C., two of the most prestigious radio stations in this area.
15. Mike and Rhoda have submitted applications to AT&T, IBM, RCA, and other major corporations.

B. Find and correct all the errors in the following sentences. Write *OK* if a sentence has no error.

1. Of course, we are delighted to help this worthy cause. Because we know that the needy in our area will benefit from our contribution.
2. Arthur Bancroft, who is in charge of manufacturing has negotiated long-range contracts with our major suppliers.
3. Doctor Yolanda Demerest has joined the clinic staff, she was formerly on the staff at Montclair Hospital.
4. The quantity discount is very generous, however, we have inadequate space to store the materials.
5. Upon hearing the cost estimate, Ms. Flint asked, "Why has the cost of materials increased more than 50 percent in the past year"?
6. Mr. Aaron wanted to know whether we should send the contract to the company lawyer for approval?
7. Jennifer has wrote a very convincing report supporting our need for additional clerical help.
8. During the past year market demand for italian-style furniture has increased drastically.
9. The order was supposed to have been shipped to Springfield Illinois; instead, it was shipped to Springfield Masssachusetts.
10. If you decide to take advantage of this special opportunity. Just complete the enclosed order form and return it to us before March 30.
11. Most of the managers in this company has volunteered to help in this charity drive.
12. Helen has been on the telephone all morning in an effort to collect money from several past-due accts.
13. Marla said "Does anyone know the procedures for requesting reimbursement for tuition?"

14. "Look in Chapter 3 of the official policy manual," Nancy replied, "For information concerning the company's tuition-refund program."

15. Max Edwards, the district manager for Ontario, will be in the office on May 12. To discuss the development of some potential new products.

C. Revise the following paragraph.

The personal computer market is growing tremendously each year. I.B.M., Radio Shack, Apple, and other companies, are predicting increased sales of personal computers for this year and the next. We have decided therefore, to study the potential of a new magazine for owners of personal computers, we have tentatively called this magazine The Home Computer. The Harrison Agency will conduct a feasibility study to determine the potential, of such a magazine. By September 30 we expect to have, all the information necessary to make our decision.

VOCABULARY AND SPELLING STUDIES

A. These words are often confused: *continual, continuous; magnificent, munificent.* Explain the differences.

B. For each of the following words, name an *antonym*—a word that is opposite in meaning.

1. different
2. complicated
3. sensible
4. objective
5. receive
6. careful

C. Add *el* or *le* to each of the following words.

1. lab___
2. mod___
3. gigg___
4. nick___
5. pick___
6. whist___

COMMUNICATING FOR RESULTS

Pompous Prose. A co-worker wrote the following paragraph copying the style she had read in an old report. How would you rewrite this to make it sound clear and natural?

Henry Marcusi terminated his employment with our organization as of the first day of August, A.D. 1983, citing as his reason the acquisition of another position with a firm also headquartered in this city. The same Mr. Marcusi performed exceptionally well in his position here, which was as media planner in our advertising department. In his tenure with our firm (the extent of which was precisely three years six months) he always achieved the established goals within budget and on schedule. Our consensus is that we would consider reemploying him if he were to apply to us at some future time for a position with us.

U · N · I · T

33 Numbers

Numbers provide our communications with specific information—quantities, dollar amounts, percentages, measurements, dates. The importance of numbers and the precision with which they are used are obviously critical to accurate communication. Begin, then, to study when to write numbers in words and when to write them in figures.

Numbers Written as Words

Generally, numbers are expressed in figures in business correspondence. However, there are occasions when numbers are written in words.

Numbers From 1 Through 10. When used in isolated instances, the numbers from 1 through 10 should be written in words.

> Each of the four speakers has *one* hour to complete his or her presentation.

> Of the *nine* proposals that were submitted to the panel, only *five* were accepted.

Numbers That Begin Sentences. Write in words any number that begins a sentence. Rephrase the sentence if the number is too awkward to express in words.

> *Thirteen* districts have reported that this new product line is a smashing success.

> *Two hundred sixty-three* sales representatives have attended our telephone techniques seminar. (Awkward.)

> Our telephone techniques seminar has been attended by *263* sales representatives. (Rephrased sentence is not awkward.)

When spelling out large numbers (numbers over 1,000), use the shortest form possible.

> *Fifteen hundred* orders were received in the first week of the sale! (Not *One thousand five hundred.*)

> *Twenty-four hundred* samples have been distributed to qualified buyers throughout the area. (Not *Two thousand four hundred.*)

Fractions Standing Alone. Write in words a fraction that stands alone without a whole number.

Nearly *one-half* of the complaints concerned the quality of the paint. (Not ½.)

Ages. Ages are spelled out unless they are considered significant statistics or technical measurements.

Blanche began working for Ms. Logan at the age of *twenty-three*. (A general reference to age.)

Employees over the age of 35 are eligible to join this pension plan. (A significant statistic.)

Periods of Time. General periods of time are usually written in words.

This product had virtually no competition for the first *fifteen* years it was on the market.

Most of the regional managers have been with the company for *fifteen* years or more.

CLASS PRACTICE 1

Find and correct any errors in the following sentences. Write *OK* if there are no errors.

1. The average discount on the used merchandise is ½ off.
2. Yes, I'll be able to meet with you to discuss this at 3 o'clock.
3. One thousand seven hundred copies of the catalog will be distributed to our regular customers.
4. If you would like 2 or 3 more copies of the brochure, just call me.
5. A change in company policy now prohibits working past the age of sixty-five.
6. 34 people have applied for this position in just one day.
7. Jeanette, who has been with our department for about twelve years, will most likely become the new supervisor.
8. Of course, we realize that there is more than 1 way to solve this problem.

Numbers Written as Figures

Writing numbers in figures is generally preferred in business writing because figures are emphatic and specific. Below are the instances in which numbers should be written in figures.

Numbers Higher Than 10. You already saw that numbers from 1 through 10 are written in words. Numbers above 10 are written in figures.

This morning *17* suppliers submitted bids to our comptroller.

More than *150* employees are currently taking courses at the company's expense.

Sums of Money. Write sums of money in figures.

The average unit cost for these manuals in $3.46.

We expect to sell Model T20 for $5; Model T25, $7.   (Note that the two zeros in *$5.00* and *$7.00* are not needed. In legal documents, however, the two zeros are usually included, and sums may be written both in figures and in words.)

Amounts smaller than $1 are expressed with the word *cents.*

The cost of engraving each person's initials on the pen is only *50 cents* for each letter.

Amounts in millions and billions are written in figures, with the word *million* or *billion* spelled out.

According to newspaper reports, the estimated cost of manufacturing each plane will exceed *$2.5 million.*   (Also acceptable: *2.5 million dollars.*)

Age in Years, Months, and Days. In the previous section you learned that general ages are expressed in words; significant ages, in numbers. Ages expressed in years, months, and days are obviously significant statistics and are therefore always expressed in numbers.

At the time this policy was approved, Mr. Kennedy's age was precisely *29 years 6 months 10 days.*   (No commas—the age is considered a single unit.)

Time. Use figures with *a.m.* and *p.m.* Use either words or figures with *o'clock:* words for greater formality; figures for less formality.

Her estimated time of arrival is *9:45* p.m.

We will leave for the airport at *9* o'clock.

We invite you to be our guest at the banquet, which will begin at *nine* o'clock. (More formal than *9 o'clock.*)

House, Street, ZIP Code Numbers. House numbers (except for the number *one*) are always written in figures. Note that the abbreviation *No.* or the sign # should not be used with house or box numbers.

The new address is *One* Wall Street.

Mail her correspondence to her home address: *191* Central Avenue, East Peoria, Illinois 61611.

Send the package under his name to Box *8989,* Indianapolis, Indiana 46227.

Spell out street names from *1* through *10.* Use figures for numbered street names over *10.* When figures are used, the ending *st, d,* or *th* may be omitted if a word such as *East* or *West* separates the house number from the street number. If there is no such word between the house number and the street number, use the original ending to prevent misreading.

1212 Fourth Street
350 West 67 Avenue
767 23d Street

Use one space before the ZIP Code number; use no punctuation after the ZIP Code in an address block.

Dr. P. J. Frawley
345 45th Avenue
St. Paul, MN 55101

Decimals. Decimals are always expressed in figures: *5.7, 11.45, 9.6454.* For clarity, use a zero before the decimal point when there is no whole number: *0.25.*

Mixed Numbers. Write a mixed number (a whole number plus a fraction) in figures, except at the beginning of a sentence.

The cost of the project was 2½ times higher than had been estimated.

When spelling out a mixed number (for example, at the beginning of a sentence), use the word *and* to separate the whole number from the fraction:

Three *and* one-half times more orders came in in July than in June.

Numbers in Series, Related Numbers. When one number in a series must be written in figures, write all the numbers in figures.

Our department consists of *one* manager, *two* secretaries, and *six* ad writers. BUT: Our department consists of *2* managers, *5* secretaries, *12* media buyers, and *13* ad writers. (Because the number *13* is above *10*, it must be expressed in figures; likewise, all other numbers in the series should be expressed in figures.)

Related numbers are numbers that refer to the same kinds of things. Treat related numbers similarly—write them either in figures or in words.

Kenneth mailed *32* brochures to his special customers and has already received *8* orders in just two weeks! (Ordinarily, *8* would be spelled out; here, however, it is related to the figure *32* and must be expressed similarly—in figures. Note that *two* is not related to the other numbers and is therefore correctly spelled out.)

Percentages. Use figures with the word *percent*.

Last week the interest rate was about *8* percent; this week the rate is fluctuating between *9* and *10* percent.

The symbol % is generally used in technical writing and in tables and invoices, not in general correspondence. Always use figures with the symbol %.

Weights and Measures. Use figures to express numbers in weights, measures, and distances.

> We need several 3-gallon containers of this lubricant.

> Each solution has precisely 4.5 grams of solvent.

Miscellaneous. When a number is considered significant it is generally expressed in figures, even when the number is under *10*.

> We allow 5 days for a check to clear; for out-of-town checks we allow 6 days. (Here, the numbers 5 and 6 are significant; they deserve the special emphasis that figures provide.)

Consecutive numbers (as in *100 twenty*-cent stamps) deserve special attention. To avoid the possibly confusing *100 20-cent stamps*, write the smaller of two consecutive numbers in words, even if that number would usually be written in figures.

CLASS PRACTICE 2

Check how well you understand the rules for writing numbers in figures. Correct any errors in the following sentences. Write *OK* if there are no errors.

1. The cost of these high-quality diskettes is only $50.00 per box.
2. The property at 575 45 Street is still for sale, but the owners have lowered their asking price to $95,000.00.
3. Territory A has the fewest number of sales representatives, six; B has nine; C has 16; and D and E have 22 each.
4. The computer automatically "flags" an account when payment is 10 days past due.
5. We asked whether the microcomputer could handle the records for all our four hundred and fifty active patients.
6. Mortgage interest has increased slightly more than one and a half times since we purchased this building.
7. Although we wanted to rent office space at 1 Park Avenue, we found that the cost was too high at this prestigious address.
8. Only nine of our staff of 17 telemarketing representatives have been with the company more than a year or two.
9. To fix these pipes, we will need two 14-inch wrenches.

Ordinal Numbers in Dates

Numbers such as *1st, 2d, 3d, 4th*, and so on, are called *ordinal numbers*. Follow these rules for using ordinal numbers in dates.

1. Do not use an ordinal ending for the date when the day follows the month: *April 1, September 3, October 13*, and so on.
2. Use an ordinal number when the date precedes the month: *the 1st of April, the 3d of September, the 13th of October*, and so on.

COMMUNICATION LABORATORY

APPLICATION EXERCISES

A. Can you find all the errors in number expression in the following sentences? On a separate sheet of paper, correct any errors. Write *OK* for any sentence that is correct.

1. Please be sure to add seven percent sales tax to the total amount.
2. We expect about ⅔ of the stockholders to vote in favor of the proposition.
3. There is no delivery charge for packages weighing under eight pounds.
4. Printing the brochures on this better-quality paper will increase the unit cost by about $.15.
5. The deadline for submitting the report to headquarters is September 30th.
6. To assemble this product, you will need 16 6-inch screws.
7. In 1983 our company spent about $1.5 million on research alone.
8. Over the past four or five years our raises have averaged about 9%.
9. Although the quality is excellent, I am convinced that this small bookcase is overpriced at $175.00.
10. To package these items, we will need 150 5-pound boxes.
11. Twelve applicants are scheduled to be interviewed this morning by our personnel staff.
12. Ask a messenger to rush this package to 1301 East 45 Street.
13. As you know, we must complete this form and submit it to the court no later than three p.m. tomorrow.
14. Please make a duplicate of Policy No. 84-756-983; send the copy to Accounts Receivable.
15. One thousand five hundred requests for more information were received in the first two days.

B. Find all the errors in the following sentences; write your corrections on a separate sheet of paper. Write *OK* for a sentence that has no error.

1. The correct price of this disk drive is $375.00.
2. Has Martin already spoke with Ms. Brando about his transfer to our Durham, North Carolina, office?
3. To prepare this mixture properly, add five grams of the powder to one and a half liters of water.
4. We sell these pads at cost (just $.89 each) as a service to our customers.
5. Yes, we are optimistic about our sales potential for the second ½ of the year.
6. Between the 2 of us, I am really bullish on Hill-Top Computers Inc.
7. The banquet will be held at the Astor Hotel, 114 23 Street.

8. 75 of our stores will feature name-brand items at 25 percent off in the month of January only.

9. The total amount of the balance must be paid within sixty days, as specified in the original agreement.

10. The 15 of April is, of course, the deadline for filing all personal income tax forms.

11. Corporate policy requires employees to retire by the age of 65; employees may retire at age 56 and still be eligible for their pensions.

12. Under the new program, we will hire high school students age 16 and older to work in our offices during the summer months.

13. The art director ordered these 12 18-inch rulers, I believe.

14. Our sales goal for this year is ten million dollars—about 11 percent higher than last year's actual sales.

15. The nine clerks, two secretaries, and sixteen sales representatives who work out of this district office may be transferred to our larger office in Fresno.

C. Edit the following excerpt from a memorandum.

At Ms. Vernon's request, we are scheduling a meeting for the 10 of July. The purpose of the meeting is to discuss sales strategies.

As you know, sales for the first ½ of the year are down about 25%. Among the topics we plan to discuss are, the ways in which we can cut our expense budgets by a total of four hundred thousand dollars. In addition, we will explore some of the reasons we predicted sales so poorly.

VOCABULARY AND SPELLING STUDIES

A. These words are often confused: *deceased, diseased; risky, risqué.* Explain the differences.

B. Among the following words are some of the words most frequently misspelled in the business office. Which words are misspelled?

1. refered
2. sincerly
3. intrest
4. applicible
5. aproximately
6. conveniance
7. comittee
8. reccomend
9. statment
10. aggreement

C. In an effort to save space and at the same time attract attention, vendors often take shortcuts in writing copy for signs. Check the following signs for correct use of numbers. Are there any errors?

1. Special Sale—½ Off!
2. 1 Day Only!
3. All 1-of-a-Kind Bargains!

COMMUNICATING FOR RESULTS

An Honest Error. You proofread twice the letter that was printed for a special mailing to customers. Now, while you are looking at one of the printed copies, you spot an error—a misspelled word that you missed for some reason. Now this error appears on all the several thousand copies that were printed!

What should you do? No one knows about the error but you. Should you tell your supervisor? If so, when?

P · A · R · T

5

UNDERSTANDING THE COMMUNICATION PROCESS

No matter how you are communicating, you are always dealing with people. Someone is always either sending or receiving a message. Even if automated equipment is used in communicating, people are still involved in the process. That is why it is important to remember that the people involved in the process may be different. Understanding something about communication psychology can help you communicate well despite any differences.

Communication psychology deals with the principles of human behavior and human motivation. Given a situation that requires understanding of these principles, your mastery of the units in this chapter will enable you to do the following:

1. *Develop an ongoing awareness of the importance of psychology in effective communication.*

2. *Select and present topics that will meet your receiver's needs, communicate your ideas effectively, and obtain the desired results.*

3. *Avoid approaches that may threaten an individual's self-image and block effective communication.*

4. *Promote goodwill and ensure understanding in all communication situations.*

U · N · I · T
34
Principles of Communication Psychology

Communication is involved in every part of our lives, from the time we wake up until the time we go back to sleep. When we are talking with family or friends, other students or our teachers, other employees or our supervisors; when we are listening to the radio or watching TV; when we are buying or selling products or services; when we are speaking, writing, listening, or "sizing up" a situation—when we do any of these things, we are involved in communication. Since communication has such a major effect on all our lives and since everyone is a communicator, it is most important for us to understand what happens when people communicate. If we look at people who are successful communicators, we find that they apply effectively the principles of human behavior.

What Do We Know About Human Behavior?

If we compare what we know about science and technology with what we know about human behavior, we can easily see that we are way ahead in science and technology. Many of our problems today arise from communication mishaps caused by a lack of understanding of human behavior. However, the application of science and technology has shown that given enough resources and knowledge, we can do almost anything, including going to the moon and back.

Yet our breakthroughs in understanding human behavior have not been nearly so significant as those in space travel and medicine. Probably a major reason is that the study of human behavior as it relates to business is only about as old as the century. If that sounds very old to you, remember that some of the science and technology fields—chemistry, physics, and engineering, for example—are centuries old! Obviously, it will take time and research for us to catch up in our understanding of human behavior, and communication is always closely tied to human behavior, since understanding behavior is a necessary foundation for being a successful communicator.

Research in psychology, sociology, and anthropology contributes to our understanding of human behavior and helps us to apply its principles to communication psychology. Psychologists study individual behavior; sociologists, group behavior; anthropologists, cultural behavior. Their studies provide us with theories that are useful in understanding human behavior. However, it is important to remember that theories are useful only to understand how and why *most* people behave as they do—there are always exceptions. Throughout history, for instance, we find examples of people who have overcome incredible obstacles that would have stopped most people. So while studying theories of human behavior in an attempt to be a better communicator, remember that we are frequently talking about the behavior of most people and that there are exceptions.

A Look at Our Needs

We all have certain needs at certain times. These needs determine our behavior and the goals we set for ourselves. A successful communicator has the ability to understand the needs of those who will receive his or her message. A successful communicator speaks and writes with the receiver's needs in mind at all times. According to Abraham Maslow, a famous psychologist, most people will respond positively to messages that will meet their particular needs at particular times.* When their primary needs have been reasonably well satisfied, then the message must be refocused on the receiver's next level of needs. In other words, there are *levels* of needs that can be compared to the rungs of a ladder. Once we are fairly well settled on one rung, we begin to turn our attention to the next rung. We can classify these needs into five levels or rungs.

Rung 1—Basic Physical Needs. What basic things do we need before we can turn our attention to other things? We need food, shelter, and clothing—physical needs. Until these needs are reasonably well met, we think of little else.

Rung 2—Safety and Security Needs. Next we think about keeping ourselves free from physical harm or mental abuse. Most of us try to avoid situations that could cause us physical harm or people that threaten our peace of mind.

   The first two rungs represent lower-level needs. Once we have met these needs, we can turn our attention to our upper-level needs.

Rung 3—The Need to Belong. Most of us want to feel that we are part of a group. During our teen years, it seems most important to be "one of the gang." Our families also provide us with a sense of belonging. When we finally go to work full time, it will become important to most of us to feel that we have friends and enjoy being with our co-workers.

Rung 4—The Need to Be "Somebody." Once we have met the needs of Rung 3, feeling comfortable in the society in which we live, most of us want to feel that we are good at doing something. If we are good at swimming or

*Abraham H. Maslow, *Motivation and Personality*, 2d ed., Harper & Row, New York, 1970.

bowling or some of our school subjects, we feel very pleased with the recognition we receive. We feel that we are "somebody." We have met the needs of our ego.

Rung 5—The Need to Help Others and to Be Creative. If we are reasonably able to meet all the previous needs, we seem to lose our anxieties and fears. Two things then happen: (1) we are more willing to help people who are still struggling on the lower rungs of the ladder, those still striving to meet their physical, safety, and security needs; and (2) we become more creative, and creative people make a better quality of life for us all.

Our Needs Determine Our Reaction

To be a successful communicator, you must try to determine the needs of the people to whom you are writing or speaking. You can do this by noticing which goals seem to motivate them. But remember that goals may change rapidly. For example, when you arrive at school in the morning, you have had a good breakfast so you are not hungry (Rung 1). You feel safe and comfortable in your surroundings (Rung 2), and you have enjoyed visiting with friends before class (Rung 3). You have just finished a class that you enjoy and do well in, so you have satisfied the need to be "somebody" (Rung 4). However, 11:30 a.m. comes and you get hungry. The lunch hour doesn't begin till 12 noon. You shift in your chair and keep looking at your watch. You find it most difficult to concentrate because you now have a basic physical need, the need for food (Rung 1). Until that need is satisfied, the only really meaningful messages you will receive concern food.

Have you ever had someone invite you into his or her office for what you thought would be a most interesting conference? Maybe you felt flattered (Rung 4) and were looking forward to the meeting. Yet while you were there, telephone calls and other interruptions were permitted. Soon you began to feel very unimportant and perhaps even wanted to leave (Rung 3). We react favorably to a situation or person who helps us satisfy our needs, but we react negatively to a situation or a person who hurts us and our ability to meet our needs.

An example of sending a positive message directed toward our needs is our government's appeal to us to use car pools. Although the main reason for car pools would be to conserve energy, we are also told that riding to work with a group is more fun (Rung 3). Our reaction is favorable because the message also appeals to our personal needs.

Thus we can learn to identify these levels of needs and relate them to all our communications. Whether we are looking for a job, buying or selling products or services, ordering supplies, or asking for information—we must always put ourselves in the place of our receiver, decide what our receiver's needs are, and then phrase our message to meet those needs. In this way, we are sure to get the reaction we want.

Nonverbal Communication

Many people believe that our nonverbal communication—facial expressions, posture, gestures—contributes much to oral communication. They believe that cultural and environmental differences contribute to conscious or unconscious body movements that communicate our true feelings. Some movements or facial expressions seem to be common to all humans. For example, people everywhere seem to turn up the corners of their mouths to show amusement. This is one of the many ways in which we use nonverbal communication.

Personal Space. We all seem to carry a sense of having personal space around us. This personal space is generally guarded against intruders. We also try not to intrude on the personal space of others. For example, the next time you sit at a table with your friends in the cafeteria, notice how each person generally seems to have about the same amount of space to eat in. You have unconsciously divided the space at the table fairly equally. If you are walking down a sidewalk next to a stranger, notice that there is an unspoken informal agreement that you will not walk too closely together.

The amount of space we allow people also relates to their status. If you went into the offices of several executives for the first time, how close would you come to their desks? You would probably find that the higher the executive is in the organization, the more timid you would be about approaching.

Here in the United States, when we talk with each other, we may stand about 2 feet apart. However, in some countries, people stand much closer. When your personal space is invaded, you may move elsewhere, or you may give signals of tension (uneasy movements) to get the intruder to move. If you back away from people because they have invaded your personal space, they may perceive it as a sign that you don't like them. Therefore, an understanding of personal space can certainly help you communicate more successfully.

Gestures and Posture. People can communicate many moods through gestures and posture. Keeping your head down and hunching your shoulders may be your way of telling people to leave you alone. Crossing your arms may indicate that you do not accept what someone is saying. Shrugging your shoulders may mean that you don't have any interest in a situation anymore. An important thing to remember about nonverbal communication, however, is that these movements should not be interpreted by themselves. You should also consider what is being said and the whole context of the situation.

Facial Expressions. Looking *away* from a person can convey as much meaning as looking *at* a person. Looking away may tell people that we would not invade their privacy. Or it may mean that we are not comfortable with what they are saying. Or it may mean that we are trying to hide something. We know that facial expressions can convey a whole range of meanings—joy, hate, love, sorrow—but as with gestures and posture, we need to consider the entire situation.

Our Language Affects Our Behavior

The words we use can make us behave in different ways. To communicate successfully, we must remember that words are only symbols; meaning is added by people. Two people may interpret the same word differently. For example, Ben's supervisor, Sylvia, told him that his sketch for a certain book was "old-fashioned." Ben understood this to be a negative comment and began to revise the sketch to make it more modern. Sylvia, however, intended her comment to be complimentary. She *wanted* the cover to have an old-fashioned look! Thus, although Ben and Sylvia fully agreed on what the book cover should look like, they did not agree on the meaning of the term *old-fashioned*. Ben's misunderstanding of Sylvia's language made him do more work—unnecessary work.

Have you ever seen dates written like this: 3-2-86? To most of us, this symbol means "March 2, 1986." However, some people (for example, workers in government agencies or in foreign countries) interpret the symbol 3-2-86 to mean "February 3, 1986." On an invoice, such a misinterpretation could be costly.

Since some symbols can be interpreted to mean two different things, a person who wishes to communicate a message successfully must look beyond the written and spoken word in order to understand how communication works.

COMMUNICATION LABORATORY

APPLICATION EXERCISES

A. Visit a department store and note five ways that appeals are made to your physical and safety needs (Rung 1 and Rung 2) through advertising, displays, and pricing.

B. Prepare an oral account of a newspaper or magazine advertisement or of a television or radio commercial that made a direct appeal to your need to be "somebody."

C. Tell which need levels the following items would appeal to (**1**) a cabin cruiser; (**2**) an athletic jacket; (**3**) shoveling snow from the walk of an elderly neighbor's home; (**4**) exercising daily; (**5**) a home fire alarm.

D. Analyze the following advertisement, using your knowledge of the various levels of needs: "When you drive up in a Decibel 700, the car itself says everything that can be said. From the bold hood ornament to the gold-plated rear bumper, the car proclaims success. All you need do is to quietly acknowledge the knowing glances."

VOCABULARY AND SPELLING STUDIES

A. Do you really know the exact order of the letters in the alphabet? In your dictionary, locate the following words, taking each one in the sequence in which it is shown. Note the exact time you start your search and the exact time you finish. How many minutes did you need? Then write the words in alphabetical order.

1. gasoline	6. absolute	11. dehumidify
2. rhubarb	7. exclusive	12. inflation
3. appreciate	8. evidence	13. ingenious
4. willful	9. deliberate	14. periodic
5. condense	10. essential	15. congregate

B. Among the following words are several common misspellings. Find and correct any words that are misspelled.

1. preparation	5. accidentally	9. technical
2. corespondence	6. beneficial	10. commiting
3. exagerated	7. dispair	11. briliant
4. seperately	8. disatisfied	12. chosing

C. Here are 12 words that you are likely to encounter frequently. If you are a typist, you must know the correct points at which to divide these words in order to make line-ending decisions. Remember that accents have a bearing on choosing the preferred division points. Without consulting your diction-ary, indicate the syllable divisions and the accent marks. Place each accent mark *before* the syllable to be accented. Then, using the dictionary, check the accuracy of your choices.

1. congratulate	5. privilege	9. conscious
2. obstacle	6. visible	10. accumulate
3. inadequate	7. utilize	11. surprising
4. repetition	8. similar	12. acquaintance

D. Ten frequently used foreign expressions are listed in Column A. Match each with its correct meaning in Column B. Then copy in your notebook the phonetic spelling of each expression.

A	B
1. esprit de corps	a. an indispensable condition
2. tempus fugit	b. good-bye
3. nom de plume	c. fashionable society
4. a la carte	d. knowledge of just what to do
5. sine die	e. each dish priced separately
6. savoir-faire	f. calmness; coolness of mind
7. beau monde	g. group spirit
8. sang-froid	h. indefinitely
9. bon voyage	i. a pen name
10. sine qua non	j. time flies

COMMUNICATING FOR RESULTS

Positive and Friendly. Positive statements are more likely to win friends than negative ones. Rewrite the statements below so they will accomplish something in a positive way.

1. All our products work well when they are used by intelligent people.
2. If you will return your toaster to us at once, we will think about giving you an adjustment.

U · N · I · T
35
Applying Communication Psychology

Knowledge of any kind is of little value unless it can be used. For example, men and women who succeed in business are knowledgeable people—but it is not knowledge alone that makes them successful; it is the intelligent *use* of what they know. There are fewer crippled children today because Dr. Jonas Salk gave the world the benefit of his research on the problem of infantile paralysis. There are fewer companies treating their employees like machines because Dr. Lillian Gilbreth gave the world the benefit of her research on the problems of increasing production. Logically, then, your success as a communicator depends not only on your understanding of the principles of communication psychology but also on your use of that knowledge.

In the preceding unit you studied the human behavior factors that must be known by any communicator who desires to rise to the top; but unless you know how to apply what you have learned, your rise will not be very fast or very far. Therefore, you need the training provided in this unit—training in using your knowledge to promote goodwill, to prevent ill will, and to stimulate desired action.

Promoting Goodwill

Goodwill is difficult to define because it is a feeling, an emotion. We know that in business it is listed as an asset and therefore can be sold—but nobody can see or touch it. Perhaps the nearest we can come to a definition is to say that goodwill is the favor or prestige that a business has which causes people to trade with—and keep coming back to—that company.

We know that goodwill results from satisfying people's needs. Whenever we do or say anything that causes people to like *themselves* better, they like *us* better. Keep in mind the workings of the need ladder as you learn how to promote goodwill in the categories being discussed.

Customer Goodwill. It is important, of course, for a business to gain new customers. It is equally important, however, to keep old customers. How will a firm profit if it gains new business but, at the same time, loses current business? Promoting customer goodwill, then, must be concerned with both the new and the old.

Most people who come into our place of business and most people with whom we correspond are either customers or potential customers. In Unit 48 you will learn how to use your writing skills to win new friends and keep old ones. In addition, you need to know the following essentials of goodwill building. Apply these basics to your oral as well as to your written communications, and you will be sure to satisfy your customers' needs.

Be Courteous. To most people, *courtesy* means saying "Please" and "Thank you." Of course, saying these words is important when dealing with all people, not just customers—but "Please" and "Thank you" merely scratch the surface of the courtesy needed to promote customer goodwill.

The basis of true courtesy is consideration for the other person. Some of us seem to develop this quality easily; others must develop it by constantly saying to themselves, "How would I feel if this were said or done to me?" For example, you would immediately greet a client who came into your office, and by doing so you would meet the client's need to feel comfortable around others. But your prompt recognition of the client could also be based on your instinctive knowledge of how *you* would feel if *you* were kept waiting. If you were talking to a customer and your telephone rang, would you excuse yourself before lifting the receiver? Would you keep taking calls while you had someone in your office? If people are behind you when you reach a closed door, do you hold the door for them or even let them precede you? These are but a few of the niceties that mark a person whose good manners come from sincere consideration for others.

Another aspect of consideration for others is a genuine desire to be of help. Suppose, for instance, a customer asks if your company sells Nordic refrigerators, but you know that they do not. Although a simple no would answer the question, a wish to help would prompt you to say something like this: "No, Nordic is carried by Reliable Appliances on East Street. But perhaps you'd like to see and compare our Aurora refrigerator over here on the right." And who knows? Maybe you'll gain a new customer. Even if you don't sell the Aurora you will have shown that you want to be of help, will have made a potential customer feel warm and important, and quite possibly will have created an atmosphere that will lead the customer back to you for future purchases.

Be Pleasant and Cordial. Being made to feel welcome and wanted is a morale builder and a source of great satisfaction to anybody's need for a sense of belonging. You can give a customer that satisfaction by being pleasant and cordial not only in the words you say but also in the facial expression you show and the tone of voice you use. If we have a professional attitude at work, we don't allow our personal troubles to show. No matter how warm and gracious our words may be, they fall flat when they come from the lips of a deadpan or indifferent face. If we really are pleased to see a customer, our facial expression and tone will project that pleasure.

Use the Customer's Name. As you know, every person considers his or her name very important; therefore, a person is pleased when recognized and called by name. Many customers favor certain stores, cleaners, restaurants, and so on, even though these stores are *not* the ones that are located closest to them. If asked why they prefer to trade with their favorites, they might say that the goods or services are superior. But often the real reason is that the business people with whom they deal show a personal interest in their customers and give them individual service, an impression created partly because they are known and greeted by name.

One of the ways in which you can promote customer goodwill, therefore, is to make a determined effort to learn and use your customer's names. If you are a salesperson and the customer has a charge card, you will be able to see the written name. Be sure to check spelling and, if it is an unusual name, like Kosieski, be sure to check pronunciation. After the customer leaves, you will make a note like this *Kosieski (Ko-'sis-ky)*. When you make a cash sale, find a tactful way of learning that customer's name. Then the next time the customer comes in, you can say, "Good morning, Mrs. Kosieski, and how are you today?" instead of the less personal "May I help you?"

Listen Attentively. An attentive listener boosts the speaker's ego; an inattentive listener deflates it. Therefore, since ego satisfaction helps build customer goodwill, we must be concerned with how to listen, as well as with how to talk. Attentive listening will also help you to identify and correct any real problems that the customer may have.

When listening to customers, regardless of the importance or the triviality of what is said, look directly at them. Show that you are following their every word; don't interrupt or try to change the subject. Even if they are talking just to pass some time, your listening techniques will make them feel so warm and important that they may very likely think of your firm first the next time they have business to transact. And if what they have to say does affect you or your employer, you may be able to increase goodwill, turn ill will into goodwill, or learn how to improve your products or services.

For example, suppose you are listening to Mr. Stenak, an angry customer who has a just complaint. You show that you are interested and concerned. You let him express his entire complaint with no comment except an occasional, "Oh, that's too bad, Mr. Stenak." When he finishes, his anger will be considerably reduced because he was able to tell his entire story to a sympathetic audience—you. Then if you have the authority to right the wrong, you should do so immediately. If not, you should make arrangements for the customer to see whoever does have the authority to help him.

Give Prompt Service. We Americans are a "now" people. We want everything right away; we are always in a hurry. Customers expect, even demand, quick service, and their trade goes to the companies that do not keep them waiting. Merely giving speedy service, however, is not enough to promote customer goodwill. After all, customers expect prompt service and therefore take it for granted. So what must we do to increase goodwill?

Without being obvious, we must impress upon customers the fact that we give "super" service. For instance, if a customer hands you a change of address, you shouldn't just say, "Thank you." Instead say, "Thank you, Ms. Pappas, I'll attend to this right away." As you make out the sales slip for a lamp, you might say to the customer, "You can expect your lamp on Tuesday, our very first delivery day to your section of the city." Take every opportunity to point out the prompt service your company gives. Make each customer feel deserving of your special attention.

In effect, we should make a conscious, sincere effort that will become a habit and perhaps result in a customer's making a remark such as this: "Never saw such good service as Lloyd's gives me!" Remember that we should not make a promise about good service unless it can be kept.

Vendor Goodwill. Vendors are individuals or companies from whom we buy in wholesale quantities; we pay them to supply us with goods that we in turn resell to our customers. If we didn't have vendors, we wouldn't be able to do business. We need them, we depend upon them; consequently, their goodwill is important to us. Yet many people do not recognize the importance of vendor goodwill. Because they pay the vendor, they see no reason for trying to cultivate a friendly relationship. They see no need to be gracious or even courteous to vendors.

For example, there are executives who would drop everything to attend to a customer but who would think nothing of keeping other firms' sales representatives cooling their heels for an hour before getting around to seeing them. And there are sales representatives who, when the roles are reversed and they are the buyers, treat others like second-class citizens.

If a customer arrives while a vendor is talking with you, the vendor may encourage you to serve the customer while he or she waits. Watch for cues from vendors, as they may be interested in seeing and hearing how a customer reacts to their merchandise.

Failure to give the same courteous treatment to everyone is not just unkind but also unintelligent. Consider some of the benefits that will come our way when suppliers are made to feel like friends: Our orders will receive prompt attention; and if we are in urgent need of a special order, we can depend on the vendor to get it to us without delay. In addition, we will be among the first to know of any special discounts or of any contemplated increase in the cost of merchandise. Thus, having vendor goodwill helps us to promote customer goodwill, for we can give customers the best of service only if we ourselves receive top service.

Co-Worker Goodwill. Football coaches stress the need for teamwork. Social organizations emphasize the necessity of having cooperation among their members. The armed forces aim for *esprit de corps*, an enthusiastic common spirit among members of a group. Business managers try to develop high employee morale. All of them know that a spirit of loyalty, willingness, and friendliness produces the best results whenever two or more people are engaged in a common enterprise. As a member of an office team, you also have a financial stake in promoting co-worker goodwill. When the company profits, you profit; and to make a profit the company must have the backing of a smooth-running, harmonious staff.

Consequently, you should make a conscious effort to be pleasant, courteous, friendly, and helpful—but above all, tactful and considerate. To be thoughtful and promote co-worker goodwill you can (1) avoid listening to or spreading gossip, (2) put away materials correctly when you have finished with them, (3) return what you borrow, and (4) be tactful in the remarks you make to others. In other words, treat others as you would like to be treated.

Credibility and Goodwill. If you are dealing with established customers and vendors, much of your credibility is based on your past performance—your "track record." Maintaining your track record includes keeping the same high-quality goods and/or services. You must also keep your established customers and vendors well informed and reassure them about changes that occur in all successful businesses—new merchandise, new employees, new owners, new facilities. Rumors often precede such changes. To avoid the dangers of rumors, be sure to share complete and accurate information with your established customers and vendors.

In dealing with new customers, your appearance may affect your credibility. *You* know the kind of person you really are, but the fact is that to other people you are what they perceive you to be. Banks, for example, are run essentially on goodwill, as banking services are about the same for all banks. Have you ever noticed that bank employees are generally neat and well groomed? Since bank employees handle people's money, people want to have a secure feeling about the bank employees with whom they leave their money.

All businesses want a prospective customer to have a secure feeling about their ability to give the customer quality service. Vendors, too, have much concern for the image presented by the businesses that handle their goods. Thus it is important to develop credibility and goodwill with all customers and vendors.

Some Personal Qualities. If you flare up easily or if you are short on patience or if you lack tact, you need to do some self-training, because temper control, patience, and tact are high on the list of personal qualities that are "musts" if goodwill is to be maintained.

Control Your Temper. Expressing anger is a luxury that business people cannot afford, because it interferes with good relations. If you receive a rude or insulting letter, your first impulse may be to sit down and "tell that person a thing or two." Well, go ahead; write a blistering letter. Then tear it up, and after you have cooled off, write the kind of smooth, polished letter that marks you as a top communicator. Spoken insults place a much greater strain on temper control, but you can get at least a partial grip on yourself by counting to ten before you say anything. Always remember that although a sharp answer may relieve *your* feelings, it definitely will not foster goodwill with others. Your customers rely on your goodwill.

Be Patient. Patience in answering questions can be one of your most valuable assets. If you think back about some of the best teachers you've had, you probably remember you could always ask them a question and know that you would receive a courteous, informative answer. You can probably remember their explaining something over and over to different students without ever getting upset or being rude. You have the same obligation to your customers and clients. They are paying for your merchandise or services. Without them you would have no job. Therefore, your customers and clients should be able to depend on you for information. You must expect to be asked the same questions by many customers even though there may be no necessity for asking. For instance, suppose there is a sign right in plain view that reads "Electric Blankets, 4th Floor"; yet customer after customer asks whether electric blankets are sold on the third floor in household furnishings. Each time the question is asked, you should answer as though it were the first time. You should also keep your tone of voice friendly. Any answer that shows your impatience would be sure to lose a customer.

Tact and Positive Tone. Very few people would be so blunt and rude as to make a remark such as, "Well, you certainly did a lousy job." On the other hand, very few people understand that what they write or say may *imply* criticism. Study the following illustrations and learn how to avoid even hinting at carelessness, negligence, or dishonesty.

Suppose a customer who places an order within two weeks is entitled to a 5 percent discount for prompt ordering. One of our customers takes three weeks to order but still deducts the discount; therefore, we must write a letter to straighten out the situation. Look at these possible ways of conveying the same message:

POOR: You are not entitled to the special discount because you did not order in time. *(Are you trying to take advantage of us?)*

BETTER: You probably overlooked the fact that the discount was available only to those who ordered by July 1. *(This is a mistake that anyone could make.)*

Suppose you are writing to a vendor to order goods that you need very soon. Note the implications in each of the following closing sentences:

POOR: We want this order right away. *(We can't wait for your usual slow service.)*

BETTER: Since we have buyers for this merchandise, your rapid delivery will allow us to keep our customers happy. *(Your prompt service will allow us to continually sell your merchandise.)*

Now that you are alerted to the dangers of implied criticism, your written communications will take on an added polish; you will see your messages as your readers see them and will have second thoughts about your wording. But what about oral communication? The moment words are spoken, they cannot be recalled or revised. Despite the fact that we speak more often than we write, training in this area of oral communication is often neglected. But you will know the fundamentals of such training if you give careful attention to the following discussion.

Mr. Rustin selects some items in a retail store and goes to a register to pay for them. Because he has gone to a closed checkout line, a sales clerk must ask him to come to another register. Note the different ways of making the request.

POOR: Hey, come over here. Can't you see that register is closed? *(Tells the cus-*

tomer to do something that he should have been alert enough to do in the first place.)

BETTER: Sir, if you will step over here, I will serve you at once. *(Ignores the customer's lack of attention and emphasizes immediate service.)*

When a service technician receives a call about a home appliance, he or she knows that something basic could have been overlooked. The technician's response can cause or present ill will.

POOR: Of course you did plug in the machine. *(Is it possible that you made this stupid error?)*

BETTER: We will be happy to look at the machine. But check to be sure that it's plugged in. Some of those plugs slip out easily. *(The plug itself might be at fault.)*

Then there is the secretary who gives the supervisor a message that Mr. Arbour called and asked to be called back. Time passes, and the supervisor still has not made the call. Various reminders might be:

POOR: Didn't you call Mr. Arbour yet? *(Is it possible that you could be so forgetful?)*

BETTER: Mr. Arbour really wanted to talk to you. Did you remember to call him? *(A little more positive.)*

BEST: Would you like me to place that call to Mr. Arbour? *(I am not criticizing. I merely want to be of service.)*

Tact and positive tone when communicating orally depends not only on *what* is said but also on *how* it is said. That is why expert communicators think before they speak and mentally rephrase any words that might be construed as criticism.

Stimulating Desired Action

To get desired action, successful communicators:

1. Identify the action desired.
2. Consider the audience.
3. Meet the audience's needs.
4. Facilitate action.

Identify the Action Desired. The first step in communicating effectively is to be clear in your own mind as to exactly what it is that you want the person or persons to do. Do you want people to buy your product? Do you want them to subscribe to a magazine, a book club, a computer service? Unless you yourself know precisely what you want, you cannot expect to evoke the action you are trying to get.

Consider the Audience. Next visualize the people at whom you are aiming your message. What is their age group? What is their income level? Even realizing that you know nothing about your audience is important, as you will learn in the following paragraph.

Meet the Audience's Needs. Now you are ready to review the audience's needs and to construct a message that will best meet those needs in order to achieve your action-getting purpose. For instance, for teenagers you might emphasize recreation; for older people, health and security; for the in-betweens, family and community. And if you are writing to get action from hundreds of people about whom you know nothing, you might concentrate on the needs that motivate many of us—financial security, comfort and convenience, leisure time, good services.

Facilitate Action. Your chances of getting people to respond favorably are much increased when you make it easy for them to act, a fact that is very important to keep in mind. For example, when Ms. Perelli is ready to sign an order, you should not only give her the order form but also hand her a good pen. If she has to take time to find a pen or if yours is not in good condition, the annoyance may be enough to call the whole deal off.

If you were composing a letter that will go to hundreds of prospective subscribers to your magazine, leave space at the bottom of your letter. In that space, type an acceptance form with a signature line. And be sure that you enclose a stamped return envelope. Thus, without moving from a chair, the prospect can sign and fold the letter and slip it into an envelope that is already stamped and addressed. If the prospect is an impulse buyer, you have a new subscriber.

By applying the fundamentals of communication psychology to your dealings with customers, vendors, and co-workers, you will promote goodwill, prevent ill will, and stimulate desired action from them. Needless to say, you will also be more successful on the job.

COMMUNICATION LABORATORY

APPLICATION EXERCISES

A. Keeping in mind the importance of promoting customer, vendor, and colleague goodwill, rate each of the following sentences as *Good* or *Poor*.

1. We very much appreciate the immediate attention given to our special order.

2. Whenever you have a problem with service, please let me know right away.
3. Drop into our showroom sometime soon.
4. I would be most happy to see you on Wednesday, April 8, at 3 p.m.
5. You will have to give us more information if you expect us to act on your complaint.
6. You had better pick up the lawn mower that you mistakenly delivered to us at once.
7. Since it took you so long to deliver our order, we don't want it anymore.
8. It is very easy to understand why our mistake upset you.
9. Unfortunately, your line of sweaters would not fit in with our other merchandise.
10. This watch has obviously been abused, so we won't take it back.

B. Now rewrite the sentences that you rated *Poor*, wording them in such a way that they will promote goodwill or prevent ill will.

C. For each of the following products (a) specify the probable audience to whom you would direct a sales letter and (b) state the need that the product would satisfy.

1. tamper-proof window locks
2. power tools
3. work shoes
4. natural fruit juices

D. Choose some real or imaginary product or service and write a sales lett__ that will put into practice your knowledge of the psychology of business communication.

E. Using your knowledge of communication psychology, write four suggestions that you would give to salespeople.

VOCABULARY AND SPELLING STUDIES

A. These words are often confused: *receipt, recipe; vein, vain, vane.* Explain the differences.

B. Each of the following sentences contains slang or an incorrect expression. Substitute a more formal word or expression for each.

1. I could of told you that this customer would complain.
2. We will really have to hustle to meet their competition.
3. I sort of think that we can improve our advertising.
4. Our salespeople should of featured the cheaper model.
5. I can't get a handle on the shipping problem.

C. Should *ei* or *ie* appear in the blank spaces in these sentences?

1. We bel___ve you will find this to be a conven___nt way to rec___ve the magazines you want each month.
2. It is a real ach___vement to become ch___f of police in a large city in such a br___f period of time.
3. Th___r fr___ght was misdelivered to a n___ghboring warehouse.

COMMUNICATING FOR RESULTS

What Should Have Been Said? Some examples of poor human relations are shown in the following incidents. Suggest (**a**) what the probable reaction was in each situation and (**b**) what should have been said to maintain or further good human relations.

1. Secretary on the telephone: "Ms. Judson's not here. I have no idea where she is. Try calling tomorrow."
2. Salesperson to customer: "I told you that the more expensive camera was a better deal. Maybe you'll listen to me next time."
3. Customer to sales clerk: "Don't you know I'm in a hurry? I've been here 20 minutes watching you fool around."
4. From a letter to a customer: "If you had read the guarantee, you would not have returned the watch to us."
5. Customer to supplier: "We would like some real speed on this order, not your usual leisurely pace."

6

WRITING MESSAGES THAT GET RESULTS

Even in this era of automated communication technology, the written word has survived. It is still the basic tool with which ideas, especially in business, are presented. Whether you are writing in longhand or typing on a word processor, you must give life to your ideas. Knowing how to use the principles of effective writing will help you to accomplish this.

The techniques mastered by successful business writers apply to all written forms of communication. This is especially true of the business letter. Given a situation that requires writing in business, your mastery of the units in this chapter will enable you to do the following:

1. *Use words, phrases, and clauses so that your messages will be interpreted correctly.*

2. *Develop your written message so that each idea flows smoothly into the next.*

3. *Avoid stiff and outdated phrases that communicate little information and detract from a positive, conversational tone.*

4. *Use balanced words, phrases, and sentences.*

36 Qualities of Effective Letters

Why do you write letters to friends and relatives who live out of town? You write because you want to keep in touch, and it isn't possible to make a trip every time you want to exchange news and information; that would be time-consuming and expensive. Telephoning, too, becomes expensive if you talk very long. Your letters, then, are substitutes for personal visits. They convey messages, and at the same time, they build new friendships or maintain old ones.

Business letters are written for many of the same reasons as personal letters. Business people can't afford the time for, nor the expense of, a personal visit each time they want to transact business in various parts of the country, so they make phone calls or write letters instead. Even telephone messages, however, must be put in writing for understanding and formal confirmation by both sender and receiver and as a source for later reference. Business people depend on the written word to keep them in touch with their customers and business associates and to preserve on paper their conversations with them. Thus their letters become their "paper representatives."

Since business letters represent business people in dealing with their customers and business associates, it is important that the letters leave the reader with a good impression of the writer and his or her company. Building goodwill—and maintaining it—is an important job of the business letter. Because many people who receive business letters never enter the place of business or talk with its managers and employees, their impressions are formed entirely through the correspondence they receive. Therefore, not only is the business letter a business representative, but it is also in many cases an ambassador of goodwill.

What Makes a Letter Effective?

On what basis do you select your friends? How do you decide what food to pick from an appetizing display in a cafeteria? How do you decide what suit or dress to buy?

In each case, the person or the article you choose possesses certain qualities or characteristics that appeal to you. The friend may be thoughtful of

Good letters don't just happen—they are
the result of knowledge, experience, and
careful planning.

**Whether you dictate directly to someone or use
dictation equipment, you should plan a written or mental
outline for your letter, memo, or report.**

When writing a routine business letter, ask yourself this important question: "What kind of letter would I like to receive if this letter were being sent to me?"

Many businesses, especially banks and department stores, welcome the opportunity to grant credit to responsible customers. Goodwill-building letters granting this credit are then sent to customers whose request for credit has been approved.

When writing a claim letter, remember to explain *carefully* and *tactfully* what is wrong.

Sales letters are written because face-to-face selling situations like the one shown here are not always necessary or possible.

Some businesses think public relations is so important to sales that they devote entire departments to it.

If, through business, you are invited to a social activity, are helped to find a job or a contact, or are granted a special favor, remember to write a social business letter to acknowledge the event and to build goodwill.

Message forms allow people to take complete, accurate messages for others quickly and help us build goodwill with both colleagues and customers.

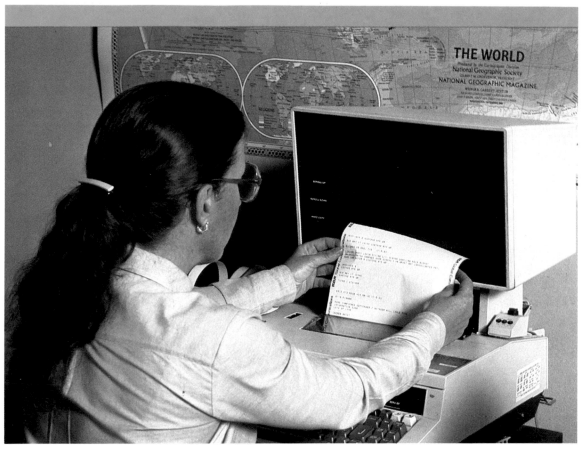

Businesses today often use teleprinter
equipment to communicate directly with
branch offices or divisions.

Whether a business meeting is formal or informal, a written record of it, in the form of minutes, must be prepared and distributed to those who attended and to other interested parties.

other people—and thoughtfulness is a trait you like. The salad may simply look appetizing—and appearance helps you make the choice. The suit or dress may be of an interesting texture—and texture influences your decision. These are only a few of the factors that help us choose one person or thing rather than another. There are many other factors. We react favorably to some characteristics and unfavorably to others.

The same is true when you read a letter. The qualities it possesses will cause you to react either favorably or unfavorably. One of the main objectives of all business letters is to prompt the recipient to react favorably.

But, you may say, every person does not like the same things, so how can a letter please everyone? All of us do not like spinach; we do not all like the color yellow; not everyone likes Beethoven's music. How, then, can one write a letter that will appeal to *every* reader?

You cannot predict exactly how your words will affect another person. From your own experience in dealing with friends and classmates, however, you know what kind of behavior and personal characteristics affect *most* people favorably. You know that friendliness usually wins friends, but sarcasm and indifference do not. You know that a "sharp" appearance, a ready smile, and good listening habits usually attract people; but shoddiness, glumness, and nervous jabber drive them away. There are certain qualities in business letters, too, that will call forth successful results.

Ten Requirements

If each of your letters meets the following ten requirements, the chances are that you will be a successful letter writer. A good letter does the following:

1. Creates a favorable first impression.
2. Appeals to the reader's point of view.
3. Is correct in every detail.
4. Is courteous, friendly, and sincere.
5. Promotes goodwill.
6. Is clear and complete.
7. Is concise.
8. Flows smoothly.
9. Is well paragraphed.
10. Avoids jargon.

Create a Favorable First Impression. When you meet people for the first time, you probably form some quick judgment of them on the basis of their appearance. Research has shown that during a job interview the first impression of a person's appearance in most cases may decide whether that person gets the job. And so it is with a letter. Your first impression is often influenced by the appearance of the letter, and that impression stays with you as you read the message. Just as an attractive platter of food stimulates your appetite to eat, an attractive letter stimulates your desire to read. If the physical characteristics of the letter create a favorable first impression, you will probably react more favorably to the contents.

But if you receive a letter that is smudged, has strikeovers or misspelled words, has erasure holes, or has been typed with a worn-out ribbon so that you can hardly make it out, you really don't feel much like reading it. However, when you receive a letter that looks prestigious, you are impressed that whoever wrote it would be writing to you. You read the letter, as you are curious to know what he or she wants.

The impression of not caring by the sender of a messy letter carries over to an impression of not caring about the quality of products or services that the sender is offering. This impression may make your readers place their orders elsewhere. To the receiver, the only reason a letter appears messy is that the writer didn't care enough to retype it or make neat corrections. Therefore, every letter you write should look inviting. The factors that help to create a favorable impression include the quality of stationery, the attractiveness of the letterhead, the neatness of the typing, and the form or setup of the letter placement.

Appeal to the Reader's Point of View. Producing an action-getting letter will be easier for writers who put themselves in the reader's place. As you compose a letter, pretend to be the reader and ask: "What do I get out of this? What will it do for me?" Then you will find that you can write from the reader's point of view. You can show how taking the desired action will be to the advantage of the reader.

Suppose you wrote the following sentence in a letter to Enrico Ortiz, a potential customer, who inquired about your magazine:

> Your $15 check will put *Financial Planning* in your mailbox next month and for the next eleven months after that.

Is there anything in this sentence that would move Mr. Ortiz to sit down, write a check, and mail it? Probably not. Certainly, he can't see any advantage in it for him. Nearly always there is a better chance of motivating the reader if he or she is definitely brought into the picture. For example, here is an appeal that is aimed at the need for leisure-time activities.

> Your $15 check will give you a year's worth of the knowledgeable articles and money-saving advice that are included in every issue of *Financial Planning*.

Be Correct in Every Detail. Errors in a letter can prevent the letter from doing the job it sets out to do. Of course, errors are never intentional; even so, there is little excuse for them. Reasons for errors fall into two main categories:

1. Carelessness, such as the following:
   Typographical errors—wrong letters, strikeovers, errors in spacing.
   Uneven typing—some letters light, others dark.

Poor margin balance—top and bottom and right and left margins out of balance.

Messy corrections—holes in paper, smudges.

2. Failure to consult reference sources, with these results:

Misspelled words and names. (All misspellings are serious, especially a misspelled name because it does not meet the reader's need to "be somebody.")

Errors in word selection.

Errors in dates and figures.

Errors in capitalization and punctuation.

Incomplete information.

Some errors, such as those involving dates and amounts of money, can cause a great deal of harm. Such errors not only irritate the reader (especially if they cause loss of time or money), but they also cause the reader to lose faith in the company sending the letter. There is a harmful effect on goodwill if your letters are not correct. Therefore, you should proofread every letter carefully and correct all mistakes before you send it.

Be Courteous, Friendly, and Sincere. Would you continue shopping in a store where your patronage was not appreciated? A famous chain of stores displays this sign at all cash registers: "Your purchases are free if we fail to say 'thank you.'" The owners claim they have never lost any money but have won thousands of friends. They do not take their customers for granted.

Of course, good manners are not reflected merely in a "please" or "thank you." The *way* in which you say or write "please" or "thank you"—the tone—makes the difference. The tone of your letter tells many things about you—your attitude, your sense of fair play, your desire to be of service. Such expressions as the following help to give your letter a desirable tone:

"You were very kind to . . . ."
"We are most grateful for . . . ."
"We very much appreciate your . . . ."
"We are very happy to know that . . . ."
"We value your . . . ."
"You are entirely correct in saying . . . ."

These phrases do not in themselves make a courteous letter. Your letter must "talk to" and treat the reader like a guest in your home.

Friendliness is an important quality of the good letter. Friendliness and courtesy are related terms, but they are not synonymous. You may use courteous words and yet not be very friendly. For example, the person who wrote the following was not actually discourteous. But the letter does not sound very friendly, does it?

We can't do a thing about your request for a discount. Our special discount offer expired a month ago. Please send us a check for an additional $11.50.

You can inject warmth into your letters by writing as you would talk, by keeping the reader's point of view, and by using friendly sounding words and expressions. Now let's try to inject a friendly tone into the previous letter:

We wish we could honor your request for a discount. However, our discount offer expired a month ago. Since the merchandise currently available was manufactured at a higher price, we must reluctantly ask you to send us your check for an additional $11.50.

Sincerity is another quality your letter should possess. Sincerity means that you really do wish to be of service to your readers—you have a genuine interest in them. False sincerity, however, will show through. If you are genuinely sincere, customers will not take the attitude that your courtesy and friendliness are prompted by a selfish desire to get what you want. Rather, your sincerity should make them feel that they will benefit by acting as you request. When you are sincere, you mean what you say and your letter reflects this feeling. To write a sincere letter, you must believe in people, in your company or organization, and in yourself. You must talk *with*, not *at*, people. Following are examples of expressions that help to reflect sincerity:

"You are correct. We did send you the wrong . . . ."
"Please accept our apology for the delayed shipment."
"Our mistake is very embarrassing to us."
"We would like very much to help you; however, we . . . ."
"I am more than happy to explain the situation."
"You have a right to better service, and we have an obligation to provide it."
"You are right in saying that three weeks is a long time."

Promote Goodwill. Every letter you write should help to promote goodwill for your firm, because goodwill is considered one of the major purposes of all business messages. Goodwill results from:

1. Good products or services.
2. Ethical conduct.
3. Superior service to customers.
4. Prompt attention to details.

Remember that every letter you write *is* the company insofar as the reader is concerned. Your letter sells—or unsells—the reader on your firm.

When you write letters for your company, you should have a thorough knowledge of that company and of the goods or services it offers. You also should have loyalty toward your company; you should believe in it and its goods and services. If you are sincere in this belief (and also a good letter writer), then your faith will show in your letters. Goodwill must necessarily follow.

Loyalty toward your company is dependent upon the company's ethical conduct—its honest and upright dealings in all situations. A company's reputation for high ethical standards must also include keeping its word, never taking advantage of any other firm or person, and paying its bills promptly. In carrying out your duties for the company, you should reflect your company's ethics in what and how you write.

It is ironic that customers expect good service, but when they receive it, they are flattered. When they get poor service, on the other hand, they react negatively, and their outrage soon makes itself felt. In no time at all their goodwill is lost and, eventually, their business. Most progressive firms make top service a company policy, for they know that consistently excellent service keeps old customers and makes new customers out of prospects. Your business letters should stress the service-mindedness of your company.

One secret for building a reputation for "super" service is prompt action. When an order comes in, it should be filled immediately. When a request comes in, it should be answered within 48 hours. If a customer has a complaint, it should be attended to without delay. Failure to reply quickly to a letter is a sure way to destroy goodwill. Such negligence implies to customers that they are not important enough to merit your attention, nor does it meet their needs for safety and security, belonging, and being "somebody." Therefore, even if you are unable to answer all the writer's questions within 48 hours, you should write anyway, giving what help you can and indicating when the remaining questions will be answered.

Be Clear and Complete. Have you ever received a message that you did not understand? How did you feel—confused, and maybe a little angry? What kept the message from being clear? Was something left unsaid? "Meet me on Wednesday at 4 p.m.," Jim writes. But Jim doesn't tell you *where* to meet him. So his message is not clear because it is not complete. You can see, then, that completeness contributes to clarity in letter writing and that a clearly written message is vital if your letter is to achieve its purpose. You can't meet Jim if you don't know where to meet him. And Miller Brothers can't fill your order for shirts if you don't tell them the size you want. Incomplete letters can be costly, for they lead to errors, often cause delays in filling orders, and call for other letters of clarification to be written. With the cost of today's business letters running between $6 and $15, it is necessary to make the *first* letter get the job done successfully.

Clarity also depends on the words you use and the way you use them. First you must have a clear idea in your own mind of what you want to say. Then you must decide how you are going to say it. In general, the writer should use the simplest everyday expressions—those the reader will surely understand. Contrast the following:

POOR: It is absolutely essential that all delinquent payments be forwarded within 15 days to avoid substantial penalty charges.

BETTER: Please pay overdue bills within 15 days to avoid added charges.

Be Concise. A concise letter—a letter that covers the subject in the fewest words possible—is more certain to convey the message than a rambling, wordy letter. But do not think that *concise* and *brief* mean the same thing; brevity is only a part of conciseness. To be concise, a message must be *both* brief and complete. Look at the following request:

> Please send me four of the shirts that you advertised in yesterday's Seattle Times. My check for $32 is enclosed.

This request certainly meets the test for brevity, but could the order be filled? No; the size (and perhaps color) desired has not been specified. Brevity is desirable, but it must not be achieved at the expense of clarity or completeness.

Conciseness means saying all that needs to be said and no more. In business, time is money—and few business people have time to read irrelevant details.

Maintain a Smooth Flow. A letter should hold together; that is, each part should be related to the other parts. This cohesiveness helps the reader to follow your thinking because each sentence flows smoothly into the next, and each paragraph connects with the one preceding and the one following. On the other hand, a rambling letter that has no guidelines—like a rambling speech—is hard to follow.

Logical sequence of thought is the most important factor in achieving cohesiveness. You will be helped in thinking logically if you first number the points you wish to make and then expand each point into a paragraph. In other words, you should make an outline of your thoughts before you begin to write your letter.

In making the transition from one sentence to another or from one paragraph to another, you will be helped by using connecting or linking words or expressions, such as the following:

however	in the first place	furthermore	next
therefore	nevertheless	at any rate	thus
of course	on the other hand	for example	finally

Don't expect these words to work miracles for you, however. Using them to link sentences that embrace disconnected thoughts will fool no one. Again, make an outline before you begin.

Use Paragraphs That Invite the Reader. Good paragraphing is an essential part of effective business letters. However, there is no formula for determining how many paragraphs a letter should have. Many believe that every letter, no matter how short, should contain at least two paragraphs. This is a pretty good rule to follow in most cases. However, the rule does not always work. Consider the following example:

> Enclosed is my $24 check for a one-year subscription to Financial Planning.

This letter is complete (assuming that the writer's name and address are included elsewhere), and there is no need to say more. If you have to contrive a message just to make two paragraphs, then you should forget about the two-paragraph rule.

There are three main guiding principles in paragraphing letters:

1. Convey only one principal idea in a paragraph.
2. Hold paragraphs to not more than six or eight typewritten lines. Long paragraphs make your message *look* hard to read, whether or not it really *is* hard to read.
3. Don't overparagraph. Too many paragraphs make a letter look choppy and detract from the smoothness of the message. The typical full-page letter contains three or four paragraphs.

Avoid Jargon. Within any trade, profession, art, or science, there develops a vocabulary of technical terms commonly called *jargon*. On the job, jargon may help you to communicate with co-workers and to save time. But when writing letters, put yourself in the receiver's place and avoid jargon: the reader may not understand it. For example, in the jargon of the printing industry, a *signature* is a large printed sheet that, when folded, usually makes 32 printed pages. Although this jargon has a special meaning for printers and publishing people, it would be confusing to those outside these industries.

COMMUNICATION LABORATORY

APPLICATION EXERCISES

A. Each of the sentences below is writer-biased; that is, each takes the writer's point of view. Rewrite each sentence so that it is reader-biased and takes the reader's point of view.

1. I would like to work for your company because of your fine benefit plans.
2. Your immediate order would allow us to reduce inventories.
3. We need your reservation by the middle of the month to avoid problems with our bookkeeping.
4. Your early confirmation will make it easier for us to hold your room.

B. The following sentences do nothing to build goodwill. Rewrite them, keeping in mind your knowledge of the psychology of business writing.

1. Please submit your order again; we can't seem to locate the original.
2. You made an error in not advising us of your room preference.
3. A careful customer would have brought this complaint to our attention much earlier.
4. You should have completed a credit application.
5. It is far too late for you to receive our special discount.
6. Because so many people fail to pay promptly, we do not ship merchandise until we receive their check.

7. Your order will be delayed because your size is so unusual.
8. All our other watch purchasers are completely satisfied.
9. It can't possibly be that we sent you the wrong batteries.
10. Our careful order clerks never make that kind of mistake.

C. Each of the following messages lacks some important information. Rewrite the message, providing the information that will make it clear and complete.

1. We would like to introduce our new line of sweaters to you at the Colony Hotel.
2. I would like to receive a copy of your schedule of upcoming events.
3. Please send six of your best white shirts to me at 81 Exeter Drive, Sunderland, Missouri 63042.
4. Would you like to attend our meeting at 10 a.m. tomorrow morning?
5. When does the plane leave?

D. Rewrite the following letter. Paragraph it correctly and use connecting words that will aid clarity and make the ideas flow better.

We received your order today for three dozen of our portable AM/FM radios. We welcome this opportunity to serve you. There has been such a great demand for our radios. We are temporarily out of stock. This fine product will again be available in eight days. Our plant is working overtime. Your order will be shipped very soon. Once again, we very much appreciate your order. We are convinced that the quality of the product will make up for the slight delay.

VOCABULARY AND SPELLING STUDIES

A. These words are often confused: *deprecate, depreciate; bow, beau, bough.* Explain the differences.

B. Many of our most frequently used words are derived from Latin or Greek roots. Using the root in the first column, add two or more words containing this root to each word in the third column.

Root	Meaning	Words Built From Root
1. dict-	say	predict
2. fer-	carry	transfer
3. scrib-	write	describe
4. geo-	earth	geography
5. voc-	call	vocal

C. Change the present-tense forms of the verbs within parentheses to the past-tense forms.

1. The clerk (tear) the invoice by mistake.
2. We (see) the new word processing system last week.
3. She (begin) the meeting on time.
4. The rest of our group (catch) the last plane for Chicago.

5. Our general manager (send) invitations to all our loyal customers.
6. Clarissa (write) a letter that explained the delay.

COMMUNICATING FOR RESULTS

Getting Away. Assume that you are a sales representative for a large manufacturer. You are visiting one of your key accounts, which is represented by Mr. Dennis Bronson, their purchasing agent. Within the hour, Mr. Bronson has placed a sizable order with you. Since it is close to lunchtime, he suggests that the two of you dine together. However, you have an appointment with a customer whom you have been trying to develop into an even larger account. It will take you approximately forty-five minutes to travel to where your appointment is. Suggest ways in which you can make your important second call without antagonizing Mr. Bronson.

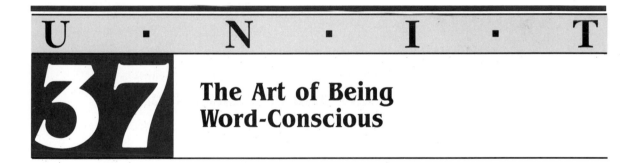

U · N · I · T

37

The Art of Being Word-Conscious

As an expert communicator, you will want to have an understanding of human behavior and recognize how people's needs relate to business writing. Words, our chief means of communication, play an important role in affecting human behavior, and the top-notch writer or speaker needs to be aware of their impact in presenting ideas.

Our Language Affects Our Behavior

It is obvious that word meanings affect human behavior. However, this question arises: "How do we determine the meanings of words?" The factual, objective dictionary meanings are called *denotations*. But denotations tell only half the story.

Each of us has had experiences with words and has developed feelings about words based upon those experiences. For example, what is *your* reaction to *spinach?* to *hamburgers?* These words undoubtedly bring to mind something other than "green leafy plant served as a vegetable" or "chopped meat served in a bun."

The reactions and feelings created by words are called *connotations.* Some words have stronger connotations than others, and many words mean different things to different people based on their past experiences. Connotations may be pleasant or hostile, as you can imagine from your reactions to the *spinach* and *hamburger* examples.

Words that carry varying associations include *labor union, management, Republicans, Democrats, freedom,* and *strike.* In the last few years, other words have taken on new connotations. For example, the words *pollution, transplant,* and *ecology* had different implications ten years ago. Through their experiences with these words, people have now developed more conflicting reactions to these terms.

Careful business writers select words that not only convey the intended meaning but also create positive images in the minds of their readers. Words with antagonistic or distasteful connotations are likely to tune out the reader and lessen the chance of obtaining goodwill. Any term or idea that threatens or does not meet the reader's needs causes a psychological withdrawal from the person who is trying to communicate. Therefore, words that may have varying or highly emotional associations should be used sparingly—and then only when the writer is confident that their use will obtain positive reactions from the reader.

Conversational Words. Some people use big, fancy words to impress others. They do impress others, but not in a favorable way. The successful writer uses conversational words—words that most people can understand. The man in the cartoon asking for another word for *"profundity, erudite, or omniscient"* is on the right track. He probably knows that few people would understand those words and that a simpler, more conversational word is needed. "The Source" gives an excellent substitute—*"smart."* "The Source's" final comment, "They get a little too smart, and they forget how to talk," could refer to the attitude of most people who receive letters loaded

B. C. by permission of Johnny Hart and Field Enterprises, Inc. Copyright © Field Enterprises, Inc., 1971.

with big, fancy words. The reader would be far more favorably impressed with clear, conversational language.

Obsolete Words. A few of today's letter writers use words that are outdated. An expert, however, realizes the importance of projecting the company's or organization's image as up to date and progressive. Therefore, as a budding expert, you must learn to refrain from using such outdated words as those given below:

advise (for *say, tell*)	kindly (for *please*)
beg	cover (for *envelope*)
duly	same ("and we will send you same")
esteemed	state (for *say, tell*)
indulgence (for *understanding*)	trust (for *hope, know, believe*)
via	

Pleasant, Warm Words. Whenever a person is made to feel pleasant and warm, that person is ready to listen to a message. A person who is ready to listen is more likely to take positive action. That is why the expert business writer knows and uses pleasant words that pave the way for stimulating a desired action on the reader's part. Here are some of these words:

admirable	comfortable	generous	secure
advantage	cordial	pleasure	success
agreeable	deserving	profit	valuable
amazing	exclusive	progress	warmth
benefit	fortunate	satisfaction	welcome

Unpleasant, Cold Words. On the other hand, there are words that can annoy, displease, or threaten your reader. These words are unpleasant in themselves, but they are much more so when prefixed by *you* or *your: you failed to send us, your error, your delay.* Depending on your purpose in writing, you may consider it necessary to use a cold word. If, however, you wish to retain the goodwill of the reader or listener, you can take away some of the sting by changing the pronoun *you* to *we* or *our* or by using an impersonal reference: *we did not receive,* instead of *you failed to send; maybe the mistake was ours,* instead of *your error.*

Some of the words that can be a source of irritation to your readers are the following:

abuse	complain—t	dissatisfied	inferior
allege—d	criticism—cize	error	mistake—n
biased	damage	fail—ure	neglect—ligence
blame	defective	fault	trouble
careless	delay	inadequate	unsatisfactory

Unnecessary Words. The number of words we use can add up. Since many people don't like to read, we must take time to rid our writing of unnecessary words. This extra effort pays off: we increase our credibility when our readers know we use words economically and concisely.

Unnecessary Words	Concise Phrases
check in the amount of $5	$5 check
at this point in time	now
I wish to take this opportunity to thank you for	Thank you for . . . .
at all times	always
for the period of a year	annually

Male and Female Words. Most of us are aware that half of our work force is female and that women share positions of responsibility and leadership in business, industry, and government. Word-conscious writers and speakers try to reflect this reality by avoiding words such as *businessmen* and *salesmen* and by using instead terms such as *business workers* (or *business people* or *business executives*) and *sales representatives* (or *salesclerks*). The list below offers other modern substitutes for such terms.

Instead of . . .	Use . . .
fireman	firefighter
mailman	mail carrier
insurance man	insurance agent
foreman	supervisor
stewardess	flight attendant
policeman or policewoman	police officer

Interesting Reading Results From Word Variety

In addition to selecting words that create a positive reaction in the mind of your reader, you will want to use a *variety* of words to hold interest. Just think how dull your communications would be if you used the same words over and over to express a variety of situations, events, or emotions.

You could, for example, describe your supervisor, last evening's TV program, the weather, or a new coat as *nice*. One of the following words substituted for *nice* would add variety and interest to your writing and would convey more meaning to your reader.

Your supervisor: *understanding, encouraging, engaging, agreeable, considerate, even-tempered*

PEANUTS by Schulz

Last evening's TV program: *compelling, dramatic, realistic, informative, suspenseful, hilarious, lighthearted*

The weather: *mild, bracing, temperate, exhilarating, seasonable*

A new coat: *comfortable, stylish, flattering, practical, smart, becoming*

Overused, Worn-Out Words. Other overused words include the following:

good	awful	little	big	think	fix	fantastic
fine	know	lovely	say	come	go	great

Now don't think that these words are entirely taboo. They are essential for many occasions, but they are abused by overuse. To prove this, in each of the following sentences, substitute for the italicized word the words in parentheses.

Management made a *bad* forecast of the company's sales and profits.   (inaccurate, misleading)

Businesses are always looking for *fine* young men and women.   (competent, motivated, diligent)

We both had a *fantastic* performance review.   (glowing, sensational, extraordinary)

The team has an *awful* record.   (uneven, inconsistent, deplorable)

"We made our quota," *said* Andrew.   (proclaimed, announced, shouted)

Sales *went* slowly but surely during the quarter.   (rose, increased, climbed, crept up)

You surely will agree that the substitution of the parenthetical words would give more accurate, interesting, and vivid pictures in these sentences.

Consider also how the improved sentences would help the reader understand precisely what the writer had in mind instead of having to infer or guess the meaning.

Concrete Words. Research has shown that readers and listeners will remember specific, concrete words rather than general ones. Therefore, we need to try to use as many concrete words as possible. Some examples include the following:

General	Concrete
pretty good profit	*14.5 percent* profit
clean offices	*spotless* offices
a *rough* month	a *profitless* month
a *huge* loss	a *$3 million* loss
a *lengthy* report	a *38-page* report

Synonyms Add Variety. What exactly is a synonym? A *synonym* is a word that has the same or nearly the same meaning as another word—*glad* is a synonym for *happy,* for example. Most synonyms, however, are not *exactly* synonymous; that is, although they have the same *basic* meaning, each synonym has a slightly different shade of meaning. Look up the word *get* in your dictionary. You will find the following listed as synonyms: *obtain, procure, secure, acquire, gain, win, earn.* Notice that each of these words, although it has the fundamental idea of *get,* has its own shade of meaning. For example, you would *obtain,* not *win* a position; you would *win,* not *acquire,* a prize. Because the English language was derived from so many other languages—Latin, Greek, French, German, Anglo-Saxon, and others—it is exceedingly rich in synonyms; therefore, it is possible to express fine shades of meaning by choosing the appropriate synonym.

A prime source of help in learning to differentiate among the meanings of synonyms is your dictionary. Form the habit of noticing whether synonyms are listed at the end of the entry under any word that you look up. If they are, try to understand the differentiations in meaning of the various synonyms. For example, suppose you have looked up *occurrence* (perhaps in order to check on the number of *c*'s and *r*'s in the word). Notice the list of synonyms: *event, incident, episode, circumstance, happening.* From the differentiations given, you can "concoct" these phrases: "The final *event* that led up to World War II," "We have completely forgotten the unpleasant *incident,*" "The *episode* of launching the first satellite," and so on.

If you will follow this plan of conscientiously learning the differences between synonyms, you will be surprised by your growing awareness of distinctions in meanings that you had never thought of before. (Also review "The Thesaurus," page 59.)

Antonyms Add Clarity. An antonym is a word that has an opposite meaning. There are two types of antonyms. In Type 1, a prefix meaning *not* is added to the word for which the antonym is desired. *In, non, un* and other prefixes are widely used to "manufacture" almost any word of opposite meaning that may be desired. For example, *incorrect,* the antonym of *correct,* is formed by joining *in* and *correct.*

However, a person who has a wide enough vocabulary can choose an entirely different word (Type 2 antonyms). For example, instead of characterizing a certain statement as *incorrect,* you might describe the statement as *erroneous.*

Type 1			**Type 2**
de	+ activate	deactivate	arrest
dis	+ appear	disappear	vanish
dis	+ ordered	disordered	cluttered
dis	+ pleased	displeased	offended
im	+ mobile	immobile	static
in	+ validate	invalidate	nullify
ir	+ regular	irregular	peculiar
non	+ conformist	nonconformist	dissenter
un	+ common	uncommon	exceptional

Avoid These Expressions

Contrast the following italicized expressions. Those on the left are stiff and outdated and are to be avoided. On the right are more appropriate expressions for the same ideas.

To Be Avoided	**Preferable**
1. *Acknowledge receipt of*	1. *Thank you for* or *I received*
"This is to acknowledge receipt of your letter."	"Thank you for writing me about . . . ."
2. *Advise*	2. *Say, tell, let us know*
"Please advise us of the action you intend to take."	"Please let us know what action you intend to take."
"I cannot advise you as to when the contract will be ready."	"I cannot tell you when the contract will be ready."
3. *Am (are) in receipt of*	3. *Thank you* or *I have received*
"We are in receipt of your check for $81.20."	"Thank you for your check for $81.20."
	"I have received your check for $81.20 and appreciate . . . ."
4. *As per*	4. *As* or *according to*
"We are crediting your account as per instructions."	"As you instructed, we are crediting your account."
	"We are crediting your account, according to your wishes."
5. *At an early date*	5. *Soon* (Or give a specific date.)
"You will hear from us at an early date."	"I will write you soon about . . . ."
	"You will hear from me by August 15 about the new delivery date."
6. *At this time, at present, at the present writing*	6. *Now* (Or omit entirely.)
"My opinion at this time (or *at present*) is that the meeting will take place."	"I now think that the meeting will take place."
	"I believe that the meeting will take place."
7. *Attached hereto*	7. *Attached, here, enclosed*
"Attached hereto is the agreement for your signature."	"Attached is the agreement for your signature."
	"Here is the agreement, which I hope you will sign."

To Be Avoided	Preferable
8. *Beg*	8. *Ask, request, hope,* and so on
"I beg your indulgence in this matter."	"I request a 30-day extension."
	"I hope you will allow me another month in which to pay this bill."
9. *Due to the fact that*	9. *As, because, since*
"Due to the fact that our factory is on strike, we cannot . . . ."	"Because our factory is on strike, we cannot . . . ."
"You have been placed on our preferred list of customers due to the fact that you always pay promptly."	"Since you always pay your bills promptly, we are pleased to list you as a preferred customer."
10. *Duly*	10. Do not use. Superfluous.
"I received your February 8 order, which I duly acknowledge."	"I appreciate your February 8 order."
11. *Enclosed please find*	11. *Enclosed* or *here*
"Enclosed please find your copy of the minutes of our last meeting."	'Enclosed are the minutes . . . ."
	"Here are the minutes . . . ."
12. *I have before me*	12. Do not use. Superfluous.
"I have before me your reminder of the deadline for my article."	"I am grateful for your reminder of the deadline for my article."
13. *Herewith*	13. Do not use.
"I am sending you a duplicate bid herewith."	"Enclosed (or *attached*) is a duplicate bid."
14. *In re*	14. *Regarding, concerning, as to*
"In re the freight charges, I believe they are high."	"Regarding the freight charges, I believe they are high."
15. *In the event that*	15. *In case* or *if*
"In the event that you cannot arrive on Tuesday evening, I will schedule the conference for Wednesday."	"If you cannot arrive on Tuesday evening, I will schedule the conference for Wednesday."
16. *In this matter*	16. Do not use. Superfluous.
"I will await your action in this matter."	"I will await your action."
17. *Kindly*	17. *Please*
"If our substitution is not satisfactory, kindly let us know."	"If the substitution we are sending is not satisfactory, please let us know."

To Be Avoided

18. *In the amount of*

"Our money order in the amount of $6 is enclosed."

19. *Party* (referring to a person)

"According to another party in your firm, our record is satisfactory."

20. *Same*

"I have received your letter and thank you for same."

21. *State*

"In response to your inquiry, I wish to state that we can furnish you with the items you specified."

"In your letter you state that you want a ripple finish on the letterheads."

22. *Take the liberty of*

"I am taking the liberty of sending you the beige, rather than the desert tan, drapery material."

"May I take the liberty of telling you how much we value your business."

23. *Thank you in advance*

"Thank you in advance for any courtesies you can extend Mr. Phillips."

24. *The writer*

"The writer wishes to acknowledge receipt of the book."

"Please send the samples to the attention of the writer."

25. *Trust*

"I trust my suggestion will be satisfactory."

"I trust you will agree with the action I have taken."

Preferable

18. *For*

"Our $6 money order is enclosed."

19. *Person* (Or use a name or title.)

"According to your credit supervisor (or *another person*, or *Mrs. Black*), our record is satisfactory."

20. *It, they, them,* or omit.

"Thank you for your letter."

21. *Say, tell,* or omit.

"We can furnish you with the steel plates you need."

"In your letter you say (or *you mentioned*) that you want a ripple finish on the letterheads."

22. Omit.

"Therefore, I am sending you the beige, rather than the desert tan, drapery material."

"Many thanks for your business."

23. Do not use. It is presumptuous to thank a person in advance.

"I would appreciate any courtesies you can extend Mr. Phillips."

24. *I, me, my*

"Thank you for sending me the book."

"Please send the samples to me."

25. *Hope, know, believe*

"I hope my suggestion will be satisfactory."

"I believe you will agree with the action I have taken."

To Be Avoided	Preferable
26. *Under date of*	26. Omit.
"I have your letter under date of May 1."	"I have your May 1 letter."
27. *Under separate cover*	27. *Will send, am sending,* and so on
"I am mailing the back issues under separate cover."	"I will send the back issues to you today."
	"The sample you requested was mailed this morning."
28. *Up to this writing*	28. *So far,* or omit.
"Up to this writing, I have had no word from the Wilson Company."	"So far, I have had no word from the Wilson Company."
	"I have not heard from the Wilson Company."
29. *Would ask, would remind, would say*	29. Do not use *would* in this way.
"I would ask that you bear with us on your delayed order."	"I hope you will understand why your order will be delayed."

COMMUNICATION LABORATORY

APPLICATION EXERCISES

A. You now know that meanings connected with words might not correspond exactly to dictionary definitions. For this laboratory practice, write a dictionary definition (denotation) for each of the following words; then explain what comes to your mind when you see the word (connotation).

1. summer
2. home
3. baseball
4. teapot
5. apple
6. beach
7. chalkboard
8. poodle

B. Give at least one synonym for each of the following italicized words. Consult a dictionary or a thesaurus if you need help in finding a good word to substitute.

1. This thermometer takes very *exact* measurements.
2. The company *commemorates* the anniversary of its founding every year.
3. Every manager must *defend* his or her budget.
4. A salesperson must always *keep* a positive attitude.

5. Andrea offered a new *slant* on our sales problem.
6. *Speed* is to be avoided on some jobs.
7. We must all work together to *shape* a new advertising campaign.
8. Ms. Cellars likes her computer assistants to *test* every program.
9. Is there really a *choice?*
10. The company's decision to cut prices was *brave.*

C. Match each word in column A with its antonym in column B.

A	B
1. discourage	a. fearless
2. errorless	b. excited
3. afraid	c. simple
4. observe	d. cheer
5. peculiar	e. ordinary
6. sensible	f. foolish
7. calm	g. faulty
8. rebellious	h. ignore
9. complicated	i. sturdy
10. frail	j. obedient

D. Substitute a more precise adjective for the overworked *little* in these examples.

1. a little town
2. a little locomotive
3. a little mind
4. a little kitten
5. a little matter
6. a little portion
7. a little wire
8. a little build
9. a little computer
10. a little issue

E. Change the following negative statements into positive statements.

1. Do not forget the sales meeting at the end of the month.
2. Don't fail to ship this order by air freight.
3. You forgot to provide a delivery date.
4. We cannot deliver your order because our plant is closed until July 15.
5. Do not lower the product's quality.
6. Don't anger customers by being late for an appointment.
7. We cannot act on your request at this time.
8. We will not forget your special request.
9. We won't know our prices until April 1.
10. Never forget a customer's preferences.

F. Rewrite the following sentences to eliminate outdated or unpleasant expressions.

  1. Kindly favor us with a note if we can help.
  2. We are in receipt of your order of May 5, and we thank you for same.
  3. Your shipping department's blunder caused us unbelievable trouble.
  4. As per our recent discussion, attached hereto is our latest price list.
  5. I have your letter under date of August 27.
  6. Please be so kind as to find a photocopy of my canceled check.
  7. We are forwarding the book you ordered under separate cover.
  8. The order will arrive late due to the fact that the railroad is on strike.
  9. This is to acknowledge the receipt of your reservation.
 10. We are crediting your account as per your wishes.

VOCABULARY AND SPELLING STUDIES

A. In each of the following groups, three of the four words have similar meanings. Which word is the intruder?

1. impartial, fervent, unbiased, objective
2. offend, entreat, beg, implore
3. blossom, bloom, forbid, flower
4. fabricate, fashion, shape, dodge
5. meddle, invent, interfere, tamper
6. revise, denounce, correct, remedy

B. These words are often confused: *morning, mourning; hail, hale*. Explain the differences.

COMMUNICATING FOR RESULTS

Gobbledygook. High-sounding words and phrases cloud the meaning of your writing and speaking. For example, "Consumers purchase when they possess sufficient funds" means, in everyday language, "People buy when they have enough money." Rewrite the following example of gobbledygook so that it is easy to understand.

> The values of equities have constantly eroded over the recent past. Nevertheless, the long-term economic prospects appear positive. We therefore suggest that long-term investors retain their positions in sound equities. Those who have additional funds to commit and those who have refrained from a committment should buy on weakness. These investors should search out sound equities that combine secure current yield with the likelihood of future price appreciation.

38

The Art of Being Explicit

One of the marks of the trained business communicator is explicitness, the ability to put down on paper a message that the reader can interpret in only one way—the way intended by the writer. The lack of such ability can cause confusion and misunderstanding, and a confused reader is in no condition to respond positively.

For instance, suppose you received a letter containing this sentence: "The manager told Mr. Edwards that he will visit your territory soon." Would you know whether to expect Mr. Edwards or the manager? If it is important for you to know which one is coming, you would have to write a letter to find out. Letters that must be written to straighten out mix-ups not only generate ill feeling but also increase the cost of doing business.

Because of garbled messages, goodwill may be lost and prestige dimmed. The purpose of this unit is to help you to be explicit. Mastery of the following principles will enable you to say exactly what you mean and to construct messages that mean the same thing to your reader as they do to you.

Placing Words, Phrases, and Clauses Clearly

Confusing and ridiculous messages often result when a writer fails to place a word, a phrase, or a clause with the unit of thought to which it belongs. As you study the following presentation, keep in mind the all-important "thought unit."

Words. The meaning of a sentence can be changed by a word carelessly placed. When the word is written with its correct thought unit, however, the intended message is clear. For instance, consider the following examples:

Only Mrs. Vilas brought her son.   (Others did not bring children.)

Mrs. Vilas brought her only son.   (Mrs. Vilas has no more than one son.)

In the first case, you know that the only person who brought a son was Mrs. Vilas. Had the word *only* been misplaced, confusion may have resulted because a different meaning would have been conveyed. In the second case, the meaning is that Mrs. Vilas brought her son, her only son. This second sentence tells the reader that Mrs. Vilas has only one son, whereas the first sentence does not make this limitation. See how by shifting the word *only* the meaning can be altered.

A college professor once received the following telephone message from Tom Jaworsky, a student:

I am ill and will not be in class again.

The professor immediately dropped the name from the class list. When the student returned to class the next day, he was amazed to learn that he had been excluded. What the telephone message was really supposed to say was:

I am ill *again* and will not be in class (today).

Placing modifying words near the words they modify is important in conveying ideas precisely. Perhaps not quite so readily misinterpreted, but nevertheless as important, are those misplaced words that give silly meanings to our writing. Now suppose the following advertisement appeared in your local newspaper:

FLANNEL BOYS' TROUSERS ON SALE TOMORROW.

Wouldn't you be amused by the thought of "flannel boys"? And how simple it would have been to write *boys' flannel trousers!*

Phrases. Incorrectly placed phrases, too, can completely change the meaning of a message:

I stood looking at the flocks of ducks at my window.

Flocks of ducks at my window presents a fantastic picture. But place the phrase *at my window* with its proper thought unit and we have:

I stood at my window looking at the flocks of ducks.

Perhaps more illustrative of how modifier placement can affect meaning are the following two statements:

With an instant camera, Darlene took a picture of a squirrel.

Darlene took a picture of a squirrel with an instant camera.

The first sentence says that it was Darlene who had the camera. But the second sentence suggests that perhaps the squirrel was holding a camera when the picture was taken! Be sure that a phrase is placed next to the element it modifies so that the reader interprets the meaning correctly.

Clauses. Errors of all kinds are more likely to be made in long sentences, and misplaced clauses are no exception. The reason may be that there is such a string of words that the writer loses sight of the thought unit. Evidently that is what happened in this sentence:

Marcia ran from the house as the fire spread through the upper floor and went next door to call for help.

What do you think of "as the fire spread through the upper floor"? The way it is positioned suggests that the fire ran for help! If the clause is properly placed, the sentence communicates its message clearly, like this:

As the fire spread through the upper floor, Marcia ran from the house and went next door to call for help.

Not quite so startling but just as inexact is the following message:

Ms. Frensen brought a clock to the meeting that had been running for over a hundred years.

What had been running for over a hundred years? According to the sentence, the meeting had been running for over a hundred years. More likely, though, the writer was referring to the clock, not the meeting. The sentence, of course, should have been written as follows:

Ms. Frensen brought to the meeting a clock that had been running for over a hundred years.

Which *Clauses*. There is nothing wrong with using *which* clauses, provided they are explicit in meaning. A *which* clause is not essential to a sentence, and therefore is *always* set off by commas. When used to refer to an entire thought or when incorrectly placed, *which* clauses can confuse the message. As is the case with any other kind of thought-unit violation, misplaced clauses can be confusing in written and oral communication.

We neglected to turn off the word processor, which really annoyed the office manager.

The meaning of this sentence is not entirely clear. Was it the machine itself that annoyed the office manager, or was it the fact that someone had neglected to turn off the machine? Because in this case the *which* clause refers to the entire idea of *We neglected to turn off the word processor*, one of the following revisions should have been used to make the meaning explicit:

The office manager was really annoyed by our failure to turn off the word processor.

We neglected to turn off the word processor that the office manager hated.

Only the untrained or the careless writer is guilty of the *which*-clause error. Good writers are aware that a grotesque meaning may be conveyed when a *which* clause is not written with its proper thought unit. See what happens in this sentence:

The wood has been stored in a metal container, which burned brightly in the stove.

A metal container, which burned brightly in the stove sounds pretty silly, doesn't it? The following revision makes clear that the wood burned brightly and that it had been stored in a metal container.

The wood, which had been stored in a metal container, burned brightly in the stove.

The *which* clause simply provides an extra bit of information about where the wood had been kept.

That *Clauses. That* clauses are essential to the sentence because they are needed for identification. They arc *never* set off by commas.

The wood that had been stored in a metal container burned brightly in the stove.

Using *that* instead of *which* means that only the wood that had been stored in a metal container burned—no other wood.

CLASS PRACTICE 1

Stop now and see how well you understand the presentation so far. Discuss and revise the following sentences:

1. Ms. Hanson's secretary found a memo that her supervisor had written on the floor.
2. Sara found a faded invoice in the file cabinet that was twenty years old.
3. We looked at the tall buildings walking down the street.
4. Memos were given to all employees announcing the changes.
5. Sam finished reading his report on improving sales while flying to San Francisco.

Who and What

Another way to be explicit is to state clearly *who did what, or who will do what.* To do so, be sure to observe the thought-unit principle when writing sentences. In the following sentence, for example, is it clear *who did what?*

Having finished all the correspondence and having done all the filing, the supervisor praised Anne's efficiency.

Precisely who finished the correspondence and did the filing? As this sentence is now written, it means either that the supervisor finished the correspondence and did the filing or that Anne finished the correspondence and did the filing. Had the writer followed the *who did what* principle, the meaning of this sentence would have been clear:

After Anne had finished all the correspondence and had done all the filing, the supervisor praised her efficiency.

Although the original sentence was worded very awkwardly, it was nevertheless logical to assume that it was Anne, not the supervisor, who finished the correspondence and did the filing. However, *who did what* is not always so obvious:

Hoping to improve sales, a new advertising agency was hired by the corporation.

Who was hoping to improve sales? The advertising agency? The corporation? Make it absolutely clear to the reader.

Hoping to improve sales, the corporation hired a new advertising agency.

In some cases, the *who did what* confusion can be amusing, as you will see in the following example.

The tourists looked at the tall office buildings driving down the avenue.

The buildings, of course, are not driving down the avenue—the tourists are. The sentence should read:

Driving down the avenue, the tourists looked at the tall office buildings.

Pinpointing the Pronoun Reference

The last part of your training in the art of being explicit concerns pronoun reference. When you use *it, he, she, they, this,* or another pronoun to refer to somebody or something, you must pinpoint the person or the thing meant by that pronoun. Do not make the reader guess at your meaning.

To be definite, you must avoid the indefinite. Some of the specific pronoun reference pitfalls that you must learn to avoid are the following:

Indefinite *It.* Inexperienced writers use the pronoun *it* as a sort of vague catchall word. They frequently use *it* as a substitute for something that should be clearly stated. Consider the use of *it* in this sentence:

We are offering a special discount to new customers, because it will mean more business for us.

Do you see that the *it* in this sentence forces the reader to stop and think of what *it* stands for? A person with writing know-how would have used a definite reference.

We are offering a special discount to new customers because an *introductory offer* will mean more business for us.

Even more indefinite and confusing is the use of the *it* in the following illustration:

If you can keep a ledger, please show it to Andy and Bill.

As you read the following revision, note that the writer is much more explicit.

If you can keep a ledger, please show Andy and Bill how it is done.

Indefinite *He, She,* and *They.* Vagueness in the use of these pronouns, in all their different forms, is also a common writing fault. Sometimes their references are so uncertain that the reader is faced with a serious interpretation problem:

> Ms. Golden told Paula that her sister had applied for a position.

Whose sister had applied for a position? Is it Ms. Golden's sister or Paula's sister? Now look at two possible revisions, either of which would be explicit:

> Paula learned from Ms. Golden that the latter's sister had applied for a position.

> Ms. Golden told Paula that her, Paula's, sister had applied for a position.

Then, too, there is the favorite, but slipshod, *they say* expression.

> They say that the demand for housing will continue to grow in the future.

Who is meant by the *they* in this sentence? A person who knew what he or she was talking about would have been specific about who said what.

> Economists (or housing experts or mortgage bankers) say that the demand for housing will continue to grow in the future.

Indefinite *This.* Even professional writers are sometimes careless about using *this* to refer to an entire preceding thought. In such an event, the reference is so hazy that the reader may have to reread in order to be sure of the meaning.

> When the stock market opened yesterday morning, orders to buy flooded the exchange. This created a hectic trading day.

The above message exemplifies sloppy, as well as inexact, writing. A moment's reflection would produce something like the following:

> When the stock market opened yesterday morning, the flood of orders to buy created a hectic trading day.

CLASS PRACTICE 2

Test your ability to handle *who did what* and *indefinite pronoun reference* situations by discussing and revising the following sentences.

1. Mr. Hendricks told Phil that his plan had worked.
2. They say that interest rates might drop this fall.
3. We are advertising more because it brings us to the attention of more people.
4. If the cats will not stay off the chairs, put them in the cellar.
5. Seeking to improve her efficiency, an experienced secretary was hired by Ms. Cowell.
6. While studying the figures, the phone rang.

7. When the changes were announced, the salespeople were confused. This lost us some time.

COMMUNICATION LABORATORY

APPLICATION EXERCISES

A. All the following sentences contain phrases that are confusing because they're in the wrong place. On a separate sheet of paper, copy the phrase that you think is confusing.

1. The supervisor watched the driver pick up passengers from the back of the bus.
2. There is a report on the secretary's desk that contains the information we need.
3. A production chart is on the wall that includes all the critical dates.
4. The purchasing agent bought the machinery who was here last week.
5. Many home owners buy fire insurance for their houses that they don't need.
6. My brother works for a company that repairs automobiles three evenings a week.
7. Mr. Thornton promised after lunch that he would see us.
8. I could hear the rain beating on the roof while talking to my supervisor.
9. I could see the order clerks working through my office window.
10. If you take advantage of our offer, you will receive a watch that keeps excellent time for two dollars.

B. Now revise the sentences in Exercise A so that they are clear and correct.

C. The following sentences also need revision. Rewrite each one, making the meaning explicit.

1. They say that sales always decrease in June.
2. On the news last night, it said that the economy was improving.
3. Ms. Suarex told Nancy that she had been promoted.
4. Our new advertising campaign will begin in May.
5. Some word processing operators are assigned to equipment they don't like.
6. The manager refused to approve the request, which made the office staff unhappy.
7. Three new branch offices were opened last March, which ought to improve customer service.
8. This should have been known by everyone in the company.
9. The accountant told Mr. Blair that his deduction has been disallowed.
10. They claim that lack of lubrication causes the part to fail.

VOCABULARY AND SPELLING STUDIES

A. How are the following words spelled when the suffixes indicated are added?

1. direct- or
2. mile- age
3. prefer- ed
4. perform- ance
5. sunny- er
6. shake- y
7. jealous- y
8. true- ly
9. forget- ing
10. know- ledge

B. Which words in the following groups are misspelled? Respell them correctly.

1. ment, apply, sought, sord
2. ferce, gallon, chanel, panel
3. lawyer, maner, wisper, tennis
4. ballance, relief, secure, acept
5. document, difficult, paralel, citys
6. atractive, storege, reveal, similar
7. grammar, iner, conect, admire
8. suggest, discus, oppose, confus
9. shalow, polish, selfish, sesion
10. decrese, obtain, occupy, ocur

C. Add a suffix pronounced *shun* to each of the following.

1. miss_____
2. men_____
3. mo_____
4. cau_____
5. satisfac_____
6. affcc_____
7. instruc_____
8. except_____
9. explor_____

D. Choose *ize, ise,* or *yze* to complete each of the following.

1. notar_____
2. anal_____
3. advert_____
4. adv_____
5. disgu_____
6. rev_____
7. critic_____
8. organ_____
9. exerc_____

E. How are the following spelled when the *uhble*-sounding suffix is added?

1. respons_____
2. cap_____
3. imposs_____
4. vis_____
5. wash_____
6. pass_____
7. sens_____
8. lov_____
9. reli_____

F. Which of the following words ending with the sound of *seed* are misspelled? Spell them correctly.

1. proced
2. succeed
3. exced
4. receed
5. sede (yield or grant)
6. intercede
7. conceed
8. secede
9. superceed
10. acceed

COMMUNICATING FOR RESULTS

Write as You Talk. Saying something aloud before writing it often helps to give naturalness to your expression. Rewrite the following paragraph as you would *say* it. See how much your writing can be improved.

> In compliance with the regulations governing such matters, your recent complaint about the malfunctioning of your kitchen appliance has been referred to our engineering staff. It is currently being analyzed. After the analysis has been concluded, one of our engineering representatives will contact you directly.

U · N · I · T

39

The Art of Being Polished

The expert communicator must be able (1) to select and place words carefully and (2) to arrange ideas so that they flow smoothly. Notice, for example, the television commercials or magazine ads that hold your interest. After appealing to your needs, they take you smoothly from one idea to the next, each idea building upon and growing out of the previous one. Such continuity provides the polish needed for understanding and acceptance.

To become an expert writer, then, you must learn to write fluent, well-explained messages. In business communications, polish is a secret ingredient that may make a very important contribution to increased profits. For example, the business message that is clearly understood promotes goodwill and inspires confidence; it conveys the *image* of a top-quality firm. Confusion and misunderstanding, on the other hand, can only destroy the company's image in the eyes of the public.

Mastery of the principles that govern this phase of the art of writing—the principles that you will study in this unit—will help you become a polished writer.

Messages That Flow

Each type of communication—letter, report, news release—usually develops one main thought; consequently, the entire communication should flow from beginning to end, showing the logical development of that thought.

Sentences within each paragraph must be written so the paragraph hangs together, and all paragraphs must glide along the main-thought track.

One way to help your messages flow is to learn how to use transitional, or "bridging," words and phrases. These are simply the conjunctive adverbs and the introductory expressions that you have studied previously. Note the following examples:

accordingly	for this purpose	on the contrary
after all	furthermore	on the other hand
as a result	hence	otherwise
at the same time	however	similarly
besides	in addition	still
consequently	meanwhile	therefore
for example	moreover	yet
for instance	nevertheless	

Making Sentences Flow Smoothly. To understand the importance of bridging expressions within sentences, study carefully the following illustration and explanation:

> We have four strategically located warehouses; delivery delays are common.

Can you see any connection between having four warehouses and having delivery delays? A transitional word is needed to tie this sentence into a smooth, meaningful message. Let's try *nevertheless*.

> We have four strategically located warehouses; nevertheless, delivery delays are common.

Now you can see that the word *nevertheless* bridges the meaning of the second clause to the meaning of the first clause.

Remember that a comma usually follows an introductory transitional, or bridging, expression that contains more than one syllable. *Nevertheless* is considered introductory because it introduces the second clause.

Making Paragraphs Hang Together. Failure to use transitional expressions to introduce new paragraphs can affect the flow of the entire message exactly as such failure affected the smoothness of the single sentence you have just studied. With bridging thought in mind, consider the following paragraphs taken from a report from a marketing manager to a company's president.

> Yes, we have catered to a select group of customers over the years. These people appreciated the finest and did not complain about paying high prices.
>
> We believe that the market for our quality products has increased dramatically. Over the past year we have been flooded with requests for our products from people we have never approached directly.
>
> We believe that sizable numbers of people whom we have never thought of as our customers have suddenly become our customers. These people cannot pay our standard prices as easily as our regular clientele. If our sales volume can increase

by 20 percent, we will be able to lower our prices by at least 10 percent. We believe that both of these goals can easily be met.

Let's polish this report by using transitional expressions to introduce the second and third paragraphs and to link the first and second sentences of the third paragraph.

Yes, we have catered to a select group of customers over the years. These people appreciated the finest and did not complain about paying high prices.

At the same time, we believe that the market for our quality products has increased dramatically. Over the past year we have been flooded with requests for our products from people we have never approached directly.

As a result, we believe that sizable numbers of people whom we have never thought of as our customers have suddenly become our customers. These people cannot pay our standard prices as easily as our regular clientele. *However,* if our volume can increase by 20 percent, we will be able to lower our prices by at least 10 percent. We believe that both these goals can easily be met.

Some Pitfalls

Boring, repetitious, and incorrect use of the word *and* is a common writing fault that you should learn to avoid. The *and* pitfalls are the following:

And, And, And. And is one of the most important conjunctions. There is no reason for a writer to avoid using it, but there is good reason to be cautious of overusing it. A message consisting of sentence after sentence containing two or more clauses joined by *and* is monotonous and boring. The expert writer adds sparkle by (1) using many synonyms and (2) varying sentence structure. For instance, consider this sentence: "We will control our careless expenses, and profits will improve greatly." Use of the *and* connective makes this a wishy-washy message. Now see how the sentence could be strengthened and polished.

GOOD: After we control our careless expenses, profits will improve greatly.

BETTER: The control of our careless expenses will allow us to improve profits greatly.

BEST: Profits will improve greatly when our careless expenses are controlled.

While the *and* construction has its place in writing, notice how constant use of this sentence structure results in monotonous writing.

Last month our ten new service technicians completed their training, and they began working on June 1. Customer response to these added people has been tremendous, and the better service should lead to more sales. Current sales are already far ahead of budget, and we'd better think about adding more service personnel. We are developing a fine product reputation, and we can't afford to damage it through poor service.

Now let's vary the sentence structure. Study the following revision and note how much more interesting the writing appears.

> Our ten new service technicians who completed their training last month began working on June 1. The tremendous customer response to these added people suggests that better service should lead to more sales. We'd better think about adding more service personnel, since current sales are already far ahead of budget. We are building up a fine product reputation which we cannot afford to damage through poor service.

And So. Using *and so* to introduce a clause is using the expression as a conjunction; yet *and so* does not appear in any list of conjunctions. This incorrect expression is another common writing fault. Some writers constantly use *and so* to introduce a reason-giving clause; they do not know that there are other expressions that would be just right for reason-giving. Some transitional words that may properly be used for this purpose are *hence, therefore, consequently,* and *accordingly.* Now study the following illustrations and revisions:

> POOR: When we tested the product, the customer response was tremendous, and so we began manufacturing it.
>
> BETTER: When we tested the product, the customer response was tremendous; therefore, we began manufacturing it.
>
> POOR: Your bids were accepted, and so we signed a contract with you.
>
> BETTER: Your bids were acceptable; consequently, we signed a contract with you.
>
> POOR: Your payment record has not been good, and so we cannot extend additional credit.
>
> BETTER: Your payment record has not been good; therefore, we cannot extend additional credit.

Written without the *and,* however, *so* is an acceptable conjunction. Like any other conjunction, it must not be overused. The following sentence illustrates the *so* usage; but *therefore* or *consequently* would be just as effective.

> Hard work is always necessary for success; so prepare yourself for a significant effort.

Balanced Sentences

When you want to emphasize a comparison or contrast or when you want to emphasize a particular idea in a forceful way, you may want to use a "balanced" sentence. This type of sentence is one in which ideas of equal value are expressed in parallel, or similar, constructions.

Balancing Comparisons. To be balanced, comparisons must contain all necessary words; omitting necessary words causes lopsided comparisons. Look at the following sentence:

> Mr. Alden appreciates your work just as much, and maybe more, than I do.

You know that words set off by commas are considered excess baggage and can be omitted without affecting the basic meaning of the sentence. In the above illustration, however, omission of the words enclosed in commas would produce this meaning: Mr. Alden praises your efforts just as much *than* I do. The use of *than* in this sentence is inappropriate; therefore, the meaning of the sentence is obscured.

If, however, you correctly insert the second *as*, and if you place the commas correctly, you will have the following balanced comparison:

Mr. Alden praises your efforts just as much as, and maybe more than, I do.

To fix this principle in your mind, study one more illustration and explanation.

Do you believe that the office staff is less interested in profits than salespeople?

As written, this question is a request for your opinion as to whether the office staff is less interested in profits than they are in salespeople. For balance and clarity the comparison should be phrased this way:

Do you believe that the office staff is less interested in profits than salespeople are (interested)?

Balancing Modifiers. Although you would say *a boat*, you would not say *a apple*. When writing words in a series, do not omit modifying adjectives if the first adjective will not serve for the entire series.

We looked at a personal computer, word processor, and automatic letter opener.

Because *a* is used only before the first item in the series, the meaning is that we looked at a personal computer, a word processor, and *a* automatic letter opener. However, the first modifier is not correct for all members of the series; so the sentence should be changed to read: "a personal computer, a word processor, and *an* automatic letter opener."

Balancing Verbs. Some sentences contain verb phrases such as *will make, have sent, was shipped,* and so on. Other sentences may contain two verb phrases, as does this sentence:

We *will go* to the airport and (*will*) *take* a flight to Dayton.

Note that the *will* is omitted before take, because the *will* in the first verb phrase serves correctly for the second part of the compound verb phrase.

Verbs will not balance, however, if a sentence has two verb phrases and any part of one of them is omitted or if the tense or number of both is not the same.

POOR: Your successful bids were received last week, and the contract (were) approved today.

These verb phrases do not balance because the *were* that is correct for *received* is not correct for *approved*. *Bids* requires a plural verb; *contract* requires a singular verb. Correctly written, this is the sentence:

Your successful bids were received last week, and the contract was approved today.

Now consider balance in relation to a compound verb:

POOR: I never have, and never will, see a better worker.

While only one form of the main verb phrase, *will see*, is expressed, the two forms are not the same. Adding the unexpressed *see* to the first part of the compound would give this awkward construction: "I have never see." Thus omission of part of a verb phrase destroys verb balance. The sentence should have been written this way:

I never *have seen*, and never *will see*, a better worker.

Balancing Prepositions.
Different words call for different prepositions to go with them. For instance, you would say *conform to*, but *in compliance with*. Balancing prepositions means that if different prepositions are required to accompany words used in a compound, each preposition must be stated. Consider the preposition *in* as used in this sentence:

Our employees have respect and belief in the company's goals.

Respect and belief in means *respect in* and *belief in*. But *respect in* does not make sense. Omission of a preposition, therefore, caused a mismatch; the sentence should have been written like this:

Our employees have *respect for* and *belief in* the company's goals.

Now study this second illustration:

I can't figure out why some of our workers have no appreciation or interest in our mutual problems.

Can you see that *appreciation (in) or interest in* is not balanced? The sentence must be written like this:

I can't figure out why some of our workers have no appreciation *of* or interest *in* our mutual problems.

Incomplete Clauses.
Although omitting part of a clause may be good writing, in many cases such an omission can really confuse a reader. In the sentence "Kelley is more outgoing than I," for example, the meaning "than I (am)" is clear.

But read the following sentence and see what an omission in a clause can do to the clarity of a message:

Did Anderson lose the sale or his manager?

What do you suppose this writer means? The question may be whether Anderson or his manager lost the sale. The polished writer would have asked clearly and simply:

Which one lost the sale, Anderson or his manager?

Now see how absurd the following illustration is as a result of the incomplete clause:

Did Laura mail the package or her secretary?

The sentence can be interpreted to mean: "Did Laura mail the package or did she mail her secretary?" To make this sentence clear, the complete clause should be included:

Did Laura mail the package, or did her secretary do it?

Balancing Items in Lists. Balance is especially important in lists. Note, for example, the following list:

The salary committee decided:

1. To study pay scales in local companies.
2. To study salaries in the industry.
3. That employees be informed of the studies.

For balance, the last item in the list should match the other items:

3. To inform the employees of the studies.

When listing items, be sure to use the same structure for all items. Compare the following example of a poor list with the better example that follows. Note how the better list is easier to read.

POOR: When you are traveling, be sure to follow these guidelines:

1. Tell someone in the company where you plan to be.
2. Call in each day for messages.
3. A number should be left where you can be reached.
4. Your office should be notified if plans change.

BETTER: When you are traveling, be sure to follow these guidelines:

1. Tell someone in the company where you plan to be.
2. Call in each day for messages.
3. Leave a number where you can be reached.
4. Notify your office if plans change.

As you see, in both examples the items listed are complete sentences, but in the poor example the sentences are not balanced. Notice how the words *Tell, Call, Leave,* and *Notify* create a balanced list. Each item now begins with an imperative verb.

COMMUNICATION LABORATORY

APPLICATION EXERCISES

A. Rewrite the following sentences, avoiding the *and* pitfalls.

1. Our warehouse will be closed for summer vacation, and no orders will be shipped between July 1 and July 15.
2. Our office staff serves coffee and doughnuts on Friday mornings, and just about everyone attends.
3. These word processors are just what we need, and we want to order five as soon as possible.
4. The advertising is being prepared now, and the sale will be held.
5. Experts forecast an increase in consumer spending, and our company will continue to open new branch stores.
6. We made some changes in our billing operation, and payments came in more quickly.
7. Our representatives manage to make more calls than before, and there are fewer of them now.
8. We showed your suggestion to Mr. Ordin, and he liked it very much.

B. With the principle of balance in mind, rewrite the following sentences.

1. The new procedure was adopted yesterday and the new regulations published today.
2. To equip the office, we have ordered a word processor, minicomputer, and electronic typewriter.
3. I never have, and never will, see a successful disorganized salesperson.
4. A customer has little faith and respect for a representative who is always late.
5. This is the simple procedure: push the button, wait one minute, any number of copies can now be made.
6. Did the general manager give you those instructions or his secretary?
7. Ms. Willard called the airline, made a reservation, and she has driven to the airport.
8. Purchasing, billing, and the maintenance of the books are all done in the home office.
9. Each participant will be responsible for joining in the discussion and for questions.
10. It will take quite a while to update our bookkeeping, to check accounts, and for examining the salespeople's daily reports.

C. Use transitional expressions to show a closer relationship between the following pairs of ideas.

1. We are making too many billing errors. We must check invoices twice from now on.

2. The recession has very much affected our performance. We do have a chance of bettering last year's performance.
3. You are invited to suggest an office improvement. The deadline is tomorrow at 5 p.m.
4. The mail room closes at 4 p.m. This package will have to go out tomorrow morning.
5. Experienced people are scarce. Ms. Johns will have to start a training program.
6. The computer terminals frighten the staff. Mr. Osmond uses his 10 hours a day.
7. She was hired mainly because of her accounting background. She is also extremely intelligent and able.
8. This collection service is very expensive. It seems to be much more efficient than our present service.

D. Rewrite the following paragraph so that it flows smoothly.

Last year we closed four branch offices to conserve funds. This decision saved about 8 percent on our operating budget. Sales decreased by 14 percent. A large portion of this decrease can be traced to the closing of the offices. A portion is due to the general decline in the economy. I would suggest that we reopen these offices. Their closings cost us more than we saved.

VOCABULARY AND SPELLING STUDIES

A. These words are often confused: *threw, through, thorough*. Explain the differences.

B. Three of the four words in each line below are synonyms. The fourth is an antonym. Spot the intruder in each group.

1. frighten, calm, alarm, terrify
2. conform, correspond, deviate, match
3. enthusiasm, eagerness, zeal, indifference
4. happy, miserable, distressed, pitiable
5. forceful, weak, strong, mighty

C. Complete the following by adding *ar*, *er*, or *or*—whichever is correct.

1. supervis___
2. lawy___
3. regul___
4. direct___
5. monit___
6. sweep___

COMMUNICATING FOR RESULTS

"Prepositionitis." "Prepositionitis" is the condition of writers who fall into the trap of using too many prepositions, thereby making their sentences long and unwieldy. Some prepositions, of course, are necessary. Rewrite the following sentences eliminating unnecessary prepositions.

1. The supervisor of our branch office in St. Louis has asked for additional workers for the summer.
2. The efficient use of our computer equipment depends upon careful scheduling.
3. At the meeting of our Ohio representatives held in May, we decided upon a special promotion for that territory.

CHAPTER 8

In your job, you will quite frequently have to deal with business letters. Business letters are perhaps the most common form of written communication. They are so common that at one time or another you, like everyone, will be asked to write one. To do so, you need to know something about language structure, psychological principles, writing techniques, and different kinds of letters.

Because there are different kinds of letters, you will need some guidelines on how to write them. The message plans in the following units include these guidelines. They are simple, logical, easy to follow, and easy to remember. In fact, you will find that you automatically think of these guidelines when you plan and write your business letters. Given a situation that requires you to write business letters, your mastery of the units in this chapter will enable you to do the following:

1. *Select which of the three basic letter-writing plans best helps you organize your ideas.*

2. *Identify appropriately placed letter parts, classify kinds of business letters, and plan and dictate successful business letters.*

3. *Write routine letters that request, transmit, acknowledge, or respond.*

4. *Write letters with unpleasant news or refusal decisions but still maintain goodwill.*

5. *Write effective claim and fair adjustment letters.*

6. *Write needed credit and appropriate collection letters.*

7. *Write persuasive sales letters, attention-getting public relations letters, and thoughtful social business letters.*

40 Business-Letter Format and Letter Style

Almost everything that you use is available in a wide variety of styles or models. Clothing, for example, is available in a "Western Look," an "Italian Look," and so on. Therefore, when buying a suit or a dress, you try to select the style that meets your preference and that best reflects *you*.

The same is true of styles for business letters. There is no standard by which the appropriateness or inappropriateness of a specific style can be firmly established. However, some companies adopt one particular style, and employees are expected to use that style. In all other situations, the choices are for you to make from the styles discussed in this unit.

Since the differences among formats and styles concern the placement of letter parts, you will first review the various parts of business letters; then you will review the different arrangement styles of letters. In this way, you will be better able to present your ideas within an acceptable framework, leave the reader with a positive impression, and keep the reader's goodwill.

Letter Parts

The letter writer works with many letter parts: the address, the salutation, the message, and the complimentary closing, to mention some. These parts must be arranged in a sequence that will make the letter meaningful and will contribute to attaining the purposes of the message. See, for example, the letter on page 364.

Usually a letter is divided into four sections. These sections, each of which contains several essential and a few optional parts, are the following:

1. The heading
2. The opening
3. The body
4. The closing

The Heading. Except in unusual situations—when proof of the mailing date is important, for example—envelopes are not retained and filed in business offices. Therefore, information that the reader needs to answer a letter must be included in a *letterhead* and *date line*. These are the essential heading parts referred to when the reply is written and, frequently, after the letter has been filed.

The content and design of a company's letterhead identify the company and project the company's image.

The Company or Organization Letterhead. Almost every company uses high-quality stationery with its name, address, and telephone number printed on it. These identifying items, and often such additional data as the names of the company's top executives, its slogan, and so on, are referred to collectively as the letterhead. Some examples are shown above.

In addition to providing identification of the writer's company, the content and design of the letterhead help to project the company's image. While the reader is primarily interested in getting to the writer's message as quickly as possible, the letterhead is almost sure to be glanced at first. An opinion of the company may be formed (perhaps subconsciously) because of its letterhead: It's old-fashioned or it's modern; it's futuristic or it's ultraconservative; it's middle-of-the road or it's progressive; and so on.

For these reasons practically every company hires a professional artist to design its letterhead. Various styles and sizes of type and different layouts serve to project different images. Naturally, every company wants to make the most favorable impression that it can—even if only for a fleeting second in a reader's mind.

The Date Line. It is often *very* important to know when a letter was written—important to both reader and writer. With the flood of mail that every business office receives and sends, it is unwise to assume that you or your reader will remember the exact order of events related to a particular

Letterhead: The company's printed name and address.

Date Line: The date (month, day, year) the letter is typed; starts on line 15 or three lines below letterhead (whichever is lower).

Inside Address: The name and address of the person to whom you are writing.

Salutation: An opening greeting.

Subject Line: Indicates what the letter is about.

Message: The text of the letter; paragraphs are typed single-spaced.

Complimentary Closing: A parting phrase.

Company Signature: Emphasizes that the writer is acting on behalf of the company.

Writer's Identification: The signer's name or title or both.

Reference Initials: The initials of the writer and/or typist.

Enclosure Notation: A reminder that the letter has an enclosure.

Carbon Copy Notation: The names of those who will receive copies of this letter.

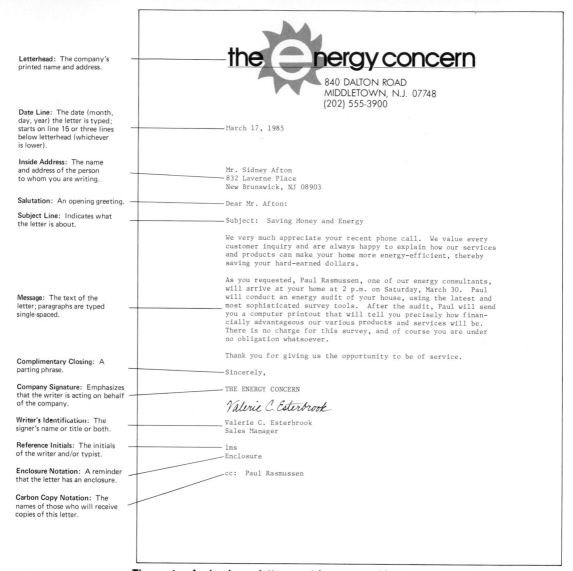

the energy concern

840 DALTON ROAD
MIDDLETOWN, N.J. 07748
(202) 555-3900

March 17, 1985

Mr. Sidney Afton
832 Laverne Place
New Brunswick, NJ 08903

Dear Mr. Afton:

Subject: Saving Money and Energy

We very much appreciate your recent phone call. We value every customer inquiry and are always happy to explain how our services and products can make your home more energy-efficient, thereby saving your hard-earned dollars.

As you requested, Paul Rasmussen, one of our energy consultants, will arrive at your home at 2 p.m. on Saturday, March 30. Paul will conduct an energy audit of your house, using the latest and most sophisticated survey tools. After the audit, Paul will send you a computer printout that will tell you precisely how financially advantageous our various products and services will be. There is no charge for this survey, and of course you are under no obligation whatsoever.

Thank you for giving us the opportunity to be of service.

Sincerely,

THE ENERGY CONCERN

Valerie C. Esterbrook

Valerie C. Esterbrook
Sales Manager

lms
Enclosure

cc: Paul Rasmussen

The parts of a business letter must be arranged in a sequence that will make the parts meaningful.

matter. Every letter should therefore carry a date line consisting of the month, day, and year.

There are two widely used date line styles—one for general business correspondence and one for military correspondence. In neither style is it acceptable to use a number to indicate the month—even if the letter is written to a military organization or an individual. Do not use *st, nd, rd, th,* or *d* after the day of the month.

Business	Military
February 3, 1985	3 February 1985
November 14, 1985	14 November 1985

Personal or Confidential Notation. A personal or confidential notation is typed below the date at the left margin to indicate that a letter is of a private nature. The notation may be typed in all-capital letters or initially capped and underscored.

PERSONAL OR <u>Personal</u>   CONFIDENTIAL OR <u>Confidential</u>

The Typed Heading. Office people become so accustomed to using printed letterheads, which are return addresses, that they sometimes forget to type this information when they write personal business letters on plain paper. A personnel manager once remarked: "I received a splendid letter of application today. I'd certainly hire that woman if only I knew her address."

For a typed heading, use one of the following forms:

932 Wyncrest Drive
Manchester, Missouri 63011
January 18, 1985

OR:

YOLANDE P. LADOWSKI
932 Wyncrest Drive
Manchester, Missouri 63011

January 18, 1985

The Opening. The functions of the opening are to direct the letter to a specific individual, company, department, or whatever, and to greet the reader. The *inside address* directs the letter, as does an *attention line*, if used; and the *salutation* greets the reader. Both the inside address and the salutation are essential in the most commonly used letter styles.

From your point of view as the reader, the opening is assurance that the letter is intended for you and that the writer is thoughtful enough to say "hello" before beginning to talk business. In addition to serving a practical need, the opening serves the purpose of courtesy and helps establish the overall letter tone.

The Inside Address. The name of the addressee, which should always be preceded by a courtesy title (except when followed by *M.D.* or another abbreviation), is usually the first line of the inside address. It is also common courtesy to include the person's job title when it is known—either on the same line as the name or on a separate line in the inside address. The name of the addressee's company; the street address; and the city, state, and ZIP Code number are also included. The following are examples of accepted inside-address styles:

Mr. David L. Grosshans, President
Grosshands Furniture Company
1746 Laurel Road
Ogden, Utah, 84401

Amanda P. Rodriguez, M.D.
(or Dr. Amanda P. Rodriguez)
6002 Exchange Avenue
Albuquerque, New Mexico 87101

Ms. Miriam E. Deem, Chairperson
Business Education Department
Riddner High School
981 West Wisconsin Avenue
Milwaukee, Wisconsin 53203

Mrs. Lee Ming
83 Sansome Street
San Francisco, California 94111

The Attention Line. When a letter is addressed to a company or to a department within a company rather than to a specific person, an attention line may be used to speed up handling of the letter. This line is typed below the inside address and above the salutation. The following are various styles of attention lines:

ATTENTION MS. CARRIE J. ADLER
ATTENTION MARKETING DEPARTMENT

Attention Ms. C. J. Adler
Attention General Manager

Notice that they are typed in all-capital letters or in underlined upper- and lowercase letters. Remember to use one of the following salutations with an attention line: *Ladies:* or *Gentlemen:* or *Ladies and Gentlemen:*.

The Salutation. There are several accepted forms of salutations, and each form reflects a different tone. The following are examples of salutations and descriptions of their use:

Singular Form	Plural Form	Use
Dear Bob:		Used for informal business letters—implies a personal friendship.
Dear Dominica:		
Dear Mr. Chambers	Dear Messrs. Chambers	Used in routine business correspondence
Dear Mr. Traut:	and Traut:	addressed to one or
Dear Ms. Shapiro:	Dear Ms. Shapiro and	several individuals—
Dear Mrs. Anthony:	Mrs. Anthony:	formal but cordial.
	Ladies and Gentlemen:	Used for correspondence addressed to a
	Gentlemen:	company or to a
	Ladies:	group.
Dear Madam:	Dear Mesdames:	Used only for *very formal* correspondence;
Dear Sir:	Dear Sirs:	avoid in most correspondence
Dear Madam or Sir:	Dear Mesdames or Sirs:	spondence
Madam:	Mesdames:	
Sir:	Sirs:	
Madam or Sir:	Mesdames or Sirs:	

If you know the name of the person to whom you are writing, then use the name in the salutation. This approach is more human and meets the receiver's ego needs since we all like to see our name in print (spelled correctly of course). If you don't know the person's name, use an attention line with the person's job title (*ATTENTION PERSONNEL MANAGER*). Then use a salutation such as *Ladies and Gentlemen*.

The Body. The body of the letter is, of course, the most important section of the letter—from both the writer's and the reader's point of view. Here the writer makes every effort to get his or her thoughts across to the reader effectively. The important thing to remember is that the body of the letter consists essentially of the *message* and may optionally include a *subject line*.

The Subject Line. The writer can give the reader advance notice of what the letter is about by including a subject line immediately *below* the salutation (so that it precedes the message). Like the attention line, the subject line is typed in all-capital letters or in underlined upper- and lowercase letters. The word *Subject* may be omitted, but when it is used it is followed by a colon:

SUBJECT: ANNUAL STOCKHOLDERS' MEETING
Subject: Annual Stockholders' Meeting

In legal correspondence or when referring to policy or project numbers, the term *In re* may be used in place of *Subject*.

The Message. The message is the "body and soul" of the whole letter—all the other parts are appendages, arms and legs, that support and help make the message work. By using the letter-writing principles discussed in Units 42-50, the writer gives the message a purpose that is meaningful to both the writer and the reader.

The message of every business letter usually consists of at least two paragraphs—even if the second paragraph is nothing more than "Thanks and best wishes to you," or something along that line.

The Closing. Just as a person usually says "Good-bye" or "So long" when finishing a conversation, so a writer usually uses a *complimentary closing* in a business letter. The only thing that is different is the way in which "So long" or "Good-bye" is said.

The Complimentary Closing. Complimentary closings, like salutations, vary in form and tone. The important thing to remember is to match the tone of the complimentary closing with that of the salutation as closely as possible. *Dear Bob* and *Very truly yours,* for example, obviously would make a rather absurd combination in a letter. Forms that are commonly used are shown at the top of page 368.

Formal	Informal
Yours very truly,	Sincerely,
Very truly yours,	Cordially,
Very sincerely yours,	Sincerely yours,
Very cordially yours,	Cordially yours,
Respectfully yours,	Best regards,

The Company Signature. The company signature, the typed name of the company, is usually considered an optional part of the closing. Some companies prefer having their typewritten names in the closing on the theory that the company, not the writer, is legally sending the letter. Most companies, however, do not use a company signature.

When a company signature is used, it is usually typed in all-capital letters on the second line below the complimentary closing:

Sincerely yours,   Very truly yours,
THE GREEN ISLAND COMPANY   ADVENT DISTRIBUTORS

The Writer's Signature. This is simply the handwritten signature of the person who has written the letter.

The Writer's Identification. In most instances, the writer's name and job title (and/or department) are typed below the signature. Sometimes only the writer's title and/or department are used. Here are several examples of styles:

Laura C. Angelis, General Manager   Carlton C. Westlake
                                       Executive Vice President
C. W. Chase, Manager
Estimating Section   Assistant Manager
Marketing Department   Service Department

Reference Initials. The reference initials serve an administrative pupose only. If the writer's name is included in the writer's identification, then his or her initials may be omitted in the reference initials. Remember that when used, the writer's name or initials are written first, followed by the typist's initials. The following are widely used reference-initials styles:

FCBorstal/laj	FCB/laj	FCB/crn/laj	(Three initials indicate
FCB/LAJ	laj		that FCB signed the letter,
FCB/laj	FCB		crn wrote it, and laj typed it.)

Enclosure Notation. When something is included with the letter in the same envelope or package, this fact should be indicated by an *enclosure notation*. Such a notation helps writers, recipients, and secretaries confirm that all the enclosures are included when the letter is sent and received. The following are widely used enclosure-notation styles:

Enclosure	Enclosure: Contract	Enclosures:
Enc.	2 Enclosures	1. Contract
Enclosures (2)	1 Enc.	2. Check
Enc. 2	2 Enc.	3. Envelope
		4. Memo

Mailing Notation. When some special postal service, such as *registered mail* or *certified mail,* is to be used in mailing a letter, a note indicating the special service should appear on all copies of the letter. Such notations are typed below the reference initials (or below any enclosure notations). A sample notation is shown in the letter on page 375.

Carbon Copy Notations. When the writer wishes to send a copy of the letter to one or more persons and wishes the addressee to know, a *carbon copy (cc) notation* is indicated on the original and all duplicate copies of the letter. The *cc* may be typed in lowercase letters or in all-capital letters, and it may be followed by a colon:

cc Public Relations Department   cc: Mr. Bruce Patco
CC Mrs. Nancy Fells   CC: Ms. Francine Dollar

Other acceptable carbon copy notations are as follows: *c, pc, copy to,* or *copies to.*

Note that *cc* applies both to carbon copies and to copies that are duplicated photographically.

Blind Carbon Copy Notation. The *blind carbon copy (bcc) notation* never appears on the original copy of a letter. It appears only on carbon copies and is used only when the writer wishes to send a copy to a person other than the addressee but does not want the addressee to know. It is typed in the upper left corner so it will be quickly noticed when referring to any carbon copies. All *cc* and *bcc* notations should appear on the writer's file copy.

Postscript (PS). The writer who has unintentionally forgotten to mention something in the message can add a *PS* rather than have the letter completely retyped. In fact, some writers deliberately add postscripts to draw the reader's attention to a particularly important point. A postscript therefore functions as part of the *body,* but it is always positioned in the closing section of the letter. The letters *PS* may be omitted, but when they are used, they are followed by a period or a colon.

Positioning of Letter Parts

The sequence in which the letter parts occur in a business letter follows the order in which they have just been discussed. Their horizontal positioning—whether typed to begin at the left margin or the center, for example—is determined by the letter's arrangement style, which will be discussed later in this unit. The vertical spacing of the letter parts, however, is relatively fixed.

The placement of the whole letter on the page can do much to enhance or destroy the impact of the message on the reader. If the left and right margins are approximately even, the letter looks balanced horizontally; if not, it looks as though it is ready to fall sideways off the page. The same is true of vertical placement. If the letter ends too high on the page, it looks as though it is hanging at the top of a cliff. If it ends too low, it looks as though it is sliding right off the page. The letter should be balanced visually.

To balance your letters visually on a page you must set your margins according to the size of the type your typewriter has (pica or elite) and the size of the stationery you are using. *Pica* type fits 10 strokes to the inch; slightly smaller, *elite* type fits 12 strokes to the inch. The most commonly used stationery sizes and their metric equivalents are as follows:

Customary-Size Stationery		Metric Equivalent	
Standard:	8½″ × 11″	A4:	210 × 297 mm (approx. 8¼″ × 11¾″)
Baronial:	5½″ × 8½″	A5:	148 × 210 mm (approx. 5⅞″ × 8¼″)
Monarch:	7¼″ × 10½″	———	
Official:	8″ × 10½″	———	

Knowing the size of type and the size of the stationery, then, you can determine your margin settings using the chart below.

If the Stationery You Are Using Is . . .	Start Date on . . .	Use Line Length of . . .	Set Margins at . . .*
Standard, A4	Line 15	50 spaces (pica)	25-80
		60 spaces (elite)	20-85
Monarch and Official	Line 14	50 spaces (pica)	25-80
		60 spaces (elite)	20-85
Baronial, A5	Line 12	40 spaces (pica)	30-75
		50 spaces (elite)	25-80

Spacing. On standard 8½- by 11-inch stationery, the date is usually typed on line 15, with the inside address typed five lines below it. (See the preceding chart for the positioning of these parts when using other sizes of stationery.) One blank line is left before the salutation, each paragraph, and the complimentary closing. If an attention line or a subject line is included, one blank line precedes and follows these parts.

The writer's identification should be preceded by at least three blank lines to allow room for the signature, and at least one blank line usually separates the writer's identification from the reference initials. Generally, no blank lines are left to separate the reference initials from the enclosure and carbon copy notations.

A postscript, if used, would be preceded by one blank line, and a *bcc* notation would be typed about 1 inch from the top of the (carbon copy) page.

*The additional five spaces added to the right margin setting avoids overusing the margin release key.

All these parts except the blind copy notation are shown in the sample letters on pages 364 and 374–376.

ZIP Code Numbers. The postal ZIP Code follows the state in an address, with no punctuation preceding or following the number. In the inside address, in a typed letterhead, on an envelope, and in running text material, the ZIP Code number is preceded by only one space.

The state may be spelled out, or it may be abbreviated, using the official two-letter abbreviations recommended by the United States Postal Service.

Sharon Service Company	Mr. Andrew Bestor
760 Hanson Avenue	318 Harrison Avenue
Oklahoma City, Oklahoma 73111	Canton, OH 44708

Using these official abbreviations will aid handling by an optical character reader (OCR).

The Second Page

Sometimes letters cannot be completed on one page and the message must be continued on a second, and sometimes even a third, page. When this happens, *plain* (not printed letterhead) paper of the same size and quality as the letterhead sheet should be used for continuation pages.

Side Margins. All continuation pages should have the same side margins as the first page. Since there would be over 200 words in the body of a two- or three-page letter, the right and left margins would be about 1 inch each.

Top and Bottom Margins. The top margin of a continuation page should be 1 inch (start typing on line 7). At least 1 inch—no more than 2 inches—should be left blank at the bottom of each continuation page. The last page of a letter may, of course, have a much deeper bottom margin.

Continuation-Page Heading. A heading consisting of the name of the addressee, the page number, and the date should appear at the top of each continuation page. Two of the commonly used arrangements for such headings are illustrated next. Remember that three blank lines should be left between the last line of the heading and the first line of the continued message.

Ms. F. C. Wilkins   2   October 20, 1986

Ms. F. C. Wilkins
Page 2
October 20, 1986

When dividing a paragraph at the bottom of the first page, leave at least the first two lines on the page and carry at least two lines to the continuation page. If this isn't possible, carry the whole paragraph over to the continuation page. Avoid dividing the last word on any page.

The Envelope

Envelopes should be of the same quality and color as the letterhead paper, as illustrated below. Here are some points to remember when addressing envelopes.

1. On a small (No. 6¾, 7, 5⅜, C6, or C⅞) envelope, start the address on line 12 about 2 inches from the left margin; on a large (No. 10 or DL) envelope start the address on line 14 about 4 inches from the left margin.
2. Single-space all addresses and use block style.
3. Always type the city, state, and ZIP Code number on the last line.
4. Leave one space between the state and ZIP Code number.
5. Type the attention line or any personal notation below the return address. Begin on line 9 or on the third line below the return address, whichever is lower. Capitalize each word, and underscore the entire notation.

The Green Island Company
• 191 ANDERSON AVENUE • ARLINGTON, VIRGINIA 20559 •

The Green Island Company
• 191 ANDERSON AVENUE • ARLINGTON, VIRGINIA 20559 •

A company's envelopes should be of the same quality and color as the letterhead.

6. If special mailing services are required, type the service in all-capital letters on line 9 in the upper right corner of the envelope.

7. If the envelope does not contain a printed return address, be sure to type a return address in the upper left corner—it should not be typed on the back of the envelope.

Arrangement Styles of Letters

The arrangment style of a letter depends upon the *horizontal* placement of the various letter parts. The order or sequence in which the parts are positioned is, as indicated in this unit, fixed in a logical pattern that is normally not altered to suit individual tastes.

Block Style. Letters in which *all* the parts begin at the left margin are written in block style. This style, which is illustrated on page 374, saves typing time since the typist doesn't have to use the tabulator in setting up the letter.

Modified-Block Style. In arranging a letter in modified-block style, the typist usually changes only the position of the date line, the complimentary closing, and the writer's identification. All these parts usually start at the horizontal center of the page. However, the date may be aligned to end at the right margin, and the subject line may be centered or indented five spaces. A letter in modified-block style is illustrated on page 375.

Modified-Block Style With Indented Paragraphs. These letters are exactly the same as the modified-block style except that the first line of each paragraph is indented five spaces. This style is illustrated on page 376.

Social Business Style. The social business style differs from regular business letter styles in a number of ways. Instead of opening the letter, the inside address may be typed at the left margin five lines below the signature line. Reference notations, enclosure notations, carbon copy notations, and often the writer's typewritten signature are omitted. Informal salutations, often followed by a comma instead of a colon, characterize the social business style. Complimentary closings such as *Cordially, Regards, Sincerely, Best wishes,* and *Yours* also maintain the informality of this letter format. An example of the social business letter style is shown on page 476.

Punctuation Style for Business Letters

The message part of the business letter is punctuated, of course, using the standard rules of punctuating sentences. Two parts that get special punctuation treatment are the salutation and the complimentary closing. The complimentary closing traditionally ends with a comma, and the salutation traditionally ends with a colon:

Dear Janet:	Cordially,
Dear Mr. Buntin:	Sincerely,
Ladies:	Yours truly,

SSC

STEADFAST
SERVICE CORPORATION
819 Laurelton Road, Newark, Delaware 19711

February 6, 1985

Ms. Geneva Clauson
Investment Properties Company
708 Talton Avenue
San Antonio, TX 78285

Dear Ms. Clauson:

Subject: Form of a Block Letter

This letter style is fast becoming the most popular style
in use today. Efficiency is the main reason for its popu-
larity. The typist can save time and eliminate the necessity
of working out placement. Some organizations are even de-
signing letterheads to accommodate this style. A few years
ago, some people felt the block style looked odd. That
complaint is seldom heard today, however. As more organizations use a block style, people have become accustomed to
its appearance.

This letter also illustrates the subject line. A subject
line may be typed with initial caps or all in caps. It should
start at the left margin. It always appears after the salutation and before the body of the letter.

Sincerely,

George P. Webcor

George P. Webcor
Manager, Customer Services

nkm
Enclosure

The block letter is the fastest one to type, because each line begins at the left margin.

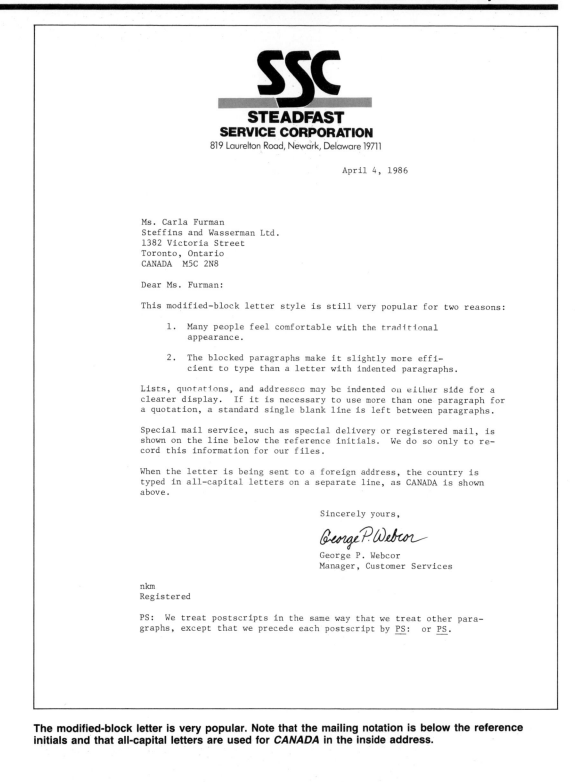

SSC
STEADFAST
SERVICE CORPORATION
819 Laurelton Road, Newark, Delaware 19711

April 4, 1986

Ms. Carla Furman
Steffins and Wasserman Ltd.
1382 Victoria Street
Toronto, Ontario
CANADA M5C 2N8

Dear Ms. Furman:

This modified-block letter style is still very popular for two reasons:

1. Many people feel comfortable with the traditional
    appearance.

2. The blocked paragraphs make it slightly more effi-
    cient to type than a letter with indented paragraphs.

Lists, quotations, and addresses may be indented on either side for a
clearer display. If it is necessary to use more than one paragraph for
a quotation, a standard single blank line is left between paragraphs.

Special mail service, such as special delivery or registered mail, is
shown on the line below the reference initials. We do so only to record this information for our files.

When the letter is being sent to a foreign address, the country is
typed in all-capital letters on a separate line, as CANADA is shown
above.

Sincerely yours,

George P. Webcor

George P. Webcor
Manager, Customer Services

nkm
Registered

PS: We treat postscripts in the same way that we treat other paragraphs, except that we precede each postscript by PS: or PS.

**The modified-block letter is very popular. Note that the mailing notation is below the reference
initials and that all-capital letters are used for *CANADA* in the inside address.**

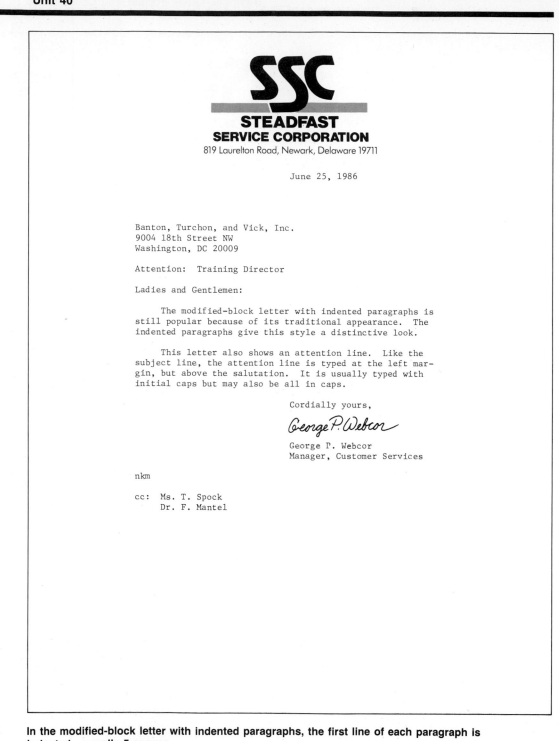

SSC
STEADFAST
SERVICE CORPORATION
819 Laurelton Road, Newark, Delaware 19711

June 25, 1986

Banton, Turchon, and Vick, Inc.
9004 18th Street NW
Washington, DC 20009

Attention: Training Director

Ladies and Gentlemen:

     The modified-block letter with indented paragraphs is
still popular because of its traditional appearance. The
indented paragraphs give this style a distinctive look.

     This letter also shows an attention line. Like the
subject line, the attention line is typed at the left margin, but above the salutation. It is usually typed with
initial caps but may also be all in caps.

Cordially yours,

George P. Webcor

George P. Webcor
Manager, Customer Services

nkm

cc: Ms. T. Spock
     Dr. F. Mantel

In the modified-block letter with indented paragraphs, the first line of each paragraph is indented—usually 5 spaces.

All display lines in the other parts of business letters end with no punctuation unless, of course, the line ends in an abbreviation:

Mr. Bryon Landesman	Mrs. Donna Bellman
700 Gaston Ferry Road	CDE Limited
Hicksville, New York 11802	91 Vestry Avenue
	Coventry, Connecticut 06238
Enc.	Enclosure
cc Miss Claudia Renfrew	cc Mr. Ralson W. Brown, Jr.

A Final Word . . .

Knowing all the letter parts and the arrangement styles will help you to prepare successful letters. However, you must also be sure that the typewriting quality helps foster the positive image of your letters.

The quality of the typescript is governed by three factors: the evenness of touch, the quality of the typewriter ribbon, and the neatness of corrections. An even touch will produce typescript of even density—not a sprinkling of light and dark letters across the page. A well-adjusted electric typewriter guarantees consistent density of typescript, since each key strikes the paper with the same force, regardless of how much or how little pressure is used by the typist. Cleaning the type keys regularly prevents dust-and-ink-clogged letters from marring the appearance of the typescript.

A good-quality ribbon should be used, one that is suited to the kind of typewriter—standard or portable, manual or electric. When the ribbon has been used so frequently that there is insufficient ink to produce clear typescript, the ribbon should be replaced. Ribbons come in a variety of colors, but black is the color most frequently used.

Corrections should be kept to a minimum, of course, and they should be made so neatly that they are not noticeable. Good correction tools are as essential to the typist as a good set of carpentry or plumbing tools is to the carpenter or the plumber. If corrections are noticeable, the letter should be retyped.

Erasable typing paper can prove to be both expensive and disappointing. Easily erased paper is also smudged, and it will pick up old ink as it travels around the platen of your typewriter. Simply brushing your fingers across it or touching it with something can easily smudge a typewritten page and ruin it.

COMMUNICATION LABORATORY

APPLICATION EXERCISES

A. Many of the following letter parts contain errors. Rewrite each, correcting the errors wherever they occur.

    1. Dear Ms. Merrill,

    2. Paul Carstairs
       738 Spencer Court
       Columbia, MD 21045

    3. 8/6/1985

    4. lms/HEK

    5. Mr. Harland Planter
       2768 Tipton Road
       Jericho, NY

    6. Bollinger Roofing Co., Inc.
       1302 Carroll Street
       Baltimore, MD 21230

       SUBJECT: ORDER #788
       Dear Mr. Bollinger:

B. Write the salutation and complimentary closing for each of the following.

1. A letter to a competitor, Ms. Carla Weinberg, who has just received a promotion in her firm.

2. A letter to a state senator, Paul Sprague, inviting him to speak to a monthly meeting of a trade association.

3. A letter to your state's department of economic development inquiring about plant sites.

4. A letter to a good customer, Mr. Nicholas Costa, that includes an invitation to a formal dinner party.

5. A letter to a sales representative, Ms. Diane George, congratulating her for exceeding her monthly quota by a large margin.

C. Bring to class some business letters that you or a member of your family has received. Be prepared to discuss the appropriateness of format, style, and letterhead for each letter.

D. Design a letterhead that you believe would be appropriate for a local business in your area. Use pencil, pen, typewriter—whatever tools you need.

VOCABULARY AND SPELLING STUDIES

A. These words are often confused: *pursue, peruse; populous, populace.* Explain the differences.

B. Which of the words that follow each of these sentences is nearest in meaning to the italicized word in the sentence?

1. We *partitioned* the office to give each worker some quiet. (**a**) restored (**b**) divided (**c**) examined (**d**) scattered

2. We developed a *calculating* plan for expanding our share of the furniture market. (**a**) secret (**b**) unusual (**c**) reckless (**d**) deliberate

3. I remained *impassive* as the customer enumerated how inferior our product was. (**a**) distressed (**b**) intense (**c**) composed (**d**) defiant
4. If we *consolidate* our warehouses, our costs will drop. (**a**) integrate (**b**) separate (**c**) organize (**d**) abolish
5. She is the most *methodical* manager in the division. (**a**) petty (**b**) indifferent (**c**) orderly (**d**) prosperous

COMMUNICATING FOR RESULTS

Each morning before she begins working, Jennifer prepares a list of all the things she must do. She then numbers the items in the order of their importance and begins working on the first item. Ted, her co-worker, thinks that Jennifer wastes valuable time organizing her day this way. He prefers to start working. With whom do you agree? Discuss.

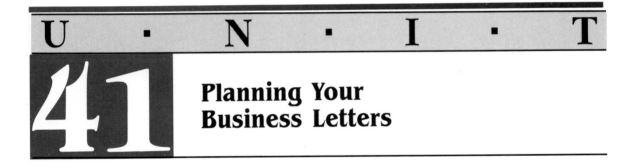

UNIT 41

Planning Your Business Letters

Using the formats and arrangement styles discussed in Unit 40, you will be sure to send letters that look attractive and modern. As inviting as your letters may look, however, they cannot be effective and promote goodwill if your writing is not well organized and your ideas are not well planned.

In this unit you will preview the major kinds of business letters and learn how to plan these letters from the reader's point of view. Three basic plans are offered that are sure to help you organize any kind of business letter—and write it effectively.

Kinds of Business Letters

The employee in business writes many types of letters—to ask for information, advice, or favors; to send information; to collect money; to apologize for a mistake; to refuse a request that cannot be granted; to apply for a job; or to sell the company's products or services.

Business letters, though, are written not only by the business employee. They are also written by others to conduct *personal* business. Parents, students, bill payers, and consumers are just a few of the others who have occasion to write personal business letters. A parent may write to the school board requesting better courses; a student may write to several colleges requesting catalogs; a bill payer may write to Nash's Department Store to clarify charges on the last statement; a consumer may write to an automobile manufacturer to request a new car adjustment.

One could hardly name all the kinds of letters written—the list is practically endless. However, the following are among those most frequently in use.

Request Letters. Request letters may also be called "please send me" letters. They are the simple requests for information, literature, favors, appointments, reservations, and so on. Secretaries and stenographers often write such letters for their employers.

Another type of request letter is written to order merchandise or services. It is commonly called an *order letter*. Many large companies use a form called a *purchase order* for this purpose, but thousands of small companies place orders for goods and services by means of letters.

Letters Answering Requests. Just as a business firm often writes letters asking for something from another organization, it also receives a great many letters of request. Form letters and postal cards are often used to acknowledge routine requests if the reply does not require a personal message.

If a letter is needed to convey a personal message, it may not be so easy to write. You may sometimes have to tell a customer that the order will be delayed because the merchandise is out of stock, or you may have to refuse a customer's request for a special favor simply because you cannot possibly grant it. These letters require the utmost tact and courtesy.

Letters answering requests give the letter writer an excellent opportunity for making friends and building goodwill. They are, therefore, among the most important communications in business.

Claim and Adjustment Letters. However hard people try to avoid them, mistakes will occur in business. A furniture store receives a shipment of lamps and several are broken. A disappointed parent feels that the tricycle she ordered for her child does not look new—the paint has been scratched in several places. A shoe store manager receives too many shoes in size 6A and too few in size 5B. These are typical situations in which the person who has been inconvenienced or offended writes a letter in protest. Although these letters are called *claim letters*, they really are *complaint letters*. All businesses receive—and send—them.

Letters written in response to claims are called *adjustment letters*. When the adjustment asked for is not granted (it isn't always; the claim may be unreasonable or unjustified), you must write the claimant a letter refusing to make the adjustment. To retain goodwill you must always give a logical reason for the refusal. Because adjustment letters are among the most difficult to write, they require special understanding of people, plus extensive knowledge of the company the writer represents.

Credit and Collection Letters. A large percentage of business transactions in this country are handled on a credit basis. Letters must be written in response to requests for credit. Usually, the responses are favorable: "We are pleased to welcome you as a new charge customer at Elliot's." Sometimes, however, requests for credit must be declined because the applicants are not good credit risks. These are perhaps the most difficult of all letters to write. People don't want to be told that they are a poor credit risk!

Collection letters are written because a very small percentage of those who are given the privilege of credit violate that privilege. Therefore, they must be reminded, reasoned with, and sometimes threatened before they will pay what they owe. Collection letters are among the most challenging to the letter writer—their effectiveness is measured by the amount of money they bring in from forgetful or careless customers.

Sales Letters. In a sense, every letter business people write is a sales letter because it automatically becomes a showcase for the writers and their firms. However, there are letters written for the specific purpose of selling a product or a service. You probably have received a great many of these. A publisher wants to sell you a subscription to a magazine; a record company tries to persuade you to join its record club; an insurance company asks you to buy a policy. Millions of such letters are written every year.

Other sales letters come under the heading of *promotion letters*. These don't attempt to make *direct* sales; their primary purpose is to make friends and to create a good feeling between the company and its customers. In the long run, of course, the desired outcome is an increase in customers—and in sales.

Employment Letters. Employment letters deal with getting a position. They are written by everyone, not only by those who expect to work in business. Employment letters include letters inquiring about a position, letters of application, letters thanking an employer for an interview, and letters of resignation.

Social Business Letters. Many letters of a social business nature are written to maintain friendly relationships with customers and business acquaintances. Typical social business correspondence includes letters of congratulation, letters of sympathy, invitations, letters of friendship, and thank-you letters. Since they show thoughtfulness on the part of the writer, social business letters do a great deal to build goodwill.

Classifying the Kinds of Business Letters

No matter what kind of business letter your write, you must consider its effect on the reader's needs. How you put your ideas on paper and in what order you present your thoughts will in large part determine how your reader will react to your message.

While there are many different *kinds* of business letters, these kinds of letters can be handled simply in terms of the reader's anticipated reaction. Three basic letter patterns enable the business writer to solve problems with request, order, claim, adjustment, credit, collection, sales, employment, and social business letters. By putting ideas together according to the basic patterns, you can work within the framework of the reader's needs and minimize the possibility of creating ill will.

Some everyday letters may be matter of fact or may share good news. Persuasive letters, on the other hand, attempt to convince the reader to do something not previously considered or something that might be inconvenient.

Letters that refuse (say "no") or convey bad news have the potential of alienating the reader. It is the business writer's task to transmit the bad news and still maintain the reader's goodwill. The following discussion of the three organizational plans will help you in planning your business letters. Each plan considers the reader's needs in presenting its message.

Everyday Letters. In your role as an effective writer, you will face a variety of communication situations. In some cases your writing tasks will be pleasant. You may tell a reader that the charge account she has requested has been opened; that your company will be able to donate 500 pens for a charity benefit; that you will be able to ship the requested merchandise today; that you will be able to attend the sales convention next week. These "yes" letters are easy to write because they tell your reader good news. The reader's needs are met in this type of correspondence by the positive answer that the request will be granted.

Other everyday letters include order letters, acknowledgments of orders, simple requests, simple claims, and friendly collection reminders. Because of their routine nature, everyday letters use a direct approach in conveying their messages. The business writer usually starts the letter by telling the reader the good news, by granting the request, or by stating the claim. After the opening statement come the necessary details and then a friendly statement designed to maintain or generate goodwill. The organizational pattern for everyday letters is outlined below.

1. Direct statement indicating purpose of the letter.
2. Necessary details (if any) to carry through the purpose of the letter.
3. Goodwill statement that brings the letter to a close.

If you wanted information from the San Diego Chamber of Commerce for a class report, you would organize your letter according to the plan for everyday letters.

1. Request information about the city of San Diego for class report.
2. Indicate specific kinds of information needed—population trends, industrial growth patterns, unemployment figures, building trends, and recreational facilities.

3. Close with a statement of appreciation for any help that can be given in gathering information.

Persuasive Letters. Everyday letters take a direct approach and are simple to write. More skillful writing techniques are needed, however, when you show Mrs. Ramon why she should purchase your product; when you convince the Landon Candy Company that it should send you a complimentary display; when you ask Illuminare Company to replace your batteries because they leaked in the flashlight, or when you request Mr. Ramon to pay his past-due account of $48.23. What particular needs must be met for each situation? How can our ability to meet our reader's needs be stated so that the reader acts positively?

The organization of persuasive writing is important in getting your reader to act positively. By using an indirect approach in persuasive writing, you can show your reader *why* he or she should take a desired action before you actually ask that action be taken.

The needs for financial gain, status, health, security, family, leisure time, and comfort and convenience provide bases upon which to organize the persuasive letter. A general organizational pattern that relies on the needs is presented below.

1. Attention-getting statement or device that encourages the reader to continue reading the letter.
2. Statements that present facts that show the writer's ability to meet the reader's needs.
3. Presentation of request in terms of how it will benefit the reader, if possible.
4. Request for action.

If your electric shaver broke just two days after the warranty had expired, you might want to write a persuasive claim letter. In this case you would probably use the following organizational pattern:

1. Praise company for its reputation for quality and dependability.
2. Explain that the electric shaver broke two days after warranty expired. Appeal to pride by indicating you know that this is not a usual occurrence with the company's products.
3. Indicate that you wish to have the razor repaired under terms of warranty.
4. Ask company to let you know if it will comply with your request.

Bad-News Letter. Probably the most difficult communication situation involves saying "no." But you must say "no" when you refuse requests, refuse adjustments, and refuse credit. Conveying bad news is just as difficult as saying "no." We find it hard to explain order delays or announce price increases—and still maintain the customer's goodwill. How can you avoid losing a customer when sending bad or negative news?

Like the persuasive letter, the bad-news letter should take an indirect approach. If you were to say "no" or relate the bad news in the opening sentence, you would immediately lose your reader.

To maximize the amount of potential goodwill in a bad-news situation, you should begin your letter with a neutral statement upon which both you and the reader can agree. Then you should present the reasons for the refusal (as positively, tactfully, and courteously as possible) before actually stating the refusal. Offer an alternative, if possible, and then close your letter with a goodwill-building statement. This organizational pattern for bad-news letters is outlined below.

1. Neutral opening statement upon which the reader and the writer can agree.
2. Reasons for the refusal stated in positive, tactful, and courteous terms.
3. Statement of refusal.
4. Suggested alternatives, if any.
5. Statement to retain goodwill of reader.

The bad-news letter organizational plan might be used to tell a customer that the bank for which you work is unable to lend him or her the $3,000 requested:

1. Thank customer for the credit request.
2. Discuss the need for collateral. Discuss the income requirements for a $3,000 loan without collateral.
3. Compare customer's qualifications with requirements and courteously refuse request (or combine refusal with alternative proposal).
4. Indicate amount you can lend, if any.
5. Indicate that you look forward to hearing from customer if the alternative is satisfactory *or* invite customer to take advantage of one of your other banking services.

Planning Leads to Better Results

If you were going to take a long trip, would you just get into your car and take off? Not very likely. Your car might break down shortly after you started, you might run out of money before you reached your destination, and you might waste much valuable time by traveling on the wrong routes. Many things could go wrong because you had not planned ahead.

A blueprint helps the carpenter to build a house; a pattern helps the dressmaker to make a dress. Without the blueprint and the pattern, the builder and the dressmaker would be lost. When you write a letter, your "blueprint" can be of great help to you, for an effective letter does not just happen—it combines knowledge, experience, and careful planning.

How to Plan. The first step in any planning process is to gather all the materials you will need to do the job. In writing a letter, these materials may include the letter to which you are replying, a good dictionary, and pertinent information, such as prices and delivery dates. Only when you have all the necessary tools and information at hand can you plan an effective letter.

Using this information, you may wish to make brief notes—either on a scratch pad or on the letter to which you are replying. From these notes you can prepare a rough draft of your letter.

First, however, you should prepare an outline of what you wish to say, for an outline will help you to organize your thoughts. This practice will save you time and money, and it should prevent the necessity for writing follow-up letters to add information or explain something that was not clear in the original.

Using your outline, you should next prepare a rough draft of the letter. Then, check this draft for correct spelling and grammar and for completeness and accuracy of details. You may wish to improve the wording or change the order of some sentences so that your meaning is clear, your words are vivid, and your ideas flow. This is the process of revising, or editing, your letter.

Probably you will want to prepare another draft, and perhaps still another, before you arrive at a final draft. In each, you will incorporate the changes made in the preceding draft. This procedure is time-consuming, but it results in a better letter.

As you gain experience in letter writing, you will find that you need to spend less and less time in detailed planning; in time, many facets of the letter-writing process will become almost automatic.

A Successful Example. An outline for a letter quoting wholesale prices on personal computers to a retail store might look like that given below. Notice how this outline follows the organizational plan for everyday letters.

1. Send catalog of complete line of Computab computer products.
2. Appreciate interest in the Computab line.
3. Recommend economical Basic 4 model for Laramie Electronics' special anniversary sale.
4. Quote price of $139.95 each in lots of less than 25 and $134.95 each in lots of 25 or more.
5. Promise delivery one week after order is received.
6. Reassure retailer that Computab products are good sellers because of their low prices and fine values.

Eventually, when you have had more experience in planning and writing business letters, you will need only brief notations to direct you. Your condensed outline then might look like this:

1. Send catalog; acknowledge inquiry.
2. Basic 4 model $139.95 each in lots of less than 25 and $134.95 each in lots of 25 or more.
3. Delivery in a week.
4. Goodwill closing.

Here is the letter written from this outline:

Dear Mr. Hulton:

As you requested, I enclose our current Computab catalog that describes our complete line of personal computers and accessories. We appreciate the opportunity to acquaint you with our products.

For Laramie Electronics' special anniversary sale, we recommend the economical Basic 4 model that is described on page 7 of the catalog. The Basic 4 wholesales at $139.95 each in lots of fewer than 25 and at $134.95 each in lots of more than 25. You can expect delivery one week after you place your order.

We predict that the Basic 4 will be a big seller for you, because, at a little over $200 retail, it represents a fine value and meets the growing demand for this kind of equipment. Like many other retailers throughout the country, you will have great success with this fine product.

Sincerely yours,

Dictating Effectively

If you were scheduled to speak to a group of people on a certain topic, would you simply wait until you were standing before your audience to decide what you were going to say? Obviously not. You would certainly want to outline your message beforehand, gather any pertinent facts, estimate the length of your presentation, and so on. Only by planning your speech can you be sure that it will be effective. Dictating letters and memos also requires advance planning.

Whether you dictate directly to a secretary or employ dictating equipment such as the machines used in word processing centers, you should plan a written or a mental outline of your letter, memo, or report and have at hand all the data you will need. As you dictate, be sure to:

1. Speak clearly—enunciate each syllable.
2. Specify the spelling of any proper names, unusual words, and words that may be confused, such as homonyms.
3. Indicate the beginning of each new paragraph and the placement of any tables or lists.
4. Include proper punctuation marks.
5. List specifically any enclosures to be included, carbon copies to be made, or mailing service to be used.
6. Mention whether a rough draft is required.
7. State when the typed copy is needed.

In addition, when dictating to a secretary, ask the secretary to let you know whether you are speaking too quickly or too slowly. And be sure not to move around the room as you speak.

Before dictating to a machine, read the instructions for operating the machine. Then practice using it for a few minutes to make sure that your speech is clear and that your voice is neither too loud nor too soft.

Following these guidelines will help you not only to write more effective letters but also to save time and increase your productivity.

COMMUNICATION LABORATORY

APPLICATION EXERCISES

A. List all the types of letters that you have received during the past year.

B. List and describe the types of letters that the following people might write in a typical month:

1. Electronics store owner
2. Police chief
3. High school or college teacher
4. Automobile dealer
5. Librarian
6. Physician or dentist

C. Bring to class at least four examples of different types of letters that you are able to collect at home or from people in business. Be prepared to discuss:

1. The kind of letter.
2. The reason the letter was written.
3. The organizational plan used to write the letter.

D. For each of the following situations, tell the kind of business letter you would write. Then indicate which organizational plan you would use to write the letter. For example, if the situation is to replace a defective product, your answer would be an adjustment letter using the everyday plan.

1. To send a customer a requested price list.
2. To order 3000 pens imprinted with the company's name.
3. To request payment on a long overdue account.
4. To interest a potential vacationer in a resort.
5. To thank the Richmond Corporation for an interview.
6. To sell a lawn maintenance service.
7. To congratulate a competitor on a promotion.
8. To invite potential customers to a plant tour.
9. To complain about a long overdue shipment.
10. To reject someone who has applied for a job.

E. For each of the following situations, plan the letter you would write. Outline the letter, using one of the three basic organizational plans.

1. Maria Ramirez wants to attend Castleton College after she graduates from high school. In order to pay her tuition and expenses, she will need a part-time job on campus. Outline the letter Maria would write to the Student Aid Director at Castleton College requesting information about part-time clerical jobs on campus. Be sure to ask about the kinds of jobs

that are usually available and about what the pay scale is. Maria would like to have any available literature describing such jobs and whatever application forms that might be required. She has enclosed a résumé.

2. Assume that you are the assistant to the Director of the Student Aid Office at Castleton College. You have been asked to reply to Maria Ramirez's letter. Outline the letter that you might write in response to her inquiry. Be sure to answer all her questions.

3. Assume that Maria Ramirez has forwarded her completed applications to you. After reviewing it and noting that she has fine clerical and secreterial skills, you feel that, even though no full-time position is available, she would be qualified for a part-time position with one of the two companies near campus. She would have a better opportunity for advancement and her rate of pay would be higher. Outline your letter telling Maria that she would probably do better working off campus. Tell her about the two possibilities and provide her with all the information she will need to apply.

VOCABULARY AND SPELLING STUDIES

A. These words are often confused; *intense, intents; insoluble, insolvable, insolvent.* Explain the differences.

B. Use either *raise* or *rise* to complete each of the following sentences. (Some sentences require the past tense or past participle forms.)

1. No matter what I propose, my boss will _____ objections to it.
2. If our costs continue to _____, our prices must soon follow.
3. The prices of raw materials have _____ dramatically.
4. The technician _____ the top of the machine to service it.
5. The cost of living _____ steadily last year.

C. Which of the following frequently used words are misspelled? Spell each correctly.

1. application
2. apointment
3. akward
4. necessary
5. lisence

6. posess
7. sincerely
8. unconcious
9. privlege
10. anual

COMMUNICATING FOR RESULTS

Correcting an Error. In checking a cash register tape, a food shopper notices that he has been charged $11.90 for a $1.19 item. The customer comes to you, the manager on duty. What will you say to the customer to correct the error and maintain his goodwill?

42

Everyday Business Letters

Everyday business letters comprise most of the correspondence that flows into and from a business organization. These letters are routine in nature. They ask for information, respond to simple requests, transmit documents, order goods or services, make reservations, request appointments, inform customers and clients, and further the simple, routine operations of a business organization.

Everyday business letters are considered routine because they have a neutral effect on the reader. Such letters are very common and do not present special problems. They do not attempt to persuade the reader to take an inconvenient action, nor do they refuse to grant a request. These kinds of letters usually grant requests graciously, provide needed information, or contain inquiries the reader is eager to answer. The positive or neutral aspects of the everyday letter are the basis for its routine handling.

Writing everyday letters is usually quite simple, but they are not unimportant and deserve no less attention than more difficult letters. Regardless of its purpose or length, every letter requires careful planning and thoughtful writing to do the job it is intended to do.

Characteristics of Everyday Letters

When writing a routine letter, ask yourself this important question: "What kind of letter would I like to receive if this letter were being sent to me?" You would probably decide that you would want the writer to be as *brief* as possible—to avoid wasting your time. On the other hand, you would want the writer to give you *complete* information so that you wouldn't need to write for more details. And you would probably expect the writer to be *courteous* and *tactful*. While these characteristics are applicable to any kind of business letter, they are especially important in routine letters where miscommunication can lead to additional cost and ill will.

Brevity. Some people are inclined to ramble in a simple letter. Consider the aimless verbiage in the letter that follows:

Gentlemen:

I have been a subscriber of your magazine for nearly ten years. Well, maybe it's been twelve years. During this time I have not missed reading a single issue, at least not that I can remember. Golfing is one of my favorite sporting activities so your magazine articles are of interest to me.

Anyway, I was wondering if I could take advantage of your offer to extend my subscription to Golf Magazine for the next two years. I wish to take advantage of your special two-year rate so I am enclosing a check for $14 to cover the cost of this subscription for that period.

Please continue to send the magazine to me at the following address: Richard Rodriguez, 814 Barneston Street, Duluth, Minnesota 55803.

Sincerely yours,

Ridiculous? Of course it is. But the letter serves to illustrate the pitfall into which many writers fall: *going into unnecessary detail.* You have already seen that the entire first paragraph of this letter could have been omitted—with much better results! The remaining part of the letter could have been expressed in fewer words too.

Look at the following letter. Note that it says what needs to be said—no more, no less—and then stops.

Gentlemen:

I wish to take advantage of your offer to extend my Golf Magazine subscription. A check for $14, your special two-year rate, is enclosed.

Please continue sending the magazine to me:

Richard Rodriguez
814 Barneston Street
Duluth, Minnesota 55803

Sincerely yours,

Completeness. In striving for brevity, the writer should not overlook the need to give complete information. Business firms often receive letters that contain no return address (and frequently the writers of such letters are the most vocal about the poor correspondence habits of the firms to which they have written!). Other important information may be lacking too. Suppose you were the reservations clerk of a hotel that received a letter requesting a room for April 10 but neglected to indicate whether a single or double was needed. What if you were an order clerk who received a letter requesting a blue shirt, but no size was stated? No doubt in both situations another letter would be needed to gather all the necessary information. The cost of business letters is rising all the time. An incomplete letter only calls for another letter, which means more expense.

Tact and Courtesy. Pleasant words like *please, thank you, appreciate, pleasure,* and *grateful* do more to create goodwill than brusque statements and demands. These kinds of words set the scene for building a positive business relationship.

Place yourself in the reader's position. Write the kind of letter you would like to receive. Use positive words and pleasant expressions. Make your reader feel important and convince that person this letter was written with his or her needs specifically in mind. Although you may be writing a routine business letter, do not let your reader feel unimportant for even one minute.

Organization of Everyday Letters

Because most everyday letters are routine and tend to have a positive or neutral effect on the reader's needs, they take a direct approach. Therefore, their organization is patterned after the plan for everyday letters:

1. Direct statement indicating the purpose of the letter.
2. Necessary details (if any) to carry through the purpose of the letter.
3. Goodwill or other statement that brings the letter to a close.

Notice how the following letter uses the everyday letter plan outlined above.

Dear Ms. Dillion:

Please send me the name of a dealer in the Chicago area from whom I can purchase your Casa Grande bedroom suite.

After seeing your advertisement in this month's American Homes and Gardens, I called several Thomas dealers in our area. None of them stock the Casa Grande line.

I would appreciate receiving this information as soon as possible. I have always enjoyed the luxury of your fine furniture and am looking forward to the possibility of owning some additional pieces.

Sincerely yours,

Organizational plans, such as the plan for everyday letters, help the business writer place ideas in a meaningful sequence. The organizational plan is only a guide, however, and the writer must tailor the letter to make sure that it will accomplish its purpose as simply, as clearly, and as completely as possible.

Sometimes a routine letter will not require a presentation of details to accomplish its purpose, so the second step in the organizational plan may be omitted. Other situations may occur when no goodwill closing is needed to carry out the sequence of ideas. In these cases the business writer may close with a statement relating to the contents. Notice in the following letter, for example, how the writer concludes courteously with a request for additional information.

Dear Mr. Samuels:

Please send me your complete portfolio of Italian, French, Spanish, and other furniture that you advertised in this month's issue of American Homes and Gardens. Enclosed is my check for $2.

I would also appreciate receiving the names of Thomas dealers in the Chicago metropolitan area.

Sincerely yours,

Enclosure

Routine Requests

Have you ever answered magazine or television advertisements that invited you to send for something free? If you yielded to those temptations, you probably wrote a routine request letter (unless you merely filled out a coupon). Routine request letters are letters that ask for something the reader is eager to give.

Many routine requests are written in every business. A business executive's administrative assistant writes to a supplier, asking for a catalog or a price list; to a publisher, asking for reprints of an article or to be listed as a subscriber; to a hotel, asking that a conference room be reserved for a meeting or to make reservations; to another executive, asking for an appointment; and so on. All these routine requests follow the organizational plan for everyday letters.

Requesting Information, Literature, or Free Service. Most letters requesting information, literature, or free service are short. They should give only the information needed by the reader to fulfill the request. Of course, they should also contain a return address so the recipient knows where to respond.

Dear Miss Renko:

Please send me the copy of Beauty Magic for Modern Home Owners advertised in your June issue of Today's Home. I am also interested in a booklet you published several months ago, which I recently saw at a friend's home. It was Make Your Own Rug. Do you have a copy to send me?

I have learned a great deal about home decoration from your various publications; and I, as well as my friends, appreciate this wonderful service.

Sincerely yours,

Often a postal card will serve as well as a letter in making routine inquiries; in fact, many companies prefer postcards.

Dear Mr. Wykowski:

Please send me Proper Telephone Techniques, the booklet advertised in this month's Management Methods magazine. My address is 260 Carter Avenue, S.E., Atlanta, Georgia 30317.

I certainly appreciate your distributing this valuable publication.

Sincerely yours,

Ordering a Product or a Service. Most business firms of medium and large size use a purchase order form when ordering goods. Such a form centralizes in the hands of one department the responsibility for ordering merchandise and helps to eliminate the possibility of employees' ordering goods on their own initiative. Also, a purchase order form is quicker to prepare than a letter.

Orders may also be placed on an order blank supplied by the company from which goods are being bought. Some companies supply such order forms.

A third way of ordering merchandise, used widely in small companies, is by means of letters and postal cards.

In preparing order letters, accuracy is extremely important. Figures and items must be checked and rechecked. To make an order letter easier to read and to check, the smart typist places each order item on a separate line in tabular form.

Dear Miss O'Neill:

Please send us the following hand stamps:

Quantity	Item	Price	Amount
2	No. 613B (PAID)	$2.10	$ 4.20
4	No. 721X (Company name: ARNESON NOVELTIES INC.)	3.25	13.00
1	No. 41 (Name: BARRY LASK)	3.00	3.00
1	No. 41 (Name: CORA LAMBERT)	3.00	3.00
Subtotal			$23.20
5% Sales Tax			1.16
TOTAL			$24.36

Our check for $24.36 is enclosed. Please let us know when we may expect delivery of this order.

Sincerely yours,

Enclosure

It is important that every order letter contain all the necessary information to process the order. Besides quantity, price, and amount, the order letter should pay careful attention to additional specifications. If applicable, is color and size information included? Has the method of payment been discussed? Is a specific date of shipment important? Are both the customer and the supplier in agreement on who will pay the freight charges and the method of shipment? All these items need to be considered in composing the order letter.

Requesting Appointments. In business the usual practice is to make an appointment by telephone or letter when you wish to call on an executive at his or her office. Of course, if you are requesting an appointment with someone nearby, the use of the telephone is quicker and less expensive. Out-of-town appointments are often made by letter.

Dear Mr. Cassella:

I am planning to spend April 14 in Fort Wayne and would like very much to talk with you or one of your associates while I am there. We are setting up a wage-incentive program in our organization, and I have been told that you have a very effective plan at Hoffman Industries.

Would you find 10 a.m. on the 14th a convenient time to see me? An hour of your time should be sufficient and would mean a great deal to me.

Cordially yours,

Making Reservations. While hotel reservations may be made by telephone, many persons prefer writing letters so that they are assured all the information has been conveyed correctly. What kinds of information need to be included? Of course, the dates of arrival and departure are paramount, but other kinds of information are important too. The hotel needs to know the name of the person who is to occupy the room. If there are other persons in the party, their names should be given too. Does the guest want a single room or a double room? What will be the arrival time? (Rooms are usually not held after 6 p.m. unless the person making the reservation asks that it be held for late arrival.) Is payment for the first night included so as to guarantee that the room will be held? Other information that might be given—although it is not always essential—is the guest's preference for a room location, the expected price, and any special required services.

Ladies and Gentlemen:

Please reserve a single room for Mr. George Vernon, sales manager of our company, for April 10 and 11.

Mr. Vernon will arrive around 7:30 p.m. on April 10, so please hold the reservation for late arrival. If possible, Mr. Vernon would like to have a room facing Lake Michigan.

Please confirm this reservation.

Sincerely yours,

Letters of Transmittal

A check, a money order, or an important business paper sent by mail should always be accompanied by a letter. A letter helps to identify what is being sent so that the recipient knows exactly what you *intended* to send. The letter also provides a valuable record for future reference. When remittances or business papers are accompanied by a letter, the carbon copy answers the question: "I wonder whether I sent that salary survey to Johnson as I promised?" or "How many copies of the Mayberry agreement did I send to Lawford and Hines?"

Good transmitting letters should be able to accomplish the following:

1. Identify *what* is being sent and *how many* (if money, the *amount*).
2. Specify any action necessary on the part of the recipient.
3. If transmitting money, identify the purpose for which the money is to be used—to apply on account, in payment of a certain invoice number, for services rendered, or for purchases made.

Note the following example:

Dear Professor Gabriel:

Enclosed are the original and one copy of the contract for your manuscript, <u>Starting Your Own Business</u>. Please sign both copies, return the original to me, and retain the copy.

The review of your manuscript in <u>Retailing</u> magazine was extremely complimentary. As you know, our target date for publication is October 15. I'll be in touch with you when editing begins.

Sincerely yours,

Letters of Acknowledgment

A usual business practice—and always a very good one—is to acknowledge by letter receipt of any money or business papers, orders, favors, appointments, and oral agreements. Letters are important in acknowledging such business matters to avoid misunderstandings, to provide a record, and to show courtesy.

Letters of acknowledgment help to avoid misunderstandings or mistakes. If you have received an order and will make shipment as soon as possible, the customer will want to know. If you do not acknowledge the order, the customer may assume that you did not receive it or wonder what you are doing about it if you did. A written acknowledgment should state that you have the merchandise in the requested quantity and tell the customer when you are going to fill the order. In this way, misunderstandings and mistakes can be avoided.

Written acknowledgment letters provide a record, and records provide the internal control and memory of business. You would not want to trust your own memory as to the date on which you promised delivery of an order, especially if you are responsible for hundreds of orders. The copy of your acknowledgment, therefore, provides the information. A written record may also be needed for legal proof.

Courtesy builds goodwill in a business organization, and acknowledgment letters are one way to show courtesy. By reassuring the reader that you have received the order and are doing something about it, you show courtesy and build goodwill.

Acknowledgment letters, because they are routine letters, generally follow the everyday letter plan. After you have expressed appreciation for the reader's action, you may then supply the necessary details before giving your goodwill closing.

Acknowledging Receipt of Money. When money is received on a regular basis, such as monthly in the payment of an account, usual business practice calls for acknowledging the current month's payment on the next month's statement. Isolated payments or payments received on an irregular basis, however, require individual attention and should be acknowledged through a form or letter. Remember these special considerations when writing letters that acknowledge the receipt of money:

1. Express thanks for the money, even though payment may be long over-due.
2. Be sure to mention the amount that is received. This letter provides a valuable record for the future. Rather than just saying, "Thank you for your check," say, "Thank you for your check for $88.95."
3. When appropriate, mention how the money is to be used—to apply on account, to be used as full payment for merchandise or services, or whatever the purpose of payment.
4. If you can think of something pleasant to say to the sender, do so. "We appreciate your prompt payment," or "Doing business with you is always a pleasure," or "I hope you will enjoy your new Easy-View floor lamp."

Following is a typical example of a letter acknowledging the receipt of money.

Dear Ms. Irwin:

Thank you for your check for $33.50. This amount has been applied to your account, leaving a balance of $67.

We appreciate your promptness in making your payments, Ms. Irwin, and we are always pleased to serve you.

Sincerely yours,

Acknowledging Business Papers. Important business papers—such as contracts, securities (stocks and bonds), notes, insurance policies, bids, and the like—should always be acknowledged promptly, since they are often just as important as money. In writing such letters, be specific as to just what was received and the identifying number. If any action is required, your acknowledgment should state clearly that you have taken such action.

Dear Mr. Cooke:

Your life insurance policy, No. BFLS1003468, arrived today. As you requested, we will cancel the policy and send you the cash surrender value, $3,912. You will receive a check within 30 days.

May we recommend, Mr. Cooke, that you consider the possibility of maintaining your current protection through the purchase of term insurance. Considerably less expensive than ordinary life, this kind of insurance would enable you to retain the same amount of protection with up to 70 percent less in premium payments.

If you are interested in looking into this program or if we can be of further service, please call Arnold Harrison at 555-8921.

Sincerely yours,

Acknowledging Orders. Some business firms acknowledge all orders they receive for goods or services. Automation makes possible the easy use of form letters or postal cards for this purpose. However, to welcome a new customer, to acknowledge an unusually large order, or to remind longtime customers how much you appreciate their business, individually written letters are much more effective. Customers, especially, appreciate the "extra touch" of a personal letter, such as the one illustrated on page 398.

Letters acknowledging orders follow the same plan as other acknowledgment letters. Because the customer is primarily interested in when the merchandise will arrive, this information is supplied in the opening sentence. Once you have expressed the main idea, you may then follow up with a statement of appreciation and other necessary details pertaining to the order.

Individually written acknowledgment letters provide the writer with an excellent opportunity to create goodwill. In the concluding sentences of the letter, you may reassure the reader that the purchase was a wise one. On the other hand, if your customer just purchased golf clubs, you might conclude the letter by giving a low-pressure pitch for your golf balls. Other kinds of goodwill closings might include a hearty welcome to a new customer or a statement of appreciation for the business given you by a longtime customer.

The general plan for organizing order acknowledgments would include the following:

1. A statement concerning the time and method of delivery.
2. A statement of appreciation for the business received.
3. Special instructions related to the order.
4. A goodwill closing.

Notice how the general plan is put to work in the following letter:

Dear Mrs. Hanover:

Your Power House outboard motor is being shipped today by prepaid freight. Thank you for your order.

Would you do us—and yourself—a favor? Just as soon as your Power House "37 Plus" arrives, please fill out the card attached to the motor and mail it back to us. Receipt of this card will tell us that the motor arrived in good condition and will also serve as a record of our special two-year guarantee.

FRANKLIN PORCELAIN

FRANKLIN CENTER, PENNSYLVANIA 19091

215-459-6553

January 24, 1984

Mrs. Claire Marcil
35 Foster Street
New Haven, CT 06511

Dear Mrs. Marcil:

I am very pleased to tell you that your porcelain sculpture by Ronald Van Ruyckevelt, "The Queen Elizabeth Rose," has been handcrafted to your commission and is ready to be sent to you.

This original work of art is the premiere issue in the Royal Horticultural Society's first collection of flower sculptures in porcelain. And when you actually have this exquisite work before you, I think you will agree that it is a triumph of realism. Each of the 15 individual petals has been formed by hand and then assembled carefully by hand to form the complete flower. And no fewer than 12 ceramic colors were hand-applied, achieving a range of subtly beautiful, authentic shades.

When you entered your commission for "The Queen Elizabeth Rose," you instructed us to bill you for the deposit as soon as your sculpture was ready for shipment. The invoice for that initial payment is enclosed, and the balance will be billed in three equal monthly installments after your sculpture is sent to you.

We wish to thank you for commissioning this beautiful work. It is, I am sure, a work that will give you much pleasure for many years to come.

If you wish to pay in full for this purchase, you may do so by remitting the total order amount as shown on the enclosed invoice.

Sincerely,

Jonathan Strauss

Jonathan Strauss

sm
Enclosure

Customers appreciate the "extra touch" of a personal letter of acknowledgment.

I hope you have many happy hours of motor boating. Let us know if we can help you further. Incidentally, Neptune Marina in Norfolk carries a complete line of parts and accessories for your Power House "37 Plus."

Sincerely,

Confirming Appointments and Agreements. Appointments and agreements, whether made orally (in person or by telephone) or in writing, should be confirmed by letter. A letter will clarify any possible misunderstandings—especially for appointments and agreements made orally.

Dear Marion:

I very much enjoyed meeting with you last Tuesday at the Civic Club meeting in Butte. It was interesting and helpful to learn how you have improved correspondence procedures in your office.

I was especially pleased when you suggested we get together for lunch on the 16th. Unless I hear from you, may I assume that our appointment is still on? I'll plan to arrive at your office about 12:15.

Sincerely,

Writing Acknowledgments While the Manager Is Away. When managers are out of the office, their administrative assistants or secretaries are expected to acknowledge important letters and explain any delays caused by the managers' absence. These acknowledgment letters are usually brief, courteous, and noncommittal. *Noncommittal* means that the administrative assistant or secretary should be careful neither to reveal private company matters in acknowledgments—not saying, for example, where the manager is—nor to commit the company in any way. For example, if a secretary works for a magazine publisher and receives an article in the editor's absence, the following letter would *not* be appropriate.

Thank you for sending us your article, "Ceramic Magic." It is extremely good, and I know Miss Talbert will want to publish it in the next issue of <u>Handcrafts</u> magazine.

If the editor feels differently about the article, this letter will put her in an embarrassing position. The noncommittal, but courteous, letter the secretary might write is as follows:

Dear Mrs. Kessler:

Thank you for your article, "Ceramic Magic," which you wish to have considered for publication in an early issue of <u>Handcrafts</u>.

The editor, Miss Ida Talbert, is out of the office on a short business trip. When she returns, I will be sure to give her your article.

Sincerely yours,

Note that the secretary has said that Miss Talbert "is out of the office on a short business trip." It is usually best not to reveal more than this. Such information as "Miss Talbert is in Miami on vacation" or "Miss Talbert is in Akron this week visiting a new printing plant" would not be appropriate. The safest phrase, when in doubt, is "Miss Talbert is out of the office this week."

When the employer is away and the correspondence cannot wait, letters are often referred to another individual in the company. Before referring letters to another executive, however, the administrative assistant or the secretary must be sure that it is permissible to do so. Only the urgent or highly important letters will usually deserve this action.

Dear Ms. McGinnis:

Thank you for your April 17 letter to Mrs. Kent.

Mrs. Kent will be out of the office for about two weeks, so I am referring your letter to our sales manager, Mr. T. J. Loring. You will be hearing from Mr. Loring just as soon as he has had an opportunity to study your proposal.

Cordially yours,

Simple Responses

There is nothing that says "we are interested in you" better than a prompt reply to an inquiry. For this reason, some companies insist that all mail be acknowledged within 48 hours after it is received; others set 24 hours as the maximum. Although simple letters of response may be a daily routine in many offices, such letters should not be handled in a routine, mechanical fashion. Each inquiry should be given individual attention to ensure that all questions have been answered and that the inquirer's goodwill has been retained.

Businesses that receive many inquiries of the same type usually develop a form letter (either printed or typed and stored on a word processor) to send to all those who request information. In addition, to save money and to present the product in the most favorable light, the company will probably prepare special booklets containing photographs, descriptive information, and sales features. Some type of letter, however, is needed to accompany the booklet. Even if generated on automated equipment, the more personal the letter can be made to look, the more successful it will be.

Many inquiries, of course, cannot be answered by a form letter or a postal card. And even if they could, some companies consider inquiries important enough to deserve individually written replies. Routine letters of response fall under the classification of everyday letters. Letters telling the reader that you can accept an invitation to speak at a banquet, that you can provide favors for the charity bazaar, or that you can attend a 9 a.m. Wednesday morning meeting are treated like all other everyday letters. Because they convey the good news the reader is waiting for, these letters of response use a direct organizational plan. Like other everyday letters, the routine answering letter grants the request or provides the important information in the opening sentence because the answer is what the reader wants most. Details related to the main idea and a goodwill closing follow.

Notice how the everyday letter plan is used to accept an invitation.

Dear Ms. Stowe:

It will be a pleasure to speak to the Detroit chapter of NBMA on Thursday, November 18. Thank you for inviting me to address your group on Awards Night, the highlight of your year's meetings.

As you requested, I will plan a 30-minute demonstration, "New Office Equipment," slanting the presentation toward what secretaries and executives can use to make their time most productive. In addition to the ideas given in my recent article, "Using New Technology to Make Your Time More Productive," I will cover two or three other important areas.

I am looking forward to attending your meeting, Ms. Stowe. When you have confirmed the details concerning the time and place, please let me know.

Sincerely,

The following response was written as a result of an inquiry. Mrs. Gantry asked about replacement seats for her child's swing set. Notice how the everyday letter plan is used to answer Mrs. Gantry's questions. In closing, the writer took advantage of this opportunity to introduce Mrs. Gantry to another one of the company's products.

Dear Mrs. Gantry:

Replacement seats for Gym Dandy swing sets are available in three sizes. The 18-inch bench sells for $3.40, the 24-inch bench sells for $2.80, and the saddle seat sells for $4.35. You may have your choice of yellow or white molded plastic.

All orders should be accompanied by a money order. Also, please include a 50-cent handling charge for each seat requested. The new seats will reach you within three weeks after we receive your order.

Perhaps you might be interested in our new line of sandboxes, Mrs. Gantry. As you can see by the enclosed brochure illustrating the various sizes and shapes, these sandboxes have been designed to complement your Gym Dandy swing set. Your local toy center has a complete display of this new line and would be pleased to help you select a sandbox for your child's enjoyment.

Sincerely yours,

COMMUNICATION LABORATORY

APPLICATION EXERCISES

A. In a magazine or a newspaper, find an advertisement offering a free pamphlet or booklet that you might like to have. Clip the advertisement. Then write a letter requesting the booklet or pamphlet and attach the advertisement to your letter. After your letter has been returned to you by your teacher, you may want to send for the booklet or pamphlet.

B. You have been offered a summer job with North County Community College, which you will attend in the fall. You will work in the student records office, processing applications from entering freshmen. To get the job, you need three letters of reference. Your business English teacher, Dolores Ruiz, has moved to this address: 2234 Elm Street, Topeka, Kansas

66604. Write Ms. Ruiz asking her if she would send a letter of recommendation to Mr. P. D. Latimer, Personnel Director, North County Community College, P.O. Box 749, San Diego, California 92109.

C. Assume that you are employed by a small legal firm and have been asked to update its filing system. While reading *Office Management*, a professional magazine, you notice an advertisement for "Suspen-sion" filing. The Dorado Paper Company, 2087 Western Avenue, Topeka, Kansas 66604, requests interested people to send $1 for its booklet, *Records Management Simplified*. Write the letter you would send to obtain a copy of this booklet.

D. Write a letter to the Del Coronado Hotel, Coronado, California 92118, to make a reservation for your five-day vacation. Request a room in the Ocean Towers at the lowest possible rate. You will need a room with two double beds. Because this motel is in a resort area, a deposit is required; include with your letter a $100 check. Supply dates and other details.

E. You receive a signed contract from a client, Gus Andrea, Quality Industries, 1876 Magnolia Boulevard, Detroit, Michigan 48233. The contract is very important and is placed in a safe immediately. The contract is to service all of Quality's office machines for the next three years, which makes Mr. Andrea a major client. Acknowledge receipt of this contract and use this opportunity to generate continued goodwill for your company.

F. A regular customer, George Mulhauser, writes to renew a contract with your company. Your supervisor, Alice Haberman, who is in charge of such contracts, will be out of town until October 5, and you have no authorization to renew contracts. Ms. Haberman has asked you to acknowledge receipt of all correspondence in her absence. Write a noncommittal letter acknowledging receipt of this customer's letter.

G. Eugene Ellsworth, an industrial client whom your company represents, called to request a Friday, April 10, appointment at 3 p.m. He inquired as to whether you have a carousel slide projector available since he wishes to show the sales staff some slides illustrating the features of his new product line. Write a letter acknowledging the appointment and confirming the availability of the equipment. Mr. Ellsworth's address is 4288 Irving Street, N.E., Portland, Oregon 97213.

H. Last week Mrs. Agnes Streebing, a counselor from nearby Hillsdale College, visited your school. Just as she was leaving, you managed to ask her for an appointment to see about enrolling at Hillsdale College. You will graduate from Kennedy High School in June and would like to continue your education in some field of business, possibly computers. Mrs. Streebing suggested that you drop by her office after school a week from Thursday to discuss Hillsdale's business curriculum and the possibility of your attending this college. Write the letter you would send to Mrs. Streebing confirming your appointment. Hillsdale College is located at 3800 Hillsborough Street, Raleigh, North Carolina 27611.

I. Assume you work in the Visitor's Bureau of the Ocean Wave National Wildlife Preserve, Rocky Point, North Carolina 28457. You receive a letter from Ms. Sally DeGroot, Reiss & DeGroot Travel Agency, 1221 Foxpoint Street, Huntsville, Alabama 35801. Ms. DeGroot asks for literature and any other information needed to plan a trip through the preserve. Send her several pamphlets. In your letter point out that this preserve is one of the few places that has red-tailed twitter geese. The best time to visit the preserve is during the spring and fall. Food facilities are available, but she may also bring her own box lunches and take advantage of the picnic grounds or indoor dining facilities.

J. Assume you work in the offices of the Miami Chamber of Commerce. Kym Freeman, a student at Washington High School, has written a letter requesting information about Miami for her term report. She would like to have up-to-date information about population, industrial growth, housing, and recreational facilities. Answer Ms. Freeman's inquiry. Include various pamphlets published by the Chamber of Commerce and other civic groups. In your letter point out one or two interesting facts about Miami. Address the letter to Ms. Freeman at 1350 Shawnee Avenue, Des Moines, Iowa 50313.

VOCABULARY AND SPELLING STUDIES

A. These words are often confused: *elicit, illicit; key, quay.* Write each in a sentence that illustrates its meaning.

B. Are these statements truthful?

1. Two adjectives that precede a noun are always connected by a hyphen.
2. In typewritten material, words referred to as words are either underscored or enclosed in quotation marks.
3. Words that interrupt a direct quotation are also enclosed in quotation marks.
4. Slang is capitalized for emphasis.
5. Commas and periods are always placed inside, never outside, quotation marks.

C. In which of the following words should an *e* appear in the blank space?

1. d__scriminate
2. d__scribe
3. d__sease
4. exist__nce
5. restaur__nt
6. bull__tin

COMMUNICATING FOR RESULTS

Planning a Meeting. Your company has named you as head of a task force. Your job is to develop a plan for employees to spend one afternoon a month tutoring high school students who are having problems with certain subjects. Prepare a memo to the other task force members announcing the first meeting and listing a few of the items that will be discussed. Be sure to let them know that their ideas are needed and most welcome.

U · N · I · T
43
Persuasive Request Letters

Most request letters can be handled routinely because they are everyday business letters. A letter ordering a product or service makes money for the business organization to which it is sent. Likewise, written communications requesting hotel reservations improve the profit picture of the receiver. Even letters requesting appointments, although they may not directly result in sales, simplify the business operation from either a selling or a purchasing viewpoint. All these kinds of letters are eagerly awaited by the recipient. They improve the recipient's position and lead directly to goal fulfillment.

Other request letters, however, do not directly benefit the receiver. In fact, these requests may cause an inconvenience, cost money, or take up valuable time. How, then, can the business writer expect the receiver to comply with his or her request? While some request letters, and other types of persuasive letters, may attempt to spur an action that the reader is not necessarily inclined to pursue, the well-written persuasive request shows how this action will benefit the reader. If no direct benefit can be seen, the successful persuasive letter appeals to pride, fair play, fear, recognition, or self-worth—any of the motivators that stimulate human responses.

The job of the persuasive letter is to convince the reader to take an action that on the surface is not directly beneficial. A letter designed for action, then, should use the psychology of communication to achieve its goals.

Qualities of Request Letters

Request letters, especially those persuasive in nature, need to be planned carefully. Close attention must be given to the reader's needs, and any attempt to relate the reader's needs to the request will bring the writer a step closer to accomplishing the purpose of the letter. By placing yourself in the reader's position, you can more easily see how the request could fulfill one of the reader's personal needs.

The request letter should be exceptionally well written, with ideas stated in as little space as possible. At the same time, the ideas should be presented completely and clearly. The writer must also be courteous and tactful—and definitely make it as easy as possible for the reader to carry through the desired action.

Be Concise. Have you ever received a letter that just rambled on and on? What did you do with it? More than likely you glanced through it briefly and set it aside. Most other readers would do the same.

A letter that is written to persuade a reader to take an action must be worded so that the reader has no opportunity to become bored. Each word must contribute to the meaning of the message and hold the reader's attention. Only by making every word count can you accomplish this goal.

To achieve conciseness, avoid the needless repetition of words and ideas. Make sure that every sentence in your letter contributes specifically to accomplishing its purpose. Avoid including any unnecessary ideas that do not contribute to the reader's understanding of your request.

Develop Ideas Clearly and Completely. To promote understanding, you need to develop your ideas clearly and completely. The reader needs to be taken step by step through your reasoning process. Be sure that each idea follows logically from the previous one. Incoherent writing places stumbling blocks in the path of the reader and makes it difficult to interpret your request.

Test your own writing for coherence. If you were to remove a sentence, would the paragraph still make sense? If it would, your writing is too wordy. Another test for coherence is to assess the availability of all the necessary information. Have enough details been supplied to give a vivid, concrete picture persuasive enough for the reader to take the desired action? Omissions of important information and descriptive words provide a dull perspective. Test the following for coherence:

> Please attend a retraining session on Friday at 9 a.m. The session will end by noon.

Some concrete information has been supplied here: the type of session the reader is being asked to attend and the time during which the session will take place. But what concrete information is *missing?* The reader may want to attend the retraining session but should be told the following: What is the retraining for? On which Friday will it take place? And, most importantly, where is the session being held?

Idea development should not revolve around the needs of the writer, but instead should take into consideration the needs of the reader. For example, in writing to alumni of the local high school to request donations for a gymnasium, appeal to their sense of pride in their alma mater. Offer them recognition for their tax-deductible contributions of $100 or more by having their names appear on a plaque.

Request letters can very often offer psychological or other nonmonetary rewards for compliance. But these compensations must be presented from the reader's viewpoint and carefully woven into the persuasive request. Where possible, the request should be paired with the psychological appeal.

To keep your alma mater the best in the city, send your tax-deductible contribution in the enclosed envelope while this letter is before you.

Be Courteous and Tactful. If you have a special request, write to a particular individual, if possible, rather than to a company. Using a person's name makes your letter more personal and starts you off properly with the person whom you are addressing.

Be sure you have spelled all names correctly and have written them exactly as the addressee prefers to have them written. Correct titles and proper spelling get your letter off to a good start and set a receptive stage for your special request.

If you do not know the name of the person who would handle your request, you can at least speed up its handling by indicating the department you think will respond. For example, if your letter concerns employment, you would address the personnel department; if it concerns an order, you would address the sales department; if it concerns advertising or customer relations, you would probably address the advertising department or public relations department.

Expressions of appreciation are always in good taste, but do not write "Thank you in advance," or worse yet, "Thanking you in advance." You cannot be sure that the reader will take the action you request. To thank in advance takes the reader for granted and may be the phrase that defeats the purpose of your letter. Here are some expressions, though, that exhibit tact and courtesy when used with requests:

"May I please . . . ."

"I will be grateful if you would . . . ."

"Will you please . . . ."

'I would appreciate having . . . ."

"Please send me . . . ."

Expressions of expectation such as the following are appropriate in anticipating a favorable response to a special request.

"I hope that we can count on your cooperation."

"Your suggestions would be genuinely appreciated."

"I would appreciate this help."

"We will be grateful for this special service."

Make It Easy to Respond. Courtesy copies are frequently used to make it easy for those who receive them to grant favors. Of course, a self-addressed, stamped envelope should be enclosed too. For example, in a letter requesting a company to participate in a word processing survey, a copy may accompany the original so that the recipient may simply check and return the copy. Following is an example of a letter that was accompanied by a courtesy copy.

Dear Mrs. Basil:

Have you had the time, along with your other duties as word processing supervisor, to keep abreast of all the new developments in word processing during the last year? Have you wondered what other companies are doing to upgrade their equipment and procedures?

If so, you are among hundreds of other word processing supervisors throughout the country. That is why the Executive Board of the National Word Processing Association has undertaken as its major project for this year a research study to assess the status of word processing in business, government, and industrial organizations in the United States.

You will receive a copy of the research results to provide you with an up-to-date picture of word processing installations throughout the country. But before we can send you this information, we will need you to spend approximately an hour of your time filling out a questionnaire about word processing equipment and practices in your company. This information, as well as information from other leading organizations, will be used as the basis for this study.

May we count on your assistance to complete this project? For your convenience, I am sending you an extra copy of this letter. Please indicate your answer in the space provided and return the copy to me in the enclosed envelope.

Sincerely yours,

Teresa Caruana
Project Director

Please
Check (✔)

1. Yes, I will participate in the research project; please send me the questionnaire. As soon as the results have been compiled, I wish to receive a copy of the study. _____

2. I personally am unable to complete the questionnaire. Please contact (Name) _____, (Title) _____ of our company, who may be able to assist you. _____

3. Our company is unable to participate in this research project now. _____

The courtesy carbon is just one mechanism to induce favorable responses. Stamped return envelopes and postal cards also make it easier for the reader to say "yes." Separate response forms that are easy to fill out and return are another kind of convenient mail reply. Where faster or more personal replies are desired, invitations to call a certain number, collect if toll charges apply, simplify even further the response process.

Organization of Persuasive Requests

Before actually writing a persuasive request, you must determine the approach you will take. First of all, ask yourself, "In what way *will* or *can* my request benefit the reader?" Look at your request from the reader's viewpoint to determine if it can benefit him or her in any way.

Do not limit your analysis to profit motives, but view your request in terms of satisfying one or more of the reader's psychological needs. Fulfillment of the need for recognition (having one's name appear on a plaque) or the need for self-actualization (keeping up to date on developments in one's field) or one of the other psychological needs is a powerful motivator. Therefore, develop your persuasive request around fulfilling the needs of your reader, and write the letter as much as possible from the reader's viewpoint.

The organizational plan for persuasive letters assists in developing a letter that will present your request in its most favorable light. Once you have gained your reader's attention with a stimulating or provocative opening, you continue to build interest by relating the discussion of your request to the reader's needs. Then, by allowing the reader the opportunity to respond easily, you have used the appropriate motivational techniques to stimulate your reader to take the desired action. Specifically, the persuasive organizational plan uses the following outline to accomplish its purpose.

1. Attention-getting statement or device that encourages the reader to continue reading the letter.
2. Statements that (a) present facts or (b) meet the reader's needs.
3. Presentation of request in terms of how it will benefit the reader, if possible.
4. Request for action.

Notice how the letter on page 409 uses the persuasive letter plan to accomplish its purpose. As an attention-getter, a real X ray was enclosed with the letter.

Kinds of Persuasive Requests

Among the array of persuasive letters are sales letters to prospective customers, the first several collection letters in a series, persuasive claims, job-application letters, requests for donations, letters requesting favors, and responses to inquiries with sales potential. Each of these types of letters attempts to convince the reader to take a specific action, one toward which the reader presently has a neutral attitude or one that may cost money, require time, or result in inconvenience.

Sales, collection, claim, and application letters are all covered in detail in separate units. Requests for donations, letters requesting favors, and responses to inquiries with sales potential are described in the remaining part of this unit.

Requests for Donations. Donations of money, products, and time for worthy causes are often solicited through business letters. These letters generally use the persuasive letter plan, since their purpose is to motivate the reader to take an unselfish action. See how the following letter attempts to secure a food donation for a function to benefit senior citizens.

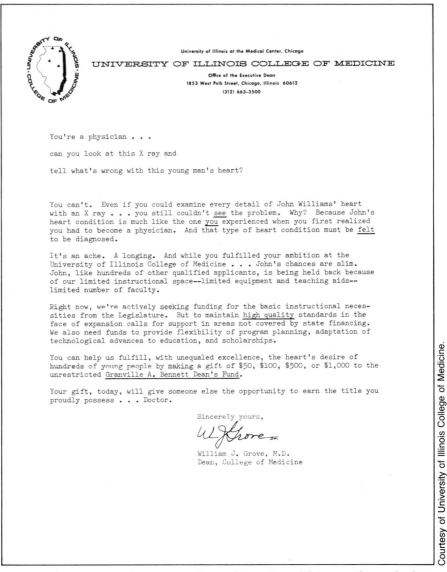

University of Illinois at the Medical Center, Chicago

UNIVERSITY OF ILLINOIS COLLEGE OF MEDICINE

Office of the Executive Dean
1853 West Polk Street, Chicago, Illinois 60612
(312) 663-3500

You're a physician . . .

can you look at this X ray and

tell what's wrong with this young man's heart?

You can't. Even if you could examine every detail of John Williams' heart
with an X ray . . . you still couldn't see the problem. Why? Because John's
heart condition is much like the one you experienced when you first realized
you had to become a physician. And that type of heart condition must be felt
to be diagnosed.

It's an ache. A longing. And while you fulfilled your ambition at the
University of Illinois College of Medicine . . . John's chances are slim.
John, like hundreds of other qualified applicants, is being held back because
of our limited instructional space--limited equipment and teaching aids--
limited number of faculty.

Right now, we're actively seeking funding for the basic instructional neces-
sities from the Legislature. But to maintain high quality standards in the
face of expansion calls for support in areas not covered by state financing.
We also need funds to provide flexibility of program planning, adaptation of
technological advances to education, and scholarships.

You can help us fulfill, with unequaled excellence, the heart's desire of
hundreds of young people by making a gift of $50, $100, $500, or $1,000 to the
unrestricted Granville A. Bennett Dean's Fund.

Your gift, today, will give someone else the opportunity to earn the title you
proudly possess . . . Doctor.

Sincerely yours,

William J. Grove, M.D.
Dean, College of Medicine

This persuasive request letter uses a human-interest appeal to spur the reader into responding.

Dear Mr. Gresham:

Just as your commercials advertise, "All family members—from toddler to grandpa—love the smooth, zesty flavor of Stern's macaroni and cheese." And Stern's is easy to prepare too, either for lunch or dinner.

Many of us in the Diablo Valley Youth Association are big eaters of your macaroni and cheese, and that is why we thought of Stern's in connection with our forthcoming Senior Citizens Hoedown on August 10. DVYA, a nonprofit community youth group, is sponsoring a hoedown for 50 less fortunate senior citizens who reside in convalescent homes in our city. We plan to transport the senior citizens to our center, serve them lunch, and then provide a show with old-fashioned Western music and entertainment.

DVYA is financed solely through contributions from community members; therefore, our budget is quite limited. To provide a delicious and nutritious lunch for the senior citizens, we are asking manufacturers like yourself to donate sufficient quantities of their food products. Would you be able to send us 12 boxes of macaroni and cheese to help highlight an afternoon in the lives of these individuals?

Of course, your contribution is tax-deductible. Special thanks will also be given to Stern's in our monthly newsletter, which is distributed to over 600 families in Diablo Valley.

May we count on you to help brighten the day for 50 less fortunate senior citizens? I would appreciate receiving your answer by July 6 so that we can confirm our menu plans.

Sincerely yours,

Letters Asking Favors. Another type of persuasive letter that sometimes must be written is one requesting a special favor. Of course, these letters should have the same characteristics as any other persuasive letter, and they are organized according to the persuasive letter plan.

Dear Mrs. Milton:

Your very interesting article in the August issue of The Administrative Assistant magazine prompted me to write you.

The Denver chapter of PSI is having its annual Administrator-Secretary Night on Thursday, November 18. Our members and their administrators (we expect about 80 people in all) have expressed a particular interest in hearing a lively talk on letters secretaries can send in their administrators' absence. We are especially interested in having our administrators hear something about what the secretary can do to help the employer with communication problems. Our program calls for a 30-minute presentation from the speaker.

Would you be able to address our group on November 18? You can build your speech along the same lines as your article, if you wish. As you know, this night is the highlight of our year's meetings, and we would be pleased to have you as our guest speaker.

I hope you can accept this invitation, Mrs. Milton. If you can, I will write you again giving you all the details—time, place, and complete program plans.

Sincerely yours,

Responses to Inquiries With Sales Potential. One of the main purposes of advertising is to get readers and listeners so interested in a product that, if it isn't readily available, they will make a trip to their dealer for a closer look or they will write a letter asking for more information. Inquiries received as a direct result of advertising have a great deal of sales potential. So when a writer shows interest, some companies respond with a polished, sales promotion letter instead of a simple response to an inquiry.

Letters of response with direct sales potential need to show the reader *why* the desired action should be taken—that is, why the product should be purchased. Persuasive letters written from the reader's point of view stimulate action—to purchase the new car, the aluminum siding, the air conditioner, or the stereo. Therefore, the persuasive letter plan is used in responding to inquiries with sales potential.

Notice how the first two paragraphs of the following letter get the reader's attention and develop interest. The presentation of the request and the request for action are carried out in the concluding paragraph.

Dear Mr. and Mrs. Tyre:

Naturally, we are delighted that you are interested in the Porpoise. Thank you for giving us a chance to tell you more about this fine new sports car that has just received Sports Car National's "Best Newcomer of the Year" award.

The enclosed booklet, Continental Sports Cars, was prepared especially for you and others like you whose taste runs to the bold, the daring, the unusual—the discriminating. Only in the Porpoise does the true sports car lover find that dreams can come true! You will be thrilled with its sleek lines, its handling, its economy.

May I suggest that you visit your dealer, Lyle's Sports Car Center, to test drive the new Porpoise. Only when you get behind the wheel of the Porpoise can you fully appreciate the sensational advantages of this little masterpiece.

Sincerely,

Here is still another example of how a response to an inquiry can be used to bring a potential customer closer to the sale.

Dear Ms. Stango:

We are so pleased that you thought of Starr's Town House for the annual Awards Night of the Detroit chapter of the National Business Managers Association.

We have two excellent private dining rooms—the Colonnade Room and the Garden Court. Each is decorated in a distinctive motif, and each is perfectly suited to a group such as yours. Each banquet room seats 100 to 125 people and is equipped with a loudspeaker system, a piano, and a movie projector and screen. The Colonnade Room also has a raised dais where the speaker's table may be placed. Both rooms are still available for November 18.

The decor of both the Colonnade Room and the Garden Court will give you a delightful, absolutely private dining atmosphere. Each is air-conditioned and sound-conditioned. As you know, Starr's Town House has an excellent reputation for the finest meals and service. I am enclosing our banquet menu, featuring full-course dinners ranging from $9 to $14.95.

I would be happy to show you these two lovely dining rooms, Ms. Stango, when it is convenient for you to visit Starr's Town House. Would it be possible for you to have lunch here with me one day next week? Just telephone me at 555-2491.

Sincerely yours,

COMMUNICATION LABORATORY

APPLICATION EXERCISES

A. Your boss, Marla Bergstrom, is the convention chairman for the National Information Processing Association convention to be held in Madison, Wisconsin, from March 21 to 24 at the Lafayette Hotel. You expect nearly 1,200 people—word and information processing managers and supervisors—from throughout the United States to attend this convention. For many of these people, this will be their first visit to Wisconsin. Ms. Bergstrom would like to provide as favors at the March 22 banquet samples of various Wisconsin cheeses. A small (perhaps 1-ounce) individually wrapped packet to be placed at each seat would suffice. Write the Wisconsin Cheese Manufacturers Association requesting them to donate 1,200 packages of cheese. One of your members in Madison would be able to pick up the cheese several days before the convention. Of course, you would publicize that the cheeses were donated by the Wisconsin Cheese Manufacturers Association. Address your letter to Mr. Barry Haskell, Director of Public Relations, Wisconsin Cheese Manufacturers Association, 666 Wisconsin Avenue, Madison, Wisconsin 53701.

B. For one of your classes, assume that you have been given the assignment of interviewing a person who presently is working in an occupation in which you are interested. To complete this assignment, you will need to inquire about duties, qualifications, educational background, opportunities for employment, salary, benefits, work schedules, and opportunities for advancement. Such an interview could take from 45 minutes to an hour, since you need to obtain a comprehensive picture of the position for a report you must write. Select an individual whom you might like to interview and write him or her a letter requesting an interview.

C. Answer the following letter of inquiry. Use this letter as an opportunity to persuade the reader to purchase and install your Carson live oak kitchen cabinets. Address the letter to Mr. Edward Young, 3129 Miller Road, Flint, Michigan 48507.

Gentlemen:

Please send me a copy of your pamphlet Modern Kitchenry, which was advertised in Decorator's World magazine. I am interested in replacing my present kitchen cabinets with Carson live oak cabinets.

While I am at it, I am also thinking of having my kitchen floor recovered. Do you have any suggestions for colors that would blend with live oak?

Sincerely yours,

D. You are employed by Crickton Realty, 1732 Henway Drive, Des Moines, Iowa 50318. You receive a letter from Henry T. Bonner, 2231 Treadway Street, Los Angeles, California 90069, requesting information about available housing in Des Moines for a family of six. Respond to his letter, referring to an enclosed list of suitable dwellings. You would very much like to sell Mr. Bonner a house, so make your letter as friendly and persuasive as possible.

VOCABULARY AND SPELLING STUDIES

A. These words are often confused: *raise, raze, rays; costume, custom.* Write each in a sentence that illustrates its meaning.

B. Indicate the prepositions that should be used in these sentences.

1. Our salary increases are retroactive _____ May 1.
2. The office is adjacent _____ the cafeteria.
3. Are you sure that these specifications are identical _____ those?
4. Did Mr. Mandac give his approval _____ the new training program?
5. Ms. Olinger was satisfied _____ the last shipment.
6. *Rug* is synonymous _____ *carpet.*

C. Add an *e* to the end of the following:

A Word Meaning:	To Result in a Word Meaning:
1. Pertaining to or characteristic of people	Kind, merciful, tender
2. Relating to a choir or chorus	A simple tune sung in unison
3. Ethical	A confident state of mind
4. Melodious, harmonious	A social entertainment featuring music
5. Characteristic of cities	Smoothly polite

COMMUNICATING FOR RESULTS

Say It Better. Rewrite the following letter. Simplify the content and keep it friendly.

Some time ago we were forced to discontinue Wearwell tires as a stock item in our inventory owing to the dissolution of the Wearwell Company last month and are therefore unable to fill your kind order for four of them. In consequence of this, therefore, we regretfully return your check made in our favor for $168.35 and request that you write us again.

U · N · I · T

44

Refusal Letters

As a business writer, you have a relatively easy job when you are sharing good news with customers. After all, there is little or no danger that such letters will alienate customers or will cause them to take their business elsewhere. All you need do is tell the customers exactly what they want to hear.

Sometimes, however, you cannot comply with a request because some information you may need is missing, the request is unreasonable, a product is sold out, or other circumstances prevent your granting the request. In situations like these, you must write refusal or bad-news letters—letters that say "no."

The word *no* can cause more ill will than any other word in the English language. Therefore, letters that refuse requests or convey bad news are very difficult to write. Care must be taken not to offend readers when you are unable to satisfy their needs. Customers must be led to understand the logic behind and the reasons for the refusal. Every letter you write has as its secondary purpose the promoting or retaining of goodwill. But the ill-will potential of a refusal letter is so great that only by drawing on your knowledge of human behavior can you write a "no" that gives your reader the feeling of "yes."

Qualities of the Refusal Letter

All the principles of good business writing are essential in writing letters that say "no." The following four guidelines, however, are of particular importance to bad-news and refusal letters.

Be Prompt. As you learned in Unit 41, most business firms consider it good practice to answer letters of inquiry within 48 hours. Whether the letter carries good or bad news, this policy should be carried out. Delayed negative responses can only offend the reader even more and lessen your chance of retaining goodwill. It is, of course, tempting to avoid writing the refusal letter and to handle more pleasant duties instead. But the longer the letter is delayed, the more difficult it will be to write and the more likely you are to compound the problem.

Be Positive. Avoid using negative words such as *fault, refuse, unfair,* and *unreasonable.* Maintain a positive tone in your writing and use words that convey pleasant images. Always try to phrase your refusal in a positive way by emphasizing what you *can* do for your readers instead of what you cannot do. How much more positive it is to say, "Your order will be shipped in two weeks" rather than "Your order will be delayed for two weeks." "We sell only through authorized dealers" is more friendly than "We refuse to sell directly to the public." Review "Pleasant, Warm Words" and "Unpleasant, Cold Words" on page 331.

Be Helpful. In writing a refusal or bad-news letter, you can occasionally provide an alternative solution. Although you cannot comply with the original request, you may be able to suggest some other plan that may help the reader. For example, if you cannot accept an invitation to speak at a certain meeting, you may recommend someone who can. Or if you cannot accept an appointment for March 13, you may suggest the reader see you on March 15. When possible, you should try to help the reader by providing a substitute plan.

If you had to refuse to donate door prizes to the Little League's fundraising breakfast, you might include the following sentence in your letter to give it a "yes" slant.

> We will, however, be glad to support your project by displaying your poster in our store window.

Or when refusing to give space in your store for a display of frozen foods, you might be able to offer an alternative date.

> We would be pleased to speak with your demonstrator, Miss Marcus, sometime in January to arrange for a demonstration early in the spring.

Be Tactful. While the inquirer's request may be unreasonable or the tone insistent, always respond with a tactful letter. Do not insult the reader or indicate that the request is unreasonable. Avoid accusations and other discourtesies in writing your letter. Be careful to explain the circumstances fully and in such a way that the reader understands and accepts the refusal or bad news as being necessary. Study the following pairs of tactful and tactless responses.

> TACTFUL: We wish we could send you the personnel information breakdown requested in your April 3 letter, but we do not have the data readily available. As a business executive, you can see that the time and money involved in preparing such a pamphlet would be prohibitive.

> ABRUPT: We cannot send you the personnel information breakdown requested in your April 3 letter. The time and money involved in preparing such a pamphlet would be prohibitive, a fact that you, as a business executive, should have taken into consideration before making your request.

TACTFUL: We would like very much to accommodate you by accepting the return of the clothing purchased from us on January 4 of last year, but we are unable to do so. To protect all our customers who may purchase returned merchandise, we place a two-week limit on the return of all wearing apparel.

SARCASTIC: Surely you cannot seriously expect us to accept return of the clothing you purchased from us on January 4 of last year. We are sending the items back to you today and will notify you whenever we decide to go into the used-clothing business.

Organizing the Refusal Letter

Because refusal letters contain information antagonistic to the reader's needs, the writer must take care not to alienate the reader and thereby lessen the chance of retaining goodwill. If readers can be shown why you must refuse the request, delay the order, or refuse the invitation *before* they are told "no," they may be more tolerant and understanding. Their self-images may not be as threatened since they have been taken step-by-step through the reasoning process that led to the refusal or bad news. Consequently, the following indirect organizational plan should be used for refusal letters and letters conveying bad news:

1. Neutral opening statement upon which both the reader and the writer can agree.
2. Reasons for the refusal stated in positive, tactful, and courteous terms.
3. Statement of refusal.
4. Suggested alternatives, if any.
5. Statement to retain goodwill of reader.

Notice how the bad-news organizational plan is used to refuse the following request:

Dear Mr. Eggert:

Your new line of heavy-duty machinery is certainly of interest to me. I appreciate your contacting me about an appointment to discuss how this equipment can improve our production and increase sales.

On Monday, March 25, I am scheduled to fly to New York for a two-week sales conference. Consequently, I will not be able to meet with you on March 27. Perhaps you might be free on April 10 and could come to my office at 10 a.m. that day.

I look forward to hearing from you as to when we might get together to discuss your new machinery.

Sincerely,

Explaining Refusals and Delays

Many kinds of requests are directed to a business organization. People ask for appointments, special favors, literature, service, information, and jobs. Sometimes you must ask for additional information before complying with a request. At other times you must refuse the request completely, as in the case in the letter illustrated on the next page.

Carnation

World Headquarters

5045 Wilshire Boulevard
Los Angeles, California 90036
Telephone: (213) 932-6000

August 9, 1985

Mr. David Avila
3519 Carlson Boulevard
El Cerrito, CA 94530

Dear David:

Thank you for taking the time to meet with us regarding
career opportunities with Carnation Health and Nutrition
Centers.

While we are impressed with your background and believe
that you have a great deal to contribute to an organization, the limited number of available positions forces
us to select only a relatively small number of the many
talented applicants we see. Unfortunately, we cannot
offer you a position at this time.

We appreciate your interest in Carnation Health and Nutrition Centers and wish you much success in whatever career
you select.

Very truly yours,

Roseann B. Perrotti

Roseann B. Perrotti
Director of Store Operations
Health and Nutrition Department

lg

Courtesy of Carnation Company—Health and Nutrition Division.

The letter of refusal must be written in such a way as to retain goodwill.

Refusing Orders. The primary purpose of any business is, of course, to sell goods or services for profit. Usually nothing makes a business happier than to receive an order. Under some circumstances, however, orders must be refused. Sometimes customers have poor credit ratings or do not have the legal qualifications to purchase the product sold. In other cases the product has been discontinued. The most common instances involve consumers who try to purchase directly from a wholesaler or manufacturer. The wholesaler or manufacturer must, of course, refer them to a retail store. This type of letter is not so much a refusal as it is an explanation and a referral.

Following is a typical letter refusing an order. The letter was sent by a national manufacturer to a customer who ordered directly from the warehouse. Notice how the letter uses the bad-news plan to achieve its goal.

Dear Mrs. Warren:

Thank you for your order for a Worksaver steam iron. We are delighted that you chose this fine product. Worksaver does indeed live up to its motto, "Takes the dread out of ironing."

Since we distribute our products through local dealers only, we are unable to serve you directly, Mrs. Warren. I am pleased, however, to refer you to the Lincoln Appliance Center at 115 West Main Street in River Grove. The Lincoln people will be delighted to show you their complete line of steam irons and many other fine Worksaver appliances.

I am returning your check for $25.95 and hope that you will make a trip to Lincoln Appliance Center right away for your new Worksaver. You will find our steam iron to be one of the wisest investments you have ever made.

Sincerely yours,

Why not take this opportunity to build goodwill with the retail store? Send Lincoln Appliance Center a copy of the letter so the Lincoln management will (1) know you are living up to your agreement of selling only on a wholesale basis, (2) appreciate your effort in helping make the sale, and (3) contact the customer about the specific merchandise.

Refusing Unreasonable Requests. Businesses sometimes receive information requests that must be refused. The request may be unreasonable or the information sought may be confidential. For example, a physician or a hospital employee cannot divulge medical information about a patient; a bank will not give information regarding a depositor except to those authorized by the depositor to receive such information. Letters refusing to give information follow the bad-news plan. Study the following example:

Dear Ms. Frosch:

I appreciate your letter in which you ask for information concerning markup rates on drug products sold in our store. Markup rates vary considerably, Ms. Frosch, and it is impossible for me to give you a figure that would apply to all drug products. Putting together detailed information would require more time than we can afford just now.

May I refer you to Service Bulletin 16, Markups in the Drug Industry, issued by the State Bureau of Commerce and Industry. This 50-cent booklet contains markup rates for the drug industry as a whole, and I am sure it will be helpful to you. You can obtain a copy by writing to the State Bureau of Commerce and Industry, 3001 Central Avenue, Hartford, Connecticut 06103.

Cordially yours,

Refusing Invitations. A business organization and its employees receive numerous invitations to participate in exhibits, to speak before groups, to take part in various kinds of community activities. Most business executives feel that it is wise to participate in these affairs—they help to build goodwill for the business. However, not all such invitations can be accepted because of time or financial limitations. In writing a letter refusing an invitation, you may adapt the bad-news plan to include the following three points:

1. Express appreciation for the invitation.
2. Give a logical reason for having to refuse.
3. Keep open the possibility of accepting a similar invitation in the future (if desirable).

Note the following example of a letter refusing an invitation to speak:

Dear Mr. Milchak:

I was pleased and complimented by your invitation to speak at the October Senior Citizens Meeting of the Paxton Civic Club.

Because I plan to be out of town during the last week in October, unfortunately I will not be able to accept your invitation. An important company business trip is scheduled for that time and it cannot be postponed. I am genuinely sorry that I cannot be with you.

It would be a pleasure to appear before your group at some later date. If you wish me to do so, I hope you will let me know at least a month in advance. Incidentally, the subject "How to Make Your Retirement Income Go Further" suits me just fine.

Sincerely,

Delays in Filling Orders. Delays may occur because the customer has not given you enough information to fill the order or because the goods ordered are temporarily out of stock or for some other reason. In any case, be sure to open your letter with a statement of appreciation for the customer's order.

When writing letters concerning delays because you are temporarily out of stock, explain why the merchandise is not being shipped immediately and tell the reader when the order will be delivered. For both the incomplete order and the out-of-stock acknowledgment, conclude with a statement designed to reinforce confidence in your company and products.

In the following example, notice how the bad-news plan described on page 000 is used to tell a customer about a shipping delay.

Dear Mr. Hensel:

We were naturally very pleased to have your first order for Tempo sports shirts. You are most thoughtful to comment on our advertisement in Men's Wear magazine. Apparently a good many others saw the ad too, because we have been swamped with orders for the Tempo line.

I am sending you today two dozen each of small, medium, and large sizes in assorted colors. The remaining four dozen of each will be shipped on Monday, March 4.

I regret, Mr. Hensel, that you should be inconvenienced on your very first order, but I hope you will understand that we were not prepared for the large quantity of orders received. You may be sure that our factory is now geared for round-the-clock production to keep all our dealers supplied.

I hope you find it just as hard to keep Tempo sports shirts in stock—they are so very popular! We look forward to doing business with you on a regular basis and promise our usual prompt service on your next order.

Sincerely yours,

In writing letters of this type, observe the following rules of tact, courtesy, and goodwill:

1. Always tell the customer first what you *can* do; then what you *can't* do. ("We are sending some shirts now; the rest will have to be sent later.")
2. Keep the tone positive. Even though you must apologize for the delay, don't overdo it. Assume that the customer understands. ("This rush of business naturally caught us unprepared.")
3. Reestablish customers' confidence in your firm by encouraging them to place additional orders. ("We look forward to future business. We will give you our usual prompt service.")

Delays Caused by Incomplete Requests. Suppose you receive the inquiry shown on the facing page. Obviously, this letter is neither clear nor complete. When possible, try to answer the customer's inquiry on the basis of your first letter. Sometimes you can answer it by providing more information than the customer needs. To answer this letter, you would have to know the kinds and quantities of gifts the customer desires; and the customer may not be able to answer these questions until you send the prices. In this case the entire price list should be sent to the customer with an everyday covering letter. Naturally, you could conclude such a letter with a sales appeal urging the customer to visit your shop.

Other inquiries may not be handled so easily, however. Any attempt on your part to answer some letters on the basis of the initial inquiry would probably fail to satisfy the customer. What you must do, then, is write the customer to ask for the information you need. Such a situation must be handled tactfully, without giving correspondents the impression that they were negligent or careless. If the order is incomplete, ask the customer in a positive way for the additional details. A statement such as "Before we ship your order, Mr. Jones, can you tell us whether you prefer your shirt in white or blue?" tactfully indicates to the reader that he did not provide you with sufficient information.

November 4, 1985

Ladies and Gentlemen:

I would like to buy some unusual gifts for the holidays. I am unable, however, to come to Tampa until late this month, and I would like to know in advance of my trip how much the gifts would cost.

Sincerely yours,
John R. Lyons

A letter that is unclear and incomplete may lead to a delay in fulfilling a request.

Make it easy for the customer to reply so as to increase your chance of completing the sale. Consider, for example, the following reply to a letter requesting a copy of a company's "booklet on gardening."

Dear Mrs. Petito:

We appreciate your interest in our service publications on gardening.

At present we publish over 300 booklets on every aspect of home gardening. In this way we hope to help our customers solve their special gardening problems.

Enclosed is a complete list of our publications. Just check the ones you want and mail your list in the enclosed stamped envelope. If you will let us know which booklets are of interest to you, we will forward them to you immediately.

Sincerely yours,

COMMUNICATION LABORATORY

APPLICATION EXERCISES

A. The Center Halfway House, 383 Trellis Road, Johnstown, Pennsylvania 15909, requests a donation from your company for a minibus. Your company, Cross-Country Vans, makes a large donation each year to the Johnstown Community Fund for distribution. You cannot possibly make donations for all the requests you receive. Write a refusal letter. Suggest that the Center Halfway House contact the Johnstown Community Fund. Try to write the letter so that the Center Halfway House staff will not be offended. They are highly respected in the community.

B. What is wrong with the following letter? Note several specific errors; then rewrite the letter.

Dear Ms. Callahan:

We are returning your check for $89.90. We stopped carrying Neato lawn trimmers when the manufacturer went out of business last year.

Yours truly,

C. You are a public relations associate at Sabel Electronics. You receive a request from Ms. Janet Ronstedt of the Summer Day Camp, P.O. Box 12, Kansas City, Missouri 64141, for a plant tour. Your plant is not set up to give tours. However, you do provide speakers for young people's groups on the topic of careers in electronics. Write a letter refusing the request for a plant tour but retaining Summer Day Camp's goodwill.

D. You work for Heeber's Discount Store, 121 Lenox Avenue, Columbia, South Carolina 29208. You receive an order from Larry Lucas, 1706 Huldy Avenue, Greenville, South Carolina 29611, for a Minisnack Model 6 office refrigerator. This model had a lock, which increased the cost by 10 percent. The manufacturer found there was not enough demand for this model and discontinued it. You now carry Model 8, which has no lock but is 15 percent larger than Model 6. Recommend your Model 8. It sells for $12 more than Model 6 and has a five-year guarantee.

E. You are employed by LTU Precision Valves. You receive an order from Vandock Oil Tools, 1200 Elmer Street, Missoula, Montana 59801, for 125 No. 81A7 valves. You welcome the business; but unfortunately, because of a recent steel strike, you are out of stock on these valves. It will take about ten days to fill this order. Write the kind of letter you would like to receive if you were the company that had placed the order.

F. You are a purchase order clerk at Handy Kitchen Supplies, 15 Grant Street, Minneapolis, Minnesota 55455. Mrs. Trudy Hilliard, 876 Willers

Road, Rochester, Minnesota 55901, sends you an order for a vegetable grater. You carry several sizes and models made from different materials. Send her a pamphlet that illustrates the kinds you have available. Make it easy for her to reply.

VOCABULARY AND SPELLING STUDIES

A. These words are often confused: *appraise, apprise; pretend, portend.* Write each in a sentence that illustrates its meaning.

B. Correct the capitalization in these sentences:

1. The president left the white house on Wednesday.
2. The Bordens will celebrate their Tenth Wedding Anniversay at Vanda's steak house.
3. She is qualified to take recordkeeping II next Semester.
4. He enjoyed his Tour of the west.
5. Have you read *Better Health through exercise?*

C. What are the plurals of the following?

1. harness
2. century
3. 1970
4. moose
5. a
6. cupful

COMMUNICATING FOR RESULTS

Getting the Facts. John Rickert, a customer who is behind in his installment payments, has been threatened by letter with repossession of his furniture. He comes to you, a credit clerk at the company, waving the letter and shouting, "You can't take my furniture back unless you return the $150 in payments I've made." His installment contract reads: "I, the lessee, hereby rent from the Ace Furniture Company the goods listed above. . . . The lessors agree that, if at the end of the term of the lease, the lessee has fulfilled all covenants, they will convey a free and clear title to the above articles to the lessee." You are an experienced credit clerk and have dealt with this kind of situation before. Because of this, you know that you should select your words carefully. What will you say to this customer? Be sure you understand the contract. HINT: Your company does not want to take back the furniture.

U · N · I · T

45

Claim and Adjustment Letters

No matter how efficient a business firm tries to be, mistakes will happen. A customer may receive the wrong merchandise, slow service, invoices or statements that contain errors, or even discourteous treatment at the hands of employees. Letters in which complaints are expressed—that is, letters in which customers make a claim against the company—are called *claim letters*.

The company for which you work undoubtedly will receive some claim letters; in turn, the company will have occasion to write claim letters to those from whom it buys. As a consumer you will also have many opportunities to write such letters. Therefore, to promote the company's and your own best interests, you need to be familiar with claim situations and with the principles of writing effective claim letters.

Preparing to Write Claim Letters

People writing claim letters are interested in one thing: satisfaction. If the merchandise is faulty, they want it replaced at no cost or inconvenience to themselves. If the service is poor, they want an apology and assurance that service will improve; they may even want some compensation for the inconvenience caused them. If an error has been made, they want it corrected.

To get satisfaction, claimants must present their cases carefully and thoughtfully to the people they feel are at fault. Suppose you ordered a gold identification bracelet from a mail-order house, specifying that the bracelet be engraved with your name. When the bracelet arrives, you are disappointed to find that a silver bracelet was sent. You become quite upset and a little angry. "How could they make such a stupid mistake?"

How would you begin your letter? In the first place, you should not write the letter while you are angry. Cool off first. You can do a much more convincing job when you are calm and can see the situation in a reasonable light. The mistake was not intentional; mistakes never are. If your letter were written in anger, it might begin like this:

> It was certainly carelessness on somebody's part to send me a silver bracelet when I asked for a gold one. Don't your order clerks know how to read? I simply do not understand . . . .

Such a letter might do more harm than good.

You would surely get much more willing cooperation from the seller if you had been courteous. Imagine how much sympathy you would get from the order clerks with your insulting remarks! A letter like the following would accomplish your purpose and do it much more successfully.

Gentlemen:

Today I received a silver identification bracelet (your Invoice 753291) instead of the gold identification bracelet specified in my May 25 order, a copy of which is enclosed.

I am returning the silver bracelet to you in a separate mailing. Please substitute a gold one with the name "Karen" engraved in script.

The quality of these identification bracelets is superb, and I am looking forward to receiving my gold bracelet as soon as possible.

Sincerely yours,

Writing Claim Letters

When writing a claim letter, remember to explain *carefully* and *tactfully* what is wrong. Avoid negative accusations or threats such as "I demand," "I must insist," "you will have to," "unless you," "why can't you," and so on. Discourteous statements such as these only tune out the reader. In addition, they lessen the likelihood of your obtaining the best possible service that you could possibly receive.

Avoid lecturing the reader about the ethics of the situation. You can't change the reader's values in one letter. And you only add more words. You want readers to read the specific points of your claim—not to be distracted or to begin skimming the letter because of words that seem to have no bearing on the specific situation from the reader's point of view.

So that your claim can be processed quickly, be sure to include any details necessary for identifying your claim—dates, catalog numbers, styles, order numbers, invoice numbers, and so on. If appropriate, also indicate the loss or inconvenience you have suffered—but, by all means, don't exaggerate!

Another important consideration in stating your claim is to let the company know specifically what you wish them to do about the situation. Remember, though, do not be unreasonable in your request. If the electric toothbrush you received as a gift breaks a month before the one-year warranty expires, don't ask the company to send you a new toothbrush. All you can expect is a repair of the one you have.

All the considerations described in the preceding paragraphs are important in writing a successful claim letter. The way you present your ideas in the letter, however, may vary. The nature of the claim itself will determine whether you will need to write a simple or a persuasive claim letter.

Simple Claims. Companies recognize that errors will occur occasionally, and they are prepared to handle them to the customer's satisfaction. Therefore, most claim letters may be written using the everyday letter plan. A simple and tactful statement of the situation in the opening paragraph brings the claim letter off to a direct start. Details needed to process the claim and the specific action the customer desires should follow the direct statement. Of course, skillful letter writers will conclude their letters with a statement that builds goodwill or one that shows they anticipate satisfaction of the claim. Notice how the everyday letter plan is used in the following letter:

Ladies and Gentlemen:

The wood-grained radio I ordered from your store arrived broken. Apparently, no packing had been placed in the box before it was sent from the warehouse.

This radio was purchased on June 25 and charged to my account under your Sales Check PL538795. I am returning the broken radio to your store and would appreciate your replacing it with a new one in the same size and wood-grained finish.

The radio is to be a birthday gift, so I would appreciate receiving the replacement by July 28.

Sincerely yours,

Persuasive Claims. Occasionally claim situations may not be so obvious. If your travel alarm clock stops working two weeks after the warranty expires, you may wish to convince a reputable company that it should repair the clock free of charge. After all, you used it on only one vacation! Or you may wish to return clothing you purchased over a month ago because it shrank when you washed it, even though the tag is marked "Machine Washable." Many situations require an explanation before requesting an adjustment, and for these situations you must write persuasive claim letters.

Like other persuasive letters, the persuasive claim begins with an attention-getting statement. In some cases this statement may begin to explain the situation; in other cases it may relate to the good reputation of the company or ask a question to stimulate the reader's interest. Then a presentation of facts and details leads the reader to the request for an adjustment. A closing that anticipates receiving the adjustment rounds out the persuasive claim letter. Notice how the following letter uses this approach.

Gentlemen:

Harmon's has always represented quality service and quality merchandise. That is why I know you will be interested in this letter.

Last month I purchased a Velda tennis dress (your Sales Check 8739621 dated April 9) from your better sportswear selection. The beauty and durability of my other Velda dress prompted me to purchase this one.

Because of the embroidered design, I decided to hand-wash the dress, in spite of its machine-washable label. Much to my dismay, though, the dress shrank 3 inches. I know you will agree that a Velda dress should not shrink, especially when it has been carefully hand-washed. Therefore, I am returning the dress to your store and would appreciate your crediting my account for $39.95.

Since Harmon's always stands behind its reputation for quality, I look forward to receiving credit for this merchandise.

Sincerely yours,

Preparing to Write Adjustment Letters

In writing answers to claim letters, you are on the other side of the fence. Your customers wish to present a claim, and they write to you. They may be dissatisfied with your merchandise, your service, or your general efficiency. You will respond to their claim with an *adjustment letter*.

Opportunity to Remedy Faults. A good company welcomes customer comments because they create opportunities to identify and remedy faulty products or poor services that may exist. It is your job to see that customers receive fair treatment—fair to them, of course, but also fair to your firm. Since adjustment letters sell satisfaction too, they are really sales letters.

Policies Differ. Most firms have established broad policies for making adjustments. Some are very generous and practice the motto "The customer is always right." Others are not so eager to please customers, especially if the customer is wrong. Even in the most generous organizations, there will be numerous occasions when claims cannot be granted. Regardless of the fact that established policies exist for most adjustment situations, there will always be exceptions. For example, an old customer who has dealt with a firm faithfully over the years is likely to receive a little more consideration than a new customer who is merely shopping around for the best buy. Many factors enter into the decision as to whether or not an adjustment will be granted. Often there is simply no policy to cover an adjustment situation, so letter writers must weigh all the evidence and then do what they think is fairest to their customers and to their employers. However, the writer must have or must get authority for any adjustment that is out of the ordinary.

Writing Adjustment Letters

When writing adjustment letters, under all circumstances be patient, tactful, and diplomatic. Always be sure to observe these four principles:

1. Reply promptly.
2. Show the customer that you understand the problem.
3. Tell the customer exactly what you are going to do about the problem.
4. Avoid negative words and accusations.

Reply Promptly. The longer customers wait for replies to their claims, the angrier they get and the harder it is to soothe their feelings. Show customers that they are important enough to warrant your immediate attention to their problems and that they are getting fast action.

"Right after I finished reading your June 10 letter, I looked into the matter of . . . . "

"We lost no time tracing the discrepancy in the invoice you wrote about . . . . "

"Good news! The lawn mowers arrived this morning, and they are already on their way to you."

"To make sure that there would be no slipup this time, I personally saw to it that your order . . . . "

"Your letter arrived this morning, and we have already put a tracer on your shipment."

Show Understanding. Those who make claims want, first of all, to have someone understand why they feel as they do. Your letter will be more effective if it expresses empathy.

"We can imagine how you feel about . . . . "

"You are entirely right about . . . . "

"Indeed, we can understand that . . . . "

"Your point is well taken, and . . . . "

"We ourselves have been in the same situation, and . . . . "

"Surely you have a right to feel that . . . . "

Be Exact. Tell customers exactly what you are going to do about their claim. If you are in a position to grant it, say so immediately and describe how you are going about it.

"Our check for $38.62, which is a refund on Invoice A1428, will be sent to you this week."

"Within a day or two you will have your new green blanket to replace the blue one you received . . . . "

"You have been given $184 credit for the eight dead batteries. Although these batteries were carefully inspected before they left our warehouse, they . . . . "

"We are pleased to replace the plastic hose on your Loyal vacuum cleaner with a new 'Tite-Nit' hose made of nylon."

"You are entirely right. The discount to which you were entitled was not shown on your February statement. You may be sure, however, that . . . . "

Even if you are not able to grant the claim, you should be exact in telling the customer why.

"We wish we could offer you an adjustment on this clothing, but our inspection shows that the suit has been worn several times and is soiled. You can understand, of course, that . . . . "

"Time slips by so fast that we can understand how it happened that your May 8 check contained a discount deduction of $32.70—although the 10-day discount period had expired. Would you like to send us a check for $32.70, or should we add this amount to your next statement?"

"Nothing would please us more than to accept your Jolly Jack guitar for refund, but we are bound by the terms of the guarantee that you received with your instrument."

Avoid Negatives. Negative words tend to put an unhappy claimant in an even more irritable frame of mind. On the other hand, positive, pleasant words help to soothe the claimant's irritation. Thus, you should try to conclude your letter with a positive statement that will build goodwill. In the following examples, notice the difference in tone between the positive statements and the negative ones.

POSITIVE: We appreciate receiving your helpful June 3 letter.

NEGATIVE: We have received your complaint of June 3.

POSITIVE: We are glad that you called our attention to the late arrival of your Purchase Order 4286.

NEGATIVE: We are sorry to hear of the unfortunate delay in the delivery of your Purchase Order 4286.

POSITIVE: Thank you for the friendly suggestion made in your July 8 letter.

NEGATIVE: Your July 8 criticism has been received.

POSITIVE: We will check all your future orders even more carefully than usual.

NEGATIVE: Please accept our apologies for sending you unsatisfactory goods.

POSITIVE: Our driver returned your parcel to our store because the house number was omitted from the address.

NEGATIVE: Because of your failure to give us your house number, our driver had to bring back the parcel, thus delaying delivery for three days.

Kinds of Adjustments

Adjustment letters answer claim letters. As the writer of adjustment letters, you may grant fully the requests of the claimant or reject totally the writer's proposals. Many times you may not grant the claim as the writer suggested, but instead you may seek to rectify the situation through an alternative procedure. Whatever method of adjustment you choose, you must organize your response carefully and seek to retain, as much as the circumstances permit, the goodwill and future business of the claimant.

Full Reparation. Full reparation adjustment letters are easy to write because they do exactly as the claimant asks. These "yes" letters follow the everyday letter plan to solve the problem described in the claim. Each begins with a statement granting the adjustment. Only the details in subsequent paragraphs vary, depending on whether the seller is at fault, the fault is divided, or the customer is at fault but the claim is granted to retain goodwill.

Seller at Fault. If you are the seller of goods or services and you are entirely at fault in an adjustment situation, you will usually, of course, grant the claim. And you should do so willingly. Just as you have greater respect for persons who readily admit their mistakes, your customer will respect your company when it cheerfully fulfills its responsibilities without quibbling. When you must grant a claim because it is your fault, follow an outline such as this:

1. Tell the customer the good news immediately—preferably in the first sentence.
2. Explain how the mistake happened (if you have an explanation). Don't be afraid of embarrassment—it is folly to try to save face when you are unquestionably wrong.
3. Express appreciation for the customer's understanding, and tell the customer that you will do your best to assure better treatment in the future.

The letter might read:

Dear Ms. Groskin:

This Friday we will send you by parcel post, special handling, 200 "Cougar" pennants to replace those that were printed in white instead of yellow. There will be, of course, no additional charge for these.

We have tried to find out what caused the confusion, but we have no explanation—or excuse. The only possible reason we can offer is that two members of our production department were ill last week, and we had to use inexperienced help for two or three days.

Please excuse us this time, Ms. Groskin. We can take a little solace from this situation: we have started a new training program for all those who are likely to be called into emergency service in the production area. We expect that this precaution will help us give you better service.

You may dispose of the 200 pennants that you received. It is not necessary to return them to us. Thank you for giving us an opportunity to serve you.

Sincerely yours,

Fault Is Shared. Occasionally the seller and customer share the responsibility for error. For example, the customer may have misunderstood your policy because it was not stated clearly or because the sales representative gave the wrong impression. In another case, one of your products may have malfunctioned and been damaged even further because the customer attempted to repair it. Of course, you should cheerfully acknowledge your part of the blame. At the same time, you may try to convince the customer to share some of the responsibility too. The following letter uses a form of the everyday letter plan to accomplish this purpose:

Dear Mr. Petrofsky:

Your American Home pinball machine has been restored to working order and is being returned to you today by parcel post.

The trigger device jammed because one of the bolts holding it in place had come loose. To prevent this situation from recurring, we have used special lock bolts to hold the trigger in place.

It was also necessary for us to replace the spring-feed mechanism. Apparently a screwdriver or other sharp instrument had been used in an attempt to free the jammed trigger. Instead, the spring feed was bent so severely that it was no longer operable. Although there is no charge this time for this replacement, please understand that such repairs are not included under the terms of the warranty. May I suggest that in the future any needed repairs be left solely to our well-trained service staff.

Enclosed is a copy of our latest catalog describing the newest in American Home electronic games. See for yourself the additional hours of enjoyment you can receive from these exciting, challenging entertainments.

Sincerely yours,

Goodwill Adjustment. As a goodwill gesture, you will sometimes grant adjustments even though the customer is clearly at fault. The risk of turning down a good customer may be too great, or the amount in question may be so small that refusing to make the adjustment would be poor business. In such a case, you should take full advantage of the opportunity to give in gracefully and build goodwill.

Dear Mrs. Renz:

It is a pleasure to write about the Stellar stereo recordings that you returned on November 8. I am sending you a replacement for the first record; the other two have been checked by our inspectors and are in excellent condition.

Upon examination of the records, our inspectors found that both sides of the first record were apparently played with a blunt needle. May I suggest that you examine the needle of your stereo before playing any records. A record is only as good as the needle playing it.

The enclosed booklet describes the various needles recommended by Stellar— available at any authorized Stellar record dealer.

Sincerely yours,

Partial Adjustment. Sometimes customers may request adjustments that are unreasonable or that are not covered under the warranty agreement. Instead of refusing the adjustment, you can reach a compromise by attempting to meet the customer halfway.

For example, suppose a customer returned to you a piece of luggage that was badly scratched and requested a replacement under the terms of the warranty. "After all," states the customer, "you guarantee this luggage against damage." You guarantee the luggage against *breakage*, not necessarily damage, under normal travel conditions. While you cannot replace the luggage, you can repair the scratch so that it will not be noticeable.

What if a customer writes you that one of your Lastever tires is threadbare after only 24,000 miles of service? Your 40,000-mile warranty does not guarantee the customer a full refund or even a new tire, as the claim letter suggested. You can, however, prorate the cost of the tire and issue a credit toward the purchase of a replacement.

Situations such as these two require partial adjustments. Since you are not doing exactly what the customers requested, you are in fact writing a "bad-news letter." The task of the effective communicator is not to convey the bad news, but to present the circumstances in such a positive, thoughtful light that the customer is able to understand and accept graciously the partial adjustment.

Adapt the bad-news plan to the writing of partial adjustments. Use the following outline to organize your ideas:

1. Refer to the claim and its circumstances in a neutral manner.
2. Explain the circumstances for refusing the requested adjustment; tactfully weave in the refusal with the explanation.
3. Present your alternative for rectifying the situation.
4. Close with resale of your company or its products.

The following claim letter was received by a mail-order nursery. The warranty on the bulbs had expired. How would you handle this claim?

Gentlemen:

The catalog you mailed to me last spring attracted my attention. Excited about the beautiful photos, I purchased an order of begonia tubers.

Even though I did everything the planting and caring manual prescribed, all I got were some sad-looking plants, without even a trace of a flower. Since my garden is landscaped with plenty of trees and an excellent sprinkling and misting system, I know it was not because of a lack of water or shade that the begonias didn't bloom.

I relied on Spring Valley's Triple-Tested Seal of Approval, which ensured that the begonias would grow and bloom to my full satisfaction. I have great confidence in Spring Valley and would like to maintain it. Therefore, would you please stand behind your guarantee and refund to me the purchase price of these begonias—$19.20. A copy of my credit card statement is enclosed.

Sincerely,

Ella Larsen

The company that received this letter chose to make a partial adjustment. Notice how the bad-news plan was used to retain the business and goodwill of this customer.

Dear Ms. Larsen:

We appreciate hearing from you about your experience with our begonia tubers.

The guarantee period for the plants you purchased expired on August 1. Although we are unable to grant a refund after the guarantee period, we do wish to make an adjustment. Because we value you as a customer, we are enclosing a gift certificate for $19.20 for use on your next order.

You should be receiving our new spring catalog within the next six weeks. In it you will find many beautiful selections for the planting season, which is rapidly approaching.

Sincerely,

Adjustment Refusals. In many instances the customer's request for an adjustment is not justifiable and you must refuse the claim. Of course, this fact must be established conclusively before a letter is sent. You cannot automatically *assume* that the customer is wrong; therefore, all the facts should be obtained and weighed carefully. "Make sure you are right, and then go ahead" is good advice in writing letters of this type. Even though you know you are right and the customer is wrong, however, this type of letter is still one of the most difficult to write. Somehow you must convey to the customer the idea that you are following the only course open to you and that, as a reasonable person, the customer will agree with you. You will have to rely on your best skills as a business writer!

Nonreturnable Merchandise. Suppose a customer writes wanting to return for credit some items of merchandise purchased several months ago. The reason given for the return is that the merchandise received was not that specified in the order. Of course, you are immediately skeptical. Why did the customer wait so long before reporting the error to you? After looking up the original order, you find that the correct merchandise was definitely sent; the bill was even paid. You conclude that the customer is merely trying to unload some unwanted stock and may be trying to take advantage of your company's very fair adjustment policies. In this particular case, you cannot accept the merchandise for credit.

In writing the reply to this claim, use the bad-news letter plan, which may follow an outline like the one shown below:

1. Thank the customer for writing you, restating the adjustment he or she believes should be made.
2. Explain why it is not possible to grant the adjustment.
3. Offer helpful advice, if possible.
4. Assume that the customer accepts your position as fair, and close the letter on a friendly note.

The letter might read:

Dear Mrs. Kamen:

Thank you for writing us about the "Key Comfort" hassocks that you wish to return for credit.

Immediately after receiving your letter, I rechecked your May 11 order. The order specified 12 "Key Comfort" hassocks in beige; the bill of lading matches your order in every respect. In fact, you have already paid the invoice for this shipment. Under the circumstances, we are unable to accept these hassocks for credit.

The "Key Comfort" line was discontinued by the manufacturer in July, and we are now featuring "Royal Rest" hassocks. Several of our dealers, however, reported considerable success in moving the "Key Comfort" line. Premier Furniture, in Oceola, found that one of the biggest sales features is that the hassocks can be used with both indoor and outdoor furniture. The plastic cover included with each hassock makes this a genuine all-purpose item. Have you tried running an ad on these hassocks in connection with your summer furniture clearance sales? I think you will find doing so profitable.

Several new items of furniture for fall have arrived. Particularly exciting is the new line of Radwick Maple originals for every room in the house. Look over the enclosed folder describing some of these authentic period pieces. People everywhere are talking about Radwick furniture. This line promises to be one of the best sellers we have had in years.

Sincerely yours,

Buyer at Fault. Sometimes you must refuse to grant an adjustment because the product is no longer under warranty or it has been abused. Customers may request unwarranted repairs, replacements, or refunds. In any of these cases, the effective communicator must show the claimant why the request is not justified and minimize any resulting ill will.

Suppose a customer returned to you an electric typewriter that "will not turn on" and asks that it be repaired under the terms of the one-year guarantee. You find that the typewriter had apparently been dropped and three components in the motor were broken; such repairs are not covered under the terms of the guarantee. You would need to write this customer a refusal letter using the bad-news letter plan.

Dear Ms. Phillips:

Your Wizard electric typewriter, along with your letter, arrived at our repair center yesterday. We appreciate your calling this condition to our attention.

Upon its arrival your Wizard was checked by one of our repair supervisors. Apparently the typewriter had been dropped or severely jarred because the carriage return mechanism was broken, the cylinder feed was cracked, and the wires to the power switch were torn loose. Since your typewriter is guaranteed against defects in parts and work quality only under normal-use conditions, the needed repairs are not covered under the terms of the warranty. We can, however, put your typewriter in good working order for $98.40, which is the actual cost of parts and labor.

Please let us know if you wish us to make the repairs. A postage-paid card is enclosed for your convenience in replying.

Sincerely yours,

Unearned Discounts. Occasionally customers may figure the discount on a bill incorrectly or may attempt to take advantage of a discount when they are not entitled to it. The company may do one of three things:

1. Return the remittance and request a check for the correct amount.
2. Accept the remittance and ask for an additional remittance to make up the difference.
3. Accept the remittance and add the difference to the customer's next bill.

In any event, a letter must be written to the customer. Under no circumstances should the situation be ignored. In fairness to other customers who abide by the rules, the business cannot afford to make exceptions. In writing to customers, point out the error tactfully and appeal to their sense of fair play—but do both without offending them.

Dear Mr. DeWitt:

Thank you for your check for $2,450 in payment of your March invoice. We appreciate the many opportunities you have given us to serve you.

We notice that in the past you have always paid your invoices within the discount period to take advantage of the saving. As you know, we can afford to give this discount because prompt payment enables us to make a similar saving on our purchases.

When a customer does not make payment within the discount period, we do not make any saving either. In this instance, 17 days passed before we received payment. Of course, this is 7 days beyond the maximum allowed.

Because you are a good customer and because this is the first time you have gone beyond the discount period, we would like to allow the discount. However, if we did so, we would be unfair to our customers who pay within the 10-day period. They would lose confidence in us, and so would you.

Therefore, Mr. DeWitt, will you please send us with your next remittance the $50 remaining on your account.

Very sincerely yours,

Third Party at Fault. Quite often the roots of a claim lie neither in the customer's nor in the seller's actions but in the carrier's. Since the carrier assumes responsibility for safe delivery of any shipment accepted, the customer's claim is usually against the carrier rather than against the seller. The seller should have a receipt showing that the merchandise was in good condition at the time it was released to the carrier. When a shipment arrives in damaged condition or is "short," the company to whom the claim is made may do one of two things:

1. Take the responsibility for the adjustment; then make a claim against the carrier.
2. Suggest that the customer enter a claim with the carrier, since the matter is really between the buyer and the carrier.

Following is an example of a letter from a supplier to a dealer who received a badly damaged television set. The bad-news letter plan is used to write this kind of adjustment letter.

Dear Miss Malcolm:

We appreciate your calling to our attention the damage done to the Tru-Color television that you ordered from us recently.

When the television left our warehouse in Toledo, it was in perfect condition, as substantiated by a signed receipt from the Ohio Western Railroad. Evidently the television was damaged in transit, and your claim is with the railroad. The shipment was fully insured so you should have no difficulty recovering the cost of the set.

Would you like us to send a duplicate shipment to replace the television damaged in transit? If so, please sign and mail the enclosed postal card and we will ship the replacement immediately.

Sincerely yours,

COMMUNICATION LABORATORY

APPLICATION EXERCISES

A. Assume that you had bought a set of tires from your service station. You paid for them in six equal installments that were added to your monthly gasoline bill. Even though you have paid all six installments in full, you now receive two additional monthly bills for them. Write to Edward Harmon,

Fleet Oil Company, P.O. Box 170, New York, New York 10004, requesting that the company (1) stop billing you for the tires and (2) write you confirming that your credit rating has not been damaged.

B. Now suppose you work for the Fleet Oil Company (see Exercise A). You are asked to write the adjustment letter in response to the claim. Address the letter to Karen Harlow, 717 Cedar Road, Macon, Georgia 31206. After checking, you find that Ms. Harlow has continued receiving a bill because of a computer error. Tell Ms. Harlow that you have corrected the error, apologize, and assure her that her credit rating is unchanged.

C. A box of grapefruit you ordered from All-Pink Grapefruit, Route 6, Fort Lauderdale, Florida 33314, arrives with some of the fruit spoiled. The grapefruit was crated poorly and was marked "Keep in a Cool Place." Write a letter making your claim.

D. Compose the adjustment letter you would write if you were employed by All-Pink Grapefruit, who found that the Laraway Shipping Company was at fault in carelessly transporting the grapefruit (see Exercise C). Address the letter to yourself.

E. Suppose you had purchased a Bell-Tone tape recorder from Good Sounds Inc., 2703 Callaway Street, Pittsburgh, Pennsylvania 15229. After you had used the recorder four or five times, it failed to record properly and required adjustment. Now Good Sounds bills you $22.50 for the adjustment. Naturally you feel the charge is not justified since this is a new recorder. Write the claim letter, addressed to Vincent Way, you would send to the store. Indicate several possible ways that Good Sounds might adjust your claim.

F. Assume that you are answering the claim in Exercise E. Because the recorder had been improperly loaded, its winding mechanism was bent. Write a refusal letter to Peter C. Hale, 1811 Holiday Road, Sante Fe, New Mexico 87501.

VOCABULARY AND SPELLING STUDIES

A. These words are often confused: *disposition, deposition; disprove, disapprove*. Write each in a sentence that illustrates its meaning.

B. Substitute the correct forms for any incorrect number style in these sentences.

1. The candidate needs only ⅔'s of the vote.
2. Aviation has changed our lives during the 20th century.
3. This historic oak tree is 10½ feet high.
4. 32 tons were shipped yesterday.
5. The company retirement fund now has over two million dollars.

C. Should one or two *l*'s be used in the blank spaces in these words?

1. ba___sistics
2. cau___iflower
3. co___ection
4. cu___ture
5. mai___able
6. mi___eage
7. para___el
8. we___come

COMMUNICATING FOR RESULTS

A Delivery Error. You place an order by telephone to a local stationery store for ten columnar pads of a particular size for use by the accounting staff. Two weeks later a messenger brings in ten *cartons*, each carton containing ten pads. Of course, it is a mistake, but you know the messenger is not to blame—the delivery ticket shows ten *cartons*. How would you handle this problem?

U · N · I · T
46   Credit and Collection Letters

Today millions of Americans enjoy credit privileges. Perhaps the house you live in, the family automobile, your television set, and much of your clothing were purchased on credit. A conservative estimate reveals that a majority of all business in the United States is transacted on credit. The consumer buys merchandise on credit from the retail store; the retail store purchases its stock on credit from a wholesaler; the wholesaler buys on credit from the factory; the factory purchases its raw materials, also on credit, from various suppliers. The chain is almost endless, and the use of credit continues to grow. Many Americans travel, dine, and obtain hotel accommodations on a credit basis merely by producing a convenient credit card.

Even though millions of dollars' worth of business is done on credit each year, the losses from bad debts are surprisingly small. Most businesses estimate that of their total charge accounts, fewer than 1 percent will be uncollectible. One reason for this small percentage of "bad debts" is that credit privileges are not granted in a hit-or-miss fashion. Before businesses grant credit, they make reasonably sure that they will be paid for the goods they sell. Thus each prospective charge account customer is investigated carefully before credit is extended. Another reason for the small number of uncollectible accounts is, of course, that most people are honest.

Credit Letters

A person wishing to establish credit will usually go to a store's credit department or will write or telephone for a credit application form. Such an application is illustrated on page 440.

When the store receives a credit application, the credit manager will begin immediately to investigate the references that have been supplied or in some cases will ask the local retail credit bureau to investigate. When asking for a reference from stores where the applicant has been a credit customer, the credit manager will usually use a form letter like this:

Dear Mr. Payson:

Mr. Frank Gordon, 1010 Franklin Street, Hampton, has requested credit privileges from us and has given your firm as a reference.

We would very much appreciate your answering the following questions about Mr. Gordon:

1. How long has the applicant had an account with you? _____

2. Was there a maximum amount allowed? _____ If so, how much? _____

3. Did the applicant make payments according to your terms? _____

4. Does the applicant still owe you money? _____ If so, how much? _____

5. Do you consider the applicant:

   _____ An excellent credit risk?

   _____ An average credit risk?

   _____ A poor credit risk?

A stamped return envelope is enclosed for your convenience in replying. Of course, any information you give us will be kept confidential.

Sincerely yours,

Letters Granting Credit. If the decision regarding an applicant's request for credit is favorable, the letter writer faces a pleasant writing task—that of telling the customer the welcome news. The following outline, using the everyday letter plan, may be used as a guide in writing letters granting credit.

1. Welcome the customer, expressing your wish for a pleasant association.
2. Describe the special privileges available.
3. Explain the terms of payment.
4. Encourage use of the new charge account and offer any special assistance.

JCPenney Charge Application

Signature

Your Signature(s) mean(s) that you have read and agree to the terms of our Charge Account Agreement.

Applicant's Signature: *Sarah Brown*
Co-Applicant's Signature:
Date: 2/16/85
Date:

For Office Use Only
Store Number: 196901
Account Number:

General Information — (Please Print All Information)

Type Of Account You Want (Check One): ☑ Individual ☐ Joint

Have You Applied For A JCPenney Account Before? Applicant ☐ Yes ☑ No   Co-Applicant ☐ Yes ☐ No

Where: When: Where: When:

Name Of Applicant To Whom Our Billing Statements Should Be Sent
(First) SARAH (Initial) (Last) BROWN

Social Security Number: 054-19-8718   Date of Birth: 5/22/51   No. Of Dependent Children: 0

Name of Co-Applicant (If Joint Account Requested)
(First) (Initial) (Last)

Social Security Number: Date Of Birth: / /   Relationship To Applicant:

Name And Relationship(s) To Applicant(s) Of Any Other Person(s) You Will Allow To Charge Purchases To Your Account
(First) (Initial) (Last)   (Relationship)

For Office Use	
FLC	RI
CBC	
JCP-12	
J	I
CL	Audit Code
CBSC	
Date	TB
ID	
CCA	
CCAB	Date
CCID	
For Office Use Only	

Information About Applicant To Whom Our Billing Statements Should Be Sent

Present Residence Address—Street: 1131 S. PRINCE ST.
City, State: PALMYRA, PA   Zip: 17078
Area Code & Phone Number: 717 555-9811   How Long At This Address: Yrs. 8 Mos. 2   Monthly Mtge./Rent: $450
Do You: ☐ Own ☑ Rent ☐ Own Mobile Home ☐ Live With Parents ☐ Other (Please Specify)
Former Address — Street: 338 W. 77th ST.   How Long: 5 YRS.
City, State: NEW YORK, NY   Zip: 10024
Employer (Give Firm's Full Name): WILSON + WILSON, INC.   How Long: 5 YRS.
Employer's Address (Street/City/State): 2 MAIN ST., HARRISBURG, PA   Business Telephone: 555-1144
Type Of Business: STEEL MFG   Present Position: EXEC SECRETARY   Monthly Salary: $1,250

Information About Co-Applicant (If Joint Account Requested)

Present Residence Address—Street:
City, State: Zip:
Area Code & Phone Number: ( )   How Long At This Address: Yrs. Mos.   Monthly Mtge./Rent:
Do You: ☐ Own ☐ Rent ☐ Own Mobile Home ☐ Live With Parents ☐ Other (Please Specify)
Former Address — Street: How Long:
City, State: Zip:
Employer (Give Firm's Full Name):   How Long:
Employer's Address (Street/City/State):   Business Telephone:
Type Of Business: Present Position: Monthly Salary:

You Need Not Furnish Alimony, Child Support or Separate Maintenance Income Information If You Do Not Want Us To Consider It In Evaluating Your Application

Other Income — Source(s): NONE   Amount (Monthly):
Other Income — Source(s):   Amount (Monthly):

Bank Accounts (Include Co-Applicant's, If Joint Account Requested)

1. Bank — Branch: PENN STATE NAT'L   Account In The Name Of: SARAH BROWN   Checking & Savings ☑   Checking ☐   Savings ☐   Loan ☐
2. Bank — Branch: Account In The Name Of: Checking & Savings ☐   Checking ☐   Savings ☐   Loan ☐

Credit References (Include Co-Applicant's, If Joint Account Requested)

Credit Cards (Include Loan Or Finance Companies)

	Firm Name	Location	Account/Loan Number	Account/Loan In The Name Of
1.	MASTERCARD	PENN STATE NAT'L	8766000698338765	SARAH BROWN
2.				
3.				

Personal Reference

Name Of Person Not Living At Address of Applicant Or Co-Applicant: RONALD J. STOKES   Relationship To Applicant: SUPERVISOR   Present Residence Address (Street/City/State): 42 DEVON ST, ICKESBURG, PA

JCP-8600 (Rev. 5/82)   After completing application, detach at perforation, fold down from top, moisten flap, fold and seal. Postage paid by JCPenney.

Courtesy of JC Penney Company, Inc.

A credit application usually requests personal as well as business information.

Dear Mrs. Chang:

We take great pleasure in opening a charge account at Hapwell's in your name. I feel sure that this will be the start of a long and mutually pleasant association.

As a charge customer, you will enjoy many privileges at Hapwell's. For instance, our charge customers receive advance notices of special sales so that they may take advantage of these bargains before they are offered to the general public. Charge customers, too, are entitled to free gift wrapping on any purchase of $5 or more. You may also use your charge card at our Terrace Restaurant, at our Calorie Watchers' Bar, and in our Book Rental Department. Your charge card is accepted for all our services!

By the 1st of each month, you will receive an itemized statement of your purchases made through the 25th day of the preceding month; purchases made after the 25th appear on the following month's bill. Payments are due by the 10th, and a monthly charge of 1½ percent will be made on the balance remaining at that time.

We hope you will make regular use of your charge account. Remember, everyone at Hapwell's is dedicated to the slogan that is taken from the first three letters of our name—HAP: "Hapwell's Always Pleases."

Sincerely yours,

Many stores notify acceptance of applications for credit by a printed announcement card.

Letters Refusing Credit. If the credit manager determines from the information gathered that an applicant is a poor credit risk, a letter turning down the request must be written. No other letter is more difficult to write. Regardless of the wording, the writer is in effect saying the customer does not warrant the store's faith. A letter refusing credit must be very tactful, as is the one on page 442. Remember, you want the customer to continue buying from you on a cash basis.

To write a letter refusing credit, use an indirect approach that follows the bad-news plan. Notice how the following letter leads the reader on a step-by-step basis to the refusal and then offers the alternative plan of purchasing on a cash basis.

Dear Mr. McBride:

You have paid us a compliment by requesting credit privileges at Young's. Thank you for submitting your application.

As in the case of all those who apply for credit, we have made a careful investigation of your resources and credit obligations. Since you have a number of loan commitments, may we suggest that you continue to allow Young's to serve you on a cash basis until such time as you are able to reduce your present obligations.

You may be sure, Mr. McBride, that we will welcome the opportunity of considering your application again when circumstances are more favorable toward your receiving additional credit.

Sincerely yours,

Letters Stimulating Credit Business. Business firms welcome the opportunity to grant credit to the right people—those who will use it wisely. In fact, because they know that credit customers are bigger buyers and generally more loyal customers, stores often put on special campaigns to encourage credit customers to make more frequent or larger purchases. These letters are combined sales-goodwill letters because they stimulate both interest in and sales for the firm.

Retail stores will often invite steady cash customers to open charge accounts on the theory that they will like the convenience of shopping in this manner and will, of course, be encouraged to make more frequent pur-

willamette
DEPARTMENT STORES
2105 East 30th Avenue   Eugene, Oregon 97405

November 18, 1986

Ms. Arlene Craven
1504 Olive Street
Eugene, Oregon 97401

Dear Ms. Craven:

Thank you for requesting a credit account with Willamette.
Willamette believes that people who have not yet established
credit certainly deserve the opportunity to do so, and we
would like to help you.

To establish your first credit account, then, we suggest
that you ask someone to act as a cosigner with you on the
credit application. Perhaps one of your relatives or
friends who has already established credit would be willing
to help you do this.

As soon as you and your cosigner have completed the enclosed
form, please return it to us, and we will reevaluate your
request.

All of us at Willamette are eager to welcome you to our
store again--soon!

Sincerely yours,

Terry Patria

Terry Patria
Credit Department

nw
Enclosure

A letter refusing credit should be tactful.

chases. The following letter, using the everyday letter plan, encourages a
cash customer to avail herself of a charge account.

Dear Ms. Mosca:

You are cordially invited to open a charge account at Benson and Black.

Hundreds of our customers enjoy the convenience of a charge account. They are
able to shop without having to carry large sums of money, and often, too, they
enjoy the convenience of shopping more easily by mail or by telephone. Merchan-

dise that you really need can be purchased now, and you will not have to defer the pleasure of using it.

Benson and Black pampers its charge customers in many ways, and you will be delighted with the personal attention you will receive. Why not come in and let us show you how easy it is to open an account—and use it immediately.

Sincerely yours,

Collection Letters

Most of the people who have been granted credit pay their bills faithfully and on time. Some people, however, need to be reminded when their accounts are past due. The person who writes collection letters must assume that customers are fundamentally honest and fair and intend to pay their bills. This attitude is necessary to maintain the basic principle of credit— mutual faith. Therefore, the experienced credit manager assumes that "the customer is trustworthy until proven otherwise."

Collection-Letter Series. Collection letters are often written in a series. There may be as many as six letters in a series, beginning with the first reminder and ending with the final ultimatum. Many large department stores and mail-order houses have developed several series of collection letters—as many as five or six different series. Each series may be independent of the others, or letters in one series may be used interchangeably with one or more in the others.

Collection-letter series are usually duplicated form letters; the typist merely fills in the date, inside address, and salutation. Some firms, however, prefer to give their collection letters a more personal touch (these command more attention) by having them typed on word processing equipment. Each letter in a series is given a code number, and a careful record is kept of those that have been sent to the customer.

Statements of Account. Most stores send out statements each month to those who have charge accounts. These statements serve as reminders to pay. At the same time, they furnish customers with a record of their purchases.

At one time charge customers looked upon the statement as a *dun*—a demand for payment. Today, however, we expect to receive a statement of our account each month and use it as a basis for payment.

A statement of account is all that most people need to pay their bills. No additional reminders are necessary. But sometimes statements are mislaid or forgotten. If the store does not receive payment within a specified number of days after the statement is sent, it may simply send a second statement and hope this will be sufficient. The second reminder may be a form letter or a card reminder, such as the one shown on page 444.

You will notice that form reminders are very impersonal and very gentle. There is a good reason for this. At this stage of collection, the credit manager

AN OPPORTUNITY . . .

TO THANK YOU FOR YOUR BUSINESS AND TO REMIND YOU
OF THE BALANCE (SHOWN ON THE ENCLOSED STATEMENT
FOR YOUR CONVENIENCE) FOR YOUR RECENT PURCHASES.

IF YOU HAVE SENT US YOUR PAYMENT WITHIN THE LAST
FEW DAYS, PLEASE ACCEPT OUR THANKS. IF YOU HAVE
NOT, PLEASE TAKE THIS OPPORTUNITY TO DO SO.

PIERCE'S

The second reminder that payment is due may be in the form of a printed card.

doesn't want the customer to feel singled out. Otherwise, the customer's attitude may be "Why are they picking on me? I'm only a few days late." Because of this possible attitude, a personalized message in this situation is not so effective as a printed notice or a form letter.

The Collection Process. If the various notices just discussed do not bring results, additional reminders will be necessary. The procedures to be followed from this point depend greatly on the customers. If their credit records are good, the store may continue reminding them with gentle hints that use the everyday letter plan. If there is some past history of tardiness in paying, the next reminder may be more persuasive. If the store suspects, because of past dealings, that a customer will be difficult to collect from, stiffer reminders may be written earlier. Also, the number of days allowed between reminders will depend on the store's experience with the customer; quick-paying customers are usually given more time between reminders. There is no standard pattern for all customers or for all businesses; many factors determine the frequency and the types of letters sent to collect past-due accounts. A typical pattern in a collection system may be as follows:

Step	Number of Days After Regular Billing
1. Reminder	30
2. Inquiry letter	45
3. Mild appeal	60
4. Strong appeal	75
5. Ultimatum	90–100

To illustrate a collection situation, let us assume that Lisa Jones has a charge account with Willamette Department Store. Willamette records show that Ms. Jones has had an account for about a year. She has made frequent purchases during that time and has always paid her bills, but several times reminders were necessary before the account was paid.

During June Ms. Jones purchased a rattan chaise longue and a redwood dining set for outdoor use. The amount of her purchase was $187.88. A statement was sent on July 1.

The Reminder Stage. Because Ms. Jones did not pay the $187.88 statement sent to her on July 1, a routine form reminder was mailed on August 1. If Ms. Jones does not respond to this routine reminder, the credit manager may choose to send her a more personal reminder or advance to the next stage of collection, depending upon what kind of customer he or she judges Ms. Jones to be.

If the credit manager considers her merely careless or forgetful, rather than deliberately slow, the manager will send a second, more personal reminder, somewhat like the one on page 446. Care will be taken not to offend Ms. Jones since she is still considered a profitable customer. The letter to Ms. Jones may sound something like this.

Dear Ms. Jones:

Haven't you overlooked something? According to our records, you received a statement of your account in early July. On August 1 we sent you a reminder that your balance of $187.88 had not been paid.

I believe that this matter is merely an oversight and that you will mail us your check right away. Better still, why not come to the store in person to take care of the account. While you are here, stop in to see the new shipment of barbecue grills we have just received. These aluminum grills are as handsome as they are practical.

Cordially yours,

Notice that this letter uses a variation of the everyday letter plan and gently chides the customer for her oversight. Note, too, that she is indirectly complimented by the implication that there is no cause for worry on your part—you know she will pay. The letter ends with a sales message because at this stage you wish merely to plant an idea, not to offend the customer by overemphasizing your plea.

If this letter does not get results (but in most cases it will), you will have to use a different approach. Again, the time elapsed between the letter just illustrated and the next one will depend upon the customer and the store. In most cases, the time between letters grows progressively shorter. If there is a problem in receiving payment, the store does not wish to drag the matter

THE
WALL
STREET
JOURNAL.

DOW JONES & COMPANY, INC. Publishers.
THE WALL STREET JOURNAL · BARRON'S

THE EDUCATIONAL SERVICE BUREAU
200 Burnett Road
Chicopee, Massachusetts 01021

Myrtle White
Manager, Subscriber Services

October 20, 1986

Mr. George Vandenburg
15 Summit Avenue
Providence, Rhode Island 02906

Dear Mr. Vandenburg:

We know how busy college life can be, with classes, studies
and extracurricular activities. So we'd like to remind you
that we have not yet received payment for your Wall Street
Journal subscription. Here is a second copy of the invoice
for your convenience.

No doubt by now you've had an opportunity to become familiar
with The Journal, to use it as an adjunct to your studies,
and to recognize what an important part of the American
business scene it is. We hope you'll come to find, as many
students have, that The Journal provides indispensable information for the campus and the business communities alike.

Your invoice is made out for the term you selected. If you
chose less than a year, you can take this opportunity to
extend your subscription to a full year and save even more
at our special educational rate. Simply check the appropriate box on the invoice and enclose your payment.

To make sure you don't miss a day of your subscription, we
are always happy to accept changes of address, whether on or
off campus. Just give us two weeks' notice.

Thank you.

Sincerely,

Carole Brinkman

Carole Brinkman
Subscriber Services

an
Enclosures

PS: If you've sent payment, please excuse this request.
Your payment and our letter probably crossed in the mail.

Credit managers may send a personal reminder letter to customers whose failure to pay may be accidental rather than deliberate.

out; the customer may get the impression that prompt payment really isn't important.

Inquiry Letter. If Ms. Jones still does not pay, you begin to suspect that something is wrong—and that is exactly the approach you take in the next collection stage. The inquiry stage still assumes the customer wishes to pay but that something is preventing his or her prompt payment.

Reasons people hold up payment may be that they are dissatisfied with the merchandise, the service has been unsatisfactory, or they are in temporary financial difficulty. Whatever the case may be, you wish to take this opportunity to say, "Let's sit down and talk about it." Of course, if there is no such problem, you wish the customer to send a check for the overdue balance to clear up the account.

Dear Ms. Jones:

You have always in the past paid your account promptly. That is the reason we cannot understand why we have not received your check for $187.88 or an explanation why your account remains unpaid.

Is something wrong? We have no reason to believe anything other than that you are completely satisfied with the chaise longue and redwood dining set you purchased last June. Perhaps there is some other reason that prevents you from sending your payment for these purchases. Whatever the circumstances may be, please let us know. We would like to work out a solution with you. However, we cannot do so unless we hear from you.

Write me personally, Ms. Jones, or give me a call at 555-8733 to discuss this situation. I am eager to hear from you. However, if there is no reason for nonpayment, won't you please take a moment now to write a check for $187.88 and mail it so that your account can be marked "paid in full."

Sincerely yours,

Mild Appeal. There are several appeals the store may use in writing the next letter if the "let's-talk-about-it" approach does not get results. Since most people like to have others think well of them and are uncomfortable if their image is in danger of blemish, the appeal to pride is often successful. "We are confident your reputation for prompt payment and fair business practices will not allow you to permit this balance to remain unpaid any longer" says what is needed to implement this mild appeal.

The one most often used mild appeal is the appeal to fair play. This appeal tells the customer, "We have kept our part of the bargain—now won't you keep yours?" The appeal to fair play uses the persuasive letter plan to convince the reader to pay, as illustrated in the following letter.

Dear Ms. Jones:

Suppose a good friend of yours wanted to borrow your new outdoor redwood dining set for a lawn party she was giving. Because you like her and wish her party to be a success, you gladly consent—even offer to help her move the furniture to her house for the occasion. Of course, it is understood that the furniture will be returned promptly after the party.

How would you feel if your friend kept the furniture and said nothing about returning it? If she even ignored several reminders from you that it should be returned? My guess is, Ms. Jones, that you would be somewhat bewildered—and a little annoyed.

We find ourselves in a similar position regarding your account. We granted you credit because we felt you would not abuse the privilege. Yet you have not paid for your June purchases, and you have not responded to the four notices we have sent you. We are naturally curious to know why. We sold you a chaise longue and a redwood dining set in good faith, and we have tried to see that you were pleased in every way. But we believe you also have a responsibility to show us that our faith in you was justified.

Won't you use the enclosed envelope to send us your check (the amount is $187.88) right now—this minute, while the matter is fresh in your mind. This will substantiate our faith in you.

Sincerely yours,

Strong Appeal. If this appeal to the customer's sense of fair play does not bring the desired results, the credit manager has reason to be worried about the intentions of the customer. What will the next step be? If the firm's collection policy permits (some firms have more lenient collection policies than others), a second appeal may be made before sending the customer a "pay-or-else" ultimatum. The second appeal letter, which also follows the persuasive letter plan, may make a strong appeal to fear.

Fear of losing one's credit rating and fear of losing one's credit privileges are the main motivators in this appeal stage. The resulting letter is positively worded but firm in its position. Sentences such as "To protect your credit rating, your account must be cleared up immediately" and "You would not want to lose your credit privileges by allowing this account to go unpaid" are typical statements that might appear in the strong appeal letter. The following letter illustrates fully how the appeal to fear can be carried out in the persuasive letter plan.

Dear Ms. Jones:

If we received an inquiry concerning your credit, we would like to say, "Of course, Ms. Jones is an excellent charge customer. She always pays her account and, what's more, she pays on time." If we received such an inquiry today, however, we unfortunately would not be able to be so positive.

You have been a good Willamette customer, Ms. Jones, and we value your friendship. But we do have some question about your intention of settling your current account. Frankly, we cannot imagine what is wrong.

Please help us to help you. Your credit reputation is a valuable asset, and we do not want to see it damaged. Your credit reputation is in danger, however, unless you send us your check immediately. The amount is $187.88

Sincerely yours,

"Last-Chance" Ultimatum. If the appeal letters do not elicit immediate payment, the credit manager has no alternative but to assume that the customer does not intend to pay. Usually, however, the customer will be given one last chance before the matter is placed in the hand of a collection agency

When listeners spend too much time taking notes, they miss the heart of the message. Use note-taking as an aid to remembering, not as a substitute for listening.

Habits of efficient listening contribute greatly to one's success in life, but particularly in one's professional life.

A speaker can help create a favorable first impression with attractive dress and grooming, good posture and carriage, pleasant facial expressions, good manners, and lack of distracting mannerisms.

Your success in giving a speech depends on how carefully you plan it and how effectively you deliver it.

Almost all business people in offices and stores have some contact with the public, either face-to-face or on the telephone.

The rules for meeting the public—in person or on the telephone—are based on courtesy, consideration, and friendliness.

To chair a meeting effectively and responsibly, one should know how to plan and conduct it.

After completing your formal education, consult
school placement offices, newspaper ads,
employment agencies, government offices, colleges and universities, and individual businesses
to find a job suited to your training, interests,
and ambitions.

An employer will make a decision about your employability on the basis of how you respond on the application form and how you act in a personal interview, among other things.

Make your appearance speak
favorably for you at an interview.
Trained interviewers will
recognize a direct relation
between personal habits and
work habits.

All your communication skills—speaking, writing, listening,
and reading—will be tested at an employment interview.

or an attorney, who will bring suit against the customer. (A collection agency is an organization whose business is to collect delinquent accounts for other firms. The agency makes its income by retaining a percentage of the money it collects on each account. Therefore, to recover the full amount due it, a store or other business may sue the customer for the amount of the account *plus* collection costs.) This "last chance" is a letter of ultimatum. It is courteous, but quite matter-of-fact and to the point. A letter of this type, which follows the everyday letter plan, may read as follows:

Dear Ms. Jones:

Will you please mark the date of September 15 on your calendar. This is an important date to you because unless your account is paid by that time (the amount is $187.88), we will be forced to place your account in the hands of a collection agency. I am sure you realize that this is a drastic step, and it is taken only when we have reason to believe that a customer does not intend to pay his or her account.

Of course, such a step will damage your credit reputation, and we hope it will not be necessary for us to take it. There is only one way you can stop us: send us your check immediately, or at least let us know your intentions. This is the last notice you will receive from us.

Sincerely,

Acknowledging Payment.

When a customer responds to a collection letter by making full payment, some stores write a special thank-you letter.

Dear Mrs. Fowler:

I was pleased to receive your check for $116.20. It has been credited to your account, which is now completely clear.

All of us at Roth's appreciate your cooperation, Mrs. Fowler. We hope you will continue to let us serve you in every way we can.

Sincerely yours,

Sometimes a customer sends only a portion of the amount due. This payment should be acknowledged by letter. At the same time, the customer should be asked very tactfully when the balance may be expected. Since the partial payment indicates a willingness to pay, drastic steps should not be necessary to recover the remainder due.

Dear Mr. Kennedy:

Thank you for your check of $100 to apply on your July 11 invoice for $156.25.

Your account has been credited for $100, leaving a balance of $56.25. We hope you will send us your check for this balance very soon. Would you let us know when we may expect it.

Cordially yours,

Sometimes recipients of collection letters admit frankly that they cannot pay. Of course, the credit manager is not greatly concerned about retaining such customers but is very much interested in getting the money due. Writing an angry response to such an admission will have no results. Bringing suit will be costly and unpleasant. The only alternatives are either to grant a delay and request small weekly or monthly payments or to have the customer sign a note for the amount due. Sometimes both are demanded. The following is an example of such a letter:

Dear Mr. Kennedy:

Thank you for writing us about your inability to pay your $150 account. I appreciate your being so frank with us.

I know you are sincere in wanting to meet your obligations, and I want to be just as sincere in helping you do so. We can arrange for you to make monthly payments of $50 until your account is settled in full. If you will sign the enclosed 90-day promissory note, we will set up your account in three monthly payments.

Sincerely yours,

COMMUNICATION LABORATORY

APPLICATION EXERCISES

A. You work in the credit office of Loopdale's Department Store. You have been granting credit to customers simply by mailing them a card with a form message. Your boss has decided that a more personal approach should be used. Design a letter granting credit that the store could have typed on word processing equipment and personally signed for each new credit customer.

B. You are credit manager for Oakland Industries. Canton Products Inc., 4280 Selwyn Street, Saint Paul, Minnesota 55106, requests $2,500 credit. After checking the credit references, you find that Canton Products is very slow in paying bills and is considered a poor risk. In fact, one of the credit references indicated that this store appears to be having severe financial difficulties. You decide to refuse the credit request. Write a letter to Mrs. Rose Gorshen, treasurer of Canton, trying to persuade Canton Products to buy from your company on a cash basis.

C. Oakland Industries has received three substantial orders from Hilliard Building Supplies, 16 Newly Road, Lincoln, Nebraska 68509, for metal kitchen cabinets. You know that Hilliard is well established and has an excellent reputation. You would like to add this company to your list of charge customers. Write a letter to Henry Behar, the vice president, acknowledging his latest order and inviting Hilliard to open an account with you.

D. You work for A-V Electronic Networks, a local retail store that specializes in the sale and repair of televisions, radios, stereos, video and cassette recorders, video games, electronic calculators, and microcomputers. Jeremiah Strovant, 3131 Welton Street, Denver, Colorado 80205, purchased from you a video recorder for $689. He paid $239 down and promised to pay the rest in six monthly installments of $75 each. Mr. Strovant paid the first two installments but has not made any further payments. He is presently two payments ($150) behind. You have sent two reminders and a letter of inquiry. Now write a letter appealing to his sense of fair play. Try to collect the $150 past due and remind him about his next payment, which is due early next week.

E. Oakland Industries has received a $350 check from Mr. Étienne Hébert, owner of Trendmaker Interior Designs, P.O. Box 810, High Point, North Carolina 27260, in partial payment of a long overdue account for $700. Write Mr. Hébert, thanking him for the check and inquiring tactfully when you may expect to receive the balance.

VOCABULARY AND SPELLING STUDIES

A. These words are often confused: *conscious, conscience; cereal, serial.* Write each in a sentence that illustrates its meaning.

B. For what words or phrases do the following frequently used abbreviations stand? Be sure to consult the abbreviations section of your dictionary if necessary.

1. bal.
2. Ltd.
3. nt. wt.
4. SW
5. bbl
6. ft
7. ETA
8. kg

C. The following "words" appear as they are pronounced. How are they spelled?

1. ruf	3. wimin	5. līt	7. nok
2. stā	4. rīt	6. nē	8. lēv

COMMUNICATING FOR RESULTS

Obtaining Information. As assistant manager of a hotel, you are responsible for authorizing all checks cashed for guests. The cashier has sent Mr. Lester to you. He wishes to cash a personal check for $50. What questions will you ask Mr. Lester before you approve his check for payment? With another student, enact the scene as you think it might happen. Remember, you must get the information you need yet retain the goodwill of the guest.

U · N · I · T

47

Sales Letters

All business letters have something to sell—whether it is merchandise, service, a point of view, an idea, or simply goodwill. When you write a letter telling your customers how much you appreciate their business, you are selling goodwill. When you write collection letters, you are hoping to sell the customers the idea of paying their accounts. A letter explaining why you cannot grant a request sells a point of view. Even a letter applying for a job is a sales letter—the writer is selling abilities.

Usually, however, the term *sales letter* is used in connection with selling merchandise or service. "Experience the thrill of stepping from your bath and wrapping yourself in a luxuriously fluffy, absorbent Marcan towel" and "Your family is in safe, reliable hands when you trust your insurance program to State Mutual" are typical of the sales statements you are accustomed to hearing or reading. As you study this unit, which emphasizes the writing of letters selling merchandise or service, you should keep in mind that many of the same principles apply to writing letters that sell ideas, goodwill, or points of view.

Steps in Planning

A sales letter is effective if it achieves its purpose. The purpose may be to get prospects to come to your place of business, to think of your firm when they are in the market for your product, or to get them to place an order by return mail. In any event, the effective sales letter requires careful planning. In planning a sales letter, you should:

1. Determine your market—the people to whom you are writing. Are all your readers office workers, or do they represent all types of occupations?
2. Determine the aim of your letter. What do you want the reader to do?
3. Select the appeals that are appropriate to your readers. Why would people want to buy your product? What will it do for them?
4. Organize the facts according to a logical, effective, clear, and easy-to-follow plan.

Determine Your Market. For whom is the sales message intended? A mass audience—*all* the people in a particular area, regardless of occupation, income, and educational background—or a selected audience whose tastes and interests are known to be similar? The kind of person who will receive and read the sales letter should determine to a large extent the kind of letter you will write. If you are selling air conditioners, are you selling them to consumers who want the comfort and convenience of air conditioners, to retailers who want to make a profit in reselling the air conditioners, or to industrial users who may be more concerned with the economies to be effected by using your particular brand of air conditioner? The same sales letter could not be used very effectively for all three groups, even though the product is the same. Therefore, the first step in the sales process is to identify the people to whom the letter is to be sent.

The following sales letters were sent by the same furniture store. Letter 1 was sent to all customers who previously had made purchases at the store. Letter 2 was sent to business executives in the community. Notice how each letter is geared for its particular market.

Letter 1

Dear Friend:

Put a red circle around May 2 on your calendar! On May 2 our spectacular May Furniture Sale begins—and you will want to be at our store when the doors open at 9 a.m.

Every piece of bedroom furniture will be reduced in price from 10 to 60 percent. Just to give you two examples of the savings in store for you: a beautiful four-piece Mediterranean bedroom suite that originally sold for $1,275 has been reduced to $995. Mattresses and box springs that sold for $150 each will be sold for $99 each. Every item you purchase during this week-long sale will represent a substantial saving to you.

You won't want to miss this sensational sale, so be here early on May 2. Remember, our Home Furnishings Account calls for only 10 percent down, with the remainder budgeted over a period of up to 36 months.

Sincerely yours,

Letter 2

Dear Ms. Tyler:

Have you taken a good look around your office lately? Is your furniture drab and shabby-looking? Does your office give your firm the appearance of success and prosperity—or does it make your clients think that your business is not doing very well at all?

If your office does not project the image you wish to present, now is a good time for you to see our line of office furniture. Every item is reduced 10 percent during the month of July. Our decorators are specialists in office layout and furnishings. They can help you select appropriate matching furniture, rugs, and draperies— and give free advice for the asking. You will be under no obligation to make your purchases from us, but you can't beat our low prices and large selection anywhere else.

You can't afford to miss this once-a-year sale of office furniture and furnishings. So—to take advantage of our expert, free advice and substantial savings—call 555-9371 and ask for Mr. Draper. He will be happy to make an appointment to visit your office and help you with your redecorating problems.

Sincerely yours,

Determine Your Aim. Why are sales letters written? Sales letters are written because face-to-face selling is not always necessary or possible. A sales letter may be written to accomplish any one of five purposes: (1) to get new customers to buy your product now, (2) to develop an interest in your product that will induce them to buy later, (3) to keep the name of your organization in each customer's mind, (4) to get customers to visit your place of business, or (5) to get customers to try your product or ask questions about it. Once you have determined the market for your letter, you must decide which of these purposes you would like your sales letter to accomplish—and build your letter around this one purpose.

If your aim is to get the customer to buy now, you will build your letter around the idea of getting the customer to take *immediate* action. If the aim of your letter is to get customers to visit your place of business, then you will make it inviting and advantageous for them to do so. For example, to get new customers, the Fashion Hut offered a gift (most of the gifts were small items like handkerchiefs, socks, or neckties) to everyone who entered the store. Here is the letter that Fashion Hut sent:

We have a gift for you! At the bottom of this letter is a number—your gift number. Everybody with a numbered letter receives a gift from us—without obligation. Nothing to write and no purchase required. How do you get this gift?

In our store window we have posted a list of numbers, and each number is followed by a handsome gift—a man's suit, a raincoat, a complete woman's ensemble, to mention but a few. Just compare your letter number with those posted in our store window. Then present your letter to me, and I will give you your gift. Come in any time between now and Friday, April 14.

While you are at our store, you will want to get acquainted with the "wonderful difference" in buying clothing in our big, beautiful, exciting house of values. You have never seen such a large selection of men's, women's, and children's clothing! Everything from the top of your toes (shoes) to the top of your head (hats).

Come in for your free gift on or before April 14. It will be a pleasure to meet you personally and to present your free gift to you.

Cordially yours,
FASHION HUT

Oyhane Lee, Manager,

Your gift number is:
14896

INSTANT HELP
T E M P O R A R I E S

893 South Loop,
Atlanta, Georgia 30312

Every once in a while it happens:
your work gets the best of you.
Perhaps it's inventory time. Or
your secretary is on vacation.
Or you're busy finishing that
special report. Whatever the
reason, your desk gets piled higher and higher with papers. It
seems as if the pile will never end--and maybe it won't, if you
don't ask for help.

Help is precisely what you'll get from Instant Help Temporaries.
Professional help. At Instant Help Temporaries, we always match
the skills of our personnel to your needs. We select the people
you need from our exclusive computerized list of more than 3,000
experienced office workers. Whether your business is advertising,
publishing, banking, or importing; whether you need a typist, a
bookkeeper, a secretary, or a filing clerk--call Instant Help
for experienced people who will help you get out from under that
pile of papers.

Instant Help Temporaries' number is 555-1111, an easy number to
remember and an important one. We'll be waiting.

Cordially,

Joshua Braun

Joshua Braun
Director

rp

The unique format of this sales letter is designed to attract the reader's attention so that further inquiry will be made.

In the letter above, the aim of the unique format is to get the reader to make further inquiry about the service offered. Here is another letter written to attract a new customer:

Dear Mr. Adkins:

Congratulations on your appointment to the position of office manager for the Rego Oil Company in Cincinnati. We enjoyed reading the announcement in last night's *Evening Bulletin*.

Like most people, you probably dread the chore that accompanies moving from one locality to another. First, the hours of wrapping and packing, and then additional hours of unpacking and unwrapping. Well, put your mind at ease—Wide World Moving Company is at your service to help make moving painless and easy.

Just tell us your moving date, and 24 hours before the date, our corps of courteous, efficient packers will come to your home with all the necessary equipment and supplies. They will carefully wrap and pack every item—from your most delicate china to your grand piano. Although we are insured for any loss or damage, our packers and movers do their jobs so well that our claims are phenomenally small and infrequent.

On moving day our movers arrive promptly at the designated hour and carefully and quickly load all your belongings into our moving vans. You don't have a care or a worry. When the van reaches its destination with your belongings, another crew takes over to help you with your unpacking.

Wide World really makes moving a pleasure. So telephone us at 555-3686 and ask our representative to call on you to discuss our low rates and to determine your specific needs.

Very sincerely yours,

Each of these preceding letters had one specific goal, and the letter was built around the goal. A letter that tries to accomplish too many things at the same time usually winds up accomplishing nothing.

Select Appropriate Appeals. When the writer of a sales letter has determined the purpose of the letter and the market to be reached, he or she must then determine the appeals the product will have for the reader. Although the air conditioner discussed in the following letter will do the same thing for everyone who uses it, different people will buy it for different reasons. The home consumer probably is concerned primarily with comfort and relaxation; the office or industrial user, with increased efficiency of employees. Some appeals, however, are effective for every kind of audience. Most people like to save money, so the thrift of operation of the air conditioner may appeal to both the home consumer and the office or industrial user.

A sales letter for air conditioners sent to home consumers might read like the following letter. Notice that several appeals—pleasure, comfort, health, and thrift—are used in this letter. The central or main appeal, though, emphasizes the comfort of the prospective buyer.

Dear Mrs. Gottbaum:

Do you remember the prolonged heat and humidity of last summer? For five nights in a row, the temperature did not go below 87 degrees!

Another "long, hot summer" is coming, bringing with it many uncomfortable days and nights. But this year you don't have to let the hot weather get you down. Relax and enjoy life this summer!

The new Icecap air conditioner has just arrived at our store. It is not only beautiful—but also beautifully cool! The 2-ton model will comfortably cool the average five-room home, providing 24 hours of relaxing comfort and permitting restful sleep. In addition, you breathe pure air, free of the dust and pollen to which so many of us are allergic. Its quiet operation and low-voltage consumption make the Icecap a pleasure to own.

Why sacrifice comfort when for a few cents a day you can own and operate the Icecap? Come in today. You'll want to see and try the Icecap, the ultimate in modern air conditioning.

Cordially yours,

From the appeals used to sell a product, buying points must be developed. Notice how in the previous letter an appeal was used to develop a buying point.

Appeal	Buying Point Developed
Comfort	Helps you to get a restful night's sleep
Pleasure	Helps you to relax and enjoy your home
Health	Purifies your air; especially helps people with allergies
Thrift	Costs you little to own and to operate

A letter attempting to sell air conditioners for office use might read this way:

Dear Ms. Braxton:

How would you like to increase the efficiency of your office staff by 10 percent this summer?

Tests in over 100 business offices using Icecap air conditioners have proved that worker efficiency increased 10 percent after the Icecap was installed. Since increased worker efficiency means greater profits for your organization, the Icecap will pay for itself in just a few short years. And if you would like to spread the cost, you have 36 months in which to pay. In addition, improvements in the new model make your operating costs low. A 3-ton unit consumes only $1.80 worth of electricity each working day. Isn't that a small sum to pay for the comfort and increased working efficiency of your employees?

Won't you call and ask us to send our engineer to determine the air conditioning needs of your office? Each day's delay costs you money.

Very sincerely yours,

Notice that the emphasis here is upon increased worker efficiency, low initial cost, and low operating cost. Since one primary purpose of a business is to make a profit, increasing worker efficiency and keeping costs low contribute to this profit motive. The following buying points are developed by these appeals:

Appeal	Buying Point Developed
Thrift	Low initial cost
Thrift	Low operating cost
Profit	Increased worker efficiency

The writer of sales letters has a choice of many different appeals. Those used depend upon the aim of the letter, the nature of the product, and the market—the people who will receive the letter. People usually spend their money for these reasons:

For comfort (air conditioners)
To make money (stocks)
To save money (storm windows)
To save time (microwave oven)
To imitate others (sunglasses)
To be different (exclusive hat)
For health (toothpaste)
For enjoyment (television set)
For cleanliness (soap)
To avoid effort (power lawn mower)
To be popular (dancing lessons)
To safeguard possessions (fire insurance)
To be attractive (jewelry)
To be adventurous (travel)

To attract the opposite sex (after-shave lotion)
To escape physical pain (corn and callous remedy)
To gratify curiosity (new gadget)
To protect family (smoke detector)
To be in style (new coat)
To avoid trouble (casualty insurance)
To take advantage of opportunities (investment property)
To enhance reputation (charitable contribution)
To satisfy appetite (candy)
For beautiful possessions (colored telephone)

Of course, some products may be used to satisfy a number of desires. For example, a fur coat has several appeals—to keep warm, to appear attractive, to be in style, and to impress others. Health insurance may be sold to satisfy the multiple needs for financial security, good health, and peace of mind, as in the letter on page 459.

Organize the Facts. Once writers of sales letters have selected the appeals that are most suitable to their audience, they must then organize their ideas into an effective letter plan such as the persuasive letter plan explained below.

An Effective Letter Plan

You are now ready to begin composing your sales letter. You must, therefore, gather all the facts about your product and the various appeals that may be used and organize them according to the persuasive letter plan. This plan, as adapted to the sales message, calls for four steps, the ABCDs of sales letters:

Attracting attention
Building interest and desire
Convincing the reader
Directing favorable action

Let's take a look at what is involved in each of these steps.

CAL FED ENTERPRISES

September 5, 1985

Ms. Jean McGrory
5902 Franklin Avenue
Los Angeles, California 90028

Dear Ms. McGrory:

We've seen it happen so many times. A family invests money with
us, starts to earn more money, and then--suddenly--all their savings
are gone.

Why? An unexpected illness has placed a family member in the hospital and created a severe family financial burden on the others to
meet the sudden overwhelming expenses of a hospital stay.

That's why we decided to recommend the Group Hospital Cash Insurance Plan enclosed with this letter. Underwritten by Continental American Life Insurance Company, this benefit guarantees all of our customers
supplemental hospital cash protection at economical rates.

With hospital costs rising faster than ever, the insurance you now
own is probably not keeping pace. This Group Hospital Cash Insurance
Plan was designed with these additional hospital expenses in mind.

As a customer of California Federal Savings, you are guaranteed
acceptance. You will not be turned down.

We feel that our most valuable asset is you, and that's why we are
pleased to announce this important service for our customers. Please
read the enclosed material immediately. It provides complete details
on how you can take advantage of this exclusive offer.

And remember . . . your acceptance is guaranteed.

Sincerely,

Peter D. Singer
Customer Representative

ls
Enclosure

5670 Wilshire Boulevard / Los Angeles, California 90036
An Affiliate of CALIFORNIA FEDERAL SAVINGS AND LOAN ASSOCIATION

**The writer of a sales letter has a choice of many appeals, depending on the aim
of the letter, the nature of the product, and the people who will receive the letter.**

Attracting Attention. A sales letter can attract the reader's attention even
before it has been removed from the envelope. The envelope may be a color
instead of the traditional white. It may contain a phrase or a picture, as does
the one shown on page 460.

When the letter has been removed from the envelope, it can continue to
attract attention through these devices:

```
THE CYCLE SHOP
4100 Graham Boulevard, Houston, Texas 77052




                        Mr. Daniel Lockhart
                        1130 Willow Lane
                        Euless, TX 76039
```

A sales letter can attract attention even before it is opened if the envelope containing it is creative and colorful.

1. Tinted stationery.
2. An unusual letterhead design.
3. A colored typewriter ribbon.
4. An unusual style of type, such as a script type.
5. Typing certain words or sentences in all capitals.
6. Underscoring key words or phrases.
7. Using italicized words for emphasis.
8. Using dashes or exclamation points for emphasis, such as "Call us today—tomorrow may be too late!"

All these devices are aimed at attracting attention. However, be sure not to "gimmick" the letter to the extent that these eye-catchers get in the way of the message.

The opening paragraph of the letter—in fact, the very first sentence—should excite curiosity or start a train of thought or attract attention in some way that will make the reader continue reading the letter. These opening sentences may be either questions or statements, and they should be original and concise. Questions should not be phrased so that they can be answered by a mere "yes" or "no." Statements should contain a startling, new, interesting, or different fact that leads the reader to the major buying point. Here are some examples of opening sentences that have proved effective.

Pertinent Questions
"How can you become the most fashionably dressed individual in town?"
"Where can you save 8 cents on each gallon of fuel oil you buy for your home?"
"How much is your family's health worth to you?"
"If you lost your job today, how would you pay your bills?"

Startling or Significant Statements
"They said it couldn't be done, but *we* did it!"
"Word processing equipment can increase production up to 40 percent!"

"You can't afford to be without one!"
"Three out of four families use hospital services at least once each year."

To select which device would best attract attention, the writer should consider one or more of these factors:

1. The kind of firm sending the letter. (Is it a conservative bank? a store selling gardening supplies?)
2. The nature of the product. (Is it a religious book? a lawn mower?)
3. The kind of audience to receive the letter. (Are they doctors? plumbers?)

Building Interest and Desire. When you have succeeded in getting the reader's attention, you must hold that attention. The best way to hold it is to build interest—by vividly describing your product so that your readers can virtually experience it. With colorful, descriptive words and expressions like those listed below, you can make readers feel, taste, or smell it as well as see it—and you can also make readers "see" themselves using your product and getting satisfaction from it. To stimulate readers to buy your product, you must use descriptions that will activate their emotions.

Objectives	Suggested Descriptions
To sell no-wax flooring	"It's a bright shine. A tough shine. An easy-to-wipe-up shine."
To sell canned frozen oyster stew	"Savory oyster stew with plump, pampered oysters."
To sell laundry detergent	"Softness—you can feel it in the *powder* . . . feel it in the *clothes!*"
To convince readers to send for a catalog from a plant nursery	"Lifelike illustrations you can almost smell and touch!"
To sell oranges	"Big, plump wedges . . . . "
To sell hardwood paneling	"The soft beauty and warmth of fine hardwoods."
To sell porcelain bathroom fixtures	"The porcelain finish is glass-smooth."
To sell small cars	"The driver who is fed up with bigger, thirstier cars switches to ____."
To sell air travel	"For travel elegance, fly with ____."
To sell electronic typewriters	"Letters that are a pleasure to type, a pleasure to sign, a joy to read."
To sell soft drinks in cans	"And cans chill so fast, keeping the flavor fresh and full of zip."
To sell a station wagon	"From a frisky, sturdy little workhorse to the jauntiest little sedan of them all!"

To sell a soft drink	"You'll really welcome the cold, crisp taste that so deeply satisfies . . . the cheerful lift that's bright and lively."
To sell a deodorant	"New spray-on deodorant with staying power."
To sell an air deodorant	"Makes air smell flower-fresh."
To sell mustard	"A mustard that is shy and retiring is no mustard at all; a great mustard should manage to be a delightful contradiction of emphatically hot and delicately mild."
To sell fruit punch	"The circus-red color, the candy-and-ice-cream taste."
To sell shampoo	"Hair so satin-bright—airy-light!"

Suppose you write a letter to sell stereo tape decks. You attract the reader's attention in the first paragraph by asking, "How would you like to bring the concert hall into your living room?" You hope that the reader is interested—or at least curious enough—to find out how this can be done. So you vividly describe your product, appealing to the desire for relaxation. You continue your letter as shown.

> You have just come home after a tiring day at the office. You relax your body in the comfort of your favorite chair. But you must relax your mind, too, freeing it of the many tensions of the day. You flip the switch on your Magnasound Stereo. Suddenly the room is filled with the soft tones of your favorite music. You are carried away to the concert hall—every note, every tone is as clear as though the orchestra were performing in your living room. Soon both your mind and your body are completely at ease, and the cares and tensions of the day are forgotten.

Notice how the paragraph builds interest by emphasizing the desire for relaxation.

Convincing the Reader. If you have done your work well to this point, the reader is already strongly interested and partially convinced. The readers who really want to buy can certainly find reasons for doing so. Nevertheless, you must still convince readers that it will be to their advantage to own the Magnasound. In fact, you must be able to convince them that they really cannot afford NOT to buy it. Therefore, you are ready now to bring out other features of the product that will convince them. You have attempted to sell readers on the beautiful performance they can expect from the Magnasound and the effect that performance will have on their pleasure and relaxation. Now, what other features might appeal to them? They certainly would like to have a piece of furniture that will enhance the beauty of their living room and win praise from others, so you tell the reader:

Your guests, too, will appreciate the true state-of-the-art sound when you invite them to your home for an evening of listening pleasure. You will win praise for the unit's sleek styling. Both inside and out, you will own the finest stereo tape deck anywhere at this low price.

Now some readers may think, "Well, this Magnasound is going to cost more than I can afford." You must convince them that this is not so. Therefore, your letter might continue:

The magnificent Magnasound can be yours for only $100 down and $45 a month for 24 months, and your monthly payments will not begin until August.

Directing Favorable Action. You have now reached the point where if each of the preceding steps has accomplished its purpose, you must move the reader to act. Some action-getting suggestions that you might use are these:

1. Enclose a return envelope or postal card.
2. Imply that the reader "act now before it is too late."
3. Offer special inducements for prompt action.

The letter you write to sell the Magnasound stereo tape deck, therefore, might conclude as follows:

If you act before May 15, you may select $25 worth of tapes from those we have in stock as a FREE addition to your music library. Won't you come in today and listen to the Magnasound?

A Typical Sales Letter. Below is an example of an outstanding sales letter showing each of the steps in the ABCDs of sales letter writing.

Dear Mrs. Kramden:

ATTRACTING ATTENTION

Graduation is the perfect time to make a wise investment in your child's future. By giving a Richmond typewriter for graduation, you will be providing the key to success, both for college and the years that follow.

A survey of 3,000 college professors revealed that 90 percent viewed typewritten work as a vital factor in earning high grades. And here are 7½ reasons why Richmond is the typewriter best suited to help your future college student be successful:

BUILDING INTEREST AND DESIRE

1. Richmond's full standard keyboard allows the individual to type in an easy and comfortable manner.
2. Richmond's Stroke Control adjusts to suit a particular touch.
3. Richmond's Eze-Margin lever allows margins to be set with the touch of a finger.
4. Richmond's Line Meter indicates the exact number of lines remaining on the page.
5. Richmond's Magic Column-Set Key allows quick and easy tabulations.

6. Richmond's Correcting Cartridge allows errors to be corrected with a flick of the finger.
7. Richmond's attractive aluminum cast-metal base is built to withstand all the wear and tear your child can give it.
8. Yes, Richmond's portable model, at 16 pounds, is one half the weight of standard typewriters—it can be taken anywhere typing needs to be done.

CONVINCING
THE READER

Compare these features with other brands and see if you don't agree that it is the best electric portable typewriter on the market. In addition, Richmond's one-year warranty assures you of quality materials and workmanship. So for $249.50 (or $24 a month for 12 months), make your graduation gift a Richmond.

DIRECTING
FAVORABLE
ACTION

Come to our store today for a free demonstration, or call me at 555-3946 to arrange for a home demonstration. A Richmond typewriter is a gift your child will remember long after graduation has passed.

Sincerely yours,

Follow-Up Sales Letters

Frequently, more than one sales letter will be sent to prospective customers to convince them to buy. In selling higher priced items, for instance, more than one letter may be necessary to do the job. If no action results when the first letter is sent, one or more additional letters may follow. These follow-up letters often make up what is called a sales campaign or a "wear-out" series. Sometimes as many as six letters will be sent, depending upon the product, its cost, and the nature of the market. Letters in the series are spaced about ten days apart. An attempt is made to vary the appeal in each letter with the hope that one of the appeals will ultimately convince the reader to take action. Preferably, the letters will be short, and each will concentrate on one principal sales feature.

If possible, the opening paragraph of each letter should be constructed so that the additional letter seems a natural development. Suppose that in the first letter attempting to sell the Magnasound stereo, you enclosed a postal card for prospective customers to let you know that they would like to have a five-day home trial. Since the postcard was not returned, the second letter in the series might begin:

We note that you have not yet taken advantage of our five-day no-obligation trial of the wonderful Magnasound. Perhaps you feel that you will be obligated to buy. May we assure you that this will not be the case. At the end of five days, just telephone us to pick up the Magnasound. No questions will be asked; no sales pressure will be exerted. If the trial use of the Magnasound does not convince you, we don't want you to buy it.

Another letter in the series might appeal to the economical side of the reader by stating:

After March 1, all tape players will increase 10 percent in price. If you act now, you will save yourself $60, a saving that will enable you to buy several of your favorite stereo tapes.

COMMUNICATION LABORATORY

APPLICATION EXERCISES

A. For each reason for buying given on page 458, name at least one other product or service that might be bought.

B. Bring to class ten different sales letters or magazine advertisements. Identify the sales appeal used in each letter or advertisement and evaluate the effectiveness of the appeal.

C. Assume that you have been asked to work on the school football program committee and have been placed in charge of getting advertisements from local businesses. Half-page ads sell for $25; full-page ads, $50. Proceeds from ads are to be used partially for financing the cost of the program and partially for student transportation to out-of-town games. The ads will be read by all the high school students, as well as by many of their parents. Since the community really turns out for games, the ads will be seen by many people. Write a form letter that can be sent to the businesses in your community, requesting that they purchase an ad in your school football program. If they consent to purchase an ad, tell them a student will call to arrange a visit to obtain information regarding ad content and layout. Be sure to make it easy for the businesses to give a "yes" response.

D. Assume that during the summer you wish to earn some extra money. You decide to start a home-care service for your vacationing neighbors. You can water lawns, feed and care for pets, bring in mail and newspapers, and perform other minor jobs that need to be done while people are on vacation. Write a form letter that can be distributed to your neighbors within a four-block radius. Tell them about your services and assure them of your dependability.

E. Assume that your class is going to put on the play *Shenandoah* in the school auditorium to raise money to buy lights for the school stadium. Evening performances are scheduled for Friday, April 18, and Saturday, April 19. Ticket prices are $2 for adults and $1 for anyone under 18. Write a letter that could be sent to PTA members urging them to attend the play.

F. Suppose that you work part time for a photographer in your community. Marcy Studios, your employer, specializes in wedding photographs. Write a form letter to be sent to women who have announced their engagements in your local newspaper. Sell them on having Marcy Studios take their wedding pictures.

G. Choose a product (such as a clock radio, a camera, a video game, a set of cookware, a video recorder, a home computer, or an electronic calculator) and gather sufficient information to write a sales letter. Define the group to whom you will write, select an appeal for that group, and write the appropriate letter.

VOCABULARY AND SPELLING STUDIES

A. These words are often confused: *detract, distract; carton, cartoon.* Write each in a sentence that illustrates its meaning.

B. Should *a* or *an* precede these words?

1. opposite
2. half
3. appetite
4. egg
5. ulcer
6. harvest

C. Which of the following commonly used words are misspelled?

1. canidate
2. omitted
3. liesure
4. anilize
5. occasionally
6. seperate

COMMUNICATING FOR RESULTS

A Club Project. The Community Service Club in your company plans to take orders for Christmas trees from employees in the plant. The proceeds are to be used for food baskets to be given to needy families. Write an announcement to go into your monthly employee magazine describing the why, what, where, when, how, and who (make up your own set of circumstances) for purchasing a tree. Appeal to the employees to purchase their trees from the club. Do this by describing the plight of the needy in the community, citing statistics about their number, and emphasizing their needs. Remember, however, to be tactful about the needy in the community. Be sure to include all information that the employees will need to purchase a tree from your club.

48

Public Relations Letters

Although effectively written sales letters help to convince the reader to buy, they are not the only letters that help to make sales. In addition to sales letters such as those discussed in Unit 47, alert businesses use letters to build public relations—and good public relations ultimately create sales. Some businesses think public relations is so important to sales that they devote entire departments to it; other businesses hire special public relations firms to help them.

The term *public relations* is a difficult one to define. In essence, a firm has created good public relations when its customers and clients think highly of it—highly enough to feel that the firm is more interested in a satisfied customer than it is in just making a sale. A business that has conveyed this feeling to its customers does not have to worry about sales. Public relations letters, then, such as the one shown on page 468, are letters written to show the firm's concern for its customers and for people in general.

Characteristics of Public Relations Letters

Although the underlying motive of public relations letters is to increase sales, they do not "push" a product or service. Instead, they act subtly to build goodwill. The writer hopes to impress the firm name and its product or service on the mind of the reader so that when the need arises for this product or service in the future, the customer will think of the writer's firm.

Public relations letters (sometimes called *business promotion letters*), then, are a special type of sales letter that sells indirectly. In fact, the chief difference between public relations and sales letters is that public relations letters *seem* to be selling nothing at all. Instead, they are written with an eye to the future; that is, with the thought that if you treat your customers well today, they will perhaps buy from you tomorrow. Therefore, most public relations letters use an everyday letter organizational plan rather than the persuasive plan characteristic of sales letters.

Public relations letters are generally written to accomplish one of the following purposes:

1. To express appreciation to customers for their business. ("Thank you for your business during the past year.")

CAMBRIDGE SAVINGS BANK

114 Forest Street, Cambridge, Massachusetts 02140

December 4, 1986

Mr. and Mrs. Nathan Washington
17 York Street
Watertown, Massachusetts 02172

Dear Mr. and Mrs. Washington:

Thank you for keeping your savings at Cambridge. You
are a valued depositor, and all of us at Cambridge appreciate your banking with us.

Your personal banker, Anne Cortez, and all the tellers
and personnel at our 14 branches very much enjoy working
for you, and we are eager to continue to service your
account. At Cambridge, we work every day to maintain
your trust and to provide you with the most pleasant,
most convenient banking services available. If you have
enjoyed banking with us--and we hope you have!--please
recommend us to your friends.

Mr. and Mrs. Washington, please do let us know whenever
we can be of service to you.

Sincerely,

Patrice G. Mason

Patrice G. Mason
Chief Operating Officer

bt

Goodwill letters help companies maintain good relations with their customers.

2. To capitalize on some special occasion—a holiday or a birthday, for example. ("We wish you and your family a joyous holiday season.")
3. To offer service to the customer. ("We have opened a branch bank in your neighborhood, and you will find that banking with us will be even more convenient.")
4. To show concern not only for customers but also for people everywhere. ("We have invested over $50,000 in new antipollution equipment this year.")

Expressing Appreciation. You may not feel that you are accomplishing much when you write to thank a customer for business. However, a courteous "thank you" serves as a gesture of goodwill and paves the way for future business with the customer. Don't you like to feel appreciated? When someone thanks you for something you have done, don't you feel an inner glow of satisfaction? So it is when a firm takes the time to thank you for your patronage; you certainly feel more kindly toward that firm. The next time you need its type of product or service, you will be more likely to think of dealing with this firm than with any other.

How do you think the recipient of the following letter might react to it?

Dear Mrs. Merritt:

As another year draws to a close, Foster's feels very grateful for having customers like you.

Thank you for the business you have given us during the past year. We certainly appreciate your friendship and hope that you have derived much satisfaction from your purchases.

Please remember that we are here to be of service to you. During the coming year we hope that you will continue to give us the opportunity to serve you.

Sincerely yours,

A letter such as this will not sell a specific item, but it will certainly cement good relations. Notice that the letter is written in a friendly style and does not "push" the reader in any way.

Capitalizing on Special Occasions. A holiday, the beginning of a new season, a birthday or an anniversary, the arrival of new merchandise, a new type of product, a new service, or some other special event—any of these may prompt writing a letter to customers. Of course, in letters of this type, you do not attempt to sell a specific item. However, by making customers aware of the new service or product—or by calling attention to some special event—you may be indirectly stimulating their desire to buy. In these letters you are attempting to give customers the impression of doing them a favor rather than of trying to sell them something.

Note, for example, the following letter announcing a sale especially for charge customers:

Dear Mr. Ambrose:

Hensen's is now preparing for its annual summer clearance sale. As you can see by the enclosed brochure, all our summer merchandise—women's dresses, men's sportswear, children's play clothes, patio tables and chairs, and a host of other merchandise—has been drastically reduced.

Before we offer these bargains to the general public, however, Hensen's wishes to say "Thank you" to our charge account customers by giving them an exclusive opportunity to take advantage of these savings. On Monday, August 30, our store hours will be extended from 6 p.m. to 10 p.m. This extra time will give you and our other special customers an opportunity to shop before the general sale begins on August 31.

Just give the enclosed ticket to our representative at the door, who will admit you to Hensen's special preview. If you wish to take advantage of these bargains, though, do plan to come early, as many sizes, styles, and colors are limited.

Sincerely yours,

Offering to Be of Service. Offering to be of service to the customer is another important function of the public relations letter. Whereas the sales letter says "Buy," this letter says "Let us be of service to you."

The following letter was written by a department store to let customers know about a new type of charge account for home furnishings. Again, no particular item is being sold. Instead, the letter gives the impression that here is something new the store is doing for the convenience of its customers—and it is doing them a favor by telling them about it.

Dear Mr. Jaeckel:

Martin and Richards has added a new service to make it more convenient for you to buy home furnishings on a deferred-payment plan. May we tell you about it?

Whenever you buy home furnishings totaling $100 or more, ask the salesperson to open a Home Furnishings Account for you. This will automatically spread your payments over a 12-month period, with each month's payment added to your regular monthly charge account.

For example, suppose you purchase new living room tables totaling $300. You pay nothing down; but each month when you receive your regular monthly statement, you will find a charge for $25, plus a small carrying charge, to apply on your home furnishings payment. Isn't this an easy way to handle your home furnishings charges? No separate payments or payment books to worry about. All your payments are included on your regular monthly statement.

The next time you need any home furnishings costing $100 or more, remember to say, "Please open a Home Furnishings Account for me."

Sincerely yours,

When a new family moves into the community, some progressive businesses send a welcome to the new residents and offer to be of service. If the service is not a costly one, an invitation to try the service with no charge or at a reduced cost is not an uncommon gesture. For example, here is a letter written by a dry-cleaning establishment to new residents who move into the community it serves:

Welcome to the Palmier family . . .

It is a pleasure to have you as residents of Fanwood, and we hope you enjoy the community as much as we do.

Will you give us an opportunity to show you the excellent dry-cleaning, pressing, and laundering service we make available to Fanwood residents? And at low cost, too! Our courteous drivers will pick up and deliver your clothing, or you may prefer to bring it to either our Market Street store or our Randolph Avenue store. Both have convenient drive-in windows, so that you don't need to get out of your car—and you save 10 percent by using our cash-and-carry service.

We are enclosing an introductory card that entitles you to a 50 percent discount on your first order—no matter how large or how small. Won't you come in to see us and let us give you a personal welcome to Fanwood?

Sincerely yours,

Showing Concern for People. All businesses must make a profit in order to survive. Besides their profit goals, however, most organizations also establish "people goals"—to provide equal employment opportunities for all, meet employees' needs, treat customers honestly, provide safe products and services, support projects that improve the quality of life in their communities, and so on. They know that their concern for people not only will help their employees and their customers but also will improve their productivity and profitability. Thus organizations use a variety of means to let the public know about their people-oriented activities. One of the most commonly used—and most effective—means is the public relations letter.

The following public relations letter offers to be of service. At the same time, it might attract good future employees and more customers because it shows concern for people.

Dear Mrs. Beech:

As principal of Oakwood High School, you have a great responsibility for the education of our youth. Malor Industries thanks you for your efforts.

We hope the following invitation will help you give students more insight into how products are manufactured, packaged, and distributed to dealers. You are invited to send your senior class to spend the day with us. We will plan a full schedule of activities for them and have them as guests for lunch in our cafeteria. You may choose a date that is most convenient for you.

Please call Sylvia Campbell, our public relations director, at 555-3434 to make arrangements.

Sincerely yours,

COMMUNICATION LABORATORY

APPLICATION EXERCISES

A. List occasions when public relations letters might be written.

B. Assume that you work for Bouquet Florists. At the end of each year, you mail a calendar to all customers who have ordered flowers from you that year. Write a letter of transmittal to accompany these calendars. Use this opportunity to build goodwill for Bouquet Florists by making this transmittal letter a public relations letter.

C. Assume that you work for Carter's Country Store, which will open a specialty and gourmet foods department next month. This department will offer imported teas, fresh pastries, and exotic fruits. Write an appropriate letter telling Carter's customers about the enlarging of the store and the new department.

D. As an employee of your town library, write a letter to welcome new people who move into your growing community. Enclose a card that lists library hours, information services, and activities for children.

VOCABULARY AND SPELLING STUDIES

A. These words are often confused: *annul, annual; emigrant, immigrant.* Write each in a sentence that illustrates its meaning.

B. Select from the pronouns within the parentheses the one that is correct in each sentence.

1. Is Peter as qualified as (she, her)?
2. The winner was (he, him).
3. Invitations will be issued to (whoever, whomever) is willing to go.
4. She asked that the merchandise be sent only to (myself, me) and the Wainwrights.
5. Everyone got the message but (they, them).

C. Using standard spellings, respell these well-known brand names that manufacturers have devised for their products.

1. Ry-Krisp Crackers
2. Spic and Span Cleanser
3. Cut-Rite Waxed Paper
4. My-T-Fine Pudding Mix
5. Pepomint Lifesavers
6. Sunkist Oranges

COMMUNICATING FOR RESULTS

Helping a New Employee. A new employee is assigned to the desk next to yours. Your supervisor, Frank Hart, was called to a meeting before he could introduce the new employee to you or to any of the other employees. Courtesy demands that you take action. What are your responsibilities? Enact a typical introduction. Make a list of other things you could do to introduce this person to the new situation.

U · N · I · T

49

Social Business Letters

The use of social business correspondence has become increasingly important in today's business world. No longer do people think that social life should be distinctly separate from business life. In fact, many times the social lives of business and professional people closely involve their customers, vendors, associates, and even competitors. Social relations contribute to the success of a business by fostering a warm friendship and developing goodwill between the company and its public. Social business letters are frequently the means by which friendship and goodwill are created.

Why Social Business Correspondence?

If a friend invites you to spend a weekend, you write a thank-you note upon returning home. When someone presents you with a gift for your birthday, Christmas, graduation, or some other special occasion, you always write a letter of appreciation. Likewise, acts of kindness while you are hospitalized or during periods of personal grief are always acknowledged by letter. If someone helps you obtain a job, secures hard-to-get concert or theater tickets, or goes out of the way to be thoughtful, you write a letter of appreciation. Yes, you already know that all special favors should be acknowledged by a personal letter. In business, the same courtesies should be shown.

Business executives receive invitations from business associates outside the company to attend social functions. They also receive favors or gifts from close business friends. From time to time, they hear of promotions or special honors awarded to other executives or of personal tragedies (serious illness, an operation, or a death in the family) that strike them. These situations call for letters to be written and provide opportunities for building friendly relations.

Social business letters are just as appropriate as letters to your personal friends who have been especially thoughtful. Business people who take the time to write social business letters will be remembered, and their letters will add to their personal credit. They will undoubtedly also build goodwill for their company, even though this is not the underlying purpose of social business letters.

Kinds of Social Business Letters

Many executives who every day write effective business letters dealing with business matters find it difficult to compose social business letters. As a correspondent, you may be asked to write some of these social business letters. Here is an excellent opportunity to reveal your abilities.

Although any acceptable letter style may be used for social business correspondence, many such letters call for the social business format discussed in Unit 40. In this letter style the inside address may appear at the bottom of the page, and the signature lines and reference notations are usually omitted. Also, a comma rather than a colon is often used after the salutation. Other kinds of social business correspondence—such as announcements, invitations, and replies to invitations—may take a printed or handwritten formal format.

Letters Expressing Thanks. People in business who receive gifts or are granted special favors should acknowledge the gifts or favors and express their appreciation. The following are examples of the kinds of thank-you letters frequently written by business executives and other employees. Note the direct approach used in each of these examples, as well as the brevity of the letters.

For a Gift

Dear Barbara,

I was pleased to receive the Old World maps you so thoughtfully sent me. They are going to be framed for my office and will look very handsome with the new mahogany paneling.

Thank you for your thoughtfulness. The next time you visit us, you can see to what good use I am putting your gift.

Cordially,

Ms. Barbara Phillips
Continental Portrait Company
833 Bay Lane
Muskegon, Michigan 49445

For a Favor

Dear Bill,

I appreciate very much your thoughtfulness in getting tickets for Catherine and me to The Nutcracker. We enjoyed this ballet enormously—and the seats were just perfect.

Thank you for helping to make our visit to New York this Christmas an enjoyable one.

Cordially,

Mr. William Inez
322 East 72 Street
New York, NY 10021

For Business Referrals

Dear Elizabeth,

Thanks for telling Joe Ferris of Consolidated Savings and Loan Association how pleased you are with the computer system we installed for your company. He called me last week, and we met today to discuss the possibility of installing a similar system at Consolidated.

I certainly appreciate your referring a new business prospect our way. If at any time we can help you in a similar way, we will do so.

Sincerely,

Ms. Elizabeth Langley, Manager
Accounting Department
Fillmore Oil Company
2800 Amherst Avenue
Dallas, Texas 75225

Letters of Congratulation. As with all social business letters, the style of a letter of congratulation is designed to make the letter warm and personal, as is the one shown on page 476. The following are also examples of letters of congratulation. This kind of letter is usually written by the person who is to sign it, especially when the writer is a personal friend of the individual who is being congratulated.

To a Business Acquaintance

Dear Russ,

I was pleased to hear that you have been promoted to sales manager of Simon & Dunn Enterprises. Congratulations! Simon & Dunn is certainly fortunate to have such a dynamic and hardworking person in charge of its marketing operations.

If ever I can be of assistance to you in making contacts on the West Coast, please let me know.

Sincerely,

Whenever business executives take the time to recognize a milestone in the career of one of their employees, the thoughtfulness is certain to be rewarded in terms of a more productive employee. How do you think Maria would react to the following letter from her employer?

To an Employee

Dear Maria,

In the ten years you have been with Ford's, you have seen our company grow from a small local factory to a nationwide organization. Responsible for this

The Evening Courier

2510 SOUTH WALNUT STREET
SPRINGFIELD, ILLINOIS 62704
(217) 555-6891

May 3, 1985

Dear Lou:

Congratulations on being named State Journalist of the
Year by the State Association of News Journalists. All
of us at The Evening Courier agree that your superb coverage in our weekend magazine section of the construction
of the new State Center deserved the Association's top
honors. We know that this is just the first of many
awards that you will receive for your outstanding creative
work.

To celebrate your winning this award, we'd like very much
to have you as our guest for dinner on June 5. Will you
be free?

Cordially,

Don Zubick

Donald Zubick
Managing Editor

Mr. Louis Leone
14 Hanover Road
Springfield, Illinois 62707

hw

As with all other social business letters, a letter of congratulations should be warm and personal.

remarkable growth are highly productive and loyal employees like you. It is a pleasure for me to write this congratulatory letter on your tenth anniversary, for it gives me an opportunity to thank you for your contribution to our success.

As supervisor of our filing staff, you have set up a highly flexible and effective system for handling the increasing volume of records. I am sure you have heard the often-repeated statement around the office, "If you don't know, ask Maria." This statement is indeed a tribute to your efficiency.

I look forward to working with you in the years ahead. When I think of the slogan "Ford's is people," I can't help calling to mind a picture of you and all those like you who help to make our firm the congenial, effective group it is today.

Sincerely yours,

Formal Invitations and Replies. Occasionally business people receive formal invitations—to an open house, to a special party honoring a distinguished person, to a special anniversary celebration, or to a formal social gathering. These invitations, such as those shown on page 478, are usually engraved or printed and are written in the third person. When these invitations are handwritten, however, they are placed on plain white notepaper.

Replies to formal invitations are often requested by stating *Please reply* or *R.S.V.P.* (an abbreviation of the French *Répondez, s'il vous plaît,* which means "Please answer"). Even if such a notation is not placed on the invitation, there is an unwritten obligation to respond. If the invitation is written in the third person, the reply is also written in the third person and follows the wording and arrangement of the invitation, as shown in the replies on page 478. If the invitation includes a formal reply card and return envelope, the reply card may simply require a check (✔) to indicate whether the receiver will attend.

Announcements. Many companies send printed announcements to business associates to publicize the affiliation of a new partner or executive. Companies also use these notices to inform customers or potential customers of new sales representatives. Formal announcements also publicize new services, new branch offices, new locations, and company mergers. A typical announcement is shown on page 479.

Letters of Condolence. Letters of condolence are among the most difficult letters to write. Such letters should be brief and dignified. Obviously, the writer should not be maudlin or recall too vividly the grief recently suffered. These letters should be written by the person signing them—not by a secretary or an assistant. Following is an example of a letter of condolence:

Dear Lila,

Please accept my sincere sympathy in the passing of your mother last week. I understand the difficult time you are going through since I, too, lost my mother last year.

My thoughts are with you and your family in this hour of grief.

Sincerely,

The Local Bank Tellers Club
requests the pleasure of your company
at a tea
in honor of
Nancy Fitzgerald
on Saturday, May the sixth
at four o'clock
Suite 13 of the Howard Building
Please reply

Formal invitations

Mr. and Mrs. John Shensa
request the pleasure of the company of
Mr. and Mrs. Barry Greenberg
at dinner
on Monday, the fourth of April
at eight o'clock
8106 Keats Road

R.S.V.P.

Mr. William Gregory
accepts with pleasure
the kind invitation of
The Local Bank Tellers Club
to attend a tea on
Saturday, May the sixth
at four o'clock
Suite 13 of the Howard Building

Formal acceptance

Mr. and Mrs. Barry Greenberg
regret that a previous engagement
prevents their accepting
the kind invitation to dinner
at the home of
Mr. and Mrs. John Shensa
on Monday, the fourth of April

Formal refusal

Formal invitations and replies may be handwritten, printed, or typed.

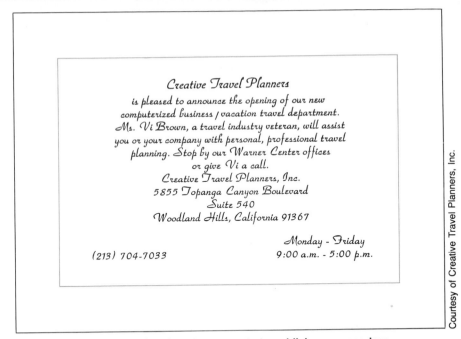

Courtesy of Creative Travel Planners, Inc.

Many companies send printed announcements to publicize new services.

For a more personal touch, the letter should be handwritten rather than typewritten. However, except in the case of a close personal friend, a typewritten message is acceptable.

COMMUNICATION LABORATORY

APPLICATION EXERCISES

A. While driving to work one day, you see a good customer, Lynn Merrick, having car trouble. You take Ms. Merrick to a nearby service station for help. Three days later you receive a letter thanking you and saying that arrangements have been made for you and a guest to have dinner at a very fine restaurant. You have a delicious meal and a delightful evening at the restaurant. Write a thank you letter to Ms. Merrick, Merrick's Personnel Agency, 12 Hunter Avenue, Memphis, Tennessee 38122.

B. Police Sergeant Terry Keyes spoke to your Employees' Service Club on the topic "Making Your Home Burglarproof." Write Sergeant Keyes a thank-you letter. Two employees have mentioned to you that Sergeant Keyes' advice may already have saved their homes from being robbed.

C. You read in the paper that a friend of yours, Chris Adams, is being given a three-month leave of absence from work to help with the summer job program for underprivileged youth. Write a letter congratulating your friend and offer your help.

D. You read in the newspaper that your friend Mildred DeForrest has been promoted and is now a word processing supervisor for Woolen Mills, Inc. Write Mildred a congratulatory letter.

E. Paul Bohannon's father passed away yesterday. Paul works in your department. Write him a letter of condolence.

F. You are employed by Adams, Howe, and Whitehead, an insurance and investment counseling firm. Prepare a formal announcement about Diana Lalinga's joining your firm. The announcement will be sent to Ms. Lalinga's prospective clients and friends.

G. Prepare a formal invitation to attend a reception honoring the new president of the Civic Service Club. The reception is being sponsored by the Clean-Air Club. Invitations are to be sent to all local service organization members.

H. You have received a formal dinner invitation for the Saturday after next. Either accept or reject it. Supply all the necessary details.

VOCABULARY AND SPELLING STUDIES

A. These words are often confused: *liable, libel; ingenious, ingenuous.* Write each in a sentence that illustrates its meaning.

B. Which of the three words following each of these phrases is closest in meaning to the italicized word in the phrase?

1. *Unobtrusive* lighting. Precise, regular, unnoticed.
2. *Volatile* temper. Violent, changeable, stable.
3. *Provincial* attitude. Positive, elevated, narrow.
4. *Articulate* speaker. Distinct, humorous, controversial.
5. *Minute* detail. Tiny, simple, unnecessary.

C. Where are apostrophes needed in the following sentences?

1. Theres no way we can believe that the estate is completely theirs.
2. Its about time for the jury to announce its decision.
3. Theyre all taking their books. Where are yours?
4. Whose pen is this?
5. Theres a three-week trial period before the warranty goes into effect.

COMMUNICATING FOR RESULTS

Safe-Driving Course. You have been asked to arrange a safe-driving course for all interested employees in your company. Make a list of the information you will need to give and receive as you telephone the local automobile association to ask for an instructor.

CHAPTER 9

Business letters are not the only type of business writing you will need to master. Some situations may call for formal records, such as reports. Other situations may call for informal records, such as interoffice memos.

Whatever the form of business record, you must be able to communicate effectively. Given a situation that requires writing business records, your mastery of the units in this chapter will enable you to do the following:

1. *Write interoffice memorandums.*

2. *Write informational messages and analytical reports.*

3. *Use telephone messages and routing slips effectively.*

4. *Select appropriate telegraphic services.*

5. *Write newsletters.*

6. *Write news releases.*

7. *Write minutes of meetings.*

U · N · I · T

50 Memos and Other Form Messages

In business, a letter is used to communicate with someone outside the company. When you wish to write to someone within your own company, you will send a memorandum. Memos are used to communicate with other employees, regardless of where the employees may be located—whether in the same office, in the same building, or in a branch office many miles away.

Because the interoffice memorandum form was developed to save time, the formality of an inside address, salutation, and complimentary closing is omitted. In other respects, however, office memos and letters have a great deal in common, as you will see from the following discussion.

The Tone of Memorandums

In most companies and organizations, memorandums are written in the first person, just as business letters are. The trend is decidedly away from the stiff, formal writing style that characterized the business letters and memos of several years ago. The tone of the memo is influenced by the position held by the writer in relation to that held by the receiver. Also, the topic under consideration plays an important part in determining tone. Obviously a person writing to a company official to report the results of a financial audit will be more formal than a person writing a co-worker about the company bowling league.

An important factor is the personality of the individual receiving the memorandum. The president, for example, may insist on informality, whereas a peer might like a formal, impersonal tone. Therefore, the effective business writer must evaluate the position of the reader, the topic under consideration, and the personality of the reader when setting the tone of the memo.

Writing Memorandums

There are usually three main parts to a memorandum:

1. The heading
2. The subject and date
3. The message

484

Occasionally, when official approval or authority is required, the memorandum may be concluded with a line for the signature of the person originating the correspondence.

The Heading. The heading of a memorandum is usually printed. One example is shown at the bottom of the page.

In the *To* and *From* sections, the business title of each person is often included, particularly when the memorandum is being sent to a person whose office is in another city. In the *To* section, a courtesy title—*Miss, Mrs., Ms., Mr., Dr.*—is sometimes included. However, in the *From* section, the writer does not use a courtesy title. (This principle also applies when you introduce yourself to someone: "Good morning, Miss Bloom—I'm Roy Vecchione," *not* "I'm *Mr.* Vecchione.")

> TO: Mr. Ramon Ortega, Accounting Supervisor
>
> FROM: Theresa Nibi, Accounts Receivable Manager

The memo forms used in large companies may also include *Department* and *Location* sections to facilitate communication among co-workers in various branches of the firm. These sections need not be filled in if reader and writer work in the same location or department.

The Subject and Date. The subject, a brief statement telling what the memo is about, helps the reader to prepare for the contents and aids in filing the correspondence for future reference. The subject line is not a complete sentence but rather a concise phrase that includes some specific information. For example, the subject may read:

> SUBJECT: Changes in Travel Advance Form

Complete dates are just as important on memos as they are on letters. Dates are necessary for future reference to prevent oversights and miscommunication.

ARNESS
PETROLEUM CORPORATION
Interoffice Memorandum

TO: FROM:

SUBJECT: DATE:

On some interoffice memo forms, the company's logo—as well as the standard heading—is printed.

The Message. The presentation of the message closely follows one of the three patterns presented for writing business letters. Like business letters, most memos follow a direct organizational plan. These messages present the main idea in the first paragraph and then follow with the necessary details to support the opening statements. Finally, the everyday memo concludes with suggestions for future action or requests guidance on future action.

Occasionally, however, you may find it necessary to write a persuasive or bad-news memorandum. Rather than take a direct approach, you are likely to be more successful if you present your details first and lead the reader on a step-by-step method to your request or bad news. In this way, the receiver is more likely to complete reading the memo and come to the conclusion of bad news along with the writer. By allowing the reader to see the reasoning that supports or leads to the idea you are conveying, you are better able to maintain goodwill.

Note the various memo parts in the everyday memorandum that is illustrated on the facing page.

When Are Memorandums Written?

Many business firms tell their employees to put in writing all important information that crosses their desks. Written records help to (1) determine responsibility, (2) clear up inconsistencies, and (3) record needed information. If you are sending important papers or documents to another person, for example, it is best to transmit them by memorandum so that if they become lost, there will be a record—your file copy—proving when they were actually sent, and recording exactly what they were.

TO:	Francis Heffron	FROM:	Joyce Holtzclaw
SUBJECT:	Home Burglar Alarm Effectiveness Report	DATE:	August 3, 1986

The Home Burglar Alarm Effectiveness Report that you asked to see is attached.

I would appreciate it if you would return it to me within ten days. Incidentally, Ms. Dalton has requested that the report not be circulated outside the company until its reliability can be checked.

JH

The following is an example of a request correctly written in the form of a memorandum.

TO:	Mr. Charles Werner	FROM:	Cynthia Lewis
SUBJECT:	Request to Carry Over Vacation Time	DATE:	May 12, 1986

I would like to request that I be given permission to carry over into next year the two weeks that remain of my vacation time for this year.

VIGILANT INSURANCE COMPANY

Interoffice Memorandum

TO: Gloria Ambrusco   **FROM:** Sidney Parton

SUBJECT: Loss From December Storm   **DATE:** February 9, 1985

The analysis of the company's losses as a result of the storm that hit the northeast states on December 11 and 12 of last year is now complete. This is the study that you requested in your memo of January 19.

As you are aware, most of the damage was suffered by the coastal New England states. This is the one area of the country where our company has relatively few policies in force. Our approximate losses in each of the states affected by the storm are given below:

Massachusetts	$1,025,800
Connecticut	723,100
Rhode Island	324,000
New Hampshire	182,300
	$2,255,200

Very slight losses were also sustained in eastern Vermont and southern Maine, but the total for these states is insignificant. Of the total amount of our New England loss, 82 percent comes from wind damage claims under the "Extended Coverage" provision of our standard homeowner's policy. The balance comes from claims filed by owners of marine policies.

Since some policyholders are late in filing claims, the above total could rise by as much as 10 percent. I will provide you with a final report in three months.

SP

mn

Labels (left margin):
- Brief, specific subject
- Why the memo is being written
- Information the memo is to convey
- Future action

The various parts of an interoffice memorandum are illustrated here.

I am well aware of the company's policy that vacation time be taken between June 1 and May 31 in the year that it is earned. However, I have been involved this year in a number of busy projects that simply did not allow me to take the time that I was owed. I had hoped to squeeze in my vacation this month, but the delay in the Hartmann project has made that impossible. We are now running three weeks behind. If we ever hope to catch up, I will simply have to stay with it.

Ms. Lydia Jason, my immediate supervisor, is aware of my request and has acknowledged her support of it.

CL

Displaying Detailed Matter

A memorandum containing a great many details will be easier to read if each point is numbered in 1-2-3 order, each number starting a new paragraph. Enumerations also help readers to refer by number to specific points when they are replying.

When the memorandum contains statistical matter, the writer should display this material in tabulated form for easier reading, as in the memorandum below. When there is a full page or more of detailed material, it may be

TRICOUNTY AIRLINES

MEMORANDUM

TO: Benjamin Spitzer   **FROM:** T. A. Arthur

SUBJECT: Monthly Boardings for Last Year: Cranston-Titusboro   **DATE:** January 7, 1984

Following are the monthly boarding tables for last year on all our flights operating between Cranston and Titusboro. As you will recall, we began this service on January 1. The seat-occupancy rate, which is based on the total of 1,000 seats that are available monthly between these two points is also included.

Month	Number	Occupancy Rate
January	362	36%
February	427	43%
March	512	51%
April	598	59%
May	673	67%
June	718	71%
July	640	64%
August	639	64%
September	720	72%
October	810	81%
November	830	83%
December	710	71%
TOTAL	7639	AVERAGE 64%

As you can see, this service has grown steadily since we began it, largely as a result of our effective promotion in the area. Since the break-even point for our aircraft is 42 percent, it has been a profitable service as well. The only decrease in growth came in July and August, when many of our business passengers were on vacation. The December decrease was due to the storm at the beginning of the month.

These figures do not report on the increase in our service between Titusboro and Wheeling, which is obviously affected by the Cranston-Titusboro route. I am gathering this information, and you shall receive it within ten days.

TAA

wp

When a memorandum contains statistical material, the writer should display this material in tabulated form for easier reading.

displayed on separate pages and accompanied by a brief covering memo explaining the material.

In any case, outside sources of information should be specifically and completely identified so that the reader could go back to the original source if necessary. Complete and accurate source identification enhances your credibility and helps your memo gain acceptance.

Routing Slips

Routing slips are sheets of paper that are used to send materials to several people. The routing slip may be a small (3″ × 5½″) sheet that lists the names of the people who are to get certain articles or magazines. The routing slip is stapled to the first page, and after each person reads the material and crosses out his or her name, the magazine or article is passed on to the next person on the list. See the example illustrated below.

A routing slip may also travel along with an important document—a contract, for example—that must be approved by several people. As each per-

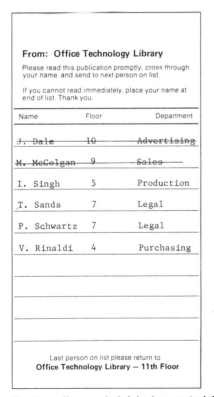

From: Office Technology Library

Please read this publication promptly, cross through your name and send to next person on list.

If you cannot read immediately, place your name at end of list. Thank you.

Name	Floor	Department
~~J. Dale~~	~~10~~	~~Advertising~~
~~M. McColgan~~	~~9~~	~~Sales~~
I. Singh	5	Production
T. Sands	7	Legal
P. Schwartz	7	Legal
V. Rinaldi	4	Purchasing

Last person on list please return to
Office Technology Library — 11th Floor

Routing slips are helpful when material must be sent to several people.

son approves the contract, he or she initials and dates the routing slip. The completed routing slip is filed as a one-page record showing that everyone did approve the document.

Routing slips that are used frequently may have names printed on them and a standard instruction at the bottom: "Return to P. Daniel, 29th Floor" or "Return to Library" or "Return to _____." Of course, a routing slip may also be individually typed as the need for one arises.

Obviously routing slips can save much time and money by reducing the need to duplicate the same information over and over again and by ensuring that all the people who *must* see a document or a magazine *will* see it.

Message Forms

Message forms allow people to take complete, accurate messages for others quickly. Thus they help us and our co-workers to build goodwill with customers and to work more efficiently with one another.

Since the forms usually include printed guide words (*To, Phone No., Date,* and so on) and easy-to-check boxes, the person who takes the message writes very few words. In the example below, note that the check-off boxes make this form useful both for telephone messages and for messages from visitors.

To: *Harvey Lentz*

Here is a Message for You

Helen Sturgis

of *Sturgis + Wells*

Phone No. *555-7229*   Ext. _____

☑ Telephoned   ☐ Will Call Again
☐ Returned Your Call   ☐ Came To See You
☑ Please Phone   ☐ Wants To See You

She wants to inform you of the progress made on the Fuller case.

Taken By *Andy*   Date *10/28*   Time *3:40 p.m.*

Message forms help people to take complete, accurate messages.

Mailgrams and Other Telegraphic Services

Telephone and telegraph companies offer several services for sending messages. Perhaps the best known is the telegram, a fast (but costly) way to send a message anywhere in the world. To send a telegram, you can call Western Union, give the name and address of the person who is to receive the message, and dictate an exact message. Western Union will send your message by teleprinter to the branch office that is closest to the recipient, and the branch office will then deliver it. The cost of the telegram, which is based on the number of words in your message, and its destination, can be charged to your telephone account.

Businesses today often use teleprinter equipment to communicate directly with branch offices or divisions. For example, a company with branches in San Francisco, Dallas, Chicago, and New York can facilitate communications among its branches by installing a teleprinter in each location. Two such services offered by Western Union are called *TWX* (*teletypewriter exchange* service) and *Telex*.

Western Union also offers Mailgram service, which is actually a joint service of Western Union and the United States Postal Service. Western Union wires a Mailgram message to the post ofice that is closest to the person who will receive the message. Since the post office gives Mailgrams special delivery service, they are usually received the day after they are sent. Mailgrams can be used successfully for advertising campaigns and for other volume mailings when a special effect is desired, because their distinctive blueand-white envelopes command the readers' attention and the telegraphic format impresses readers.

COMMUNICATION LABORATORY

APPLICATION EXERCISES

A. You are the secretary of your high school's Career Club. Gladys Enright, a partner in a local advertising agency, has accepted an invitation to speak to your club about job opportunities in the advertising field. She is a knowledgeable and effective speaker and has a genuine interest in informing others about her field. Prepare a memo that will be posted in each classroom announcing Ms. Enright's speech, "Advertising—A Field We All Need." The program is scheduled for 3:45 p.m. on February 7 in Room 119.

B. Your office manager, Henry Washington, wants to set up a standard routing slip so that useful publications can circulate among those who need to see them. Draw up a sample form and send it to him, along with a memorandum that explains the standards you followed. List at least five names and titles of people who should be on a routing slip.

C. A friend who works for another firm has shown you a copy of a new monthly magazine called *Tomorrow's Office Today*. Since the publication features the latest advances in office machinery and procedures, you believe it would be useful to several people in your office. Write a memo asking your supervisor for permission to subscribe to the magazine in your company's name. It is issued monthly and costs $26 for twelve issues.

D. Write a memo to Claudia Ortiz, your supervisor, asking for funds to attend a weekend communication conference in a city 150 miles away from your own. The conference, which will be held on November 8 and 9, will focus upon ways of improving employee efficiency through better internal communication. The conference leaders are people of established reputation in the field. Your estimate of the cost is about $250, an amount that includes mileage allowance, a hotel room for one night, meals, and a $75 registration fee for the conference.

E. Employees have been using the office postage meter as well as pre-stamped envelopes for personal correspondence. Write a memo to employees explaining that postage and stationery costs have risen greatly and that personal correspondence simply cannot be paid for by the company.

F. Fred Halliwell, one of the sales representatives located in your office, has been with a customer all morning. Two recent orders from this customer have been poorly handled and have arrived very late. Fred has spent the morning soothing the customer and promising that service will improve dramatically. He has guaranteed the customer that he will personally deliver the last order no later than 2 p.m. today. But the warehouse has just called to explain that the order won't be ready for Fred until 4 p.m. You must leave for the airport in five minutes, but you know that Fred is on his way back to the office. Write a telephone message that explains the development to him.

G. Write a congratulatory message that your regional manager can send as a Mailgram to all sales personnel in the region. It has just been announced that the revenue budget has been exceeded by 23 percent. The message should contain 50 words or fewer.

H. A long-time employee from a branch office has called for information about early retirement. He would like to know what his monthly combined pension and social security payments would be if he retired at age 62 instead of age 65. He would also like to know how much notice the company needs if he plans to take early retirement. Leave a telephone message for the personnel director.

VOCABULARY AND SPELLING STUDIES

A. These words are often confused: *marital, martial, marshal; charted, chartered*. Use each word in a sentence that illustrates its meaning.

B. Match each definition in the left-hand column with a word in the right-hand column.

1. a travel outline
2. showing great abundance
3. sturdy
4. to remove
5. to overthrow

a. delete
b. profuse
c. subvert
d. itinerary
e. stalwart
f. vivid
g. derive

C. What are the superlative forms of the following adjectives and adverbs?

1. clear
2. complicated
3. good
4. less
5. carefully
6. few

COMMUNICATING FOR RESULTS

Former Supervisor. You have been promoted to the position of sales correspondent. In this position you work closely with 15 sales representatives in coordinating their schedules, making many of their appointments, providing sales support materials, tracking all advertising and promotion for their products, and writing letters to customers and potential customers. Before your promotion, you were secretary to the employee benefits supervisor, Ms. Carla Newhouse, who trusted your judgment and who relied upon you completely. She always praised your work and had supported your promotion. In fact, your working relationship was so close that she still comes to you for help and advice several times a day. This takes up time you really don't have and also interferes with your transition to the new job and your relations with your new supervisor. You do not want to offend Ms. Newhouse, for whom you have great respect, or your supervisor, with whom you are trying to establish an effective relationship. You realize that you must do something before the situation becomes worse. What should you say or do?

51 Informational And Analytical Reports

Owners or managers of small businesses are able to keep in touch personally with everything that goes on in the firm. Whenever executives of a small company need information, they can go directly to the appropriate person and ask, "Michael, will we be able to fill the Levering order by December 12?" Michael could probably base his answer on readily available data.

In larger business, however, the owner, manager, or president cannot personally keep in touch with all operations of the company. Even department heads in very large operations are not able to directly supervise all the activities under their direction. Many businesses are so large and complex thaat a firm may be scattered throughout a particular section of the country or throughout the United States. In fact, many businesses now operate worldwide. Therefore, when business executives need information, they often ask for a written report.

The Need for Business Reports

Business reports are written to communicate facts and ideas to others. Without facts and ideas, without data on costs and expenses, and without statistics that indicate trends, businesses could not operate. The flow of information and ideas is necessary for business executives to make their decisions. The quality and accuracy of their decisions determine the future of the company. To make successful decisions, executives, managers, and supervisors rely heavily on the information that is reported to them.

Information is reported on all levels of business. The board of directors studies the reports from presidents and vice presidents, who in turn rely on reports from their department heads and assistants. Managers and supervisors rely on reports from their sales staff, their accounting department, and so on. The information reported may be complex and detailed, or it may be simple and straightforward.

A complex and detailed report may be written to explain the results of a lengthy study on topics such as (1) whether the company should close its three outdated plants and open one modern plant, (2) whether the company should expand its product line, or (3) whether the company should merge with another firm. Reports that require a long period of research and investigation to analyze a major topic in depth are called *analytical reports*. The format and the language used for such a report are usually formal.

Most of the reports written in business are simpler and more straightforward than analytical reports. They are called *informational reports* because their purpose is to communicate facts, ideas, statistics, or trends in a direct manner. Informational reports are less formal than analytical reports—in fact, informational reports are generally typed on standard memo paper or on printed forms.

Informational Reports

The average business worker writes many, many informational reports each year. For an informational report, the writer will generally have to gather and organize facts and figures, and perhaps make recommendations. The report illustrated on page 488 was written to inform the company's president of the flight boardings on an airline's new route. The writer of the report, the marketing director, will prepare similar reports for other routes that the airline flies. These are likely to be issued at regular intervals. *Periodic reports*, reports that are submitted at regular intervals, are common in business. Sales representatives may submit their sales reports on a daily basis. Production managers may submit their reports on a weekly basis. Executives usually submit their expense reports on a monthly basis or upon the completion of a major trip. For an example of a common periodic report, see the completed expense report form on page 496.

In addition to periodic reports, other informational reports are frequently submitted. If you were asked, for example, to provide estimates of the cost of janitorial and maintenance services for a new office building and warehouse, you might submit an informational report such as the one on page 497.

Writing Informational Reports. Like a business letter (or any other business message), an informational report must be clear, complete, correct, and concise. However, the wording of an informational report will be different from that used in a business letter. The wording for an informational report follows the style used for any other memorandum—that is, it is direct and to the point. The following paragraph, for example, might be used in a business letter informing a customer that a product that was ordered is no longer available.

> We were most happy to receive your June 3 order for ten of our 5-gallon gasoline drums. Since Associated Industries is always working to improve its products, we no longer manufacture this container. It has been replaced by a seamless aluminum container with a special no-spill top. This container sells at retail for only 2 percent more than our former model and wins immediate customer approval everywhere.

In a report, the same information would be worded in a more straightforward style, as follows:

Expense Report Summary				Entertainment & Miscellaneous Expense Record			
Name Marilyn Rosenfeld			Date	Place	Misc.—Explain expense Entertainment—List guests & affiliation	Business purpose & Business discussion	Total expended
Period Ending January 31 19 85			1/4	Luciano's	Lunch with Phoebe Spitzer of Spitzer and Wilson.	March advertising schedule.	29 45
	Due Co.	Due Me	1/8	The Cabin	Dinner with P. C. Wong and Jean Hayes of Marketing Association.	Annual conference plans.	75 50
Last Month's Closing Balance		46 95					
Error corrections—use this line only when notified							
Cash advances Date	50 00		1/15	Chez Pierre	Lunch with Hal Greene.	Discussed sales in his territory.	35 56
"							
"							
"							
Travel advances Date							
"							
"							
Travel Refunds Date							
Month's expenses		140 51					
Amount of remittance enclosed or surrendered to cashier							
Total Each Column	50 00	187 46					
Insert difference between totals above into proper box	Due Co.	Due Me					
Closing Balance		137 46					
Audit correction (accounting use only)							
☐ Check this box if remittance is enclosed							
I Certify This Report To Be Correct *Marilyn Rosenfeld*							
Dept. Head Approval *Robert Kranty*							
Additional Approval			If this space is insufficient, use a plain sheet of paper and staple to this form.			Total for period	140 51

Periodic reports such as this expense summary are usually submitted at regular intervals. They are usually completed on printed forms.

Associated Industries no longer manufactures its former line of gasoline containers. Here is a list of our discontinued models and the improved models that we suggest as replacements:

Discontinued Models	Suggest Replacement
2-721—2 gallon	A-802
5-722—5 gallon	A-805
10-723—10 gallon	A-810

The replacements are superior to the discontinued models and retail for almost the same price. I enclose a copy of our current catalog.

Analytical Reports

An analytical report (1) defines a problem, (2) presents relevant data to analyze the problem, (3) draws conclusions from the data, and (4) makes recommendations based on the conclusions. Since it is a thorough, extensive re-

WILCOX CORPORATION

Interoffice Memorandum

TO: Corinne Calvert   **FROM:** Henry Bester

SUBJECT: Maintenance Estimates--   **DATE:** September 27, 1984
St. Louis Branch Office

At your request, I asked the Purchasing Department to secure estimates from outside suppliers to provide janitorial and maintenance services for our new St. Louis office building and warehouse. The estimates are based upon the service specifications that were drawn up by our purchasing staff. They match in all essential respects the specifications established for our home office facility.

Supplier	Monthly Cost	Yearly Cost
Aspen Cleaning	$10,632	$127,584
Rogers Associates	11,812	141,744
Republic Services	9,112	109,344
Wheelwright Company	12,005	144,060

In spite of the fact that the Wheelwright Company's bid is the highest, the Purchasing Department is recommending that we contract with that firm. Sources in the area that are known to us are enthusiastic about their services, which are reported to be superior. The firm is well established and most reliable.

Please let me know is you agree with the Purchasing Department's assessment. If you do, I will advise Purchasing to enter into an agreement with them.

                                        HB

rd

An informational report must be accurate and complete, but also direct and to the point.

port, it may take months (even a year or more) to complete the research, investigation, and analysis for the report and to submit it. In fact, because of the importance and the scope of such a report, several people may be asked to contribute to its preparation.

Obviously, an analytical report is not an everyday task for most business workers. It will be required only for special projects—projects that deserve detailed research, investigation, and analysis. Any company that is considering an expensive proposal (such as the possibility of installing a computer system or of opening a new branch office) or a major change (such as expanding its line of products or reorganizing its accounting system) will ask for an analytical report to help make a sound decision. A company specializing in market analysis (product testing, plant location, advertising media, and the like) has need for many analytical reports. Actually, the report is the end product of the business. Chemical, petroleum, drug, and similar manufacturing companies require analytical reports from research and laboratory personnel who are conducting experiments on new products.

Writing Analytical Reports. The pattern of the analytical report varies with the type of business for which it is prepared. Memorandum forms (such as those discussed in Unit 50) may be used for reports as long as five or six pages. Longer reports will require a more formal format. Many companies adopt their own standard pattern for reports. The longer report will usually contain the following parts:

1. Memo or letter of transmittal
2. Summary
3. Body
4. Conclusions and recommendations
5. Appendixes

Letter of Transmittal. Since longer reports are more formal, a memorandum or letter of transmittal usually accompanies the report. The letter of transmittal serves several purposes:

1. It tells why the report is being submitted. The report may be the result of a project that was assigned several months earlier. Therefore, readers should be reminded of the reason for the report.
2. It identifies the report. Since executives receive many reports, it is important to identify each one so that it is easily recognizable.
3. It acknowledges sources of information and help. The people who helped gather and analyze data for the report should be acknowledged, of course.

Summary. Reports are presented to busy executives who will make decisions based on them. Many executives will not read an entire report. Since they are interested in getting directly to the heart of the material, they will be favorably impressed with the writer who provides a well-done summary. A report that does not contain a summary is not a welcome sight to a busy executive!

The summary includes (1) the purpose for writing the report, (2) the methods for collecting data, (3) the conclusions based on the data, and (4) the recommendations based on the conclusions. Some executives prefer a summary that begins with the recommendations. As a general rule of thumb, the summary is about one-tenth the length of the body of the report.

Body. The body begins with a brief introductory paragraph stating why there was interest in the topic. Then the main sections of the body (in order of appearance) are labeled as follows:

1. Purpose—explains what the writer hopes to accomplish.
2. Scope—tells what the report does include and what topic areas are to be covered.
3. Limitations—tells what the report does *not* include; usually specifies geographic locations and dates on information that is included.
4. Justification—lists those who will benefit from the report and explains why.
5. Related Publications—lists any articles the writer may have read before gathering the data.
6. The Present Study—presents the pertinent facts that have been gathered for this particular report.

In the "Related Publications" section, the writer will probably summarize the most relevant points of published articles on the subject. By showing what experts have said on the subject, this section adds credibility to the entire report. More important, these readings often provide direction for the writer in gathering and analyzing data. Report writers generally find appropriate articles in trade magazines, professional journals, and newspapers and periodicals. A complete bibliography of the articles should appear at the end of the report for those who are interested in reading more on the subject.

The facts offered in "The Present Study" section must be carefully assembled and clearly presented. Since there is no excuse for carelessness in a written report, the writer must be sure of the accuracy of the data presented. Careless errors will damage the writer's reputation for accuracy.

Conclusions and Recommendations. Up to this point, the writer has explained why the report was written and what was discovered. Sometimes this is all that is required, and the writer's conclusions and recommendations may not be necessary. In some cases, however, the report may be incomplete without conclusions—especially if the report writer has been asked to include them. By asking for the writer's conclusions and recommendations, the executive is showing (1) faith in the writer's judgment and (2) interest in what the writer will say. The writer's conclusions and recommendations should be based strictly on the "Related Publications" and "The Present Study" sections of the report. Writing the "Conclusions and Recommendations" section gives the writer a prime opportunity to show his or her ability to think. In fact, good writing ability combined with the skills to prepare a successful report have in many cases brought the writer favorable attention and promotions.

Appendix. The appendix may include working papers that show statistical computations; visual aids (tables, pie charts, trend lines, maps, graphs) that were too numerous to include in the body; and computer printouts—in other words, any kind of material that supports the report. A report may have a relatively short body with a long appendix. If the appendix is very long, it may be divided into sections, each with its own title page. The appendix material should be fully identified in the table of contents. A good appendix can lend much credibility to a report.

Writing Headings and Subheadings

Headings and subheadings are important communication tools—especially in reports. They (1) form an outline for your report, (2) improve your organization, (3) prepare your readers for the next topic, and (4) help readers to keep on track. Like signs on freeways, headings and subheadings help readers proceed smoothly to their destination. Remember the principle of balanced structure (see Unit 39) when using headings and subheadings. Within a chapter, the wording of headings should be balanced; the wording of the subheadings below each heading should be balanced; and so on.

Choosing the Right Tone

Shorter reports—those submitted on memo forms—use a conversational tone. Longer analytical reports generally adopt a formal (but not a stiff) tone. Contractions and the personal pronoun *I* are avoided, although they may be used correctly in other kinds of writing. Avoiding *I* gives the report a certain objectivity. For example, "I gathered the following evidence as I conducted a survey of . . . " sounds too much as if the report is based on the writer's personal feelings. Instead, "The evidence gathered during the survey proved that . . . " makes the report objective—based on facts, not on personal opinions.

Using Visual Aids

Statistical information should be presented as visual aids—tables, charts, graphs, trend lines, and so on. Statistical data is much easier for the reader to comprehend when presented in visual form rather than in paragraph form. Since visual aids are usually grouped in the appendix, they should be mentioned in the body of the report. However, do *not* repeat all the data in the body; emphasize only the most significant points.

When developing the kinds of visual aids listed above, be sure to follow these guidelines:

1. Use a title that is clear and complete. The title of each visual aid should identify it precisely. The visual aid should be able to stand alone—away from the report—and still be understandable. See, for example, the table shown at the top of the facing page.

YEARS OF SERVICE OF EMPLOYEES IN BRANCH OFFICES AS OF JUNE 30, 1984						
		YEARS OF SERVICE				
OFFICE	TOTAL EMPLOYEES	OVER 20	OVER 15	OVER 10	OVER 5	FEWER Than 5
Atlanta	36	1	3	4	17	11
Chicago	21	1	4	6	5	5
Dallas	46	0	2	7	6	31
Denver	14	1	1	10	1	1
San Francisco	29	3	3	12	7	4
TOTALS	146	6	13	39	36	52

2. Identify the original source of the data. Give the full source for each visual aid. List whatever information would help the reader identify and find the visual aid: author's name, publisher's name, place of publication, date of publication, volume number, and page numbers for magazines, books, and periodicals; dates, locations, and names for interviews; and so on.
3. Explain the meaning of any graphic devices. Graphic devices such as colors, shaded areas, and stick figures must be explained. For example, in a graph comparing expenses for three different years, three different lines may be used to identify the years. The reader must therefore be told that the dotted line represents 1984, the solid line represents 1985, and the wavy line represents 1986. If a graphic device has a specific purpose, be sure to let the reader know that purpose.

Typing Analytical Reports

Expert typing and setting up of a report will increase the forcefulness of the communication by helping the reader to absorb the main points quickly. The long analytical report usually consists of the following parts:

1. Cover
2. Title page
3. Letter of transmittal
4. Table of contents
5. Summary
6. Body
7. Conclusions and recommendations
8. Bibliography
9. Supplementary material or appendix

Reports should be typed on plain white bond paper, 8½ by 11 inches. Each page should be typed on only one side of the sheet. All reports should be double-spaced, and each page after the first should be numbered. A left margin of approximately 1½ inches should be allowed for the binding. Top, bottom, and side margins of all but the first page should be 1 inch.

Most analytical reports require a title page. The illustration below shows the title and contents pages for a report on advertising needs.

Typing Headings and Subheadings. In typing headings and subheadings, observe the following points:

1. Use the same typing format for each level of headings.
2. Main headings are usually (**a**) typed in capital and small letters, (**b**) underscored, and (**c**) displayed on separate lines. Two blank lines are used above main headings and one blank line below them.
3. Subheadings, a secondary level of headings, are typed at the left margin in all-capital letters. They are not underscored. Two blank lines are used above these headings and one blank line below them. However, if a main heading directly precedes the subheading, then only one blank line is used above the subheading.
4. If a third level of heading is needed, the headings are usually run in with the text. They are (**a**) indented (like paragraphs) five spaces from the left margin, (**b**) typed in capital and small letters, (**c**) underscored, and (**d**)

SURVEY OF CUSTOMER REACTIONS

TO THE BENEDICT CORPORATION'S

ADVERTISING PROGRAM

Prepared for A. F. Furman
Director of Public Relations
by Janice Loew

October 14, 1984

CONTENTS

Summary   1

Purpose   2

Scope   4

Limitations   5

Justification   7

Related Publications   9

The Present Study   11

Conclusions and Recommendations   16

Bibliography   19

Appendixes   20

A title page (left) and a table of contents (right) are standard parts of any analytical report.

followed by a period (or a question mark or exclamation point, if appropriate). Two spaces are used after the period.

If all three levels of headings are required in a report, the headings would then be structured as follows:

Main Heading

SECONDARY HEADING

    Third-Level Heading. Text copy follows this run-in heading.

NOTE: Some writers prefer typing the main heading in all-capital letters and the secondary heading in capital and small letters. The main heading would still be centered (but not underscored), and the secondary heading would still be typed at the left margin. In either style the heading typed in capital and small letters is underscored; the heading typed in all-capital letters is not.

Binding the Report. When the report is completed, it may be bound at the side with staples (usually three vertical staples close to the left edge) or fastened at the top with a paper clip. Some reports are placed inside a special folder made for the purpose; others are bound by special backing paper of a heavy stock.

COMMUNICATION LABORATORY

APPLICATION EXERCISES

A. Assume that you have been asked by your office manager, Sharon Rosenberg, to prepare a report on the types of mailings done by your firm. She would like to know how many pieces of the various categories of mail are processed each week: how many are first-class letters, how many are bulk-rate sales pieces, how many are packages. She is especially interested in the package shipments that must be received by the addressee on the following business day. She needs information on the postage that the firm spends during a typical week and during a particularly busy week.

1. Prepare an outline for the proposed report, even though you will not actually gather the information.
2. Describe the procedures you would use in gathering the information and preparing the report.
3. List the sources of information that you would use.

B. Your supervisor has asked you to investigate the methods used to conserve energy in five firms in your area. Assume that you have interviewed five employees of different firms. Prepare a report of your findings.

C. Survey your class or a group of about 20 students to determine what kinds of jobs in what kinds of businesses they hope to have by the time they are thirty years old. Prepare a visual aid—a table, a chart, a graph, or trend line—that would display your data most effectively. Discuss the visual aid briefly.

VOCABULARY AND SPELLING STUDIES

A. These words are often confused: *suit, suite, sweet; rout, route, root.* Use each word in a sentence that illustrates its meaning.

B. Find and correct the errors in the following sentences.

1. The duties will be divided between Donna and I.
2. I can not understand this computer printout.
3. The new letterheads have all ready been designed.
4. This calculator has it's correction key in an inconvenient place.
5. That machine don't need much maintenance.
6. We chartered all the sales figures on this graph.

C. In each of the following words, the sound of "sh" occurs at the point indicated by the blank spaces. Fill in the missing letters.

1. auc___on
2. op___on
3. divi___on
4. conclu___on
5. defi___ent
6. permis___on

COMMUNICATION FOR RESULTS

Writing a Public Announcement. Each Monday morning students announce upcoming events over the school's public address system. Write a one-minute announcement about the monthly meeting of the school's Junior Achievement Club. The club will use this meeting to introduce several local business people, who will speak on topics relevant to starting a new job in their respective businesses. The club would like a large attendance at such an important and useful meeting. Tell when and where the club will meet and who the special guests will be.

U · N · I · T

52

Minutes and News Releases

In business, you will probably have frequent opportunities to attend meetings. Whether a meeting is formal or informal, a written record of the meeting will usually be prepared and distributed to everyone who attended the meeting and, perhaps, to other interested people as well. This written record, called the *minutes* of the meeting, is discussed in this unit.

This unit will also introduce you to news releases—a form of business communication that has a very special purpose.

Preparing Minutes of Meetings

In a typical business, many committees and task forces operate within the company. The purpose of committees is to discuss various problems and to make recommendations to management. A *standing committee* is one that operates permanently year after year, although its members may change. A *task force* is a group of people who are appointed to solve a specific problem; when they make their recommendation on the "task" assigned to them, the task force is disbanded. Each department may have several committees that meet periodically—usually once a week, every two weeks, or monthly. If you are working in a sales department, for example, there may be committees on advertising, sales conferences, commissions, forms control, product development, public relations, and so on.

Minutes of Informal Meetings. The written record of the proceedings of a meeting is called the *minutes* of the meeting. Since most meetings in business are informal (that is, do not follow the rules of parliamentary procedure), the minutes are also informal. The minutes usually include the date, time, and place of the meeting; the name of the presiding officer; a list of those present (and frequently those absent); and the time of adjournment. Discussions are usually summarized.

Usually the minutes are signed by the person who took them and sometimes by the presiding officer as well. Minutes are usually duplicated, and copies are sent to each person present at the meeting and to other desig-

```
                The Market Watchers Investment Club

                  MINUTES OF THE MONTHLY MEETING

                         May 6, 1985


Presiding:  Claire Natallia, President

Present:    Anne Barton            Frederick Lamont
            Eugene Entmann         Barbara Masters
            Sara Guarino           Janet Olliphant
            Jonathan Habbib        Cynthia Regan
            Spencer Haeman         Felix Samuelson

Absent:     Carlton Fields         Robert Noonan
            Joseph Imperato        Helen Prescott
            Valerie Kasper         Donald Zimmerman

After calling the meeting to order at 3:15 p.m., the president asked
the treasurer for a brief report.  The treasurer distributed to each
member a statement that indicated the member's present investment in
the club's holdings.  She noted that a share was currently worth $23.60
and that this month's contributions plus accumulated dividends amounted
to a total of $372.40 that the club could invest.

The president asked Sara Guarino, chairperson of the investment committee,
for the committee's recommendation.  Ms. Guarino said that the committee
had studied stocks of building supply companies.  She reported that the
committee believed that the depressed housing market would improve even-
tually and that these companies were bound to do better when the improve-
ment came.  She said that her committee had located three companies whose
shares were very low and would probably benefit most from a rebound:  the
Benton Water Meter Company, the Aramo Forest Products Corporation, and
the Monarch Wire Company.

The president asked Felix Samuelson of Lauder, Bennet, and Laser, the
club's broker, to comment.  Mr. Samuelson said that he agreed with the
committee's analysis and suggested Aramo Forest Products as the best buy.
He noted that the firm was diversified and that the 7 percent dividend
was rather secure.  Ms. Guarino then moved that Aramo be purchased.  Ms.
Regan seconded.  The motion was approved unanimously.

Mr. Habbib announced that the club's annual picnic is scheduled for Sat-
urday, June 23, at Forest Park in Afton.  Each member is entitled to
bring one guest.  More details will be available at next month's meeting.

The meeting was adjourned at 5:30 p.m.

                                  Respectfully submitted,

                                  Spencer Haeman

                                  Spencer Haeman, Secretary
```

The minutes of an informal meeting include summaries of discussion as well as standard information such as date, opening and closing times, and the names of presiding officers and present and absent members.

nated officials. The minutes of a meeting of an investment club committee are shown above.

Minutes of Formal Meetings. Minutes of meetings that follow parliamentary procedure are somewhat different in form from the informal minutes illustrated here. Formal minutes do not include discussions. Only motions, reso-

```
                The Historical-Commercial Club of Springfield

                     MINUTES OF THE MONTHLY MEETING

                           February 8, 1986


TIME AND PLACE   The regular monthly meeting of the Historical-Commercial
                 Club of Springfield was called to order by the president,
                 Sanders Ransome, on Friday, February 8, 1986, at 2 p.m.,
                 in the Lincoln Room of the Pioneer Hotel.

MINUTES          The minutes of the last meeting were read and approved.

TREASURER'S      The following report was given by Angela Asbach, the
REPORT           treasurer:

                    Balance on hand, January 1, 1986      $2,372.38
                                                           1,816.40
                                                Total     $4,188.78
                    Paid out in January                     863.40
                    Balance on hand February 1            $3,325.38

                 The treasurer's report was accepted.

OLD BUSINESS     It was moved, seconded, and voted that a booklet describ-
                 ing local commercial sites of historic interest be writ-
                 ten and published by the club and distributed to local
                 schools (Claudia Lawson, Bill Travers).

NEW BUSINESS     After a discussion about improving the club's ability to
                 advise the local media about its activities, a committee
                 consisting of Angela Fairchild, chairperson; Francis
                 Aaron; Julia Fletcher; and Sandra Toller was appointed
                 to report to the next meeting.

PROGRAM          Sanders Ransome introduced Mary Beth Stillman, an archae-
                 ologist at Springfield University. Ms. Stillman's topic
                 was "Establishing a Partnership Between Business and
                 Archaeology." Her remarks are summarized briefly here:
                 Successful partnerships are being established between ar-
                 chaeologists and businesses. When companies build or re-
                 build in downtown areas, they allow archaeologists to ex-
                 amine the excavation sites for a period of time. Professors
                 and their students gather artifacts that shed considerable
                 light upon the history of our cities. Companies receive
                 publicity from these partnerships, and they may display
                 what was collected at the building sites in their completed
                 buildings.

                 The meeting was adjourned at 4:15 p.m.

                                   Respectfully submitted,

                                   Walter A. Frampton

                                   Walter A. Frampton, Secretary
```

The minutes of a formal meeting do not include summaries of discussions leading up to votes.

lutions, committee assignments and reports, and other specific accomplishments are included. Note in the example above how topical headings are used for easy reference and how the recorder has briefly summarized a speaker's remarks. Note, too, that motions should be worded specifically as shown and should be followed by the name of the person who made the motion and the name of the seconder.

Resolutions. Resolutions to express sympathy, appreciation, congratulations, and the like are often passed at formal meetings. The form of resolutions follows a rather definite pattern, as illustrated on the facing page.

Notice that the paragraphs giving the reasons for the resolution are introduced by the word *WHEREAS* (followed by a comma) and that the paragraphs stating the action to be taken are introduced by the word *RESOLVED* (also followed by a comma).

News Releases

All businesses are eager to get as much favorable publicity as possible in newspapers and magazines, on radio or television—wherever there is a reading or listening audience. Larger businesses—even colleges—employ publicity directors whose job is to attract favorable public attention to the organization. The old saying attributed to a movie star, "I don't care what you say about me as long as you spell my name correctly," indicates how valuable publicity is to some people. Businesses, however, want only stories that show them in a favorable light, for public confidence is at stake. Unfavorable publicity can lose customers and lower stock values.

The physical form in which the planned news or publicity is given to news outlets is called a *news release*. Any subject that the business executive thinks may be of public interest or may bring the company name before the public may be the basis for a news release. It may be an announcement of a new product or service, the promotion of a major executive, a retirement, a death, an honor for an employee, the election of employees to civic posts, company anniversary celebrations, and so on. News releases are usually written, or at least approved, by one executive in an organization. In larger firms, a public relations department or publicity department handles such releases. In smaller firms, releases may be written by various executives. To prevent inaccurate or conflicting information from leaking out, however, these releases are usually channeled through one executive.

The purpose of the news release is to get a story into print or on the air. Newspaper, magazine, radio, and television editors receive hundreds of news releases every day from all types of businesses and individuals. The editor appraises these releases by one basic rule: "Is this item of current, specific interest to our readers or listeners?"

Form of the News Release. The style in which releases are written is highly important. Since news editors cannot accept for publication every news release they receive, everything else being equal, they will usually choose those that require the least amount of additional checking and editing.

R E S O L U T I O N

WHEREAS our beloved colleague Robert Embers passed away on
April 8, 1984, and was one of the most sympathetic and hardest-working
members of the Executive Committee; and

WHEREAS his wise counsel and unselfish services will be
missed not only by the employees of the Piedmont Specialty Company but
also by the community at large; therefore, be it

RESOLVED, that we, his fellow committee members, take this
means of expressing our deep appreciation for his untiring and unselfish
service to the Piedmont Specialty Company and to the community; and be it

RESOLVED, further, that we extend our sincerest sympathies to
his widow, Mrs. Mara Embers; to his son, Mr. Larry Embers, of Northampton,
Vermont; and to his brother, Mr. F. D. Embers, of Houston, Texas; and be it

RESOLVED, further, that a copy of this resolution be included in
the minutes of the Executive Committee of the Piedmont Specialty Company,
that a copy be sent to the members of the immediate family, and that a
copy be supplied to the press of the city.

ADOPTED, unanimously, by the Executive Committee of the Piedmont
Specialty Company, this ninth day of April, 1984.

David Lee

David Lee
Director

P. A. Trazinski

P. A. Trazinski
Secretary

The form of a resolution follows a definite pattern, including the use of the words *WHEREAS* and *RESOLVED*.

Therefore, a release should give complete information and follow as closely as possible the newspaper style of writing, as does the one on the facing page.

News releases must be typed and reproduced (usually by stencil or photo-offset). Carbon copies should never be sent to an editor. Releases should be kept as brief as possible—rarely should they be more than a page and a half. The shorter and more interesting the news release, the better its chance of getting into print.

Companies that issue a great many news releases have special forms on which to write them. Reporting a story on a special news release form is much more effective than writing a letter. Editors like to be able to read quickly; they cannot waste time going through the formalities of a letter. Like a letterhead, a news release form usually contains the name, address, and telephone number of the company. This information, however, may be placed at the bottom of the form. In addition, the name of the person who issued the release is included so that the editor can call for more information.

When writing or issuing news releases, be sure to observe all the points outlined here:

1. Always double-space the news release. Double-spacing is a must for all news releases so that the editor has room to make changes in the copy.

2. Use generous side margins and leave plenty of space at both top and bottom. This permits room for the editor to add typesetting instructions.

3. At the beginning of the story, give a brief headline so that the editor may learn quickly what the release is about; for example, "New Plastic Skin-Diving Equipment Announced" or "New Vice President Appointed" or "Printing Press Handles Sheets 110 Inches Wide." (Editors will nearly always write their own headlines; nonetheless, news release writers should include a suggested headline.)

4. At the top of the form indicate when the news release may be made public. "For Release Upon Receipt" means that the story may be printed immediately upon receipt. Sometimes a news release may be issued several days in advance of the time it is to be used, in which case it will be marked, "To Be Released on July 1" or "Not to Be Released Before July 1."

5. Indicate the end of the release by typing the word *END* in parentheses or by typing three *x*'s: —*xxx*—. (The three *x*'s stand for "30," the signal telegraphers once used to signify "the end.")

6. If there is more than one page, add the word *more* in parentheses at the end of each page except the last page.

7. If the news release is long, insert subheads between paragraphs of the text to help break the monotony of type.

N E W S   R E L E A S E

Conway Medical Supply Company
San Antonio, Texas 78207

Release: Immediate

From: P. D. Seymour
          Public Relations Officer

ARROYO NAMED SALES MANAGER AT CONWAY MEDICAL SUPPLY COMPANY

SAN ANTONIO, Nov. 10--Antonio F. Arroyo has been appointed national sales manager of the Conway Medical Supply Company of San Antonio, according to the announcement made yesterday by Phyllis Sherman, president.

Mr. Arroyo succeeds Rosemary H. Chevalier, who retired October 1 after 30 years of service.

The new sales manager joined the firm in 1976 as a sales representative in the surgical instrument division. In 1979 he was made executive assistant to the sales manager, and in 1982 he was appointed assistant sales manager.

Mr. Arroyo lives in northwest San Antonio with his wife, Francesca Arroyo, a production supervisor at the Danvers Printing Company. The Arroyos have three children.

In commenting on his new post, Mr. Arroyo paid tribute to the fine work done by his predecessor. "We shall continue to promote our fine products throughout the United States. We shall continue to develop the fine reputation for quality and service that we have built over the last fifty years." (END)

Any subject that a business thinks may be of public interest or may bring the company name before the public may be the subject of a news release.

Writing the News Release. Whether your story heads for the wastebasket or the composing room may depend upon the words you use in your first paragraph. The first paragraph should summarize the basic idea of the story. It should stand by itself if need be, giving the *who, what, why, when,* and *where,* as stories appearing in newspapers generally do. Some examples follow:

> Appointment of Martha G. Stein as controller of the Clauson Construction Company, Clarkson, West Virginia, has been announced by Percy T. Lavalle, president.

This release may be revised by the editor of the newspaper or magazine as follows:

> Martha G. Stein has been named controller of Clauson Construction Company, Clarkson, West Virginia.

In any case, the news angle to the story is Ms. Stein's appointment rather than Mr. Lavalle's participation. Put the accent on Stein; don't write this:

> Percy T. Lavalle, president of Clauson Construction Company, Clarkson, West Virginia, has announced the appointment of Martha G. Stein as controller.

After the lead paragraph is written, move on to the background facts:

> She succeeds A. Frederick Falls, who retired October 1.

Additional background worth noting may then be given:

> The new controller joined the firm in 1978 as an auditor. In 1980 she was made accounting supervisor and in 1982 was appointed assistant controller.

A well-written news release follows all the guidelines on the previous page.

COMMUNICATION LABORATORY

APPLICATION EXERCISES

A. Write the minutes for a class session or for a meeting of a club that you belong to. Use the informal form discussed in this unit.

B. Prepare a formal set of minutes for an actual meeting that you have attended. The minutes might come from a club meeting or from the meeting of a local governmental agency. If you have not attended such a meeting, you may make up the necessary information.

C. Prepare a news release for your school or for a club or group that you belong to. If the release is for your school, it might announce a graduation, an athletic schedule, special student awards, or an annual play. If the release is for a club or group, it might announce an important upcoming meeting, a special activity or speaker, or a fund or membership drive.

VOCABULARY AND SPELLING STUDIES

A. These words are often confused: *wave, waive; bearing, baring, barring.* Explain the differences.

B. Substitute a modern word or phrase for each of the following expressions:

1. We advise you herewith.
2. We beg your indulgence.
3. We trust . . .
4. Under separate cover . . .
5. At an early date . . .
6. In the event that . . .

C. Write the present participial (ending in *ing*) form of each of the following verbs:

1. plan
2. develop
3. duplicate
4. sit
5. occur
6. believe

D. Three of the four words in each group are synonyms. The fourth is an antonym. Spot the intruder.

1. skilled, awkward, expert, efficient
2. just, unbiased, objective, partial
3. prohibit, ban, permit, enjoin
4. exhibit, disguise, cloak, camouflage
5. authenticate, confirm, invalidate, verify
6. submit, yield, surrender, resist
7. lively, animated, dull, sprightly
8. fulfill, initiate, commence, begin
9. append, add, attach, detach
10. constrict, expand, compress, contract

COMMUNICATING FOR RESULTS

Solving a Customer's Problem. Anita Felix is a sales representative for an auto parts manufacturer. As part of her normal customer contact program, she visits Mr. Henry Vaughan, the owner of an auto parts retail outlet. Mr. Vaughan is very happy to see her. He tells her that he is in the midst of a special promotion and that his sale still has a week to go. Unfortunately, he is virtually out of one of Anita's line of spark plugs that has been selling better than expected. He begs her for an immediate shipment from her nearby warehouse and wants to order three times his normal amount. Anita realizes that supplies of the product have just about vanished and will not be available for another month. The only way that she can supply the amount that Mr. Vaughan needs is to deliver to him three smaller orders already promised other customers.

What should Anita say to Mr. Vaughan?

P · A · R · T

7

DEVELOPING LISTENING AND SPEAKING SKILLS

Listening is a complex communication activity. It is more than just being quiet and courteous when someone else is speaking. It involves remembering what you hear, recording what you hear, and following instructions. It is no surprise, then, that listening skills are valued highly in business.

How well you listen indicates a lot about your communication skills. Given a situation that requires listening, your mastery of the units in this chapter will enable you to do the following:

1. *Take brief—but complete—written notes at meetings, demonstrations, and lectures, and of telephone instructions.*

2. *Remember more of what you hear.*

3. *Remember the names of people to whom you are introduced.*

4. *Eliminate the common misunderstandings that can result from spoken conversations.*

5. *Improve your ability to follow instructions on the job.*

U · N · I · T

53

The Importance of Listening

Communication is a two-way process: *sending* a message and *receiving* a message. The sending device may be written words (written communication) or spoken words (oral communication). In written communication, the *writer* is the *sender* and the *reader* is the *receiver*. In oral communication, the *speaker* is the *sender* and the *listener* is the *receiver*. In both written and oral communication, there is no communication unless the message has been received. A letter that has been lost in the mail does not communicate. The best speech communicates nothing to you if you do not listen to it. How many lost messages have resulted in lost benefits to you?

The effectiveness of every communication depends first upon the proper functioning of the sending process and then upon the proper functioning of the receiving process. This unit stresses the importance of the receiving process in oral communication—listening—because listening skill is too often taken for granted and ignored.

How Listening Differs From Hearing

Too often people think that listening and hearing are the same thing, but there is a big difference. Hearing depends upon the ears, but listening uses the mind as well—and may even require the eyes. The ears permit you to hear sounds; the mind enables you to interpret these sounds, to recognize some of them as words, and to fashion the words into thoughts or ideas. With your mind, you are able to determine that an oral message is important, interpret the message, and react to it.

Interpreting the message is a *thinking* act. It is dependent on both the listener's vocabulary and attitude. The listener must *want* to grasp the meaning of the words.

You may not have considered the eyes to be an important tool in listening. Yet what you see when a person is speaking is sometimes as important as what you hear. A smile, a quizzical glance, the appearance of boredom or exhilaration—all the facial expressions and mannerisms of a speaker may alter the meaning of the message.

The problem of improving listening is not one of improving the physical tools. Rather, it is a problem of improving the use of these tools so they become more effective in receiving messages.

518

Why Improve Listening Efficiency?

Surveys have shown that listening occupies more time than any other communication activity: we spend more time listening than we spend talking, reading, or writing. Obviously, then, we can greatly improve our ability to receive communications by improving our listening skills.

The rewards of listening are great: they include increased knowledge, broadened experience, more and deeper friendships, increased job opportunities and promotions, development of facility in using language, and an increased appreciation of the spoken word.

On the other hand, ineffective listening may have a disastrous effect on any of these rewards, resulting in disappointments and failure. Frequently, potential school dropouts fail in their studies not because they can't learn but because they don't know how to listen. Snobs or bores may not want to be unfriendly; perhaps they just haven't mastered the listening requirements necessary for successful social relations. Employees may be fired not because they are unable to perform their jobs well but because they don't know how to listen to instructions.

Tests have shown that immediately after most people have listened to someone talk, they remember only about half of what they heard. Two months later, they remember only about a fourth of what was said. In other words, the average person is only 25 percent efficient in listening skills. This fact means, then, that the average person has the potential for greatly increasing listening efficiency.

What does all this mean to you? Well, suppose you are one of these "average" persons. But, through instruction and practice, you are able to double your listening efficiency. You become 50 percent efficient in listening rather than just 25 percent. Consider what this improvement will mean in relation to your learning, your social life, your job. Consider how this improvement will increase your pleasure when you are with other people.

Listening and Your Social Life. Improved listening is certain to pay dividends in your social life. We find it easy to listen attentively to a good conversationalist, but courtesy demands that we *always* be good listeners. We should listen to others not only out of courtesy but also so that we can understand *what* the speaker is saying and *why*. In this way, good listeners gain new friends and enrich and deepen their existing friendships.

Listening and Your Education. In high school today, many class hours are devoted to lectures and discussions, so doubling your listening effectiveness would greatly increase your learning productivity. It might eliminate "burning the midnight oil" when you cram for exams. Efficient listening—resulting in improved learning and remembering—also would give you more time for other subjects and for extracurricular activities.

Listening and Your Job. The rewards of improved listening are more tangible when you have a job, for often the rewards are in money. Beginning employees must listen to instructions and directions from their supervisors and co-workers. They must listen to suggestions and criticisms in order to improve their job performance. To advance in a job, they must have an awareness of what's going on in their department and in the company, and this awareness results in part from intelligent listening. You can easily see that improved listening will enhance your chances of success in business.

The Effect of Listening on Other Communication Skills

Each medium of communication can reinforce the other media to produce a higher degree of learning. For example, listening can be reinforced with reading, with speaking, and with writing to produce better understanding and longer remembering.

Listening and Reading. Listening, like reading, is a message-receiving skill. But listening is more difficult than reading because, generally, you cannot relisten to a spoken message as you can reread a written one. You must get the message right the first time or you lose it.

Reading about a topic in advance will enable you to listen more effectively to the speaker's message because you bring more knowledge to the topic and thus derive greater benefit from it. When planning to attend an important committee meeting, if you examine the agenda and reread the minutes of previous meetings beforehand, you will be able to listen much more effectively during the meeting.

Listening and Speaking. Speaking reinforces listening in various ways. Good listeners repeat to themselves the speaker's important points, and they mentally rephrase these points in their own words; this process adds to the listeners' understanding. In addition, good listeners ask questions to clarify what a speaker is saying.

Speaking is often an aid to memory, thus helping the listener to remember. When you are introduced to people, for example, you will be more likely to remember their names if you repeat the name orally and use the name as much as you can in talking with the person or in talking with others about the person.

Listening and Writing (Note-Taking). Writing, perhaps more than any other communication skill, contributes to good listening. Frequently, the listener must take written notes in order to retain for future reference the information he or she hears. The student attending a lecture, the secretary taking a telephone message, and the accountant receiving oral instructions from a supervisor are but a few of the persons who write notes to reinforce their listening.

However, notes should be made with discretion. A listener who spends too much time taking notes may miss the heart of the message. A listener who is too dependent upon note-taking may be using these notes as a crutch to avoid real listening rather than as a reinforcement to listening. In the next unit you will be given specific suggestions for note-taking.

Listening and Job Success

Habits of efficient listening contribute greatly to one's success in all areas of life, but particularly in business and industry. So important are habits of good listening that many large corporations—American Telephone and Telegraph, General Electric, and General Motors among them—provide listening training for many of their executives and supervisory personnel.

Supervisors Must Know How to Listen. These corporations know that management must be able to listen properly if it is to be effective. They know that successful supervisors or managers don't just give orders; they also do a lot of listening. They listen to their employees to find out what they think so that management can help to settle grievances and establish good employee relationships. They also listen to their employees because they know that their employees often contribute time- and money-saving ideas to those employers who prove to be sympathetic and appreciative audiences.

All Employees Must Know How to Listen. Listening is extremely important at all levels of employment. Many employees in business and industry rely on listening skills to help them carry out their daily assignments. The telephone operator must listen carefully in order to handle the requests of hundreds of callers. The salesperson must listen just as carefully to determine the wishes of customers.

One large retailing organization found that two out of every three former customers had taken their business elsewhere because its sales personnel were indifferent to customers' needs. Moreover, the organization found that much of the indifference was expressed through poor listening.

Have you ever had an experience like this one? In a shoe store, you ask the salesclerk to show you a pair of brown loafers in size 8C. The clerk appears to have understood and proceeds to select from the shelves two or three boxes of shoes. To your annoyance, the clerk brings you back dress oxfords in size 9C. Now you must again describe the shoes you want. Poor listening habits have caused you unnecessary delay and have made extra work for the clerk. Such incidents are much too frequent in business.

Among others who are greatly dependent upon effective listening for success in their jobs are service department managers. When a customer brings a car into an automobile service center, the service manager must listen and record what the customer thinks is wrong with the automobile. The service manager must even listen to the motor for clues to the difficulty. Then, the manager must listen to learn if, when, and where the repaired vehicle is to be delivered. After the work has been completed, the manager must listen to the mechanics to find what repairs have been made and whether they have been made satisfactorily. The success of all service department managers depends greatly upon how well they listen in their roles as liaisons between customers and the employees making the repairs.

All employees who provide service of any kind—and that includes most—are partially, if not mainly, dependent upon their listening ability to carry out their duties. No one in business and industry is immune to the need for effective listening. Every worker—every secretary, accountant, shipping clerk, machine operator, maintenance person—receives much information and many instructions orally from co-workers, from supervisors, and from customers. Failure to listen results in errors and misunderstandings, and these are costly in terms of time, money, and goodwill.

Because effective listening is so important to you in every aspect of your life—social, school and work—you should be eager to begin the listening improvement program suggested in the next unit.

COMMUNICATION LABORATORY

APPLICATION EXERCISES

A. Choose a business position that you would someday like to hold. In a paragraph, describe some of the listening activities that you would have to engage in when carrying out the duties of the position.

B. How much time do you spend listening during a typical day in school? Take a guess at the total time in hours and minutes. Then keep an hour-by-hour log of the listening activities that you engage in during one school day. Total the time spent. Then compare the actual time with your original estimate. Compare your log of one day of school listening with the logs of your classmates.

C. Play a game of introductions. Divide the class into groups of five or six. Prepare a card for each person in each group. On each card will be a person's name and business title. Each person is to assume the name and title on the card and to introduce himself or herself to the others in the group. After all introductions are made, how many members of your group can you introduce by name and title? Missing one name in a group of five or six is normal. If you missed more than one, you weren't listening.

D. Plan a 1-minute skit to enact in class with another student. In the skit, two friends are conversing. One is a poor listener who prefers to do all of the talking. The other person, although considerate, is obviously annoyed. Write a script for the skit and perform it as it is written. Then reenact the skit, showing both people as considerate and attentive conversationalists.

E. Prepare to enact for 2 minutes another kind of listening skit in class. Assume that you are a job applicant who is discussing a position with a personnel supervisor. As the supervisor describes the job's duties and requirements, you show obvious signs that you are a poor listener. Instead of listening to the supervisor, you are thinking about what you are going to say next. You interrupt. You fiddle with your hands. You look about the room.

The skit ends when the supervisor escorts you, the unsuccessful applicant, out of the office. After the skit has been performed, list specific listening techniques that you *should* have used during the interview. Then reenact the scene, practicing sound listening techniques during the job interview.

VOCABULARY AND SPELLING STUDIES

A. The following words appeared in this unit. Read through the unit, locate each word, and guess its meaning from the way in which it is used in its sentence. Check the meaning of the word in a dictionary. Then use each word in a sentence of your own.

1. device
2. functioning
3. interpret
4. quizzical
5. disastrous
6. dividends
7. attentively
8. relation
9. reinforce
10. indifferent
11. immune
12. aspect

B. In each of the following sentences, choose the word in parentheses that correctly expresses the meaning.

1. In the next (addition, edition), the publishers will make changes.
2. The slugger hit the ball into the upper (tier, tear) of seats.
3. (Immortal, Immoral) books should be in every library.
4. Mr. Haggerty could test anyone's (patients, patience).
5. All agreed that the supervisor had made a (judicial, judicious) decision.
6. When the hours were shortened, the (moral, morale) improved.
7. My boss (inferred, implied) that I could go to the conference.
8. The judge asked two (disinterested, uninterested) parties to decide the dispute.
9. A large (amount, number) of customers were awaiting their orders.
10. The company's decision will (affect, effect) all employees.

COMMUNICATING FOR RESULTS

Vocabulary Game. Sometimes it is better to know big words than to use them. Consider the following: "Individuals who inhabit dwellings made of translucent or transparent silicate materials should refrain from hurling concretions of earthy or mineral matter." This statement means that people who live in glass houses should not throw stones. The game of changing ordinary sayings into difficult-to-understand sayings by substituting complicated words for common words is fun and will improve your ability to recognize words. Use a dictionary to find difficult and uncommon synonyms for words in three popular sayings or proverbs. Try them out on your class. Discuss why you should know words that are not in your everyday speaking vocabulary.

U · N · I · T

54 Improving Your Listening Skills

Our ears are assaulted with sounds continually. We *hear* these sounds, but we don't *listen* to all of them. We can't; we would be overrun with sound if we did. In self-defense, we block off many sounds from our consciousness—we "tune out" unwanted sounds.

Blocking off sounds is a useful device, as it often aids concentration. But too often we also block off sounds to which we *should* be listening. Most of us have acquired bad habits of nonlistening, even when we are with our best friends, and these habits are very hard to break.

Fortunately, they can be unlearned and replaced by good listening habits. The first step in this process is to become *aware* of your deficiencies in listening and of your need for good listening habits. When you have made this awareness a habit, you will be well on your way to becoming a good listener.

How to Prepare for Listening

In order to prepare yourself for listening, you should follow these guidelines:

Determine Your Purpose. We have said that the chief difference between hearing and listening is that listening involves both the mind and the ears. Another way of expressing this difference is to say that *listening has a purpose*. This point is important because different purposes in listening imply different *kinds* of listening.

Your purpose in listening may be to act friendly and sociable, as would be the case in a party conversation; to obtain information, as in listening to a lecture; or to analyze critically, as in listening to a political debate.

Listening to a pep talk at a football rally is not the same as listening to a formal speech. Listening to a friend introduce you to someone is not the same as overhearing a conversation on a bus. In an introduction you would want to listen carefully for the person's name, as well as make note of any specific details that you can use as a basis for conversation. When listening to a speech, you would listen for main ideas and supporting facts. In a pep talk, you would listen for the general tone of the meeting, which you could easily anticipate, and the the overheard conversation you might want to tune out after a few minutes.

Listening in each situation calls for different skills and for different degrees of attentiveness. In each situation the demands are different because the purpose is different, so you must decide on your purpose for listening in every listening situation. You will be a better listener as a result of knowing *why* you are listening.

Get Ready to Listen. Good listening implies a *readiness* to listen. This means that you prepare yourself for listening—physically, mentally, and emotionally. Literally turn your back on distracting sights and sounds, if necessary, and always give yourself maximum opportunity for listening by sitting near enough to the speaker to see and hear easily. If possible, read about a topic in advance, because the more you know about a topic, the more interested you will be in what the speaker has to say about it. Mental preparation, because it invariably supplies you with a purpose for listening, automatically leads to emotional involvement. And this involvement, in turn, increases your readiness to listen.

Accept Your Share of Responsibility. Too often listeners approach speakers with an "I dare you to interest me" attitude. Such an attitude is tough on the speaker and is obviously discourteous. Remember that you, as a listener, share the responsibility for communicating with the speaker and therefore must be courteous to the speaker. By doing so you will notice that the quality of your listening can affect the speaker's talking—it may even control it!

The reason is simple: we all crave good listeners, and we react accordingly. For example, imagine for a moment that you are in the midst of telling an interesting story. One of your "listeners" is flipping the pages of a magazine; two others are whispering to each other; another is openly yawning. How would you react? Would you go on with your story? As you can see, then, an audience can influence the delivery, and even the length, of a speech.

| **How to Listen— Basic Rules** | **Listen With Understanding.** Be sure you understand the speaker's ideas fully and completely; don't jump to conclusions about a false or half-true idea. To understand the speaker's ideas, you might listen *carefully*. If necessary, ask questions to clarify anything that is vague. |

Listen With an Open Mind. Keep your mind open when you listen. Forget your biases and prejudices for the moment, and be ready to receive new ideas. Don't refuse to listen to new ideas just because they may *conflict with* those you believe. Hear the speaker out; don't tune in only what you want to hear. Of course, it is possible that your point of view may be changed somewhat as a result, but you should be courageous enough to take that chance. After all, the change may be for the better.

Listen Actively. Listening actively implies work on your part. Primarily, it means three things: concentrating, relating what you hear to what you already know, and reading between the lines.

To concentrate, you must be selective about the sounds you hear. Focus your attention on what a speaker is saying and disregard the noises coming from the street outside. Being an active process, concentration takes both willpower and energy.

Relating ideas and facts just heard to your existing store of knowledge means that change will take place. No change, no learning. And naturally, learning takes concentrated effort.

Reading between the lines—or sensing the implications of a speaker's message—is another rule of good listening. The good listener analyzes the speaker's word choice and observes closely the speaker's posture, facial expressions, tone of voice, manner, general appearance, and so on.

Listen With Empathy. Listening with empathy means putting yourself in the speaker's place—making an extra effort to understand the speaker's point of view. Naturally, such listening requires imagination. However, because it results in attentiveness that is very flattering to most speakers, listening with empathy serves to draw them out and to help eliminate any shyness, suspicion, or hostility they may have. Thus listening with empathy aids communication and usually results in many rewards for the listener.

How to Listen Critically

Critical listening is a special kind of listening—listening with a view toward analyzing and evaluating what speakers say and how they say it. It involves all the basic rules of listening, plus a few others: listening for main ideas and supporting details; reviewing points already made and anticipating what is coming next; and finally, analyzing the evidence and accepting or rejecting the speaker's conclusions on the basis of this evidence.

To listen critically may seem to be a large order in view of the fact that you are expected to listen intently at the same time. However, it's entirely possible and reasonable, and good listeners do so all the time. They use their *spare listening time* to reflect on the words they have just heard.

All of us have this spare listening time because we think at a much faster rate than the average speaker talks. The rate of speech for most Americans is around 125 words a minute, but we think at a rate four or five times that fast.

The half-listener or nonlistener generally uses this time to daydream or to turn his or her attention elsewhere. Although you do have spare listening time, using it to daydream will not work out well. The reason is that daydreamers usually find their attention focused more on distractions than on the words of the speaker. By missing certain portions of the speech, the listener becomes less interested in the topic and more interested in the distractions, making the speech harder and harder to follow. Finally, the listener gives up completely and tunes out the speaker.

Good listeners, on the other hand, use their spare listening time to engage in thought processes that are closely related to what the speaker says; in other words, they listen *actively*. Such active listening results in increased understanding and longer remembering. Following are some rules for using your spare listening time.

Note Major Points. A well-prepared speech usually consists of a few major points. Often a good speaker may indicate these points near the beginning of the talk.

Suppose the speaker says the following:

> There has been a major technological revolution in the past 15 years: a revolution in automated equipment and business practices that makes many traditional practices obsolete. Today, we shall deal with the effects of automation on the classroom in school. We shall discuss this technological upheaval as it relates to the preparation of young men and women to work in the automated world of work. As we discuss desirable changes in the preparation, let us consider three main topics. First, the power of automation in changing the way that work is performed. Second, the changing purposes for preparing people for work in automated business. And third, the changing classroom methods required to teach young people to learn.

Thus the speaker reveals an outline, and you grasp it by noting these three main points:

1. The changing methods of performing work
2. The changing purposes of education and training
3. The changing methods of teaching

Recognize Details. As soon as you grasp the speaker's major ideas, you should recognize that everything else that is said is, or *should be*, designed to support these main ideas. The details will help you to fill in the structure of the speech and lead you to a better understanding of the speech as a result. Details will also tell you a lot about the way a speaker thinks.

In the following portion of a speech, note that while the sidelights add color and interest to the main idea, they are not separate ideas in themselves; the main idea is comprised of only the italicized words.

> *One of the most important factors in locating a manufacturing facility these days is the availability of trained workers.* For example, Wellington in the northern part of the state would be a suitable site for our new computer manufacturing facility except for one thing. There is no ready supply of workers nearby. There is no university in the area which produces engineering and administrative personnel. There are no technical institutes or training schools. The high schools in the vicinity lack both comprehensive vocational training programs and developed business courses. While transportation facilities are adequate, taxes are low, land is inexpensive, and the climate is outstanding, it would be extraordinarily difficult to staff such a facility in Wellington. Our only choice would be to institute training programs, and those are always tremendously expensive.

In the above paragraph, note the words *for example*. Speakers often provide the listener with cues to indicate whether an idea is a new one or whether it merely adds support to an idea already presented.

Rephrase and Review. The effective listener works to retain the message of the speaker in two ways: by *rephrasing* silently the speaker's words and by *reviewing* the major points of the speech from time to time. Using both methods will reinforce your understanding of the speech and help you to remember the principal ideas.

The rephrasing process is similar to taking notes, except that you rephrase mentally: you concentrate on main ideas and summarize them as briefly as possible. Note in the following illustration how you can mentally rephrase a speaker's words:

WHAT THE SPEAKER IS SAYING	WHAT YOU ARE SAYING TO YOURSELF
The good salesperson tries to determine the customer's real needs and then caters to those needs. The successful salesperson always tries to figure out what the customer really wants. The customer is often unaware of his or her desires. The good salesperson brings these desires out into the open. For example, someone looking for an automobile might very well put price above all else, because we are all conditioned to be careful about money. But the skillful salesperson soon determines that the customer yearns for those additional options that add comfort to the vehicle. The customer says, "It would be sort of nice to have air conditioning, but I really don't think it is worth $600." Detecting what the customer really wants, the salesperson says, "You know, it really costs very little in the end, since it adds about $300 to the value of the car at trade-in time. So you are only paying about $300 for it. If you keep the car for three years, that's about $100 a year, or 28 cents a day." The salesperson isn't doing anything dishonest. He or she is merely helping the customer to get what the customer truly wants.	The good salesperson meets the customer's real needs. Once a customer lets it be known that he or she would really like something, the salesperson does everything possible to make it appealing. The good salesperson fulfills the customer's needs and desires.

Detect Bias and Determine Motives. A biased viewpoint is a partial, or prejudiced, viewpoint. In business, bias and preconceived opinions are natural because a company wants to sell its product or service; this desire then becomes its primary motive. But the critical listener must learn to recognize this bias and this motive.

For example, people who sell automobiles may focus all their attention on the favorable features of a particular make of car; it is natural to do so. But you, as a good listener, must recognize this bias and also the fact that what you hear from the seller may not be the whole truth. Automobile salespeople would be foolish to let you know all the weaknesses of their cars, since their motive is to sell them; nor would they rave about other cars.

The customary warning *caveat emptor,* which means "let the buyer beware," applies as well to listeners: let the listener beware of the words of biased or emotional speakers.

Take Notes. Note-taking should be used as an aid to remembering, not as a substitute for listening. When listeners spend too much time taking notes, they miss the heart of the message. Therefore, notes should be made with caution. Here are specific suggestions for note-taking:

1. Have plenty of notepaper, a good pen, and an extra pencil or two.
2. Use an uncluttered writing surface that provides backing for the paper.
3. Label your notes for easy identification later.
4. Listen for such speaker's cues as "first," "second," and "third"; "another important consideration"; "finally"; "the most significant thing"; "on the other hand"; "in summary"; as well as questions posed by the speaker, pauses, changes of emphasis in voice and gestures.
5. Flag important parts of your notes with brackets, underscores, arrows, or indentions.
6. Listen for special instructions.
7. Go over your notes promptly after the speech to fix the major points more firmly in your mind.

Practice, Practice, Practice. Efficient listening, like other communication skills, requires practice. To become a good listener, take every opportunity to put the techniques presented in this unit into practice. In other words—practice, practice, practice!

COMMUNICATION LABORATORY

APPLICATION EXERCISES

A. On a separate sheet of paper answer each of the numbered questions on page 530 by writing *yes, sometimes,* or *no.* The questions are designed to help you evaluate your own listening habits.

1. When your teacher or others are speaking, do you pay close and considerate attention to what they say?
2. Before a class on a given topic, do you read and think about the topic before the class meets?
3. When you enter an auditorium to listen to a speech, do you deliberately seat yourself where you can easily see and hear the speaker?
4. When listening, do you carefully watch the speaker's facial expressions?
5. When in class, do you alertly listen to and accurately follow all the instructions and directions of the teacher?
6. When you receive instructions or directions that must be carefully followed, do you write them on a piece of paper?
7. When another person is introduced to you, do you mentally practice saying and spelling the name to fix it in your memory?
8. Do you take notes during all class presentations and discussions?
9. As soon as possible after an introduction, do you use the new name when speaking to the person just met to help fix it in your memory?
10. When listening in class, do you mentally rephrase in your own words what you have heard?
11. Do you suspect that you have a hearing or vision problem that a physician should check?
12. When you do not understand what a teacher or another student has said in class, do you ask questions to make the message clear?
13. When speaking on the telephone, do you try to picture the other person's facial expressions in order to more fully participate in the conversation?
14. Do you deliberately make a mental note of oral messages you need to remember?
15. In listening to a speech or lecture, do you mentally repeat to yourself important points that the speaker makes?

B. Using your answers to the questions in the previous exercise, prepare a 200-word written analysis of your listening skills. Your analysis should focus on the following points: (1) your listening weaknesses and (2) what you can do to improve your listening.

C. Using the suggestions for taking notes (page 529), evaluate your own note-taking skills. In what specific ways can you improve your skills?

D. Assume that instead of reading this unit on how to improve your listening skills, you had listened to a lecture on the topic. The major points and discussion were identical to those in your textbook. Describe to the class one or more of the details you would have heard about one of the major points discussed.

E. Be prepared to report to the class on the *major ideas* you would have learned had you listened to a lecture based on this unit.

F. Write a 30-second radio or television commercial for a product or service. Present the commercial orally in class. Then lead a discussion of the commercial that analyzes the motives and biases of its sponsor.

G. Join with the other members of your class in developing a list of rules and sound practices that will promote good classroom listening.

VOCABULARY AND SPELLING STUDIES

A. Match each verb in the left-hand column with its correct synonym in the right-hand column. Use a dictionary to find the meanings of words you do not know.

1. *condone* a bad practice	**a.** postpone
2. *scrutinize* an expense report	**b.** shorten
3. *curtail* a meeting	**c.** implant
4. *revoke* a license	**d.** waste
5. *impede* progress	**e.** cancel
6. *defer* benefits	**f.** hinder
7. *dilute* earnings	**g.** allow
8. *instill* confidence	**h.** abandon
9. *repudiate* a decision	**i.** inspect
10. *squander* funds	**j.** weaken

B. Use each of the following nouns in the sentence that it best completes: *discretion, involvement, motive, bias, empathy, retention.*

1. The firm was criticized for its active _____ in a political campaign.
2. My supervisor has a _____ for people who work hard.
3. The _____ of workers allows a company to avoid expensive training programs.
4. I had great _____ for the suffering heroine in that film.
5. The judge questioned the suspect's _____ for requesting a postponement.
6. At the manager's _____, the staff might be dismissed early if a storm threatens.

COMMUNICATING FOR RESULTS

Listening. Your teacher will read a short passage. Listen carefully and try to absorb every important detail. Be prepared to give an accurate oral summary of the passage.

Your speaking skills are always being put to use. At home, at school, at social activities, at work, *what* you say and *how* you say it are equally important. You want to be sure to communicate verbally in such a way that your receiver understands your messages without the benefit of a written record.

It is easy to see how effective speaking skills influence business situations. Given a situation that requires speaking skills, your mastery of the units in this chapter will enable you to do the following:

1. *Address an audience confidently.*

2. *Participate both as a speaker and as a member of the audience.*

3. *Learn to use the telephone efficiently.*

4. *Plan and manage successful meetings.*

U · N · I · T

55

Qualities of Effective Speaking

Although you make some use of all the means of communicating, you spend most of your time communicating with your voice. In school you ask and answer questions, contribute to discussions, participate in debates, and give oral reports. Those who are successful in extracurricular activities often depend upon their ability to express ideas orally. In your relationships with friends and family, social conversation plays an important role as you talk about the events of the day and your plans for the future. Whether you work in an office, a store, or a gasoline station, you certainly spend much time in talking—giving instructions or explanations, asking questions or answering them, promoting good business relations, selling ideas, or selling your personal qualities.

Since most of us talk much more than we write, we are judged more by our speech than by our writing. Speech is an important part of your personality—it is individually and particularly yours. To many people, your speech is *you*. The words you use, the way you put them together, the sound of your voice (tone, pitch, volume, and rate), and your enunciation and pronunciation all add up to the *you* that others hear. You can't separate your voice from your personality; they contribute to each other in many ways. On the telephone, for example, your voice represents your entire personality. Therefore, you should be as concerned about speech improvement as you are about personality improvement.

Creating a Favorable Impression: Dress, Posture, Expression, Manners, and Mannerisms

Effective speech, whether in a formal or an informal situation, depends upon factors other than the words spoken. The setting, or atmosphere, in which words are used often determines how they are received by the listener. Just as a successful play or motion picture must have the proper setting, musical background, and costumes, so must successful speaking have the appropriate atmosphere. Therefore, before learning the elements of effective speaking, you need to learn how to create a favorable impression that will set the stage for the best reception of what you say.

534

An impression is the sum total of many factors. Each of these factors needs to be studied and mastered. After these factors are learned, they must be practiced. Among the elements that help a speaker make a favorable first impression are the following:

1. Attractive dress and good grooming
2. Good posture and carriage
3. Pleasant facial expressions
4. Good manners
5. Lack of distracting mannerisms

Attractive Dress and Good Grooming. It is impossible to prescribe a set of dress standards that will apply to every business situation today. In recent years standards of acceptable dress and grooming have changed quite drastically. Indeed, by the time you read these words, they may no longer apply. Therefore, the best advice one can give is to suggest that you first determine who will be the judge of your dress and grooming in a particular situation and how important this judgment is to you. If it is important to you, then determine what is acceptable in terms of dress and grooming to that individual or group and dress accordingly.

Although business dress standards tend to be somewhat conservative, many offices have relaxed these standards and permit employees to follow some of the current fads. However, extremes in clothing, hairstyles, or makeup are not likely to be acceptable to those businesses that wish to convey a feeling of conservatism to their customers. To determine what will be acceptable, you should observe other employees in your company and read employee manuals that describe dress and grooming codes.

Regardless of what dress standards are followed, two aspects of grooming that are always important are cleanliness and neatness. Your overall appearance makes a strong impression. If you are well-groomed and neatly dressed, your appearance will inspire a basic confidence in your work habits.

Both men and women in business should wear clothing that is becoming to their physical size and age. Accessories should harmonize with the rest of your outfit. You want to be attractive but not showy. Above all, you want to convey a certain amount of maturity and good judgment—and one way to do so is to show that you know how to dress for business, for work.

Lack of cleanliness is offensive to most people. Therefore, skin, teeth, hair, breath, fingernails, and hands should be checked frequently to see that they are as clean as possible. Clothing that is clean and pressed will help you to make a better impression too. Furthermore, your clothing should fit well and be in good repair. If your shoes have heels that are run down and you are wearing clothing that has holes or is torn, you will attract attention—but it will be unfavorable attention. Instead, your goal should be to do everything possible in terms of dress and grooming to create the best impression of yourself in the minds of those with whom you come in contact.

Good Posture and Carriage. The positive effect you wish to create by wearing carefully chosen clothing and practicing good grooming can be completely destroyed if you do not sit, stand, and walk correctly. The fit and the hang of an article of clothing are best when posture and carriage are good. Therefore, if you take pride in your appearance, you should analyze your sitting, standing, and walking habits and make any necessary improvements.

Your Posture Tells. The main reason for studying correct posture and carriage, however, is that the way you carry yourself seems to reveal traits of personality and character. Do you sprawl when you sit? Then you are lazy. When you stand, do you always rest all your weight on one leg and hip? Then you tire or lose interest quickly and have no drive. When you walk, do you shuffle along with your head down? If so, you must be the kind of person who does not work well with others, and you very definitely show that you have no force of character.

"Not so," you say? Well, perhaps the tales told by your posture and carriage are false. For instance, although you do have the habit of lolling in a chair, you are not lazy. But such is the impression you give, and erasing the impression of laziness will be very difficult. Accordingly, you need to study the following discussion of good posture and carriage so that you will be able to make an impression that is favorable—and true!

When you get ready to sit, bend your joints and sit. Do not fall into a chair as a rag doll would. Once in the chair, sit up straight—not rigidly, but not slumped either. For correct sitting posture, the best practice is to be sure that the end of your spine touches the back of the chair. A little practice in taking a seat and in sitting correctly will pay dividends. And if you like to sit with your legs crossed, make sure that you do not look awkward.

Stand Tall, but Not Stiff. People who stand correctly stand tall. Their shoulders are in line with the rest of their body—not far back, not caved in toward the chest. They hold themselves erect, but not stiff. They have formed the habit of standing with their weight distributed evenly on both feet to avoid having to shift position continually. Standing tall will make you look self-confident and will give others a good impression of you.

There are as many variations in the manner of walking as there are people. You will find that it is impossible to change completely your own distinctive style of walking. You can, however, learn just one thing that will help. With steps neither too long nor too short, neither too fast nor too slow, walk as though you have somewhere to go and you intend to get there without stopping at way stations! Walking purposefully, you will give an impression of being ambitious, industrious, and self-directing.

Pleasant Facial Expressions. Part of the education of an aspiring young actor or actress consists of practicing the different facial expressions that reflect various emotions—joy, fear, pleasure, sorrow, and so on. If, through intelligent practice, actors can change their facial expressions, you, too, can change yours if you so desire. First, of course, you need to know what kind of expression creates a favorable impression. You need some pointers on how to assume such an expression. You need, too, to know where your own short-comings are. And you need to practice before a mirror.

Look Interested. A pleasant, interested, alive-looking expression is a winning expression. Even a hasty glance at an expression like this would generate a feeling of warmth, of liking. In an interview, a meeting, a conference, or any other working situation, pleasant facial expressions promote pleasant relationships. Fortunate indeed are those of you who naturally and habitually have this type of facial expression. You are the extroverts, the ones who are interested in and enjoy other people; and you let your interest and enjoyment shine through. However, you represent a very small minority of our population.

Too many persons tell a story of indifference, boredom, or discontent with their expressions. Possibly they tell nothing at all. Some very intelligent people are afflicted with shyness, which they try to hide behind a "deadpan" or a bored facial expression. These are the ones who will profit by a study of the following discussion.

The eyes are the focal point of facial expression, as you can prove by doing this: stand in front of a mirror and think of something very pleasant that has happened to you recently. See how your eyes light up your whole face? Now pretend that your are shopping for a car and a dealer is showing you some interesting models. If you are good at make-believe, your eyes will reflect your intense interest. With practice, you will find that it is not necessary to smile or grin in order to look pleasant but that it *is* necessary to *feel* pleasant. However, if you have a warm, attractive smile, use it whenever you can.

Really Look at People. Suppose that you are shy and that you do not look at those who are talking to you. Since they cannot see your eyes, they are unable to form a favorable opinion of your personality and disposition, and you run the risk of being judged as undesirable. For instance, there are interviewers who will not hire an applicant who looks everywhere but at the interviewer. They think that this habit indicates that the applicant is shy and shifty. So after you have worked to acquire a facial expression that will contribute to your advancement, be sure to look at people. Otherwise, your efforts will have been wasted.

Learning to look pleasant, interested, and alert is purely an individual problem. Only you can study your own expression, and only you can put in the practice time necessary to achieve the results you wish. You are the one who must consciously assume the facial expression that produces a favorable impression. It is you who must remember to look at people when you talk to them. The rewards, also, are yours alone. One of the rewards is that in a relatively short time, your improved facial expression will become your habitual expression.

Good Manners. Another very important factor in creating a favorable impression is showing good manners. The atmosphere of polish created by those who do and say the correct thing at the correct time earns the respect and admiration of all. These models of good taste and breeding, however, did not reach the state of being natural without learning and practicing and without brushing up from time to time. Your own manners may be excellent, but even you may need to study the following discussion and the suggestions given.

The Basis Is Courtesy. The basis of good manners is courtesy, and the basis of courtesy is consideration for others. Without courtesy, good manners are only a false front.

However, natural courtesy, while basic, is not enough for correct behavior. Do not minimize the importance of knowing and observing the rules of etiquette. You must know such things as how to make and acknowledge introductions properly. You should, in short, be familiar with all the rules that govern correct social and business relationships. This means that you need to know and to review periodically the contents of an etiquette book. There are some slight differences between social and office etiquette, and these you can learn by studying a book on office etiquette.

Introductions. There are many aspects of social correctness, but only two that are frequently important in business usage will be discussed—introductions and handshaking. Although numerous rules apply to making introductions, they may all be simplified by determining quickly which of the two or more people being introduced you wish to honor or which has the more important position. Then say that person's name *first*. By so doing, you will find your introduction procedures automatically correct. For instance, if you were introducing anybody at all to your mother, you would say, "Mother, may I present . . . ," "Mother, I'd like you to know . . . ," or "Mother, this is . . . ." If you wished to introduce your boss, Mr. Martin, and a young man who is with you, you would say, "Mr. Martin, this is . . . ." You might call this a Quick Trick that will prevent those first embarrassing moments of silence that occur while you are trying to remember the various methods of presentation.

The second suggestion is that you learn to shake hands in a manner that will give an impression of decision and determination, of having a mind of your own. Clasp hands firmly, and shake hands once, without overdoing the up-and-down motion. *Firmly* does not mean "bone crushing." You should use just enough hand pressure to show some strength. Your handclasp may be more important to you than you realize. You may be shaking hands with one of those people who believe strongly that a handclasp tells all about character and ability. If this act tells a story, let that tale be favorable to you.

Lack of Distracting Mannerisms. The person who sits at the desk next to yours may be first-rate in grooming, posture, manners, and pleasant facial expressions. But what about that annoying habit of knuckle cracking? And what about the person who comes to tell you something, stands behind you, and breathes down your neck? or chews gum? And so on. Often, ambitious young people may work very hard to improve themselves but are still defeated because they have overlooked some mannerism that will annoy others.

Logically, then, as a finishing touch to your study on creating a favorable impression, study your own mannerisms. To appear favorably to others, you must let nothing detract from the impression you have worked so hard to produce. You will find it quite difficult to study yourself because you may not realize that you have distracting or annoying habits. For best results, first study the people around you. Watch to see if they have any behavior quirks. Whenever you observe a mannerism that you think is objectionable, say to yourself, "Do I do that?" After you have had practice in looking for these faults in others, you will be more likely to see your own faults.

Studying your own personal mannerisms and eliminating any that are undesirable are necessary tasks if you wish to protect your position. There is little profit in presenting a fine appearance and in being polite and well mannered if you consistently do something that annoys your colleagues

Factors of Voice Quality

How you say something can be as important as what you say and how you look while saying it. Your voice qualities play a very important role in determining how your words affect the listener. For example, your voice can soothe people or make them angry, thus helping or hindering a situation. The first time people hear you, they are likely to classify you as cheerful or solemn, interesting or dull, lively or lazy.

Since most people in business communicate more frequently by speaking than by writing, voice quality can work for or against you and your company. For example, what is the effect on public relations of a switchboard operator with a voice quality that is irritatingly loud? of a receptionist whose voice is so low that visitors cannot hear half of what has been said? of a salesperson who speaks so slowly that the listener becomes exasperated?

Voice quality is determined by four principal factors: volume, pitch, tone, and tempo. The effectiveness of your voice depends also upon enunciation and pronunciation, as well as upon breath control.

In order to improve your voice, you must be able to control your breathing. Breath control depends both on correct posture and on deep breathing. Good posture enables a person to breathe into the lungs the maximum amount of air and also to control the amount of air expended. Deep breathing adds to the resonance of your tones because you have more air with which to vibrate the vocal chords. Be sure to breathe from the diaphragm, the muscle partition that separates the chest from the abdominal cavity.

Volume. Intensity, force, and volume are all similar words that describe the quality in your voice that enables people to hear you. Speakers must be heard, or they will lose their audience. Since good breath control is so important in providing volume, you should practice correct breathing so that you will not have trouble being heard.

Pitch. Pitch refers to the degree of highness or lowness of a sound. A shrill voice is much too high. A moderately low voice is usually the most pleasing. If your voice is unpleasantly high, you can lower it by making a conscious effort to do so over a long period of time.

If possible, record your voice on a tape recorder and listen to it several times. Try to hear your voice as others hear it, and ask your friends or classmates to criticize it. Practice lowering your voice and then record the same material a second time to see if there has been any improvement.

Tone. It is your tone that reveals your attitudes and feelings to your listeners. In business relations, as well as in social life, try to use a pleasant and cheerful tone whenever possible. However, variations in tone, as well as in volume and pitch, will add interest to your speech. Think about what you are saying when you are talking or reading orally; then adapting your tone to your meaning will not be difficult.

Tempo. The rate of speed at which you talk is the tempo of your voice. Since your tempo often determines whether your speech is understandable, you should speak at an appropriate rate of speed. Use pauses to stress major points, for they add variety to a speech and also give emphasis to the points you want the listener to remember. By speaking important words slowly and less important words or phrases more rapidly, you contribute to both variety and clarity in your speaking.

Saying Words Correctly and Distinctly

A person applying for a position may be carefully groomed and may give the outward appearance of being a promising employee. But faulty pronunciation and poor enunciation may cost the applicant the position, particularly if the job calls for frequent oral communication with the public, either in person or over the telephone.

Pronunciation means saying words *correctly*, while enunciation means saying words *distinctly*. Both are necessary if you are to be understood and wish to make a good impression on others.

To some of us, English is a second language, for we were raised in an area where some other language was spoken primarily. Some of us were brought up in parts of the United States where the language pattern is different from that where we are now living. We should not be ashamed if we speak with an accent. An accent may add character to one's speech and make the voice more colorful and interesting to the listener. Remember that the principal purpose of communication—in whatever form—is to be understood by the person or persons with whom you are communicating. As long as the listener understands you, you are achieving this goal.

Even those brought up in an English-speaking environment make mistakes in enunciation and pronunciation, usually because of carelessness. So regardless of background, everyone needs to make every effort to improve the speaking voice, particularly in the enunciation and pronunciation of words.

Enunciation

Listen to yourself. Do you run words together, leaving out some sounds? Do you say "dijago" for *did you go?* "meetcha" for *meet you?* "gawna" *for going to?* Poor enunciation results from running words together, from leaving out letters or syllables, or from adding letters or syllables. Let us look first at a group of useful and common words that are sadly mistreated when letters or even whole syllables are dropped.

Lost Consonants. The final consonants most often dropped are *t, d,* and *g* when they are in combination with some other consonant. Thus *fact* becomes "fac," *yield* becomes "yiel," and *going* becomes "goin." The *wh* sound, too, frequently is carelessly pronounced; for example, "wat" for *what.* Practice saying the following phrases aloud until you are sure you do not slight the sounds of the underlined consonants.

recognized candid	the second of February
tourist list	three hundred thirty-three
factual arrangement	through thick and thin
current account	lingering and longing
collect payment	being a typist
competent party	test of strength
demand payment	assistant management
trust fund	seemingly strict
next payment	bonded debt outstanding
kept a strict accounting	judgment for the tenant
arranging pictures	attempted bankruptcy
earned discount	outstanding print
consigning the prints	whistle while thinking
width and length	why white wheels

Lost Vowels. When two vowels occur together in a word, the sound of one often tends to be slighted. Thus *li-on* becomes an indistinct "line." A single vowel used as a syllable is frequently overlooked and not sounded. A careless person will say "captal," completely ignoring the single-vowel syllable *i.* Pronounce the word correctly: "cap-i-tal." In the list below, be sure to notice each vowel, and be sure you do not lose any vowel sounds when you practice these phrases:

metropolitan area	especially positive
federal cabinet	terrible sophomore
ridiculous accident	indirect but definite
municipal regulation	generally separate

cru<u>e</u>l li<u>o</u>n   var<u>i</u>able reg<u>u</u>lation
exc<u>e</u>llent fam<u>i</u>ly   fam<u>i</u>ly hist<u>o</u>ry
acc<u>u</u>rate and reg<u>u</u>lar   us<u>u</u>ally int<u>e</u>resting
alph<u>a</u>betical list of li<u>a</u>bilities   pop<u>u</u>lar batt<u>e</u>ry
<u>e</u>leven man<u>u</u>facturers   sep<u>a</u>rate po<u>e</u>m
var<u>i</u>able cap<u>i</u>tal   or<u>i</u>ginal comp<u>a</u>ny
temp<u>o</u>rarily sep<u>a</u>rated   ind<u>i</u>rectly responsible
iv<u>o</u>ry t<u>o</u>w<u>e</u>r   pos<u>i</u>tive ver<u>i</u>fication
vet<u>e</u>ran gen<u>e</u>ral   partic<u>u</u>larly qui<u>e</u>t

Lost Syllables. People who drop consonant and vowel sounds often drop syllables from words too. Such a person "c'lecs stamps" instead of "col-le<u>c</u>ts." It is as though the speaker wished to make a contraction (shortened form like *it's*) out of every word spoken. Try to avoid losing syllables as you practice saying these phrases:

perhaps (not *praps*)   five-year *guarantee* (not *garntee*)
little people (not *lil*)   detailed *itinerary* (not *itinree*)
laboratory technician (not *labatory*) *generally* acceptable (not *genrally*)
just *obligation* (not *obgation*)   *occasionally* wrong (not *occasionly*)

Addition of Letters or Syllables. The frequent mistake of adding extra sounds is another enunciation fault. As you say aloud the following italicized words, listen carefully to see if you ordinarily add extra incorrect sounds to them.

a fine *athlete* (not *ath<u>a</u>lete*)   pop *singer* (not *sing-g<u>e</u>r*)
the *height* of fashion (not *heigh<u>th</u>*) fourth *finger* (not *fing-g<u>e</u>r*)
across the street (not *acros<u>t</u>*)   *disastrous* results (not *disast<u>e</u>rous*)
broken *umbrella* (not *umb<u>e</u>rella*)   *entrance* examination (not *ent<u>e</u>rance*)
one roll of *film* (not *fil<u>u</u>m*)   a *hindrance* to progress (not *hind<u>e</u>rance*)
drowned duck (not *drown<u>d</u>ed*)   a *mischievous* child (not *mischiev<u>i</u>ous*)
grievous fault (not *griev<u>i</u>ous*)   a good *preventive* (not *prevent<u>a</u>tive*)
rhythm for dancing (not *rhyth<u>u</u>m*)   a *burglar* alarm (not *burg<u>u</u>lar*)

One remedy for these types of enunciation errors is giving attention to spelling. If you spell these words correctly, you will be more likely to pronounce them correctly and enunciate them distinctly. If you misspell them, you may also mispronounce them.

Some Troublemakers. Some words are more difficult to enunciate than others. They require an even slower rate of speech, to allow maximum use of jaw, lips, and tongue. You will be surprised to know that most of these words are short three- to five-letter words. They usually include one or more sounds that are difficult to distinguish. Thus, *ache* requires both the long *a* sound and a definite hard *k* sound.

Most of your practice so far has been with phrases and sentences. Now practice pronouncing the following words out of context so that each one of them is clear.

ache	corn	fine	kit	nap	peat	tang
at	darn	gas	kite	nick	race	tent
balk	earn	grow	lay	oils	scab	very
big	else	heed	map	our	sign	wag
climb	fill	jam	nab	path	tan	wield

Pronunciation

All of us learned to talk by imitating the speech of those around us: first, of members of the family; then, of neighbors and friends; later, of schoolmates, teachers, co-workers, and others with whom we came in contact. Of course, many of us have moved from one part of the country to another and have changed our original pronunciation and other speech habits to conform to those characteristic of the region in which we now live. Thus our present speech patterns reflect the wide variety of social, cultural, regional, and other influences to which we have been exposed.

Variations in Pronunciation. Who decides whether a particular pronunciation is correct? Your answer most likely will be "the dictionary." However, this answer is only partially correct.

As indicated in the preface or explanatory notes of the dictionary, it is impractical and unnecessary for a dictionary to show all the pronunciations that are in use for a particular word. Most dictionaries show only the one or two pronunciations that occur with the greatest frequency among educated speakers. Since all of us can understand those pronunciations and agree that they are not incorrect, even though many of them may not be the pronunciations that we ourselves use, all of us tend to view them as the standard, or correct, pronunciations.

Pronunciation Difficulties

In addition to regional and other differences in speech, certain types of incorrect pronunciations are quite common. They may be grouped according to the following categories.

Incorrect Vowel Sounds. Many words are not pronounced correctly because certain vowels are sounded wrong.

The Sound of Long U. The use of the $\overline{oo}$ sound instead of the correct long *u* sound (heard in *human*) is a common error. It makes a decidedly unpleasant impression on listeners who are speech-conscious.

Read the following words aloud, concentrating on using the long *u* sound.

annuity	latitude	New York
culinary	multitude	numerous
due	neuralgia	revenue
duke	neuritis	student
duty	neurotic	substitution
institution	new	tube

Troubles With A. In another group of words, the sound of long *a* (the sound in *hate*) is incorrectly replaced by the sound of short *a* (the sound in *hat*).

The following words are typical of this group. Again, read the list aloud.

āviator	gāla	stātus
blātant	ignorāmus	tenācious
dāta	lātent	ultimātum
flāgrant	rādiator	verbātim

In the following words, the short *a* should be used instead of the long *a*.

Ărab	păgeant	păgination
deprăvity	măltreat	Spokăne

Troubles With I. In some words, the sound of long *i*, as heard in *wide*, is incorrectly replaced by the short *i* sound head in *hit*.

alumnī   grīmy   stīpend

On the other hand, in the following words, the short *i* rather than the long *i* should be used.

Ĭtalian   respĭte

Substituting One Vowel for Another. In another type of mispronunciation, an entirely different vowel is substituted for the correct one. In the following words, the underscored letters are often replaced. Read the list aloud, clearly enunciating the underlined letters. If in doubt about any pronunciation, consult your dictionary. The mispronunciations involved here are often closely linked with misspellings.

accurate	just	preparation
description	mathematics	privilege
despair	optimistic	restaurant
divide	particular	sacrilegious
escalator	percolator	separate
existence	permanent	

Incorrect Accent. Many pronunciation errors are caused by placing the stress, or accent, on the wrong syllable of a word.

In the following words, the accent should be on the *first* syllable.

'ad-mirable	'dic-tionary	'in-teresting
'am-icable	'for-midable	'pref-erable
'ap-plicable	'in-famous	'the-ater
'com-parable		

In these words, the accent should be on the *second* syllable.

con-'do-lence	ir-'rev-ocable	om-'nip-otence
de-'mon-strative	ob-'lig-atory	su-'per-fluous
ex-'traor-dinary		

In these words the accent should be on the *final* syllable.

automo-'bile   di-'rect   rou-'tine (*n.*)
bou-'quet   po-'lice

Silent Letters. Among the chief stumbling blocks to correct spelling are silent letters, which occur in many of our most frequently used words. Because we do not hear these letters, they do not constitute a serious threat to correct pronunciation. However, there are a few important words in which letters that should be silent are often sounded. As you read aloud the following words, make a special effort *not* to sound the letters that are underscored.

a_l_mond	mor_t_gage	sa_l_mon	ve_h_ement
corp_s_	of_t_en	sa_l_ve	ve_h_icle
indi_c_t	post_h_umous	s_w_ord	

Just Plain Tricky. Many words often mispronounced cannot be classified under any of the above listings. There is only one way of mastering the correct pronunciations of these offenders. Concentrate on each one, first looking up the word in your dictionary and then repeating the word many times. Here are sample words of this type.

absorb	deaf	once
absurd	denunciate	partner
apron	err	peremptory
associate	gist	perhaps
association	homogenous	perspiration
attorney	hundred	possess
bona fide	library	prerogative
clothes	luxurious	quay
censure	luxury	reservoir
codicil	martial	soot
column	medieval	strength
congratulations	mercantile	suppose
coupon	Nebraska	tremendous

Some Tips to Help You

These miscellaneous suggestions will help you in your battle against mispronunciation and poor enunciation.

1. Be especially careful in pronouncing personal names. People resent having their names mispronounced just as they resent having them misspelled. Make an effort to learn the correct pronunciation of a person's name and to follow that preference.
2. Likewise, be careful in pronouncing geographic names. Often, the spelling is no guide to pronunciation. If you are uncertain, check the gazetteer

in your dictionary. Following are a few geographic names that bear watching. You may be surprised when you verify their pronunciations.

Abilene	Edinburgh	Lima (Peru)	Southampton
Worcester	Haverhill	Marseilles	Valparaiso
Cannes	Houston	Norfolk	Versailles
Cherbourg	Illinois	Salina	Ypsilanti

3. Be especially careful with foreign words and phrases. Some very amusing (and embarrassing) mistakes can be made by pronouncing them, especially French words, as they are spelled. The dictionary gives the closest approximation possible to the English sounds.

4. Guard against running words together, making such sounds as "wotcha doon?" (what are you doing?), "shoulda" (should have), "willyuh?" (will you?), or "jeet?" (did you eat?). Nothing more quickly brands a person as careless, if not illiterate, as does slovenly enunciation.

5. When you learn a new word, learn its correct pronunciation at once. In other words, when you look up the spelling and meaning of a word, notice also its pronunciation and practice saying it correctly.

6. When you speak to a group of people, speak more slowly than you do in ordinary conversation and enunciate carefully.

If you faithfully carry out the suggestions outlined in this unit, you will soon find that your improved speaking qualities will improve your relations with people.

COMMUNICATION LABORATORY

APPLICATION EXERCISES

A. Ask yourself the following questions to determine how you set your stage for speaking. Answer each question with *usually, sometimes,* or *rarely.* Compare your answers with other members of the class to see whether they agree with you. Then make a list of the items needing improvement.

My Personality

1. Do I like to be with other people and make the first move to gain other acquaintances?
2. Do I look for ways to say complimentary things about people to them and others?
3. Am I understanding of the ways other people act or think, and do I avoid direct criticism and argument?
4. Am I positive and optimistic instead of gloomy and pessimistic when presented with a new problem or situation?
5. Do other people like to be in my company because I am likable and congenial?

First Impressions

1. Do I try to find ways of being helpful to other people and sympathetic to their problems?
2. Do I steer clear of controversial topics when I enter into a conversation with a new acquaintance?
3. Do I consciously think about other people's interests and their comforts when I converse with them?
4. Do I take the first step to meet, greet, and introduce strangers?
5. Do I avoid talking about personal problems, strong personal likes or dislikes, rumors, and personal prejudices when I first meet someone?

My Personal Appearance

1. Do I know what appropriate dress is?
2. Am I careful about cleanliness and good grooming?
3. Do I usually feel well dressed?
4. Are my clothes clean, pressed, and in good repair?
5. Do my personal health habits contribute to my appearance?

My Facial Expressions

1. Do I avoid showing indifference or nervousness toward others in my facial expressions?
2. Do I refrain from allowing my facial expression to reflect my personal problems or sad feelings?
3. When I first meet people, does my facial expression reveal genuine interest?
4. Do my facial expressions reveal the way I want to be understood?
5. Am I willing to allow my facial expression to reflect how I think instead of remaining deadpan and noncommittal?

My Mannerisms

1. Does the way I move about suggest alertness rather than lack of interest?
2. Is my posture straight without being stiff?
3. When I walk, is my weight well distributed on both legs?
4. Do I control meaningless gestures when I talk?
5. Do my movements suggest control rather than uncertainty, fright, and nervousness?

B. Ask some people you know who work in business offices to explain the dress and grooming rules that are observed there. Develop a list of these practices and be ready to contribute your findings in a class discussion of dress and grooming customs in offices in your city.

C. In pantomime, express before the class some mannerisms (walking, hand movements, facial expressions) that would distract and limit communication. Then express the opposite positive characteristics. Was the class able to identify the points you were trying to make?

D. Francis Larkin, your employer, calls you on a Friday morning for a list of people who have called the office since he left on a business trip last Monday. As you read the following names and telephone numbers, remember to make maximum use of your jaw, lips, and tongue in pronouncing each name. You may want to spell difficult names. For example: "Choctaw Trading Company (Choctaw—C-h-o-c-t-a-w) of Richmond, Indiana. Mr. Samuel Bodine (B-o-d-i-n-e), the sales manager, would like you to call him at (317) 555-4193."

Company and City	Person Calling	Telephone Number
Gurston Supply Co. Haverhill, Massachusetts	Pamela Sage	(617) 555-7213
Clauswitz and Byron Elko, Nevada	Sandra Byron, partner	(702) 555-6400
McElkiney Corp. Severna Park, Maryland	Joseph Wilton	(301) 555-7815
Marketing Assistance Co. Oswego, New York	Barton Brandt	(315) 555-2777
Excello Corporation Olympia, Washington	Judson Sims	(206) 555-3004

E. In the shipping department, you are reading the quantities and stock numbers of an order as the shipping clerks checks the merchandise to be delivered to customers. Work with a partner. One of you reads from the packing slips, and the other checks the merchandise. Be sure to speak clearly. Be sure that the packing slips agree with the merchandise that is ready to be shipped. Make a note of any errors in numbers or quantities of merchandise as you read the following information.

From the Packing Slips		Merchandise Ready for Shipping	
Quantity	*Stock Numbers*	*Quantity*	*Stock Numbers*
6 cartons	73X1177	70 yards	91X3613
70 yards	91X3614	25 feet	11XR9197
12 dozen	73X6621	12 each	1SX6216Y
25 feet	11XXR9197	12 dozen	73X6621
10 each	1SX6215Y	6 cartons	73X1177

F. Each of the following words means one thing when accented on the first syllable and something else when accented on the final syllable. Write definitions for the words in each pair and then indicate the part of speech of each word.

1. contract   4. digest   7. project
2. combine   5. absent   8. progress
3. contest   6. object   9. extract

VOCABULARY AND SPELLING STUDIES

A. These words are often confused: *later, latter; biannual, biennial; lesson, lessen; incite, insight.* Explain the differences.

B. Which of the following place names are misspelled?

1. Chatanoga, Tennessee   4. Debuke, Iowa
2. Cincinati, Ohio   5. Lubock, Texas
3. Ashville, North Carolina   6. Poughkeepsie, New York

C. What letter should appear in the blank space in each of these words?

1. pers__ade   3. fradul__nt   5. fa__ilitate
2. perform__nce   4. ex__rbitant   6. ex__aust

D. The following words are spelled incorrectly; a letter or syllable has been added or dropped. Spell each word correctly:

1. paralel   4. probly   7. brillant
2. suprise   5. strenth   8. temperture
3. canidate   6. surender   9. labratory

E. Match the definitions in the left-hand column with the foreign words and phrases in the right-hand column. Then look up the pronunciation of each of the foreign words or phrases.

1. cognoscenti   a. the common people
2. a priori   b. an actress who plays a naive young girl
3. ennui   c. the best possible
4. ne plus ultra   d. boredom
5. hoi polloi   e. a council that governs
6. troika   f. presupposed through experience
7. junta   g. the knowledgeable
8. ingenue   h. three who govern

COMMUNICATING FOR RESULTS

You receive this telephone message from someone whom your boss has just left the office to meet: "Please tell Ms. Kim that there has been a death in my family and I won't be able to meet with her until next Wednesday at the earliest." Ms. Kim has already left the office for the airport to board a plane to meet with the caller. The flight is scheduled to depart in 45 minutes. How would you relay this urgent message to her? List alternative possibilities in case your first attempt fails.

U · N · I · T

56

Giving a Talk

You will probably have to talk before an audience sometime, if you have not already done so. Does this idea bother you? Many people have a fear of getting up before a group of people and giving a talk. Instead, they should feel complimented by any invitation to speak. The very fact that you are asked to give a talk indicates that someone believes that your ideas or experiences will be of interest and value to others and that you will do a good job.

The length and nature of talks vary. You may be asked for some brief remarks to introduce another speaker, or you may be asked to be a member of a panel discussion group. On the other hand, you may be invited to give a five- or ten-minute talk or even to present a longer speech at a meeting. Your success in any one of these roles will depend upon how carefully you plan your presentation. Only with careful planning will you be able to develop the feeling of confidence that will enable you to communicate your ideas to others, for an effective talk is the result of more than just knowing your subject. Not only do good speakers know what they are talking about, but also they know how to prepare and deliver the speech. Effective speakers have learned the best techniques of preparing and giving a talk, the techniques that you learn in this unit.

Guides to Effective Preparation

Every good talk requires careful preparation. The speaker-to-be must be ready to cover the subject thoroughly and must carefully organize the presentation. Use the following guidelines to help you prepare your talk.

Determine Your Purpose and Topic. First of all, you must know the purpose of your talk. Are you going to inform, explain, convince, entertain, or combine two or more of these purposes? Only when you know *why* you are going to talk will you be able to select the subject of the talk. Ask yourself these questions: Why was I asked to speak to this audience? What is the occasion and reason for this meeting? How long am I expected to talk? What does the group expect to gain from listening to me? Am I personally in harmony with the interests and background of this group? How can I capture the audience's interest? The answers to these questions will guide you in selecting a topic that will be timely and interesting.

Adapt Your Talk to the Audience. Who is your audience? What is their age range, sex, educational and social background, economic status, experience? What are their interests? A talk presented before one group may have little appeal for another group. For example, a discussion of microcomputers that would be exciting to office workers might cause a group of plumbers and pipe fitters to go to sleep. Failure to know and to consider the audience can destroy the effectiveness of the talk.

Limit Your Subject. Don't select a 4-hour subject for a 10-minute speech! It is better to make two or three specific points in a talk—and do the job well—than to ramble on about too broad a topic. The secretary who talked about "Office Automation" would have presented a more interesting talk on a more limited topic, such as "How the Microcomputer Affects My Job." Limit your subject so that you can emphasize two or three important points in the time allotted to you.

Collect and Organize Your Materials. Collect much more information about your subject than you will use. Use 3-by-5 cards to jot down ideas. Use your own personal experiences; talk with people who can help you; read newspapers, magazines, and books. Take good notes from as many sources as you can. As you organize the material you have collected, you will be able to select the most important ideas to include in your outline.

If the use of visual materials (transparencies, for example) or handouts (duplicated materials) will make your presentation more effective, carefully prepare these materials and determine at what point they may best be used.

Prepare Your Outline. A good outline is a "must" in preparing a talk. Prepare notes on cards first. Then arrange and rearrange them according to major ideas and order of importance. In the following example, note that only important ideas are included in the outline.

<u>How to Determine Career Interests</u>

   I.   Introduction.
         A. Thank presiding officer for introduction.
         B. Explain personal interest in topic.
         C. Explain importance of topic to all young people.
         D. Preview the major points to be made:
            1. Do an inventory of interests and abilities.
            2. Learn about jobs that are of interest.
            3. Observe people doing these jobs.

  II.   Do an inventory of interests and abilities:
         A. Indoor person or outdoor person?
         B. Working with people or alone?
         C. Concentration or action?

    III. Learn about jobs that are of interest:
        A. Read about the jobs.
        B. Talk with people who do such jobs.

    IV. Observe people doing these jobs:
        A. Ask to be an observer.
        B. Observe a typical day.
        C. Ask questions.
        D. Honestly judge your reactions to what you saw.

    V. Conclusion:
        A. Summary of talk.
        B. Thank audience for attention.

Arouse and Hold Interest. The success of your talk will depend on how well you are able to arouse and hold the interest of your audience. Make sure that you have variety and pep in your talk. Insert an amusing story here and there. Emphasize new ideas. You can hold interest by using personal experiences and examples. Your talk should have a certain element of suspense as the plot unfolds. Complicated ideas, such as figures or statistics, should be omitted, simplified, or supplemented by charts and graphs. As you prepare your talk, consider carefully how you will arouse and hold the group's interest.

Talk; Don't Read or Recite. How should you prepare your talk? Should you write your speech word for word? use only your outline? use notes on 3-by-5 cards? plan to talk without notes? These methods are all used by speakers to prepare their talks. Some people prefer not to speak from a written manuscript because they feel that their talk will sound stilted. Whatever method you select, be sure that your talk will sound natural—not like an oral reading or a class recitation.

    A written talk will be of value as you practice your presentation. It will enable you to fix each idea in your memory and to time your delivery. Having memorized the *what* and *how* of your talk, you can then use brief notes when you deliver it.

Practice, Practice, Practice. As you practice, try to anticipate the conditions of the actual talk. Imagine your audience in front of you. Stand tall and look at the audience. Talk loud enough for the person in the farthest corner of the auditorium to hear you. Make slow and deliberate movements. Use hand gestures sparingly, and then only if they seem natural to you. If a mirror is available, practice your talk in front of it. The person you see there should be the severest critic of your facial expressions and your platform appearance. Perhaps you can enlist the help of family and friends, too, to listen and offer suggestions. Don't be satisfied with your practice until the talk flows along from idea to idea without the aid of a written script.

Guides to Effective Delivery

Now that you have planned and practiced your talk, are you ready to deliver it to the audience? Study carefully the following tips. These pointers will help you to present most effectively the thoughts and ideas that you have so carefully prepared. They represent the principles of effective speaking to groups; and if you know them and use them, your audiences will say, "What a fine speaker!"

Hide Your Nervousness. Face the fact that you will be nervous as you wait for your introduction. But remain confident, knowing that you have carefully prepared your talk. If you find that you have stage fright, take a deep breath before opening your mouth. The deep breath will help relax your vocal cords. Speakers who are not at all anxious are either those who give talks often or those who do not know enough to be nervous. Controlled nervous anticipation is good for you. It will key you up and give your delivery some sparkle and liveliness.

Check Your Volume. You know how annoyed, disinterested, and bored listeners become if they can't hear the speaker. Don't create this problem for your audience. If possible before the meeting, check your volume in the room where you are to speak. Have someone stand in the back of the room to tell you if you can be heard perfectly. If you cannot make this test or if you sense that the audience cannot hear you, ask at the beginning of your talk if everyone can hear; then adjust your volume accordingly.

Keep Your Head Up. Good speakers hold their heads high. This position gives an appearance of authority and helps the speaker project the voice better. Your words are more likely to reach your listeners instead of being lost as they fall to the floor.

Use a Conversational Tone. Remember that you are talking to an audience, not giving an oration. Your voice should reflect the warm, easy, conversational tone that you would use if you were talking to a group of your very good friends. Also, remember that you will destroy any warmth created by your tone if you allow a critical, scolding, or sarcastic note to creep in.

Look at Your Audience. An audience responds favorably to a speaker who seems to be talking directly to each person in the audience. One way of making your listeners feel that you are talking to each one individually is to look directly at the assembled people. Look at those in the middle section, then those to the right, and then those to the left. As you look, you may see nothing but a blur, a mass of faces. Let your eyes rest on different sections of the blur, and the audience will feel that you are giving a person-to-person talk. And, with experience, you will begin to see the faces and expressions of individual listeners.

Stand at Ease. How you stand and what you do with your hands will help or hinder your presentation. If possible, stand behind a lectern (a speaker's stand). The lectern will provide a place for you to put your notes. Avoid holding them, for nervousness may cause the papers to rattle like leaves in a storm. To keep your hands from getting in the way, grasp the lectern on each side or occasionally hold your hands behind your back. If you shift your weight from one hip to the other when you are nervous, train yourself to stand with your weight evenly distributed on both feet.

Avoid Mannerisms. Mannerisms such as playing with objects, clearing the throat or wetting the lips, repeating "uh" or "and" frequently, and overusing slang expressions are objectionable to audiences. If you do not know whether you have such mannerisms, ask some of your friends to watch and listen and report any they observe. A speaker with even one annoying habit cannot give the best possible talk, for mannerisms distract the audience and obstruct the thoughts the speaker is trying to convey.

Use Only the Time Allotted. If you are asked to talk for five minutes, don't talk for six minutes. A program with several speakers is usually timed to the last minute; anyone who does not keep to the time limit forces other speakers to shorten their talks. Not only are long-winded talkers thought inconsiderate; they are also marked as egotistical. They think that what they have to say is so important that the other speakers can be disregarded. To avoid going over the time limit, you might ask the presiding officer of the meeting to give you warning when you have only one minute left.

Observe Audience Reaction. You can and should train yourself to watch the audience as you speak and to be sensitive to its changing moods. If, as you talk, you see blankness or boredom on the faces before you, this signal tells you that your listeners need perking up. You might then tell one of the amusing stories you keep in reserve. Remember, however, that jokes are only effective if used intelligently.

If your audience seems tired, if the hour is late, or if the previous talks have been overlong, you have two choices: accept the situation as a challenge and give such an interesting and sparkling performance that everyone perks right up, or have pity on your audience and cut your talk to the bare essentials. Sometimes it is better to omit part of a speech rather than give it before a weary audience.

Carefully Select the Closing Words. Inexperienced talkers often give themselves away by lowering their voices as they say the last few words or by dashing off the ending in a hurried rattle. Of course, a beginner is happy to see the end in sight and is eager to get the ordeal over. What a pity, though, to spoil the effect of an otherwise fine talk with a poor ending! Remember to keep your pitch up and to observe good timing to the very end.

COMMUNICATION LABORATORY

APPLICATION EXERCISES

A. The following major topics were taken from notes for a talk entitled "The Importance of Effective Speaking in a Business Organization." Assume that you are going to give the talk to an audience that has done little or no prior thinking about the importance of effective speaking in business. Arrange the notes in order of increasing importance. Place the least important idea first and the most important idea last. Be prepared to justify your selection of the three least important ideas and the three most important ideas.

The good speaker can motivate others; the good speaker can avoid mistakes and misunderstandings; good speaking skills impress customers; the good speaker gains personal satisfaction by being listened to; the good speaker can easily explain to co-workers what has to be done; the ability to express oneself brings one to the attention of management; a good speaker can get others to act on his or her ideas; the good speaker can help the company make a favorable impression upon the public.

B. List the three most important topics you selected in Exercise A. Then explain how you would go about preparing information that would allow you to develop each point.

C. From the following job classifications, select one that you are particularly interested in. Collect information about the job, specifically the duties performed by someone who holds the job and has the skills the job demands. Prepare an outline for a 5-minute talk. Prepare your talk and give it in class.

Accountant or auditor	Computer programmer
Paralegal worker	Sales representative
Service technician	Word processing operator
Administrative assistant	Sales correspondent
Systems analyst	Public relations assistant

VOCABULARY AND SPELLING STUDIES

A. These words are often confused: *sole, soul*. Explain the differences.

B. Use either *sometime, some time,* or *sometimes* to complete each of the following sentences.

1. Every worker needs _____ to relax.
2. I _____ go shopping during my lunch hour.
3. We will check those invoices _____ this morning.
4. It has been _____ now since the telephone rang.

C. Each of the following sentences contains an error in the use of a word. Correct each.

1. I haven't used this machine for sometime.
2. Your loan payment is long overdo.
3. John made a vein effort to correct the mistake.
4. Ms. Harcourt is the soul owner of this company.
5. The new vacation policy goes into affect in March.

COMMUNICATING FOR RESULTS

Storyteller. A good conversationalist has a knack for relating an incident that is of interest to listeners: a strange or unusual happening, an embarrassing moment, a humorous occurrence, a recounting that sheds some light on human nature. From your own personal experience, select one such event to describe to your class. Limit yourself to 1 minute.

U · N · I · T

57

Meeting the Public

Almost all business employees in stores and offices have some contact with the public, either face-to-face or by telephone. As a business employee, you will probably meet and talk with the public often—to make reservations at a travel agency, airline, railroad, or theater; to receive money from or pay money to stores, banks, and other companies; to receive or place orders for services or repairs; to receive complaints and make adjustments; to provide information to garages, office appliance companies, and other service organizations; and so on. Millions of people earn their livings primarily by meeting the public in person or on the telephone.

In a business office, the receptionist or switchboard operator usually makes the first contact with the public, transferring a call or referring a caller or visitor to the appropriate person or department. In smaller offices, clerical employees may be asked to help callers in addition to performing their other duties. And just about everyone in an office has a telephone to use in connection with work being done. Therefore, everyone planning to work in business can expect to have some contact with the public.

Your first step in preparing yourself to meet the public is to give careful attention to the basic rules for dealing with callers. In addition, you need to learn how these rules may be applied to meeting a caller in person and to meeting the public by telephone.

Basic Rules for Meeting the Public

The rules for meeting the public—in person or by telephone—are based on courtesy, consideration, and friendliness. These are the same qualities that make a visitor in your home feel welcome, comfortable, and at ease. Applied specifically to business callers, the rules include those discussed below.

Give Prompt Attention to Callers. A caller's presence should be recognized immediately. Telephones should be answered promptly, before the second ring if possible. Have you ever waited and waited for a telephone call to be answered? Have you ever had to stand and wait for someone to attend to you in a store and felt completely ignored? If so, you know that you became increasingly uncomfortable, even angry, as you waited. You hung up the telephone, or you turned on your heel and walked out of the store. In a well-run business, this does not happen. Salespeople, for example, are trained to recognize a caller immediately. A clerk busy with one customer will glance and nod at a waiting customer or say pleasantly, "I'll be with you in a moment." Then callers know that they are not being overlooked. As you meet the public, you must follow the same procedure and give prompt attention to all callers.

Greet Callers Pleasantly. The tone of voice you use to greet people should be cheerful and friendly. Even an angry caller will feel better hearing your pleasant, "Good morning, Mr. Lawton. How nice of you to call." Of course, if you don't mean what you say, it is best not to say it; your tone of voice and your facial expressions will often reveal that you are not sincere.

If possible, vary your greeting to fit the visitor. Treat all visitors as though they were special in some way—as they are! Try also to make the greeting fit the occasion. For example, a car dealer approaching a customer behind the wheel of a new demonstrator might say, "It's a comfortable feeling to sit behind the wheel of a new car, isn't it?" One of the following greetings may fit other situations: "Good morning." "What may I show you?" "Whom do you wish to see?" "How may I help you?" "What a pleasant surprise!" "We were expecting you." "How nice of you to call." "How are you today?" Just adding the name of the person, if you know it, will tailor the greeting for each caller. Often, too, the same words may be varied by a change in emphasis or in the way they are said.

Treat All Callers as Honored Guests. Be friendly and courteous to everyone. Never let a caller's voice or appearance influence what you say. Some very important people do not dress expensively, and not everyone has had the advantage of voice training. All callers deserve the same courteous and considerate treatment.

Prepare yourself for an occasional irritable or even rude caller. Treat such people with an understanding smile and gloss over their discourtesies. You represent the firm, and these people are your guests. If you must make some response, express sympathy: "I'm sorry you feel that way." Your own graciousness will often soften the caller's anger and might even make the caller friendly again toward you and your company.

Obtain Needed Information. Before you can refer to a caller to someone else, you must find out the caller's name and the reason for the call. You can then relay this information to your boss, who will determine specifically who will handle the call.

Because people sometimes resent being asked about their business, it takes considerable tact to get the needed information without harming pleasant relations. To a telephone caller, you might say, "May I tell Miss Benemo who is calling, please?" When greeting a caller in person, you might point a pen over a pad and say pleasantly, "Your name is . . . ?" And, as you write the name on the pad, you will probably repeat, "Oh, yes, Mr. Lee Kim." Next you would ask, "And you would like to see Mrs. Polisky about . . . ?" and also write his answer on your pad. Filling in a leading question is a natural thing to do, so your caller usually will freely and willingly supply the information you need.

Save the Caller's Time. Let callers know if they have to wait. On the telephone, if the wait is to be longer than two or three minutes, it is usually better to take the number and call back. You can say: "I'll have to get the information from the files, Mr. Stratton. It will take about five minutes to do so. May I have your number and call you back?"

Let callers know how long they must wait, even if it is a relatively short time. You might say: "I'm sorry, but Mr. Stamas will not be available for at least another hour. Would you like to make an appointment for later?" or "Mr. Stamas is in a meeting but should be free in about 5 minutes." Callers will appreciate this.

Be Discreet. Protect your employer in what you say—and in what you don't say. If your boss is late in arriving at the office, for example, don't say, "Mr. Rosenberg has not come in yet this morning." The tactful thing to say is: "Mr. Rosenberg is not in the office just now. I expect him in a few minutes." Make certain that your remarks reflect favorably on your employer.

Protect your employer's business, also. Certain business information is confidential, and you must keep it so. Imagine what a visitor would think of your company (and you) if you were indiscreet enough to say, "Business is so poor that Mr. Rosenberg had to let some workers go last week." A prospective customer would not be favorably impressed! So be discreet in what you say on the telephone and in person.

Keep Within Your Authority. Know the limits of your authority and don't exceed them. If you think your company will replace a defective part, for example, but it is not your responsibility to make adjustments, don't say: "Certainly we'll replace this for you. Just take it to the service manager." Both you and your company will be embarrassed if for some reason the service manager is unable to make the adjustment. Keep within your authority by saying, "Why don't you talk with Ms. Ortega, the service manager?" Be sure you know the names of the people in your company who are authorized to make various kinds of decisions. You can then help callers by referring them to the appropriate person, and you will be keeping within your authority.

Say "No" Gracefully. Some decisions you must convey to callers will be unfavorable to them. Be pleasant but firm. Your knowledge of how to say "no" in a letter will help you. Review Unit 44 so that when you must refuse a caller, you can do so without losing goodwill.

Show a Genuine Desire to Serve. An extra courtesy or some thoughtful touch should be extended to guests to make their visit memorable. In business, too, you should be on the lookout for the little extra that makes the difference. Think, for example, how much an out-of-town visitor might appreciate your offer to reconfirm a returning flight. "While you're talking with Mr. Puggi, I'll call the airline to reconfirm your reservation." This kind of added service helps to make new customers and helps to keep current customers coming back.

With these basic rules in mind, you are ready to receive the public—in person or by telephone. In greeting callers, however, you need to know certain additional techniques.

Telephone Techniques

Telephone techniques differ somewhat from techniques for greeting callers in person because of the nature of telephone conversation and the technical equipment used.

A telephone caller is unable to see the other person's facial expressions or surroundings and must depend entirely upon the voice at the other end of the line. In voice-to-voice meetings, therefore, you should remember the guidelines given below.

Identify Yourself Immediately. Callers cannot see you. They need to know whether they have the right number, company, or person. A switchboard operator usually identifies only the firm's name: "Brennan and Goldstein" or "This is Stammerman's Furniture Company." In answering an office or departmental telephone, identify both the office and yourself. You might say: "Dr. Silver's office, Joan O'Loughlin speaking"; "Personnel, Saul Shapiro "; or "Good morning. This is the Sales Department, Lily Giesen speaking." "Accounting, Bromberg" is technically correct, but the abruptness of the identification might confuse some people, and the purpose of this identification is to indicate who you are. Whatever greeting you use, remember that on the telephone you must identify yourself at once.

Keep the Caller Informed. Telephone callers can't see what is happening, so you must tell them. If you must leave the line to get some information, excuse yourself, saying, "I can find that information in just a few moments, if you wish to hold the line." Of course, all delays must be explained, and best business practice requires that you report to the caller every minute. You can make an appropriate remark, such as: 'We're still trying to locate Mrs. Lamotta" or "I'm sorry, Mrs. Lamotta is still talking on the other line. Do you wish to wait, or shall I have her call you?"

You must also let your callers know that you are following what they are saying. In person, you might nod your head; on the telephone, your voice must do the notifying. You can show that you are listening attentively by simple responses such as "Yes" or "I see."

Be Ready to Write Information. Have pencil, paper, and message forms ready for use near the telephone. Then you won't delay the caller with, "Will you wait while I get a pencil?" Be sure, too, to verify the message. For example, after taking the message "Wants refrigerator serviced free under CS contract—wants service *today*," you would verify the information by saying: "You would like Mr. Madsen to call you regarding free servicing of your refrigerator under our company service contract, Mrs. Cassell—and you want service today. Let's see, you spell your name C-A-S-S-E-L-L? And your number is 555-1372? Thank you. Good-bye."

How to Use the Telephone. The telephone is a sensitive instrument. Knowing how to use it correctly will enable you to greet telephone callers courteously and efficiently. Follow these suggestions:

1. Hold your lips from about an inch from the mouthpiece. Don't let the mouthpiece slip down under your chin, and don't cut off your voice by holding your hand over the mouthpiece.
2. Adjust your voice to the equipment. Remember, you don't have to shout over the telephone. Use your natural voice. But enunciate clearly so that you will be understood.
3. Transfer calls efficiently and quickly. To transfer a call from the outside to another extension within the company, say to the caller, "If you will hold for just a moment, I'll have your call transferred." How you get the attention of the operator depends on the phone system in your company. Usually you should simply depress the cradle button once—firmly. When the operator answers, say, "Please transfer this call to Mr. Domey on Extension 2317."
4. Avoid irritating mechanical noises. If you must leave the line, place the receiver on a book or magazine. The noise made when the receiver is bumped or dropped on a desk is magnified over the wire and will not be

appreciated by the caller. At the completion of a call, place the receiver gently in the cradle. Of course, the courteous person will allow the caller to replace the receiver first.

COMMUNICATION LABORATORY

APPLICATION EXERCISES

A. Your office manager asks you to write a one-page memo that summarizes the correct procedures to be followed by all office workers who receive telephone calls. As you plan your memorandum, give special attention to the following points:

1. Promptness in answering calls
2. Proper identification
3. Treating callers as honored guests
4. Practices for handling delays
5. Obtaining needed information from callers

B. Assume that you work as an assistant to the marketing manager of a large firm. Your job is to contact dealers in order to assess customer response to new products. You visit the large dealers in person. You contact the smaller dealers by phone. Discuss the different techniques you would use in gathering reactions—by telephone and in person.

C. Ms. Alvaro has left word that she has an important report to complete and is not to be disturbed by calls. But a telephone caller insists: "I need to talk with Ms. Alvaro right away. I would like to discuss an important contract with her, and the deadline for bids is tomorrow." What would you say? Select one of the following. Then defend you answer in a paragraph. Be prepared to discuss your answers in class.

1. "I'm sorry. I simply cannot disturb Ms. Alvaro."
2. "If it's important, I'll transfer your call to her right away."
3. "Please give me a number where I can reach you within a half hour. I will get your message to Ms. Alvaro."
4. "Ms. Alvaro is not in the office today."

D. Select one of the following situations to enact in front of the class. Decide how you would communicate the unfavorable decision to the caller. Write a script for your skit.

1. The caller's application for a mortgage has been rejected because the down payment was 10 percent below the minimum.
2. The caller's bid to supply typewriters to your firm has been rejected in favor of another's, which was 7 percent lower.

3. Your employer does not wish to see a caller because the caller has provided poor service to your firm on three prior occasions.

VOCABULARY AND SPELLING STUDIES

A. These words are often confused: *cooperation, corporation; eligible, illegible*. Explain the differences.

B. Write the nouns that can be formed from these verbs.

1. renovate
2. invert
3. invest
4. offend
5. revoke
6. expand

C. Complete the following by adding *ary*, *ery*, or *ory*—whichever ending is correct.

1. vocabul_____
2. regulat_____
3. green_____
4. ordin_____
5. art_____
6. laborat_____

COMMUNICATING FOR RESULTS

Handling a Difficult Caller. Mrs. Seaton, a stockholder in the company for which you work, telephones and asks to speak with Mr. Edmunson, your boss and the company's public relations director. After you tell the caller that Mr. Edmunson is out of the office for the day, she explains her problem to you. She says that she has just been very rudely treated by the manager of your firm's retail store in Seattle. She had tried to return some defective merchandise and was told that she had misused it. She characterizes the manager as "abusive," and she threatens not only to sell her stock, but to tell all her friends and acquaintances about how she has been treated. You recognize that Mrs. Seaton is highly agitated and needs to feel as if prompt attention to her complaint is assured. You want to preserve her goodwill in your response to her. Exactly what would you say to the caller? Write a summary of the conversation for your employer, so he will know how you handled the call.

U · N · I · T
58
Conferences and Meetings

You probably are active in one or more social, civic, religious, or school clubs. Participating in group activities is good training for the person who hopes someday to work in business or industry.

More and more, in all walks of life, decisions are made as a result of group thinking. Many business groups and committees are organized to make the best use of the talents and ideas of employees. Often the work of each person in the group—participating members as well as leaders—is carefully considered by the people who help determine who should be promoted. Why? Management can observe how well a person works in a group and how well that person communicates with others—an important basis for advancement into leadership positions. Therefore, every person who plans to enter business should know how to participate effectively in a group.

The Group Member

For every leader in a group there are many more working members. You, therefore, will probably serve more often as a member than as a leader. Every person who is invited to join a group discussion has an obligation to contribute his or her best. Time and money are wasted when employees take meetings for granted and do not contribute their maximum efforts to the discussion.

Principles to Follow. Some rules for participating effectively in a meeting are discussed below. Knowing and practicing these rules will help you to be a valuable group member.

Respect the Opinions of Others. It is easy to respect the opinions of people whom you like and whose ideas agree with yours. Good group members, however, respect the opinions of all others in their group and are courteous to everyone, even though they may not agree with them.

Because good group members are open-minded, they listen attentively to each member of the group and respond with appropriate comments. Discourteous behavior—fidgeting, gazing into space, or trying to start an unrelated private conversation—marks the group member as a poor risk for promotion. The courteous person, on the other hand, is considerate of everyone at all times. You may have strong convictions, but you do not close your mind to a different point of view. You know that by considering the ideas and beliefs of others, you will grow and learn, you will gain a new respect for the thinking of others, and you will become a more effective person.

Use Only Your Share of Talking Time. Every member has a contribution to make to a group. Some people, however, have an exaggerated opinion of the value of their ideas, and they attempt to monopolize a meeting. Good group members know that everyone has an equal right and responsibility to talk. By limiting their own talking, they make sure that others are not robbed of their fair share of talking time.

Help to Harmonize Differences of Opinion. Good group members try to see the value in each opposing view and to balance these views to keep peace in the group. They recognize good ideas and encourage others in the group to make compromises that will help get results. Such a member might say, for example: "That's a good idea, and I can see how it would work under some conditions; but the other plan is good too. Shall we take the best from each?" Thus, by emphasizing the good aspects of all ideas, the effective group member is able to harmonize differences of opinion.

Help to Keep Discussion Relevant. It's easy in a group for some members to let their talking wander from the discussion at hand. However, good group members stick to the subject and also help direct the ideas of others to the topic at hand. They may do so by reminding the group of their goal or purpose: "As I understand it, our purpose is to . . . ." Or when the discussion begins to wander, "Let's see now, what is it we hope to accomplish in this meeting?" Summarizing the progress made or pointing out stumbling blocks to reaching the goal may also help to keep group thinking on track. Thus the good group member takes action to let the group know whether it is reaching its goal.

Attitudes to Avoid. To be sure, you must know the positive principles that constitute good group membership; but it is just as important for you to understand the attitudes and practices that *prevent* effective group work. An understanding of these attitudes and practices will help you avoid pitfalls and make you better able to harmonize differences of opinion and keep a discussion on the main track. The attitudes and practices of the following types of people hinder the smooth progress of a group.

Selfish-Interest Pleader. "I don't care what the rest of you think—what I want to see is . . . ," says the selfish-interest pleader. John has decided what *he* wants. Everything he says and does is intended to help him get his way despite the good ideas of others.

The Blocker. The blocker is opposed to every new idea. "That isn't the way to do it. Here's what we've been doing for years . . . ." or "That's an idiotic idea. It won't work." Whatever the idea is, Martha is against it. She often displays a negative, stubborn resistance. She opposes in a disagreeable manner and frequently without reason.

The Aggressor. The aggressor is usually unaware of the feelings of others. Harry may try to build his own importance by deflating the ego of others: "That's a silly thing to do. If I were doing it, here is how I'd go about it." But, alas, Harry usually avoids doing much! He may attack the group, its purposes, or the importance of the topic. He usually attempts to assert his superiority by trying to manage the group. As the name implies, the aggressor want to take command.

The Sympathy Seeker. Frank, the sympathy seeker, may accept responsibility to do something for the group, but then he doesn't carry it through. He says: "I thought Joe was supposed to do that" or "I was just so busy that I couldn't get that done." Alibis, confessions of shortcomings, and exaggeration of personal problems are all used to gain the sympathy of the group. Such a person would like the group to compliment him for his weaknesses!

The Disinterested Bystander. Kitty, the disinterested bystander, may make a display of her lack of involvement. Through childish tactics, she may attempt to disrupt. Or she may patronize the group with a frozen smile that permits her to escape mentally from the boring proceedings.

Success as a Group Member. Study your role in a group. Make sure that you practice the principles that contribute to group success and eliminate all actions that might prevent you from being a good group member. Remember: A leader is usually selected from among the good group members.

The Group Leader

People who consistently block group action will not need to know how to lead a group. They won't be given the opportunity. However, people who know and practice the positive principles that help a group to work together, will soon be selected for a leadership post—an honor, but also a serious obligation. Before you take on the responsibility of chairing a group, therefore, make sure that you know the duties involved in planning and conducting a meeting.

Planning a Meeting. When you chair a group, you will usually plan all meetings—whether they are programs or business meetings. If the group does not have a constitution or bylaws to define your responsibilities, you can usually assume that you are responsible for all aspects of planning—place and time, publicity, pattern of the program, and speakers and other participants.

The Program. The first step is to write a plan for the program. This plan should answer the following questions: (1) What is the purpose of the meeting? (2) What theme or topic is to be considered? (3) Where and when will the meeting be held? Should reservations for a room or hall be made now? (4) Who will attend? (5) How many will attend? (6) What publicity will be needed? (7) How much money is available for speakers, arrangements, decorations, and so on? (8) What persons or committees should be appointed to make arrangements, sell tickets, publicize, act as hosts? (9) What form or pattern should the program take—speaker or symposium of speakers? demonstration? panel discussion? mock television or radio program? panel, with audience questions and answer? debate? small group discussions? brainstorming? other?

Delegating Authority. At this point in planning, you may feel overwhelmed by the size of the job ahead of you. Don't be, however, for an important characteristic of the leader is an ability to delegate authority. Specific tasks are assigned, usually in writing, to other people. Delegate as many details as you can, but be sure to follow up on each assignment. Carbons of letters of committee appointments or of letters written to the speakers can be used as a tickler (reminder) file. To avoid any last minute slip-up, send reminders to all committees and speakers at least two weeks before the meeting. If you have carefully planned and effectively delegated responsibility, you can go before the group with a feeling of confidence that the meeting you conduct will be a good one.

The Agenda. In an agenda for a business meeting, like the one shown on page 567, the discussion items should be listed in the order of increasing controversy. For instance, the first item will be the one most likely to meet with almost total agreement. Next will come the item on which the leader expects less agreement, and so on. A sound psychological principle is behind this practice. If a group starts by agreeing, the members will be in a friendly and positive frame of mind that will carry over to succeeding discussion topics. Untrained leaders who start their meetings with the "big question"—the topic likely to provoke the widest difference of opinion—should not wonder why nothing is accomplished at their meetings.

Conducting a Meeting. You, the leader, set the tone for the meeting as you follow the agenda or program. If you are stiff and formal, the other people on

```
                    TEMPLETON MANUFACTURING COMPANY

                   Meeting of the Employee Awards Committee

                        June 8, 1984, 9:30 a.m.
                          East Conference Room


                                AGENDA


        1.  Call to order by Chairperson Edwards.

        2.  Approval of the minutes of the May meeting.

        3.  Approval of the agenda.

        4.  Announcements.

        5.  Old Business:

                A.  Report of the subcommittee on employee
                    morale.

                B.  Discussion of awards for money-saving
                    suggestions.

        6.  New Business:

                A.  Plans for the annual retirement dinner.

                B.  Discussion of employee incentive plan.

                C.  Subcommittee appointments.

                D.  Other items.

        7.  Adjournment.
```

In an agenda for a business meeting, the discussion items should be listed in the order of increasing controversy.

the program are likely to be stiff and formal too. If you are natural and informal (but in good taste, of course), the others on your program will probably be natural and informal too. Most audiences today prefer a moderator who conducts an informal kind of meeting, whether or not parliamentary procedure is followed.

Parliamentary Procedure. The bylaws of most clubs state that business will be conducted according to Robert's *Rules of Order*. Robert's *Rules* are to parliamentary procedure what Emily Post and Amy Vanderbilt are to etiquette; and, as presiding officer, you will need to know some of the basic principles of Robert's *Rules* and how to apply them. For example, you should know how to call a meeting to order and how to determine whether a quorum is present; how to make and follow an agenda; how to recognize members who wish to make a motion; what an appropriate motion is and how it is seconded, amended, and voted upon; and how to adjourn a meeting. Most organizations will appoint a parliamentarian to help the group leader, but the leader who possesses a working knowledge of the rules is that much ahead.

Introducing a Speaker. An introduction should be short and simple and should include (1) some gracious remark that will make the speaker feel warmly welcome, (2) a statement of the speaker's topic, (3) a brief summary of the speaker's background or special interests, and (4) presentation of the speaker by name. The announcement of the name of the speaker is usually made last, so that it serves as a signal for the speaker to come forward and begin the talk.

Responding to a Speech. The leader, of course, wishes the meeting to end on a high note. After an effective talk, there is little to say. Even after a poor speech, the leader shouldn't say too much. One or two comments about the importance of the talk or a short anecdote to leave the audience in good spirits is all that is needed. You should thank the speaker, express appreciation to those who helped plan the meeting, and adjourn.

COMMUNICATION LABORATORY

APPLICATION EXERCISES

A. Which of the following statements were made by people who practice principles of good group membership? Do any of the statements represent an attitude that is likely to hinder group progress?

1. "I think there is a way to combine the two ideas we have been discussing into one workable plan."
2. "Everyone realizes that this foolish scheme won't work."
3. "As far as I can see, our purpose is simply to make a proposal."
4. "My years at the Rodney Corporation taught me that there is only one way to do this."

B. Write a plan for an important meeting of a group to which you belong. Include a speaker in the meeting plan. Use the questions on page 566 to guide your plan. Finally, write the introduction that you will use to present the speaker.

C. Write a letter to the person you have selected to be the speaker. Invite him or her to address the group. Be sure that the speaker gets all needed information, including a description of your group and its interests.

D. Write a letter appointing a presiding officer for one of the following committees: (1) program, (2) publicity, (3) arrangements, (4) membership.

VOCABULARY AND SPELLING STUDIES

A. These words are often confused: *censor, censure; read, reed, red.* Explain the differences.

B. From each pair of words in parentheses, select the one that correctly completes the sentence.

1. I was (real, really) pleased to learn that Sara received a promotion.
2. Do you use (that, those) kinds of correction tapes?
3. In order to make the contract deadline, we will have to rush (some, somewhat).
4. Jennifer is (sure, surely) qualified for this position.
5. I prefer the (smaller, smallest) of the two calculators.

C. Choose the item that answers each of the following questions correctly.

1. Which of the following compound nouns *should* be hyphenated? vice president, trade in, notary public
2. Which one of the following compound nouns *should not* be hyphenated? tie-up, follow-up, building-contractor
3. Which one of the following expressions *should not* contain hyphens? up-to-date equipment, first-rate salesperson, data-processing equipment
4. Which one of the following words that contain prefixes *should not* be hyphenated? co-worker, ex-president, semi-independent, non-neutral

COMMUNICATING FOR RESULTS

Small-Group Discussion Technique. The small-group discussion technique is often used to solve problems. It is based on the idea that two heads are better than one. Here is the way it works. Divide your class into small groups of four, five, or six. Then, in each group: (1) Elect a presiding officer. (2) Agree quickly on a secretary or recorder who will take notes and later report the major points of the discussion to the entire class. (3) Make sure that everyone understands the problem you are to discuss. (4) Be sure that everyone enters into the discussion. When you are through, evaluate the discussion process.

Select one of these problems: (1) How can students improve their knowledge of career possibilities? (2) What kind of program can be established that would allow students to obtain actual work experience in interesting jobs?

P · A · R · T

8

COMMUNICATING TO GET A JOB

Effective communication skills will influence all aspects of your life, but never more so than when you get a job. Even the most basic business situations involve speaking, listening, reading, and writing.

Your command of communication skills will benefit you in a job situation. Given a situation that requires communicating on the job, your mastery of the units in this chapter will enable you to do the following:

1. *State your qualifications for employment in a complete, attractive résumé.*

2. *Complete employment application forms accurately and thoroughly.*

3. *Organize and write effective letters of application.*

4. *Prepare letters requesting others to serve as your references.*

5. *Write letters accepting or refusing positions offered to you.*

6. *Prepare yourself for a successful interview.*

U · N · I · T
59

Résumés and Job Applications

When you have completed your formal education, you will look for a job suited to your training, interests, and ambitions. In most cases, you will visit a prospective employer's office and complete an application form for the position in which you are interested. The employer may then make a decision regarding your employability on the basis of the application form and a personal interview. This employment process is the simplest one and probably the one most commonly used for obtaining a first job.

Throughout your lifetime, however, you may find yourself in other job-seeking situations in an attempt to improve your position. As you gain experience, you are likely to become ambitious for better and better jobs. These better jobs very often call for written letters of application and summaries of your background and experience. Your writing skills may very well play an important part in obtaining the job you desire.

In any job-seeking situation, there are a number of ways you may use your writing skills: to complete an application blank, prepare a résumé (a summary of your qualifications), write an application letter, or write employment follow-up letters. To obtain your first job, you may need to complete only an employment application form. However, you may also need to prepare a letter of application and a résumé. As an ambitious job-seeker, therefore, you should be able to prepare all the written material that will help you obtain the job you want.

What Abilities Do You Have to Offer an Employer?

You will be hired because you have a skill that an employer needs. Before you start your campaign for a job, you must decide for which specific jobs you are qualified and in which jobs you are interested. On the basis of your personal and educational background, you begin by listing specific skills and knowledge that would benefit an employer. Then you decide which specific job titles need the skills and knowledge you possess.

Which of the positions you have listed interest you most? Which ones interest you least? Direct your job-seeking efforts to the most interesting positions for which you are qualified.

For example, suppose your high school major is a general clerical program. Courses in the program may include typewriting, accounting, general business, business English and communication, filing, business mathematics, and office practice. At the end of your high school training, you will probably be able to type at least 50 words a minute, perform basic record-keeping functions, operate various calculating and duplicating machines, and compose business letters. Some of the job classifications for which you will have received preparation include clerk-typist, payroll clerk, teller, file clerk, general office clerk, correspondence clerk, or credit clerk.

Once you have assessed your skills and knowledge and determined the various jobs for which you are qualified, your most important decision involves selecting the job that interests you most. How can you locate such a position?

What Are Good Job Sources?

How do you find the job in which you are interested? Where do you look for the job for which you are qualified? Several employment sources may be investigated to find a job suitable for you.

School Placement Offices. Your school placement office may be a good place to begin looking for your first job. To employers, graduating seniors are a good source of personnel. If your school has established a reputation for providing training in occcupational areas, then you may be able to obtain a job through your school placement office. In addition, your teachers may be able to supply specific names of employers who are looking for graduates in your particular field of interest.

Newspaper Advertisements. Newspaper advertisements placed by local businesses are a good source of employment opportunities. These advertisements may request you to apply in person for the positions listed, or they may request that you submit an application letter accompanied by a résumé.

Sometimes local professional journals or newspapers contain job listings. For example, the *Los Angeles Daily Journal,* a publication for the legal profession, is a good source of legal secretarial positions in the Los Angeles area.

Employment Agencies. Both state employment agencies and private employment agencies list job openings. Your local state agency places applicants in positions that have been referred to its office. Of course, this service is performed without cost to either the employee or the employer.

Private employment agencies charge either the employer or the applicant a fee for filling an opening that has been referred to them by the employer. Positions listed as "fee paid" are the ones employers pay for. Some companies prefer to refer all their openings to private employment agencies to save themselves the trouble and expense of screening applicants. In the long run, it may prove less expensive for them to use an employment agency than to maintain their own personnel recruitment facilities.

Federal, State, County, and City Offices. Opportunities in civil service employment should not be overlooked, as salaries and opportunities for advancement are competitive with those in industry. Local federal, state, county, and city employment offices regularly publish announcements of job opportunities in their levels of government. Persons interested in working in civil service should consult local government employment offices to learn about the jobs available and to inquire about taking the civil service examinations for the jobs in which they are interested. Often, too, officials from various government offices will visit high schools to recruit qualified applicants and to administer civil service examinations right on campus.

College and University Offices. All institutions of higher education have business offices that employ many clerks, secretaries, managers, and administrators. Colleges and universities offer their employees some major advantages. Some, for example, permit their employees to take one course during working hours. In addition, of course, employees have the advantage of working in a different environment—the college campus.

Individual Companies. Many companies do not actively recruit prospective employees through newspaper advertisements or employment agencies. Sufficient numbers of applicants present themselves to the company and directly request employment. While companies may not always have immediate openings in every area, a qualified applicant's résumé is usually filed for future reference.

Larger companies with hundreds or thousands of employees are constantly busy recruiting and placing personnel. Therefore, contacting these companies directly may often lead to obtaining employment.

The Résumé

Once you have decided what you have to sell an employer, you should prepare a written summary of your qualifications. This summary—called a *résumé*—is a description of your qualifications. It usually includes a statement of your education, your employment record (experience), a list of references, and other data that will help you obtain the job you wish.

A résumé is highly useful. You may use it to accompany a letter of application, present it to an employer at the interview, mail it to a prospective employer without a formal letter of application, or use it to assist you in filling out an employment application form.

Since résumés are sales instruments, they must be prepared just as carefully as sales letters. They must present the best possible impression of you. The act of preparing the résumé is just as valuable as the résumé itself, for it forces you to think about yourself—what you have to offer an employer and why you should be hired. Thus it becomes a self-appraisal. Everyone brings unique talents to a position, but usually only after you prepare a résumé do you realize your true worth.

Make the Résumé Attractive. Because the résumé is a sales instrument, it should be as attractive as you can make it. Of course, it should be typewritten, perfectly balanced on the page, and free from errors and noticeable corrections. Résumés vary in length from one page to several pages, depending on how much you have to say about yourself. Your first résumé should probably fit on one page or at the most two, but as you gather experience and obtain more education, your résumés may get longer and more detailed.

Make the Résumé Fit the Employer's Needs. A résumé is tailored carefully to meet the employer's needs for the job for which you are applying. Thus it is an individual thing. Never try to copy someone else's résumé or to use the same one over and over. You must find out what the job you are seeking demands and then tailor your résumé accordingly. For example, if you apply for a job where you will be required to take dictation at a high speed, you will want to emphasize your skill in shorthand. You will make absolutely sure that the employer knows you are a highly skilled shorthand writer and transcriber. On the other hand, if the secretarial job you want requires little in the way of shorthand but a good deal of talent in writing, you will mention your shorthand skill but emphasize your writing ability.

The Main Categories of a Résumé

The form of the résumé varies according to your individual taste and, more importantly, according to the job for which you are applying. If you were applying for a job with a bank or an accounting firm, you would probably want to use white paper and a conservative format. But if you were applying for a job with an advertising agency you would probably want to exhibit creativity, and might want to use a tinted paper and a more creative format.

The résumé illustrated on page 578 is an example of an effective arrangement. Notice that it contains four main headings: "Position Sought," "Experience," "Education," and "References." The information at the top of the form includes the name, address, and telephone number of the applicant. This is all the personal data needed here; you will supply other personal details on the application.

Position Sought. The employer wants to know, first of all, the specific job for which you are applying. It is best to find out in advance whether there is a vacancy in the company and to specify that position by its correct title, such as "Secretary to the Assistant Credit Manager." If you don't know the specific job title, it is satisfactory to write "Payroll Clerk," "Sales Trainee," "Receptionist," and so on. Whichever résumé format you use—conservative or creative—be sure to include all the necessary details.

Experience. If you are a recent high school graduate, the employer will not expect you to have had a lot of experience that is related directly to the job for which you are applying. Employers understand that you have been in

```
                              Laura A. Stern
                              6732 Fraser Court
                         San Diego, California 92126
                         Telephone (603) 555-1239


POSITION SOUGHT     Executive Assistant


EXPERIENCE          La Jolla Engineering Company, La Jolla, California.
                    July 1981 to present.  Assistant Office Manager.
                    Supervisor: Ms. Antonia Quarles.  Duties include
                    preparing weekly and monthly work schedules, pre-
                    paring and distributing payroll, maintaining all
                    office records, securing temporary help, and moni-
                    toring use and service of all office machinery.

                    Chula Vista Supply Company, Chula Vista, California.
                    June 1979 to July 1981.  Secretary to Sales Manager.
                    Supervisor: Mr. Miguel Rodriguez.  Duties included
                    typing, filing, arranging travel schedules, tele-
                    marketing, and assisting sales personnel.

                    Samson's Stationery, San Diego, California.  Summers
                    of 1977 and 1978.  Salesperson.  Supervisor: Mrs.
                    Doris Samson.


EDUCATION           San Diego Business Academy, San Diego, California.
                    Awarded certificate upon completion of twelve-month
                    secretarial program in June 1979.  Skills: short-
                    hand, 120 wpm; typing 70 wpm.  Major subjects included
                    office automation and modern office procedures.  Re-
                    ceived First Class Secretarial Award.

                    El Centro High School, San Diego, California.  Gradu-
                    ated with honors in June 1978.  Served as President of
                    Business Club in 1977 and 1978 and as Secretary of
                    Junior Achievement Club in 1978.


REFERENCES          Ms. Rosa Gonzago, Instructor, San Diego Business Acad-
                    emy, 73 Cabot Drive, San Diego, California 92126

                    Mr. Joseph Turrell, Vice President, The Ames Company,
                    949 Bennett Avenue, Oklahoma City, Oklahoma 73125

                    Mr. Frederick Lapatta, Principal, El Centro High School,
                    San Diego, California 92126
```

A résumé should give specific details about the applicant's experience and education.

school and have used most of your summers for vacation. Nevertheless, any paid work experience, regardless of its nature, will impress an employer because the fact that you have worked reveals that you have some initiative. Therefore, be sure to mention such experience as temporary, part-time, after-school, Saturday, or Christmas vacation work—mowing lawns, baby sitting, delivering newspapers, and so on. Even volunteer typing or clerical work for a teacher or a community agency should be listed.

Include the following facts about your experience:

1. Name and address of your employer (including the telephone number is always very helpful).
2. Type of work you performed. Give not only the title of the position but also a brief description of the work.
3. Dates of employment. Employers usually prefer that you start listing your work experience with your *last* job and work back to your first job. When listing full-time experience by dates, it is important to leave no obvious, unaccounted-for time gaps:

January 1980–September 1981	Did not work during this period; I cared for my mother, who was recovering from surgery.

OR:

August 1982–July 1983	During this period I was a part-time student at the Franklin Music School. I was not employed.

If you have held one or more full-time positions prior to making the application, you may wish to state why you left each position. For example: "I left this position because I was needed at home."

Education. For most high school students, the education section of the résumé will be the most important, since work experience will at this point be limited. Therefore, give specific details about your training that qualify you for the position. Study the information presented in the résumé illustrated on page 578. Note that the courses emphasized are those that have particular bearing on the position being applied for. Note also that special skills and interests are described. Be sure, on your résumé, to list any honors you have received in school, even though they may not appear to be of great significance to you. Employers *are* interested.

Some people who take part in out-of-school activities mention their hobbies as indications of their broad interests. Mentioning outside interests is a good idea, especially if these hobbies give the prospective employer a clue to your personality and talents. For example, the hobby of working on cars will impress the manager of an automobile agency or an auto parts store. The hobby of reading will be of interest to a publisher. If art is your main hobby, this talent will appeal to a large number of employers.

References. At the end of your résumé, list the names of people whom the employer can contact for information about you. Common courtesy requires that you obtain permission before using a person's name for reference. (The letter requesting such permission is discussed in Unit 60.) Ordinarily, only three or four names need be listed, but others should be available to attest to your experience, education, and character. If possible, select your references according to the job for which you are applying. And let your references know what kind of position you are applying for so that they will be guided in their replies. If you are applying for a position as an accounting clerk, for example, a reference from someone in that type of work would be more appropriate than one from your family doctor. When you ask someone to write a letter of recommendation for you, include a stamped envelope to the prospective employer.

The following information should be given about each and every reference you include on your résumé:

1. Full name (check spelling) with appropriate title (such as *Mr., Miss, Ms., Mrs., Professor, Dr.*).
2. Business title (such as *President, Director, Data Processing Manager*).
3. Name of company or organization and complete address.
4. Telephone number (with area code).

Filling Out Employment Applications

Most business firms like to have a standardized record for each employee. You will probably be asked to fill out the company's application form either before or after you have been hired. Frequently, personnel interviewers use the application form as they interview you. Since interviewers are familiar with this form, they can quickly select from it items about which to question you. The application form also provides a great deal of information about the applicant other than the answers to the questions asked—information regarding the legibility of handwriting, accuracy and thoroughness, neatness, and ability to follow written directions.

Here are some helpful suggestions to follow when you must fill out application forms:

1. Bring with you:
   a. A reliable pen. Many pens provided for public use are not dependable. An ink-blotched or unevenly written application form will reflect on your neatness.
   b. Two or more copies of your résumé, one or more for the interviewer and one for you to use in filling out details on the application blank.
   c. Your social security card.
2. Write legibly. Your handwriting does not need to be fancy, but it must be legible. You should take particular care that any figures you write are clear. If the interviewer has difficulty reading your writing, you will start your interview with one strike against you—that is, if you get as far as an interview!
3. Be accurate and careful. Double-check all the information you have included. Have you given your year of birth where it is asked for, and not this year's date? Are your area code and telephone number correct? Be careful to avoid any obvious carelessness.

4. Don't leave any blanks. If the information asked for does not apply to you, draw a line through that space or mark it "Does not apply."

5. Follow directions exactly. Since you have the opportunity to reread the directions to make sure you are completing the form correctly, reread them. If you ask unnecessary questions, you show that you cannot follow simple written instructions. The interviewer will then wonder how you would follow complicated oral instructions once you are on the job! If the directions say to print, then do not write. If the instructions call for your last name first, then do not give your first name first. If you are asked to list your work experience with your last job first, then be sure you do not list your first job first.

COMMUNICATION LABORATORY

APPLICATION EXERCISES

A. Investigate the kinds of jobs that are available in your community by studying the advertisements published in your local newspaper. List specific jobs that are of interest to you. Then list the kinds of jobs for which there are many ads.

B. Prepare a résumé for yourself. Assume that you will graduate from high school within the next two months.

C. Obtain application forms from two local business firms. Complete them just as you would if you were going to apply for a position. Be prepared to discuss in class the kinds of information that the forms required you to supply.

VOCABULARY AND SPELLING STUDIES

A. These words are often confused: *born, borne; coarse, course.* Explain the differences.

B. What are the adjective forms of these verbs?

1. spend
2. supplement
3. harm
4. despair
5. predict
6. investigate

C. Add either *ant* or *ent* to each of the following to form a correctly spelled word.

1. penn_____
2. quoti_____
3. remn_____
4. differ_____
5. radi_____
6. defend_____

COMMUNICATING FOR RESULTS

Innocent Bystander. You answer the office phone and hear the familiar voice of your boss's teenage daughter. The daughter calls frequently. Although she has a reputation in the office of being a "pest," your boss always loves to hear from her and seems to enjoy her calls. This is a very busy day, however, and your boss is working on a report that must be finished within hours. Your boss has given you strict orders not to be disturbed under any circumstances. You must honor your boss's wishes. What do you think you should say to the daughter?

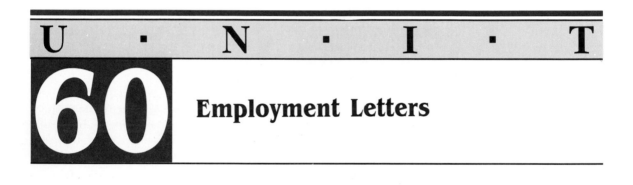

U · N · I · T
60 Employment Letters

Your ability to write an effective employment letter will help you compete successfully against others who want the same job you want. At some point in your career, you will surely have occasion to write one or more of the following types of employment letters:

1. A letter of application. This letter may be written (**a**) in response to a newspaper advertisement; (**b**) at the suggestion of a relative, friend, teacher, or business acquaintance; or (**c**) on your own initiative, even though you do not know of a specific job opening in the business to which you write.
2. Letters to various persons requesting their permission to give their names as reference.
3. A follow-up letter to thank an employment interviewer for the time given you and to reemphasize some of your qualifications that particularly suit you for the job.
4. A letter accepting the position.
5. A letter refusing a position.
6. A thank-you letter to each person who helped you in your job-seeking campaign.
7. A letter resigning from a position.

Letters of Application

Employers often receive hundreds of applications for one job, and they cannot possibly interview each person who applies. Therefore, the personnel recruiter uses the letter of application and other written documents as a basis on which to select those who will be called for a personal interview. An effective application letter can open doors to a bright future; a poor one could quickly close those doors. However, an application letter alone will rarely get you a job. Obviously, an employer needs more than your letter to decide whether to hire you. But your letter can make you stand out from other applicants. It can get your foot in the door—its main purpose.

Appearance. The appearance of your application letter gives the employer a first clue to your personality and work habits. A sloppy letter suggests that you may not be careful about your own appearance or about your work habits—and this is not the kind of impression you want your letter to make.

Appearances *do* matter. Imagine, for example, getting caught in the rain before you are to meet—for the first time—an important person. Even though you explain that you have been caught in the rain and are excused, your bedraggled appearance will create a negative first impression of you. Likewise, a sloppy letter will give a prospective employer an impression of you—but a sloppy letter cannot be excused. It says, "I didn't care enough to do it over." Employers are interested only in applicants who care enough to do the job properly.

Thus, in writing your application letter you want the prospective employer to be favorably impressed and to grant you an interview. The physical appearance of your letter can do much to help create this favorable impression. Follow these instructions, therefore, in preparing your letter:

1. Use a good grade of 8½- by 11-inch bond paper (white). Be certain that it is clean and free from smudges and finger marks both before and after you write your letter. Be careful of paper that is specially treated so that it erases easily. "Erasable" paper is generally expensive. Moreover, you may be paying for extra smudges, because erasable paper tends to pick up old ink from your typewriter platen (roller). Since this paper erases so easily, you can blur the words merely by rubbing your finger across your paper. A good grade of bond paper is usually the best choice.
2. Type your letter of application. Here are some suggestions to follow when typing your letter:
   a. Make no strikeovers.
   b. Make very neat erasures. If an erasure can be detected easily, retype the letter.
   c. Use a black ribbon that is not so worn that the type is too light or so new that the type is too dark and smudgy.
   d. Balance your letter neatly on the page, allowing plenty of white space in the margins (at least 1½ inches all around).
   e. Clean your keys so that letters appear sharp and clear.

3. Address your letter to a specific person in the organization if it is possible to obtain his or her name.
4. Don't expect to get your letter exactly right the first time. Be willing to rewrite it until it represents you in the best possible light.
5. Never copy an application letter out of a book. Let your letter express your own personality.

Organizing the Letter. An application is usually accompanied by a résumé, such as the one illustrated on page 578. It is neither necessary nor desirable to describe fully your education and experience in the letter. This is the job of the résumé. The letter's main purpose is to transmit the résumé and to supplement it with a personal sales message:

> Could you use a sales representative who is hard-working, conscientious, and ambitious? who understands people and who has a knack for knowing what they are looking for? who has sold successfully even while still a student? who wants to build a career in your organization? If your answer to these questions is "Yes," I think I can help you.

> Can your word processing operators produce flawless work hour after hour, documents that pass every test for accuracy? I can—and I can prove this ability to you.

> Is there a place in your organization for a bookkeeper whose work is accurate and meticulous and who accepts a demanding atmosphere as a challenge?

> Can you use a secretary who takes flawless dictation and who transcribes quickly and accurately?

Another good beginning for an application letter that sells is a summary statement of your special qualifications. This type of beginning gives the prospective employer an immediate indication of your ability and training. If these qualifications seem to be what is needed, the employer will read further. Here are some examples:

> My four years of telemarketing experience, plus my proven record of assisting a district sales staff, should qualify me for the position of sales correspondent in your regional office.

> A sound background in secretarial training at Midland High School combined with three years of summer typing in the policy loan department of the Atlas Insurance Company have given me the knowledge and experience necessary for the secretarial position advertised in the May 3 edition of the Post-Dispatch.

> My two years as a receptionist at the Zumwalt Corporation has given me the experience in working with people that your customer service position demands.

When you have been told about a vacancy by another person—an employee of the organization or a friend of the person to whom you are writing or a teacher or guidance counselor—it is often effective to use that person's name (with permission) in your opening paragraph.

Mr. Edgar Schuster, a family friend, has told me that you need a secretary that you can rely on. I have been an executive secretary for two years, and I believe I have the qualifications that you need.

Ms. Sylvia Clarke, who works as order fulfillment supervisor, has told me that you are seeking someone who is used to working with detail. Would two years of experience as a statistical clerk in the U.S. Labor Department's regional office be of interest to you?

My accounting teacher, Mr. Fred Santaro, has told me that you are looking for an accounting assistant. If you are looking for someone whom you do not have to train from the ground up, I believe that my qualifications would be of interest to you.

Developing the Body of the Letter. In the body of the letter, you should offer support for the statements made in the opening paragraph. Emphasize the highlights of your educational background and business experience that are specifically related to the job. You may also indicate why you would like to be employed by the firm to which you are applying. To impress the company favorably, get some of their literature and learn about their locations and activities. The *Funk and Scott Index* lists newspaper and magazine articles that have appeared about companies. Read some, and then you may be able to give specific reasons for being interested in a particular company. Following this suggested plan, the second paragraph of your application letter might read like one of the following:

I routinely take dictation at 110 words per minute. I can also operate a switchboard without becoming flustered during even the busiest periods. I can type accurately and quickly and can answer routine letters reliably. I also have a solid background in modern recordkeeping procedures. I have practiced and sharpened these skills for the last two years in the offices of Acorn Industries.

My enclosed résumé sets forth the training and experience that I have had during my first four years in business. I believe that it equips me for the position of assistant buyer with your firm.

Concluding the Letter. A good conclusion in any letter tells readers what you wish them to do. In a letter of application, you would like the reader to grant a personal interview. Therefore, ask for an interview and make your request easy to grant. Here are some suggested ways to accomplish this:

May I explain my background further during a personal interview? I can be reached at 555-5079.

I believe that I can tell you why I am a likely candidate for your position in just a few minutes. May I have an interview? Just note a convenient date and time on the enclosed postal card.

To a prospective employer some distance away, the applicant may write:

I will be in the Edgartown area from June 27 to June 29. May I talk to you on any of those three days? My phone number is (314) 555-6318.

Sample Letters. The following letter of application for a position as stenographer was written by a soon-to-be-graduated high school business student.

632 Sunrise Highway
Fort Lauderdale, Florida 33322

April 17, 1984

Mr. Elton Saunders
Personnel Director
Global Radio Corporation
84 Industrial Parkway
Pompano Beach, Florida 33062

Dear Mr. Saunders:

Ms. Florence Cranshaw, the business education chairperson at Sunnydale High School, has told me that you have an opening for a secretary. I would be most grateful if you would allow me to quickly explain why I believe I have the necessary qualifications for the position.

As the enclosed résumé points out, I have had two years of shorthand training and transcription at Sunnydale High School and have developed a high rate of speed and accuracy in both shorthand and typing. In addition, for the last two summers I have had the opportunity to improve both skills as a full-time summer replacement at the main office of the Bank of Broward County. This experience also served to acquaint me with the daily routine of a busy office. I have enjoyed both my training and my work experience and believe that I can satisfactorily fill the position that you have.

I can begin work anytime after July 1.

You can reach me at 555-7287 any day after 3:30 p.m. May I have a personal interview at your convenience?

Sincerely yours,

The following letter was written by a graduating student applying for an accounting position in reply to a blind newspaper ad:

73 David Lane
Collegeville, Minnesota 56321

May 30, 1984

The Register
Box 777
Collegeville, Minnesota 56321

Dear Sir or Madam:

Two years of high school accounting, supplemented by summer work at an accounting firm and strengthened by an evening program in accounting at the

Abrams Institute, have equipped me to handle the general demands of accounting work. I would therefore appreciate it if you would consider me for an accounting position in your firm.

I am presently employed as a tax clerk with the Arvida Manufacturing Corporation. But I am looking for a position that would make greater use of my broad training. I would also value the opportunity to get into a more advanced phase of accounting. I plan to continue my accounting education through a night school program at our local community college.

The enclosed résumé summarizes my education and experience. It also includes the names of three people from whom you may obtain information about my character and ability.

I would very much like to talk to you in person. I may be reached by phone at 555-3000, Ext. 342, from 9 a.m. to 5 p.m. or at 555-3894 after 6 p.m.

Sincerely yours,

Letters Requesting References

Almost every prospective employer likes to have information regarding the character, training, experience, and work habits of job applicants. You may need to supply only the names, titles, and addresses of references, leaving to the interested prospective employer the task of obtaining the desired references. Under some circumstances, you may request that the person speaking on your behalf write a letter of reference directly to the prospective employer. (In most cases, a letter of reference that you carry with you is not too effective.)

Before using a person's name as a reference, you should request permission to do so. This permission may be obtained in person, by telephone, or by a letter such as the following:

Dear Ms. Dalton:

I am applying for the position of assistant order clerk that is currently open at the Dennings Corporation in Afton.

As a student in your office practice class two years ago, I received the background that is needed for this position. I would like very much to use your name as a reference.

I enclose a return postal card for your reply.

Sincerely yours,

You might use a courtesy carbon and return envelope instead of the postal card.

If you are writing to request that a reference be sent directly to a prospective employer, you may say:

Dear Mr. Domboski:

I am applying for an assistant auditor's position at Dixon's Department Store.

Since I worked under your supervision for two years in the claims department of the Northwest Insurance Company, I believe that you are in a position to evaluate my character and ability. Would you be willing to send a letter of reference for me to Ms. Helen Salton, Personnel Director at Dixon's? I am enclosing a stamped and addressed envelope for your convenience.

Sincerely yours,

Follow-Up Letters

Application letters and letters requesting references are written before the interview with a prospective employer. After the interview, there are several types of follow-up letters you may write. Here are some examples.

The Interview Follow-Up. If your application letter has succeeded in obtaining a personal interview for you, the next letter you should write will follow the personal interview. This letter may serve to satisfy one or more of the following purposes:

1. To thank the interviewer for the time and courtesy extended to you.
2. To let the interviewer know you are still interested in the position.
3. To remind the interviewer of the special qualifications you have for this particular position.
4. To return the application form that the interviewer may have given you to take home to complete.
5. To provide any additional data requested by the interviewer that you may not have had available at the time of the interview.

Notice how the interview follow-up uses the everyday letter plan by directly thanking the reader for the interview and then following up with details related to the interview.

Dear Mr. Lewes:

Thank you for discussing with me yesterday afternoon the position that you have available in your billing office. You told me exactly what would be demanded of me in that position.

I am more interested than ever in this job. I believe that the position I have held for the last two years at Lyon's Service Company has given me the background I would need to perform the work required.

I have completed the application form that you gave me, and it is enclosed. I have asked my references to write to you directly.

I hope that you will look positively upon my application. Please let me know if I can supply you with any additional information.

                                        Sincerely yours,

Letters of Acceptance. If you are notified by mail that you are being offered the position for which you applied, you should write a letter of acceptance. This letter does the following:

1. Notifies your employer-to-be of your acceptance.
2. Reassures the employer that she or he has chosen the right person.
3. Informs the employer when you can report for work.

The letter of acceptance, which follows the everyday letter plan, may read as follows:

Dear Miss Sands:

It is a pleasure to accept your offer of a secretarial position at Standard Embroidery. You can be sure that I will do everything possible to justify confidence you have expressed in me.

Since June 24 is my graduation day, Monday, June 27, will certainly be a convenient starting date for me. I will report to your office ready to work at 8:30 a.m.

Thank you for the opportunity that you have given me.

                                        Sincerely yours,

Letters of Refusal. Perhaps you have been offered a position for which you applied, but you have also received another offer that you believe is better. You should return the courtesy extended to you by writing a tactful, friendly letter of refusal. You may want to reapply to this same company in the future. Structure your letter according to the bad-news plan. Refuse the position only after you have expressed appreciation for being offered the job.

Dear Mr. Sauter:

Thank you for offering me the position of inventory clerk at the Atlantic Company's warehouse.

It would have been a pleasure working with you and the other fine people at Atlantic. However, just two days before receiving your offer, I accepted a position at another company.

I very much appreciate the time that you gave me.

                                        Sincerely yours,

Thank-You Letters. When you have obtained your position, remember that the people who have written reference letters for you undoubtedly helped you. You should be courteous enough to let them know that you have accepted the position. You might write a letter such as this:

Dear Mrs. Keno:

Thank you for the letter of reference that you sent on my behalf to the Ridgeville Trust Company. You will be pleased to know that I have accepted the position of secretary to Mr. Francis Easterly, Assistant Treasurer.

I want you to know how very much I appreciate your support.

Sincerely yours,

Resignation Letters

Occasionally you may need to write a letter resigning from a position. (Of course, you should discuss your resignation with your supervisor before writing a letter.) Regardless of your reason for resigning, your letter should be friendly in tone and tactful. Someday you may want this employer to give you a reference, and you want the employer to remember you favorably. The following letter, which follows the bad-news plan, is a good example of a letter of resignation.

Dear Mr. Connolly:

I want you to know how much I have enjoyed my last two years at the Ridgeland Tool Company. I have learned a great deal here and have made many permanent friends as well.

Because I would like to make greater use of my sales background, I have accepted a position at the Lufkin Investment Company. I would therefore appreciate it if you would accept my resignation effective July 31.

Thank you for all that you have done to make my work here both interesting and enjoyable.

Sincerely yours,

COMMUNICATION LABORATORY

APPLICATION EXERCISES

A. The following advertisements appeared in a recent edition of your local newspaper. Write a letter of application answering one of these advertisements.

SECRETARY: Small office needs someone capable of doing everything. Good position for the right person. Apply to Mr. Charles Kim, 72 Delaware Street.

CLERK-TYPIST: Must be quick and accurate. Opportunity to learn real estate business in convenient downtown location. Salary open—fringe benefits. Ms. Donna Madden, Edgemont Building.

TRAVEL COORDINATOR: Entry-level position. Work for a busy manufacturing firm with people who are always on the go. Will teach the use of official Air Line Guide and routing maps. Much telephone work. No typing. Personnel Director, Massey Corp., Eagleton Mall.

B. Write a letter to a teacher or acquaintance requesting permission to use his or her name as a reference.

C. Assume that you have had a personal interview for one of the jobs in Exercise A. Write a follow-up letter to the person who interviewed you.

D. You have received a letter notifying you that you have been selected to fill the vacancy for which you had applied. Write a letter accepting the position.

E. Suppose that you have decided not to accept the position offered to you in Exercise D. Write a letter of refusal.

F. Write a letter to the person who wrote a letter of reference for you, notifying him or her that you have accepted a position.

G. You have been employed in the office of the Reliance Electrical Supply company for two and a half years. A friend who works for the Pennington Advertising Agency has told you of a vacancy there, and you have applied for and have been offered the position. The job that you have been offered pays more than your current salary; the opportunities to learn and advance seem better; there are many more benefits, including a college tuition plan and a dental plan; and the firm is much closer to your home. You decide to leave your present position. Assume that you have already discussed this new job with your present supervisor. You must now put your resignation into writing. Write the letter.

VOCABULARY AND SPELLING STUDIES

A. These words are often confused: *decent, descent, dissent; imitate, intimate.* Use each word in a sentence that illustrates its meaning.

B. From each pair of words within parentheses, select the one that correctly completes the sentence.

1. A city (ordnance, ordinance) prohibits parking in this area.
2. I have no (illusions, allusions) about my capabilities.
3. The (aisles, isles) in this hall must be kept clear at all times.
4. The marketing people will (canvas, canvass) the food stores for customer preferences.
5. Its expense is the (loan, lone) reason for rejecting your plan.

C. A letter is missing from each of the following words. Spell the words correctly.

1. remitance
2. misaprehension
3. knowledgable
4. prefered
5. transmited
6. embarass

COMMUNICATING FOR RESULTS

You Feel Responsible. Anthony Forbes, a close friend of yours, was looking for a job and asked you to speak to your supervisor about a data processing position with your firm. You did this, Anthony was interviewed, and he was eventually hired, partly because of your recommendation. He has been working in your department for about a month now. You have noticed that he is always late, both in the morning and after lunch. Moreover, he takes constant breaks during the day. Worst of all, he makes several mistakes that are due mainly to inattentiveness and lack of concentration. Because you helped him to get his job, you feel responsible for his performance. What, if anything, should you do?

In preparation for a class discussion of the problem, jot down some of the various things that you might do and identify what you believe would be the best course of action.

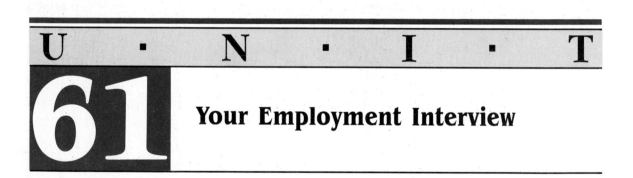

U · N · I · T
61 Your Employment Interview

For any job opening, an applicant is required to have a personal interview. This interview may be the most important use you make of oral communication, for your future may depend upon your success in selling yourself during this interview. The employment interview is also one of the best examples of total communication because it is in the interview that job applicants reveal whether they possess the communication skills required for the position for which they are applying. Does the applicant *speak* well, *listen* attentively, *read* and follow instructions carefully, *write* an effective résumé?

Getting Ready for the Interview

An interviewer judges job applicants by the degree to which they know their own qualifications and the requirements of the job and by their ability to relate their qualifications to the requirements. Careful planning and preparation for the interview are required. Study the following suggestions thoroughly, for the way you apply them will be a big factor in determining your standing among the other applicants.

Know Your Qualifications. Before the interview, be sure you have collected and reviewed the necessary information about your personal qualifications. If you wrote a letter of application (as discussed in Unit 60), refresh your memory about what you said. If you prepared a résumé (Unit 59), memorize the facts you included. Have a transcript of school credits at hand and review the names of subjects you have taken. Have available, too, a list of class activities in which you have participated, clubs and organizations to which you have belonged, honors you have won, and your hobbies and favorite sports. Know your school average and your attendance record. How embarrassing to be asked about your personal qualifications and not be able to remember exactly!

Interviewers will generally have on their desk your application letter or form, your résumé, school records, statements from previous employers, and letters of reference. Using these materials as a base, they will ask you questions. They may ask you to clarify or expand upon some information, and as you answer they will probably note how closely your reply agrees with the written records. Prepare yourself, therefore, by collecting and reviewing all the data on your qualifications. Have the information on the tip of your tongue so that you can answer questions readily and accurately.

Know the Job. Many employers advertise for experienced applicants to fill a position because they believe an experienced person is more likely to know the job—what is expected and how to perform. But the requirement of experience is not the handicap it may at first seem. An inexperienced applicant may be able to make up for a lack of experience by learning everything possible about that job. Thus prepared, the applicant can show the interviewer that a realistic understanding of what the job involves may make up for the lack of experience.

To learn about a job, you can talk with employees in that field. Before you leave school, you might ask a recent graduate who is now working in the company of your choice to talk about the job. If you have an opportunity to do so, take a field trip through the offices or plant. Read about the products manufactured or about the services or goods sold. Through friends, you may even be able to learn something about the people who own or operate the company and about the particular person who will interview you. The more you know about the job, the company, and the people you will meet, the better you will be able to relate your abilities to the specific job.

Match Your Qualifications to the Job. Well-intentioned, well-qualified applicants have been known to enter a personnel office with a general statement such as "I want to apply for a job." This shows lack of wisdom and immaturity. Such people might as well say that they have not considered what job they wish to apply for, what qualifications are needed, or how their own qualifications are related to the needs of the job. These applicants usually do not get past the receptionist. To avoid such a disappointment, you must prepare for the employment interview by considering how your abilities fit you for the specific job for which you are applying.

Conducting Yourself During the Interview

If you have prepared carefully for the interview, you should make a favorable first impression. Your dress and behavior will be correct for the situation, and you will appear self-confident and poised.

Your Appearance. Care in grooming and in the selection of clothing, as discussed in Unit 55, is of major importance to every applicant. The clothing you wear to the interview should be neat, clean, comfortable, and, of course, appropriate. As interviewers talk with you, they will notice such details as your nails, teeth, and hair. A full night's sleep will contribute to your fresh, alert appearance. Any detail of appearance and dress that attracts unfavorable attention will count against you. Trained interviewers know that there is a direct relationship between personal habits and work habits—sloppy appearance, sloppy work; neat appearance, neat work. Therefore, make your appearance speak favorably for you at the interview.

Your Manner and Manners. Good manners are often taken for granted, but any lack of good manners is noticed immediately. Follow these tips on common courtesy and etiquette during job interviews.

Arrive on Time or Early. It is rude to be late for any appointment. If you are late for a job interview, you may make the interviewer wonder how often you will be late if you are hired. The interviewer might also conclude that you do not really want the job, since you are late. Rushing to arrive on time will leave you breathless, however; so start early enough to allow for any possible delays.

Meet the Unexpected With Poise, Tact, and Humor. If the interviewer is not ready to see you, take a seat and occupy yourself while you're waiting. Imagine the childish impression a person makes who says, "But Mr. O'Toole told me that he would see me at ten o'clock."

Follow the Interviewer's Lead. Remember that you are a guest. Shake hands if the interviewer offers to do so, and give a firm handshake. A limp handshake indicates weakness. Wait for an invitation before seating yourself, and let the interviewer tell you where to be seated. You are being a good guest if you follow the lead of the interviewer.

Be Tactful and Gracious in Conversation. Listen carefully. Don't interrupt, even if the interviewer is long-winded and you think of something to say right away. Follow the interviewer's conversation leads and show that you understand the importance of what has been said. Don't bore the interviewer with long, overdetailed answers; but do reply with more than a meek "yes" or "no" to questions. Never contradict the interviewer or imply that an error has been made, under any circumstances. Such lack of tact is rude and will do nothing to help you in the interview.

Show Appreciation for the Interviewer's Time and Interest. At the close of the interview remember to express appreciation, just as you would thank any host as you take your leave. Don't let the excitement and tension of the interview make you forget this courtesy. Failing to show appreciation could spoil an otherwise effective interview.

Your Speech and Conversation. The speech principles you have studied will aid you in demonstrating your oral communication. Have you worked to improve your voice? How is your enunciation? vocabulary and pronunciation? Do you still say "yeah" when you mean "yes"? If you have worked hard and applied all you have learned, your voice and speech will do you credit. You can concentrate on what you say.

What you say reflects your attitudes and tells what kind of person you are. During the interview, for example, if you betray that you are overly interested in salary, your lunch hour, vacation, sick leave, or short working hours, you may reveal that you are more interested in loafing than in working. Interviewers have a responsibility to employ people who want to work!

Typical Interview Questions. Understanding the intent of the interviewer's questions will help you answer more intelligently. Here are some typical interview questions, with the reasons behind them and suggestions as to what you might say in reply.

Why Have You Selected This Kind of Work? The interviewer wishes to know how interested you are in the work and what your goals are. An answer like "Oh, I just need a job" shows lack of purpose. Isn't the following a better answer? "I've wanted to be a secretary ever since I started school. That was my reason for taking the stenographic course. I believe I'll like this type of job too." This type of answer tell the interviewer that you know what you want from a job, that you have interest, and that you have a purpose.

If You Had Your Choice of Job and Company, What Would You Most Like to Be Doing and Where? Watch your answer to this question! The interviewer is trying to gauge just how satisfied you will be working in this job and in this company. The best answer, if you can truthfully say so, is: "Ms. Vargas, the job I want is the one for which I am now applying. The company? Yours. Before too long, I hope to have proved myself and to have been promoted to greater responsibility."

What Are Your Hobbies? The interviewer is not interested in swapping information about your stamp collection. What the interviewer really wants to know is whether you have broad interests, for a person who has few outside interests is likely to become restless. Be ready to list briefly your major interests in hobbies and sports.

In What Extracurricular Activities Have You Participated? To what clubs do you belong? What offices have you held? What honors have you received? These and similar questions are asked to determine the scope of your interest in people—whether you are able to work with people and whether you have leadership qualities. These are the characteristics of a well-rounded, well-adjusted individual. In preparing for the interview, review your extracurricular activities so that you can give the facts without hesitation.

Would You Be Willing to Work Overtime? Employers like to see a willingness, even an eagerness, to perform well in a job. Overtime may be required seldom, but if it is, employers want to have people who will accept this responsibility. You would be entering a job with the wrong attitude if you were not willing to work overtime when necessary.

COMMUNICATION LABORATORY

APPLICATION EXERCISES

A. Make a list of your personal and educational qualifications to fill one of the following positions: receptionist, accounting clerk, secretary, word processing operator, clerk-typist, retail sales clerk. From the standpoint of an interviewer, make a list of qualifications for the job, including some that you may not currently have.

B. Make a list of your leisure-time activities. Include all extracurricular activities, clubs, offices held, and awards received. The completed list will include things that you might mention in an employment interview.

C. Make a list of grooming and dress standards that you might consult before going to an employment interview.

D. Assume that you are the personnel manager for one of the largest employers in your community. You have an opening for a general clerical worker. Make a list of questions that you might ask an applicant. Explain what each answer would tell you about the potential employee. In class, use your questions to enact the interview in the form of a skit.

VOCABULARY AND SPELLING STUDIES

A. These words are often confused: *breath, breathe, breadth; indignant, indigent, indigenous.* Explain the differences.

B. Select the word in parentheses that best completes each of the following sentences.

1. The prefix *re-* in *reconsider, return, reunite,* and *remit* gives these words the meaning of (beyond, again, under, after).
2. The prefix *mis-* in *misguide, misapply, misuse,* and *misdirect* gives these words the meaning of (wrongly, throughout, partly, before).
3. The suffix *-ician* in *musician, technician,* and *electrician* gives these words the meaning of (specialist in, the service of, the quality of, the state of).
4. The suffix *-ist* in *journalist, pianist, economist,* and *specialist* gives these words the meaning of (the study of, the act of, the science of, one who).

C. Replace the italicized words with correctly formed contractions.

1. *Who is* going to do the work?
2. You *should not* guess about such an important number.
3. *It is* impossible to determine when we will finish this job.
4. Fred *did not* catch the error in time.
5. *Let us* recheck this column of figures.

COMMUNICATING FOR RESULTS

Supervising People. You are a department head in a large firm. At salary-review time, you receive the following written report from one of your managers: "I cannot recommend either Ms. Denning or Mr. Isaacson for the normal budgeted salary increases. For their first few months with the firm, they learned quickly and worked well and conscientiously. For the last couple of months, however, their work seems to have taken second place to long coffee breaks, lengthy personal visits with other employees, and continual inattentiveness. During this past week, Ms. Denning was unable to complete a three-page report. Mr. Isaacson fell further behind in the routine posting of invoices. I think you ought to talk with both of them."

You have asked each of these employees to come to your office. What will you say when each comes to see you?

A · P · P · E · N · D · I · X

The following list includes almost 700 commonly used—and frequently misspelled—business words. By mastering this short list of business words, you can reduce the number of times you must refer to a dictionary and, at the same time, increase your efficiency and accuracy in writing business communications.

A

absence
accede
accept
accessible
accidentally
accommodate
accordance
accrual
accumulate
accurate
acknowledge
acquire
acquisitive
across
adaptability
address
adequate
adhere
adjacent
adjoining
adjourn
adjunct
adjustment
admissible
advantageous
advertise

advice (n.)
advisability
advise (v.)
adviser
advisory
affiliate
aggressive
agreeable
agreement
allege
allocated
almost
already
altogether
amateur
among
amortize
analysis
analyze
annual
anxious
apologize
apparatus
apparel
applicable
appointment
appraisal
appreciable
appropriate

approximately
aptitude
around
arrears
article
artificial
ascertain
assignment
assistance
assumption
attention
attorneys
auditor
authenticity
authoritative
authorize
auxiliary
available

B

bankruptcy
bargain
basis
becoming
beginning
belief

believe
beneficial
benefited
bookkeeper
boundary
brilliant
brochure
budget
bulletin
business

C

calendar
campaign
cancel
canceled
cancellation
cannot
capacity
career
careful
carried
carrying
catalog
centralized
certificate
changeable
chargeable
chemical
chief
choice
choose
chose
chronological
coincidence
collapsible
collectible

college
collision
column
coming
commensurate
commercial
commission
commitment
committed
committee
comparable
comparative
comparison
compel
compelled
competent
competition
competitive
compilation
complete
comptroller
computer
concede
conceit
conceive
concise
concur
concurred
confer
conference
conferred
conscientious
conscious
consensus
conspicuous
contingency
continuous
contract
control
controlled

convenience
coolly
cooperate
cordially
corporation
correspondence
correspondents
corroborate
council
courtesy
coverage
credentials
criticism
criticize
crystallize
current
customer
cycle
cylinder

D

dealt
debtor
deceased
deceit
deceive
decision
deductible
defensible
defer
deferred
deficit
definite
definition
delinquent
dependent
depreciation

desirable
develop
development
differed
difference
differential
differing
dilemma
director
disappear
disappoint
disapprove
discernible
discipline
discretion
disillusion
dissatisfied
dissension
dissolution
distribution
distributor
dividend
duly
durable

E

economical
education
effect
efficiency
either
electrical
elementary
eligible
eliminate
embarrass
eminent
emphasis

employee
endeavor
endorsement
enforceable
enterprise
enumerate
envelop (v.)
envelope (n.)
environment
equaled
equalize
equally
equip
equipment
equipped
equipping
equivalent
erroneous
especially
essence
essential
exaggerate
exceed
excellent
except
excessive
exhaust
exhibit
exhibitor
existence
exorbitant
expeditiously
expendable
expense
experience
explanation
extension
extraordinary
extravagance
extremely

F

facilitate
facilities
facsimile
familiarize
fascinate
favorable
favorite
feasible
February
finally
financial
financier
flexible
flourishing
fluorescent
forcibly
foreign
forfeit
forty
forward
fourteen
fourth
fragile
franchise
fraudulent
freight
friend
fulfill

G

garnishee
gasoline
gauge
generalize

genuine
government
governor
gram
granite
grateful
grievance
griping
(complaining)
gripping
(holding)
guarantee

H

handicapped
handled
handsome
harass
hardware
hazardous
heretofore
hesitant
hinder
hindrance
hygiene

I

identical
illegible
imaginary
immediately
imminent
impel
impelled
imperative

implement
impossible
impromptu
inadvertent
incandescent
incapable
incessantly
incidentally
inconceivable
inconvenience
incredible
incredulous
incur
incurred
indebted
indefensible
indelible
indemnity
indispensable
individual
inducement
industry
inexhaustible
inference
inferred
inflationary
initial
inquiry
inspector
installation
insurable
intelligence
intelligible
intercede
interested
interference
interpretation
interrupt
intricate
invalidate
invaluable

investigator
invoicing
irreconcilable
irrelevant
irreparable
irresistible
itemize
itinerary
its (possessive)
it's ("it is")

J

janitor
jeopardize
judgment

K

kilometer
knowledge
knowledgeable

L

label
labeled
laboratory
lavatory
legible
leisure
lessen (decrease)
lesson (in school)
liaison
license

likable
likelihood
linoleum
liquefy
liter
loose
lose
lucrative
luncheon
luxurious

M

machinery
magazine
mailable
maintain
maintenance
manageable
managing
mandatory
manufacturer
marketable
marvelous
material
mathematics
measurable
measurement
mechanical
mechanism
mediator
medical
mediocre
memorandum
memorize
merchandise
meter
mileage
millimeter

minimum
misapprehension
miscellaneous
modernize
monopolize
moreover
mortgage
movable
mutually

N

naive
necessarily
necessary
negative
negligible
negotiate
neutralize
nickel
nineteen
ninety
ninth
notarize
noticeable
nucleus
numerical

O

obedient
objectionable
obligatory
observant
obsolete
obtainable
occupant

occurred
occurrence
omission
omitted
operator
opportunity
option
ordinarily
organization
original
outstanding
overrated

P

paid
pamphlet
parallel
paralleled
pardonable
parity
participant
particularly
pastime
patience
patronize
payroll
percent
perceptible
perforate
permanent
permissible
permit
permitted
perseverance
personal
personnel (staff)
persuasive
pertinent

phenomenal
piecework
Pittsburgh (Pa.)
planning
plausible
pleasure
pneumatic
politician
possession
potential
practical
practice
precede
precise
precision
preferable
preference
preferred
premium
prerogative
previous
privilege
probably
procedure
proceed
processing
progress
prohibition
promissory
prosperous
psychology
purchase

Q

quantity
questionnaire
quite

R

readily
realize
receipt
receive
recently
reciprocate
recognize
recollect
recommend
reconciliation
recurrence
reducible
reference
referred
reimburse
relevant
relief
relieve
reluctant
remember
remembrance
remittance
repetition
representative
resources
responsibility
responsible
restaurant
returnable
revenue
routine

S

safety
salary
schedule
scientific

scrutinize
seize
sense
sensible
separate
serviceable
shipment
shipping
similar
sincerely
sizable
solely
specialize
specifically
specimen
sponsor
standardize
statement
statistical
statistician
status
submitted
substantial
successful
sufficient
summarize
supersede
superficial
superfluous
supervisor
surmise
surname
surprise
survey
susceptible
symmetry

T

tariff
technical

technician
tenant
their (possessive)
there (place)
they're
 ("they are")
thorough
throughout
to (*prep.*)
too ("also")
totaling
traceable
transmit
transmitted
traveler
traveling
truly
two (2)

U

unduly
unique
unnecessary
until
urgent
usable
useful

usually
utilize

V

vacancy
vacuum
vague
valid
validate
valuable
various
velocity
vendor
ventilator
vertical
visualize
volume
voluntary
volunteer

W

waive
warehouse
warranty

weather
Wednesday
whereas
wherever
whether
wholly
wield
withhold
writing

Y

yield

Z

zealous
zeros

I · N · D · E · X

A

D

J

L

M

Q